Database Processing

Fundamentals, Design,
and Implementation

14TH EDITION

Database Processing

Fundamentals, Design, and Implementation

14TH EDITION

David M. Kroenke

David J. Auer
Western Washington University

PEARSON

Boston   Columbus   Indianapolis   New York   San Francisco   Hoboken
Amsterdam   Cape Town   Dubai   London   Madrid   Milan   Munich   Paris   Montréal   Toronto
Delhi   Mexico City   São Paulo   Sydney   Hong Kong   Seoul   Singapore   Taipei   Tokyo

Vice President, Business Publishing: Donna Battista
Editor in Chief: Stephanie Wall
Acquisitions Editor: Nicole Sam
Program Manager Team Lead: Ashley Santora
Program Manager: Denise Weiss
Editorial Assistant: Olivia Vignone
Vice President, Product Marketing: Maggie Moylan
Director of Marketing, Digital Services and Products:
  Jeanette Koskinas
Executive Product Marketing Manager: Anne Fahlgren
Field Marketing Manager: Lenny Ann Raper
Senior Strategic Marketing Manager: Erin Gardner
Product Marketing Assistant: Jessica Quazza
Project Manager Team Lead: Jeff Holcomb
Project Manager: Ilene Kahn
Operations Specialist: Diane Peirano
Senior Art Director: Janet Slowik

Text Designer: Integra Software Services Pvt. Ltd.
Cover Designer: Integra Software Services Pvt. Ltd.
Cover Art: Donna Auer
Vice President, Director of Digital Strategy &
  Assessment: Paul Gentile
Manager of Learning Applications: Paul Deluca
Digital Editor: Brian Surette
Digital Studio Manager: Diane Lombardo
Digital Studio Project Manager: Robin Lazrus
Digital Studio Project Manager: Alana Coles
Digital Studio Project Manager: Monique Lawrence
Digital Studio Project Manager: Regina DaSilva
Full-Service Project Management
  and Composition: Integra Software Services Pvt. Ltd.
Printer/Binder: RRD Willard
Cover Printer: Phoenix Color/Hagerstown
Text Font: 10/12 Mentor Std Light

Credits and acknowledgments borrowed from other sources and reproduced, with permission, in this textbook appear on the appropriate page within text.

Microsoft and/or its respective suppliers make no representations about the suitability of the information contained in the documents and related graphics published as part of the services for any purpose. All such documents and related graphics are provided "as is" without warranty of any kind. Microsoft and/or its respective suppliers hereby disclaim all warranties and conditions with regard to this information, including all warranties and conditions of merchantability, whether express, implied or statutory, fitness for a particular purpose, title and non-infringement. In no event shall Microsoft and/or its respective suppliers be liable for any special, indirect or consequential damages or any damages whatsoever resulting from loss of use, data or profits, whether in an action of contract, negligence or other tortious action, arising out of or in connection with the use or performance of information available from the services.

The documents and related graphics contained herein could include technical inaccuracies or typographical errors. Changes are periodically added to the information herein. Microsoft and/or its respective suppliers may make improvements and/or changes in the product(s) and/or the program(s) described herein at any time. Partial screen shots may be viewed in full within the software version specified.

Microsoft® Windows®, and Microsoft Office® are registered trademarks of the Microsoft Corporation in the U.S.A. and other countries. This book is not sponsored or endorsed by or affiliated with the Microsoft Corporation.

MySQL®, the MySQL Command Line Client®, the MySQL Workbench®, and the MySQL Connector/ODBC® are registered trademarks of Sun Microsystems, Inc./Oracle Corporation. Screenshots and icons reprinted with permission of Oracle Corporation. This book is not sponsored or endorsed by or affiliated with Oracle Corporation.

Oracle Database 12c and Oracle Database Express Edition 11g Release 2 2014 by Oracle Corporation. Reprinted with permission. Oracle and Java are registered trademarks of Oracle and/or its affiliates. Other names may be trademarks of their respective owners.

Mozilla 35.104 and Mozilla are registered trademarks of the Mozilla Corporation and/or its affiliates. Other names may be trademarks of their respective owners.

PHP is copyright The PHP Group 1999–2012, and is used under the terms of the PHP Public License v3.01 available at *http://www.php.net/license/3_01.txt*. This book is not sponsored or endorsed by or affiliated with The PHP Group.

Many of the designations by manufacturers and sellers to distinguish their products are claimed as trademarks. Where those designations appear in this book, and the publisher was aware of a trademark claim, the designations have been printed in initial caps or all caps.

Library of Congress Cataloging-in-Publication Data

Kroenke, David M.
  Database processing: fundamentals, design, and implementation/David M. Kroenke, David J. Auer.–Fourteenth edition.
    pages cm
  Includes bibliographical references and index.
  ISBN 978-0-13-387670-3 (student edition)–ISBN 978-0-13-387676-5
  (instructor's review copy)
  1. Database management.   I. Auer, David J.   II. Title.
  QA76.9.D3K76 2016
  005.74–dc23

                                                                            2015005632

10 9 8 7 6 5 4 3 2 1

ISBN 10:   0-13-387670-5
ISBN 13: 978-0-13-387670-3

Brief Contents

Contents

PART 2 ■ Database Design   133

Chapter 3: The Relational Model and Normalization   134

Chapter 4: Database Design Using Normalization   177

Chapter 5: Data Modeling with the Entity-Relationship Model   196

Chapter 6: Transforming Data Models into Database Designs   248

PART 3 ■ Database Implementation   301

Chapter 7: SQL for Database Construction and Application Processing   302

Chapter 8: Database Redesign   396

PART 4 ■ Multiuser Database Processing   423

Chapter 9: Managing Multiuser Databases   424

Chapter 10: Managing Databases with Microsoft SQL Server 2014, Oracle Database, and MySQL 5.6 458

ONLINE CHAPTER: SEE PAGE 463 FOR INSTRUCTIONS

Chapter 10A: Managing Databases with Microsoft SQL Server 2014

PART 5 ■ Database Access Standards   465

Chapter 11: The Web Server Environment   466

Chapter 12: Big Data, Data Warehouses, and Business Intelligence Systems   533

Appendices

Appendix E: Getting Started with the MySQL Workbench Data Modeling Tools

Chapter Objectives
What Is the Purpose of This Appendix?
Why Should I Learn to Use the MySQL Workbench Data Modeling Tools?
What Will This Appendix Teach Me?
What Won't This Appendix Teach Me?
How Do I Start the MySQL Workbench?
How Do I Create a Workspace for the MySQL Workbench Files?
How Do I Install the MySQL Connector/ODBC?
How Do I Create Database Designs in the MySQL Workbench?
How Do I Create a Database Model and E-R Diagram in the MySQL Workbench?

Key Terms • Review Questions • Project Questions

Appendix F: Getting Started with Microsoft Visio 2013

Chapter Objectives
What Is the Purpose of This Appendix?
Why Should I Learn to Use Microsoft Visio 2013?
What Will This Appendix Teach Me?
What Won't This Appendix Teach Me?
How Do I Start Microsoft Visio 2013?
How Do I Create a Database Model Diagram in Microsoft Visio 2013?
How Do I Name and Save a Database Model Diagram in Microsoft Visio 2013?
How Do I Create Entities/Tables in a Database Model Diagram in Microsoft
Visio 2013?
How Do I Create Relationships Between Tables in a Database Model Diagram
in Microsoft Visio 2013?

Key Terms • Review Questions • Project Questions

Appendix G: Data Structures for Database Processing

Chapter Objectives
What Is the Purpose of This Appendix?
What Will This Appendix Teach Me?
What Are Flat Files?
　　Processing Flat Files in Multiple Orders • *A Note on Record Addressing* • *How Can Linked Lists
　　Be Used to Maintain Logical Record Order?* • *How Can Indexes Be Used to Maintain Logical
　　Record Order?* • *B-Trees* • *Summary of Data Structures*
How Can We Represent Binary Relationships?
　　A Review of Record Relationships • *How Can We Represent Trees?* • *How Can We Represent
　　Simple Networks?* • *How Can We Represent Complex Networks?* • *Summary of Relationship
　　Representations*
How Can We Represent Secondary Keys?
　　How Can We Represent Secondary Keys with Linked-Lists? • *How Can We Represent Secondary
　　Keys with Indexes?*

Key Terms • Review Questions

Appendix H: The Semantic Object Model

Chapter Objectives
What Is the Purpose of This Appendix?
Why Should I Learn to Use the Semantic Object Model?

The 14th edition of *Database Processing: Fundamentals, Design, and Implementation* refines the organization and content of this classic textbook to reflect a new teaching and professional workplace environment. Students and other readers of this book will benefit from new content and features in this edition.

New to This Edition

Content and features new to the 14th edition of *Database Processing: Fundamentals, Design, and Implementation* include the following:

- The SQL topics in Chapter 2 have been reorganized and expanded to provide a more concise presentation of SQL queries. New material on SQL set operators (UNION, INTERSECTION, and EXCEPT) has been added to ensure that nearly all SQL query topics are covered in one chapter (the exception is correlated subqueries, which are still reserved for Chapter 8).
- The material on *Big Data* and the evolving *NoSQL movement* is summarized in Chapter 12 and then expanded upon in a new Appendix K–*Big Data*. This is an important topic that is constantly developing and changing, and the new appendix provides room for an extended discussion of the topic. Material on virtualization and cloud computing is updated in Chapter 12.
- Online chapters on Microsoft SQL Server 2014 (Chapter 10A), Oracle Database (Chapter 10B), and MySQL 5.6 (Chapter 10C) now have a section on importing data from Microsoft Excel 2013 worksheets.
- The book has been updated to reflect the use of Microsoft SQL Server 2014, the current version of Microsoft SQL Server. Although most of the topics covered are backward compatible with Microsoft SQL Server 2012 and Microsoft SQL Server 2008 R2 Express edition, all material in the book now uses SQL Server 2014 in conjunction with Office 2013 exclusively.
- Oracle's Oracle Database is now updated to Oracle Database 12*c*, and Oracle Database Express Edition 11*g* Release 2 (Oracle Database XE) is introduced as the preferred Oracle Database product for use on personal computers. The current version of the Oracle SQL Developer GUI tool provides a common interface to both versions of Oracle Database, and we provide detailed examples of how to use it.
- Microsoft Windows Server 2012 R2 is the server operating system and Windows 8.1 is the workstation operating system generally discussed and illustrated in the text. These are the current Microsoft server and workstation operating systems.
- We have updated online Appendix I–*Getting Started with Web Servers, PHP and the NetBeans IDE*. We are now using the NetBeans IDE instead of the Eclipse PDT IDE. This provides a better development environment with a much simpler set of product installations because the Java JDK and NetBeans are installed in one combined installation. This new material provides a simplified (but still detailed) introduction to the installation and use of the Microsoft IIS Web server, PHP, the Java JDK, and the NetBeans in Appendix I. All of these tools are then used for Web database application development as discussed in Chapter 11.

Fundamentals, Design, and Implementation

With today's technology, it is impossible to utilize a DBMS successfully without first learning fundamental concepts. After years of developing databases with business users, we have developed what we believe to be a set of essential database concepts. These are augmented by the concepts necessitated by the increasing use of the Internet, the World Wide Web, and commonly available analysis tools. Thus, the organization and topic selection of the 14th edition are designed to:

- Present an early introduction to SQL queries.
- Use a "spiral approach" to database design.
- Use a consistent, generic Information Engineering (IE) Crow's Foot E-R diagram notation for data modeling and database design.
- Provide a detailed discussion of specific normal forms within a discussion of normalization that focuses on pragmatic normalization techniques.
- Use current DBMS technology: Microsoft Access 2013, Microsoft SQL Server 2014, Oracle Database 12c (and alternately Oracle Database Express Edition 11g Release 2), and MySQL 5.6.
- Create Web database applications based on widely used Web development technology.
- Provide an introduction to business intelligence (BI) systems.
- Discuss the dimensional database concepts used in database designs for data warehouses and online analytical processing (OLAP).
- Discuss the emerging and important topics of server virtualization, cloud computing, Big Data, and the NoSQL (Not only SQL) movement.

These changes have been made because it has become obvious that the basic structure of the earlier editions (up to and including the 9th edition–the 10th edition introduced many of the changes we used in the 11th, 12th, and 13th editions and retain in the 14th edition) was designed for a teaching environment that no longer exists. The structural changes to the book were made for several reasons:

- Unlike the early years of database processing, today's students have ready access to data modeling and DBMS products.
- Today's students are too impatient to start a class with lengthy conceptual discussions on data modeling and database design. They want to do something, see a result, and obtain feedback.
- In the current economy, students need to reassure themselves that they are learning marketable skills.

Early Introduction of SQL DML

Given these changes in the classroom environment, this book provides an early introduction to SQL data manipulation language (DML) SELECT statements. The discussion of SQL data definition language (DDL) and additional DML statements occurs in Chapters 7 and 8. By encountering SQL SELECT statements in Chapter 2, students learn early in the class how to query data and obtain results, seeing firsthand some of the ways that database technology will be useful to them.

The text assumes that students will work through the SQL statements and examples with a DBMS product. This is practical today because nearly every student has access to Microsoft Access. Therefore, Chapters 1 and 2 and Appendix A–*Getting Started with Microsoft Access 2013*, are written to support an early introduction of Microsoft Access 2013 and the use of Microsoft Access 2013 for SQL queries (Microsoft Access 2013 QBE query techniques are also covered).

If a non-Microsoft Access-based approach is desired, versions of Microsoft SQL Server 2014, Oracle Database, and MySQL 5.6 are readily available for use. Free versions of the three major DBMS products covered in this book (SQL Server 2014 Express Edition, Oracle Database Express Edition 11g Release 2 (Oracle Database XE), and MySQL 5.6 Community Edition) are available for download. Thus, students can actively use a DBMS product by the end of the first week of class.

> **BY THE WAY** The presentation and discussion of SQL are spread over four chapters so students can learn about this important topic in small bites. SQL SELECT statements are taught in Chapter 2. SQL data definition language (DDL) and SQL data manipulation language (DML) statements are presented in Chapter 7. Correlated subqueries and EXISTS/NOT EXISTS statements are described in Chapter 8, while SQL transaction control language (TCL) and SQL data control language (DCL) are discussed in Chapter 9. Each topic appears in the context of accomplishing practical tasks. Correlated subqueries, for example, are used to verify functional dependency assumptions, a necessary task for database redesign.
>
> This box illustrates another feature used in this book: BY THE WAY boxes are used to separate comments from the text discussion. Sometimes they present ancillary material; other times they reinforce important concepts.

A Spiral Approach to the Database Design Process

Today, databases arise from three sources: (1) from the need to integrate existing data from spreadsheets, data files, and database extracts; (2) from the need to develop new information systems projects; and (3) from the need to redesign an existing database to adapt to changing requirements. We believe that the fact that these three sources exist presents instructors with a significant pedagogical opportunity. Rather than teach database design just once from data models, why not teach database design three times, once for each of these sources? In practice, this idea has turned out to be even more successful than expected.

Database Design Iteration 1: Databases from Existing Data

Considering the design of databases from existing data, if someone were to email us a set of tables and say, "Create a database from them," how would we proceed? We would examine the tables in light of normalization criteria and then determine whether the new database was for a production system that allows new data to be inserted for each new transaction, or for a business intelligence (BI) data warehouse that allow users to only query data for use in reports and data analysis. Depending on the answer, we would normalize the data, pulling them apart (for the production transaction processing system), or denormalize the data, joining them together (for the BI system data warehouse). All of this is important for students to know and understand.

Therefore, the first iteration of database design gives instructors a rich opportunity to teach normalization, not as a set of theoretical concepts but rather as a useful toolkit for making design decisions for databases created from existing data. Additionally, the construction of databases from existing data is an increasingly common task that is often assigned to junior staff members. Learning how to apply normalization to the design of databases from existing data not only provides an interesting way of teaching normalization, it is also common and useful!

We prefer to teach and use a pragmatic approach to normalization and present this approach in Chapter 3. However, we are aware that many instructors like to teach normalization in the context of a step-by-step normal form presentation (1NF, 2NF, 3NF, then BCNF), and Chapter 3 now includes additional material to provide more support for this approach as well.

In today's workplace, large organizations are increasingly licensing standardized software from vendors such as SAP, Oracle, and Siebel. Such software already has a database design. But with every organization running the same software, many are learning that they can gain a competitive advantage only if they make better use of the data in those predesigned databases. Hence, students who know how to extract data and create read-only databases for reporting and data mining have obtained marketable skills in the world of ERP and other packaged software solutions.

Database Design Iteration 2: Data Modeling and Database Design

The second source of databases is from new systems development. Although not as common as in the past, many databases are still created from scratch. Thus, students still need to learn data modeling, and they still need to learn how to transform data models into database designs that are then implemented in a DBMS product.

The IE Crow's Foot Model as a Design Standard

This edition uses a generic, standard IE Crow's Foot notation. Your students should have no trouble understanding the symbols and using the data modeling or database design tool of your choice.

IDEF1X (which was used as the preferred E-R diagram notation in the 9th edition of this text) is explained in Appendix C–E-R *Diagrams and the IDEF1X Standard*, in case your students will graduate into an environment where it is used or if you prefer to use it in your classes. UML is explained in Appendix D–E-R *Diagrams and the UML Standard*, in case you prefer to use UML in your classes.

> **BY THE WAY** The choice of a data modeling tool is somewhat problematic. Of the two most readily available tools, Microsoft Visio 2013 has been rewritten as a very rudimentary database design tool, while Oracle's MySQL Workbench is a database design tool, not a data modeling tool. MySQL Workbench cannot produce an N:M relationship as such (as a data model requires) but has to immediately break it into two 1:N relationships (as database design does). Therefore, the intersection table must be constructed and modeled. This confounds data modeling with database design in just the way that we are attempting to teach students to avoid.
>
> To be fair to Microsoft Visio 2013, it is true that data models with N:M relationships can be drawn using the standard Microsoft Visio 2013 drawing tools. Unfortunately, Microsoft has chosen to remove many of the best database design tools that were in Microsoft Visio 2010, and Microsoft Visio 2013 lacks the tools that made it a favorite of Microsoft Access and Microsoft SQL Server users. For a full discussion of these tools, see Appendix E—*Getting Started with the MySQL Workbench Data Modeling Tools*, and Appendix F—*Getting Started with Microsoft Visio 2013*.
>
> Good data modeling tools are available, but they tend to be more complex and expensive. Two examples are Visible Systems' Visible Analyst and CA Technologies' CA ERwin Data Modeler. Visible Analyst is available in a student edition (at a modest price), and a one-year time-limited CA Technologies' ERwin Data Modeler Community Edition suitable for class use can be downloaded from *http://erwin.com/products/data-modeler/community-edition*. CA Technologies has limited the number of objects that can be created by this edition to 25 entities per model and disabled some other features (see *http://erwin.com/content/products/CA-ERwin-r9-Community-Edition-Matrix-na.pdf*), but there is still enough functionality to make this product a possible choice for class use.

Database Design from E-R Data Models

As we discuss in Chapter 6, designing a database from data models consists of three tasks: representing entities and attributes with tables and columns; representing maximum cardinality by creating and placing foreign keys; and representing minimum cardinality via constraints, triggers, and application logic.

The first two tasks are straightforward. However, designs for minimum cardinality are more difficult. Required parents are easily enforced using NOT NULL foreign keys and referential integrity constraints. Required children are more problematic. In this book, however, we simplify the discussion of this topic by limiting the use of referential integrity actions and by supplementing those actions with design documentation. See the discussion around Figure 6-29.

Although the design for required children is complicated, it is important for students to learn. It also provides a reason for students to learn about triggers as well. In any case, the discussion of these topics is much simpler than it was in prior editions because of the use of the IE Crow's Foot model and ancillary design documentation.

Database Implementation from Database Designs

Of course, to complete the process, a database design must be implemented in a DBMS product. This is discussed in Chapter 7, where we introduce SQL DDL for creating tables and SQL DML for populating the tables with data.

> **BY THE WAY** David Kroenke is the creator of the semantic object model (SOM). The SOM is presented in Appendix H—*The Semantic Object Model*. The E-R data model is used everywhere else in the text.

Database Design Iteration 3: Database Redesign

Database redesign, the third iteration of database design, is both common and difficult. As stated in Chapter 8, information systems cause organizational change. New information systems give users new behaviors, and as users behave in new ways, they require changes in their information systems.

Database redesign is by nature complex. Depending on your students, you may wish to skip it, and you can do so without loss of continuity. Database redesign is presented after the discussion of SQL DDL and DML in Chapter 7 because it requires the use of advanced SQL. It also provides a practical reason to teach correlated subqueries and EXISTS/NOT EXISTS statements.

Active Use of a DBMS Product

We assume that students will actively use a DBMS product. The only real question becomes "which one?" Realistically, most of us have four alternatives to consider: Microsoft Access, Microsoft SQL Server, Oracle Database, and MySQL. You can use any of those products with this text, and tutorials for each of them are presented for Microsoft Access 2013 (Appendix A), SQL Server 2014 (Chapter 10A), Oracle Database 12*c* and Oracle Database Express Edition 11*g* Release 2 (Chapter 10B), and MySQL 5.6 (Chapter 10C). Given the limitations of class time, it is probably necessary to pick and use just one of these products. You can often devote a portion of a lecture to discussing the characteristics of each, but it is usually best to limit student work to one of them. The possible exception to this is starting the course with Microsoft Access and then switching to a more robust DBMS product later in the course.

Using Microsoft Access 2013

The primary advantage of Microsoft Access is accessibility. Most students already have a copy, and, if not, copies are easily obtained. Many students will have used Microsoft Access in their introductory or other classes. Appendix A–*Getting Started with Microsoft Access 2013* is a tutorial on Microsoft Access 2013 for students who have not used it but who wish to use it with this book.

However, Microsoft Access has several disadvantages. First, as explained in Chapter 1, Microsoft Access is a combination application generator and DBMS. Microsoft Access confuses students because it confounds database processing with application development. Also, Microsoft Access 2013 hides SQL behind its query processor and makes SQL appear as an afterthought rather than a foundation. Furthermore, as discussed in Chapter 2, Microsoft Access 2013 does not correctly process some of the basic SQL-92 standard statements in its default setup. Finally, Microsoft Access 2013 does not support triggers. You can simulate triggers by trapping Windows events, but that technique is nonstandard and does not effectively communicate the nature of trigger processing.

Using Microsoft SQL Server 2014, Oracle Database, or MySQL 5.6

Choosing which of these products to use depends on your local situation. Oracle Database 12*c*, a superb enterprise-class DBMS product, is difficult to install and administer. However, if you have local staff to support your students, it can be an excellent choice. Fortunately, Oracle Database Express Edition 11*g* Release 2, commonly referred to as Oracle Database XE, is easy to install, easy to use, and freely downloadable. If you want your students to be able to install Oracle Database on their own computers, use Oracle Database XE. As shown in Chapter 10B, Oracle's SQL Developer GUI tool (or SQL*Plus if you are dedicated to this beloved command-line tool) is a handy tool for learning SQL, triggers, and stored procedures.

Microsoft SQL Server 2014, although probably not as robust as Oracle Database, is easy to install on Windows machines, and it provides the capabilities of an enterprise-class DBMS product. The standard database administrator tool is the Microsoft SQL Server Management Studio GUI tool. As shown in Chapter 10A, SQL Server 2014 can be used to learn SQL, triggers, and stored procedures.

MySQL 5.6, discussed in Chapter 10C, is an open source DBMS product that is receiving increased attention and market share. The capabilities of MySQL are continually being upgraded, and MySQL 5.6 supports stored procedures and triggers. MySQL also has excellent GUI tools in the MySQL Workbench and an excellent command-line tool (the MySQL Command Line Client). It is the easiest of the three products for students to install on their own computers. It also works with the Linux operating system and is popular as part of the AMP (Apache–MySQL–PHP) package (known as WAMP on Windows and LAMP on Linux).

BY THE WAY   Because we only present currently available software products in this book, we cover MySQL 5.6 instead of MySQL 5.7. However, MySQL 5.7 is currently in release candidate status, which means that it will be generally available in the near future. All discussion of MySQL 5.6 in this book will also apply to MySQL 5.7.

BY THE WAY   If the DBMS you use is not driven by local circumstances and you do have a choice, we recommend using Microsoft SQL Server 2014. It has all of the features of an enterprise-class DBMS product, and it is easy to install and use. Another option is to start with Microsoft Access 2013 if it is available and switch to SQL Server 2014 at Chapter 7. Chapters 1 and 2 and Appendix A are written specifically to support this approach. A variant is to use Microsoft Access 2013 as the development tool for forms and reports running against an SQL Server 2014 database.

If you prefer a different DBMS product, you can still start with Microsoft Access 2013 and switch later in the course. See the detailed discussion of the available DBMS products in Chapter 10 for a good review of your options.

Focus on Database Application Processing

In this edition, we clearly draw the line between *application development* per se and *database application processing*. Specifically, we have:

- Focused on specific database dependent applications:
    - Web-based, database-driven applications
    - XML-based data processing
    - Business intelligence (BI) systems applications
- Emphasized the use of commonly available, multiple-OS-compatible application development languages.
- Limited the use of specialized vendor-specific tools and programming languages as much as possible.

There is simply not enough room in this book to provide even a basic introduction to programming languages used for application development such as the Microsoft .NET languages and Java. Therefore, rather than attempting to introduce these languages, we leave them for other classes where they can be covered at an appropriate depth. Instead, we focus on basic tools that are relatively straightforward to learn and immediately applicable to database-driven applications. We use PHP as our Web development language, and we use the readily available NetBeans integrated development environment (IDE) as our development tool. The result is a *very* focused final section of the book, where we deal specifically with the interface between databases and the applications that use them.

> **BY THE WAY**   Although we try to use widely available software as much as possible, there are, of course, exceptions where we must use vendor-specific tools. For BI applications, for example, we draw on Microsoft Excel's PivotTable capabilities and the Microsoft PowerPivot for Microsoft Excel 2013 add-in and on the Microsoft SQL Server 2012 R2 Data Mining Add-ins for Microsoft Office. However, either alternatives to these tools are available (OpenOffice.org DataPilot capabilities, the Palo OLAP Server) or the tools are generally available for download.

Business Intelligence Systems and Dimensional Databases

This edition maintains coverage of business intelligence (BI) systems (Chapter 12 and Appendix J). The chapter includes a discussion of dimensional databases, which are the underlying structure for data warehouses, data marts, and OLAP servers. It still covers data management for data warehouses and data marts and also describes reporting and data mining applications, including OLAP.

Appendix J includes in-depth coverage of two applications that should be particularly interesting to students. The first is RFM analysis, a reporting application frequently used by mail order and e-commerce companies. The complete RFM analysis is accomplished in Appendix J through the use of standard SQL statements. This chapter can be assigned at any point after Chapter 8 and could be used as a motivator to illustrate the practical applications of SQL mid-course. Finally, Appendix K provides additional material on Big Data and NoSQL databases to supplement and support Chapter 12.

Overview of the Chapters in the 14th Edition

Chapter 1 sets the stage by introducing database processing, describing basic components of database systems, and summarizing the history of database processing. If students are using Microsoft Access 2013 for the first time (or need a good review), they will also need to study Appendix A–*Getting Started with Microsoft Access 2013* at this point. Chapter 2 presents SQL SELECT statements. It also includes sections on how to submit SQL statements to Microsoft Access 2013, SQL Server 2014, Oracle Database, and MySQL 5.6.

The next four chapters, Chapters 3 through 6, present the first two iterations of database design. Chapter 3 presents the principles of normalization to Boyce-Codd normal form (BCNF). It describes the problems of multivalued dependencies and explains how to eliminate them. This foundation in normalization is applied in Chapter 4 to the design of databases from existing data.

Chapters 5 and 6 describe the design of new databases. Chapter 5 presents the E-R data model. Traditional E-R symbols are explained, but the majority of the chapter uses IE Crow's Foot notation. Chapter 5 provides a taxonomy of entity types, including strong, ID-dependent, weak but not ID-dependent, supertype/subtype, and recursive. The chapter concludes with a simple modeling example for a university database.

Chapter 6 describes the transformation of data models into database designs by converting entities and attributes to tables and columns, by representing maximum cardinality by creating and placing foreign keys, and by representing minimum cardinality via carefully designed DBMS constraints, triggers, and application code. The primary section of this chapter parallels the entity taxonomy in Chapter 5.

Chapter 7 presents SQL DDL, DML, and SQL/Persistent Stored Modules (SQL/PSM). SQL DDL is used to implement the design of an example introduced in Chapter 6. INSERT, UPDATE, MERGE, and DELETE statements are discussed, as are SQL views. Additionally, the principles of embedding SQL in program code are presented, SQL/PSM is discussed, and triggers and stored procedures are explained.

Database redesign, the third iteration of database design, is described in Chapter 8. This chapter presents SQL statements using correlated subqueries and the SQL EXIST and NOT EXISTS operators, and uses these statements in the redesign process. Reverse engineering is described, and basic redesign patterns are illustrated and discussed.

Chapters 9, 10, 10A, 10B, and 10C consider the management of multiuser organizational databases. Chapter 9 describes database administration tasks, including concurrency, security, and backup and recovery. Chapter 10 is a general introduction to the online Chapters 10A, 10B, and 10C, which describe SQL Server 2014, Oracle Database (both Oracle Database 12c and Oracle Database XE), and MySQL 5.6, respectively. These chapters show how to use these specific products to create database structures and process SQL statements. They also explain concurrency, security, and backup and recovery with each product. The discussion in Chapters 10A, 10B, and 10C parallels the order of discussion in Chapter 9 as much as possible, though rearrangements of some topics are made, as needed, to support the discussion of a specific DBMS product.

BY THE WAY   We have maintained or extended our coverage of Microsoft Access, Microsoft SQL Server, Oracle Database, and MySQL (introduced in *Database Processing: Fundamentals, Design, and Implementation,* 11th edition) in this book. In order to keep the bound book to a reasonable length and to keep the cost of the book down, we have chosen to provide some material by download from our Web site at *www.pearsonhighered .com/kroenke*. There you will find:

- Chapter 10A—*Managing Databases with Microsoft SQL Server 2014*
- Chapter 10B—*Managing Databases with Oracle Database*
- Chapter 10C—*Managing Databases with MySQL 5.6*
- Appendix A—*Getting Started with Microsoft Access 2013*
- Appendix B—*Getting Started with Systems Analysis and Design*
- Appendix C—*E-R Diagrams and the IDEF1X Standard*
- Appendix D—*E-R Diagrams and the UML Standard*
- Appendix E—*Getting Started with MySQL Workbench Data Modeling Tools*
- Appendix F—*Getting Started with Microsoft Visio 2013*
- Appendix G—*Data Structures for Database Processing*
- Appendix H—*The Semantic Object Model*
- Appendix I—*Getting Started with Web Servers, PHP, and the NetBeans IDE*
- Appendix J—*Business Intelligence Systems*
- Appendix K—*Big Data*

Chapters 11 and 12 address standards for accessing databases. Chapter 11 presents ODBC, OLE DB, ADO.NET, ASP.NET, JDBC, and JavaServer Pages (JSP). It then introduces PHP (and the NetBeans IDE) and illustrates the use of PHP for the publication of databases via Web pages. This is followed by a description of the integration of XML and database technology. The chapter begins with a primer on XML and then shows how to use the FOR XML SQL statement in SQL Server.

Chapter 12 concludes the text with a discussion of BI systems, dimensional data models, data warehouses, data marts, server virtualization, cloud computing, Big Data, structured storage, and the Not only SQL movement.

Supplements

This text is accompanied by a wide variety of supplements. Please visit the text's Web site at *www.pearsonhighered.com/kroenke* to access the instructor and student supplements described below. Please contact your Pearson sales representative for more details. All supplements were written by David Auer, Scott Vandenberg, Bob Yoder, and Darren Lim.

For Students

Many of the sample databases used in this text are available online in Microsoft Access, Microsoft SQL Server 2014, Oracle Database, and MySQL 5.6 formats.

For Instructors

At the Instructor Resource Center, *www.pearsonhighered.com/irc*, instructors can access a variety of print, digital, and presentation resources available with this text in downloadable format. Registration is simple and gives instructors immediate access to new titles and new editions. As a registered faculty member, you can download resource files and receive immediate access to and instructions for installing course management content on your campus server. In case you ever need assistance, our dedicated technical support team is ready to help with the media supplements that accompany this text. Visit *http://247.pearsoned.com* for answers to frequently asked questions and toll-free user support phone numbers.

The following supplements are available for download to adopting instructors:

- Instructor's Resource Manual (including database files)
- Test Bank
- TestGen® Computerized Test Bank
- PowerPoint Presentations

Acknowledgments

We are grateful for the support of many people in the development of this 14th edition and previous editions. Thanks to Rick Mathieu at James Madison University for interesting and insightful discussions on the database course. Professor Doug MacLachlan from the Marketing Department at the University of Washington was most helpful in understanding the goals, objectives, and technology of data mining, particularly as it pertains to marketing. Don Nilson, formerly of the Microsoft Corporation, helped us understand the importance of XML to database processing. Kraig Pencil of Western Washington University helped us refine the use of the book in the classroom. Recently David Auer and Xiaofeng Chen team-taught a database class together at Western Washington University, and our interaction and discussions with Professor Chen resulted in several modifications and improvements in this book. Professor Chen also graciously allowed us to adopt some of his classroom examples for use in the books. Thanks are also due to Harold Wise of East Carolina University, Barry Flachsbart of Missouri University of Science and Technology, and Don Malzahn of of Harper College for their comments and SQL code checking. Finally, thanks to Donna Auer for giving us permission to use her painting *Lake Samish (Looking Into Water)* as the cover art for this book.

In addition, we wish to thank the reviewers of this edition:

Ann Aksut, *Central Piedmont Community College*
Allen Badgett, *Oklahoma City University*
Rich Beck, *Washington University*
Jeffrey J. Blessing, *Milwaukee School of Engineering*
Alan Brandyberry, *Kent State University*
Larry Booth, *Clayton State University*
Jason Deane, *Virginia Polytechnic Institute and State University*
Barry Flachsbart, *Missouri University of Science and Technology*

Andy Green, *Kennesaw State University*
Dianne Hall, *Auburn University*
Jeff Hassett, *University of Utah*
Barbara Hewitt, *Texas A&M, Kingsville*
William Hochstettler, *Franklin University*
Margaret Hvatum, *St. Louis Community College*
Nitin Kale, *University of Southern California, Los Angeles*
Darrel Karbginsky, *Chemeketa Community College*
Johnny Li, *South University*
Lin Lin, *New Jersey Institute of Technology*
Mike Morris, *Southeastern Oklahoma State University*
Jane Perschbach, *Texas A&M University–Central Texas*
Catherine Ricardo, *Iona College*
Kevin Roberts, *DeVry University*
Ioulia Rytikova, *George Mason University*
Christelle Scharff, *Pace University*
Julian M. Scher, *New Jersey Institute of Technology*
Namchul Shin, *Pace University*
K. David Smith, *Cameron University*
M. Jane Stafford, *Columbia College-Jefferson City*
Marcia Williams, *Bellevue Community College*
Timothy Woodcock, *Texas A&M University-Central Texas*

Finally, we would like to thank Nicole Sam, our editor; Denise Weiss, our Program Manager Ilene Kahn, our Project Manager; and Sue Nodine, our Production Project Manager; for their professionalism, insight, support, and assistance in the development of this project. We would also like to thank Scott Vandenberg and Bod Yoder (both of Siena College) for their detailed comments on the final manuscript–this book would not be what it is without their extensive input. Finally, David Kroenke would like to thank his wife, Lynda, and David Auer would like to thank his wife, Donna, for their love, encouragement, and patience while this project was being completed.

David Kroenke
Seattle, Washington

David Auer
Bellingham, Washington

David M. Kroenke

Work Experience

David M. Kroenke has more than 35 years' experience in the computer industry. He began as a computer programmer for the U.S. Air Force, working both in Los Angeles and at the Pentagon, where he developed one of the world's first DBMS products while part of a team that created a computer simulation of World War III. That simulation served a key role for strategic weapons studies during a 10-year period of the Cold War.

From 1973 to 1978, Kroenke taught in the College of Business at Colorado State University. In 1977, he published the first edition of *Database Processing*, a significant and successful textbook that, more than 30 years later, you now are reading in its 14th edition. In 1978, he left Colorado State and joined Boeing Computer Services, where he managed the team that designed database management components of the IPAD project. After that, he joined with Steve Mitchell to form Mitchell Publishing and worked as an editor and author, developing texts, videos, and other educational products and seminars. Mitchell Publishing was acquired by Random House in 1986. During those years, he also worked as an independent consultant, primarily as a database disaster repairman helping companies recover from failed database projects.

In 1982, Kroenke was one of the founding directors of the Microrim Corporation. From 1984 to 1987, he served as the Vice President of Product Marketing and Development and managed the team that created and marketed the DBMS product R:base 5000 as well as other related products.

For the next five years, Kroenke worked independently while he developed a new data modeling language called the *semantic object model*. He licensed this technology to the Wall Data Corporation in 1992 and then served as the Chief Technologist for Wall Data's SALSA line of products. He was awarded three software patents on this technology.

Since 1998, Kroenke has continued consulting and writing. His current interests concern the practical applications of data mining techniques on large organizational databases. An avid sailor, he wrote *Know Your Boat: The Guide to Everything That Makes Your Boat Work*, which was published by McGraw-Hill in 2002.

Consulting

Kroenke has consulted with numerous organizations during his career. In 1978, he worked for Fred Brooks, consulting with IBM on a project that became the DBMS product DB2. In 1989, he consulted for the Microsoft Corporation on a project that became Microsoft Access. In the 1990s, he worked with Computer Sciences Corporation and with General Research Corporation for the development of technology and products that were used to model all of the U.S. Army's logistical data as part of the CALS project. Additionally, he has consulted for Boeing Computer Services, the U.S. Air Force Academy, Logicon Corporation, and other smaller organizations.

Publications

- *Database Processing*, Pearson Prentice Hall, 14 editions, 1977–present (coauthor with David Auer, 11th, 12th, 13th, and 14th editions)

- *Database Concepts*, Pearson Prentice Hall, seven editions, 2004–present (coauthor with David Auer, 3rd, 4th, 5th, 6th, and 7th editions)
- *Using MIS*, Pearson Prentice Hall, eight editions, 2006–present (coauthor with Randall J. Boyle, 8th edition)
- *Experiencing MIS*, Pearson Prentice Hall, six editions, 2007–present (coauthor with Randall J. Boyle, 6th edition)
- *MIS Essentials*, Pearson Prentice Hall, four editions, 2009–present
- *Processes, Systems, and Information: An Introduction to MIS*, Pearson Prentice Hall, two editions, 2013–present (coauthor with Earl McKinney)
- *Essentials of Processes, Systems, and Information*, Pearson Prentice Hall, 2013 (coauthor with Earl McKinney)
- *Know Your Boat: The Guide to Everything That Makes Your Boat Work*, McGraw-Hill, 2002
- *Management Information Systems*, Mitchell Publishing/Random House, three editions, 1987–1992
- *Business Computer Systems*, Mitchell Publishing/Random House, five editions, 1981–1990
- *Managing Information for Microcomputers*, Microrim Corporation, 1984 (coauthor with Donald Nilson)
- *Database Processing for Microcomputers*, Science Research Associates, 1985 (coauthor with Donald Nilson)
- *Database: A Professional's Primer*, Science Research Associates, 1978

Teaching

Kroenke taught in the College of Business at Colorado State University from 1973 to 1978. He also has taught part time in the Software Engineering program at Seattle University. From 1990 to 1991, he served as the Hanson Professor of Management Science at the University of Washington. Most recently, he taught at the University of Washington from 2002 to 2008. During his career, he has been a frequent speaker at conferences and seminars for computer educators. In 1991, the International Association of Information Systems named him Computer Educator of the Year.

Education

B.S., Economics, U.S. Air Force Academy, 1968
M.S., Quantitative Business Analysis, University of Southern California, 1971
Ph.D., Engineering, Colorado State University, 1977

Personal

Kroenke is married, lives in Seattle, and has two grown children and three grandchildren. He enjoys skiing, sailing, and building small boats. His wife tells him he enjoys gardening as well.

David J. Auer

Work Experience

David J. Auer has more than 30 years' experience teaching college-level business and information systems courses and for the past 20 years has worked professionally in the field of information technology. He served as a commissioned officer in the U.S. Air Force, with assignments to NORAD and the Alaskan Air Command in air defense operations. He later taught both business administration and music classes at Whatcom Community College and business courses for the Chapman College Residence Education Center at Whidbey Island Naval Air Station. He was a founder of the Puget Sound Guitar Workshop (now in its 41st year of operations). He worked as a psychotherapist and organizational development consultant for the Whatcom Counseling and Psychiatric Clinic's Employee Assistance Program and provided training for the Washington State Department of Social and Health Services. He taught for Western Washington University's College of Business and

Economics from 1981 to June 2015, and served as the college's Director of Information Systems and Technology Services from 1994 to 2014. Now a Senior Instructor Emeritus at Western Washington University, he continues his writing projects.

Publications

- *Database Processing*, Pearson Prentice Hall, four editions, 2009-present (coauthor with David Kroenke)
- *Database Concepts*, Pearson Prentice Hall, five editions, 2007-present (coauthor with David Kroenke)
- *Network Administrator: NetWare 4.1*, Course Technology, 1997 (coauthor with Ted Simpson and Mark Ciampa)
- *New Perspectives on Corel Quattro Pro 7.0 for Windows 95*, Course Technology, 1997 (coauthor with June Jamrich Parsons, Dan Oja, and John Leschke)
- *New Perspectives on Microsoft Excel 7 for Windows 95—Comprehensive*, Course Technology, 1996 (coauthor with June Jamrich Parsons and Dan Oja)
- *New Perspectives on Microsoft Office Professional for Windows 95—Intermediate*, Course Technology, 1996 (coauthor with June Jamrich Parsons, Dan Oja, Beverly Zimmerman, Scott Zimmerman, and Joseph Adamski)
- *Microsoft Excel 5 for Windows—New Perspectives Comprehensive*, Course Technology, 1995 (coauthor with June Jamrich Parsons and Dan Oja)
- *Introductory Quattro Pro 6.0 for Windows*, Course Technology, 1995 (coauthor with June Jamrich Parsons and Dan Oja)
- *Introductory Quattro Pro 5.0 for Windows*, Course Technology, 1994 (coauthor with June Jamrich Parsons and Dan Oja)
- *The Student's Companion for Use with Practical Business Statistics*, Irwin, two editions 1991 and 1993

Teaching

Auer taught in the College of Business and Economics at Western Washington University from 1981 to June 2015. From 1975 to 1981, he taught part time for community colleges, and from 1981 to 1984, he taught part time for the Chapman College Residence Education Center System. During his career, he has taught a wide range of courses in Quantitative Methods, Production and Operations Management, Statistics, Finance, and Management Information Systems. In MIS, he has taught Principles of Management Information Systems, Business Database Development, Computer Hardware and Operating Systems, Telecommunications, Network Administration, and Fundamentals of Web Site Development.

Education

B.A., English Literature, University of Washington, 1969
B.S., Mathematics and Economics, Western Washington University, 1978
M.A., Economics, Western Washington University, 1980
M.S., Counseling Psychology, Western Washington University, 1991

Personal

Auer is married, lives in Bellingham, Washington, and has two grown children and four grandchildren. He is active in his community, where he has been president of his neighborhood association and served on the City of Bellingham Planning and Development Commission. He enjoys music, playing acoustic and electric guitar, five-string banjo, and a bit of mandolin.

Getting Started

The two chapters in Part 1 provide an introduction to database processing. In Chapter 1, we discuss the importance of databases to support Internet Web applications and smartphone apps. We then consider the characteristics of databases and describe important database applications. Chapter 1 discusses the various database components, provides a survey of the knowledge you need to learn from this text, and also summarizes the history of database processing.

You will start working with a database in Chapter 2 and use that database to learn how to use Structured Query Language (SQL), a database-processing language, to query database data. You will learn how to query both single and multiple tables. Together, these two chapters will give you a sense of what databases are and how they are processed.

PART

1

1

Introduction

Chapter Objectives

- To understand the importance of databases in Internet Web applications and smartphone apps
- To understand the nature and characteristics of databases
- To survey some important and interesting database applications
- To gain a general understanding of tables and relationships
- To describe the components of a Microsoft Access database system and explain the functions they perform
- To describe the components of an enterprise-class database system and explain the functions they perform
- To define the term *database management system* (DBMS) and describe the functions of a DBMS

- To define the term *database* and describe what is contained within the database
- To define the term *metadata* and provide examples of metadata
- To define and understand database design from existing data
- To define and understand database design as new systems development
- To define and understand database design in database redesign
- To understand the history and development of database processing

This chapter discusses the importance of databases in the Internet world, and then introduces database processing concepts. We will first consider the nature and characteristics of databases and then survey a number of important and interesting database applications. Next, we will describe the components of a database system and then, in general terms, describe how databases are designed. After that, we will survey the knowledge that you need to work with databases as an application developer or as a database administrator. Finally, we conclude this introduction with a brief history of database processing.

To really understand databases and database technology requires that you actively use some database product. Fortunately, in today's computer environment, easily obtainable versions of most major database products are available, and we will make use of them. However, this chapter assumes a minimal knowledge of database use. It assumes that you have used a basic database product such as Microsoft Access to enter data into a form, to produce a report, and possibly to execute a query. If you have not done these things, you should obtain a copy of Microsoft Access 2013 and work through the tutorial in Appendix A.

The Importance of Databases in the Internet and Smartphone World

Let's stop for a moment and consider the incredible information technology available for our use today.

The **Personal Computer (PC)** became widely available with the introduction of the **Apple II** in 1977 and the **IBM Personal Computer (IBM PC)** in 1981. PCs were networked into **Local Area Networks (LANs)** using the **Ethernet networking technology** which was developed at the Xerox Palo Alto Research Center in the early 1970's and adopted as a national standard in 1983.

The **Internet**—the global computer network of networks—was created as the **ARPANET** in 1969, and then grew and was used to connect all the LANs (and other types of networks). The Internet became widely known and used when the **World Wide Web** (also referred to as **the Web** and **WWW**) became easily accessible in 1993. Everyone got a computer software application called a **Web browser** and starting *browsing* to **Web sites**. Online retail Web sites such as Amazon.com (online since 1995) and "brick-and-mortar" stores with an online presence such as Best Buy appeared, and people started extensively *shopping online*.

In the early 2000s, **Web 2.0**[1] Web sites started to appear—Web sites that allowed users to add content to Web sites that had previously held static content. Web applications such as Facebook, Wikipedia, and Twitter appeared and flourished.

In a parallel development, the **mobile phone** or **cell phone** was demonstrated and developed for commercial use in the 1970s. After decades of mobile phone and cell phone network infrastructure development, the **smartphone** appeared. Apple brought out the **iPhone** in 2007. Google created the **Android operating system**, and the first Android based smartphone entered the market in 2008. Seven years later, in 2015 (as this is being written), smartphones and **tablet computers (tablets)** are widely used, and thousands of application programs known as **apps** are widely available and in daily use. Most Web applications now have corresponding smartphone and tablet apps (you can "tweet" from either your computer or your smartphone)!

What many people do not understand is that in today's Web application and smartphone app environment, most of what they do depends upon databases.

We can define **data** as recorded facts and numbers. We can initially define a *database* (we will give a better definition later in this chapter) as the structure used to hold or store that data. We process that data to provide *information* (which we also define in more detail later in this chapter) for use in the Web applications and smartphone apps.

Do you have a Facebook account? If so, all your posts, your comments, your "likes," and other data you provide to Facebook (such as photos) are stored in a *database*. When your friend posts an item, it is initially stored in the *database* and then displayed to you.

Do you have a Twitter account? If so, all your tweets are stored in a *database*. When your friend tweets something, it is initially stored in the *database* and then displayed to you.

Do you shop at Amazon.com? If so, how do you find what you are looking for? You enter some words in a Search text window on the Amazon home Web page (if you are using a Web browser) and click the Go button. Amazon's computers then search Amazon's *databases* and return a formatted report on screen of the items that matched what you searched for.

The search process is illustrated in Figure 1-1, where we search the Pearson Higher Education Web site for books authored by *David Kroenke*. Figure 1-1(a) shows the upper portion

---

[1] The term Web 2.0 was originated by Darcy DiNucci in 1999, and introduced to the world at large in 2004 by publisher Tim O'Reilly. See the Wikipedia article **Web 2.0** (accessed January 2015).

The Pearson Higher Education Web site Home Page

The **Search catalog** button

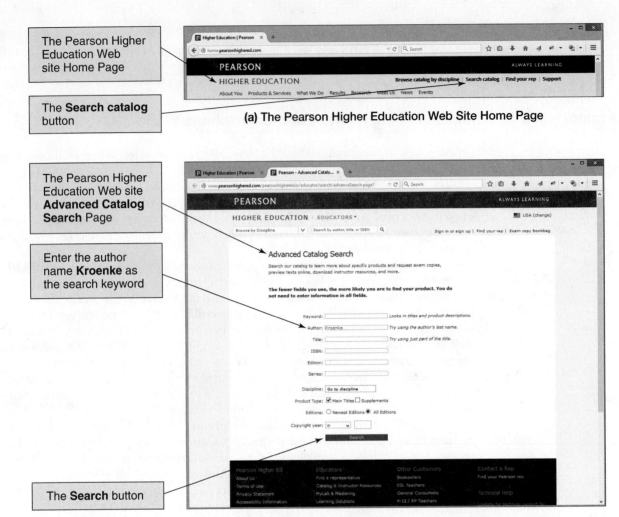

(a) The Pearson Higher Education Web Site Home Page

The Pearson Higher Education Web site **Advanced Catalog Search** Page

Enter the author name **Kroenke** as the search keyword

The **Search** button

(b) Entering Author Name *Kroenke* as The Search Keyword

The **Search Results** Web page

Each block of text is the data on one book by **Kroenke** as found in the database

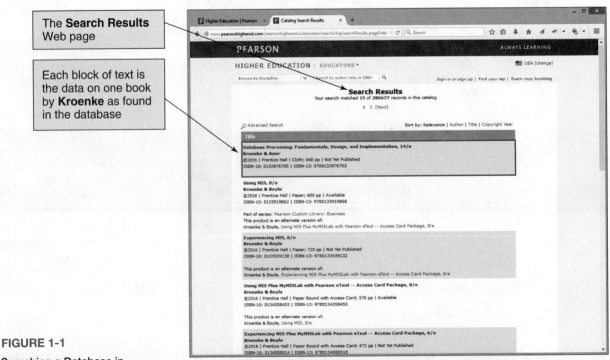

FIGURE 1-1

Searching a Database in a Web Browser

(c) Books by Author *Kroenke* Found in the Database

of the Pearson Higher Education Web site Home page. While many Web sites (including Amazon.com, REI, and Best Buy) have a text box for entering search key words on the Home page itself for immediate use, at the Pearson site we have to click on a **Search catalog** button to access the search function on the *Advanced Catalog Search* page shown in Figure 1-1(b). On this page, we enter the author name *Kroenke* in the Author text box, and then click the **Search** button. The Pearson catalog database is searched, and the Web application returns a *Search Results* page containing a listing of books authored by David Kroenke (appropriately starting with the listing for *this* book), as shown in Figure 1-1(c).

> **BY THE WAY**   It is much more effective to see this process then to just read about it. Take a minute, open a Web browser and go to Amazon.com (or any other online retailer, such as Best Buy, Crutchfield, or REI). Search for something you are interested in, and watch the database search results be displayed for you. You just used a *database*.

> **BY THE WAY**   Even if you are simply shopping in a local grocery store (or a coffee shop or pizzeria), you are interacting with databases. Businesses use **Point of Sale (POS) systems** to record every purchase in a database, to monitor inventory, and, if you have a sales promotion card from the store (the one you use to get those special prices for "card holders only"), to keep track of everything you buy for marketing purposes. All the data POS systems gather is stored in, of course, a *database*.

The use of databases by Web applications and smartphone apps is illustrated in Figure 1-2. In this figure, people have computers (desktop or notebook) and smartphones, which are examples of **devices** used by people, who are referred to as **users**. On these devices are **client** applications (Web browsers, apps) used by people to obtain **services** such are searching, browsing, on-line purchasing, and tweeting over the Internet or cell phone networks. These services are provided by **server** computers, and these are the computers that hold the databases containing the data needed by the client applications.

This structure is known as **client-server architecture**, and it supports most of the Web applications in use today. The simple fact is that without databases, we could not have the ubiquitous Web applications and apps that are currently used by so many people.

The Characteristics of Databases

The purpose of a database is to help people keep track of things, and the most commonly used type of database is the **relational database**. We will discuss the relational database model in depth in Chapter 3, so for now we just need to understand a few basic facts about how a relational database helps people track things of interest to them.

A relational database stores data in tables. A **table** has rows and columns, like those in a spreadsheet. A database usually has multiple tables, and each table contains data about a different type of thing. For example, Figure 1-3 shows a database with two tables: The STUDENT table holds data about students, and the CLASS table holds data about classes.

Each **row** of a table has data about a particular occurrence or **instance** of the thing of interest. For example, each row of the STUDENT table has data about one of four students: Cooke, Lau, Harris, and Greene. Similarly, each row of the CLASS table has data about a particular class. Because each row *records* the data for a specific instance, rows are also known as **records**. Each **column** of a table stores a characteristic common to all rows. For example, the first column of STUDENT stores StudentNumber, the second column stores LastName, and so forth. Columns are also known as **fields**.

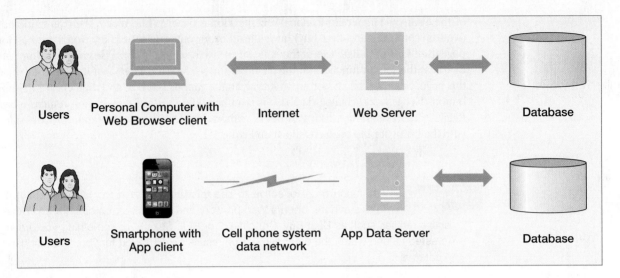

FIGURE 1-2

The Internet and Mobile
Device World

> **BY THE WAY** A table and a *spreadsheet* (also known as a *worksheet*) are very similar in that you can think of both as having rows, columns, and cells. The details that define a table as something different from a spreadsheet are discussed in Chapter 3. For now, the main differences you will see are that tables have column names instead of identifying letters (for example, *Name* instead of *A*) and that the rows are not necessarily numbered.
>
> Although, in theory, you could switch the rows and columns by putting instances in the columns and characteristics in the rows, this is never done. Every database in this text and 99.999999 percent of all databases throughout the world store instances in rows and characteristics in columns.

A Note on Naming Conventions

In this text, table names appear in capital letters. This convention will help you to distinguish table names in explanations. However, you are not required to set table names in capital letters. Microsoft Access and similar programs will allow you to write a table name as STUDENT, student, Student, or stuDent or in some other way.

FIGURE 1-3

The STUDENT and CLASS
Tables

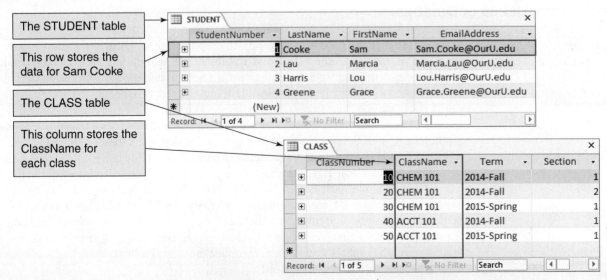

Additionally, in this text column names begin with a capital letter. Again, this is just a convention. You could write the column name Term as term, teRm, or TERM or in any other way. To ease readability, we will sometimes create compound column names in which the first letter of each element of the compound word is capitalized. Thus, in Figure 1-3 the STUDENT table has columns StudentNumber, LastName, FirstName, and EmailAddress. Again, this capitalization is just a convenient convention. However, following these or other consistent conventions will make interpretation of database structures easier. For example, you will always know that STUDENT is the name of a table and that Student is the name of a column of a table.

A Database Has Data and Relationships

Figure 1-3 illustrates how database tables are structured to store data, but a database is not complete unless it also shows the relationships among the rows of data. To see why this is important, examine Figure 1-4. In this figure, the database contains all of the basic data shown in Figure 1-3 together with a GRADE table. Unfortunately, the relationships among the data are missing. In this format, the GRADE data are useless. It is like the joke about the sports commentator who announced: "Now for tonight's baseball scores: 2–3, 7–2, 1–0, and 4–5." The scores are useless without knowing the teams that earned them. Thus, a database contains both data and the relationships among the data.

Figure 1-5 shows the complete database that contains not only the data about students, classes, and grades but also the relationships among the rows in those tables. For example, StudentNumber 1, who is Sam Cooke, earned a Grade of 3.7 in ClassNumber 10, which is Chem101. He also earned a Grade of 3.5 in ClassNumber 40, which is Acct101.

Figure 1-5 illustrates an important characteristic of database processing. Each row in a table is uniquely identified by a **primary key**, and the values of these keys are used to create the relationships between the tables. For example, in the STUDENT table StudentNumber serves as the primary key. Each value of StudentNumber is unique and identifies a particular student. Thus, StudentNumber 1 identifies Sam Cooke. Similarly, ClassNumber in the CLASS table identifies each class. If the numbers used in primary key columns such as

FIGURE 1-4

The STUDENT, CLASS, and GRADE Tables

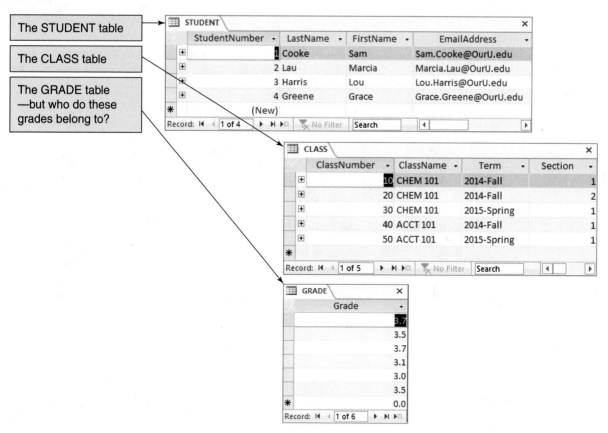

The STUDENT table

The CLASS table

The GRADE table —but who do these grades belong to?

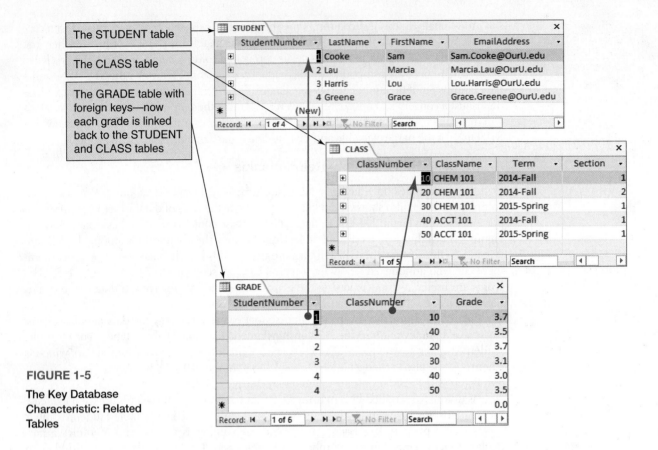

FIGURE 1-5

The Key Database
Characteristic: Related
Tables

StudentNumber and ClassNumber are automatically generated and assigned in the database itself, then the key is also called a **surrogate key**.

By comparing Figures 1-6 and 1-3, we can see how the primary keys of STUDENT and CLASS were added to the GRADE table to provide GRADE with a primary key of (StudentNumber, ClassNumber) to uniquely identify each row. When more than one column in a table must be combined to form the primary key, we call this a **composite key**. More important, in GRADE StudentNumber and ClassNumber each now serves as a **foreign key**. A foreign key provides the link between two tables. By adding a foreign key, we create a **relationship** between the two tables.

Figure 1-6 shows a Microsoft Access 2013 view of the tables and relationships shown in Figure 1-3. In Figure 1-6, primary keys in each table are marked with key symbols, and connecting lines representing the relationships are drawn from the foreign keys (in GRADE) to the corresponding primary keys (in STUDENT and CLASS). The symbols on the relationship line (the number 1 and the infinity symbol) mean that, for example, one student in STUDENT can be linked to many grades in GRADE.

Databases Create Information

In order to make decisions, we need information upon which to base those decisions. Because we have already defined *data* as recorded facts and numbers, we can now define[2] **information** as:

- Knowledge derived from data
- Data presented in a meaningful context
- Data processed by summing, ordering, averaging, grouping, comparing, or other similar operations

---

[2]These definitions are from David M. Kroenke's books *Using MIS*, 8th ed. (Upper Saddle River, NJ: Prentice-Hall, 2016) and *Experiencing MIS*, 6th ed. (Upper Saddle River, NJ: Prentice-Hall, 2016). See these books for a full discussion of these definitions as well as a discussion of a fourth definition, "a difference that makes a difference."

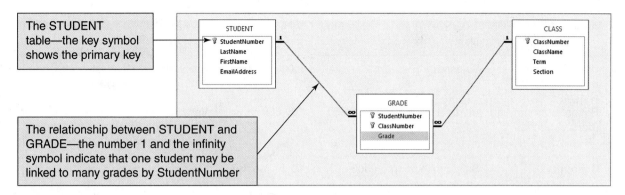

The STUDENT table—the key symbol shows the primary key

The relationship between STUDENT and GRADE—the number 1 and the infinity symbol indicate that one student may be linked to many grades by StudentNumber

FIGURE 1-6

Microsoft Access 2013 View of Tables and Relationships

Databases record facts and figures, so they record data. They do so, however, in a way that enables them to produce information. The data in Figure 1-3 can be manipulated to produce a student's GPA, the average GPA for a class, the average number of students in a class, and so forth. In Chapter 2, you will be introduced to a language called Structured Query Language (SQL) that you can use to produce information from database data.

To summarize, relational databases store data in tables, and they represent the relationships among the rows of those tables. They do so in a way that facilitates the production of information. We will discuss the relational database model in depth in Part 2 of this book.

Database Examples

Today, database technology is part of almost every information system. This fact is not surprising when we consider that every information system needs to store data and the relationships among those data. Still, the vast array of applications that use this technology is staggering. Consider, for example, the applications listed in Figure 1-7.

Single-User Database Applications

In Figure 1-7, the first application is used by a single salesperson to keep track of the customers she has called and the contacts that she's had with them. Most salespeople do not build their own contact manager applications; instead, they license products such as GoldMine or ACT!.

Multiuser Database Applications

The next applications in Figure 1-7 are those that involve more than one user. The patient-scheduling application, for example, may have 15 to 50 users. These users will be appointment clerks, office administrators, nurses, dentists, doctors, and so forth. A database like this one may have as many as 100,000 rows of data in perhaps 5 or 10 different tables.

When more than one user employs a database application, there is always the chance that one user's work may interfere with another's. Two appointment clerks, for example, might assign the same appointment to two different patients. Special concurrency-control mechanisms are used to coordinate activity against the database to prevent such conflict. You will learn about these mechanisms in Chapter 9.

The third row of Figure 1-7 shows an even larger database application. A customer relationship management (CRM) system is an information system that manages customer contacts from initial solicitation through acceptance, purchase, continuing purchase, support, and so forth. CRM systems are used by salespeople, sales managers, customer service and support staff, and other personnel. A CRM database in a larger company might

Application	Example Users	Number of Users	Typical Size	Remarks
Sales contact manager	Salesperson	1	2,000 rows	Products such as GoldMine and Act! are database centric.
Patient appointment (doctor, dentist)	Medical office	15 to 50	100,000 rows	Vertical market software vendors incorporate databases into their software products.
Customer relationship management (CRM)	Sales, marketing, or customer service departments	500	10 million rows	Major vendors such as Microsoft and Oracle PeopleSoft Enterprise build applications around the database.
Enterprise resource planning (ERP)	An entire organization	5,000	10 million+ rows	SAP uses a database as a central repository for ERP data.
E-commerce site	Internet users	Possibly millions	1 billion+ rows	Drugstore.com has a database that grows at the rate of 20 million rows per day!
Digital dashboard	Senior managers	500	100,000 rows	Extractions, summaries, and consolidations of operational databases.
Data mining	Business analysts	25	100,000 to millions+	Data are extracted, reformatted, cleaned, and filtered for use by statistical data mining tools.

FIGURE 1-7

Example Database Applications

have 500 users and 10 million or more rows in perhaps 50 or more tables. According to Microsoft, in 2004 Verizon had an SQL Server customer database that contained more than 15 terabytes of data. If that data were published in books, a bookshelf 450 miles long would be required to hold them.

Enterprise resource planning (ERP) is an information system that touches every department in a manufacturing company. It includes sales, inventory, production planning, purchasing, and other business functions. SAP is the leading vendor of ERP applications, and a key element of its product is a database that integrates data from these various business functions. An ERP system may have 5,000 or more users and perhaps 100 million rows in several hundred tables.

E-Commerce Database Applications

E-commerce is another important database application. Databases are a key component of e-commerce order entry, billing, shipping, and customer support. Surprisingly, however, the largest databases at an e-commerce site are not order-processing databases. The largest databases are those that track customer browser behavior. Most of the prominent e-commerce companies, such as Amazon.com and Drugstore.com, keep track of the Web pages and the Web page components that they send to their customers. They also track customer clicks, additions to shopping carts, order purchases, abandoned shopping carts, and so forth.

E-commerce companies use Web activity databases to determine which items on a Web page are popular and successful and which are not. They also can conduct experiments to determine if a purple background generates more orders than a blue one, and so forth. Such Web usage databases are huge. For example, Drugstore.com adds 20 million rows to its Web log database each day!

Reporting and Data Mining Database Applications

Two other example applications in Figure 1-7 are digital dashboards and data mining applications. These applications use the data generated by order processing and other operational systems to produce information to help manage the enterprise. Such applications do not generate new data, but instead summarize existing data to provide insights to management. Digital dashboards and other reporting systems assess past and current performance. Data mining applications predict future performance. We will consider such applications in Chapter 12. The bottom line is that database technology is used in almost every information system and involves databases ranging in size from a few thousand rows to many millions of rows.

> **BY THE WAY**   Do not assume that just because a database is small that its structure is simple. For example, consider parts distribution for a company that sells $1 million in parts per year and parts distribution for a company that sells $100 million in parts per year. Despite the difference in sales, the companies have similar databases. Both have the same kinds of data, about the same number of tables of data, and the same level of complexity in data relationships. Only the amount of data varies from one to the other. Thus, although a database for a small business may be small, it is not necessarily simple.

The Components of a Database System

As shown in Figure 1-8, a **database system** is typically defined to consist of four components: users, the database application, the database management system (DBMS), and the database. However, given the importance of **Structured Query Language (SQL)**, an internationally recognized standard language that is understood by all commercial DBMS products, in database processing and the fact that database applications typically send SQL statements to the DBMS for processing, we can refine our illustration of a database system to appear as shown in Figure 1-9.

Starting from the right of Figure 1-9, the **database** is a collection of related tables and other structures. The **database management system (DBMS)** is a computer program used to create, process, and administer the database. The DBMS receives requests encoded in SQL and translates those requests into actions on the database. The DBMS is a large, complicated program that is licensed from a software vendor; companies almost never write their own DBMS programs.

A **database application** is a set of one or more computer programs that serves as an intermediary between the user and the DBMS. Application programs read or modify database data by sending SQL statements to the DBMS. Application programs also present data to users in the format of forms and reports. Application programs can be acquired from software vendors, and they are also frequently written in-house. The knowledge you gain from this text will help you write database applications.

Users, the final component of a database system, employ a database application to keep track of things. They use forms to read, enter, and query data, and they produce reports to convey information.

FIGURE 1-8

The Components
of a Database System

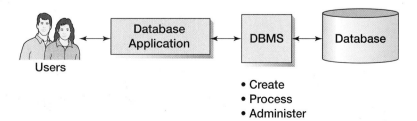

FIGURE 1-9

The Components of a
Database Systems with SQL

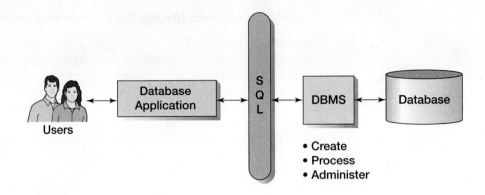

Database Applications and SQL

Figure 1-9 shows that users interact directly with database applications. Figure 1-10 lists the basic functions of database applications.

First, an application program creates and processes forms. Figure 1-11 shows a typical form for entering and processing student enrollment data for the Student-Class-Grade database shown in Figures 1-5 and 1-6. Notice that this form hides the structure of the underlying tables from the user. By comparing the tables and data in Figure 1-5 to the form in Figure 1-11, we can see that data from the CLASS table appears at the top of the form, while data from the STUDENT table is presented in a tabular section labeled Class Enrollment Data.

The goal of this form, like that for all data entry forms, is to present the data in a format that is useful for the users, regardless of the underlying table structure. Behind the form, the application processes the database in accordance with the users' actions. The application generates an SQL statement to insert, update, or delete data for any of the tables that underlie this form.

The second function of application programs is to process user queries. The application program first generates a query request and sends it to the DBMS. Results are then formatted and returned to the user. Applications use SQL statements and pass them to the DBMS for processing. To give you a taste of SQL, here is a sample SQL statement for processing the STUDENT table in Figure 1-5:

```
SELECT    LastName, FirstName, EmailAddress
FROM      STUDENT
WHERE     StudentNumber > 2;
```

This SQL statement is a query statement, which asks the DBMS to obtain specific data from a database. In this case, the query asks for the last name, first name, and e-mail address of all students having a StudentNumber greater than 2. The results of this SQL statement are shown (as displayed in Microsoft Access 2013) in Figure 1-12. As shown in Figure 1-12, running this SQL statement will produce the LastName, FirstName, and EmailAddress for students Harris and Greene.

FIGURE 1-10

Basic Functions of
Application Programs

Basic Functions of Application Programs
Create and process forms
Process user queries
Create and process reports
Execute application logic
Control the application itself

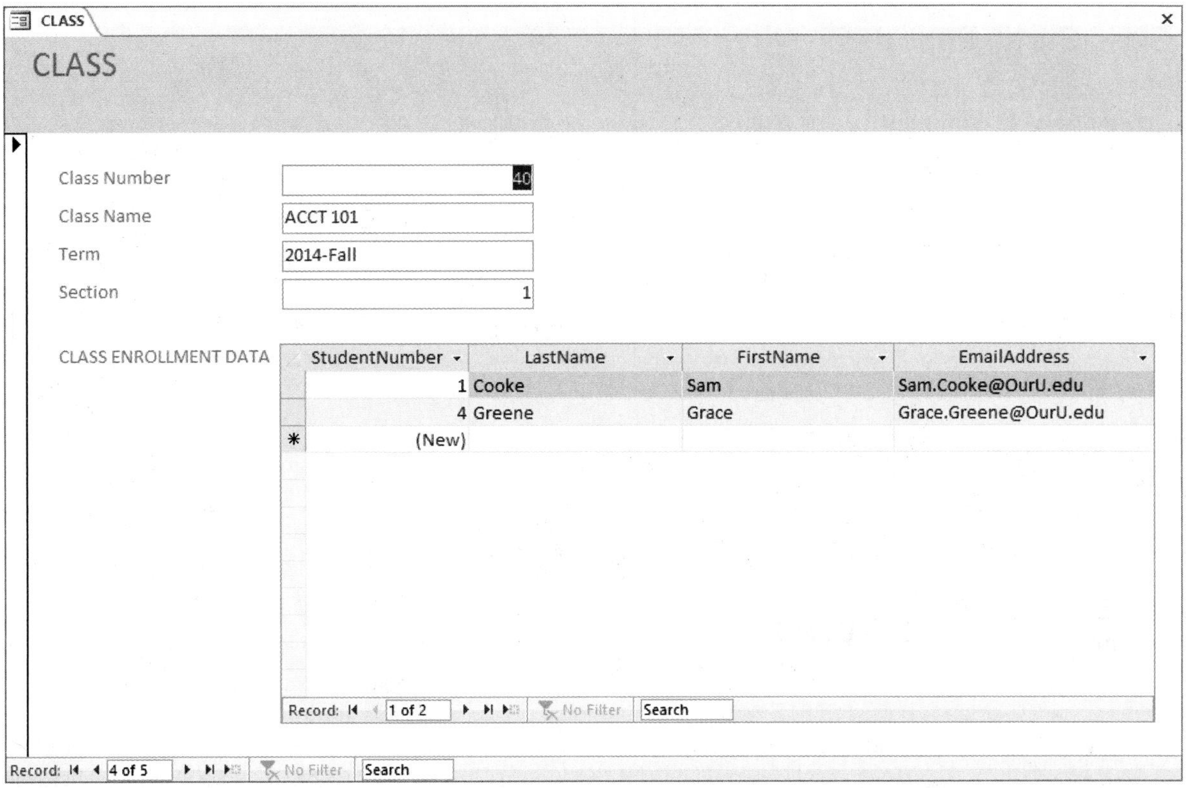

FIGURE 1-11

An Example Data Entry Form

The third function of an application is to create and process reports. This function is somewhat similar to the second because the application program first queries the DBMS for data (again using SQL). The application then formats the query results as a report. Figure 1-13 shows a report that displays all the Student-Class-Grade data shown in Figure 1-5 sorted by ClassNumber and LastName. Notice that the report, like the form in Figure 1-11, is structured according to the users' needs, not according to the underlying table structure.

In addition to generating forms, queries, and reports, the application program takes other actions to update the database in accordance with application-specific logic. For example, suppose a user using an order entry application requests 10 units of a particular item. Suppose further that when the application program queries the database (via the DBMS), it finds that only 8 units are in stock. What should happen? It depends on the logic of that particular application. Perhaps no units should be removed from inventory, and the user should be notified, or perhaps the 8 units should be removed and 2 more placed on backorder. Perhaps some other action should be taken. Whatever the case, it is the job of the application program to execute the appropriate logic.

Finally, the last function for application programs listed in Figure 1-10 is to control the application. This is done in two ways. First, the application needs to be written so that only logical options are presented to the user. For example, the application may generate a menu with user choices. In this case, the application needs to ensure that only appropriate choices are available. Second, the application needs to control data activities with the DBMS. The application might direct the DBMS, for example, to make a certain set of data changes as a unit. The application might tell the DBMS to either make all these changes or none of them. You will learn about such control topics in Chapter 9.

FIGURE 1-12

Example SQL Query Results

Class Grade Report

ClassNumber	ClassName	Term	Section	LastName	FirstName	Grade
10	CHEM 101	2014-Fall	1			
				Cooke	Sam	3.7
20	CHEM 101	2014-Fall	2			
				Lau	Marcia	3.7
30	CHEM 101	2015-Spring	1			
				Harris	Lou	3.1
40	ACCT 101	2014-Fall	1			
				Cooke	Sam	3.5
				Greene	Grace	3.0
50	ACCT 101	2015-Spring	1			
				Greene	Grace	3.5

FIGURE 1-13

Example Report

The DBMS

The DBMS, or database management system, creates, processes, and administers the database. A DBMS is a large, complicated product that is almost always licensed from a software vendor. One DBMS product is Microsoft Access. Other commercial DBMS products are Oracle Database and MySQL, both from Oracle Corporation; SQL Server, from Microsoft; and DB2, from IBM. Dozens of other DBMS products exist, but these five have the lion's share of the market. Figure 1-14 lists the functions of a DBMS.

A DBMS is used to create a database and to create the tables and other supporting structures inside that database. As an example of the latter, suppose that we have an EMPLOYEE table with 10,000 rows and that this table includes a column, DepartmentName, that records the name of the department in which an employee works. Furthermore, suppose that we frequently need to access employee data by DepartmentName. Because this is a large database, searching through the table to find, for example, all employees in the accounting department would take a long time. To improve performance, we can create an index (akin to the **index** at the back of a book) for DepartmentName to show which employees are in which departments. Such an index is an example of a supporting structure that is created and maintained by a DBMS.

The next two functions of a DBMS are to read and modify database data. To do this, a DBMS receives SQL and other requests and transforms those requests into actions on the

FIGURE 1-14

Functions of a DBMS

Functions of a DBMS
Create database
Create tables
Create supporting structures (e.g., indexes)
Modify (insert, update, or delete) database data
Read database data
Maintain database structures
Enforce rules
Control concurrency
Perform backup and recovery

database files. Another DBMS function is to maintain all the database structures. For example, from time to time it might be necessary to change the format of a table or another supporting structure. Developers use a DBMS to make such changes.

With most DBMS products, it is possible to declare rules about data values and have a DBMS enforce them. For example, in the Student-Class-Grade database tables in Figure 1-5, what would happen if a user mistakenly entered a value of 9 for StudentNumber in the GRADE table? No such student exists, so such a value would cause numerous errors. To prevent this situation, it is possible to tell the DBMS that any value of StudentNumber in the GRADE table must already be a value of StudentNumber in the STUDENT table. If no such value exists, the insert or update request should be disallowed. The DBMS then enforces these rules, which are called **referential integrity constraints**.

The last three functions of a DBMS listed in Figure 1-14 have to do with database administration. A DBMS controls **concurrency** by ensuring that one user's work does not inappropriately interfere with another user's work. This important (and complicated) function is discussed in Chapter 9. Also, a DBMS contains a security system that ensures that only authorized users perform authorized actions on the database. For example, users can be prevented from seeing certain data. Similarly, users' actions can be confined to making only certain types of data changes on specified data.

Finally, a DBMS provides facilities for backing up database data and recovering it from backups when necessary. The database, as a centralized repository of data, is a valuable organizational asset. Consider, for example, the value of a book database to a company such as Amazon.com. Because the database is so important, steps need to be taken to ensure that no data will be lost in the event of errors, hardware or software problems, or natural or human catastrophes.

The Database

A database is a *self-describing collection of integrated tables*. **Integrated tables** are tables that store both data and the relationships among the data. The tables in Figure 1-5 are *integrated* because they store not just student, class, and grade data but also data about the relationships among the rows of data.

A database is **self-describing** because it contains a description of itself. Thus, databases contain not only tables of user data but also tables of data that describe that user data. Such descriptive data is called **metadata** because it is *data about data*. The form and format of metadata vary from DBMS to DBMS. Figure 1-15 shows generic metadata tables that describe the tables and columns for the database in Figure 1-5.

You can examine metadata to determine if particular tables, columns, indexes, or other structures exist in a database. For example, the following statement queries the Microsoft SQL Server metadata table SYSOBJECTS to determine if a user table (Type = 'U') named CLASS exists in the database. If it does, then the metadata about the table is displayed.

```
IF EXISTS

     (SELECT     *

      FROM       SYSOBJECTS

      WHERE      [Name]='CLASS'

      AND        Type='U');
```

Do not be concerned with the syntax of this statement. You will learn what it means and how to write such statements yourself as we proceed. For now, just understand that this is one way that database administrators use metadata.

BY THE WAY   Because metadata is stored in tables, you can use SQL to query it, as just illustrated. Thus, by learning how to write SQL to query user tables, you will also learn how to write SQL to query metadata. To do that, you just apply the SQL statements to metadata tables rather than user tables.

FIGURE 1-15

Typical Metadata Tables

USER_TABLES Table

TableName	NumberColumns	PrimaryKey
STUDENT	4	StudentNumber
CLASS	4	ClassNumber
GRADE	3	(StudentNumber, ClassNumber)

USER_COLUMNS Table

ColumnName	TableName	DataType	Length (bytes)
StudentNumber	STUDENT	Integer	4
LastName	STUDENT	Text	25
FirstName	STUDENT	Text	25
EmailAddress	STUDENT	Text	100
ClassNumber	CLASS	Integer	4
Name	CLASS	Text	25
Term	CLASS	Text	12
Section	CLASS	Integer	4
StudentNumber	GRADE	Integer	4
ClassNumber	GRADE	Integer	4
Grade	GRADE	Decimal	(2, 1)

In addition to user tables and metadata, databases contain other elements, as shown in Figure 1-16. These other components will be described in detail in subsequent chapters. For now, however, understand that indexes are structures that speed the sorting and searching of database data. User-defined functions, triggers, and stored procedures are programs that are stored within the database. Triggers are used to maintain database accuracy and consistency and to enforce data constraints. Stored procedures are used for database administration tasks and are sometimes part of database applications. You will learn more about these different elements in Chapters 7, 10, 10A, 10B, and 10C.

Security data define users, groups, and allowed permissions for users and groups. The particulars depend on the DBMS product in use. Finally, backup and recovery data are used to save

FIGURE 1-16

Database Elements

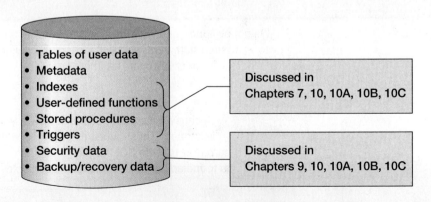

- Tables of user data
- Metadata
- Indexes
- User-defined functions
- Stored procedures
- Triggers
- Security data
- Backup/recovery data

Discussed in
Chapters 7, 10, 10A, 10B, 10C

Discussed in
Chapters 9, 10, 10A, 10B, 10C

database data to backup devices as well as to recover the database data when needed. You will learn more about security and backup and recovery data in Chapters 9, 10, 10A, 10B, and 10C.

Personal Versus Enterprise-Class Database Systems

We can divide database systems and DBMS products into two classes: personal database systems and enterprise-class database systems.

What Is Microsoft Access?

We need to clear up a common misconception: Microsoft Access is *not* just a DBMS. Rather, it is a **personal database system**: a DBMS *plus* an application generator. Although Microsoft Access contains a DBMS engine that creates, processes, and administers the database, it also contains form, report, and query components that are the Microsoft Access application generator. The components of Microsoft Access are shown in Figure 1-17, which illustrates that the Microsoft Access form, report, and query applications create SQL statements and then pass them to the DBMS for processing.

Microsoft Access is a low-end product intended for individuals and small workgroups. As such, Microsoft has done all that it can to hide the underlying database technology from the user. Users interact with the application through data entry forms like the one shown in Figure 1-11. They also request reports and perform queries against the database data. Microsoft Access then processes the forms, produces the reports, and runs the queries. Internally, the application components hidden under the Microsoft Access cover use SQL to call the DBMS, which is also hidden under that cover. At Microsoft, the current DBMS engine within Microsoft Access is called the Access Database Engine (ADE). ADE is a Microsoft Office-specific version of Microsoft's Joint Engine Technology (JET or Jet) database engine. Jet was used as the Microsoft Access database engine until Microsoft Office 2007 was released. Jet itself is still used in the Microsoft Windows operating system, but you seldom hear about Jet because Microsoft does not sell Jet as a separate product.

> **BY THE WAY** Although Microsoft Access is the best-known personal database system, it is not the only one. OpenOffice.org Base is a personal database system distributed as part of the OpenOffice.org software suite, and the personal database system LibreOffice Base is distributed as part of the related LibreOffice software suite.

FIGURE 1-17

Components of a Microsoft Access Database System

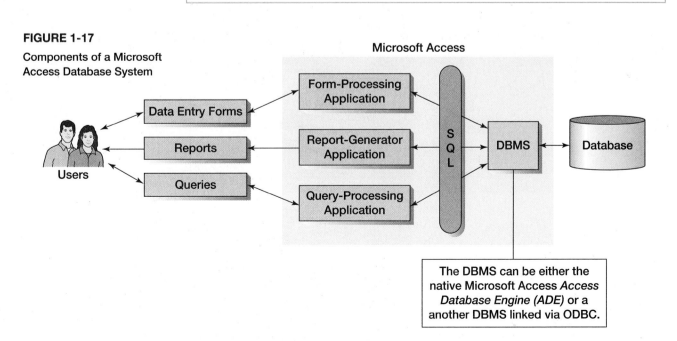

The DBMS can be either the native Microsoft Access *Access Database Engine (ADE)* or a another DBMS linked via ODBC.

Although hiding the technology is an effective strategy for beginners working on small databases, it will not work for database professionals who work with applications, such as most of those described in Figure 1-5. For larger, more complex databases, it is necessary to understand the technology and components that Microsoft hides.

Nonetheless, because Microsoft Access is included in the Microsoft Office suite, it is often the first DBMS used by students. In fact, you may have already learned to use Microsoft Access in other classes you have taken, and in this book we will provide some examples using Microsoft Access 2013. If you are not familiar with Microsoft Access 2013, you should work through Appendix A, "Getting Started with Microsoft Access 2013."

> **BY THE WAY**   With Microsoft Access 2000 and later versions, you can effectively replace the Microsoft Access database engine (either Jet or ADE) with another DBMS (typically Microsoft's enterprise-class DBMS product, Microsoft SQL Server). Microsoft Access 2013 uses the ODBC standard to make these connections, and ODBC is discussed in Chapter 11. You would do this if you wanted to process a large database or if you needed the advanced functions and features of Microsoft SQL Server.

What Is an Enterprise-Class Database System?

Figure 1-18 shows the components of an **enterprise-class database system**. Here, the applications and the DBMS are not under the same cover as they are in Microsoft Access. Instead, the applications are separate from each other and separate from the DBMS.

Database Applications in an Enterprise-Class Database System

Earlier in this chapter, we discussed the basic functions of an application program, and these functions are summarized in Figure 1-10. However, as exemplified by the list in Figure 1-7, dozens of different types of database applications are available, and database applications in an enterprise-class database system introduce functions and features beyond the basics. For example, Figure 1-18 shows applications that connect to the database over a corporate network. Such applications use the *client-server architecture*, described earlier in this chapter, and are called *client-server applications*. In this situation, the application program

FIGURE 1-18

Components of an Enterprise-Class Database System

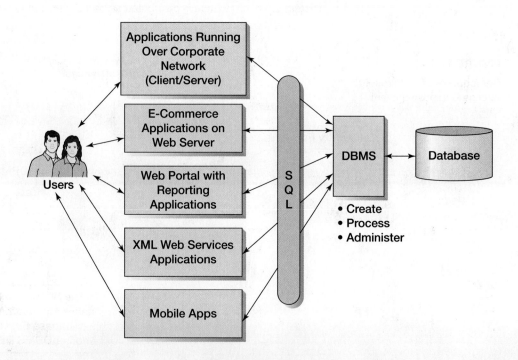

is a client that connects to a database server. Client-server applications are often written in programming languages such as VB.NET, C++, or Java.

A second category of applications in Figure 1-18 is e-commerce and other applications that run on a Web server. Users connect to such applications via Web browsers such as Microsoft Internet Explorer, Mozilla Firefox, and Google Chrome. Common Web servers include Microsoft's Internet Information Server (IIS) and Apache. Common languages for Web server applications are PHP, Java, and the Microsoft .NET languages, such as C#.NET and VB.NET. We will discuss some of the technology for such applications in Chapter 11.

A third category of applications is reporting applications that publish the results of database queries on a corporate portal or other Web site. Such reporting applications are often created using third-party report generation and digital dashboard products from vendors such as IBM (Cognos) and MicroStrategy (MicroStrategy 9). We will describe these applications in Chapter 12.

The fourth category of applications is XML Web services. These applications use a combination of the XML markup language and other standards to enable program-to-program communication. In this way, the code that comprises an application is distributed over several different computers. Web services can be written in Java or any of the .NET languages. We will discuss this important new class of applications in Chapter 12. The final category of applications is mobile apps, such as those used on smartphones. While we will not discuss mobile apps in this book, they are becoming increasingly important in today's connected world.

All of these database applications read and write database data by sending SQL statements to the DBMS. These applications may create forms and reports, or they may send their results to other programs. They also may implement application logic that goes beyond simple form and report processing. For example, an order entry application uses application logic to deal with out-of-stock items and backorders.

The DBMS in an Enterprise-Class Database System

As stated earlier, the DBMS manages the database. It processes SQL statements and provides other features and functions for creating, processing, and administering the database. Figure 1-19 presents the five most prominent DBMS products. The products are shown in order of increasing power, features, and difficulty of use.

Microsoft Access (really the Microsoft ADE) is the easiest to use and the least powerful. Oracle MySQL is a powerful, open source DBMS frequently chosen for Web applications. Microsoft SQL Server has far more power than its stablemate Microsoft Access—it can process larger databases faster, and it includes features for multiuser control, backup and recovery, and other administrative functions. DB2 is a DBMS product from IBM. Most people would agree that it has faster performance than SQL Server, that it can handle larger databases, and that it is also more difficult to use. Finally, the fastest and most capable DBMS is Oracle Database from Oracle Corporation. Oracle Database can be configured to offer very high performance on exceedingly large databases that operate 24/7, year after year. Oracle Database is also far more difficult to use and administer than Microsoft SQL Server.

FIGURE 1-19

Common Professional View of DBMS Products

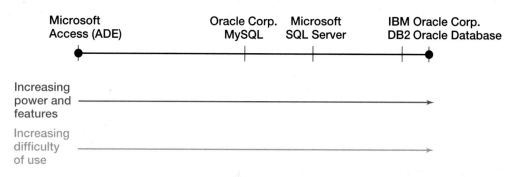

> **BY THE WAY** DBMS products, whether on a personal computer or a server, do not simply run by themselves. Like all other applications, they require that the computer have an **operating system (OS)** installed to handle the basic system operations (writing and reading files, printing, and so on).
>
> Therefore, when you are selecting a DBMS product, you must be aware of which OS will support the use of that product. Today, the main OS products are **Microsoft Windows** (for desktop and notebook computers), **Microsoft Windows Server** (for servers), **Apple OS X** for Mac (previously MacIntosh) desktops and notebooks, and various versions of **Linux** (notable for the shareware development environment of the product).
>
> Microsoft DBMS products (Microsoft Access and Microsoft SQL Server) run *only* on Microsoft operating systems. Oracle Database products will run on both the Windows OS and the Linux OS but not on Apple OS X. MySQL is the only DBMS product that runs on *all* of the three operating systems.

Database Design

Database design (as a process) is the creation of the proper structure of database tables, the proper relationships between tables, appropriate data constraints, and other structural components of the database. Correct database design is both important and difficult. Consequently, the world is full of poorly designed databases. Such databases do not perform well. They may require application developers to write overly complex and contrived SQL to get wanted data, they may be difficult to adapt to new and changing requirements, or they fail in some other way.

Because database design is both important and difficult, we will devote most of the first half of this text to the topic. As shown in Figure 1-20, there are three types of database design:

- Database design from existing data
- Database design for new systems development
- Database redesign of an existing database

Database Design from Existing Data

The first type of database design involves databases that are constructed from existing data, as shown in Figure 1-21. In some cases, a development team is given a set of spreadsheets or a set of text files with tables of data. The team is required to design a database and import the data from those spreadsheets and tables into a new database.

FIGURE 1-20

Types of Database Design Process

Types of Database Design Process
• From existing data (Chapters 3 and 4)
Analyze spreadsheets and other data tables
Extract data from other databases
Design using normalization principles
• New systems development (Chapters 5 and 6)
Create data model from application requirements
Transform data model into database design
• Database redesign (Chapter 8)
Migrate databases to newer databases
Integrate two or more databases
Reverse engineer and design new databases using normalization principles and data model transformation

Note: Chapter 7 discusses database implementation using SQL. You need that knowledge before you can understand database redesign.

FIGURE 1-21

Databases Originating from
Existing Data

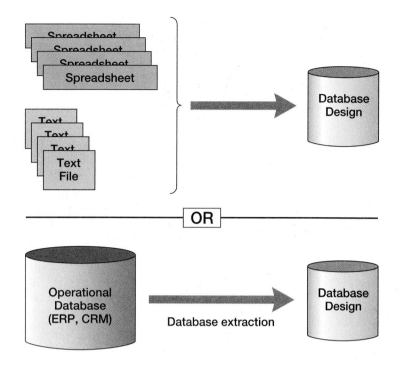

Alternatively, databases can be created from extracts of other databases. This alternative is especially common in business intelligence (BI) systems, which include reporting and data mining applications. For example, data from an operational database, such as a CRM or ERP database, may be copied into a new database that will be used only for studies and analysis. As you will learn in Chapter 12, such databases are used in facilities called **data warehouses** and **data marts**. The data warehouse and data mart databases store data specifically organized for research and reporting purposes, and these data often are exported to other analytical tools, such as SAS's *Enterprise Miner*, IBM's *SPSS Data Modeler*, or TIBCO's *Spotfire*.

When creating a database from existing data, database developers must determine the appropriate structure for the new database. A common issue is how the multiple files or tables in the new database should be related. However, even the import of a single table can pose design questions. Figure 1-22 shows two different ways of importing a simple table of employees and their departments. Should this data be stored as one table or two?

FIGURE 1-22

Data Import: One or Two
Tables?

EmpNum	EmpName	DeptNum	DeptName
100	Jones	10	Accounting
150	Lau	20	Marketing
200	McCauley	10	Accounting
300	Griffin	10	Accounting

(a) One-Table Design

OR?

DeptNum	DeptName
10	Accounting
20	Marketing

EmpNum	EmpName	DeptNum
100	Jones	10
150	Lau	20
200	McCauley	10
300	Griffin	10

(b) Two-Table Design

FIGURE 1-23

Databases Originating from
New Systems Development

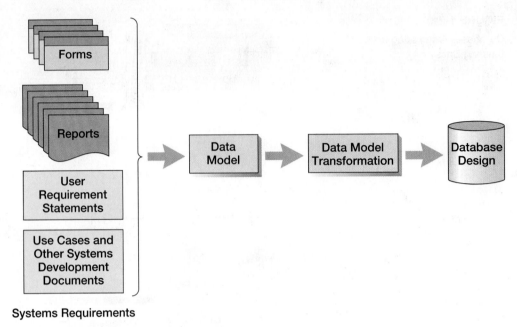

Systems Requirements

Decisions such as this are not arbitrary. Database professionals use a set of principles, collectively called **normalization**, or **normal forms**, to guide and assess database designs. You will learn those principles and their role in database design in Chapter 3.

Database Design for New Systems Development

A second way that databases are designed is for the development of new information systems. As shown in Figure 1-23, requirements for a new system, such as desired data entry forms and reports, user requirements statements, use cases, and other requirements, are analyzed to create the database design.

In all but the simplest system development projects, the step from user requirements to database design is too big. Accordingly, the development team proceeds in two steps. First, the team creates a **data model** from the requirements statements and then transforms that data model into a database design. You can think of a data model as a blueprint that is used as a design aid on the way to a **database design (as a product)**, which is the basis for constructing the actual database in a DBMS product.

Note that we have just given a second meaning to the term *database design*—previously we used it to mean the *process of designing a database*, and now we are using it to mean *the annotated diagram that is the result of that process*. The term is used both ways, so be careful that you understand how it is being used in a particular context! In Chapter 5, you will learn about the most popular data modeling technique: **entity-relationship (ER) data modeling**. You also will see how to use the entity-relationship model to represent a variety of common form and report patterns. Then, in Chapter 6, you will learn how to transform entity-relationship data models into database designs.

Database Redesign

Database redesign also requires that databases are designed. As shown in Figure 1-24, there are two common types of database redesign.

In the first, a database is adapted to new or changing requirements. This process sometimes is called **database migration**. In the migration process, tables may be created, modified, or removed; relationships may be altered; data constraints may be changed; and so forth.

The second type of database redesign involves the integration of two or more databases. This type of redesign is common when adapting or removing legacy systems. It is also common for enterprise application integration, when two or more previously separate information systems are adapted to work with each other.

FIGURE 1-24

Databases Originating from
Database Redesign

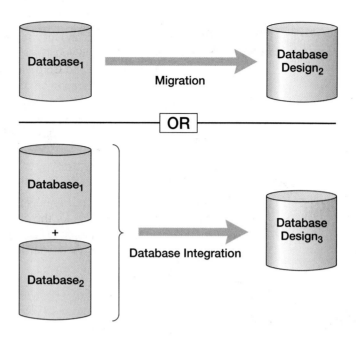

Database redesign is complicated. There is no getting around that fact. If this is your first exposure to database design, your instructor may skip this topic. If this is the case, after you have gained more experience you should reread this material. In spite of its difficulty, database redesign is important.

To understand database redesign, you need to know SQL statements for defining database structures and more advanced SQL statements for querying and updating a database. Consequently, we will not address database redesign until Chapter 8, after we present SQL statements and techniques for creating and altering the tables that make up a database in Chapter 7.

What You Need to Learn

In your career, you may work with database technology either as a user or as a database administrator. As a user, you may be a **knowledge worker** who prepares reports, mines data, and does other types of data analysis, or you may be a **programmer** who writes applications that process the database. Alternatively, you might be a **database administrator** who designs, constructs, and manages the database itself. Users are primarily concerned with constructing SQL statements to store and retrieve the data they want. Database administrators are primarily concerned with the management of the database. The domains for each of these roles are shown in Figure 1-25.

FIGURE 1-25

Working Domains of
Knowledge Workers,
Programmers, and Database
Administrators

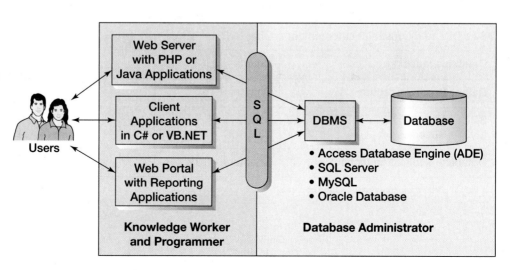

> **BY THE WAY**   The most exciting and interesting jobs in technology are always those on the leading edge. If you live in the United States and are concerned about outsourcing, a study by the Rand Corporation[3] indicates that the most secure jobs in the United States involve the adaptation of new technology to solve business problems in innovative ways. Working with databases will help you learn problem solving skills, and 4 of the top 10 jobs recently listed on the CNNMoney Web site use database knowledge and related skills (See: *http://money.cnn.com/pf/best-jobs/*).

Both users and database administrators need all of the knowledge in this text. However, the emphasis on each topic differs for the two groups. Figure 1-26 shows our opinion as to the relative importance of each topic to each group. Discuss this table with your instructor. He or she may have knowledge about your local job market that affects the relative importance of these topics.

A Brief History of Database Processing

Database processing emerged around 1970 and has been continuously evolving and changing since then. This continual change has made it a fascinating and thoroughly enjoyable field in which to work. Figure 1-27 summarizes the major eras of database processing.

The Early Years

Prior to 1970, all data were stored in separate files, most of which were kept on reels of magnetic tape. Magnetic disks and drums (magnetic cylinders that are now obsolete) were exceedingly expensive and very small. Today's 1.44-megabyte floppy disk (which is now itself

FIGURE 1-26

Priorities of What You Need to Know

Topic	Chapter	Importance to Database Administrator	Importance to Knowledge Worker and Programmer
Basic SQL	Chapter 2	1	2
The relational database model	Chapter 3	2	2
Design via normalization	Chapter 4	2	1
Data models	Chapter 5	2	1
Data model transformation	Chapter 6	2	1
SQL DDL and constraint enforcement	Chapter 7	3	1
Database redesign	Chapter 8	3	1
Database administration	Chapter 9	3	1
SQL Server, Oracle, MySQL specifics	Chapters 10, 10A, 10B, 10C	3	1
Database application technology	Chapters 11, 12	1	3

1 = Very important; 2 = Important; 3 = Less important   Warning: Opinions vary, ask your instructor for his or hers.

---

[3]Lynn A. Karoly and Constantijn W. A. Panis, *The 21st Century at Work* (Santa Monica, CA: The Rand Corporation, 2004).

FIGURE 1-27

Database History

Era	Years	Important Products	Remarks
Predatabase	Before 1970	File managers	All data were stored in separate files. Data integration was very difficult. File storage space was expensive and limited.
Early database	1970–1980	ADABAS, System2000, Total, IDMS, IMS	First products to provide related tables. CODASYL DBTG and hierarchical data models (DL/I) were prevalent.
Emergence of relational model	1978–1985	DB2, Oracle	Early relational DBMS products had substantial inertia to overcome. In time, the advantages weighed out.
Microcomputer DBMS products	1982–1992+	dBase-II, R:base, Paradox, Access	Amazing! A database on a micro. All micro DBMS products were eliminated by Microsoft Access in the early 1990s.
Object-oriented DBMS	1985–2000	Oracle ODBMS and others	Never caught on. Required relational database to be converted. Too much work for perceived benefit.
Web databases	1995–present	IIS, Apache, PHP, ASP.NET, and Java	Stateless characteristic of HTTP was a problem at first. Early applications were simple one-stage transactions. Later, more complex logic developed.
Open source DBMS products	1995–present	MySQL, PostgresQL, and other products	Open source DBMS products provide much of the functionality and features of commercial DBMS products at reduced cost.
XML and Web services	1998–present	XML, SOAP, WSDL, UDDI, and other standards	XML provides tremendous benefits to Web-based database applications. Very important today. May replace relational databases during your career. See Chapter 11 and Appendix K.
Big Data and the NoSQL movement	2009–present	Hadoop, Cassandra, Hbase, CouchDB, MongoDB, and other products	Web applications such as Facebook and Twitter use Big Data technologies, often using Hadoop and related products. The NoSQL movement is really a NoRelationalDB movement that replaces relational databases with non-relational data structures. See Chapter 12 and Appendix K.

a very limited-use technology) has more capacity than many disks of that era. Memory was expensive as well. In 1969, we were processing payroll on a computer that had just 32,000 *bytes* of memory, while the computer on which this history is being written has 16 *gigabytes* of memory.

Integrated processing was an important but very difficult problem. An insurance company, for example, wanted to relate customer account data to customer claim data. Accounts were stored on one magnetic tape, and claims were stored on another. To process claims, the data on the two tapes had to be integrated somehow.

The need for data integration drove the development of the first database technology. By 1973, several commercial DBMS products had emerged. These products were in use by the mid-1970s. The first edition of this text, copyrighted 1977, featured the DBMS products ADABAS, System2000, Total, IDMS, and IMS. Of those five, ADABAS, IDMS, and IMS are still in use, and none of them has substantial market share today.

Those early DBMS products varied in the way that they structured data relationships. One method, called **Data Language/I (DL/I)**, used hierarchies or trees (see Appendix G) to represent relationships. IMS, which was developed and licensed by IBM, was based on this model. IMS had success at many organizations, particularly among large manufacturers, and is still in limited use today.

Another technique for structuring data relationships used data structures called *networks*. The CODASYL Committee (the group that developed the programming language COBOL) sponsored a subcommittee called the Database Task Group (DBTG). This subcommittee developed a standard data model that came to bear its name: the **CODASYL DBTG** model. It was an unnecessarily complicated model (everyone's favorite idea made it into the committee's design), but several successful DBMS products were developed using it. The most successful was IDMS, and its vendor, the Cullinane Corporation, was the first software company to be listed on the New York Stock Exchange. To the best of our knowledge, no IDMS database is in use today.

The Emergence and Dominance of the Relational Model

In 1970, a then little-known IBM engineer named Edgar Frank Codd (better known as just E. F. Codd) published a paper in the *Communications of the ACM*[4] in which he applied the concepts of a branch of mathematics called relational algebra to the problem of "shared data banks," as databases were then known. The results of this work are now the **relational model** for databases, and all relational database DBMS products are built on this model.

Codd's work was at first viewed as too theoretical for practical implementation. Practitioners argued that it was too slow and required so much storage that it would never be useful in the commercial world. However, the relational model and relational database DBMS products became adopted as the best way to create and manage databases.

The 1977 edition of this text featured a chapter on the relational model (which Codd himself reviewed). Many years later, Wayne Ratliff, the creator of the *dBase* series of products for personal computers, stated that he had the idea for *dBase* while reading that very chapter.[5]

> **BY THE WAY** Today, there are as many opportunities for innovation as there were for Wayne Ratliff in 1977. Perhaps you can read Chapter 12 and Appendix K and join the NoSQL and Big Data movements to help develop alternatives to relational database technology. Just as in 1977, no product has a lock on the future. Opportunity awaits you!

---

[4]E. F. Codd, "A Relational Model of Data for Large Shared Databanks," *Communications of the ACM*, June 1970, pp. 377–387. A downloadable copy of this paper in PDF format is available at *http://dl.acm.org/citation.cfm?id=362685*.
[5]C. Wayne Ratliff, "dStory: How I Really Developed dBASE," *Data Based Advisor*, March 1991, p. 94. For more information of Wayne Ratliff, dBase II, and also his work with FoxPro (now Microsoft Visual FoxPro), see the Wikipedia article *Wayne Ratliff* at *http://en.wikipedia.org/wiki/Wayne_Ratliff*. For the history of dBase, see the Wikipedia article *dBase* at *http://en.wikipedia.org/wiki/DBASE*.

The relational model, relational algebra, and, later, SQL made sense. They were not needlessly complicated; rather, they seemed to boil down the data integration problem to a few essential ideas. Over time, Codd convinced IBM management to develop relational-model DBMS products. The result was IBM's DB2 and its variants, which are still very popular today.

Meanwhile, other companies were considering the relational model as well, and by 1980 several more relational DBMS products had been released. The most prominent and important of those was Oracle Corporation's Oracle Database (the product was originally just named *Oracle* but was renamed as *Oracle Database* after Oracle Corporation acquired other products and needed to distinguish its DBMS product from the others). Oracle Database achieved success for many reasons, one of which was that it would run on just about any computer and just about any operating system. (Some users complained, "Yes, and equally badly on all of them." Another, when asked "Should we sell it to communist Russia?" responded, "Only as long as they have to take the documentation with it.")

However, in addition to being able to run on many different types of machines, Oracle Database had, and continues to have, an elegant and efficient internal design. You will learn aspects of that design in the concurrency-control section in Chapter 10B. That excellent design, together with hard-driving and successful sales and marketing, has pushed Oracle Database to the top of the DBMS market.

Meanwhile, Gordon Moore and others were hard at work at Intel. By the early 1980s, personal computers were prevalent, and DBMS products were developed for them. Developers of microcomputer DBMS products saw the advantages of the relational model and developed their products around it. dBase was the most successful of the early products, but another product, R:base, was the first to implement true relational algebra and other operations on the PC. Later, another relational DBMS product named Paradox was developed for personal computers. Eventually, Paradox was acquired by Borland.

Alas, it all came to an end when Microsoft entered the picture. Microsoft released Microsoft Access in 1991 and priced it at $99. No other PC DBMS vendor could survive at that price point. Microsoft Access killed R:base and Paradox, and then Microsoft bought a dBase "work-alike" product called FoxPro and used it to eliminate dBase. Microsoft has now stopped upgrading Microsoft FoxPro, now named Microsoft Visual FoxPro, but Microsoft will continue to support it until 2015.

Thus, Microsoft Access is the only major survivor of that bloodbath of PC DBMS products. Today, the main challenge to Microsoft Access actually comes from the Apache Software Foundation and the open source software development community, who have taken over development of OpenOffice.org, a downloadable suite of free software products that includes the personal database OpenOffice.org Base and its sister product LibreOffice. LibreOffice is a related development of OpenOffice that was started when Oracle Corporation acquired Sun Microsystems in early 2013.

Post-Relational Developments

In the mid-1980s, **object-oriented programming (OOP)** emerged, and its advantages over traditional structured programming were quickly recognized. By 1990, some vendors had developed **object-oriented DBMS (OODBMS or ODBMS)** products. These products were designed to make it easy to store the data encapsulated in OOP objects. Several special-purpose OODBMS products were developed, and Oracle added OOP constructs to Oracle to enable the creation of a hybrid called an **object-relational DBMS**.

OODBMS never caught on, and today that category of DBMS products is fading away. There were two reasons for their lack of acceptance. First, using an OODBMS required that the relational data be converted from relational format to object-oriented format. By the time OODBMS emerged, billions upon billions of bytes of data were stored in relational format in organizational databases. No company was willing to undergo the expensive travail of converting those databases to be able to use the new OODBMS.

Second, object-oriented databases had no substantial advantage over relational databases for most commercial database processing. As you will see in the next chapter, SQL is not object oriented. But it works, and thousands of developers have created programs that use it. Without a demonstrable advantage over relational databases, no organization was willing to take on the task of converting its data to OODBMS format.

Meanwhile, the Internet took off. By the mid-1990s, it was clear that the Internet was one of the most important phenomena in history. It changed, forever, the ways that customers and businesses relate to each other. Early Web sites were nothing more than online brochures, but within a few years dynamic Web sites that involved querying and processing databases began to appear.

However, one substantial problem existed. HTTP is a stateless protocol; a server receives a request from a user, processes the request, and then forgets about the user and the request. Many database interactions are multistage. A customer views products, adds one or more to a shopping cart, views more products, adds more to the shopping cart, and eventually checks out. A stateless protocol cannot be used for such applications.

Over time, capabilities emerged to overcome this problem. Web application developers learned to add SQL statements to their Web applications, and soon thousands of databases were being processed over the Web. You will learn more about such processing in Chapter 11. An interesting phenomenon was the emergence of open source DBMS products. Open source products generally make the source code widely available so that a group of programmers not bound to a single company can contribute to the program. Further, some forms of these products are usually offered as free downloads, although other forms or product support must be purchased from the company that owns the product.

A good example of this is the MySQL DBMS. MySQL was originally released in 1995 by the Swedish company MySQL AB. In February 2008, Sun Microsystems bought MySQL AB, and in January 2013 Oracle Corporation completed its acquisition of Sun Microsystems. This means that Oracle Corporation now owns two major DBMS products: Oracle Database and Oracle MySQL. At present, MySQL continues to be available as an open source product, and the free MySQL Community Server edition can be downloaded from the MySQL Web site. MySQL has proven to be especially popular with Web site developers who need to run Web page queries against an SQL DBMS on a Web server running the Linux operating system. We will work with MySQL in Chapter 10C.

MySQL is not the only open source DBMS product—in fact, as this is being written there are 87 "free database management systems" listed on the Wikipedia category page for free database management systems (up from the 84 listed when the previous edition of this book went to press). Additionally, two of these DBMS have subcategories of related products—MySQL has 28 subcategories, and PostgreSQL (alternately Postgres) has 16 subcategories.

One interesting outcome of the emergence of open source DBMS products is that companies that typically sell proprietary (closed source) DBMS products now offer free versions of their products. For example, Microsoft now offers SQL Server 2014 Express, and Oracle Corporation makes its Oracle Database Express Edition 11*g* Release 2 available for free. Although neither of these products is as complete or as powerful (for example, in terms of maximum data storage allowed) as some other versions the companies sell, they are useful for projects that require a small database. They are also ideal for students learning to use databases and SQL.

In the late 1990s, **XML** was defined to overcome the problems that occur when HTML is used to exchange business documents. The design of the XML family of standards not only solved the problems of HTML, it also meant that XML documents were superior for exchanging views of database data. In 2002, Bill Gates said that "XML is the lingua-franca of the Internet Age." As you will learn in Chapter 11 and Appendix K, however, two key problems that remain are (1) getting data from a database and putting it into an XML document and (2) taking data from an XML document and putting it into a database. In fact, this is where future application programmers can enter the picture.

XML database processing was given a further boost with the definition of XML Web service standards such as SOAP (not an acronym), WSDL (Web Services Description Language), UDDI (Universal Description, Discovery, and Integration), and others. Using Web services, it is possible to expose nuggets of database processing to other programs that use the Internet infrastructure. This means, for example, that in a supply chain management application a vendor can expose portions of its inventory application to its suppliers. Further, it can do so in a standardized way.

The last row in Figure 1-27 brings us up to the present. Following the development of XML, the **NoSQL** ("Not only SQL") **movement** and **Big Data** have emerged in recent years, particularly following a 2009 conference organized around work on open source **distributed databases** (discussed in Chapter 12). The NoSQL movement should really be called a *NoRelational* movement because the work is really on databases that do not follow the relational model introduced in this chapter and discussed in Chapter 3. The Big Data movement is based on the need for information systems to handle increasing large sets of data and, together with NoSQL (nonrelational) databases, is the basis for such applications as Facebook and Twitter. We will discuss the NoSQL movement and Big Data, together with the associated topics of distributed databases, **virtualization** and **cloud computing**, in Chapter 12.

The NoSQL movement and Big Data bring us to the edge of the IT volcano, where the magma of new technology is just now oozing from the ground. What happens next will be, in part, up to you.

Summary

Today's Internet and smartphone world depends upon databases. Personal computers use Web clients to browse, shop, and communicate online. Smartphones use apps over cell phone data networks to do the same. All these applications rely on databases.

The purpose of a database is to help people keep track of things. Databases store data in tables in which each table has data about a different type of thing. Instances of the thing are stored in the rows of tables, and the characteristics of those instances are stored in columns. In this text, table names are written in all capital letters; column names are written in initial capital letters. Databases store data and the relationships among the data. Databases store data, but they are structured so that information can be created from that data.

Figure 1-7 lists many important examples of database applications. Databases can be processed by a single user or by many users. Those that support many users require special concurrency-control mechanisms to ensure that one user's work does not conflict with a second user's work.

Some databases involve just a few users and thousands of rows of data in a few tables. At the other end of the spectrum, some large databases, such as those that support ERP applications, support thousands of users and include many millions of rows in several hundred different tables.

Some database applications support e-commerce activities. Some of the largest databases are those that track users' responses to Web pages and Web page components. These databases are used to analyze customers' responses to different Web-based marketing programs.

Digital dashboards, data mining applications, and other reporting applications use database data that is generated by transaction processing systems to help manage the enterprise. Digital dashboards and reporting systems assess past and current performance. Data mining applications predict future performance. The basic components of a database system are the database, the database management system (DBMS), one or more database applications, and users. Because Structured Query Language (SQL) is an internationally recognized language for processing databases, it can be considered a fifth component of a database system.

The functions of database applications are to create and process forms, to process user queries, and to create and process reports. Application programs also execute specific application logic and control the application. Users provide data and data changes and read data in forms, queries, and reports.

A DBMS is a large, complicated program used to create, process, and administer a database. DBMS products are almost always licensed from software vendors. Specific functions of a DBMS are summarized in Figure 1-14.

A database is a self-describing collection of integrated tables. A relational database is a self-describing collection of related tables. Tables are integrated because they store data about the relationships among rows of data. Tables are related by storing linking values of a common column. A database is self-describing because it contains a description of its contents within itself, which is known as metadata. Most DBMS products carry metadata in the form of tables. As shown in Figure 1-16, databases also contain indexes, triggers, stored procedures, security features, and backup and recovery data.

Microsoft Access is not just a DBMS, but rather an application generator plus a DBMS. The application generator consists of applications components that create and process forms, reports, and queries. The default Microsoft Access DBMS product is called the Access Data Engine (ADE), which is not licensed as a separate product.

Enterprise database systems do not combine applications and the DBMS as Microsoft Access does. Instead, applications are programs separate from each other and from the DBMS. Figure 1-18 shows four categories of database applications: client/server applications, Web applications, reporting applications, and XML Web services applications.

The five most popular DBMS products, in order of power, features, and difficulty of use, are Microsoft Access, MySQL, SQL Server, DB2, and Oracle Database. Microsoft Access and SQL Server are licensed by Microsoft, DB2 is licensed by IBM, and Oracle Database and MySQL are licensed by Oracle Corporation.

Database design is both difficult and important. Most of the first half of this text concerns database design. New databases arise in three ways: from existing data, from new systems development, and from database redesign. Normalization is used to guide the design of databases from existing data. Data models are used to create a blueprint from system requirements. The blueprint is later transformed into a database design. Most data models are created using the entity-relationship model. Database redesign occurs when an existing database is adapted to support new or changed requirements or when two or more databases are integrated.

With regards to database processing, you can have one of two roles: user or database administrator. You may be a *user* of a database/DBMS as a knowledge worker or as an application programmer. Alternatively, you might be a *database administrator* who designs, constructs, and manages the database itself. The domains of each role are shown in Figure 1-25, and the priorities as to what you need to know for each role are shown in Figure 1-26.

The history of database processing is summarized in Figure 1-27. In the early years, prior to 1970, database processing did not exist, and all data were stored in separated files. The need for integrated processing drove the development of early DBMS products. The CODASYL DBTG and DL/I data models were prevalent. Of the DBMS products used at that time, only ADABAS and IMS are still in use.

The relational model rose to prominence in the 1980s. At first, the relational model was judged to be impractical, but over time relational products such as DB2 and Oracle Database achieved success. During this time, DBMS products were developed for personal computers as well. dBase, R:base, and Paradox were all PC DBMS products that were eventually consumed by the success of Microsoft Access.

Object-oriented DBMS products were developed in the 1990s but never achieved commercial success. More recently, Web-based databases have been developed to support e-commerce. Open source DBMS products are readily available, forcing commercial DBMS vendors to offer limited-capacity free versions of their enterprise products. Features and functions, such as XML and XML Web services, have been implemented to overcome the stateless nature of HTTP. The NoSQL movement, Big Data, virtualization, and cloud computing are at the leading edge of current database processing.

Key Terms

Android operating system
ARPANET
app
Apple II
Apple OS X
Big Data
cell phone
client
client-server architecture
cloud computing
CODASYL DBTG
column
composite key
concurrency
data
Data Language/I (DL/I)
data mart
data model
data warehouse
database
database administrator
database application
database design (as a process)
database design (as a product)
database management system (DBMS)
database migration
database system
device

distributed database
enterprise-class database system
entity-relationship (ER) data modeling
Ethernet networking technology
fields
foreign key
IBM Personal Computer (IBM PC)
index
information
instance
integrated tables
Internet
iPhone
knowledge worker
Linux
Local Area Network (LAN)
Metadata
Microsoft Windows
Microsoft Windows Server
mobile phone
NoSQL movement
normal forms
normalization
object-oriented DBMS (OODBMS or ODBMS)
object-oriented programming (OOP)
object-relational DBMS
operating system (OS)

Personal Computer (PC)
personal database system
Point of Sale (POS) system
primary key
programmer
record
referential integrity constraints
relational database
relational model
relationship
row
self-describing
server
service
smartphone
Structured Query Language (SQL)
surrogate key
table
tablet computer (tablet)
user
virtualization
Web (the)
Web 2.0
Web browser
Web site
Wide World Web
WWW
XML

Review Questions

1.1 Describe the historic development of Internet and smartphone technology from the early days of personal computers (PCs) to today's Internet Web application and smartphone app based information systems environment.

1.2 Why do today's Internet Web applications and smartphone apps need databases?

1.3 Read the description of the search process on the Pearson Web site. Using your own computer, find another retailer Web site (other than any of those discussed or mentioned in this chapter), and search for something of interest to you. Write up a description (with screen shots if possible) of your search.

1.4 What is the purpose of a database?

1.5 What is the most commonly used type of database?

1.6 Give an example of two related tables other than the example used in this book. Use the STUDENT and GRADE tables in Figure 1-5 as an example pattern for your tables. Name the tables and columns using the conventions in this book.

1.7 For the tables you created in Review Question 1.6, what are the primary keys of each table? Do you think that any of these primary keys could be *surrogate keys*? Are any of these primary keys *composite keys*?

1.8 Explain how the two tables you provided in Review Question 1.6 are related. Which table contains the foreign key, and what is the foreign key?

1.9 Show your two tables from Review Question 1.6 without the columns that represent the relationships. Explain how the value of your two tables is diminished without the relationships.

1.10 Define the terms *data* and *information*. Explain how the two terms differ.

1.11 Give an example of information that could be determined using the two tables you provided in your answer to Review Question 1.6.

1.12 Give examples of a single-user database application and a multiuser database application other than the ones shown in Figure 1-7.

1.13 What problem can occur when a database is processed by more than one user?

1.14 Give an example of a database application that has hundreds of users and a very large and complicated database. Use an example other than one in Figure 1-7.

1.15 What is the purpose of the largest databases at e-commerce companies such as Amazon.com?

1.16 How do the e-commerce companies use the databases discussed in Review Question 1.15?

1.17 How do digital dashboard and data mining applications differ from transaction processing applications?

1.18 Explain why a small database is not necessarily simpler than a large one.

1.19 Explain the components in Figure 1-9.

1.20 What are the functions of application programs?

1.21 What is Structured Query Language (SQL), and why is it important?

1.22 What does DBMS stand for?

1.23 What are the functions of the DBMS?

1.24 Name three vendors of DBMS products.

1.25 Define the term *database*.

1.26 Why is a database considered to be self-describing?

1.27 What is metadata? How does this term pertain to a database?

1.28 What advantage is there in storing metadata in tables?

1.29 List the components of a database other than user tables and metadata.

1.30 Is Microsoft Access a DBMS? Why or why not?

1.31 Describe the components shown in Figure 1-17.

1.32 What is the function of the application generator in Microsoft Access?

1.33 What is the name of the DBMS engine within Microsoft Access? Why do we rarely hear about that engine?

1.34 Why does Microsoft Access hide important database technology?

1.35 Why would someone choose to replace the native Microsoft Access DBMS engine with SQL Server?

1.36 Name the components of an enterprise-class database system.

1.37 Name and describe the four categories of database applications that would use an enterprise-class database system.

1.38 How do database applications read and write database data?

1.39 Name the five DBMS products described in this chapter, and compare them in terms of power, features, and ease of use.

1.40 List several consequences of a poorly designed database.

1.41 Explain two ways that a database can be designed from existing data.

1.42 What is a data warehouse? What is a data mart?

1.43 Describe the general process of designing a database for a new information system.

1.44 Explain two ways that databases can be redesigned.

1.45 What does the term *database migration* mean?

1.46 Summarize the various ways that you might work with database technology.

1.47 What job functions does a knowledge worker perform?

1.48 What job functions does a database administrator perform?

1.49 Explain the meaning of the domains in Figure 1-25.

1.50 What need drove the development of the first database technology?

1.51 What are Data Language/I and CODASYL DBTG?

1.52 Who was E. F. Codd?

1.53 What were the early objections to the relational model?

1.54 Name two early relational DBMS products.

1.55 What are some of the reasons for the success of Oracle Database?

1.56 Name three early personal computer DBMS products.

1.57 What happened to the products in your answer to Review Question 1.56?

1.58 What was the purpose of OODBMS products? State two reasons that OODBMS products were not successful.

1.59   What characteristic of HTTP was a problem for database processing applications?

1.60   What is an open source DBMS product? Which of the five DBMS products that you named in answering Review Question 1.39 is historically an open source DBMS product?

1.61   What has been the response of companies that sell proprietary DBMS products to the open source DBMS products? Include two examples in your answer.

1.62   What is XML? What comment did Bill Gates make regarding XML?

1.63   What is the NoSQL movement? Name two applications that rely on NoSQL databases.

Project Questions

To perform the following projects, you will need a computer that has Microsoft Access installed. If you have no experience working with Microsoft Access, read Appendix A before you proceed.

For this set of project questions, we will create a Microsoft Access database for the Wedgewood Pacific Corporation (WPC). Founded in 1957 in Seattle, Washington, WPC has grown into an internationally recognized organization. The company is located in two buildings. One building houses the Administration, Accounting, Finance, and Human Resources departments, and the second houses the Production, Marketing, and Information Systems departments. The company database contains data about company employees, departments, company projects, company assets (for example, computer equipment), and other aspects of company operations.

In the following project questions, we will start by creating the WPC.accdb database with the following two tables:

> DEPARTMENT (**DepartmentName**, BudgetCode, OfficeNumber, Phone)
>
> EMPLOYEE (**EmployeeNumber**, FirstName, LastName, *Department*, Phone, Email)

1.64   Create a Microsoft Access database named WPC.accdb.

1.65   Figure 1-28 shows the column characteristics for the WPC DEPARTMENT table. Using the column characteristics, create the DEPARTMENT table in the WPC.accdb database.

1.66   Figure 1-29 shows the data for the WPC DEPARTMENT table. Using Datasheet view, enter the data shown in Figure 1-29 into your DEPARTMENT table.

FIGURE 1-28

Column Characteristics
for the WPC Database
DEPARTMENT Table

1.67   Figure 1-30 shows the column characteristics for the WPC EMPLOYEE table. Using the column characteristics, create the EMPLOYEE table in the WPC.accdb database.

DEPARTMENT

Column Name	Type	Key	Required	Remarks
DepartmentName	Text (35)	Primary Key	Yes	
BudgetCode	Text (30)	No	Yes	
OfficeNumber	Text (15)	No	Yes	
Phone	Text (12)	No	Yes	

FIGURE 1-29

WPC Database
DEPARTMENT Data

DepartmentName	BudgetCode	OfficeNumber	Phone
Administration	BC-100-10	BLDG01-300	360-285-8100
Legal	BC-200-10	BLDG01-200	360-285-8200
Accounting	BC-300-10	BLDG01-100	360-285-8300
Finance	BC-400-10	BLDG01-140	360-285-8400
Human Resources	BC-500-10	BLDG01-180	360-285-8500
Production	BC-600-10	BLDG02-100	360-287-8600
Marketing	BC-700-10	BLDG02-200	360-287-8700
InfoSystems	BC-800-10	BLDG02-270	360-287-8800

1.68 Create the relationship and referential integrity constraint between DEPARTMENT and EMPLOYEE. Enable enforcing of referential integrity and cascading of data updates, but do *not* enable cascading of data from deleted records.

1.69 Figure 1-31 shows the data for the WPC EMPLOYEE table. Using Datasheet view, enter the first three rows of the data shown in Figure 1-31 into your EMPLOYEE table.

1.70 Using the Microsoft Access form wizard, create a data input form for the EMPLOYEE table and name it WPC Employee Data Form. Make any adjustments necessary to the form so that all data display properly. Use this form to enter the rest of the data in the EMPLOYEE table shown in Figure 1-31 into your EMPLOYEE table.

1.71 Using the Microsoft Access report wizard, create a report named Wedgewood Pacific Corporation Employee Report that presents the data contained in your EMPLOYEE table sorted first by employee last name and then by employee first name. Make any adjustments necessary to the report so that all headings and data display properly. Print a copy of this report.

1.72 Using the Microsoft Access form wizard, create a form that has all of the data from both tables. When asked how you want to view your data, select *by DEPARTMENT*. Choose the default options for other questions that the wizard asks. Open your form and page through your departments.

EMPLOYEE

Column Name	Type	Key	Required	Remarks
EmployeeNumber	AutoNumber	Primary Key	Yes	Surrogate Key
FirstName	Text (25)	No	Yes	
LastName	Text (25)	No	Yes	
Department	Text (35)	No	Yes	
Phone	Text (12)	No	No	
Email	Text (100)	No	Yes	

EmployeeNumber	FirstName	LastName	Department	Phone	Email
[AutoNumber]	Mary	Jacobs	Administration	360-285-8110	Mary.Jacobs@WPC.com
[AutoNumber]	Rosalie	Jackson	Administration	360-285-8120	Rosalie.Jackson@WPC.com
[AutoNumber]	Richard	Bandalone	Legal	360-285-8210	Richard.Bandalone@WPC.com
[AutoNumber]	Tom	Caruthers	Accounting	360-285-8310	Tom.Caruthers@WPC.com
[AutoNumber]	Heather	Jones	Accounting	360-285-8320	Heather.Jones@WPC.com
[AutoNumber]	Mary	Abernathy	Finance	360-285-8410	Mary.Abernathy@WPC.com
[AutoNumber]	George	Smith	Human Resources	360-285-8510	George.Smith@WPC.com
[AutoNumber]	Tom	Jackson	Production	360-287-8610	Tom.Jackson@WPC.com
[AutoNumber]	George	Jones	Production	360-287-8620	George.Jones@WPC.com
[AutoNumber]	Ken	Numoto	Marketing	360-287-8710	Ken.Numoto@WPC.com
[AutoNumber]	James	Nestor	InfoSystems		James.Nestor@WPC.com
[AutoNumber]	Rick	Brown	InfoSystems	360-287-8820	Rick.Brown@WPC.com

FIGURE 1-31

WPC Database EMPLOYEE
Data

1.73 Using the Microsoft Access report wizard, create a report that has all of the data from both tables. When asked how you want to view your data, select *by DEPARTMENT*. For the data contained in your EMPLOYEE table in the report, specify that it will be sorted first by employee last name and then by employee first name. Make any adjustments necessary to the report so that all headings and data display properly. Print a copy of this report.

1.74 Explain, to the level of detail in this chapter, what is going on within Microsoft Access in Project Questions 1.70, 1.71, 1.72, and 1.73. What subcomponent created the form and report? Where is the data stored? What role do you think SQL is playing?

2

Introduction to Structured Query Language

Chapter Objectives

- To understand the use of extracted data sets in business intelligence (BI) systems
- To understand the use of ad-hoc queries in business intelligence (BI) systems
- To understand the history and significance of Structured Query Language (SQL)
- To understand the SQL SELECT/FROM/WHERE framework as the basis for database queries
- To create SQL queries to retrieve data from a single table
- To create SQL queries that use the SQL SELECT, FROM, WHERE, ORDER BY, GROUP BY, and HAVING clauses
- To create SQL queries that use the SQL DISTINCT, TOP, and TOP PERCENT keywords
- To create SQL queries that use the SQL comparison operators including BETWEEN, LIKE, IN, and IS NULL

- To create SQL queries that use the SQL logical operators including AND, OR, and NOT
- To create SQL queries that use the SQL built-in aggregate functions of SUM, COUNT, MIN, MAX, and AVG with and without the SQL GROUP BY clause
- To create SQL queries that retrieve data from a single table while restricting the data based upon data in another table (subquery)
- To create SQL queries that retrieve data from multiple tables using the SQL join and JOIN ON operations
- To create SQL queries that retrieve data from multiple tables using the SQL OUTER JOIN operation
- To create SQL queries that retrieve data from multiple tables using SQL set operators UNION, INTERSECT, and EXCEPT

In today's business environment, users typically use data stored in databases to produce information that can help them make business decisions. In Chapter 12, we will take an in-depth look at **business intelligence (BI) systems**, which are information systems used to support management decisions by producing information for assessment, analysis, planning, and control. In this chapter, we will see how BI systems users use **ad-hoc queries**, which are essentially questions that can be answered using database data. For example, in English an ad-hoc query might be "How many customers in Portland, Oregon, bought our green baseball cap?" These queries are called *ad-hoc* because they are created by the user as needed rather than programmed into an application.

This approach to database querying has become important enough that some companies produce dedicated applications to help users who are not familiar with database structures create ad-hoc queries. One example is Open Text's Open Text Business Intelligence product (formerly known as *LiveLink ECM BI Query*), which uses a user-friendly **graphical user interface (GUI)** to simplify the creation of ad-hoc queries. Personal databases such as Microsoft Access also have ad-hoc query tools available. Microsoft Access uses a GUI style called **query by example (QBE)** to simplify ad-hoc queries.

However, **Structured Query Language (SQL)**—the universal query language of relational DBMS products—is always behind the user-friendly GUIs. In this chapter, we will introduce SQL by learning how to write and run SQL queries. We will then return to SQL in Chapter 7 to learn how to use it for other purposes, such as how to create and add data to the databases themselves.

Cape Codd Outdoor Sports

For our work in this chapter, we will use data from Cape Codd Outdoor Sports (although based on a real outdoor retail equipment vendor, Cape Codd Outdoor Sports is a fictitious company). The Cape Codd Outdoor Sports Web site is shown in Figure 2-1. Cape Codd Outdoor Sports, or just Cape Codd for short, sells recreational outdoor equipment in 15 retail stores across the United States and Canada. It also sells merchandise over the Internet from a Web storefront application and via mail order based on annual catalogs that are mailed to all recorded customers in early January of each year. All retail sales are recorded in a sales database managed by the Oracle Database 12*c* DBMS, as shown in Figure 2-2. This type of sales system is commonly known as an **online transaction processing (OLTP)** system and is used to record all sales transactions of the company (whether in a store, on the Web, or from mail order or phone order sales). OLTP systems are the backbone of businesses as they operate today.

FIGURE 2-1

The Cape Codd Retail Sales Web Site Home Page

FIGURE 2-2

The Cape Codd Retail Sales
Data Extraction Process

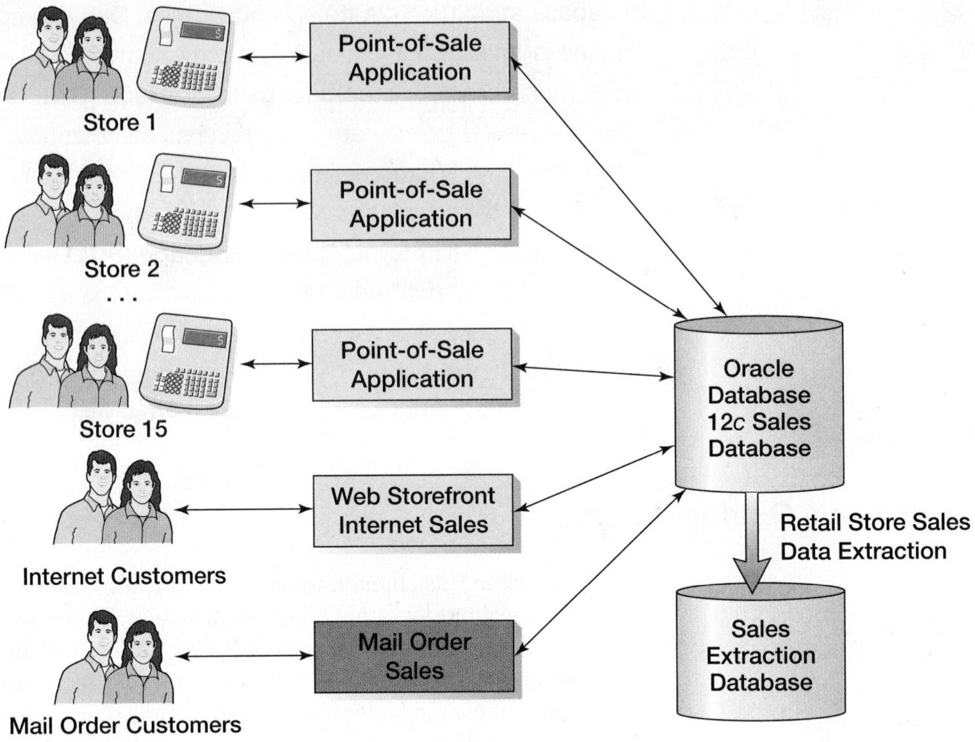

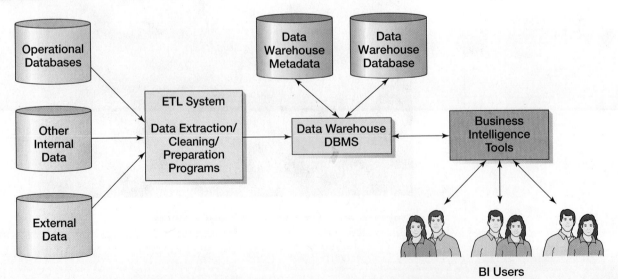

Business Intelligence Systems and Data Warehouses

You will notice in Figure 2-3 that BI systems typically store their associated data in **data ware-houses**, which are database systems that have data, programs, and personnel that specialize in the preparation of data for BI processing. Data warehouses will be discussed in detail in Chapter 12, so for now we will simply note that data warehouses vary in scale and scope. They can be as simple as a sole employee processing a data extract on a part-time basis or as complex as a department with dozens of employees maintaining libraries of data and programs.

Figure 2-3 shows the components of a typical company-wide data warehouse. Data are read from operational databases (the databases that store the company's current day-to-day transaction data), from other internal data, or from external data sources by the **Extract, Transform, and Load (ETL) system**. The ETL system then cleans and prepares the data for BI processing.

FIGURE 2-3

Components of a Data
Warehouse

This can be a complex process, but the data is then stored in the **data warehouse DBMS** for use by BI users who access the data by various BI tools. As described in Chapter 1, the DBMS used for the data warehouse stores both databases and the metadata for those databases.

> **BY THE WAY**   A small, specialized data warehouse is referred to as a **data mart**. Data marts and their relationship to data warehouses are discussed in Chapter 12. Note that the DBMS used for the data warehouse may or may not be the same DBMS product used for the operational databases. For example, operational databases may be stored in an Oracle Database 12c DBMS, while the data warehouse uses a Microsoft SQL Server 2014 DBMS.

The Cape Codd Outdoor Sports Extracted Retail Sales Data

Cape Codd's marketing department wants to perform an analysis of (1) in-store sales and (2) catalog content. Accordingly, marketing analysts ask the IT department to extract retail sales data from the operational database.

To perform the in-store sales marketing study, the marketing analysts do not need all of the order data. They want just the RETAIL_ORDER, ORDER_ITEM, and SKU_DATA tables and columns shown in Figure 2-4. Looking at this figure, it is easy to see that columns that would be needed in an operational sales OLTP database are *not* included in the extracted data. For example, the RETAIL_ORDER table does *not* have CustomerLastName, CustomerFirstName, and OrderDay columns. Similarly, not all catalog data is needed, but the market analysts do need similar data from different years to be able to compare the catalog content from year to year, so the CATALOG_SKU_2014 and CATALOG_SKU_2015 tables shown in Figure 2-4 are needed. The data types for the columns in these tables are shown in Figure 2-5.

As shown in Figures 2-4 and 2-5, five tables are needed:

- RETAIL_ORDER, ORDER_ITEM, and SKU_DATA for retail sales analysis
- CATALOG_SKU_2014 and CATALOG_SKU_2015 for catalog content analysis

The RETAIL_ORDER table has data about each retail sales order, the ORDER_ITEM table has data about each item in an order, and the SKU_DATA table has data about each **stock-keeping unit (SKU)**. SKU is a unique identifier for each particular item that Cape Codd sells. Note that these three tables are linked in a relational database structure. The relationships are shown in Figure 2-4, and the primary keys and foreign keys are clearly visible in

FIGURE 2-4

Cape Codd Extracted Retail Sales Data Database Tables and Relationships

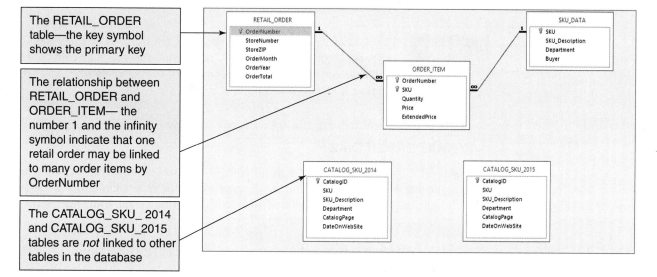

The RETAIL_ORDER table—the key symbol shows the primary key

The relationship between RETAIL_ORDER and ORDER_ITEM— the number 1 and the infinity symbol indicate that one retail order may be linked to many order items by OrderNumber

The CATALOG_SKU_ 2014 and CATALOG_SKU_2015 tables are *not* linked to other tables in the database

FIGURE 2-5

Cape Codd Extracted Retail
Sales Data Format

Table	Column	Data Type
RETAIL_ORDER	OrderNumber	Integer
	StoreNumber	Integer
	StoreZIP	Character (9)
	OrderMonth	Character (12)
	OrderYear	Integer
	OrderTotal	Currency
ORDER_ITEM	OrderNumber	Integer
	SKU	Integer
	Quantity	Integer
	Price	Currency
	ExtendedPrice	Currency
SKU_DATA	SKU	Integer
	SKU_Description	Character (35)
	Department	Character (30)
	Buyer	Character (30)
CATALOG_SKU_20##	CatalogID	Integer
	SKU	Integer
	SKU_Description	Character (35)
	Department	Character (30)
	CatalogPage	Integer
	DateOnWebSite	Date

Figure 2-6. CATALOG_SKU_2014 and CATALOG_SKU_2015 have data about the content in the annual printed catalog and the items available for sale on the Cape Codd Web site. Because some items are added to the Web site after the catalog is printed, an item on the Web site may not be in the corresponding catalog. Note that these two tables are free standing, meaning that while they do have primary keys, they are not linked to any other tables via foreign keys. The data stored in the tables is shown in Figure 2-6.

> **BY THE WAY**   The dataset shown is a small dataset we are using to illustrate the concepts explained in this chapter. A "real world" data extract would produce a much larger dataset, but our dataset is big enough for our purposes while also keeping the database easily manageable.

RETAIL_ORDER Data

As shown in Figures 2-4, 2-5, and 2-6, the RETAIL_ORDER table has columns for OrderNumber, StoreNumber, StoreZIP (the ZIP code of the store selling the order), OrderMonth, OrderYear, and OrderTotal. We can write this information in the following format, with OrderNumber underlined to show that it is the primary key of the RETAIL_ORDER table:

RETAIL_ORDER (OrderNumber, StoreNumber, StoreZIP, OrderMonth, OrderYear, OrderTotal)

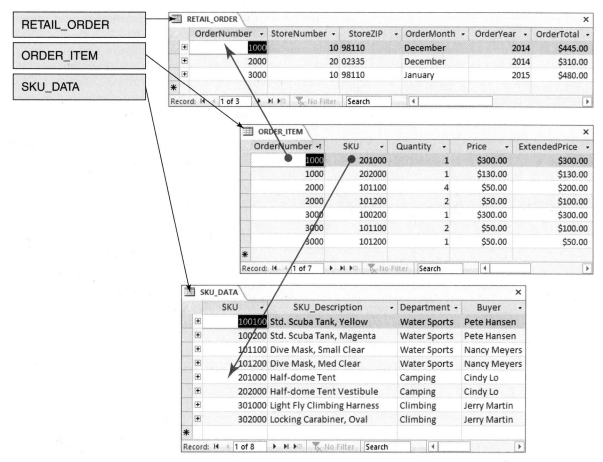

(a) The Linked RETAIL_ORDER, ORDER_ITEM and SKU_DATA Tables

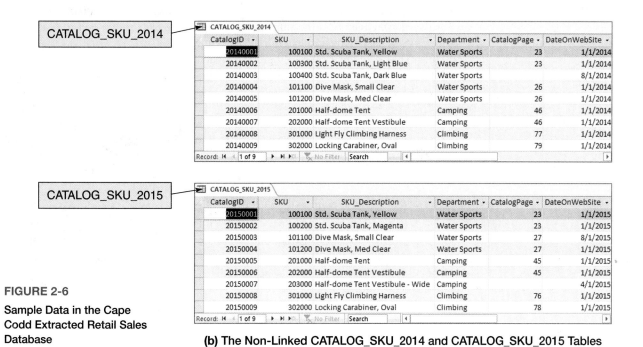

FIGURE 2-6

Sample Data in the Cape Codd Extracted Retail Sales Database

(b) The Non-Linked CATALOG_SKU_2014 and CATALOG_SKU_2015 Tables

Sample data for RETAIL_ORDER are shown in Figure 2-6. This extract includes only data for retail store sales–operational data for other types of sales (and returns and other sales-related transactions) are not copied during the extraction process. Further, the data extraction process selects only a few columns of the operational data–the Point of Sale (POS) and other sales applications process far more data than that shown here. The operational database also stores the data in a different format. For example, the order data in the Oracle Database 12*c* operational database contain a column named OrderDate that stores the data in the date format MM/DD/YYYY (e.g., 10/22/2010 for October 22, 2010). The extraction program used to populate the retail sales extracted data database converts OrderDate into two separate values of OrderMonth and OrderYear. This is done because this is the data format that marketing wants. Such filtering and data transformation are typical of a data extraction process.

ORDER_ITEM Data

As shown in Figures 2-4, 2-5, and 2-6, the ORDER_ITEM table has columns for OrderNumber, SKU, Quantity, Price, and ExtendedPrice (which equals Quantity × Price). We can write this information in the following format, with both OrderNumber and SKU underlined to show that together they are the composite primary key of the ORDER_ITEM table and with them also italicized to show that they are also foreign keys:

ORDER_ITEM (*OrderNumber*, *SKU*, Quantity, Price, ExtendedPrice)

Thus, the ORDER_ITEM table stores an extract of the items purchased in each order. There is one row in the table for each item in an order, and this item is identified by its SKU. To understand this table, think about a sales receipt you get from a retail store. That receipt has data for one order. It includes basic order data such as the date and order total, and it has one line for each item you purchase. The rows in the ORDER_ITEM table correspond to the lines on such an order receipt.

The OrderNumber Column in ORDER_ITEM relates each row in ORDER_ITEM to the corresponding OrderNumber in the RETAIL_ORDER table. SKU identifies the actual item purchased by its stock-keeping unit number. Further, the SKU column in ORDER_ITEM relates each row in ORDER_ITEM to its corresponding SKU in the SKU_DATA table (discussed in the next section). Quantity is the number of items of that SKU purchased in that order. Price is the price of each item, and ExtendedPrice is equal to Quantity × Price.

ORDER_ITEM data are shown in the bottom part of Figure 2-6. The first row relates to order 1000 and to SKU 201000. For SKU 201000, one item was purchased for $300.00, and the ExtendedPrice was $300.00. The second row shows the second item in order 1000. There, 1 of item 202000 was purchased for $50.00, and the ExtendedPrice is 1 × $50.00, or $50.00. This table structure of an ORDER table related to an ORDER_ITEM table is typical for a sales system with many items in one order. We will discuss it in detail in Chapters 5 and 6, where we will create a data model of a complete order and then design the database for that data model.

> **BY THE WAY**   You would expect the total of ExtendedPrice for all rows for a given order to equal OrderTotal in the RETAIL_ORDER table. *It does not*. For order 1000, for example, the sum of ExtendedPrice in the relevant rows of ORDER_ITEM is $300.00 + $130.00 = $430.00. However, the OrderTotal for order 1000 is $445.00. The difference occurs because OrderTotal includes tax, shipping, and other charges that do not appear in the data extract.

SKU_DATA Table

As shown in Figures 2-4, 2-5, and 2-6, the SKU_DATA table has columns SKU, SKU_Description, Department, and Buyer. We can write this information in the following format, with SKU underlined to show that it is the primary key of the SKU_DATA table:

SKU_DATA (<u>SKU</u>, SKU_Description, Department, Buyer)

SKU is an integer value that identifies a particular product sold by Cape Codd. For example, SKU 100100 identifies a yellow, standard-size SCUBA tank, whereas SKU 100200 identifies the magenta version of the same tank. SKU_Description contains a brief text description of each item. Department and Buyer identify the department and individual who is responsible for purchasing the product. As with the other tables, these columns are a subset of the SKU data stored in the operational database.

CATALOG_SKU_20## Tables

As shown in Figures 2-4, 2-5, and 2-6, all the CATALOG_SKU_20## tables have the same columns, consisting of CatalogID, SKU, SKU_Description, Department, CatalogPage, and DateOnWebSite. We can write this information in the following format, with CatalogID underlined to show that it is the primary key of each CATALOG_SKU_20## table:

CATALOG_SKU_20## (<u>CatalogID</u>, SKU, SKU_Description, Department, CatalogPage, DateOnWebSite)

CatalogID is an integer value that identifies a particular catalog item in the tables. SKU, SKU_Description, and Department have the same meaning as in the SKU_DATA table. CatalogPage is an integer that shows on which page in the printed catalog the item appeared, and DateOnWebSite shows the first date that the item could be seen on the Cape Codd Web site. As with the other tables, these columns are a subset of the CATALOG_SKU_20## data stored in the operational database.

Note that in the CATALOG_SKU_2014 table, the row with CatalogID 2014003 has *no value* for CatalogPage. Similarly, note that in the CATALOG_SKU_2015 table, in the row with CatalogID 2015007, there is again *no value* for CatalogPage. A missing data value like this is called a **null value**. We will discuss null values in detail in Chapters 4, but for now understand that we treat a null value just like any other data value, and we can search for null values in a table using the same techniques we will use to search for any other data value.

The Complete Cape Codd Data Extract Schema

A database **schema** is a complete logical view of the database, containing all the tables, all the columns in each table, the primary key of each table (indicated by underlining the column names of the primary key columns), and the foreign keys that link the tables together (indicated by italicizing the column names of the foreign key columns). The schema for the Cape Codd sales data extract therefore is:

RETAIL_ORDER (<u>OrderNumber</u>, StoreNumber, StoreZIP, OrderMonth, OrderYear, OrderTotal)

ORDER_ITEM (<u>*OrderNumber*</u>, <u>*SKU*</u>, Quantity, Price, ExtendedPrice)

SKU_DATA (<u>SKU</u>, SKU_Description, Department, Buyer)

CATALOG_SKU_2014 (<u>CatalogID</u>, SKU, SKU_Description, Department, CatalogPage, DateOnWebSite)

CATALOG_SKU_2015 (<u>CatalogID</u>, SKU, SKU_Description, Department, CatalogPage, DateOnWebSite)

Note how the composite primary key for ORDER_ITEM also contains the foreign keys linking this table to RETAIL_ORDER and SKU_DATA.

> **BY THE WAY** In the Review Questions at the end of this chapter, we will extend this schema to include three additional tables: WAREHOUSE, INVENTORY, and CATALOG_SKU_2013. Some of the figures in this chapter include these three tables in the Cape Codd database, but they are not used in our discussion of SQL in the chapter text.

Data Extracts Are Common

Before we continue, realize that the data extraction process described here is not just an academic exercise. To the contrary, such extraction processes are realistic, common, and important BI system operations. Right now, hundreds of businesses worldwide are using their BI systems to create extract databases just like the one created by Cape Codd.

In the next sections of this chapter, you will learn how to write SQL statements to process the extracted data via ad-hoc **SQL queries**, which is how SQL is used to "ask questions" about the data in the database. This knowledge is exceedingly valuable and practical. Again, right now, as you read this paragraph, hundreds of people are writing SQL to create information from extracted data. The SQL you will learn in this chapter will be an essential asset to you as a knowledge worker, application programmer, or database administrator. Invest the time to learn SQL—the investment will pay great dividends later in your career.

SQL Background

SQL was developed by the IBM Corporation in the late 1970s. It was endorsed as a national standard by the **American National Standards Institute (ANSI)** in 1986 and by the **International Organization for Standardization (ISO)** (and no, that's not a typo—the acronym is *ISO*, not *IOS!*) in 1987. Subsequent versions of SQL were adopted in 1989 and 1992. The 1992 version is sometimes referred to as SQL-92 and sometimes as ANSI-92 SQL. In 1999, SQL:1999 (also referred to as SQL3), which incorporated some object-oriented concepts, was released. This was followed by the release of SQL:2003 in 2003; SQL:2006 in 2006; SQL:2008 in 2008; and, most recently, SQL:2011 in 2011. Each of these added new features or extended existing SQL features, the most important of which for us are the SQL standardization of the INSTEAD OF trigger (SQL triggers are discussed in Chapter 7) in SQL:2008 and the support for **Extensible Markup Language (XML)** (XML is discussed in Chapter 11) added in SQL:2009. Our discussions in this chapter and in Chapter 7 mostly focus on common language features that have been in SQL since SQL-92 but do include some features from SQL:2003 and SQL:2008. We discuss the SQL XML features in Chapter 11.

> **BY THE WAY**　Although there is an SQL *standard*, that does not mean that SQL is *standardized* across DBMS products! Indeed, each DBMS implements SQL in its own peculiar way, and you will have to learn the idiosyncrasies of the SQL dialect your DBMS uses.
>
> 　In this book, we are using Microsoft's SQL Server 2014 SQL syntax, with some limited discussion of the different SQL dialects. The Oracle Database 12*c* SQL syntax is used in Chapter 10B, and the MySQL SQL 5.6 SQL syntax is used in Chapter 10C.

SQL is not a complete programming language, like Java or C#. Instead, it is called a **data sublanguage** because it has only those statements needed for creating and processing database data and metadata. You can use SQL statements in many different ways. You can submit them directly to the DBMS for processing. You can embed SQL statements into client/server application programs. You can embed them into Web pages, and you can use them in reporting and data extraction programs. You also can execute SQL statements directly from Visual Studio.NET and other development tools.

SQL statements are commonly divided into categories, five of which are of interest to us here:

- **Data definition language (DDL)** statements, which are used for creating tables, relationships, and other structures.
- **Data manipulation language (DML)** statements, which are used for querying, inserting, modifying, and deleting data.
- **SQL/Persistent Stored Modules (SQL/PSM)** statements, which extend SQL by adding procedural programming capabilities, such as variables and flow-of-control statements, that provide some programmability within the SQL framework.

■ **Transaction control language (TCL)** statements, which are used to mark transaction boundaries and control transaction behavior.

■ **Data control language (DCL)** statements, which are used to grant database permissions (or to revoke those permissions) to users and groups, so that the users or groups can perform various operations on the data in the database.

This chapter considers only DML statements for querying data. The remaining DML statements for inserting, modifying, and deleting data are discussed in Chapter 7, where we will also discuss SQL DDL statements. SQL/PSM is introduced in Chapter 7, and the specific variations of it used with each DBMS are discussed in detail in Chapter 10A for SQL Server 2014, Chapter 10B for Oracle Database 12*c*, and Chapter 10C for MySQL. TCL and DCL statements are covered in Chapter 9.

BY THE WAY Some authors treat SQL queries as a separate part of SQL rather than as a part of SQL DML. We note that the SQL/Framework section of the SQL specification includes queries as part of the "SQL-data statements" class of statements along with the rest of the SQL DML statements and treat them as SQL DML statements.

BY THE WAY The four actions listed for SQL DML are sometimes referred to as **CRUD**: create, read, update, and delete. We do *not* use this term in this book, but now you know what it means.

SQL is ubiquitous, and SQL programming is a critical skill. Today, nearly all DBMS products process SQL, with the only exceptions being some of the emerging NoSQL and Big Data movement products. Enterprise-class DBMSs such as Microsoft SQL Server 2014, Oracle Database 12*c*, Oracle MySQL 5.6, and IBM DB2 require that you know SQL. With these products, all data manipulation is expressed using SQL.

As explained in Chapter 1, if you have used Microsoft Access, you have used SQL, even if you didn't know it. Every time you process a form, create a report, or run a query, Microsoft Access generates SQL and sends that SQL to Microsoft Access's internal ADE DBMS engine. To do more than elementary database processing, you need to uncover the SQL hidden by Microsoft Access. Further, once you know SQL, you will find it easier to write a query statement in SQL rather than fight with the graphical forms, buttons, and other paraphernalia that you must use to create queries with the Microsoft Access query-by-example–style GUI.

The SQL SELECT/FROM/WHERE Framework

This section introduces the fundamental statement framework for SQL query statements. After we discuss this basic structure, you will learn how to submit SQL statements to Microsoft Access, SQL Server, Oracle Database, and MySQL. If you choose, you can then follow along with the text and process the SQL statements as they are explained in the rest of this chapter. The basic form of SQL queries uses the **SQL SELECT/FROM/WHERE framework**. In this framework:

■ The **SQL SELECT clause** specifies which *columns* are to be listed in the query results.

■ The **SQL FROM clause** specifies which *tables* are to be used in the query.

■ The **SQL WHERE clause** specifies which *rows* are to be listed in the query results.

Let's work through some examples so that this framework makes sense to you.

Reading Specified Columns from a Single Table

We begin very simply. Suppose we want to obtain the values that are in the SKU_DATA table. To do this, we write an SQL SELECT statement that contains all the column names in the table. An SQL statement to read that data is the following:

```
SELECT    SKU, SKU_Description, Department, Buyer
FROM      SKU_DATA;
```

Using the data in Figure 2-6, when the DBMS processes this statement the result will be:

	SKU	SKU_Description	Department	Buyer
1	100100	Std. Scuba Tank, Yellow	Water Sports	Pete Hansen
2	100200	Std. Scuba Tank, Magenta	Water Sports	Pete Hansen
3	101100	Dive Mask, Small Clear	Water Sports	Nancy Meyers
4	101200	Dive Mask, Med Clear	Water Sports	Nancy Meyers
5	201000	Half-dome Tent	Camping	Cindy Lo
6	202000	Half-dome Tent Vestibule	Camping	Cindy Lo
7	301000	Light Fly Climbing Harness	Climbing	Jerry Martin
8	302000	Locking Carabiner, Oval	Climbing	Jerry Martin

When SQL statements are executed, the statements transform tables. SQL statements start with a table, process that table in some way, and then place the results in another table structure. Even if the result of the processing is just a single number, that number is considered to be a table with one row and one column. As you will learn at the end of this chapter, some SQL statements process multiple tables. Regardless of the number of input tables, though, the result of every SQL statement is a single table.

Notice that SQL statements terminate with a semicolon (;) character. The semicolon is required by the SQL standard. Although some DBMS products will allow you to omit the semicolon, some will not, so develop the habit of terminating SQL statements with a semicolon.

SQL statements can also include an **SQL comment**, which is a block of text that is used to document the SQL statement while not executed as part of the SQL statement. SQL comments are enclosed in the symbols **/* and */**, and any text between these symbols is ignored when the SQL statement is executed. For example, here is the previous SQL query with an SQL comment added to document the query by including a query name:

```
/* *** SQL-Query-CH02-01 *** */
SELECT    SKU, SKU_Description, Department, Buyer
FROM      SKU_DATA;
```

Because the SQL comment is ignored when the SQL statement is executed, the output from this query is identical to the SQL query output shown above. We will use similar comments to label the SQL statements in this chapter as an easy way to reference a specific SQL statement in the text.

SQL provides a shorthand notation for querying all of the columns of a table. The shorthand is to use an **SQL asterisk (*) wildcard character** to indicate that we want all the columns to be displayed:

```
/* *** SQL-Query-CH02-02 *** */
SELECT    *
FROM      SKU_DATA;
```

The result will again be a table with all rows and all four of the columns in SKU_DATA:

	SKU	SKU_Description	Department	Buyer
1	100100	Std. Scuba Tank, Yellow	Water Sports	Pete Hansen
2	100200	Std. Scuba Tank, Magenta	Water Sports	Pete Hansen
3	101100	Dive Mask, Small Clear	Water Sports	Nancy Meyers
4	101200	Dive Mask, Med Clear	Water Sports	Nancy Meyers
5	201000	Half-dome Tent	Camping	Cindy Lo
6	202000	Half-dome Tent Vestibule	Camping	Cindy Lo
7	301000	Light Fly Climbing Harness	Climbing	Jerry Martin
8	302000	Locking Carabiner, Oval	Climbing	Jerry Martin

BY THE WAY   In the SQL SELECT statement, the SELECT clause and the FROM clause are the only *required* clauses in the statement. We will have a complete query by simply telling SQL which columns should be read from which table. In the rest of this chapter, we will discuss other clauses, such as the WHERE clause, that can be used as part of an SQL SELECT statement. All of these other clauses, however, are *optional*.

Specifying Column Order in SQL Queries from a Single Table

Suppose we want to obtain just the values of the Department and Buyer columns of the SKU_DATA table. In this case, we specify only the column names of the Department and Buyer columns, and an SQL SELECT statement to read that data is the following:

```
/* *** SQL-Query-CH02-03 *** */
SELECT      Department, Buyer
FROM        SKU_DATA;
```

Using the data in Figure 2-6, when the DBMS processes this statement the result will be:

	Department	Buyer
1	Water Sports	Pete Hansen
2	Water Sports	Pete Hansen
3	Water Sports	Nancy Meyers
4	Water Sports	Nancy Meyers
5	Camping	Cindy Lo
6	Camping	Cindy Lo
7	Climbing	Jerry Martin
8	Climbing	Jerry Martin

The order of the column names in the SELECT phrase determines the order of the columns in the results table. Thus, if we switch Buyer and Department in the SELECT phrase, they will be switched in the output table as well. Hence, the SQL statement:

```
/* *** SQL-Query-CH02-04 *** */
SELECT      Buyer, Department
FROM        SKU_DATA;
```

produces the following result table:

	Buyer	Department
1	Pete Hansen	Water Sports
2	Pete Hansen	Water Sports
3	Nancy Meyers	Water Sports
4	Nancy Meyers	Water Sports
5	Cindy Lo	Camping
6	Cindy Lo	Camping
7	Jerry Martin	Climbing
8	Jerry Martin	Climbing

Submitting SQL Statements to the DBMS

Before continuing the explanation of SQL, it will be useful for you to learn how to submit SQL statements to specific DBMS products. That way, you can work along with the text by keying and running SQL statements as you read the discussion. The particular means by which you submit SQL statements depends on the DBMS. Here we will describe the process for Microsoft Access 2013, Microsoft SQL Server 2014, Oracle Database 12*c*, and MySQL 5.6.

> **BY THE WAY**   You can learn SQL without running the queries in a DBMS, so if for some reason you do not have Microsoft Access, SQL Server, Oracle Database, or MySQL readily available, do not despair. You can learn SQL without them. Chances are your instructor, like a lot of us in practice today, learned SQL without a DBMS. It is just that SQL statements are easier to understand and remember if you can run the SQL while you read. However, given that there are free downloadable versions of Microsoft SQL Server 2014 Express edition, Oracle Database Express Edition 11*g* Release 2, and MySQL 5.6 Server Community Edition, you can have an installed DBMS to run these SQL examples even if you have not purchased Microsoft Access 2013. See Chapters 10A, 10B, and 10C for specific instructions for creating databases using each of these products. The SQL scripts needed to create the Cape Codd Outdoor Sports database used in this chapter are available at *www.pearsonhighered.com/kroenke*.

Using SQL in Microsoft Access 2013

Before you can execute SQL statements, you need a computer that has Microsoft Access installed, and you need a Microsoft Access database that contains the tables and sample data in Figure 2-6. Microsoft Access is part of many versions of the Microsoft Office suite, so it should not be too difficult to find a computer that has it.

Because Microsoft Access is commonly used in classes that use this book as a textbook, we will look at how to use SQL in Microsoft Access in some detail. Before we proceed, however, we need to discuss a specific peculiarity of Microsoft Access: the limitations of the default version of SQL used in Microsoft Access.

Does Not Work with Microsoft Access ANSI-89 SQL

As mentioned previously, our discussion of SQL is based on SQL features present in SQL standards since the ANSI SQL-92 standard (which Microsoft refers to as ANSI-92 SQL). Unfortunately, Microsoft Access 2013 still defaults to the earlier SQL-89 version—Microsoft calls it ANSI-89 SQL or Microsoft Jet SQL (after the Microsoft Jet DBMS engine used by Microsoft Access). ANSI-89 SQL differs significantly from SQL-92, and, therefore, some features of the SQL-92 language will not work in Microsoft Access.

Microsoft Access 2013 (and the earlier Microsoft Access 2003, 2007, and 2010 versions) does contain a setting that allows you to use SQL-92 instead of the default ANSI-89

The **Object Designers** button

The **SQL Server Compatible Syntax (ANSI 92)** option controls the use of SQL-89 versus SQL-92 syntax in Access queries

Use this check box to use SQL-92 syntax in just the open database

Use this check box to use SQL-92 syntax when new databases are created

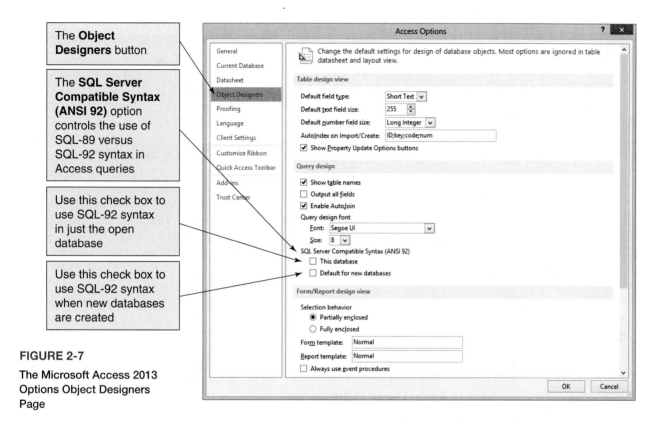

FIGURE 2-7

The Microsoft Access 2013 Options Object Designers Page

SQL. Microsoft included this option to allow Microsoft Access tools such as forms and reports to be used in application development for Microsoft SQL Server, which supports newer SQL standards. To set the option in Microsoft Access 2013, click the **File** command tab and then click the **Options** command to open the Access Options dialog box. In the Access Options dialog box, click the **Object Designers** button to display the Access Options Object Designers page, as shown in Figure 2-7.

As shown in Figure 2-7, the **SQL Server Compatible Syntax (ANSI 92)** options control which version of SQL is used in a Microsoft Access 2013 database. If you check the **This database** check box, you will use SQL-92 syntax in the current database. Or you can check the **Default for new databases** check box to make SQL-92 syntax the default for all new databases you create. When you click the **OK** button to save the changed SQL syntax option, the SQL-Syntax Information dialog box shown in Figure 2-8 will be displayed. Read the information, and then click the **OK** button to close the dialog box.

Unfortunately, very few Microsoft Access users or organizations using Microsoft Access are likely to set the Microsoft Access SQL version to the SQL-92 option, and, in this chapter, we assume that Microsoft Access is running in the default ANSI-89 SQL mode. One advantage of doing so is that it will help you understand the limitations of Microsoft Access ANSI-89 SQL and how to cope with them.

In the discussion that follows, we use "Does Not Work with Microsoft Access ANSI-89 SQL" boxes to identify SQL commands and SQL clauses that do not work in Microsoft Access ANSI-89 SQL. We also identify any workarounds that are available. Remember that the one *permanent* workaround is to choose to use the SQL-92 syntax option in the databases you create!

FIGURE 2-8

The Microsoft Access 2013 SQL-Syntax Information Dialog Box

Microsoft Access   ✕

You have chosen to alter the mode in which SQL syntax will be interpreted in this database. This will mean:

* Existing queries may return different results or not run at all.
* The range of data-types and reserved words will change.
* Different wildcards will be used.

It is recommended that you make a backup copy of this database before continuing. If you agree to continue, Access will close this database, compact it, and re-open in the new mode. Select OK to continue.

OK   Cancel   Help

Was this information helpful?

Nonetheless, two versions of the Microsoft Access 2013 Cape Codd Outdoor Sports database are available at *www.pearsonhighered.com/kroenke* for your use with this chapter. The Microsoft Access database file named *Cape-Codd.accdb* is set to use Microsoft Access ANSI-89, whereas the Microsoft Access database file name *Cape-Codd-SQL-92.accdb* is set to use Microsoft Access SQL-92. Choose the one you want to use (or use them both and compare the results!). Note that these files contain three additional tables (INVENTORY, WAREHOUSE, and CATALOG_SKU_2013) that we will not use in this chapter but that you will need for the Review Questions at the end of the chapter.

Alternatively, of course, you can create your own Microsoft Access database and then add the tables and data in Figures 2-4, 2-5, and 2-6, as described in Appendix A. If you create your own database, look at the Review Questions at the end of the chapter and create the INVENTORY and WAREHOUSE tables shown there in addition to the RETAIL_ORDER, ORDER_ITEM, and SKU tables shown in the chapter discussion. This will ensure that what you see on your monitor matches the screenshots in this chapter. Whether you download the database file or build it yourself, you will need to do one or the other before you can proceed.

Processing SQL Statements in Microsoft Access 2013

To process an SQL statement in Microsoft Access 2013, first open the database in Microsoft Access as described in Appendix A and then create a new tabbed Query window.

Opening a Microsoft Access Query Window in Design View

1. Click the **CREATE** command tab to display the Create command groups, as shown in Figure 2-9.
2. Click the **Query Design** button.
3. The Query1 tabbed document window is displayed in Design view, along with the Show Table dialog box, as shown in Figure 2-10.
4. Click the **Close** button on the Show Table dialog box. The Query1 document window now looks as shown in Figure 2-11, with the QUERY TOOLS contextual command tab and the DESIGN command tab displayed. This window is used for creating and editing Microsoft Access queries in Design view and is used with Microsoft Access QBE.

Note that in Figure 2-11 the Select button is selected in the Query Type group on the Design tab. You can tell this is so because active or selected buttons are always shown in color on the Ribbon. This indicates that we are creating a query that is the equivalent of an SQL SELECT statement.

FIGURE 2-9

The CREATE Command Tab

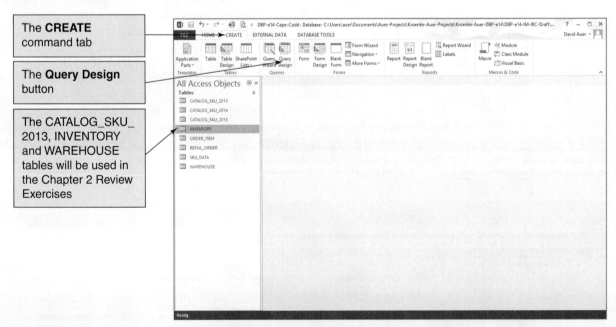

The **CREATE** command tab

The **Query Design** button

The CATALOG_SKU_2013, INVENTORY and WAREHOUSE tables will be used in the Chapter 2 Review Exercises

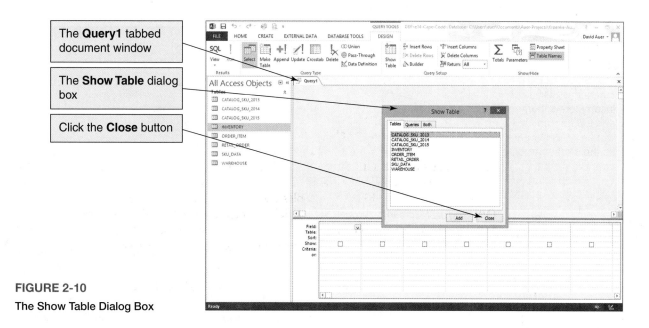

The **Query1** tabbed document window

The **Show Table** dialog box

Click the **Close** button

FIGURE 2-10

The Show Table Dialog Box

Also note that in Figure 2-11 the View gallery is available in the Results group of the Design tab. We can use this gallery to switch between Design view and SQL view. However, we can also just use the displayed SQL View button to switch to SQL view. The SQL View button is being displayed because Microsoft Access considers that to be the view you would most likely choose in the gallery if you used it. Microsoft Access always presents a "most likely needed" view choice as a button above the View gallery.

For our example SQL query in Microsoft Access, we will use SQL-Query-CH02-01, the first SQL query earlier in our discussion:

```
/* *** SQL-Query-CH02-01 *** */
SELECT      SKU, SKU_Description, Department, Buyer
FROM        SKU_DATA;
```

FIGURE 2-11

The QUERY TOOLS
Contextual Command Tab

The **QUERY TOOLS** tab

The **SQL View** button

The **View gallery** drop-down arrow button

The **Select** Query Type button

The **Query Type** command group

The **Query1** tabbed document window in Design view

The **DESIGN** command tab

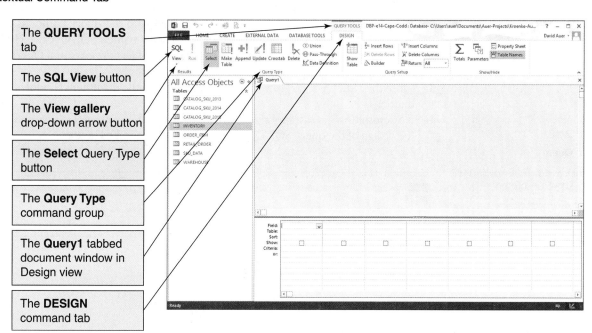

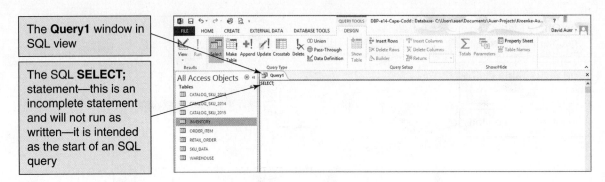

FIGURE 2-12

The Query1 Window in SQL View

The **Query1** window in SQL view

The SQL **SELECT;** statement—this is an incomplete statement and will not run as written—it is intended as the start of an SQL query

Opening a Microsoft Access SQL Query Window and Running a Microsoft Access SQL Query

1. Click the **SQL View** button in the Results group on the Design tab. The Query1 window switches to the SQL view, as shown in Figure 2-12. Note the basic SQL command **SELECT;** that's shown in the window. This is an incomplete command, and running it will not produce any results.

2. Edit the SQL SELECT command to read (do *not* include the SQL comment line):

```
SELECT      SKU, SKU_Description, Department, Buyer
FROM        SKU_DATA;
```

as shown in Figure 2-13.

3. Click the **Run** button on the Design tab. The query results appear, as shown in Figure 2-14. Compare the results shown in Figure 2-14 to the SQL-Query-CH02-01 results shown on the next page.

Because Microsoft Access is a personal database and includes an application generator, we can save Microsoft Access queries for future use. Enterprise-level DBMS products generally do not allow us to save queries (although they do allow us to save SQL Views within the database and SQL query scripts as separate files—we will discuss these methods later).

Saving a Microsoft Access SQL Query

1. To save the query, click the **Save** button on the Quick Access Toolbar. The Save As dialog box appears, as shown in Figure 2-15.

2. Type in the query name **SQL-Query-CH02-01** and then click the **OK** button. The query is saved, and the window is renamed with the query name. As shown in Figure 2-16, the query document window is now named SQL-Query-CH02-01, and a newly created SQL-Query-CH02-01 query object appears in a Queries section of the Navigation Pane.

3. Close the SQL-Query-CH02-01 window by clicking the document window's **Close** button.

4. If Microsoft Access displays a dialog box asking whether you want to save changes to the design of the query SQL-Query-CH02-01, click the **Yes** button.

FIGURE 2-13

The SQL Query

The **Run** button

The complete SQL query statement

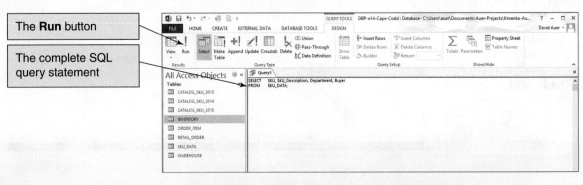

FIGURE 2-14

The SQL Query Results

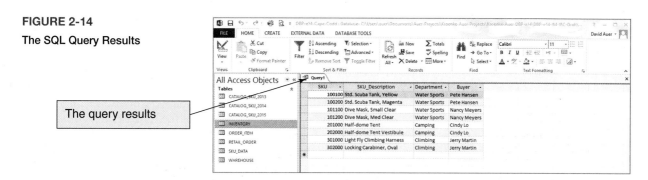

The query results

FIGURE 2-15

The Save As Dialog box

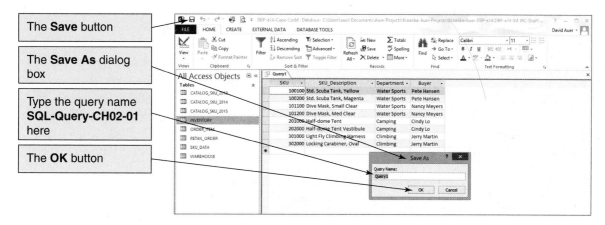

The **Save** button

The **Save As** dialog box

Type the query name **SQL-Query-CH02-01** here

The **OK** button

At this point, you should work through each of the other three queries in the preceding discussion of the SQL SELECT/FROM/WHERE framework. Save each query as SQL-Query-CH02-##, where ## is a sequential number from 02 to 04 that corresponds to the SQL query label shown in the SQL comment line of each query.

Using SQL in Microsoft SQL Server 2014

Before you can use SQL statements with Microsoft SQL Server, you need access to a computer that has SQL Server installed and that has a database with the tables and data shown in Figures 2-4, 2-5, and 2-6. Your instructor may have installed SQL Server in your computer lab and entered the data for you. If so, follow his or her instructions for accessing that database.

Otherwise, you will need to obtain a copy of SQL Server 2014 and install it on your computer. At this time, read the material in Chapter 10A about obtaining and installing SQL Server 2014.

After you have SQL Server 2014 installed, you will need to read the discussion for using SQL Server in Chapter 10A that explains how to create the Cape Codd database and

FIGURE 2-16

The Named and Saved Query

The query window is now named **SQL-Query-CH02-01**

The **Queries** section of the Navigation Pane

The **SQL-Query-CH02-01** query object

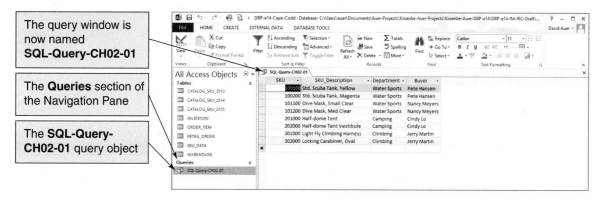

run the SQL Server scripts for creating and populating the Cape Codd database tables. The SQL Server 2014 scripts for the Cape Codd database are available on our Web site at *www.pearsonhighered.com/kroenke*.

SQL Server 2014 uses the Microsoft SQL Server 2014 Management Studio as the GUI tool for managing the SQL Server DBMS and the databases controlled by the DBMS. The Microsoft SQL Server 2014 Management Studio, which we will also refer to as just the SQL Server Management Studio, is installed as part of the SQL Server 2014 installation process and is discussed in Chapter 10A. Figure 2-17 shows the execution of SQL-Query-CH02-01 (note that the SQL comment is *not* included in the SQL statement as run–also note that the SQL comment *could* have been included in the SQL code if we had chosen to include it):

```
/* *** SQL-Query-CH02-01 *** */
SELECT    SKU, SKU_Description, Department, Buyer
FROM      SKU_DATA;
```

Running an SQL Query in SQL Server Management Studio

1. Click the **New Query** button to display a new tabbed query window.
2. If the Cape Codd database is not displayed in the Available Database box, select it in the Available Databases drop-down list, and then click the **Intellisense Enabled** button to *disable* Intellisense.
3. Check that the Cape_Codd database is selected in the Available Databases drop-down list.
4. Type the SQL SELECT command (*without* the SQL comment line shown above):

```
SELECT    SKU, SKU_Description, Department, Buyer
FROM      SKU_DATA;
```

The SQL query window now appears as shown in Figure 2-17.

FIGURE 2-17

Running an SQL Query in SQL Server Management Studio

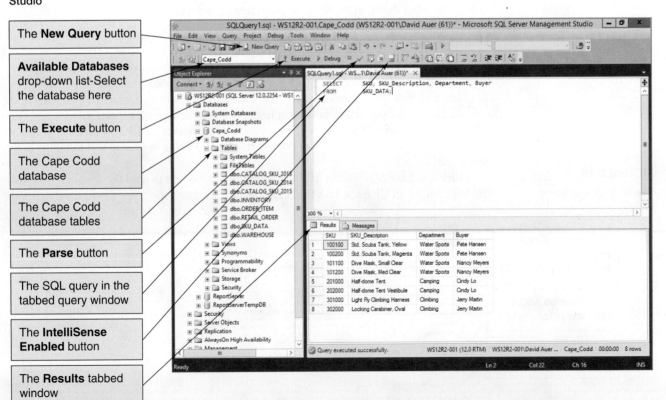

The **New Query** button

Available Databases drop-down list-Select the database here

The **Execute** button

The Cape Codd database

The Cape Codd database tables

The **Parse** button

The SQL query in the tabbed query window

The **IntelliSense Enabled** button

The **Results** tabbed window

5. At this point you can check the SQL command syntax before actually running the command by clicking the **Parse** button. A Results window will be displayed in the same location shown in Figure 2-17, but with the message "Command(s) completed successfully" if the SQL command syntax is correct or with an error message if there is a problem with the syntax.

6. Click the **Execute** button to run the query. The results are displayed in a results window, as shown in Figure 2-17.

Note that in Figure 2-17 the Cape Codd database object in the Object Browser in the left side window of the SQL Server Management Studio has been expanded to show the tables in the Cape Codd database. Many of the functions of the SQL Server Management Studio are associated with the objects in the Object Browser and are often accessed by right-clicking the object to display a shortcut menu.

> **BY THE WAY** We are using Microsoft SQL Server 2014 running in Microsoft Server 2012 Release 2. When we give specific sequences of steps to follow in the text or figures in this book, we use the command terminology used by SQL Server 2014 and associated utility programs in Microsoft Server 2012 Release 2. If you are running a workstation operating system such as Microsoft XP, Microsoft Windows 7, or Microsoft Windows 8.1, the terminology may vary somewhat.

SQL Server 2014 is an enterprise-class DBMS product and, as is typical of such products, does not store queries within the DBMS (it does store SQL Views, which can be considered a type of query, and we will discuss SQL Views in Chapter 7). However, you can save queries as SQL script files. An **SQL script file** is a separately stored plain text file, and it usually uses a file name extension of *.sql*. An SQL script can be opened and run as an SQL command (or set of commands). Often used to create and populate databases, scripts can also be used to store a query or set of queries. Figure 2-18 shows the SQL query being saved as an SQL script.

Note that in Figure 2-18 the SQL scripts are shown in a folder named *DBP-e14-Cape-Codd-Database*, as described in Chapter 10A. We recommend that you create a folder for

FIGURE 2-18

Saving an SQL Query as an SQL Script in SQL Server Management Studio

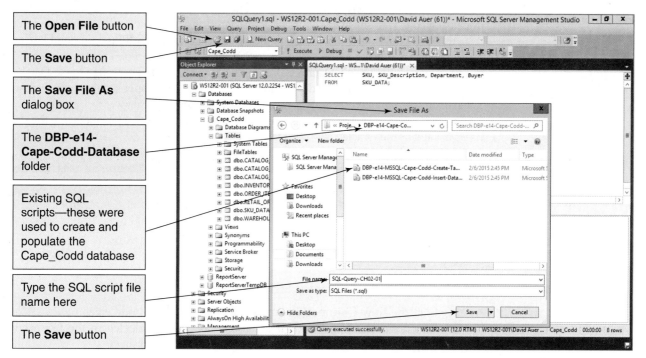

The **Open File** button

The **Save** button

The **Save File As** dialog box

The **DBP-e14-Cape-Codd-Database** folder

Existing SQL scripts—these were used to create and populate the Cape_Codd database

Type the SQL script file name here

The **Save** button

each database in the Projects folder. We have created the folder named *DBP-e14-Cape-Codd-Database* to store the script files associated with the Cape Codd database.

Saving an SQL Server Query as an SQL Script in SQL Server Management Studio

1. Click the **Save** button shown in Figure 2-18. The Save File As dialog appears, as shown in Figure 2-18.
2. Browse to the *\Documents\SQL Server Management Studio\Projects\DBP-e14-Cape-Codd-Database* folder.
3. Note that there are already two SQL script names displayed in the dialog box. These are the SQL scripts that were used to create and populate the Cape Codd database tables.
4. In the File Name text box, type the SQL script file name *SQL-Query-CH02-01*.
5. Click the **Save** button.

To rerun the saved query, you would click the **Open File** button shown in Figure 2-18 to open the Open File dialog box, open the SQL script containing the query, and then click the **Execute** button.

At this point, you should work through each of the other three queries in the preceding discussion of the SQL SELECT/FROM/WHERE framework. Save each query as SQL-Query-CH02-*##*, where *##* is a sequential number from 02 to 04 that corresponds to the SQL query label shown in the SQL comment line of each query. You can then continue working through the rest of the example SQL statements as you read the chapter.

Using SQL in Oracle Database

Before you can enter SQL statements into Oracle Database, you need access to a computer that has Oracle Database installed and that has a database with the tables and data shown in Figures 2-4, 2-5, and 2-6. Your instructor may have installed Oracle Database 12*c* or Oracle Database Express Edition 11*g* Release 2 on a computer in the lab and entered the data for you. If so, follow his or her instructions for accessing that database.

Otherwise, you will need to obtain a copy of Oracle Database Express Edition 11*g* Release 2 and install it on your computer. At this time, read the material in Chapter 10B about obtaining and installing Oracle Database Express Edition 11*g* Release 2.

After you have installed Oracle Database, you will need to read the introductory discussion for Oracle Database in Chapter 10B that explains how to create the Cape Codd database. Oracle Database scripts for creating and populating the Cape Codd database tables are available on our Web site at *www.pearsonhighered.com/kroenke*.

Although Oracle users have been dedicated to the Oracle SQL*Plus command line tool, professionals are moving to the new Oracle SQL Developer GUI tool. This application is installed as part of the Oracle Database 12*c* installation, but if you are using Oracle Database Express Edition you will need to download and install SQL Developer separately as discussed in Chapter 10B. Updated versions are available for free download at *www.oracle.com/technology/software/products/sql/index.html*. We will use it as our standard GUI tool for managing the databases created by the Oracle Database DBMS.

Figure 2-19 shows the execution of SQL-Query-CH02-01 (note that the SQL comment is *not* included in the SQL statement as run—also note that the SQL comment *could* have been included in the SQL code if we had chosen to include it):

```
/* *** SQL-Query-CH02-01 *** */

SELECT    SKU, SKU_Description, Department, Buyer

FROM      SKU_DATA;
```

Running an SQL Query in Oracle SQL Developer

1. Click the **New Connection** button and open the Cape Codd database.
2. Check that the Cape_Codd_Database connection is selected in the Connection drop-down list in the upper-right corner of the SQL Worksheet.

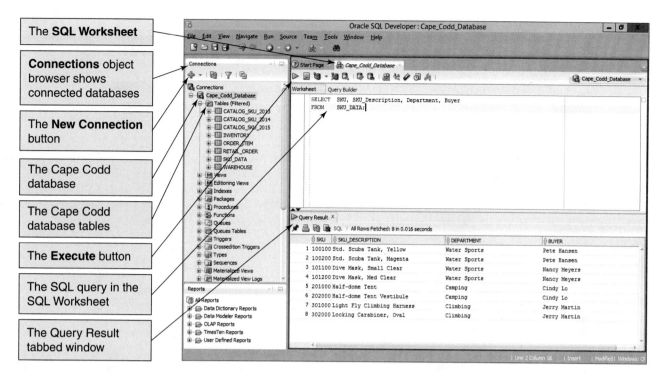

| The **SQL Worksheet** |
| **Connections** object browser shows connected databases |
| The **New Connection** button |
| The Cape Codd database |
| The Cape Codd database tables |
| The **Execute** button |
| The SQL query in the SQL Worksheet |
| The Query Result tabbed window |

FIGURE 2-19

Running an SQL Query in Oracle SQL Developer

3. In the tabbed SQL Worksheet, type the SQL SELECT command (*without* the SQL comment line shown above):

```
SELECT     SKU, SKU_Description, Department, Buyer
FROM       SKU_DATA;
```

as shown in Figure 2-19.

4. Click the **Execute** button to run the query. The results are displayed in a results window, as shown in Figure 2-19.

Note that in Figure 2-19, the *Cape-Codd-Database* object in the Object Browser in the left-side Connection object browser of the Oracle SQL Developer has been expanded to show the tables in the Cape Codd database. Many of the functions of SQL Developer are associated with the objects in the Connections object browser and are often accessed by right-clicking the object to display a shortcut menu.

BY THE WAY   We are using Oracle Database 12*c* and Oracle Database Express Edition 11*g* Release 2 running in Microsoft Server 2012 Release 2. When we give specific sequences of steps to follow in the text or figures in this book, we use the command terminology used by Oracle Database 12*c* and associated utility programs in Microsoft Server 2012 Release 2. If you are running a workstation operating system such as Microsoft Windows 7, Microsoft Windows 8.1, Microsoft Windows 10, or Linux, the terminology may vary somewhat.

Oracle Database is an enterprise-class DBMS product and, as is typical of such products, does not store queries within the DBMS (it does store SQL Views, which can be considered a type of query, and we will discuss SQL Views later in this chapter). However, you can save queries as SQL script files. An **SQL script file** is a separately stored plain text file, and it usually has a file name extension of *.sql*. An SQL script can be opened and run as an SQL command (or set of commands). Often used to create and populate databases, scripts can also be used to store a query or set of queries. Figure 2-20 shows the SQL query being saved as an SQL script.

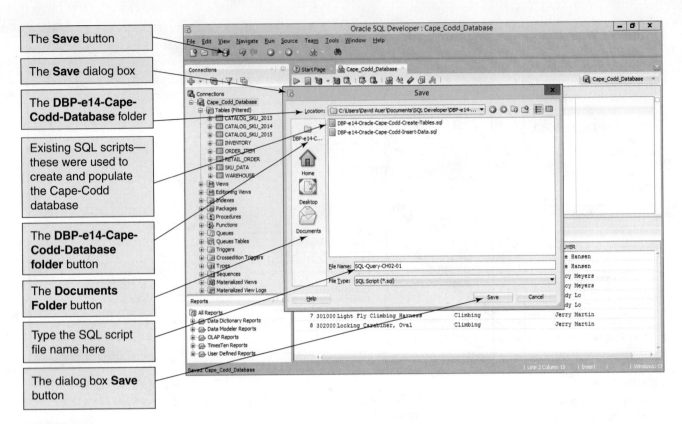

The **Save** button

The **Save** dialog box

The **DBP-e14-Cape-Codd-Database** folder

Existing SQL scripts—these were used to create and populate the Cape-Codd database

The **DBP-e14-Cape-Codd-Database folder** button

The **Documents Folder** button

Type the SQL script file name here

The dialog box **Save** button

FIGURE 2-20

Saving an Oracle SQL Query as an SQL Script in Oracle SQL Developer

Note that in Figure 2-20 the SQL scripts are shown in a folder named *{UserName}\Documents\SQL Developer\DBP-e14-Cape-Codd-Database* as described in Chapter 10B.

We recommend that you create a folder in your Documents folder named *SQL Developer* and then create a subfolder for each database in the SQL Developer folder. We have created a folder named *DBP-e14-Cape-Codd-Database* to store the script files associated with the Cape Codd database.

Saving an SQL Script in Oracle SQL Developer

1. Click the **Save** button shown in Figure 2-20. The Save dialog appears, as shown in Figure 2-20.
2. Click the **Documents** button on the Save dialog box to move to the Documents folder and then browse to the DBP-e14-Cape-Codd-Database folder.
3. Note that there are already two SQL script names displayed in the dialog box. These are the SQL scripts that were used to create and populate the Cape Codd database tables, and they are available on our Web site at *www.pearsonhighered.com/kroenke*.
4. In the File Name text box, type the SQL script file name *SQL-Query-CH02-01.sql*.
5. Click the **Save** button.

To rerun the saved query, you would click the SQL Developer **Open File** button to open the Open File dialog box, browse to the query file, open the query file, and then click the **Execute** button.

At this point, you should work through each of the other three queries in the preceding discussion of the SQL SELECT/FROM/WHERE framework. Save each query as SQLQuery-CH02-##, where ## is a sequential number from 02 to 04 that corresponds to the SQL query label shown in the SQL comment line of each query. You can then continue working through the rest of the example SQL statements as you read the chapter.

Using SQL in Oracle MySQL 5.6

Before you can use SQL statements with Oracle MySQL 5.6, you need access to a computer that has MySQL installed and that has a database with the tables and data shown in Figures 2-4, 2-5, and 2-6. Your instructor may have installed MySQL 5.6 in your computer lab and entered the data for you. If so, follow his or her instructions for accessing that database.

Otherwise, you will need to obtain a copy of MySQL Community Server 5.6 and install it on your computer. At this time, read the material in Chapter 10C about obtaining and installing MySQL Community Server 5.6.

After you have MySQL Community Sever 5.6 installed, you will need to read the discussion for MySQL Community Server 5.6 in Chapter 10C that explains how to create the Cape Codd database and run the MySQL scripts for creating and populating the Cape Codd database tables. The MySQL 5.6 SQL scripts for the Cape Codd database are available on our Web site at *www.pearsonhighered.com/kroenke*.

MySQL uses the MySQL Workbench as the GUI tool for managing the MySQL 5.6 DBMS and the databases controlled by the DBMS. This tool must be installed separately from the MySQL DBMS, and this is discussed in Chapter 10C. SQL statements are created and run in the MySQL Workbench, and Figure 2-21 shows the execution of SQL-Query-CH02-01 (note that the SQL comment is *not* included in the SQL statement as run—also note that the SQL comment *could* have been included in the SQL code if we had chosen to include it):

```
/* *** SQL-Query-CH02-01 *** */

SELECT    SKU, SKU_Description, Department, Buyer

FROM      SKU_DATA;
```

Running an SQL Query in the MySQL Workbench

1. To make the Cape Codd database the default schema (active database), right-click the cape_codd schema (database) object to display the shortcut menu and then click the **Set as Default Schema** command.

FIGURE 2-21

Running an SQL Query in the MySQL Workbench

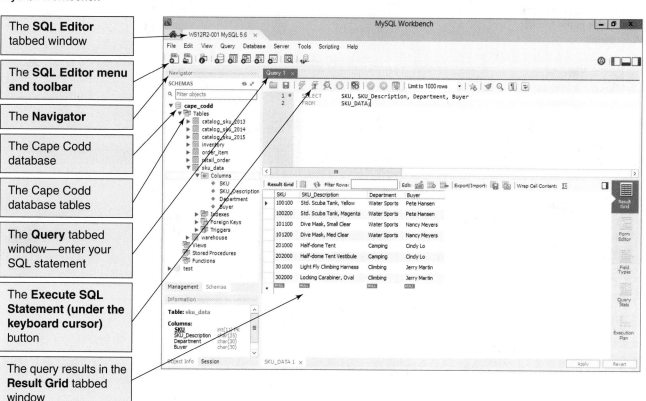

2. In the Query 1 tabbed window in the SQL Editor tabbed window, type the SQL
    SELECT command (*without* the SQL comment line shown above):

    ```
    SELECT    SKU, SKU_Description, Department, Buyer
    FROM      SKU_DATA;
    ```

    The SQL query window now appears as shown in Figure 2-21.
3. Click the **Execute Current SQL Statement in Connected Server** button to run
    the query. The results are displayed in a tabbed Query Result window, shown as the
    Query 1 Result window in Figure 2-21 (you can have more than one Query Result
    window open, and thus they need to be numbered).

Note that in Figure 2-21 the Cape Codd database object in the Object Browser in the left-
side window of the MySQL Workbench has been expanded to show the tables in the Cape Codd
database. Many of the functions of the MySQL Workbench are associated with the objects in the
Object Browser and are often accessed by right-clicking the object to display a shortcut menu.

> **BY THE WAY** We are using MySQL 5.6 Community Server running in Microsoft Server
> 2012 Release 2. When we give specific sequences of steps to follow in the
> text or figures in this book, we use the command terminology used for MySQL 5.6 and
> associated utility programs in Microsoft Server 2012 R2. If you are running a worksta-
> tion operating system such as Microsoft Windows 7, Microsoft Windows 8.1, or Linux,
> the terminology may vary somewhat.

MySQL 5.6 is an enterprise-class DBMS product and, as is typical of such products, does
not store queries within the DBMS (it does store SQL Views, which can be considered a type
of query, and we will discuss SQL Views later in this chapter). However, you can save MySQL
queries as SQL script files. An **SQL script file** is a separately stored plain text file, and it
usually uses a file name extension of *.sql*. An SQL script file can be opened and run as an SQL
command. Figure 2-22 shows the SQL query being saved as an SQL script file.

Note that in Figure 2-22 the query will be saved in a folder named *My Documents\MySQL
Workbench\Schemas\DBP-e14-Cape-Codd-Database* as described in Chapter 10C. By default,

FIGURE 2-22

Saving an SQL Query as an
SQL Script in the MySQL
Workbench

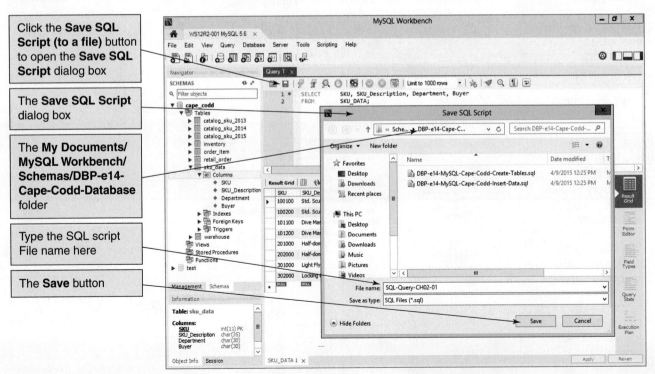

Click the **Save SQL
Script (to a file)** button
to open the **Save SQL
Script** dialog box

The **Save SQL Script**
dialog box

The **My Documents/
MySQL Workbench/
Schemas/DBP-e14-
Cape-Codd-Database**
folder

Type the SQL script
File name here

The **Save** button

MySQL Workbench stores files in the user's Documents folder. We recommend that you create a subfolder for each MySQL database. We have created the folder named *DBP-e14-Cape-Codd-Database* to store the script files associated with the Cape Codd database.

Saving a MySQL Query in MySQL Workbench

1. Click the **Save SQL Script to File** button, as shown in Figure 2-22. The Save Query to File dialog appears, as shown in Figure 2-22.
2. Browse to the *Documents\MySQL Workbench\Schemas\DBP-e14-Cape-Codd-Database* folder.
3. In the File name text box, type the SQL query file name *SQL-Query-CH02-01*.
4. Click the **Save** button.

To rerun the saved query, you would click the **File | Open SQL Script** menu command to open the **Open SQL Script** dialog box, then select and open the SQL query *.sql files, and, finally, click the **Execute the SQL Statement (under the keyboard cursor)** button.

At this point, you should work through each of the other three queries in the preceding discussion of the SQL SELECT/FROM/WHERE framework. Save each query as SQLQuery-CH02-##, where ## is a sequential number from 02 to 04 that corresponds to the SQL query label shown in the SQL comment line of each query. You can then continue working through the rest of the example SQL statements as you read the chapter.

SQL Enhancements for Querying a Single Table

Now that we know how to run SQL queries in the DBMS product that we are using, we can return to our discussion of SQL syntax itself. We started our discussion of SQL queries with SQL statements for processing a single table, and now we will add additional SQL features to those queries. As we proceed, you will begin to see how powerful SQL can be for querying databases and for creating information from existing data.

> **BY THE WAY**   The SQL results shown in this chapter were generated using Microsoft SQL Server 2014. Query results from other DBMS products will be similar but may vary a bit.

Reading Specified Rows from a Single Table

Now that we know how to designate which *columns* will be included in the results of an SQL query, we need to discuss how to control which *rows* are included in the results.

Notice that in the results to SQL-Query-CH04 some rows are duplicated. The data in the first and second row, for example, are identical. We can eliminate duplicates by using the **SQL DISTINCT keyword** as follows:

```
/* *** SQL-Query-CH02-05 *** */
SELECT     DISTINCT Buyer, Department
FROM       SKU_DATA;
```

The result of this statement, where all of the duplicate rows have been removed, is:

	Buyer	Department
1	Cindy Lo	Camping
2	Jerry Martin	Climbing
3	Nancy Meyers	Water Sports
4	Pete Hansen	Water Sports

> **BY THE WAY** The reason that SQL does not automatically eliminate duplicate rows is that it can be very time consuming to do so. To determine if any rows are duplicates, every row must be compared with every other row. If there are 100,000 rows in a table, that checking will take a long time. Hence, by default duplicates are not removed. However, it is always possible to force their removal using the DISTINCT keyword.

We can also control how many rows are displayed by using the **SQL TOP {NumberOfRows} function** (SQL Server only). For example, if we want to see only the rows one through five from SQL-Query-CH02-04, we write:

```
/* *** SQL-Query-CH02-06 *** */
SELECT    TOP 5 Buyer, Department
FROM      SKU_DATA;
```

The result of this statement displays only the first five of the eight rows in the results for SQL-Query-CH02-04. Note that because we are *not* using the DISTINCT keyword, we get some identical, duplicated rows in the result:

	Buyer	Department
1	Pete Hansen	Water Sports
2	Pete Hansen	Water Sports
3	Nancy Meyers	Water Sports
4	Nancy Meyers	Water Sports
5	Cindy Lo	Camping

The SQL TOP function can also be used to display a percentage of the resulting rows by using the **SQL TOP {Percentage} PERCENT function** (SQL Server only). For example, if we want to see 75 percent of the data from SQL-Query-CH02-04, we write:

```
/* *** SQL-Query-CH02-07 *** */
SELECT    TOP 75 PERCENT Buyer, Department
FROM      SKU_DATA;
```

The result of this statement displays only the first six of the eight rows in the results for SQL-Query-CH02-04. Note that, again, since we are *not* using the DISTINCT keyword, we get some identical, duplicated rows in the result:

	Buyer	Department
1	Pete Hansen	Water Sports
2	Pete Hansen	Water Sports
3	Nancy Meyers	Water Sports
4	Nancy Meyers	Water Sports
5	Cindy Lo	Camping
6	Cindy Lo	Camping

The DISTINCT, TOP {NumberOfRows} and TOP {Percentage} PERCENT functions provide some help in controlling which rows are displayed in a result, but the real power for controlling rows in the output to the SQL SELECT statement is in the WHERE clause. Suppose we want all of the *columns* of the SKU_DATA table, but we want only the *rows* for the Water Sports department. We can obtain that result by using the SQL WHERE clause as follows:

```
/* *** SQL-Query-CH02-08 *** */
SELECT      *
FROM        SKU_DATA
WHERE       Department = 'Water Sports';
```

The result of this statement will be:

	SKU	SKU_Description	Department	Buyer
1	100100	Std. Scuba Tank, Yellow	Water Sports	Pete Hansen
2	100200	Std. Scuba Tank, Magenta	Water Sports	Pete Hansen
3	101100	Dive Mask, Small Clear	Water Sports	Nancy Meyers
4	101200	Dive Mask, Med Clear	Water Sports	Nancy Meyers

The equal sign (=) that appears in the WHERE clause of SQL-Query-CH02-08 is an **SQL comparison operator**. A list of common SQL comparison operators is shown in Figure 2-23.

In an SQL WHERE clause, if the column contains text or date data, the comparison values must be enclosed in single quotation marks ('{*text or date data*}'). For example, in the CATALOG_SKU_2014 table, only the SKUs that were available on the Cape Codd Web site on January 1, 2014, actually appeared in the printed catalog. To see these items, we use the following query:

```
/* *** SQL-Query-CH02-09 *** */
SELECT      *
FROM        CATALOG_SKU_2014
WHERE       DateOnWebSite = '01-JAN-2014';
```

FIGURE 2-23

SQL Comparison Operators

SQL Comparison Operators	
Operator	**Meaning**
=	Is equal to
<>	Is NOT Equal to
<	Is less than
>	Is greater than
<=	Is less than OR equal to
>=	Is greater than OR equal to
IN	Is equal to one of a set of values
NOT IN	Is NOT Equal to one of a set of values
BETWEEN	Is within a range of numbers (includes the end points)
NOT BETWEEN	Is NOT within a range of numbers (includes the end points)
LIKE	Matches a set of characters
NOT LIKE	Does NOT match a set of characters
IS NULL	Is equal to NULL
IS NOT NULL	Is NOT equal to NULL

The result of this statement will be:

	CatalogID	SKU	SKU_Description	Department	CatalogPage	DateOnWebSite
1	20140001	100100	Std. Scuba Tank, Yellow	Water Sports	23	2014-01-01
2	20140002	100300	Std. Scuba Tank, Light Blue	Water Sports	23	2014-01-01
3	20140004	101100	Dive Mask, Small Clear	Water Sports	26	2014-01-01
4	20140005	101200	Dive Mask, Med Clear	Water Sports	26	2014-01-01
5	20140006	201000	Half-dome Tent	Camping	46	2014-01-01
6	20140007	202000	Half-dome Tent Vestibule	Camping	46	2014-01-01
7	20140008	301000	Light Fly Climbing Harness	Climbing	77	2014-01-01
8	20140009	302000	Locking Carabiner, Oval	Climbing	79	2014-01-01

> **BY THE WAY** When using a date in the WHERE clause, you can usually enclose it in single quotes just as you would a character string as shown in SQL-Query-CH02-09. However, when using Microsoft Access 2013, you *must* enclose dates within the # symbol. For example:
>
> ```
> /* *** SQL-Query-CH02-09-Access *** */
>
> SELECT      *
>
> FROM        CATALOG_SKU_2014
>
> WHERE       DateOnWebSite = #01/01/14#;
> ```
>
> Oracle Database 12c and MySQL 5.6 can also have idiosyncrasies when using date data in SQL statements, and this is discussed in Chapters 10B and 10C, respectively.

If the column contains numeric data, however, the comparison values need not be in quotes. Thus, to find all of the SKU rows with a value greater than 200,000, we would use the SQL statement (note that no comma is included in the numeric value code):

```
/* *** SQL-Query-CH02-10 *** */

SELECT      *

FROM        SKU_DATA

WHERE       SKU > 200000;
```

The result is:

	SKU	SKU_Description	Department	Buyer
1	201000	Half-dome Tent	Camping	Cindy Lo
2	202000	Half-dome Tent Vestibule	Camping	Cindy Lo
3	301000	Light Fly Climbing Harness	Climbing	Jerry Martin
4	302000	Locking Carabiner, Oval	Climbing	Jerry Martin

> **BY THE WAY** SQL is very fussy about single quotes. It wants the plain, nondirectional quotes found in basic text editors. The fancy directional quotes produced by many word processors will produce errors. For example, the data value 'Water Sports' is correctly stated, but 'Water Sports' is not. Do you see the difference?

Reading Specified Columns and Rows from a Single Table

So far, we have generally selected certain columns and *all* rows, or we have selected *all* columns and certain rows (the exceptions being our discussion of the DISTINCT, TOP {NumberOfRows}, and TOP {Percentage} PERCENT functions). However, we can combine these operations to select certain columns and certain rows by naming the columns we want and then using the SQL WHERE clause. For example, to obtain the SKU_Description and Department of all products in the Climbing department, we use the SQL query:

```
/* *** SQL-Query-CH02-11 *** */
SELECT     SKU_Description, Department
FROM       SKU_DATA
WHERE      Department = 'Climbing';
```

The result is:

	SKU_Description	Department
1	Light Fly Climbing Harness	Climbing
2	Locking Carabiner, Oval	Climbing

SQL does not require that the column used in the WHERE clause also appear in the SELECT clause column list. Thus, we can specify:

```
/* *** SQL-Query-CH02-12 *** */
SELECT     SKU_Description, Buyer
FROM       SKU_DATA
WHERE      Department = 'Climbing';
```

where the qualifying column, Department, does not appear in the SELECT clause column list. The result is:

	SKU_Description	Buyer
1	Light Fly Climbing Harness	Jerry Martin
2	Locking Carabiner, Oval	Jerry Martin

> **BY THE WAY**   Standard practice is to write SQL statements with the SELECT, FROM, and WHERE clauses on separate lines. This practice is just a coding convention, however, and SQL parsers do not require it. You could code SQL-Query-CH02-09 all on one line as:
>
> ```
> SELECT SKU_Description, Buyer FROM SKU_DATA WHERE Department = 'Climbing';
> ```
>
> All DBMS products would process the statement written in this fashion. However, the standard multiline coding convention makes SQL easier to read, and we encourage you to write your SQL according to it.

Sorting the SQL Query Results

The order of the rows produced by an SQL statement is arbitrary and determined by programs in the bowels of each DBMS. If you want the DBMS to display the rows in a particular order, you can add the **SQL ORDER BY clause** to the SELECT/FROM.WHERE framework. For example, to sort the rows in the ORDER_ITEM table by OrderNumber in ascending order (the default sorting order), you use the SQL statement:

```
/* *** SQL-Query-CH02-13 *** */

SELECT     *

FROM       ORDER_ITEM

ORDER BY   OrderNumber;
```

SQL-Query-CH02-13 will generate the following results:

	OrderNumber	SKU	Quantity	Price	ExtendedPrice
1	1000	201000	1	300.00	300.00
2	1000	202000	1	130.00	130.00
3	2000	101100	4	50.00	200.00
4	2000	101200	2	50.00	100.00
5	3000	101200	1	50.00	50.00
6	3000	101100	2	50.00	100.00
7	3000	100200	1	300.00	300.00

We can sort by two columns by adding a second column name. For example, to sort first by OrderNumber and then by Price within OrderNumber, we use the following SQL query:

```
/* *** SQL-Query-CH02-14 *** */

SELECT     *

FROM       ORDER_ITEM

ORDER BY   OrderNumber, Price;
```

The result for this query is:

	OrderNumber	SKU	Quantity	Price	ExtendedPrice
1	1000	202000	1	130.00	130.00
2	1000	201000	1	300.00	300.00
3	2000	101100	4	50.00	200.00
4	2000	101200	2	50.00	100.00
5	3000	101200	1	50.00	50.00
6	3000	101100	2	50.00	100.00
7	3000	100200	1	300.00	300.00

If we want to sort the data by Price and then by OrderNumber, we would simply reverse the order of those columns in the ORDER BY clause as follows:

```
/* *** SQL-Query-CH02-15 *** */

SELECT     *

FROM       ORDER_ITEM

ORDER BY   Price, OrderNumber;
```

This SQL query has the results:

	OrderNumber	SKU	Quantity	Price	ExtendedPrice
1	2000	101100	4	50.00	200.00
2	2000	101200	2	50.00	100.00
3	3000	101200	1	50.00	50.00
4	3000	101100	2	50.00	100.00
5	1000	202000	1	130.00	130.00
6	1000	201000	1	300.00	300.00
7	3000	100200	1	300.00	300.00

> **BY THE WAY** Note to Microsoft Access users: Unlike the SQL Server output shown here, Microsoft Access displays dollar signs in the output of currency data.

By default, rows are sorted in *ascending* order. To sort in *descending order*, add the **SQL DESC keyword** after the column name. Thus, to sort first by Price in descending order and then by OrderNumber in ascending order, we use the SQL query:

```
/* *** SQL-Query-CH02-16 *** */

SELECT     *

FROM       ORDER_ITEM

ORDER BY   Price DESC, OrderNumber ASC;
```

The result is:

	OrderNumber	SKU	Quantity	Price	ExtendedPrice
1	1000	201000	1	300.00	300.00
2	3000	100200	1	300.00	300.00
3	1000	202000	1	130.00	130.00
4	2000	101100	4	50.00	200.00
5	2000	101200	2	50.00	100.00
6	3000	101200	1	50.00	50.00
7	3000	101100	2	50.00	100.00

Because the default order is ascending, it is not necessary to specify ASC in the last SQL statement. Thus, the following SQL statement is equivalent to the previous SQL query:

```
/* *** SQL-Query-CH02-17 *** */

SELECT     *

FROM       ORDER_ITEM

ORDER BY   Price DESC, OrderNumber;
```

and produces the same results:

	OrderNumber	SKU	Quantity	Price	ExtendedPrice
1	1000	201000	1	300.00	300.00
2	3000	100200	1	300.00	300.00
3	1000	202000	1	130.00	130.00
4	2000	101100	4	50.00	200.00
5	2000	101200	2	50.00	100.00
6	3000	101200	1	50.00	50.00
7	3000	101100	2	50.00	100.00

SQL WHERE Clause Options

SQL includes a number of SQL WHERE clause options that greatly expand SQL's power and utility. In this section, we consider three options: compound clauses, ranges, and wildcards.

Compound SQL WHERE Clauses Using Logical Operators

SQL WHERE clauses can include multiple conditions by using the **SQL logical operators**, which include the AND, OR, and NOT operators and which are summarized in Figure 2-24

The **SQL AND operator** requires that each row in the results meets *both* of the conditions specified in the WHERE clause. For example, to find all of the rows in SKU_DATA that have *both* a Department named Water Sports and a Buyer named Nancy Meyers, we can use the SQL AND operator in our query code:

```
/* *** SQL-Query-CH02-18 *** */

SELECT     *
FROM       SKU_DATA
WHERE      Department='Water Sports'
   AND     Buyer='Nancy Meyers';
```

The results of this query are:

	SKU	SKU_Description	Department	Buyer
1	101100	Dive Mask, Small Clear	Water Sports	Nancy Meyers
2	101200	Dive Mask, Med Clear	Water Sports	Nancy Meyers

The **SQL OR operator** requires that each row in the results meets *one or the other or both* of the conditions specified in the WHERE clause. Thus, to find all of the rows of SKU_DATA for either the Camping *or* Climbing departments, we can use the SQL OR operator in the SQL query:

```
/* *** SQL-Query-CH02-19 *** */

SELECT     *
FROM       SKU_DATA
WHERE      Department='Camping'
   OR      Department='Climbing';
```

FIGURE 2-24

SQL Logical Operators

SQL Logical Operators	
Operator	Meaning
AND	Both arguments are TRUE
OR	One or the other or both of the arguments are TRUE
NOT	Negates the associated operator

This SQL query gives us the following results:

	SKU	SKU_Description	Department	Buyer
1	201000	Half-dome Tent	Camping	Cindy Lo
2	202000	Half-dome Tent Vestibule	Camping	Cindy Lo
3	301000	Light Fly Climbing Harness	Climbing	Jerry Martin
4	302000	Locking Carabiner, Oval	Climbing	Jerry Martin

The **SQL NOT operator** negates or reverses a condition set by an AND or OR operator. For example, to find all of the rows in SKU_DATA that have a Department named Water Sports but *not* a Buyer named Nancy Meyers, we can use the SQL NOT operator in our query code:

```
/* *** SQL-Query-CH02-20 *** */
SELECT      *
FROM        SKU_DATA
WHERE       Department='Water Sports'
  AND NOT   Buyer='Nancy Meyers';
```

The results of this query are:

	SKU	SKU_Description	Department	Buyer
1	100100	Std. Scuba Tank, Yellow	Water Sports	Pete Hansen
2	100200	Std. Scuba Tank, Magenta	Water Sports	Pete Hansen

Three or more AND and OR conditions can be combined, but in such cases it is often easiest to use SQL IN and NOT IN comparison operators.

SQL WHERE Clauses Using Sets of Values

When we want to include a set of values in the SQL WHERE clause, we use the **SQL IN operator** or the **SQL NOT IN operator** (Figure 2-23). For example, suppose we want to obtain all of the rows in SKU_DATA for the set of buyers Nancy Meyers, Cindy Lo, and Jerry Martin. We could construct a WHERE clause with two AND conditions, but an easier way to do this is to use the SQL IN operator, which specifies the set of values to be used in the SQL query:

```
/* *** SQL-Query-CH02-21 *** */
SELECT      *
FROM        SKU_DATA
WHERE       Buyer IN ('Nancy Meyers', 'Cindy Lo', 'Jerry Martin');
```

In this format, the set of values is enclosed in parentheses. A row is selected if Buyer is equal to any one of the values provided. The result is:

	SKU	SKU_Description	Department	Buyer
1	101100	Dive Mask, Small Clear	Water Sports	Nancy Meyers
2	101200	Dive Mask, Med Clear	Water Sports	Nancy Meyers
3	201000	Half-dome Tent	Camping	Cindy Lo
4	202000	Half-dome Tent Vestibule	Camping	Cindy Lo
5	301000	Light Fly Climbing Harness	Climbing	Jerry Martin
6	302000	Locking Carabiner, Oval	Climbing	Jerry Martin

Similarly, if we want to find rows of SKU_DATA for which the buyer is someone *other* than Nancy Meyers, Cindy Lo, or Jerry Martin, we would use the SQL NOT IN operator, which specifies the set of values to be *excluded* from the SQL query:

```
/* *** SQL-Query-CH02-18 *** */

SELECT    *

FROM      SKU_DATA

WHERE     Buyer NOT IN ('Nancy Meyers', 'Cindy Lo', 'Jerry Martin');
```

The result is:

	SKU	SKU_Description	Department	Buyer
1	100100	Std. Scuba Tank, Yellow	Water Sports	Pete Hansen
2	100200	Std. Scuba Tank, Magenta	Water Sports	Pete Hansen

Observe an important difference between the IN and NOT IN operators:

- A row qualifies for an IN condition if the column is *equal* to *any* of the values in the parentheses.
- A row qualifies for a NOT IN condition if it is *not equal* to *all* of the items in the parentheses.

SQL WHERE Clauses Using Ranges of Values

When we want to include or exclude a range of numerical values in the SQL WHERE clause, we use the **SQL BETWEEN operator** or the **SQL NOT BETWEEN operator** (Figure 2-23).

For example, suppose that we want to find all the rows in the ORDER_ITEM table where ExtendedPrice ranges from $100.00 to $200.00 including the end points of the range, $100.00 and $200.00. We could use the SQL query:

```
/* *** SQL-Query-CH02-23 *** */

SELECT    *

FROM      ORDER_ITEM

WHERE     ExtendedPrice >= 100

   AND    ExtendedPrice <= 200

ORDER BY  ExtendedPrice;
```

The SQL query produces the results sorted in order of ascending ExtendedPrice so that we can easily see the smallest and largest values:

	OrderNumber	SKU	Quantity	Price	ExtendedPrice
1	3000	101100	2	50.00	100.00
2	2000	101200	2	50.00	100.00
3	1000	202000	1	130.00	130.00
4	2000	101100	4	50.00	200.00

However, rather than specifying the range of values by using a compound SQL WHERE clause, we can accomplish the same results by using the SQL BETWEEN operator. Note how the SQL BETWEEN operator is used to create a simple, one-line WHERE clause in this SQL query:

```
/* *** SQL-Query-CH02-24 *** */

SELECT    *

FROM      ORDER_ITEM

WHERE     ExtendedPrice BETWEEN 100 AND 200

ORDER BY  ExtendedPrice;
```

The results of SQL-Query-CH02-24 are identical to those from SQL-Query-CH02-23 above, and note again that the specified end values of the range are included in the SQL query results:

	OrderNumber	SKU	Quantity	Price	ExtendedPrice
1	3000	101100	2	50.00	100.00
2	2000	101200	2	50.00	100.00
3	1000	202000	1	130.00	130.00
4	2000	101100	4	50.00	200.00

On the other hand, if we want to find all the rows in the ORDER_ITEM table *excluding* the ExtendedPrice range from $100.00 to $200.00, we can use the SQL NOT BETWEEN operator. In this case, the SQL query is:

```
/* *** SQL-Query-CH02-25 *** */

SELECT     *

FROM       ORDER_ITEM

WHERE      ExtendedPrice NOT BETWEEN 100 AND 200

ORDER BY   ExtendedPrice;
```

This gives us the results (again sorted from lowest to highest ExtendedPrice):

	OrderNumber	SKU	Quantity	Price	ExtendedPrice
1	3000	101200	1	50.00	50.00
2	1000	201000	1	300.00	300.00
3	3000	100200	1	300.00	300.00

SQL WHERE Clauses That Use Character String Patterns

There are times when we want to uses the SQL WHERE clause to find matching sets or patterns of *character stings*. **Character strings** include the data that we store in a CHAR or VARCHAR data–type column (*CHAR* columns use a fixed number of bytes to store the data, while *VARCHAR* columns adjust the number of bytes used to fit the actual length of the data) and are composed of letters, numbers, and special characters. For example, the name *Smith* is a character string, as are *360-567-9876* and *Joe#34@elsewhere.com*. To find rows with values that match or do not match specifc character string patterns, we use the **SQL LIKE operator** and the **SQL NOT LIKE operator** (Figure 2-23).

To help specify character string patterns, we use two SQL wildcard characters:

- The **SQL underscore (_) wildcard character**, which represents a single, unspecified character in a specific position in the character string.
- The **SQL percent sign (%) wildcard character**, which represents any sequence of contiguous, unspecified characters (including spaces) in a specific position in the character string.

For example, suppose we want to find the rows in the SKU_DATA table for all buyers whose first name is *Pete*. To find such rows, we use the SQL LIKE operator with the SQL percent sign (%) wildcard character, as shown in the SQL-Query-CH02-26 query:

```
/* *** SQL-Query-CH02-26 *** */

SELECT     *

FROM       SKU_DATA

WHERE      Buyer LIKE 'Pete%';
```

When used as an SQL wildcard character, the percent symbol (%) stands for any sequence of characters. When used with the SQL LIKE operator, the character string 'Pete%' means any sequence of characters that starts with the letters *Pete*. The result of this SQL query is:

	SKU	SKU_Description	Department	Buyer
1	100100	Std. Scuba Tank, Yellow	Water Sports	Pete Hansen
2	100200	Std. Scuba Tank, Magenta	Water Sports	Pete Hansen

Does Not Work with Microsoft Access ANSI-89 SQL

Microsoft Access ANSI-89 SQL uses wildcards, but not the SQL-92 standard wildcards. Microsoft Access uses the **Microsoft Access asterisk (*) wildcard character** instead of a percent sign to represent multiple characters.

Solution: Use the Microsoft Access asterisk (*) wildcard in place of the SQL-92 percent sign (%) wildcard in Microsoft Access ANSI-89 SQL statements. Thus, the preceding SQL query would be written as follows for Microsoft Access:

```
/* *** SQL-Query-CH02-26-Access *** */

SELECT      *
FROM        SKU_DATA
WHERE       Buyer LIKE 'Pete*';
```

Next, suppose we want to find the rows in SKU_DATA for which the SKU_Description includes the word *Tent* somewhere in the description. Because the word *Tent* could be at the front, at the end, or in the middle, we need to place a wildcard on both ends of the SQL LIKE phrase as follows:

```
/* *** SQL-Query-CH02-27 *** */

SELECT      *
FROM        SKU_DATA
WHERE       SKU_Description LIKE '%Tent%';
```

This query will find rows in which the word *Tent* occurs in any place in the SKU_Description. The result is:

	SKU	SKU_Description	Department	Buyer
1	201000	Half-dome Tent	Camping	Cindy Lo
2	202000	Half-dome Tent Vestibule	Camping	Cindy Lo

Sometimes we need to search for a particular value in a particular location in the column. For example, assume SKU values are coded such that a 2 in the third position from the right has some particular significance; maybe it means that the product is a variation of another product. For whatever reason, assume that we need to find all SKUs that have a 2 in the third column from the right. Suppose we try the SQL query:

```
/* *** SQL-Query-CH02-28 *** */

SELECT      *
FROM        SKU_DATA
WHERE       SKU LIKE '%2%';
```

The result of this query is:

	SKU	SKU_Description	Department	Buyer
1	100200	Std. Scuba Tank, Magenta	Water Sports	Pete Hansen
2	101200	Dive Mask, Med Clear	Water Sports	Nancy Meyers
3	201000	Half-dome Tent	Camping	Cindy Lo
4	202000	Half-dome Tent Vestibule	Camping	Cindy Lo
5	302000	Locking Carabiner, Oval	Climbing	Jerry Martin

This is *not* what we wanted. We mistakenly retrieved all rows that had a 2 in *any* position in the value of SKU. To find the products we want, we cannot use the SQL wildcard character %. Instead, we must use the SQL underscore (_) wildcard character, which represents a single, unspecified character in a specific position. The following SQL statement will find all SKU_DATA rows with a value of 2 in the third position from the right:

```
/* *** SQL-Query-CH02-29 *** */

SELECT     *

FROM       SKU_DATA

WHERE      SKU LIKE '%2__';
```

Observe that there are *two* underscores in this SQL query—one for the first position on the right and another for the second position on the right. This query gives us the result that we want:

	SKU	SKU_Description	Department	Buyer
1	100200	Std. Scuba Tank, Magenta	Water Sports	Pete Hansen
2	101200	Dive Mask, Med Clear	Water Sports	Nancy Meyers

> **BY THE WAY** While our example in SQL-Query-CH02-29 is correct, it does oversimplify this type of wildcard search a bit. In SQL-Query-CH02-29, SKU is an *INTEGER* valued column (with the values automatically converted by the DBMS to character strings during the query).
>
> If SKU had been a VARCHAR column, the same query would work. But if SKU had been a CHAR column, the query would not have worked because there would be extra spaces to the right of the characters used as padding to completely fill the CHAR length. For example, if we store the value "four" in a CHAR(8) column named *Number*, the DBMS will actually store "four____" ("four" plus four spaces). To deal with these extra spaces, we use the RTRIM function:
>
> ```
> WHERE       Number LIKE RTRIM('four');
> ```

Does Not Work with Microsoft Access ANSI-89 SQL

Microsoft Access ANSI-89 SQL uses wildcards, but not the SQL-92 standard wildcards. Microsoft Access uses the **Microsoft Access question mark (?) wildcard character** instead of an underscore (_) to represent a single character.

Solution: Use the Microsoft Access question mark (?) wildcard in place of the SQL-92 underscore (_) wildcard in Microsoft Access ANSI-89 SQL statements. Thus, the preceding SQL query would be written as follows for Microsoft Access:

```
/* *** SQL-Query-CH02-29-Access *** */

SELECT      *
FROM        SKU_DATA
WHERE       SKU LIKE '*2??';
```

Furthermore, Microsoft Access can sometimes be fussy about stored trailing spaces in a text field. You may have problems with a WHERE clause like this:

```
WHERE       SKU LIKE '10?200';
```

Solution: Use the right trim function RTRIM to eliminate trailing spaces:

```
WHERE       RTRIM(SKU) LIKE '10?200';
```

BY THE WAY   The SQL wildcard percent sign (%) and underscore (_) characters are specified in the SQL-92 standard. They are accepted by all DBMS products *except Microsoft Access.* So, why does Microsoft Access use the asterisk (*) character instead of the percent sign (%) and the question mark (?) instead of the underscore? These differences exist because Microsoft Access is, as we noted earlier, using the SQL-89 standard (which Microsoft calls ANSI-89 SQL). In that standard, the asterisk (*) and the question mark (?) are the correct wildcard characters. Switch a Microsoft Access database to SQL-92 (which Microsoft calls ANSI-92 SQL) in Access Options dialog box, and the percent sign (%) and underscore (_) characters will work.

Note that there are additional wildcard characters that can be used in Microsoft Access character string patterns. For more information on both ANSI-89 and ANSI-92 versions of Microsoft Access wildcard characters, see *https://support.office.com/en-US/Article/Access-wildcard-character-reference-af00c501-7972-40ee-8889-e18abaad12d1?ui=en-US&rs=en-US&ad=US.*

SQL WHERE Clauses That Use NULL Values

As we discussed earlier in this chapter, a missing data value is called a *null value*. In relational databases, null values are indicated with the special marker **NULL** (written as shown in uppercase letters). When we want to include or exclude rows that contain NULL values, we use the **SQL IS NULL operator** or the **SQL IS NOT NULL operator** (Figure 2-23). Note that in this situation the **SQL IS keyword** is equivalent to an *is equal to* comparison operator. However, the *is equal to* comparison operator is *never* used with NULL values, and the IS NULL and IS NOT NULL operators are *never* used with values other than NULL.

For example, suppose that we want to find all the SKUs in the CATALOG_SKU_2015 table that were *not* included in the printed catalog. Because SKUs that were not in the catalog have a CatalogPage value of NULL, we can use the IS NULL operator to find them. Thus, we can use the SQL query:

```
/* *** SQL-Query-CH02-30 *** */

SELECT      *
FROM        CATALOG_SKU_2015
WHERE       CatalogPage IS NULL;
```

This query gives us the result that we want:

	CatalogID	SKU	SKU_Description	Department	CatalogPage	DateOnWebSite
1	20150007	203000	Half-dome Tent Vestibule - Wide	Camping	NULL	2015-04-01

Similarly, if we want to find all the SKUs in the CATALOG_SKU_2015 table that *were*, we can use the IS NOT NULL operator to find them. This gives us the SQL query:

```
/* *** SQL-Query-CH02-31 *** */
SELECT    *
FROM      CATALOG_SKU_2015
WHERE     CatalogPage IS NOT NULL;
```

This query gives us the results:

	CatalogID	SKU	SKU_Description	Department	CatalogPage	DateOnWebSite
1	20150001	100100	Std. Scuba Tank, Yellow	Water Sports	23	2015-01-01
2	20150002	100200	Std. Scuba Tank, Magenta	Water Sports	23	2015-01-01
3	20150003	101100	Dive Mask, Small Clear	Water Sports	27	2015-01-01
4	20150004	101200	Dive Mask, Med Clear	Water Sports	27	2015-01-01
5	20150005	201000	Half-dome Tent	Camping	45	2015-01-01
6	20150006	202000	Half-dome Tent Vestibule	Camping	45	2015-01-01
7	20150008	301000	Light Fly Climbing Harness	Climbing	76	2015-01-01
8	20150009	302000	Locking Carabiner, Oval	Climbing	78	2015-01-01

Performing Calculations in SQL Queries

It is possible to perform certain types of calculations in SQL query statements. One group of calculations involves the use of SQL built-in functions. Another group involves simple arithmetic operations on the columns in the SELECT statement. We will consider each in turn.

Using SQL Built-in Aggregate Functions

There are five standard **SQL built-in aggregate functions** for performing arithmetic on table columns: **SUM**, **AVG**, **MIN**, **MAX**, and **COUNT**. These SQL built-in aggregate functions are summarized in Figure 2-25. Some DBMS products extend these standard built-in functions by providing additional functions. Here we will focus only on the five standard SQL built-in aggregate functions.

Suppose we want to know the sum of OrderTotal for all of the orders in RETAIL_ORDER. We can obtain that sum by using the SQL built-in SUM function:

```
/* *** SQL-Query-CH02-32 *** */
SELECT    SUM(OrderTotal)
FROM      RETAIL_ORDER;
```

FIGURE 2-25

SQL Built-in Aggregate Functions

SQL Built-in Aggregate Functions	
Function	**Meaning**
COUNT(*)	Count the number of rows in the table
COUNT ({Name})	Count the number of rows in the table where column {Name} IS NOT NULL
SUM	Calculate the sum of all values (numeric columns only)
AVG	Calculate the average of all values (numeric columns only)
MIN	Calculate the minimum value of all values
MAX	Calculate the maximum value of all values

The result will be:

	(No column name)
1	1235.00

Recall that the result of an SQL statement is always a table. In this case, the table has one cell (the intersection of one row and one column that contains the sum of OrderTotal). But because the OrderTotal sum is not a column in a table, the DBMS has no column name to provide. The preceding result was produced by Microsoft SQL Server 2014, and it names the column '(No column name)'. Other DBMS products take other, equivalent actions.

This result is ugly. We would prefer to have a meaningful column name, and SQL allows us to assign one using the **SQL AS keyword**. We can use the AS keyword in the query as follows:

```
/* *** SQL-Query-CH02-33 *** */
SELECT      SUM(OrderTotal) AS OrderSum
FROM        RETAIL_ORDER;
```

The result of this modified query will be:

	OrderSum
1	1235.00

This result has a much more meaningful column label. The name *OrderSum* is arbitrary—we are free to pick any name that we think would be meaningful to the user of the result. We could pick *OrderTotal_Total*, *OrderTotalSum*, or any other label that we think would be useful.

The utility of the built-in functions increases when you use them with an SQL WHERE clause. For example, we can write the SQL query:

```
/* *** SQL-Query-CH02-34 *** */
SELECT      SUM(ExtendedPrice) AS Order3000Sum
FROM        ORDER_ITEM
WHERE       OrderNumber=3000;
```

The result of this query is:

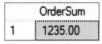

	Order3000Sum
1	450.00

The SQL built-in functions can be mixed and matched in a single statement. For example, we can create the following SQL statement:

```
/* *** SQL-Query-CH02-35 *** */
SELECT      SUM(ExtendedPrice) AS OrderItemSum,
            AVG(ExtendedPrice) AS OrderItemAvg,
            MIN(ExtendedPrice) AS OrderItemMin,
            MAX(ExtendedPrice) AS OrderItemMax
FROM        ORDER_ITEM;
```

The result of this query is:

	OrderItemSum	OrderItemAvg	OrderItemMin	OrderItemMax
1	1180.00	168.5714	50.00	300.00

The SQL built-in COUNT function sounds similar to the SUM function, but it produces very different results. The COUNT function *counts* the number of rows, whereas the SUM function *adds* the values in a column. For example, we can use the SQL built-in COUNT function to determine how many rows are in the ORDER_ITEM table:

```
/* *** SQL-Query-CH02-36 *** */
SELECT      COUNT(*) AS NumberOfRows
FROM        ORDER_ITEM;
```

The result of this query is:

	NumberOfRows
1	7

This result indicates that there are seven rows in the ORDER_ITEM table. Notice that we need to provide an asterisk (*) after the COUNT function when we want to count rows. COUNT is the only built-in function whose parameter can be the asterisk (as used in SQL-Query-CH02-36) or a column name (as used in SQL-Query-CH02-37 that follows). When used with a column name, it counts the number of rows that contain valid data–that is, data other than the NULL value.

The COUNT, MIN, and MAX functions can be used on any type of data, but the SUM and AVG functions can only be used with numeric data. Also note that the SQL DISTINCT keyword can be used with any of the SQL aggregate functions (except in Microsoft Access), but it is most commonly used with the COUNT function.

The COUNT function can produce some surprising results. For example, suppose you want to count the number of departments in the SKU_DATA table. First, we use the following query:

```
/* *** SQL-Query-CH02-37 *** */
SELECT      COUNT(Department) AS DeptCount
FROM        SKU_DATA;
```

The result of SQL-Query-CH02-37 is:

	DeptCount
1	8

However, this is the number of rows in the SKU_DATA table, *not* the number of unique values of Department, as shown in Figure 2-6. If we want to count the unique values of Department, we need to use the SQL DISTINCT keyword as follows:

```
/* *** SQL-Query-CH02-38 *** */
SELECT      COUNT(DISTINCT Department) AS DeptCount
FROM        SKU_DATA;
```

The result of SQL-Query-CH02-38 gives us the correct result:

	DeptCount
1	3

Does Not Work with Microsoft Access ANSI-89 SQL

Microsoft Access does not support the DISTINCT keyword as part of the COUNT expression, so although the SQL command with COUNT(Department) will work, the SQL command with COUNT(DISTINCT Department) will fail.

Solution: Use an SQL subquery structure (discussed later in this chapter) with the DISTINCT keyword in the subquery itself. This SQL query works:

```
/* *** SQL-Query-CH02-38-Access *** */
SELECT      COUNT(*) AS DeptCount
FROM        (SELECT DISTINCT Department
              FROM SKU_DATA) AS DEPT;
```

Note that this query is a bit different from the other SQL queries using subqueries we show in this text because this subquery is in the FROM clause instead of (as you'll see) the WHERE clause. Basically, this subquery builds a new temporary table named DEPT containing only distinct Department values, and the query counts the number of those values.

When using the COUNT function with a column name, the result is the number of rows that have valid data other that the NULL value. Thus, if we count the number of rows with page numbers in the CATALOG_SKU_2015 table, we should get eight rows as a result instead of nine because one SKU did not appear in the catalog. We can do this with the SQL query:

```
/* *** SQL-Query-CH02-39 *** */
SELECT      COUNT(CatalogPage) AS NumberOfSKUinCatalog2015
FROM        CATALOG_SKU_2015;
```

The result of SQL-Query-CH02-39 gives us the expected result:

	Catalog2015NumberOfSKU
1	8

You should be aware of two limitations to SQL built-in functions. First, except for grouping (defined later), you *cannot* combine table column names with an SQL built-in function. For example, what happens if we run the following SQL query?

```
/* *** SQL-Query-CH02-40 *** */
SELECT      Department, COUNT(*)
FROM        SKU_DATA;
```

The result in SQL Server 2014 is:

```
Messages
Msg 8120, Level 16, State 1, Line 266
Column 'SKU_DATA.Department' is invalid in the select list
because it is not contained in either an aggregate function or the GROUP BY clause.
```

This is the specific SQL Server 2014 error message. However, you will receive an equivalent message from Microsoft Access 2013, Oracle Database, or MySQL 5.6.

The second problem with the SQL built-in aggregate functions that you should understand is that you cannot use them in an SQL WHERE clause. This is because the SQL WHERE clause operates on *rows* (choosing which rows will be displayed), while the aggregate functions operate on *columns* (each function calculates a single value based on all the attribute values stored in a column). Thus, you cannot use the following SQL statement:

```
/* *** SQL-Query-CH02-41 *** */

SELECT    *
FROM      RETAIL_ORDER
WHERE     OrderTotal > AVG(OrderTotal);
```

An attempt to use such a statement will also result in an error statement from the DBMS:

```
Messages
 Msg 147, Level 15, State 1, Line 273
 An aggregate may not appear in the WHERE clause unless it is in a subquery
 contained in a HAVING clause or a select list, and the column being aggregated is an outer reference.
```

Again, this is the specific SQL Server 2014 error message, but other DBMS products will give you an equivalent error message. The desired result of the above query can be computed using an SQL subquery (discussed later in this chapter). The desired result can also be obtained using a sequence of SQL views, which will be discussed in Chapter 7.

SQL Expressions in SQL SELECT Statements

It is possible to do basic arithmetic in SQL statements. For example, suppose we want to compute the values of extended price, perhaps because we want to verify the accuracy of the data in the ORDER_ITEM table. To compute the extended price, we can use the SQL expression *Quantity * Price* in the SQL query:

```
/* *** SQL-Query-CH02-42 *** */

SELECT    OrderNumber, SKU, (Quantity * Price) AS EP
FROM      ORDER_ITEM
ORDER BY  OrderNumber, SKU;
```

The result is:

	OrderNumber	SKU	EP
1	1000	201000	300.00
2	1000	202000	130.00
3	2000	101100	200.00
4	2000	101200	100.00
5	3000	100200	300.00
6	3000	101100	100.00
7	3000	101200	50.00

An **SQL expression** is basically a formula or set of values that determines the exact results of an SQL query. We can think of an SQL expression as anything that follows an actual or implied *is equal to* (=) comparison operator (or any other comparison operator, such as greater than (>), less than (<), and so on) or that follows certain SQL comparison operator keywords, such as LIKE and BETWEEN. Thus, the SELECT clause in the preceding query includes the implied *is equal to* (=) sign as EP = Quantity * Price. For another example, in the WHERE clause:

```
WHERE      Buyer IN ('Nancy Meyers', 'Cindy Lo', 'Jerry Martin');
```

the SQL expression consists of the enclosed set of three text values following the IN keyword.

Now that we know how to use an SQL expression to calculate the value of extended price, we can compare this computed value to the value of ExtendedPrice that is already stored in ORDER_ITEM by using the SQL query:

```
/* *** SQL-Query-CH02-43 *** */
SELECT     OrderNumber, SKU,
           (Quantity * Price) AS EP, ExtendedPrice
FROM       ORDER_ITEM
ORDER BY   OrderNumber, SKU;
```

The result of this statement now allows us to visually compare the two values to ensure that the stored data are correct:

	OrderNumber	SKU	EP	ExtendedPrice
1	1000	201000	300.00	300.00
2	1000	202000	130.00	130.00
3	2000	101100	200.00	200.00
4	2000	101200	100.00	100.00
5	3000	100200	300.00	300.00
6	3000	101100	100.00	100.00
7	3000	101200	50.00	50.00

BY THE WAY   The parentheses shown enclosing the expression *Quantity * Price* are not required and do not affect the calculation, but they are useful to help us see the expression in the SQL query syntax.

Expressions can also be used in the SQL WHERE clause (but they may *not* include SQL built-in aggregate functions—see SQL-Query-CH02-41 above). For example, if we want to test whether (Quantity * Price) is equal to ExtendedPrice and then display the OrderNumber and SKU only when (Quantity * Price) is *not* equal to ExtendedPrice, we use the SQL query:

```
/* *** SQL-Query-CH02-44 *** */
SELECT     OrderNumber, SKU
FROM       ORDER_ITEM
WHERE      (Quantity * Price) <> ExtendedPrice
ORDER BY   OrderNumber, SKU;
```

The result of this statement is the **empty set** that contains no values. In terms of SQL-Query-CH02-44, this means that there are *no* rows where (Quantity * Price) is *not* equal to ExtendedPrice, which means that all the values are correct.

OrderNumber	SKU

Another use for SQL expressions in SQL statements is to perform character string manipulation. Suppose we want to combine (using the *concatenation* operator, which is the plus sign [+] in SQL Server 2014) the Buyer and Department columns into a single column named Sponsor. To do this, we can use the SQL statement:

```
/* *** SQL-Query-CH02-45 *** */
SELECT      SKU, SKU_Description,
            (Buyer+' in '+Department) AS Sponsor
FROM        SKU_DATA
ORDER BY    SKU;
```

The result will include a column named Sponsor that contains the combined text values:

	SKU	SKU_Description	Sponsor	
1	100100	Std. Scuba Tank, Yellow	Pete Hansen	in Water Sports
2	100200	Std. Scuba Tank, Magenta	Pete Hansen	in Water Sports
3	101100	Dive Mask, Small Clear	Nancy Meyers	in Water Sports
4	101200	Dive Mask, Med Clear	Nancy Meyers	in Water Sports
5	201000	Half-dome Tent	Cindy Lo	in Camping
6	202000	Half-dome Tent Vestibule	Cindy Lo	in Camping
7	301000	Light Fly Climbing Harness	Jerry Martin	in Climbing
8	302000	Locking Carabiner, Oval	Jerry Martin	in Climbing

BY THE WAY   The concatenation operator, like many SQL syntax elements, varies from one DBMS product to another. Oracle Database uses a double vertical bar (||) as the concatenation operator, and SQL-Query-CH02-45 is written for Oracle Database as:

```
/* *** SQL-Query-CH02-45-Oracle-Database *** */
SELECT      SKU, SKU_Description,
            (Buyer||' in '||Department) AS Sponsor
FROM        SKU_DATA
ORDER BY    SKU;
```

MySQL uses the concatenation string function CONCAT() as the concatenation operator with the elements to be concatenated separated by commas with the parentheses, and SQL-Query-CH02-45 is written for MySQL as:

```
/* *** SQL-Query-CH02-45-MySQL *** */
SELECT      SKU, SKU_Description,
            CONCAT(Buyer,' in ',Department) AS Sponsor
FROM        SKU_DATA
ORDER BY    SKU;
```

The result of SQL-Query-CH02-45 is ugly because of the extra spaces in each row. We can eliminate these extra spaces by using more advanced functions. The syntax and use of such functions vary from one DBMS to another, however, and a discussion of the features of each product will take us away from the point of this discussion. To learn more, search on *string functions* in the documentation for your specific DBMS product. Just to illustrate the possibilities, however, here is an SQL Server 2014 statement using the RTRIM function (which also works in Microsoft Access, Oracle Database, and MySQL) that strips the tailing blanks off the right-hand side of Buyer and Department:

```
/* *** SQL-Query-CH02-46 *** */
SELECT    SKU, SKU_Description,
          RTRIM(Buyer)+' in '+RTRIM(Department) AS Sponsor
FROM      SKU_DATA
ORDER BY  SKU;
```

The result of this query is much more visually pleasing:

	SKU	SKU_Description	Sponsor
1	100100	Std. Scuba Tank, Yellow	Pete Hansen in Water Sports
2	100200	Std. Scuba Tank, Magenta	Pete Hansen in Water Sports
3	101100	Dive Mask, Small Clear	Nancy Meyers in Water Sports
4	101200	Dive Mask, Med Clear	Nancy Meyers in Water Sports
5	201000	Half-dome Tent	Cindy Lo in Camping
6	202000	Half-dome Tent Vestibule	Cindy Lo in Camping
7	301000	Light Fly Climbing Harness	Jerry Martin in Climbing
8	302000	Locking Carabiner, Oval	Jerry Martin in Climbing

Grouping Rows in SQL SELECT Statements

In SQL queries, rows can be grouped together according to common values using the **SQL GROUP BY clause**. This is a powerful feature, but it can be difficult to understand.

To illustrate how grouping works, imagine that you are on the Cape Codd sales analysis team, and your boss asks you the question: "How many products from each department were there in the printed Cape Codd 2014 catalog?"

By simply looking at the data in the CATALOG_SKU_2014 table shown in Figure 2-26, you can easily see that the rows fall into three *groups* based on the values of Department. These groups are Water Sports (rows 1-5), Camping (rows 6-7) and Climbing (rows 8-9). A quick count of the rows in each group shows that Water Sports has 5 rows, Camping has 2 rows and Climbing has 2 rows. Checking the values of CatalogPage, you can see that only the value for row 3 is NULL, which means that all SKUs except SKU 100400 appeared in the 2014 catalog. Therefore, Water Sports had 4 items in the Cape Codd 2104 catalog, Camping had 2 items, and Climbing had 2 items.

FIGURE 2-26

Department Groups in the CATALOG_SKU_2014 Table

| This group of rows is for the **Water Sports** department |
| This SKU did not appear in the catalog |
| This group of rows is for the **Camping** department |
| This group of rows is for the **Climbing** department |

	CatalogID	SKU	SKU_Description	Department	CatalogPage	DateOnWebSite
1	20140001	100100	Std. Scuba Tank, Yellow	Water Sports	23	2014-01-01
2	20140002	100300	Std. Scuba Tank, Light Blue	Water Sports	23	2014-01-01
3	20140003	100400	Std. Scuba Tank, Dark Blue	Water Sports	NULL	2014-08-01
4	20140004	101100	Dive Mask, Small Clear	Water Sports	26	2014-01-01
5	20140005	101200	Dive Mask, Med Clear	Water Sports	26	2014-01-01
6	20140006	201000	Half-dome Tent	Camping	46	2014-01-01
7	20140007	202000	Half-dome Tent Vestibule	Camping	46	2014-01-01
8	20140008	301000	Light Fly Climbing Harness	Climbing	77	2014-01-01
9	20140009	302000	Locking Carabiner, Oval	Climbing	79	2014-01-01

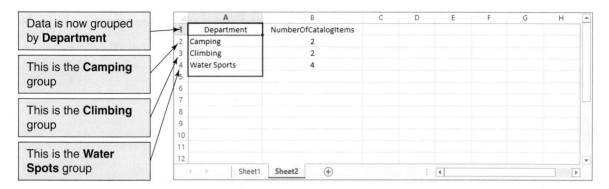

FIGURE 2-27

Grouping Data into
Department Groups

If you need to prepare a report for your boss, you could put this information into a spread-sheet, as shown in Figure 2-27. This spreadsheet clearly shows the data *grouped by Department*, with the corresponding (in alphabetical order) Camping, Climbing, and Water Sports groups.

To create the grouped data output shown in Figure 2-27 in an SQL query, we use the SQL GROUP BY clause in an SQL SELECT statement. This is shown in SQL-Query-CH02-47:

```
/* *** SQL-Query-CH02-47 *** */

SELECT      Department, COUNT(SKU) AS NumberOfCatalogItems

FROM        CATALOG_SKU_2014

GROUP BY    Department;
```

The result for this query is:

	Department	NumberOfCatalogItems
1	Camping	2
2	Climbing	2
3	Water Sports	5

The results for SQL-Query-CH02-47 display the correct grouping by Department, but there is an error in the NumberOfCatalogItems for the Water Sports department. This is because SKU 100400 is included in the count but did not appear in the catalog. To fix this problem, we revise the SQL query by adding a WHERE clause to include only the rows for SKUs that have a CatalogPage number value:

```
/* *** SQL-Query-CH02-48 *** */

SELECT      Department, COUNT(SKU) AS NumberOfCatalogItems

FROM        CATALOG_SKU_2014

WHERE       CatalogPage IS NOT NULL

GROUP BY    Department;
```

This change gives us the correct results:

	Department	NumberOfCatalogItems
1	Camping	2
2	Climbing	2
3	Water Sports	4

Now imagine that your boss asks you the question: "How many products from each department were there in the printed Cape Codd 2014 catalog where the department had three or more listed products?" We can easily answer this question: only the Water Sports department had 3 or more catalog items. Water Sports had 4 catalog items, while Camping and Climbing only had 2 each. To get the correct answer from the grouped data output in an SQL query we use the **SQL HAVING clause** in an SQL SELECT statement. Noting that *3 or more* is mathematically equivalent to *more than 2*, we can write the needed SQL HAVING clause for the SQL query. This is shown in SQL-Query-CH02-49 (note that we use *COUNT(SKU)* in the HAVING clause, *not* the alias *NumberOfCatalogItems*):

```
/* *** SQL-Query-CH02-49 *** */

SELECT     Department, COUNT(SKU) AS NumberOfCatalogItems
FROM       CATALOG_SKU_2014
WHERE      CatalogPage IS NOT NULL
GROUP BY   Department
HAVING     COUNT(SKU) > 2;
```

The result for this query is exactly the result we wanted:

	Department	NumberOfCatalogItems
1	Water Sports	4

Note that SQL built-in aggregate functions *can* be used in the SQL HAVING clause because they are working on the *set of column values in each group*. Earlier we noted that those functions *cannot* be used in the WHERE clause because the WHERE clause is applied to each *single row*. It is easy to get confused between the SQL WHERE clause and the SQL HAVING clause. The best way to understand the difference is to remember that:

- The SQL WHERE clause specifies which *rows* will be used to determine the groups.
- The SQL HAVING clause specifies which *groups* will be used in the final result.

Nonetheless, be aware that there is a potential ambiguity in statements that include both WHERE and HAVING clauses. The results vary depending on whether the WHERE condition is applied before or after the HAVING. To eliminate this ambiguity, the WHERE clause is *always* applied *before* the HAVING clause.

We can include more than one column in a GROUP BY expression. For example, imagine that your boss asks you the question: "How many SKUs is each buyer in each department responsible for?" To answer this question, we will have to group first by Department and then by Buyer. Therefore, we use the SQL statement:

```
/* *** SQL-Query-CH02-50 *** */

SELECT     Department, Buyer,
           COUNT(SKU) AS Dept_Buyer_SKU_Count
FROM       SKU_DATA
GROUP BY   Department, Buyer;
```

This groups rows according to the value of Department first, then according to Buyer, and then counts the number of rows for each combination of Department and Buyer. The result is:

	Department	Buyer	Dept_Buyer_SKU_Count
1	Camping	Cindy Lo	2
2	Climbing	Jerry Martin	2
3	Water Sports	Nancy Meyers	2
4	Water Sports	Pete Hansen	2

When using the GROUP BY clause, *any and all* column names in the SELECT clause that are *not* used by or associated with an SQL built-in function *must* appear in the GROUP BY clause. In SQL-Query-CH02-51 below, the column name SKU is not used in the GROUP BY clause, and therefore the query produces an error:

```
/* *** SQL-Query-CH02-51 *** */
SELECT     Department, SKU,
           COUNT(SKU) AS Dept_SKU_Count
FROM       SKU_DATA
GROUP BY   Department;
```

The resulting error message is:

```
Messages
Msg 8120, Level 16, State 1, Line 347
Column 'SKU_DATA.SKU' is invalid in the select list
because it is not contained in either an aggregate function or the GROUP BY clause.
```

This is the specific SQL Server 2014 error message, but other DBMS products will give you an equivalent error message. Statements like this one are invalid because there are many values of SKU for each Department group. The DBMS has no place to put those multiple values in the result. If you do not understand the problem, try to process this statement by hand. It cannot be done.

Of course, the SQL ORDER BY clause can also be used with SQL queries using the SQL GROUP BY clauses, as shown in the following query:

```
/* *** SQL-Query-CH02-52 *** */
SELECT     Department, COUNT(SKU) AS Dept_SKU_Count
FROM       SKU_DATA
WHERE      SKU <> 302000
GROUP BY   Department
HAVING     COUNT(SKU) > 1
ORDER BY   Dept_SKU_Count;
```

The result is:

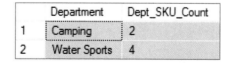

	Department	Dept_SKU_Count
1	Camping	2
2	Water Sports	4

Notice that one of the rows of the Climbing department has been removed from the count because it did not meet the WHERE clause condition and that the Climbing department itself is removed from the final results because it did not meet the HAVING clause requirement. Without the ORDER BY clause, the rows would be presented in arbitrary order of Department. With it, the order is as shown. In general, to be safe, always place the WHERE clause before the GROUP BY clause. Some DBMS products do not require that placement, but others do.

Does Not Work with Microsoft Access ANSI-89 SQL

Microsoft Access does not properly recognize the alias Dept_SKU_Count in the ORDER BY clause and creates a parameter query that requests an input value of as yet nonexistent Dept_SKU_Count! However, it doesn't matter whether you enter parameter values or not—click the OK button and the query will run. The results will be basically correct, but they will not be sorted correctly.

Solution: Use the Microsoft Access QBE GUI to modify the query structure. The correct QBE structure is shown in Figure 2-28. The resulting Microsoft Access ANSI-89 SQL is:

```
/* *** SQL-Query-CH02-52-Access-A *** */
SELECT     SKU_DATA.Department, COUNT(SKU) AS Dept_SKU_Count
FROM       SKU_DATA
WHERE      (((SKU_DATA.SKU)<>302000))
GROUP BY   SKU_DATA.Department
HAVING     COUNT(SKU) > 1
ORDER BY   COUNT(SKU);
```

which can be edited down to:

```
/* *** SQL-Query-CH02-52-Access-B *** */
SELECT     Department, COUNT(SKU) AS Dept_SKU_Count
FROM       SKU_DATA
WHERE      SKU<>302000
GROUP BY   Department
HAVING     COUNT(SKU) > 1
ORDER BY   COUNT(SKU);
```

FIGURE 2-28

Editing the SQL Query in the Microsoft Access 2013 QBE GUI Interface

Edit the query in the QBE GUI interface so that it appears as shown here

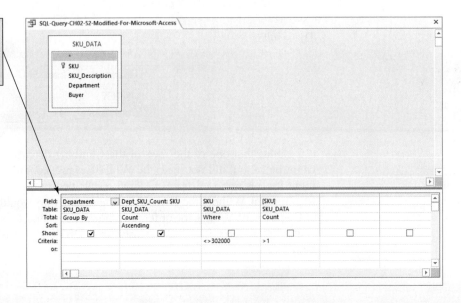

Querying Two or More Tables with SQL

So far in this chapter we've worked with only one table. Now we will conclude by describing SQL statements for querying two or more tables.

Imagine that your boss asks you the question: "What is the total revenue generated by SKUs managed by the Water Sports department?" We can compute the total revenue as the sum of ExtendedPrice, but we have a problem. ExtendedPrice is stored in the ORDER_ITEM table, and Department is stored in the SKU_DATA table. We need to process data in two tables, and all of the SQL presented so far operates on a single table at a time.

SQL provides two different techniques for querying data from multiple tables:

- The SQL subquery
- The SQL join

As you will learn, although both work with multiple tables, they are used for slightly different purposes.

Querying Multiple Tables with Subqueries

We will begin our discussion of multiple table queries with the *SQL subquery*. To understand how a subquery works, let's return to the problem of how we can obtain the sum of ExtendedPrice for items managed by the Water Sports department. Looking at the ORDER_ITEM table data structure in Figure 2-4, we can see that if we somehow knew the SKU values for the Water Sports items, we could use them in a WHERE clause with the IN keyword.

Looking at the SKU_DATA table data in Figure 2-6, we can determine that the SKU values for items in Water Sports are 100100, 100200, 101100, and 101200. Knowing those values, we can obtain the sum of their ExtendedPrice with the following SQL query:

```
/* *** SQL-Query-CH02-53 *** */

SELECT     SUM(ExtendedPrice) AS WaterSportsRevenue

FROM       ORDER_ITEM

WHERE      SKU IN (100100, 100200, 101100, 101200);
```

The result is:

	WaterSportsRevenue
1	750.00

But, in general, we do *not* know the necessary SKU values ahead of time. However, we do have a way to obtain them by using an SQL query on the data in the SKU_DATA table. To obtain the SKU values for the Water Sports department, we use the SQL statement:

```
/* *** SQL-Query-CH02-54 *** */

SELECT     SKU

FROM       SKU_DATA

WHERE      Department = 'Water Sports'
```

The result of this SQL statement is the set of SKU numbers that we need:

	SKU
1	100100
2	100200
3	101100
4	101200

Now we need only combine the last two SQL statements to obtain the result we want. We replace the list of values in the WHERE clause of the first SQL query with the second SQL statement as follows:

```
/* *** SQL-Query-CH02-55 *** */
SELECT     SUM(ExtendedPrice) AS WaterSportsRevenue
FROM       ORDER_ITEM
WHERE      SKU IN
           (SELECT   SKU
             FROM     SKU_DATA
             WHERE    Department = 'Water Sports');
```

The result of the query is the same result we obtained before when we knew which specific values of SKU to use:

	WaterSportsRevenue
1	750.00

In SQL-Query-CH02-55, the second SELECT statement, the one enclosed in parentheses, is called an **SQL subquery**. An SQL subquery is an SQL query statement used to determine a set of values that are provided (or returned) to the SQL query (often referred to as the **top level query**) that used (or called) the subquery. A subquery is often described as a *nested query* or a *query within a query*.

It is important to note that SQL queries using subqueries still function like a single table query in the sense that only the columns of the top level query can be displayed in the query results. For example, in SQL-Query-CH02-55 above, because the Department column is in the SKU_DATA table (the table used in the subquery itself), the values of the Department column *cannot* be displayed in the final results.

We can use multiple subqueries to process three or even more tables. For example, suppose we want to know the names of the buyers who manage any product purchased in January 2015. First, note that Buyer data is stored in the SKU_DATA table and OrderMonth and OrderYear data are stored in the RETAIL_ORDER table.

Now, we can use an SQL query with two subqueries to obtain the desired data as follows:

```
/* *** SQL-Query-CH02-56 *** */
SELECT     DISTINCT Buyer, Department
FROM       SKU_DATA
WHERE      SKU IN
           (SELECT   SKU
             FROM     ORDER_ITEM
             WHERE    OrderNumber  IN
                      (SELECT      OrderNumber
                        FROM        RETAIL_ORDER
                        WHERE       OrderMonth='January'
                             AND    OrderYear = 2015));
```

The result of this statement is:

	Buyer	Department
1	Nancy Meyers	Water Sports
2	Pete Hansen	Water Sports

To understand this statement, work from the bottom up. The bottom SELECT statement obtains the list of OrderNumbers of orders sold in January 2015. The middle SELECT statement obtains the SKU values for items sold in orders in January 2015. Finally, the top-level SELECT query obtains Buyer and Department for all of the SKUs found in the middle SELECT statement.

Any parts of the SQL language that you learned earlier in this chapter can be applied to a table generated by a subquery, regardless of how complicated the SQL looks. For example, in SQL-Query-CH02-56 we apply the DISTINCT keyword on the results to eliminate duplicate rows. We can also apply the GROUP BY and ORDER BY clauses as follows:

```
/* *** SQL-Query-CH02-57 *** */

SELECT      Buyer, Department, COUNT(SKU) AS Number_Of_SKU_Sold
FROM        SKU_DATA
WHERE       SKU IN

            (SELECT     SKU
             FROM       ORDER_ITEM
             WHERE      OrderNumber  IN

                        (SELECT     OrderNumber
                         FROM       RETAIL_ORDER
                         WHERE      OrderMonth='January'
                         AND        OrderYear=2015))
GROUP BY    Buyer, Department
ORDER BY    Number_Of_SKU_Sold;
```

The result is:

	Buyer	Department	Number_Of_SKU_Sold
1	Pete Hansen	Water Sports	1
2	Nancy Meyers	Water Sports	2

Does Not Work with Microsoft Access ANSI-89 SQL

This query fails in Microsoft Access ANSI-89 SQL for the same reason previously described on page 86.

Solution: See the solution described in the "Does Not Work with Microsoft Access ANSI-89 SQL" box on page 86. The correct Microsoft Access ANSI-89 SQL statement for this query is:

```
/* *** SQL-Query-CH02-57-Access *** */

SELECT      Buyer, Department, COUNT(*) AS Number_Of_SKU_Sold
FROM        SKU_DATA
WHERE       SKU IN

            (SELECT     SKU
             FROM       ORDER_ITEM
             WHERE      OrderNumber  IN

                        (SELECT     OrderNumber
                         FROM       RETAIL_ORDER
                         WHERE      OrderMonth='January'
                         AND        OrderYear=2011))
GROUP BY    Buyer, Department
ORDER BY    COUNT(*) ASC;
```

Querying Multiple Tables with Joins

Subqueries are very powerful, but as noted, they do have a serious limitation: the selected data can come only from the top-level table. Therefore, we cannot use a subquery to display data obtained from more than one table. To do so, we must use an SQL join instead.

In an **SQL join operation**, the **SQL JOIN operator** is used to combine two or more tables by concatenating (sticking together) the rows of one table with the rows of another table. If the JOIN operator is actually used as part of the SQL statement syntax, we refer to the join operation as an **explicit join**. If the JOIN operator itself does not appear in the SQL statement, we refer to the join operation as an **implicit join**.

Consider how we might combine the data in the RETAIL_ORDER and ORDER_ITEM tables. We can concatenate the rows of one table with the rows of the second table with the following SQL statement, where we simply list the names of the tables we want to combine:

```
/* *** SQL-Query-CH02-58 *** */
SELECT      *
FROM        RETAIL_ORDER, ORDER_ITEM;
```

This is known as a **CROSS JOIN**, and the result is what is mathematically known as the **Cartesian product** of the rows in the tables, which means that this statement will just stick every row of one table together with every row of the second table. For the data in Figure 2-6, the result is:

	OrderNumber	StoreNumber	StoreZip	OrderMonth	OrderYear	OrderTotal	OrderNumber	SKU	Quantity	Price	ExtendedPrice
1	1000	10	98110	December	2014	445.00	3000	100200	1	300.00	300.00
2	1000	10	98110	December	2014	445.00	2000	101100	4	50.00	200.00
3	1000	10	98110	December	2014	445.00	3000	101100	2	50.00	100.00
4	1000	10	98110	December	2014	445.00	2000	101200	2	50.00	100.00
5	1000	10	98110	December	2014	445.00	3000	101200	1	50.00	50.00
6	1000	10	98110	December	2014	445.00	1000	201000	1	300.00	300.00
7	1000	10	98110	December	2014	445.00	1000	202000	1	130.00	130.00
8	2000	20	02335	December	2014	310.00	3000	100200	1	300.00	300.00
9	2000	20	02335	December	2014	310.00	2000	101100	4	50.00	200.00
10	2000	20	02335	December	2014	310.00	3000	101100	2	50.00	100.00
11	2000	20	02335	December	2014	310.00	2000	101200	2	50.00	100.00
12	2000	20	02335	December	2014	310.00	3000	101200	1	50.00	50.00
13	2000	20	02335	December	2014	310.00	1000	201000	1	300.00	300.00
14	2000	20	02335	December	2014	310.00	1000	202000	1	130.00	130.00
15	3000	10	98110	January	2015	480.00	3000	100200	1	300.00	300.00
16	3000	10	98110	January	2015	480.00	2000	101100	4	50.00	200.00
17	3000	10	98110	January	2015	480.00	3000	101100	2	50.00	100.00
18	3000	10	98110	January	2015	480.00	2000	101200	2	50.00	100.00
19	3000	10	98110	January	2015	480.00	3000	101200	1	50.00	50.00
20	3000	10	98110	January	2015	480.00	1000	201000	1	300.00	300.00
21	3000	10	98110	January	2015	480.00	1000	202000	1	130.00	130.00

Because there are 3 rows of retail order and 7 rows of order items, there are 3 times 7, or 21, rows in this table. Notice that the retail order with OrderNumber 1000 has been combined with all seven of the rows in ORDER_ITEM, the retail order with OrderNumber2000 has been combined with all seven of the same rows, and, finally, the retail order with OrderNumber 3000 has again been combined with all seven rows.

This is illogical—what we really need to do is to select only those rows for which the OrderNumber of RETAIL_ORDER (primary key) matches the OrderNumber in ORDER_ITEM (foreign key). This is known as an **inner join**, and this is easy to do—we simply add an

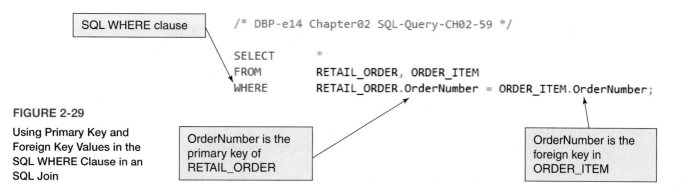

FIGURE 2-29

Using Primary Key and
Foreign Key Values in the
SQL WHERE Clause in an
SQL Join

SQL WHERE clause to the query requiring that the values in the two columns are equal to
each other as follows:

```
/* *** SQL-Query-CH02-59 *** */

SELECT    *

FROM      RETAIL_ORDER, ORDER_ITEM

WHERE     RETAIL_ORDER.OrderNumber = ORDER_ITEM.OrderNumber;
```

The result is:

	OrderNumber	StoreNumber	StoreZip	OrderMonth	OrderYear	OrderTotal	OrderNumber	SKU	Quantity	Price	ExtendedPrice
1	3000	10	98110	January	2015	480.00	3000	100200	1	300.00	300.00
2	2000	20	02335	December	2014	310.00	2000	101100	4	50.00	200.00
3	3000	10	98110	January	2015	480.00	3000	101100	2	50.00	100.00
4	2000	20	02335	December	2014	310.00	2000	101200	2	50.00	100.00
5	3000	10	98110	January	2015	480.00	3000	101200	1	50.00	50.00
6	1000	10	98110	December	2014	445.00	1000	201000	1	300.00	300.00
7	1000	10	98110	December	2014	445.00	1000	202000	1	130.00	130.00

The use of the matching primary and foreign keys in the SQL WHERE clause is shown in
Figure 2-29. While this query is technically correct, it will be easier to read if we sort the
results using an ORDER BY clause:

```
/* *** SQL-Query-CH02-60 *** */

SELECT    *

FROM      RETAIL_ORDER, ORDER_ITEM

WHERE     RETAIL_ORDER.OrderNumber=ORDER_ITEM.OrderNumber

ORDER BY  RETAIL_ORDER.OrderNumber, ORDER_ITEM.SKU;
```

The result is:

	OrderNumber	StoreNumber	StoreZip	OrderMonth	OrderYear	OrderTotal	OrderNumber	SKU	Quantity	Price	ExtendedPrice
1	1000	10	98110	December	2014	445.00	1000	201000	1	300.00	300.00
2	1000	10	98110	December	2014	445.00	1000	202000	1	130.00	130.00
3	2000	20	02335	December	2014	310.00	2000	101100	4	50.00	200.00
4	2000	20	02335	December	2014	310.00	2000	101200	2	50.00	100.00
5	3000	10	98110	January	2015	480.00	3000	100200	1	300.00	300.00
6	3000	10	98110	January	2015	480.00	3000	101100	2	50.00	100.00
7	3000	10	98110	January	2015	480.00	3000	101200	1	50.00	50.00

Looking at the statement syntax in SQLQuery-CH02-60, note that the SQL JOIN keyword is not used anywhere in the SQL statement—therefore, this is an *implicit* inner join.

If you compare this result with the data in Figure 2-6, you will see that only the appropriate order items are associated with each retail order. You also can tell that this has been done by noticing that, in each row, the value of OrderNumber from RETAIL_ORDER (the first column) equals the value of OrderNumber from ORDER_ITEM (the seventh column). This was not true for our first result.

You can think of the join operation working as follows. Start with the first row in RETAIL_ORDER. Using the value of OrderNumber in this first row (1000 for the data in Figure 2-6), examine the rows in ORDER_ITEM. When you find a row in ORDER_ITEM where OrderNumber is also equal to 1000, join all the columns of the first row of RETAIL_ORDER with the columns from the row you just found in ORDER_ITEM.

For the data in Figure 2-6, the first row of ORDER_ITEM has OrderNumber equal to 1000, so you join the first row of RETAIL_ORDER with the columns from the first row in ORDER_ITEM to form the first row of the join. The result is:

	OrderNumber	StoreNumber	StoreZip	OrderMonth	OrderYear	OrderTotal	OrderNumber	SKU	Quantity	Price	ExtendedPrice
1	1000	10	98110	December	2014	445.00	1000	201000	1	300.00	300.00

Now, still using the OrderNumber value of 1000, look for a second row in ORDER_ITEM that has OrderNumber equal to 1000. For our data, the second row of ORDER_ITEM has such a value. So, join FirstName and LastName from the first row of RETAIL_ORDER to the second row of ORDER_ITEM to obtain the second row of the join as follows:

	OrderNumber	StoreNumber	StoreZip	OrderMonth	OrderYear	OrderTotal	OrderNumber	SKU	Quantity	Price	ExtendedPrice
1	1000	10	98110	December	2014	445.00	1000	201000	1	300.00	300.00
2	1000	10	98110	December	2014	445.00	1000	202000	1	130.00	130.00

Continue in this way, looking for matches for the OrderNumber value of 1000. At this point, no more OrderNumber values of 1000 appear in the sample data, so now you move to the second row of RETAIL_ORDER, obtain the new value of OrderNumber (2000), and begin searching for matches for it in the rows of ORDER_ITEM. In this case, the third row has such a match, so you combine those rows with the previous result to obtain the new result:

	OrderNumber	StoreNumber	StoreZip	OrderMonth	OrderYear	OrderTotal	OrderNumber	SKU	Quantity	Price	ExtendedPrice
1	1000	10	98110	December	2014	445.00	1000	201000	1	300.00	300.00
2	1000	10	98110	December	2014	445.00	1000	202000	1	130.00	130.00
3	2000	20	02335	December	2014	310.00	2000	101100	4	50.00	200.00

You continue until all rows of RETAIL_ORDER have been examined. The final result is:

	OrderNumber	StoreNumber	StoreZip	OrderMonth	OrderYear	OrderTotal	OrderNumber	SKU	Quantity	Price	ExtendedPrice
1	1000	10	98110	December	2014	445.00	1000	201000	1	300.00	300.00
2	1000	10	98110	December	2014	445.00	1000	202000	1	130.00	130.00
3	2000	20	02335	December	2014	310.00	2000	101100	4	50.00	200.00
4	2000	20	02335	December	2014	310.00	2000	101200	2	50.00	100.00
5	3000	10	98110	January	2015	480.00	3000	100200	1	300.00	300.00
6	3000	10	98110	January	2015	480.00	3000	101100	2	50.00	100.00
7	3000	10	98110	January	2015	480.00	3000	101200	1	50.00	50.00

Actually, that is the theoretical result. But remember that row order in an SQL query can be arbitrary, as is shown in the results to SQL-Query-CH02-59 above. To ensure that you get the above result, you need to add an ORDER BY clause to the query, as shown in SQL-Query-CH02-60 above.

You may have noticed that we introduced a new variation in SQL statement syntax in the previous two queries, where the terms RETAIL_ORDER.OrderNumber, ORDER_ITEM. OrderNumber, and ORDER_ITEM.SKU were used. The new syntax is simply **TableName. ColumnName**, and it is used to specify exactly which table each column is linked to. RETAIL_ORDER.OrderNumber simply means the OrderNumber from the RETAIL_ORDER table. Similarly, ORDER_ITEM.OrderNumber refers to the OrderNumber in the ORDER_ ITEM table, and ORDER_ITEM.SKU refers to the SKU column in the ORDER_ITEM table. You can always qualify a column name with the name of its table like this. We have not done so previously because we were working with only one table, but the SQL statements shown previously would have worked just as well with syntax like SKU_DATA.Buyer rather than just Buyer or ORDER_ITEM.Price instead of Price.

The process of creating a result table by joining two tables via an SQL join operation is called **joining the two tables**. When the tables are joined using an inner join with an *is equal to* condition (like the one on OrderNumber), this join is called an **equijoin**. When people say *join*, 99.99999 percent of the time they mean an *equijoin*.

We can use a join to obtain data from two or more tables. For example, using the data in Figure 2-6, suppose we want to show the name of the Buyer and the ExtendedPrice of the sales of all SKU items managed by that Buyer. The following SQL query will obtain that result:

```
/* *** SQL-Query-CH02-61 *** */

SELECT      Buyer, SKU_DATA.SKU, SKU_Description,

            OrderNumber, ExtendedPrice

FROM        SKU_DATA, ORDER_ITEM

WHERE       SKU_DATA.SKU=ORDER_ITEM.SKU;
```

The result is:

	Buyer	SKU	SKU_Description	OrderNumber	ExtendedPrice
1	Pete Hansen	100200	Std. Scuba Tank, Magenta	3000	300.00
2	Nancy Meyers	101100	Dive Mask, Small Clear	2000	200.00
3	Nancy Meyers	101100	Dive Mask, Small Clear	3000	100.00
4	Nancy Meyers	101200	Dive Mask, Med Clear	2000	100.00
5	Nancy Meyers	101200	Dive Mask, Med Clear	3000	50.00
6	Cindy Lo	201000	Half-dome Tent	1000	300.00
7	Cindy Lo	202000	Half-dome Tent Vestibule	1000	130.00

Again, the result of every SQL statement is just a single table, so we can apply any of the SQL syntax you learned for a single table to this result. For example, we can use the GROUP BY and ORDER BY clauses to obtain the total revenue from each SKU managed by each buyer, as shown in the following SQL query:

```
/* *** SQL-Query-CH02-62 *** */

SELECT      Buyer, SKU_DATA.SKU, SKU_Description,

            SUM(ExtendedPrice) AS BuyerSKURevenue

FROM        SKU_DATA, ORDER_ITEM

WHERE       SKU_DATA.SKU=ORDER_ITEM.SKU

GROUP BY    Buyer, SKU_DATA.SKU, SKU_Description

ORDER BY    BuyerSKURevenue DESC;
```

The result is:

	Buyer	SKU	SKU_Description	BuyerSKURevenue
1	Pete Hansen	100200	Std. Scuba Tank, Magenta	300.00
2	Nancy Meyers	101100	Dive Mask, Small Clear	300.00
3	Cindy Lo	201000	Half-dome Tent	300.00
4	Nancy Meyers	101200	Dive Mask, Med Clear	150.00
5	Cindy Lo	202000	Half-dome Tent Vestibule	130.00

Does Not Work with Microsoft Access ANSI-89 SQL

This query fails in Microsoft Access ANSI-89 SQL for the same reason previously described on page 86.

Solution: See the solution described in the "Does Not Work with Microsoft Access ANSI-89 SQL" box on page 86. The correct Microsoft Access ANSI-89 SQL statement for this query is:

```
/* *** SQL-Query-CH02-62-Access *** */
SELECT      Buyer, SKU_DATA.SKU, SKU_Description,
            Sum(ORDER_ITEM.ExtendedPrice) AS BuyerSKURevenue
FROM        SKU_DATA, ORDER_ITEM
WHERE       SKU_DATA.SKU=ORDER_ITEM.SKU
GROUP BY    Buyer, SKU_DATA.SKU, SKU_Description
ORDER BY    Sum(ExtendedPrice) DESC;
```

You may have noticed that in SQL-Query-CH02-62 the GROUP BY clause used groupings on Buyer, SKU, and SKU_Description. Given the matching values of SKU and SKU Description, this may seem unnecessary. In fact, however, SQL syntax requires that *any* column name entered in the SELECT clause that is not used in an aggregate function *must* also be entered in the GROUP BY clause. To demonstrate this, we will run SQL-Query-CH02-62 without SKU_Description in the GROUP BY clause as SQL-Query-CH02-63:

```
/* *** SQL-Query-CH02-63 *** */
SELECT      Buyer, SKU_DATA.SKU, SKU_Description,
            SUM(ExtendedPrice) AS BuyerSKURevenue
FROM        SKU_DATA, ORDER_ITEM
WHERE       SKU_DATA.SKU=ORDER_ITEM.SKU
GROUP BY    Buyer, SKU_DATA.SKU
ORDER BY    BuyerSKURevenue DESC;
```

The result is an error message (this one is for SQL Server 2014):

Messages

```
Msg 8120, Level 16, State 1, Line 439
Column 'SKU_DATA.SKU_Description' is invalid in the select list
because it is not contained in either an aggregate function or the GROUP BY clause.
```

We can extend this implicit join syntax to join three or more tables. For example, suppose we want to obtain the Buyer, SKU, SKU_Description, OrderNumber, OrderMonth, and ExtendedPrice for all purchases of items managed by each buyer. To retrieve that data, we need to join all three tables together, as shown in this SQL query:

```
/* *** SQL-Query-CH02-64 *** */
SELECT     Buyer, SKU_DATA.SKU, SKU_Description,
           RETAIL_ORDER.OrderNumber, OrderMonth, ExtendedPrice
FROM       SKU_DATA, ORDER_ITEM, RETAIL_ORDER
WHERE      SKU_DATA.SKU = ORDER_ITEM.SKU
     AND   ORDER_ITEM.OrderNumber=RETAIL_ORDER.OrderNumber;
```

The result is:

	Buyer	SKU	SKU_Description	OrderNumber	OrderMonth	ExtendedPrice
1	Pete Hansen	100200	Std. Scuba Tank, Magenta	3000	January	300.00
2	Nancy Meyers	101100	Dive Mask, Small Clear	2000	December	200.00
3	Nancy Meyers	101100	Dive Mask, Small Clear	3000	January	100.00
4	Nancy Meyers	101200	Dive Mask, Med Clear	2000	December	100.00
5	Nancy Meyers	101200	Dive Mask, Med Clear	3000	January	50.00
6	Cindy Lo	201000	Half-dome Tent	1000	December	300.00
7	Cindy Lo	202000	Half-dome Tent Vestibule	1000	December	130.00

Comparing Subqueries and Joins

Subqueries and joins both process multiple tables, but they differ slightly. As mentioned earlier, a subquery can be used only to retrieve data from the top table, whereas a join can be used to obtain data from any number of tables. Thus, a join can do everything a subquery can do and more. So why learn subqueries? For one, if you just need data from a single table, you might use a subquery because it is easier to write and understand. This is especially true when processing multiple tables.

In Chapter 8, however, you will learn about a type of subquery called a **correlated subquery**. A correlated subquery can do work that is not possible with joins. Thus, it is important for you to learn about both joins and subqueries, even though right now it appears that joins are uniformly superior. If you're curious, ambitious, and courageous, jump ahead and read the discussion of correlated subqueries in Chapter 8.

The SQL JOIN ON Syntax

So far, we have learned to code SQL joins using implicit join syntax. However, there is another way to code join statements. In this second case, we create explicit joins using the **SQL JOIN ON syntax**. The following query is the equivalent of SQL-Query-CH02-60:

```
/* *** SQL-Query-CH02-65 *** */
SELECT     *
FROM       RETAIL_ORDER JOIN ORDER_ITEM
     ON    RETAIL_ORDER.OrderNumber = ORDER_ITEM.OrderNumber
ORDER BY   RETAIL_ORDER.OrderNumber, ORDER_ITEM.SKU;
```

The result is:

	OrderNumber	StoreNumber	StoreZip	OrderMonth	OrderYear	OrderTotal	OrderNumber	SKU	Quantity	Price	ExtendedPrice
1	1000	10	98110	December	2014	445.00	1000	201000	1	300.00	300.00
2	1000	10	98110	December	2014	445.00	1000	202000	1	130.00	130.00
3	2000	20	02335	December	2014	310.00	2000	101100	4	50.00	200.00
4	2000	20	02335	December	2014	310.00	2000	101200	2	50.00	100.00
5	3000	10	98110	January	2015	480.00	3000	100200	1	300.00	300.00
6	3000	10	98110	January	2015	480.00	3000	101100	2	50.00	100.00
7	3000	10	98110	January	2015	480.00	3000	101200	1	50.00	50.00

While these two join syntaxes are functionally equivalent, the implicit join syntax is early SQL standard syntax and is considered to have been replaced by the explicit SQL JOIN ON join syntax as of the 1992 SQL-92 standard. Most people think that the SQL JOIN ON syntax is easier to understand than the first. Note that when using the SQL JOIN ON syntax:

- The **SQL JOIN keyword** is placed between the table names in the SQL FROM clause, where it replaces the comma that previously separated the two table names, and
- The **SQL ON keyword** now leads into an **SQL ON clause**, which includes the statement of matching key values that was previously in an SQL WHERE clause.
- The SQL WHERE clause is no longer used as part of the join, which makes it easier to read the actual restrictions on the rows in the query in the WHERE clause itself.

Note that the JOIN ON syntax still requires a statement of primary key to foreign key equivalence, as shown in Figure 2-30. Also note that the SQL ON clause does *not* replace the SQL WHERE clause, which can still be used to determine which rows will be displayed. For example, we can use the SQL WHERE clause to limit the records shown to those for the OrderYear of 2014:

```
/* *** SQL-Query-CH02-66 *** */

SELECT      *
FROM        RETAIL_ORDER JOIN ORDER_ITEM
       ON   RETAIL_ORDER.OrderNumber = ORDER_ITEM.OrderNumber
WHERE       OrderYear = '2014'
ORDER BY    RETAIL_ORDER.OrderNumber, ORDER_ITEM.SKU;
```

The result is:

	OrderNumber	StoreNumber	StoreZip	OrderMonth	OrderYear	OrderTotal	OrderNumber	SKU	Quantity	Price	ExtendedPrice
1	1000	10	98110	December	2014	445.00	1000	201000	1	300.00	300.00
2	1000	10	98110	December	2014	445.00	1000	202000	1	130.00	130.00
3	2000	20	02335	December	2014	310.00	2000	101100	4	50.00	200.00
4	2000	20	02335	December	2014	310.00	2000	101200	2	50.00	100.00

You can use the SQL JOIN ON syntax as an alternate format for joins of three or more tables as well. If, for example, you want to obtain a list of the order data, order line data, and SKU data, you can use the following SQL statement:

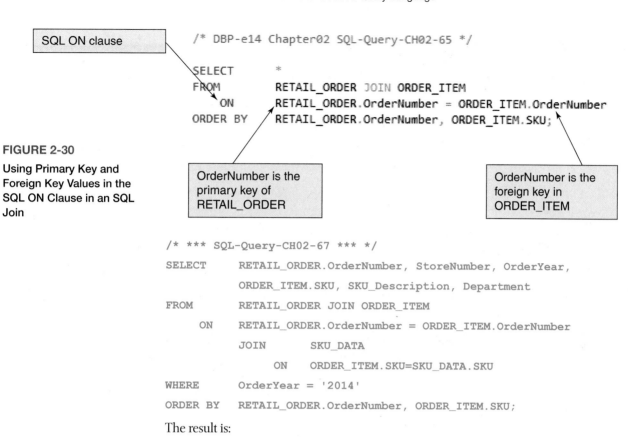

FIGURE 2-30

Using Primary Key and Foreign Key Values in the SQL ON Clause in an SQL Join

```
/* *** SQL-Query-CH02-67 *** */
SELECT      RETAIL_ORDER.OrderNumber, StoreNumber, OrderYear,
            ORDER_ITEM.SKU, SKU_Description, Department
FROM        RETAIL_ORDER JOIN ORDER_ITEM
      ON    RETAIL_ORDER.OrderNumber = ORDER_ITEM.OrderNumber
            JOIN     SKU_DATA
                ON   ORDER_ITEM.SKU=SKU_DATA.SKU
WHERE       OrderYear = '2014'
ORDER BY    RETAIL_ORDER.OrderNumber, ORDER_ITEM.SKU;
```

The result is:

	OrderNumber	StoreNumber	OrderYear	SKU	SKU_Description	Department
1	1000	10	2014	201000	Half-dome Tent	Camping
2	1000	10	2014	202000	Half-dome Tent Vestibule	Camping
3	2000	20	2014	101100	Dive Mask, Small Clear	Water Sports
4	2000	20	2014	101200	Dive Mask, Med Clear	Water Sports

You can make that statement even simpler by using the SQL AS keyword to create table aliases as well as for naming output columns:

```
/* *** SQL-Query-CH02-68 *** */
SELECT      RO.OrderNumber, StoreNumber, OrderYear,
            OI.SKU, SKU_Description, Department
FROM        RETAIL_ORDER AS RO JOIN ORDER_ITEM AS OI
      ON    RO.OrderNumber = OI.OrderNumber
            JOIN     SKU_DATA AS SD
                ON   OI.SKU = SD.SKU
WHERE       OrderYear = '2014'
ORDER BY    RO.OrderNumber, OI.SKU;
```

The result again is:

	OrderNumber	StoreNumber	OrderYear	SKU	SKU_Description	Department
1	1000	10	2014	201000	Half-dome Tent	Camping
2	1000	10	2014	202000	Half-dome Tent Vestibule	Camping
3	2000	20	2014	101100	Dive Mask, Small Clear	Water Sports
4	2000	20	2014	101200	Dive Mask, Med Clear	Water Sports

BY THE WAY   Oracle Database and MySQL create aliases in a similar manner, but Oracle Database does not allow use of the SQL AS keyword. In Oracle Database, the table name is just followed immediately by the alias to be used. This is shown in SQL-Query-CH02-68-Oracle:

```
/* *** SQL-Query-CH02-68-Oracle *** */
SELECT      RO.OrderNumber, StoreNumber, OrderYear,
            OI.SKU, SKU_Description, Department
FROM        RETAIL_ORDER RO JOIN ORDER_ITEM OI
       ON   RO.OrderNumber = OI.OrderNumber
            JOIN     SKU_DATA SD
                ON   OI.SKU = SD.SKU
WHERE       OrderYear = '2014'
ORDER BY    RO.OrderNumber, OI.SKU;
```

One final note on SQL joins: Although so far we have created SQL joins by using matching primary key and foreign key values, SQL joins are not restricted to these matches. In fact, any matching columns in two tables can be the basis for joins regardless of whether the columns are key columns or not. For example, imagine that your boss asks you the question: "Who are the buyers responsible for products in the Cape Codd 2014 catalog?"

In this case, the data on products in the 2014 catalog is in the CATALOG_SKU_2014 table, and the data on buyers is in the SKU_DATA table. A quick glance at Figure 2-4 shows that these two tables are not linked by a primary key to foreign key relationship—in fact, CATALOG_SKU_2014 is a freestanding table and not linked to any other table in the database.

Nonetheless, we can get the results we want with the SQL query:

```
/* *** SQL-Query-CH02-69 *** */
SELECT      CatalogID, CS2014.SKU, CS2014.SKU_description, Buyer
FROM        CATALOG_SKU_2014 AS CS2014 JOIN SKU_DATA AS SD
       ON   CS2014.SKU = SD.SKU
WHERE       CatalogPage IS NOT NULL
ORDER BY    CatalogID;
```

This query uses an explicit join on SKU, even though SKU is not a key in the CATALOG_SKU_2014 table. The results are exactly what we need to answer the question:

	CatalogID	SKU	SKU_description	Buyer
1	20140001	100100	Std. Scuba Tank, Yellow	Pete Hansen
2	20140004	101100	Dive Mask, Small Clear	Nancy Meyers
3	20140005	101200	Dive Mask, Med Clear	Nancy Meyers
4	20140006	201000	Half-dome Tent	Cindy Lo
5	20140007	202000	Half-dome Tent Vestibule	Cindy Lo
6	20140008	301000	Light Fly Climbing Harness	Jerry Martin
7	20140009	302000	Locking Carabiner, Oval	Jerry Martin

Outer Joins

The SQL joins we have used so far have been inner joins, where only rows that have matching values in the joined tables are displayed in the results. Suppose that we would like to see how product sales at Cape Codd Outdoor Sports are related to the buyers—are the buyers acquiring products that sell? We can start with the SQL-Query-CH02-70:

```
/* *** SQL-Query-CH02-70 *** */
SELECT      OI.OrderNumber, Quantity,
            SD.SKU, SKU_Description, Department, Buyer
FROM        ORDER_ITEM AS OI JOIN SKU_DATA AS SD
     ON     OI.SKU=SD.SKU
ORDER BY    OI.OrderNumber, SD.SKU;
```

This produces the result set:

	OrderNumber	Quantity	SKU	SKU_Description	Department	Buyer
1	1000	1	201000	Half-dome Tent	Camping	Cindy Lo
2	1000	1	202000	Half-dome Tent Vestibule	Camping	Cindy Lo
3	2000	4	101100	Dive Mask, Small Clear	Water Sports	Nancy Meyers
4	2000	2	101200	Dive Mask, Med Clear	Water Sports	Nancy Meyers
5	3000	1	100200	Std. Scuba Tank, Magenta	Water Sports	Pete Hansen
6	3000	2	101100	Dive Mask, Small Clear	Water Sports	Nancy Meyers
7	3000	1	101200	Dive Mask, Med Clear	Water Sports	Nancy Meyers

This result is correct, but it shows the names of only five of the eight SKU items in the SKU_ITEM table. What happened to the other three SKU items and their associated buyers? Look closely at the data in Figure 2-6, and you will see that the three SKU items and their buyers that do not appear in the results (SKU 100100 with buyer Pete Hansen, SKU 301000 with buyer Jerry Martin, and SKU 302000 with buyer Jerry Martin) are SKU items that have *never been sold* as part of a retail order. Therefore, the primary key values of these three SKU items do not match any foreign key value in the ORDER_ITEM, and because they have no match, they do not appear in the result of this join statement. What can we do about this case when we are creating an SQL query?

Consider the STUDENT and LOCKER tables in Figure 2-31(a), where we have drawn the two tables to highlight the relationships between the rows in each table. The STUDENT table shows the student number (StudentPK), the name of the student (StudentName), and the student's locker number (LockerFK) for students at a university. The LOCKER table shows the LockerPK (locker number) and LockerType (full size or half size) of lockers at the recreation center on campus. If we run a standard join using SQL JOIN ON syntax between these two tables as shown in SQL-Query-CH02-71, we get a table of students who have lockers assigned to them together with their assigned locker. This result is shown in Figure 2-31(b).

```
/* *** EXAMPLE CODE - DO NOT RUN *** */
/* *** SQL-Query-CH02-71 *** */
SELECT      StudentPK, StudentName, LockerFK, LockerPK, LockerType
FROM        STUDENT JOIN LOCKER
     ON     STUDENT.LockerFK = LOCKER.LockerPK
ORDER BY    StudentPK;
```

The type of SQL join is known as an **SQL inner join**, and we can also run the query using the **SQL INNER JOIN phrase**. This is shown in SQL-Query-CH02-72, which produces exactly the same result shown in Figure 2-31(b).

```
/* *** EXAMPLE CODE - DO NOT RUN *** */
/* *** SQL-Query-CH02-72 *** */
SELECT      StudentPK, StudentName, LockerFK, LockerPK, LockerType
FROM        STUDENT INNER JOIN LOCKER
     ON     STUDENT.LockerFK = LOCKER.LockerPK
ORDER BY    StudentPK;
```

FIGURE 2-31

Types of JOINS

STUDENT

StudentPK	StudentName	LockerFK
1	Adams	NULL
2	Buchanan	NULL
3	Carter	10
4	Ford	20
5	Hoover	30
6	Kennedy	40
7	Roosevelt	50
8	Truman	60

LOCKER

LockerPK	LockerType
10	Full
20	Full
30	Half
40	Full
50	Full
60	Half
70	Full
80	Full
90	Half

(a) The STUDENT and LOCKER Tables Aligned to Show Row Relationships

Only the rows where LockerFK=LockerPK are shown—Note that some StudentPK and some LockerPK values are not in the results

StudentPK	StudentName	LockerFK	LockerPK	LockerType
3	Carter	10	10	Full
4	Ford	20	20	Full
5	Hoover	30	30	Half
6	Kennedy	40	40	Full
7	Roosevelt	50	50	Full
8	Truman	60	60	Half

(b) INNER JOIN of the STUDENT and LOCKER Tables

All rows from STUDENT are shown, even where there is no matching LockerFK=LockerPK value

StudentPK	StudentName	LockerFK	LockerPK	LockerType
1	Adams	NULL	NULL	NULL
2	Buchanan	NULL	NULL	NULL
3	Carter	10	10	Full
4	Ford	20	20	Full
5	Hoover	30	30	Half
6	Kennedy	40	40	Full
7	Roosevelt	50	50	Full
8	Truman	60	60	Half

(c) LEFT OUTER JOIN of the STUDENT and LOCKER Tables

All rows from LOCKER are shown, even where there is no matching LockerFK=LockerPK value

StudentPK	StudentName	LockerFK	LockerPK	LockerType
3	Carter	10	10	Full
4	Ford	20	20	Full
5	Hoover	30	30	Half
6	Kennedy	40	40	Full
7	Roosevelt	50	50	Full
8	Truman	60	60	Half
NULL	NULL	NULL	70	Full
NULL	NULL	NULL	80	Full
NULL	NULL	NULL	90	Half

(d) RIGHT OUTER JOIN of the STUDENT and LOCKER Tables

Now, suppose we want to show all the rows already in the join, but also want to show any rows (students) in the STUDENT table that are not included in the inner join. This means that we want to see *all students*, including those who have *not been assigned a locker*. To do this, we use the **SQL outer join**, which is designed for this very purpose. And because the table we want is listed first in the query and is thus on the left side of the table listing, we specifically use an **SQL left outer join**, which uses the **SQL LEFT JOIN syntax**. This is shown in SQL-Query-CH02-73, which produces the results shown in Figure 2-31(c).

```
/* *** EXAMPLE CODE - DO NOT RUN *** */
/* *** SQL-Query-CH02-73 *** */
SELECT      StudentPK, StudentName, LockerFK, LockerPK, LockerType
FROM        STUDENT LEFT OUTER JOIN LOCKER
    ON      STUDENT.LockerFK = LOCKER.LockerPK
ORDER BY    StudentPK;
```

In the results shown in Figure 2-31(c), note that all the rows from the STUDENT table are now included and that rows that have no match in the LOCKER table are shown with NULL values. Looking at the output, we can see that the students Adams and Buchanan have no linked rows in the LOCKER table. This means that Adams and Buchanan have not been assigned a locker in the recreation center.

If we want to show all the rows already in the join, but now also any rows in the LOCKER table that are not included in the inner join, we specifically use an **SQL right outer join**, which uses the **SQL RIGHT JOIN syntax** because the table we want is listed second in the query and is thus on the right side of the table listing. This means that we want to see *all lockers*, including those that have *not been assigned to a student*. This is shown in SQL-Query-CH02-74, which produces the results shown in Figure 2-31(d).

```
/* *** EXAMPLE CODE - DO NOT RUN *** */
/* *** SQL-Query-CH02-74 *** */
SELECT      StudentPK, StudentName, LockerFK, LockerPK, LockerType
FROM        STUDENT RIGHT OUTER JOIN LOCKER
    ON      STUDENT.LockerFK = LOCKER.LockerPK
ORDER BY    LockerPK;
```

In the results shown in Figure 2-31(d), note that all the rows from the LOCKER table are now included and that rows that have no match in the STUDENT table are shown with NULL values. Looking at the output, we can see that the lockers numbered 70, 80, and 90 have no linked rows in the STUDENT table. This means that these lockers are currently unassigned to a student and available for use.

In terms of our question about SKUs and buyers, this means that we can use an SQL OUTER JOIN and specifically an SQL RIGHT OUTER JOIN to obtain the desired results:

```
/* *** SQL-Query-CH02-75 *** */
SELECT      OI.OrderNumber, Quantity,
            SD.SKU, SKU_Description, Department, Buyer
FROM        ORDER_ITEM AS OI RIGHT OUTER JOIN SKU_DATA AS SD
    ON      OI.SKU=SD.SKU
ORDER BY    OI.OrderNumber, SD.SKU;
```

This produces the following results, which clearly show the SKUs and their associated buyers that have not been part of a retail order (in particular, note that we haven't sold any of the 300000 range SKUs, which are climbing equipment—perhaps management should look into that):

	OrderNumber	Quantity	SKU	SKU_Description	Department	Buyer
1	NULL	NULL	100100	Std. Scuba Tank, Yellow	Water Sports	Pete Hansen
2	NULL	NULL	301000	Light Fly Climbing Harness	Climbing	Jerry Martin
3	NULL	NULL	302000	Locking Carabiner, Oval	Climbing	Jerry Martin
4	1000	1	201000	Half-dome Tent	Camping	Cindy Lo
5	1000	1	202000	Half-dome Tent Vestibule	Camping	Cindy Lo
6	2000	4	101100	Dive Mask, Small Clear	Water Sports	Nancy Meyers
7	2000	2	101200	Dive Mask, Med Clear	Water Sports	Nancy Meyers
8	3000	1	100200	Std. Scuba Tank, Magenta	Water Sports	Pete Hansen
9	3000	2	101100	Dive Mask, Small Clear	Water Sports	Nancy Meyers
10	3000	1	101200	Dive Mask, Med Clear	Water Sports	Nancy Meyers

> **BY THE WAY**   It is easy to forget that inner joins will drop nonmatching rows. Some years ago, one of the authors had a very large organization as a consulting client. The client had a budgetary-planning application that included a long sequence of complicated SQL statements. One of the joins in that sequence was an inner join that should have been an outer join. As a result, some 3,000 employees dropped out of the budgetary calculations. The mistake was discovered only months later when the actual salary expense exceeded the budget salary expense by a large margin. The mistake was an embarrassment all the way to the board of directors.

Using SQL Set Operators

Mathematicians use the term **set theory** to describe mathematical operations on sets, where a **set** is defined as a group of distinct items. A relational database table meets the definition of a set, so it is little wonder that SQL includes a group of **set operators** for use with SQL queries.

Venn diagrams are the standard method of visualizing sets and their relationships. As shown in Figure 2-32:

- A set is represented by a labeled circle, as shown in Figure 2-32(a).
- A **subset** is a portion of a set that is contained entirely within the set, as shown in Figure 2-32(b).
- The **union** of two sets is shown in Figure 2-32(c), and represents the two sets together to get a set that contains all values in both sets. This is equivalent to an OR logical operation (A OR B).
- The **intersection** of two sets is shown in Figure 2-32(d), and represents the area common to both sets. This is equivalent to an AND logical operation (A AND B).
- The **complement** of set B in set A is shown in Figure 2-32(e), and represents everything in set A that is not in set B. This is equivalent to a logical operation using NOT (A NOT B)

SQL provides **SQL set operators** for each of these set operations, and these are shown in Figure 2-33. Note that in order to use SQL set operators, the table columns involved in the operations *must* be the same number in each SELECT component, and corresponding columns *must* have the same or compatible (e.g., CHAR and VARCHAR) data types!

To illustrate SQL set operations, imagine that your boss asks you the question: "What products were available for sale (by either catalog or Web site) in 2014 and 2015?" Looking at Figure 2-6(b), we can see that to answer this question we must combine all the data in

FIGURE 2-32

Venn Diagrams

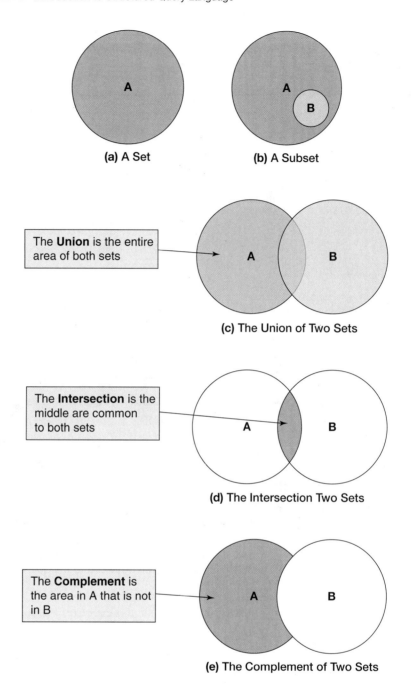

(a) A Set

(b) A Subset

The **Union** is the entire area of both sets

(c) The Union of Two Sets

The **Intersection** is the middle are common to both sets

(d) The Intersection Two Sets

The **Complement** is the area in A that is not in B

(e) The Complement of Two Sets

FIGURE 2-33

SQL Set Operators

SQL Set Operators	
Operator	**Meaning**
UNION	The result is all the row values in one or both tables
INTERSECT	The result is all the row values common to both tables
EXCEPT	The result is all the row values in the first table but not the second

the CATALOG_SKU_2014 and CATALOG_SKU_2015 tables. We do this using the **SQL UNION operator**, as shown in SQL-Query-CH02-76:

```
/* *** SQL-Query-CH02-76 *** */
SELECT      SKU, SKU_Description, Department
FROM        CATALOG_SKU_2014
UNION
SELECT      SKU, SKU_Description, Department
FROM        CATALOG_SKU_2015;
```

This produces the following results, which clearly show all the SKUs available for sale in both years:

	SKU	SKU_Description	Department
1	100100	Std. Scuba Tank, Yellow	Water Sports
2	100200	Std. Scuba Tank, Magenta	Water Sports
3	100300	Std. Scuba Tank, Light Blue	Water Sports
4	100400	Std. Scuba Tank, Dark Blue	Water Sports
5	101100	Dive Mask, Small Clear	Water Sports
6	101200	Dive Mask, Med Clear	Water Sports
7	201000	Half-dome Tent	Camping
8	202000	Half-dome Tent Vestibule	Camping
9	203000	Half-dome Tent Vestibule - Wide	Camping
10	301000	Light Fly Climbing Harness	Climbing
11	302000	Locking Carabiner, Oval	Climbing

BY THE WAY   If we compare the output of SQL-Query-CH02-76 to the data in the CATALOG-SKU_2014 and CATALOG_SKU_2015, we will note that there are no duplicate rows in the query output. For example, SKU 201000, the Half-Dome Tent, is in each table, but only appears once in the query output. If, for some reason, we wanted the duplicated rows to be displayed in the query output as well, we would simply add the **SQL ALL keyword** to the query:

```
/* *** SQL-Query-CH02-76-ALL *** */
SELECT      SKU, SKU_Description, Department
FROM        CATALOG_SKU_2014
UNION ALL
SELECT      SKU, SKU_Description, Department
FROM        CATALOG_SKU_2015;
```

Now imagine that your boss asks you the question: "What products were available for sale (by either catalog or Web site) in *both* 2014 and 2015?" Looking at the Venn diagrams in Figure 2-32 and table data in Figure 2-6(b), we can see that to answer to this question we must find the data in the CATALOG_SKU_2014 and CATALOG_SKU_2015 tables that appears in *both* tables. We do this using the **SQL INTERSECT operator** (note that MySQL does not support this operator), as shown in SQL-Query-CH02-77:

```
/* *** SQL-Query-CH02-77 *** */
SELECT      SKU, SKU_Description, Department
FROM        CATALOG_SKU_2014
INTERSECT
SELECT      SKU, SKU_Description, Department
FROM        CATALOG_SKU_2015;
```

This produces the following results, which clearly show all the SKUs available for sale in both years:

	SKU	SKU_Description	Department
1	100100	Std. Scuba Tank, Yellow	Water Sports
2	101100	Dive Mask, Small Clear	Water Sports
3	101200	Dive Mask, Med Clear	Water Sports
4	201000	Half-dome Tent	Camping
5	202000	Half-dome Tent Vestibule	Camping
6	301000	Light Fly Climbing Harness	Climbing
7	302000	Locking Carabiner, Oval	Climbing

Finally, imagine that your boss asks you the question: "What products were available for sale (by either catalog or Web site) in 2014 but *not* in 2015?" the Venn diagrams in Figure 2-32 and table data in Figure 2-6(b), we can see that to answer this question we must find the data in the CATALOG_SKU_2014 table that did *not* also appear in the CATALOG_SKU_2015 table. We do this using the **SQL EXCEPT operator** (note that Oracle Database calls this the **SQL MINUS operator**, and MySQL does not support this operation) as shown in SQL-Query-CH02-78:

```
/* *** SQL-Query-CH02-78 *** */
SELECT      SKU, SKU_Description, Department
FROM        CATALOG_SKU_2014
EXCEPT
SELECT      SKU, SKU_Description, Department
FROM        CATALOG_SKU_2015;
```

This produces the following results, which clearly show the SKUs that were available for sale in only the 2014 catalog:

	SKU	SKU_Description	Department
1	100300	Std. Scuba Tank, Light Blue	Water Sports
2	100400	Std. Scuba Tank, Dark Blue	Water Sports

This completes our discussion of SQL query statements. We have covered the needed SQL syntax to allow you to write ad-hoc SQL queries on one or more tables, displaying only the specific row, column, or calculated values that you want to see. In Chapter 7, we will return to SQL to discuss SQL DDL, some other parts of SQL DML, and SQL/PSM. In Chapter 8, we will also return to SQL to discuss correlated subqueries.

Summary

Wow! That was a full chapter!

Structured Query Language (SQL) was developed by IBM and has been endorsed by the ANSI SQL-92 and following standards. SQL is a data sublanguage that can be embedded into full programming languages or submitted directly to the DBMS. Knowing SQL is critical for knowledge workers, application programmers, and database administrators.

All DBMS products process SQL. Microsoft Access hides SQL, but SQL Server, Oracle Database, and MySQL require that you use it.

We are primarily interested in five categories of SQL statements: DML, DDL, SQL/PSM statements, TCL, and DCL. DML statements include statements for querying data and for inserting, updating, and deleting data. This chapter addresses only DML query statements. Additional

DML statements, DDL, and SQL/PSM are discussed in Chapter 7. TCL and DCL are discussed in Chapter 9.

The examples in this chapter are based on three tables extracted from the operational database at Cape Codd Outdoor Sports. Such database extracts are common and important. Sample data for the three tables is shown in Figure 2-6.

The basic structure of an SQL query statement is SELECT/FROM/WHERE. The columns to be selected are listed after SELECT, the table(s) to process is (are) listed after FROM, and any restrictions on data values are listed after WHERE. In a WHERE clause, character and date data values must be enclosed in single quotes. Numeric data need not be enclosed in quotes. You can submit SQL statements directly to Microsoft Access, SQL Server, Oracle Database, and MySQL, as described in this chapter.

This chapter explained the use of the following SQL clauses: SELECT, FROM, WHERE, ORDER BY, GROUP BY, and HAVING. By default, the WHERE clause is applied before the HAVING clause. This chapter explained the use of the following SQL keywords: DISTINCT, TOP, and TOP PERCENT. We discussed SQL comparison operators, including the SQL keywords IN, NOT IN, BETWEEN, NOT BETWEEN, LIKE, NOT LIKE, IS NULL, and IS NOT NULL. We used the SQL wildcard characters % (* for Microsoft Access) and _ (? for Microsoft Access). We learned the SQL logical operators AND, OR, and NOT. We used the SQL built-in aggregate functions COUNT, SUM, AVG, MIN, and MAX. We discussed the SQL alias operator AS, and the SQL set operators UNION, UNION ALL, INTERSECT, and EXCEPT. You should know how to mix and match these features to obtain the results you want.

You can query multiple tables using subqueries and joins. Subqueries are nested queries that use the SQL comparison operators IN and NOT IN. An SQL SELECT expression is placed inside parentheses. Using a subquery, you can display data from the top table only. An implicit join is created by specifying multiple table names in the FROM clause. An SQL WHERE clause is used to obtain an equijoin. In most cases, equijoins are the most sensible option. Joins can display data from multiple tables. In Chapter 8, you will learn another type of subquery that can perform work that is not possible with joins.

Since the SQL-92 standard, the explicit SQL JOIN ON syntax has been considered the proper syntax for SQL joins. Rows that have no match in the join condition are dropped from the join results when using a regular, or INNER, join. To keep such rows, use a LEFT OUTER or RIGHT OUTER join rather than an INNER join.

Key Terms

/* and */
ad-hoc queries
American National Standards Institute
    (ANSI)
AVG
business intelligence (BI) systems
Cartesian product
character strings
complement
correlated subquery
COUNT
CROSS JOIN
CRUD
data control language (DCL)
data definition language (DDL)
data manipulation language (DML)
data mart
data sublanguage
data warehouse
data warehouse DBMS
empty set
equijoin
explicit join
Extensible Markup Language (XML)
Extract, Transform, and Load (ETL)
    system
graphical user interface (GUI)

implicit join
inner join
International Organization
    for Standardization (ISO)
intersection
joining two tables
MAX
Microsoft Access asterisk (*) wildcard
    character
Microsoft Access question mark (?)
    wildcard character
MIN
NULL
null value
online transaction processing (OLTP)
query by example (QBE)
schema
set
set operators
set theory
SQL ALL keyword
SQL AND operator
SQL AS keyword
SQL asterisk (*) wildcard character
SQL BETWEEN operator
SQL built-in aggregate functions
SQL comment

SQL comparison operator
SQL DESC keyword
SQL DISTINCT keyword
SQL EXCEPT operator
SQL expression
SQL FROM clause
SQL GROUP BY clause
SQL HAVING clause
SQL IN operator
SQL inner join
SQL INNER JOIN phrase
SQL INTERSECT operator
SQL IS keyword
SQL IS NOT NULL operator
SQL IS NULL operator
SQL join operation
SQL JOIN keyword
SQL JOIN operator
SQL JOIN ON syntax
SQL LEFT JOIN syntax
SQL left outer join
SQL LIKE operator
SQL logical operators
SQL MINUS operator
SQL NOT BETWEEN operator
SQL NOT IN operator
SQL NOT LIKE operator

SQL NOT operator
SQL ON clause
SQL ON keyword
SQL OR operator
SQL ORDER BY clause
SQL outer join
SQL percent sign (%) wildcard character
SQL query
SQL RIGHT JOIN syntax
SQL right outer join
SQL script file
SQL SELECT clause

SQL SELECT/FROM/WHERE
    framework
SQL Server Compatible Syntax
    (ANSI 92)
SQL set operators
SQL TOP {NumberOfRows}
    function
SQL TOP {Percentage} PERCENT
    function
SQL underscore (_) wildcard character
SQL UNION operator
SQL WHERE clause

SQL/Persistent Stored Modules
    (SQL/PSM)
SQL subquery
stock-keeping unit (SKU)
Structured Query Language (SQL)
subset
SUM
TableName.ColumnName syntax
top level query
transaction control language (TCL)
union
Venn diagram

Review Questions

2.1 What is an online transaction processing (OLTP) system? What is a business intelligence (BI) system? What is a data warehouse?

2.2 What is an ad-hoc query?

2.3 What does SQL stand for, and what is SQL?

2.4 What does SKU stand for? What is an SKU?

2.5 Summarize how data were altered and filtered in creating the Cape Codd data extraction.

2.6 Explain, in general terms, the relationships among the RETAIL_ORDER, ORDER_ITEM, and SKU_DATA tables. What is the relationship of these tables to the CATALOG_SKU_2014 and CATALOG_SKU_2015 tables?

2.7 Summarize the background of SQL.

2.8 What is SQL-92? How does it relate to the SQL statements in this chapter?

2.9 What features have been added to SQL in versions subsequent to SQL-92?

2.10 Why is SQL described as a data sublanguage?

2.11 What does DML stand for? What are DML statements?

2.12 What does DDL stand for? What are DDL statements?

2.13 What is the SQL SELECT/FROM/WHERE framework?

2.14 Explain how Microsoft Access uses SQL.

2.15 Explain how enterprise-class DBMS products use SQL.

The Cape Codd Outdoor Sports sale extraction database has been modified to include three additional tables: the INVENTORY table, the WAREHOUSE table, and the CATALOG_SKU_2013 table. The table schemas for these tables, together with the RETAIL_ORDER, ORDER_ITEM, SKU_DATA, CATALOG_SKU_2014, and CATALOG_SKU_2015 tables, are as follows:

RETAIL_ORDER (<u>OrderNumber</u>, StoreNumber, StoreZip, OrderMonth, OrderYear, OrderTotal)

ORDER_ITEM (<u>*OrderNumber*</u>, <u>*SKU*</u>, Quantity, Price, ExtendedPrice)

SKU_DATA (<u>SKU</u>, SKU_Description, Department, Buyer)

WAREHOUSE (<u>WarehouseID</u>, WarehouseCity, WarehouseState, Manager, Squarefeet)

INVENTORY (*WarehouseID*, *SKU*, SKU_Description, QuantityOnHand, QuantityOnOrder)

CATALOG_SKU_2013 (CatalogID, SKU, SKU_Description, CatalogPage, DateOnWebSite)

CATALOG_SKU_2014 (CatalogID, SKU, SKU_Description, CatalogPage, DateOnWebSite)

CATALOG_SKU_2015 (CatalogID, SKU, SKU_Description, CatalogPage, DateOnWebSite)

The eight tables in the revised Cape Codd database schema are shown in Figure 2-34. The column characteristics for the WAREHOUSE table are shown in Figure 2-35, the column characteristics for the INVENTORY table are shown in Figure 2-36, and the column characteristics for the CATALOG_SKU_2013 table are shown in Figure 2-37. The data for the WAREHOUSE table are shown in Figure 2-38, the data for the INVENTORY table are shown in Figure 2-39, and the data for the CATALOG_SKU_2013 table is shown in Figure 2-40.

FIGURE 2-34

The Cape Codd Database with the WAREHOUSE, INVENTORY, and CATALOG_ SKU_2013 Tables

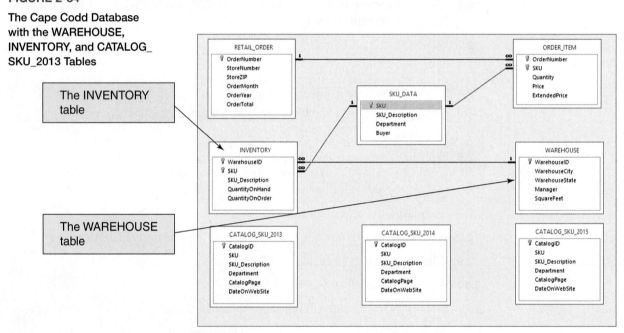

FIGURE 2-35

Column Characteristics for the Cape Codd Database WAREHOUSE Table

WAREHOUSE

Column Name	Type	Key	Required	Remarks
WarehouseID	Integer	Primary Key	Yes	Surrogate Key
WarehouseCity	Character (30)	No	Yes	
WarehouseState	Character (2)	No	Yes	
Manager	Character (35)	No	No	
SquareFeet	Integer	No	No	

FIGURE 2-36

Column Characteristics
for the Cape Codd
Database INVENTORY
Table

INVENTORY

Column Name	Type	Key	Required	Remarks
WarehouseID	Integer	Primary Key, Foreign Key	Yes	REF: WAREHOUSE
SKU	Integer	Primary Key, Foreign Key	Yes	REF: SKU_DATA
SKU_Description	Character (35)	No	Yes	
QuantityOnHand	Integer	No	No	
QuantityOnOrder	Integer	No	No	

FIGURE 2-37

Column Characteristics
for the Cape Codd
Database CATALOG_
SKU_2013 Table

CATALOG_SKU_2013

Column Name	Type	Key	Required	Remarks
CatalogID	Integer	Primary Key	Yes	Surrogate Key
SKU	Integer	No	Yes	
SKU_Description	Character (35)	No	Yes	
Department	Character (30)	No	Yes	
CatalogPage	Integer	No	No	
DateOnWebPage	Date	No	No	

You will need to create and setup a database named Cape_Codd for use with the Cape Codd review questions. You may have already created this database as suggested in Chapter 2 and used it to run the SQL queries discussed in the chapter. If you haven't, you need to do so now.

A Microsoft Access database named *Cape_Codd.accdb* is available on our Web site (*www.pearsonhighered.com/kroenke*) that contains all the tables and data for the Cape Codd Outdoor Sports sales data extract database. Also available on our Web site are SQL scripts for creating and populating the tables for the Cape_Codd database in Microsoft SQL Server, Oracle Database, and MySQL.

FIGURE 2-38

Cape Codd Database
WAREHOUSE Table Data

WarehouseID	WarehouseCity	WarehouseState	Manager	SquareFeet
100	Atlanta	GA	Dave Jones	125,000
200	Chicago	IL	Lucille Smith	100,000
300	Bangor	ME	Bart Evans	150,000
400	Seattle	WA	Dale Rogers	130,000
500	San Francisco	CA	Grace Jefferson	200,000

WarehouseID	SKU	SKU_Description	QuantityOnHand	QuantityOnOrder
100	100100	Std. Scuba Tank, Yellow	250	0
200	100100	Std. Scuba Tank, Yellow	100	50
300	100100	Std. Scuba Tank, Yellow	100	0
400	100100	Std. Scuba Tank, Yellow	200	0
100	100200	Std. Scuba Tank, Magenta	200	30
200	100200	Std. Scuba Tank, Magenta	75	75
300	100200	Std. Scuba Tank, Magenta	100	100
400	100200	Std. Scuba Tank, Magenta	250	0
100	101100	Dive Mask, Small Clear	0	500
200	101100	Dive Mask, Small Clear	0	500
300	101100	Dive Mask, Small Clear	300	200
400	101100	Dive Mask, Small Clear	450	0
100	101200	Dive Mask, Med Clear	100	500
200	101200	Dive Mask, Med Clear	50	500
300	101200	Dive Mask, Med Clear	475	0
400	101200	Dive Mask, Med Clear	250	250
100	201000	Half-Dome Tent	2	100
200	201000	Half-Dome Tent	10	250
300	201000	Half-Dome Tent	250	0
400	201000	Half-Dome Tent	0	250
100	202000	Half-Dome Tent Vestibule	10	250
200	202000	Half-Dome Tent Vestibule	1	250
300	202000	Half-Dome Tent Vestibule	100	0
400	202000	Half-Dome Tent Vestibule	0	200
100	301000	Light Fly Climbing Harness	300	250
200	301000	Light Fly Climbing Harness	250	250
300	301000	Light Fly Climbing Harness	0	250
400	301000	Light Fly Climbing Harness	0	250
100	302000	Locking Carabiner, Oval	1000	0
200	302000	Locking Carabiner, Oval	1250	0
300	302000	Locking Carabiner, Oval	500	500
400	302000	Locking Carabiner, Oval	0	1000

FIGURE 2-39

Cape Codd Database
INVENTORY Table Data

CatalogID	SKU	SKU_Description	Department	CatalogPage	DateOnWebSite
20130001	100100	Std. Scuba Tank, Yellow	Water Sports	23	2013-01-01
20130002	100500	Std. Scuba Tank, Light Green	Water Sports	NULL	2013-07-01
20130003	100600	Std. Scuba Tank, Dark Green	Water Sports	NULL	2013-07-01
20130004	101100	Dive Mask, Small Clear	Water Sports	24	2013-01-01
20130005	101200	Dive Mask, Med Clear	Water Sports	24	2013-01-01
20130006	201000	Half-dome Tent	Camping	45	2013-01-01
20130007	202000	Half-dome Tent Vestibule	Camping	47	2013-01-01
20130008	301000	Light Fly Climbing Harness	Climbing	76	2013-01-01
20130009	302000	Locking Carabiner, Oval	Climbing	78	2013-01-01

FIGURE 2-40

Cape Codd Database
CATALOG_SKU_2013
Table Data

If you are using the Microsoft Access 2013 Cape_Codd.accdb database, simply copy it to an appropriate location in your Documents folder. Otherwise, you will need to use the discussion and instructions necessary for setting up the Cape_Codd database in the DBMS product you are using:

- For Microsoft SQL Server 2014, see online Chapter 10A.
- For Oracle Database 12c or Oracle Express Edition 11g Release 2, see online Chapter 10B.
- For MySQL 5.6 Community Server, see online Chapter 10C.

Once you have setup your Cape_Codd database, create an SQL script named *Cape-Codd-CH02-RQsql*, and use it to record and store SQL statements that answer each of the following questions (if the question requires a written answer, use an SQL comment to record your answer):

2.16 There is an intentional flaw in the design of the INVENTORY table used in these exercises. This flaw was purposely included in the INVENTORY tables so you can answer some of the following questions using only that table. Compare the SKU and INVENTORY tables, and determine what design flaw is included in INVENTORY. Specifically, why did we include it?

Use *only* the INVENTORY table to answer Review Questions 2.17 through 2.39:

2.17 Write an SQL statement to display SKU and SKU_Description.

2.18 Write an SQL statement to display SKU_Description and SKU.

2.19 Write an SQL statement to display WarehouseID.

2.20 Write an SQL statement to display unique WarehouseIDs.

2.21 Write an SQL statement to display all of the columns without using the SQL asterisk (*) wildcard character.

2.22 Write an SQL statement to display all of the columns using the SQL asterisk (*) wildcard character.

2.23 Write an SQL statement to display all data on products having a QuantityOnHand greater than 0.

2.24 Write an SQL statement to display the SKU and SKU_Description for products having QuantityOnHand equal to 0.

2.25 Write an SQL statement to display the SKU, SKU_Description, and WarehouseID for products that have a QuantityOnHand equal to 0. Sort the results in ascending order by WarehouseID.

2.26 Write an SQL statement to display the SKU, SKU_Description, and WarehouseID for products that have a QuantityOnHand greater than 0. Sort the results in descending order by WarehouseID and in ascending order by SKU.

2.27 Write an SQL statement to display SKU, SKU_Description, and WarehouseID for all products that have a QuantityOnHand equal to 0 and a QuantityOnOrder greater than 0. Sort the results in descending order by WarehouseID and in ascending order by SKU.

2.28 Write an SQL statement to display SKU, SKU_Description, and WarehouseID for all products that have a QuantityOnHand equal to 0 or a QuantityOnOrder equal to 0. Sort the results in descending order by WarehouseID and in ascending order by SKU.

2.29 Write an SQL statement to display the SKU, SKU_Description, WarehouseID, and QuantityOnHand for all products having a QuantityOnHand greater than 1 and less than 10. Do not use the BETWEEN keyword.

2.30 Write an SQL statement to display the SKU, SKU_Description, WarehouseID, and QuantityOnHand for all products having a QuantityOnHand greater than 1 and less than 10. Use the BETWEEN keyword.

2.31 Write an SQL statement to show a unique SKU and SKU_Description for all products having an SKU description starting with 'Half-Dome'.

2.32 Write an SQL statement to show a unique SKU and SKU_Description for all products having a description that includes the word 'Climb'.

2.33 Write an SQL statement to show a unique SKU and SKU_Description for all products having a 'd' in the third position from the left in SKU_Description.

2.34 Write an SQL statement that uses all of the SQL built-in functions on the QuantityOnHand column. Include meaningful column names in the result.

2.35 Explain the difference between the SQL built-in functions COUNT and SUM.

2.36 Write an SQL statement to display the WarehouseID and the sum of QuantityOnHand, grouped by WarehouseID. Name the sum TotalItemsOnHand and display the results in descending order of TotalItemsOnHand.

2.37 Write an SQL statement to display the WarehouseID and the sum of QuantityOnHand, grouped by WarehouseID. Omit all SKU items that have 3 or more items on hand from the sum, and name the sum TotalItemsOnHandLT3 and display the results in descending order of TotalItemsOnHandLT3.

2.38 Write an SQL statement to display the WarehouseID and the sum of QuantityOnHand grouped by WarehouseID. Omit all SKU items that have 3 or more items on hand from the sum, and name the sum TotalItemsOnHandLT3. Show the WarehouseID only for warehouses having fewer than 2 SKUs in their TotalItemsOnHandLT3. Display the results in descending order of TotalItemsOnHandLT3.

2.39 In your answer to Review Question 2.38, was the WHERE clause or the HAVING clause applied first? Why?

Use *both* the INVENTORY and WAREHOUSE tables to answer Review Questions 2.40 through 2.52:

2.40 Write an SQL statement to display the SKU, SKU_Description, WarehouseID, WarehouseCity, and WarehouseState for all items stored in the Atlanta, Bangor, or Chicago warehouse. Do not use the IN keyword.

2.41 Write an SQL statement to display the SKU, SKU_Description, WarehouseID, WarehouseCity, and WarehouseState for all items stored in the Atlanta, Bangor, or Chicago warehouse. Use the IN keyword.

2.42 Write an SQL statement to display the SKU, SKU_Description, WarehouseID, WarehouseCity, and WarehouseState of all items not stored in the Atlanta, Bangor, or Chicago warehouse. Do not use the NOT IN keyword.

2.43 Write an SQL statement to display the SKU, SKU_Description, WarehouseID, WarehouseCity, and WarehouseState of all items not stored in the Atlanta, Bangor, or Chicago warehouse. Use the NOT IN keyword.

2.44 Write an SQL statement to produce a single column called ItemLocation that combines the SKU_Description, the phrase "is located in," and WarehouseCity. Do not be concerned with removing leading or trailing blanks.

2.45 Write an SQL statement to show the SKU, SKU_Description, and WarehouseID for all items stored in a warehouse managed by 'Lucille Smith'. Use a subquery.

2.46 Write an SQL statement to show the SKU, SKU_Description, and WarehouseID for all items stored in a warehouse managed by 'Lucille Smith'. Use a join, but do not use JOIN ON syntax.

2.47 Write an SQL statement to show the SKU, SKU_Description, and WarehouseID for all items stored in a warehouse managed by 'Lucille Smith'. Use a join using JOIN ON syntax.

2.48 Write an SQL statement to show the WarehouseID and average QuantityOnHand of all items stored in a warehouse managed by 'Lucille Smith'. Use a subquery.

2.49 Write an SQL statement to show the WarehouseID and average QuantityOnHand of all items stored in a warehouse managed by 'Lucille Smith'. Use a join, but do not use JOIN ON syntax.

2.50 Write an SQL statement to show the WarehouseID and average QuantityOnHand of all items stored in a warehouse managed by 'Lucille Smith'. Use a join using JOIN ON syntax.

2.51 Write an SQL statement to show the WarehouseID, WarehouseCity, WarehouseState, Manager, SKU, SKU_Description, and QuantityOnHand of all items with a Manager of 'Lucille Smith'. Use a join using JOIN ON syntax.

2.52 Write an SQL statement to display the WarehouseID, the sum of QuantityOnOrder, and the sum of QuantityOnHand, grouped by WarehouseID and QuantityOnOrder. Name the sum of QuantityOnOrder as TotalItemsOnOrder and the sum of QuantityOnHand as TotalItemsOnHand. Use only the INVENTORY table in your SQL statement.

2.53 Explain why you cannot use a subquery in your answer to Review Question 2.52.

2.54 Explain how subqueries and joins differ.

2.55 Write an SQL statement to join WAREHOUSE and INVENTORY and include all rows of WAREHOUSE in your answer, regardless of whether they have any INVENTORY. Run this statement.

Use *both* the CATALOG_SKU_2013 and CATALOG_SKU_2014 tables to answer Review Questions 2.56 through 2.60 (for MySQL, 2.56 and 2.57 only):

2.56 Write an SQL statement to display the SKU, SKU_Description, and Department of all SKUs that appear in *either* the Cape Codd 2013 catalog (either in the printed catalog or on the Web site) *or* the Cape Codd 2014 catalog (either in the printed catalog or on the Web site) *or* both.

2.57 Write an SQL statement to display the SKU, SKU_Description, and Department of all SKUs that appear in *either* the Cape Codd 2013 catalog (only in the printed catalog itelf) *or* the Cape Codd 2014 catalog (only in the printed catalog itself) *or* both.

2.58 Write an SQL statement to display the SKU, SKU_Description, and Department of all SKUs that appear in *both* the Cape Codd 2013 catalog (either in the printed catalog or on the Web site) *and* the Cape Codd 2014 catalog (either in the printed catalog or on the Web site).

2.59 Write an SQL statement to display the SKU, SKU_Description, and Department of all SKUs that appear in *both* the Cape Codd 2013 catalog (only in the printed catalog itelf) *and* the Cape Codd 2014 catalog (only in the printed catalog itself) *or* both.

2.60 Write an SQL statement to display the SKU, SKU_Description, and Department of all SKUs that appear in *only* the Cape Codd 2013 catalog (either in the printed catalog or on the Web site) *and not* in the Cape Codd 2014 catalog (either in the printed catalog or on the Web site).

Project Questions

For this set of project questions, we will extend the Microsoft Access 2013 database for the Wedgewood Pacific Corporation (WPC) that we created in Chapter 1. Founded in 1957 in Seattle, Washington, WPC has grown into an internationally recognized organization. The company is located in two buildings. One building houses the Administration, Accounting, Finance, and Human Resources departments, and the second houses the Production, Marketing, and Information Systems departments. The company database contains data about company employees, departments, company projects, company assets such as computer equipment, and other aspects of company operations.

In the following project questions, we have already created the WPC.accdb database with the following two tables (see Chapter 1 Project Questions):

> **DEPARTMENT (<u>DepartmentName</u>, BudgetCode, OfficeNumber, Phone)**
>
> **EMPLOYEE (<u>EmployeeNumber</u>, FirstName, LastName, *Department*, Phone, Email)**

Now we will add in the following two tables:

> **PROJECT (<u>ProjectID</u>, Name, *Department*, MaxHours, StartDate, EndDate)**
>
> **ASSIGNMENT (<u>*ProjectID*</u>, <u>*EmployeeNumber*</u>, HoursWorked)**

FIGURE 2-41

The WPC Database with the PROJECT and ASSIGNMENT Tables

The four tables in the revised WPC database schema are shown in Figure 2-41. The column characteristics for the PROJECT table are shown in Figure 2-42, and the column

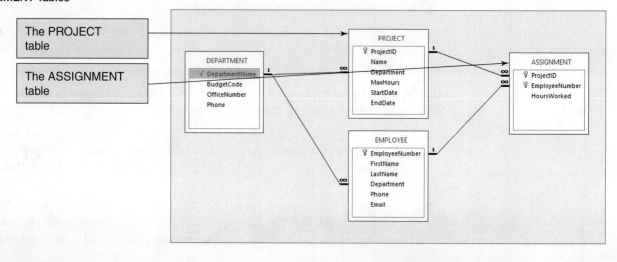

FIGURE 2-42

Column Characteristics
for the WPC Database
PROJECT Table

PROJECT

Column Name	Type	Key	Required	Remarks
ProjectID	Integer	Primary Key	DBMS supplied	Surrogate Key
Name	Character (50)	No	Yes	
Department	Character (35)	Foreign Key	Yes	REF: DEPARTMENT
MaxHours	Number (8,2)	No	Yes	
StartDate	Date	No	No	
EndDate	Date	No	No	

ProjectID	Name	Department	MaxHours	StartDate	EndDate
1000	2015 Q3 Product Plan	Marketing	135.00	10-MAY-15	15-JUN-15
1100	2015 Q3 Portfolio Analysis	Finance	120.00	07-JUL-15	25-JUL-15
1200	2015 Q3 Tax Preparation	Accounting	145.00	10-AUG-15	15-OCT-15
1300	2015 Q4 Product Plan	Marketing	150.00	10-AUG-15	15-SEP-15
1400	2015 Q4 Portfolio Analysis	Finance	140.00	05-OCT-15	

FIGURE 2-43

Sample Data for the WPC
Database PROJECT Table

characteristics for the ASSIGNMENT table are shown in Figure 2-44. Data for the PROJECT table are shown in Figure 2-43, and the data for the ASSSIGNMENT table are shown in Figure 2-45.

2.61 Figure 2-42 shows the column characteristics for the WPC PROJECT table. Using the column characteristics, create the PROJECT table in the WPC.accdb database.

2.62 Create the relationship and referential integrity constraint between PROJECT and DEPARTMENT. In the Edit Relationship dialog box, enable enforcing of referential integrity and cascading of data updates, but do *not* enable cascading of data from deleted records. We will define cascading actions in Chapter 6.

2.63 Figure 2-43 shows the data for the WPC PROJECT table. Using the Datasheet view, enter the data shown in Figure 2-43 into your PROJECT table.

2.64 Figure 2-44 shows the column characteristics for the WPC ASSIGNMENT table. Using the column characteristics, create the ASSIGNMENT table in the WPC.accdb database.

FIGURE 2-44

Column Characteristics
for the WPC Database
ASSIGNMENT Table

ASSIGNMENT

Column Name	Type	Key	Required	Remarks
ProjectID	Integer	Primary Key, Foreign Key	Yes	REF: PROJECT
EmployeeNumber	Integer	Primary Key, Foreign Key	Yes	REF: EMPLOYEE
HoursWorked	Number (6,2)	No	No	

FIGURE 2-45

Sample Data for the WPC
Database ASSIGNMENT
Table

ProjectID	EmployeeNumber	HoursWorked
1000	1	30.0
1000	8	75.0
1000	10	55.0
1100	4	40.0
1100	6	45.0
1100	1	25.0
1200	2	20.0
1200	4	45.0
1200	5	40.0
1300	1	35.0
1300	8	80.0
1300	10	50.0
1400	4	15.0
1400	5	10.0
1400	6	27.5

2.65 Create the relationship and referential integrity constraint between ASSIGNMENT and EMPLOYEE. In the Edit Relationship dialog box, enable enforcing of referential integrity, but do *not* enable either cascading updates or the cascading of data from deleted records.

2.66 Create the relationship and referential integrity constraint between ASSIGNMENT and PROJECT. In the Edit Relationship dialog box, enable enforcing of referential integrity and cascading of deletes, but do *not* enable cascading updates.

2.67 Figure 2-45 shows the data for the WPC ASSIGNMENT table. Using the Datasheet view, enter the data shown in Figure 2-45 into your ASSIGNMENT table.

2.68 In Project Question 2.63, the table data was entered after referential integrity constraints were created in Project Question 2.62. In Project Question 2.67, the table data was entered after referential integrity constraints were created in Project Questions 2.65 and 2.66. Why was the data entered after the referential integrity constraints were created instead of before the constraints were created?

2.69 Using Microsoft Access SQL, create and run queries to answer the following questions. Save each query using the query name format SQL-Query-02-##, where the ## sign is replaced by the letter designator of the question. For example, the first query will be saved as SQL-Query-02-A.

  A. What projects are in the PROJECT table? Show all information for each project.

  B. What are the ProjectID, Name, StartDate, and EndDate values of projects in the PROJECT table?

  C. What projects in the PROJECT table started before August 1, 2015? Show all the information for each project.

  D. What projects in the PROJECT table have not been completed? Show all the information for each project.

E. Who are the employees assigned to each project? Show ProjectID, EmployeeNumber, LastName, FirstName, and Phone.

F. Who are the employees assigned to each project? Show ProjectID, Name, and Department. Show EmployeeNumber, LastName, FirstName, and Phone.

G. Who are the employees assigned to each project? Show ProjectID, Name, Department, and Department Phone. Show EmployeeNumber, LastName, FirstName, and Employee Phone. Sort by ProjectID, in ascending order.

H. Who are the employees assigned to projects run by the marketing department? Show ProjectID, Name, Department, and Department Phone. Show EmployeeNumber, LastName, FirstName, and Employee Phone. Sort by ProjectID, in ascending order.

I. How many projects are being run by the marketing department? Be sure to assign an appropriate column name to the computed results.

J. What is the total MaxHours of projects being run by the marketing department? Be sure to assign an appropriate column name to the computed results.

K. What is the average MaxHours of projects being run by the marketing department? Be sure to assign an appropriate column name to the computed results.

L. How many projects are being run by each department? Be sure to display each DepartmentName and to assign an appropriate column name to the computed results.

M. Write an SQL statement to join EMPLOYEE, ASSIGNMENT, and PROJECT using the JOIN ON syntax. Run this statement.

N. Write an SQL statement to join EMPLOYEE and ASSIGNMENT and include all rows of EMPLOYEE in your answer, regardless of whether they have an ASSIGNMENT. Run this statement.

2.70 Using Microsoft Access QBE, create and run new queries to answer the questions in Project Question 2.69. Save each query using the query name format QBE-Query-02-##, where the ## sign is replaced by the letter designator of the question. For example, the first query will be saved as QBE-Query-02-A.

Case Questions

Marcia's Dry Cleaning Case Questions

Marcia Wilson owns and operates *Marcia's Dry Cleaning*, which is an upscale dry cleaner in a well-to-do suburban neighborhood. Marcia makes her business stand out from the competition by providing superior customer service. She wants to keep track of each of her customers and their orders. Ultimately, she wants to notify them that their clothes are ready via e-mail. To provide this service, she has developed an initial database with several tables. Three of those tables are the following:

> CUSTOMER (**CustomerID**, FirstName, LastName, Phone, Email)
>
> INVOICE (**InvoiceNumber**, *CustomerNumber*, DateIn, DateOut, TotalAmount)
>
> INVOICE_ITEM (***InvoiceNumber***, **ItemNumber**, Item, Quantity, UnitPrice)

In the database schema above, the primary keys are underlined and the foreign keys are shown in italics. The database that Marcia has created is named MDC, and the three tables in the MDC database schema are shown in Figure 2-46.

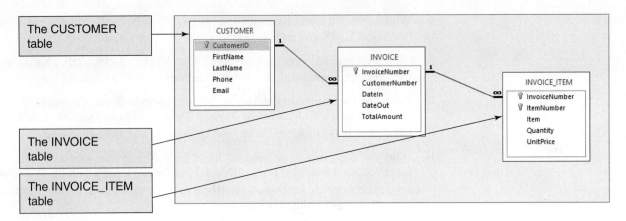

FIGURE 2-46

The MDC Database

The column characteristics for the tables are shown in Figures 2-47, 2-48, and 2-49. The relationship between CUSTOMER and INVOICE should enforce referential integrity, but not cascade updates nor deletions, while the relationship between INVOICE and INVOICE_ITEM should enforce referential integrity and cascade both updates and deletions. The data for these tables are shown in Figures 2-50, 2-51, and 2-52.

You will need to create and setup a database named MDC_CH02 for use with these case questions. A Microsoft Access 2013 database named MDC_CH02.accdb, and SQL scripts for creating the MDC_CH02 database in Microsoft SQL Server, Oracle Database, and MySQL are available on our Web site at *www.pearsonhighered.com/kroenke*.

If you are using the Microsoft Access 2013 MDC_CH02.accdb database, simply copy it to an appropriate location in your Documents folder. Otherwise, you will need to use the

FIGURE 2-47

Column Characteristics
for the MDC Database
CUSTOMER Table

CUSTOMER

Column Name	Type	Key	Required	Remarks
CustomerID	Integer	Primary Key	Yes	Surrogate Key
FirstName	Character (25)	No	Yes	
LastName	Character (25)	No	Yes	
Phone	Character (12)	No	No	
Email	Character (100)	No	No	Use Varchar

FIGURE 2-48

Column Characteristics
for the MDC Database
INVOICE Table

INVOICE

Column Name	Type	Key	Required	Remarks
InvoiceNumber	Integer	Primary Key	Yes	Surrogate Key
CustomerNumber	Integer	Foreign Key	Yes	REF: CUSTOMER
DateIn	Date	No	Yes	
DateOut	Date	No	No	
TotalAmount	Number (8,2)	No	No	

FIGURE 2-49

Column Characteristics for the MDC Database INVOICE_ITEM Table

INVOICE_ITEM

Column Name	Type	Key	Required	Remarks
InvoiceNumber	Integer	Primary Key, Foreign Key	Yes	REF: INVOICE
ItemNumber	Integer	Primary Key	Yes	Sequential number, but *not* a surrogate key
Item	Character (50)	No	Yes	
Quantity	Integer	No	Yes	
UnitPrice	Number (8,2)	No	Yes	

discussion and instructions necessary for setting up the MDC_CH02 database in the DBMS product you are using:

- For Microsoft SQL Server 2014, see online Chapter 10A.
- For Oracle Database 12c or Oracle Express Edition 11g Release 2, see online Chapter 10B.
- For MySQL 5.6 Community Server, see online Chapter 10C.

FIGURE 2-50

Sample Data for the MDC Database CUSTOMER Table

CustomerID	FirstName	LastName	Phone	Email
1	Nikki	Kaccaton	723-543-1233	Nikki.Kaccaton@somewhere.com
2	Brenda	Catnazaro	723-543-2344	Brenda.Catnazaro@somewhere.com
3	Bruce	LeCat	723-543-3455	Bruce.LeCat@somewhere.com
4	Betsy	Miller	725-654-3211	Betsy.Miller@somewhere.com
5	George	Miller	725-654-4322	George.Miller@somewhere.com
6	Kathy	Miller	723-514-9877	Kathy.Miller@somewhere.com
7	Betsy	Miller	723-514-8766	Betsy.Miller@elsewhere.com

FIGURE 2-51

Sample Data for the MDC Database INVOICE Table

InvoiceNumber	CustomerNumber	DateIn	DateOut	TotalAmount
2015001	1	04-Oct-15	06-Oct-15	$158.50
2015002	2	04-Oct-15	06-Oct-15	$25.00
2015003	1	06-Oct-15	08-Oct-15	$49.00
2015004	4	06-Oct-15	08-Oct-15	$17.50
2015005	6	07-Oct-15	11-Oct-15	$12.00
2015006	3	11-Oct-15	13-Oct-15	$152.50
2015007	3	11-Oct-15	13-Oct-15	$7.00
2015008	7	12-Oct-15	14-Oct-15	$140.50
2015009	5	12-Oct-15	14-Oct-15	$27.00

FIGURE 2-52

Sample Data for the MDC
Database INVOICE_ITEM
Table

InvoiceNumber	ItemNumber	Item	Quantity	UnitPrice
2015001	1	Blouse	2	$3.50
2015001	2	Dress Shirt	5	$2.50
2015001	3	Formal Gown	2	$10.00
2015001	4	Slacks-Mens	10	$5.00
2015001	5	Slacks-Womens	10	$6.00
2015001	6	Suit-Mens	1	$9.00
2015002	1	Dress Shirt	10	$2.50
2015003	1	Slacks-Mens	5	$5.00
2015003	2	Slacks-Womens	4	$6.00
2015004	1	Dress Shirt	7	$2.50
2015005	1	Blouse	2	$3.50
2015005	2	Dress Shirt	2	$2.50
2015006	1	Blouse	5	$3.50
2015006	2	Dress Shirt	10	$2.50
2015006	3	Slacks-Mens	10	$5.00
2015006	4	Slacks-Womens	10	$6.00
2015007	1	Blouse	2	$3.50
2015008	1	Blouse	3	$3.50
2015008	2	Dress Shirt	12	$2.50
2015008	3	Slacks-Mens	8	$5.00
2015008	4	Slacks-Womens	10	$6.00
2015009	1	Suit-Mens	3	$9.00

Once you have setup your MDC_CH02 database, create an SQL script named *MDC-CH02-CQsql*, and use it to record and store SQL statements that answer each of the following questions (if the question requires a written answer, use an SQL comment to record your answer):

A. Show all data in each of the tables.

B. List the LastName, FirstName, and Phone of all customers.

C. List the LastName, FirstName, and Phone for all customers with a FirstName of 'Nikki'.

D. List the LastName, FirstName, Phone, DateIn, and DateOut of all orders in excess of $100.00.

E. List the LastName, FirstName, and Phone of all customers whose first name starts with 'B'.

F. List the LastName, FirstName, and Phone of all customers whose last name includes the characters 'cat'.

G. List the LastName, FirstName, and Phone for all customers whose second and third digits (from the left) of their phone number are 23. For example, any phone number with an area code of "723" would meet the criteria.

H. Determine the maximum and minimum TotalAmount.

I. Determine the average TotalAmount.

J. Count the number of customers.

K. Group customers by LastName and then by FirstName.

L. Count the number of customers having each combination of LastName and FirstName.

M. Show the LastName, FirstName, and Phone of all customers who have had an order with TotalAmount greater than $100.00. Use a subquery. Present the results sorted by LastName in ascending order and then FirstName in descending order.

N. Show the LastName, FirstName, and Phone of all customers who have had an order with TotalAmount greater than $100.00. Use a join, but do not use JOIN ON syntax. Present results sorted by LastName in ascending order and then FirstName in descending order.

O. Show the LastName, FirstName, and Phone of all customers who have had an order with TotalAmount greater than $100.00. Use a join using JOIN ON syntax. Present results sorted by LastName in ascending order and then FirstName in descending order.

P. Show the LastName, FirstName, and Phone of all customers who have had an order with an Item named 'Dress Shirt'. Use a subquery. Present results sorted by LastName in ascending order and then FirstName in descending order.

Q. Show the LastName, FirstName, and Phone of all customers who have had an order with an Item named 'Dress Shirt'. Use a join, but do not use JOIN ON syntax. Present results sorted by LastName in ascending order and then FirstName in descending order.

R. Show the LastName, FirstName, and Phone of all customers who have had an order with an Item named 'Dress Shirt'. Use a join using JOIN ON syntax. Present results sorted by LastName in ascending order and then FirstName in descending order.

S. Show the LastName, FirstName, and Phone of all customers who have had an order with an Item named 'Dress Shirt'. Use a combination of a join using JOIN ON syntax and a subquery. Present results sorted by LastName in ascending order and then FirstName in descending order.

T. Show the LastName, FirstName, Phone, and TotalAmount of all customer orders that included an Item named 'Dress Shirt'. Also show the LastName, FirstName, and Phone of *all other customers*. Present results sorted by TotalAmount in ascending order, then LastName in ascending order, and then FirstName in descending order.

The Queen Anne Curiosity Shop

The Queen Anne Curiosity Shop is an upscale home furnishings store in a well-to-do urban neighborhood. It sells both antiques and current-production household items that complement or are useful with the antiques. For example, the store sells antique dining room tables and new tablecloths. The antiques are purchased from both individuals and wholesalers, and the new items are purchased from distributors. The store's customers include individuals, owners of bed-and-breakfast operations, and local interior designers who work with both individuals and small businesses. The antiques are unique, though some multiple items, such as dining room chairs, may be available as a set (sets are never broken). The new items are not unique, and an item may be reordered if it is out of stock. New items are also available in various sizes and colors (for example, a particular style of tablecloth may be available in several sizes and in a variety of colors).

Assume that **The Queen Anne Curiosity Shop** designs a database with the following tables:

> CUSTOMER (<u>CustomerID</u>, LastName, FirstName, Address, City, State, ZIP, Phone, Email)
>
> ITEM (<u>ItemID</u>, ItemDescription, CompanyName, PurchaseDate, ItemCost, ItemPrice)
>
> SALE (<u>SaleID</u>, *CustomerID*, SaleDate, SubTotal, Tax, Total)
>
> SALE_ITEM (<u>*SaleID*</u>, <u>SaleItemID</u>, *ItemID*, ItemPrice)

The referential integrity constraints are:

> CustomerID in SALE must exist in CustomerID in CUSTOMER
>
> SaleID in SALE_ITEM must exist in SaleID in SALE
>
> ItemID in SALE_ITEM must exist in ItemID in ITEM

Assume that CustomerID of CUSTOMER, ItemID of ITEM, SaleID of SALE, and SaleItemID of SALE_ITEM are all surrogate keys with values as follows:

CustomerID	Start at 1	Increment by 1
ItemID	Start at 1	Increment by 1
SaleID	Start at 1	Increment by 1

The database that The Queen Anne Curiosity Shop has created is named QACS, and the four tables in the QACS database schema are shown in Figure 2-53.

The column characteristics for the tables are shown in Figures 2-54, 2-55, 2-56, and 2-57. The relationships CUSTOMER-to-SALE and ITEM-to-SALE_ITEM should enforce referential integrity, but not cascade updates nor deletions, while the relationship between SALE and SALE_ITEM should enforce referential integrity and cascade both updates and deletions. The data for these tables are shown in Figures 2-58, 2-59, 2-60, and 2-61.

You will need to create and setup a database named QACS_CH02 for use with The Queen Anne Curiosity Shop project questions. A Microsoft Access 2013 database named QACS_CH02.accdb, and SQL scripts for creating the QACS_CH02 database in Microsoft SQL Server, Oracle Database, and MySQL are available on our Web site at *www.pearsonhigh-ered.com/kroenke*.

If you are using the Microsoft Access 2013 QACS_CH02.accdb database, simply copy it to an appropriate location in your Documents folder. Otherwise, you will need to use the discussion and instructions necessary for setting up the QACS_CH02 database in the DBMS product you are using:

- For Microsoft SQL Server 2014, see online Chapter 10A.
- For Oracle Database 12c or Oracle Express Edition 11g Release 2, see online Chapter 10B.
- For MySQL 5.6 Community Server, see online Chapter 10C.

FIGURE 2-53

The QACS Database

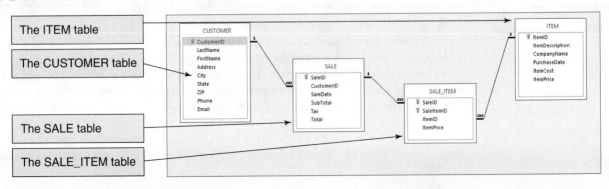

FIGURE 2-54

Column Characteristics
for the QACS Database
CUSTOMER Table

CUSTOMER

Column Name	Type	Key	Required	Remarks
CustomerID	Integer	Primary Key	Yes	Surrogate Key
LastName	Character (25)	No	Yes	
FirstName	Character (25)	No	Yes	
Address	Character (35)	No	No	
City	Character (35)	No	No	
State	Character (2)	No	No	
ZIP	Character (10)	No	No	
Phone	Character (12)	No	Yes	
Email	Character (100)	No	Yes	Use Varchar

FIGURE 2-55

Column Characteristics for
the QACS Database SALE
Table

SALE

Column Name	Type	Key	Required	Remarks
SaleID	Integer	Primary Key	Yes	Surrogate Key
CustomerID	Integer	Foreign Key	Yes	REF: CUSTOMER
SaleDate	Date	No	Yes	
SubTotal	Number (15,2)	No	No	
Tax	Number (15,2)	No	No	
Total	Number (15,2)	No	No	

FIGURE 2-56

Column Characteristics for
the QACS Database SALE_
ITEM Table

SALE_ITEM

Column Name	Type	Key	Required	Remarks
SaleID	Integer	Primary Key, Foreign Key	Yes	REF: SALE
SaleItemID	Integer	Primary Key	Yes	Sequential number, but *not* a surrogate key
ItemID	Integer	Foreign Key	Yes	REF: ITEM
ItemPrice	Number (9,2)	No	No	

FIGURE 2-57

Column Characteristics for
the QACS Database ITEM
Table

ITEM

Column Name	Type	Key	Required	Remarks
ItemID	Integer	Primary Key	Yes	Surrogate Key
ItemDescription	Character (255)	No	Yes	Use Varchar
CompanyName	Character (100)	No	Yes	
PurchaseDate	Date	No	Yes	
ItemCost	Number (9,2)	No	Yes	
ItemPrice	Number (9,2)	No	Yes	

Once you have setup your QACS_CH02 database, create an SQL script named *QACS-CH02-CQ.sql*, and use it to record and store SQL statements that answer each of the following questions (if the question requires a written answer, use an SQL comment to record your answer):

A. Show all data in each of the tables.

B. List the LastName, FirstName, and Phone of all customers.

C. List the LastName, FirstName, and Phone for all customers with a FirstName of 'John'.

D. List the LastName, FirstName, Phone, SaleDate, and Total of all sales in excess of $100.00.

E. List the LastName, FirstName, and Phone of all customers whose first name starts with 'D'.

F. List the LastName, FirstName, and Phone of all customers whose last name includes the characters 'ne'.

G. List the LastName, FirstName, and Phone for all customers whose eighth and ninth digits (starting from the left) of their phone number are 56. For example, a phone number ending in "567" would meet the criteria.

H. Determine the maximum and minimum sales Total.

I. Determine the average sales Total.

J. Count the number of customers.

K. Group customers by LastName and then by FirstName.

L. Count the number of customers having each combination of LastName and FirstName.

M. Show the LastName, FirstName, and Phone of all customers who have had an order with Total greater than $100.00. Use a subquery. Present the results sorted by LastName in ascending order and then FirstName in descending order.

N. Show the LastName, FirstName, and Phone of all customers who have had an order with Total greater than $100.00. Use a join, but do not use JOIN ON syntax. Present results sorted by LastName in ascending order and then FirstName in descending order.

CustomerID	LastName	FirstName	Address	City	State	ZIP	Phone	Email
1	Shire	Robert	6225 Evanston Ave N	Seattle	WA	98103	206-524-2433	Rober.Shire@somewhere.com
2	Goodyear	Katherine	7335 11th Ave NE	Seattle	WA	98105	206-524-3544	Katherine.Goodyear@somewhere.com
3	Bancroft	Chris	12605 NE 6th Street	Bellevue	WA	98005	425-635-9788	Chris.Bancroft@somewhere.com
4	Griffith	John	335 Aloha Street	Seattle	WA	98109	206-524-4655	John.Griffith@somewhere.com
5	Tierney	Doris	14510 NE 4th Street	Bellevue	WA	98005	425-635-8677	Doris.Tierney@somewhere.com
6	Anderson	Donna	1410 Hillcrest Parkway	Mt. Vernon	WA	98273	360-538-7566	Donna.Anderson@elsewhere.com
7	Svane	Jack	3211 42nd Street	Seattle	WA	98115	206-524-5766	Jack.Svane@somewhere.com
8	Walsh	Denesha	6712 24th Avenue NE	Redmond	WA	98053	425-635-7566	Denesha.Walsh@somewhere.com
9	Enquist	Craig	534 15th Street	Bellingham	WA	98225	360-538-6455	Craig.Enquist@elsewhere.com
10	Anderson	Rose	6823 17th Ave NE	Seattle	WA	98105	206-524-6877	Rose.Anderson@elsewhere.com

FIGURE 2-58

Sample Data for the QACS
Database CUSTOMER Table

SaleID	CustomerID	SaleDate	SubTotal	Tax	Total
1	1	12/14/2014	$3,500.00	$290.50	$3,790.50
2	2	12/15/2014	$1,000.00	$83.00	$1,083.00
3	3	12/15/2014	$50.00	$4.15	$54.15
4	4	12/23/2014	$45.00	$3.74	$48.74
5	1	1/5/2015	$250.00	$20.75	$270.75
6	5	1/10/2015	$750.00	$62.25	$812.25
7	6	1/12/2015	$250.00	$20.75	$270.75
8	2	1/15/2015	$3,000.00	$249.00	$3,249.00
9	5	1/25/2015	$350.00	$29.05	$379.05
10	7	2/4/2015	$14,250.00	$1,182.75	$15,432.75
11	8	2/4/2015	$250.00	$20.75	$270.75
12	5	2/7/2015	$50.00	$4.15	$54.15
13	9	2/7/2015	$4,500.00	$373.50	$4,873.50
14	10	2/11/2015	$3,675.00	$305.03	$3,980.03
15	2	2/11/2015	$800.00	$66.40	$866.40

FIGURE 2-59

Sample Data for the QACS
Database SALE Table

O. Show the LastName, FirstName, and Phone of all customers who have had an order with Total greater than $100.00. Use a join using JOIN ON syntax. Present results sorted by LastName in ascending order and then FirstName in descending order.

P. Show the LastName, FirstName, and Phone of all customers who who have bought an Item named 'Desk Lamp'. Use a subquery. Present results sorted by LastName in ascending order and then FirstName in descending order.

Q. Show the LastName, FirstName, and Phone of all customers who have bought an Item named 'Desk Lamp'. Use a join, but do not use JOIN ON syntax. Present results sorted by LastName in ascending order and then FirstName in descending order.

R. Show the LastName, FirstName, and Phone of all customers who have bought an Item named 'Desk Lamp'. Use a join using JOIN ON syntax. Present results sorted by LastName in ascending order and then FirstName in descending order.

S. Show the LastName, FirstName, and Phone of all customers who have bought an Item named 'Desk Lamp'. Use a combination of a join in JOIN ON syntax and a subquery. Present results sorted by LastName in ascending order and then FirstName in descending order.

FIGURE 2-60

Sample Data for the QACS
Database SALE_ITEM Table

SaleID	SaleItemID	ItemID	ItemPrice
1	1	1	$3,000.00
1	2	2	$500.00
2	1	3	$1,000.00
3	1	4	$50.00
4	1	5	$45.00
5	1	6	$250.00
6	1	7	$750.00
7	1	8	$250.00
8	1	9	$1,250.00
8	2	10	$1,750.00
9	1	11	$350.00
10	1	19	$5,000.00
10	2	21	$8,500.00
10	3	22	$750.00
11	1	17	$250.00
12	1	24	$50.00
13	1	20	$4,500.00
14	1	12	$3,200.00
14	2	14	$475.00
15	1	23	$800.00

T. Show the LastName, FirstName, and Phone of all customers who have bought an Item named 'Desk Lamp'. Use a combination of a join in JOIN ON syntax and a subquery that is different from the combination used for question S. Present results sorted by LastName in ascending order and then FirstName in descending order.

U. Show the LastName, FirstName, Phone, and Item for customers who have bought an Item named 'Desk Lamp'. Also show the LastName, FirstName, and Phone of *all the other customers*. Present results sorted by Item in ascending order, then LastName in ascending order, and then FirstName in descending order.

ItemID	ItemDescription	CompanyName	PurchaseDate	ItemCost	ItemPrice
1	Antique Desk	European Specialties	11/7/2014	$1,800.00	$3,000.00
2	Antique Desk Chair	Andrew Lee	11/10/2014	$300.00	$500.00
3	Dining Table Linens	Linens and Things	11/14/2014	$600.00	$1,000.00
4	Candles	Linens and Things	11/14/2014	$30.00	$50.00
5	Candles	Linens and Things	11/14/2014	$27.00	$45.00
6	Desk Lamp	Lamps and Lighting	11/14/2014	$150.00	$250.00
7	Dining Table Linens	Linens and Things	11/14/2014	$450.00	$750.00
8	Book Shelf	Denise Harrion	11/21/2014	$150.00	$250.00
9	Antique Chair	New York Brokerage	11/21/2014	$750.00	$1,250.00
10	Antique Chair	New York Brokerage	11/21/2014	$1,050.00	$1,750.00
11	Antique Candle Holder	European Specialties	11/28/2014	$210.00	$350.00
12	Antique Desk	European Specialties	1/5/2015	$1,920.00	$3,200.00
13	Antique Desk	European Specialties	1/5/2015	$2,100.00	$3,500.00
14	Antique Desk Chair	Specialty Antiques	1/6/2015	$285.00	$475.00
15	Antique Desk Chair	Specialty Antiques	1/6/2015	$339.00	$565.00
16	Desk Lamp	General Antiques	1/6/2015	$150.00	$250.00
17	Desk Lamp	General Antiques	1/6/2015	$150.00	$250.00
18	Desk Lamp	Lamps and Lighting	1/6/2015	$144.00	$240.00
19	Antique Dining Table	Denesha Walsh	1/10/2015	$3,000.00	$5,000.00
20	Antique Sideboard	Chris Bancroft	1/11/2015	$2,700.00	$4,500.00
21	Dining Table Chairs	Specialty Antiques	1/11/2015	$5,100.00	$8,500.00
22	Dining Table Linens	Linens and Things	1/12/2015	$450.00	$750.00
23	Dining Table Linens	Linens and Things	1/12/2015	$480.00	$800.00
24	Candles	Linens and Things	1/17/2015	$30.00	$50.00
25	Candles	Linens and Things	1/17/2015	$36.00	$60.00

FIGURE 2-61

Sample Data for the QACS
Database ITEM Table

Morgan Importing

James Morgan owns and operates Morgan Importing, which purchases antiques and home furnishings in Asia, ships those items to a warehouse facility in Los Angeles, and then sells these items in the United States. James tracks the Asian purchases and subsequent shipments of these items to Los Angeles by using a database to keep a list of items purchased, shipments of the purchased items, and the items in each shipment. His database includes the following tables:

> ITEM (<u>ItemID</u>, Description, PurchaseDate, Store, City, Quantity, LocalCurrencyAmount, ExchangeRate)
>
> SHIPMENT (<u>ShipmentID</u>, ShipperName, ShipperInvoiceNumber, DepartureDate, ArrivalDate, InsuredValue)
>
> SHIPMENT_ITEM (<u>*ShipmentID*</u>, <u>ShipmentItemID</u>, *ItemID*, Value)

In the database schema above, the primary keys are underlined and the foreign keys are shown in italics. The database that James has created is named MI, and the three tables in the MI database schema are shown in Figure 2-62.

The column characteristics for the tables are shown in Figures 2-63, 2-64, and 2-65. The data for the tables are shown in Figures 2-66, 2-67, and 2-68. The relationship between ITEM

FIGURE 2-62

The MI Database

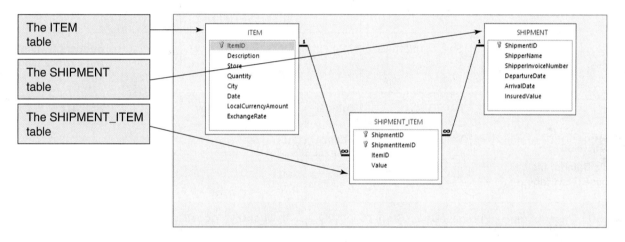

FIGURE 2-63

Column Characteristics for the MI Database ITEM Table

ITEM

Column Name	Type	Key	Required	Remarks
ItemID	Integer	Primary Key	Yes	Surrogate Key
Description	Character (255)	No	Yes	Use Varchar
PurchaseDate	Date	No	Yes	
Store	Character (50)	No	Yes	
City	Character (35)	No	Yes	
Quantity	Integer	No	Yes	
LocalCurrencyAmount	Number (18,2)	No	Yes	
ExchangeRate	Number (12,6)	No	Yes	

FIGURE 2-64

Column Characteristics
for the MI Database
SHIPMENT Table

SHIPMENT

Column Name	Type	Key	Required	Remarks
ShipmentID	Integer	Primary Key	Yes	Surrogate Key
ShipperName	Character (35)	No	Yes	
ShipperInvoiceNumber	Integer	No	Yes	
DepartureDate	Date	No	No	
ArrivalDate	Date	No	No	
InsuredValue	Number (12,2)	No	No	

FIGURE 2-64

Column Characteristics
for the MI Database
SHIPMENT Table

FIGURE 2-65

Column Characteristics
for the MI Database
SHIPMENT_ITEM Table

SHIPMENT_ITEM

Column Name	Type	Key	Required	Remarks
ShipmentID	Integer	Primary Key, Foreign Key	Yes	REF: SHIPMENT
ShipmentItemID	Integer	Primary Key	Yes	Sequential number, but *not* a surrogate key
ItemID	Integer	Foreign Key	Yes	REF: ITEM
Value	Number (12,2)	No	Yes	

FIGURE 2-66

Sample Data for the MI
Database ITEM Table

ItemID	Description	PurchaseDate	Store	City	Quantity	LocalCurrencyAmount	ExchangeRate
1	QE Dining Set	07-Apr-15	Eastern Treasures	Manila	2	403405	0.01774
2	Willow Serving Dishes	15-Jul-15	Jade Antiques	Singapore	75	102	0.5903
3	Large Bureau	17-Jul-15	Eastern Sales	Singapore	8	2000	0.5903
4	Brass Lamps	20-Jul-15	Jade Antiques	Singapore	40	50	0.5903

and SHIPMENT_ITEM should enforce referential integrity, and although it should cascade updates, it should not cascade deletions. The relationship between SHIPMENT and SHIPMENT_ITEM should enforce referential integrity and cascade both updates and deletions.

You will need to create and setup a database named MI_CH02 for use with the Morgan Importing case questions. A Microsoft Access 2013 database named *MI_CH02.accdb*, and SQL scripts for creating the MI_CH02 database in Microsoft SQL Server, Oracle Database, and MySQL are available on our Web site at *www.pearsonhighered.com/kroenke*.

If you are using the Microsoft Access 2013 MDC_CH02.accdb database, simply copy it to an appropriate location in your *Documents* folder. Otherwise, you will need to use the

ShipmentID	ShipperName	ShipperInvoiceNumber	DepartureDate	ArrivalDate	InsuredValue
1	ABC Trans-Oceanic	2008651	10-Dec-14	15-Mar-15	$15,000.00
2	ABC Trans-Oceanic	2009012	10-Jan-15	20-Mar-15	$12,000.00
3	Worldwide	49100300	05-May-15	17-Jun-15	$20,000.00
4	International	399400	02-Jun-15	17-Jul-15	$17,500.00
5	Worldwide	84899440	10-Jul-15	28-Jul-15	$25,000.00
6	International	488955	05-Aug-15	11-Sep-15	$18,000.00

FIGURE 2-67

Sample Data for the MI
Database SHIPMENT Table

FIGURE 2-68

Sample Data for the MI
Database SHIPMENT_ITEM
Table

ShipmentID	ShipmentItemID	ItemID	Value
3	1	1	$15,000.00
4	1	4	$1,200.00
4	2	3	$9,500.00
4	3	2	$4,500.00

discussion and instructions necessary for setting up the MI_CH02 database in the DBMS product you are using:

- For Microsoft SQL Server 2014, see online Chapter 10A.
- For Oracle Database 12c or Oracle Express Edition 11g Release 2, see online Chapter 10B.
- For MySQL 5.6 Community Server, see online Chapter 10C.

Once you have setup your MI_CH02 database, create an SQL script named *MI-CH02-CQ.sql*, and use it to record and store SQL statements that answer each of the following questions (if the question requires a written answer, use an SQL comment to record your answer):

A. Show all data in each of the tables.

B. List the ShipmentID, ShipperName, and ShipperInvoiceNumber of all shipments.

C. List the ShipmentID, ShipperName, and ShipperInvoiceNumber for all shipments that have an insured value greater than $10,000.00.

D. List the ShipmentID, ShipperName, and ShipperInvoiceNumber of all shippers whose name starts with 'AB'.

E. Assume DepartureDate and ArrivalDate are in the format MM/DD/YY. List the ShipmentID, ShipperName, ShipperInvoiceNumber, and ArrivalDate of all shipments that departed in December.

F. Assume DepartureDate and ArrivalDate are in the format MM/DD/YY. List the ShipmentID, ShipperName, ShipperInvoiceNumber, and ArrivalDate of all shipments that departed on the tenth day of any month.

G. Determine the maximum and minimum InsuredValue.

H. Determine the average InsuredValue.

I. Count the number of shipments.

J. Show ItemID, Description, Store, and a calculated column named USCurrencyAmount that is equal to LocalCurrencyAmountt multiplied by the ExchangeRate for all rows of ITEM.

K. Group item purchases by City and Store.

L. Count the number of purchases having each combination of City and Store.

M. Show the ShipperName, ShipmentID and DepartureDate of all shipments that have an item with a value of $1,000.00 or more. Use a subquery. Present results sorted by ShipperName in ascending order and then DepartureDate in descending order.

N. Show the ShipperName, ShipmentID, and DepartureDate of all shipments that have an item with a value of $1,000.00 or more. Use a join. Present results sorted by ShipperName in ascending order and then DepartureDate in descending order.

O. Show the ShipperName, ShipmentID, and DepartureDate of the shipments for items that were purchased in Singapore. Use a subquery. Present results sorted by ShipperName in ascending order and then DepartureDate in descending order.

P. Show the ShipperName, ShipmentID, and DepartureDate of all shipments that have an item that was purchased in Singapore. Use a join, but do not use JOIN ON syntax. Present results sorted by ShipperName in ascending order and then DepartureDate in descending order.

Q. Show the ShipperName, ShipmentID, and DepartureDate of all shipments that have an item that was purchased in Singapore. Use a join using JOIN ON syntax. Present results sorted by ShipperName in ascending order and then DepartureDate in descending order.

R. Show the ShipperName, ShipmentID, the DepartureDate of the shipment, and Value for items that were purchased in Singapore. Use a combination of a join and a subquery. Present results sorted by ShipperName in ascending order and then DepartureDate in descending order.

S. Show the ShipperName, ShipmentID, the DepartureDate of the shipment, and Value for items that were purchased in Singapore. Also show the ShipperName, ShipmentID, and DepartureDate for all other shipments. Present results sorted by Value in ascending order, then ShipperName in ascending order, and then DepartureDate in descending order.

Database Design

The four chapters in Part 2 discuss database design principles and techniques. Chapters 3 and 4 describe the design of databases that arise from existing data sources, such as spreadsheets, text files, and database extracts. We begin in Chapter 3 by defining the relational model and discussing normalization, a process that transforms relations with modification problems. Then, in Chapter 4, we use normalization principles to guide the design of databases from existing data.

Chapters 5 and 6 examine the design of databases that arise from the development of new information systems. Chapter 5 describes the entity-relationship data model, a tool used to create plans for constructing database designs. As you will learn, such data models are developed by analysis of forms, reports, and other information systems requirements. Chapter 6 concludes this part by describing techniques for transforming entity-relationship data models into database designs.

PART

2

3

The Relational Model and Normalization

Chapter Objectives

- To understand basic relational terminology
- To understand the characteristics of relations
- To understand alternative terminology used in describing the relational model
- To be able to identify functional dependencies, determinants, and dependent attributes
- To identify primary, candidate, and composite keys

- To be able to identify possible insertion, deletion, and update anomalies in a relation
- To be able to place a relation into BCNF normal form
- To understand the special importance of domain/key normal form
- To be able to identify multivalued dependencies
- To be able to place a relation in fourth normal form

As we discussed in Chapter 1, databases arise from three sources: from existing data, from the development of new information systems, and from the redesign of existing databases. In this chapter and the next, we consider the design of databases from existing data, such as data from spreadsheets or extracts of existing databases.

The premise of Chapters 3 and 4 is that you have received one or more tables of data from some source that are to be stored in a new database. The question is: Should this data be stored as is, or should it be transformed in some way before it is stored? For example, consider the two tables in the top part of Figure 3-1. These are the SKU_DATA and ORDER_ITEM tables extracted from the Cape Codd Outdoor Sports database as used in the database in Chapter 2.

You can design the new database to store this data as two separate tables, or you can join the tables together and design the database with just one table. Each alternative has advantages and disadvantages. When you make the decision to use one design, you obtain certain advantages at the expense of certain costs. The purpose of this chapter is to help you understand those advantages and costs.

Such questions do not seem difficult, and you may be wondering why we need two chapters to answer them. In truth, even a single table can have surprising complexity. Consider, for example, the table in Figure 3-2, which shows sample

FIGURE 3-1

How Many Tables?

ORDER_ITEM

	OrderNumber	SKU	Quantity	Price	ExtendedPrice
1	1000	201000	1	300.00	300.00
2	1000	202000	1	130.00	130.00
3	2000	101100	4	50.00	200.00
4	2000	101200	2	50.00	100.00
5	3000	100200	1	300.00	300.00
6	3000	101100	2	50.00	100.00
7	3000	101200	1	50.00	50.00

SKU_DATA

	SKU	SKU_Description	Department	Buyer
1	100100	Std. Scuba Tank, Yellow	Water Sports	Pete Hansen
2	100200	Std. Scuba Tank, Magenta	Water Sports	Pete Hansen
3	101100	Dive Mask, Small Clear	Water Sports	Nancy Meyers
4	101200	Dive Mask, Med Clear	Water Sports	Nancy Meyers
5	201000	Half-dome Tent	Camping	Cindy Lo
6	202000	Half-dome Tent Vestibule	Camping	Cindy Lo
7	301000	Light Fly Climbing Harness	Climbing	Jerry Martin
8	302000	Locking Carabiner, Oval	Climbing	Jerry Martin

SKU_ITEM

	OrderNumber	SKU	Quantity	Price	SKU_Description	Department	Buyer
1	1000	201000	1	300.00	Half-dome Tent	Camping	Cindy Lo
2	1000	202000	1	130.00	Half-dome Tent Vestibule	Camping	Cindy Lo
3	2000	101100	4	50.00	Dive Mask, Small Clear	Water Sports	Nancy Meyers
4	2000	101200	2	50.00	Dive Mask, Med Clear	Water Sports	Nancy Meyers
5	3000	100200	1	300.00	Std. Scuba Tank, Magenta	Water Sports	Pete Hansen
6	3000	101100	2	50.00	Dive Mask, Small Clear	Water Sports	Nancy Meyers
7	3000	101200	1	50.00	Dive Mask, Med Clear	Water Sports	Nancy Meyers

data extracted from a corporate database. This simple table has three columns: the buyer's name, the SKU of the products that the buyer purchases, and the names of the buyer's college major(s). Buyers manage more than one SKU, and they can have multiple college majors.

To understand why this is an odd table, suppose that Nancy Meyers is assigned a new SKU, say 101300. What addition should we make to this table? Clearly, we need to add a row for the new SKU, but if we add just one row, say the row ('Nancy Meyers', 101300, 'Art'), it will appear that she manages product 101300 as an Art major, but not as an Info Systems major. To avoid such an illogical state, we need to add two rows: ('Nancy Meyers', 101300, 'Art') and ('Nancy Meyers', 101300, 'Info Systems').

FIGURE 3-2

PRODUCT_BUYER—A Very
Strange Table

PRODUCT_BUYER

	BuyerName	SKU_Managed	CollegeMajor
1	Pete Hansen	100100	Business Administration
2	Pete Hansen	100200	Business Administration
3	Nancy Meyers	101100	Art
4	Nancy Meyers	101100	Info Systems
5	Nancy Meyers	101200	Art
6	Nancy Meyers	101200	Info Systems
7	Cindy Lo	201000	History
8	Cindy Lo	202000	History
9	Jenny Martin	301000	Business Administration
10	Jenny Martin	301000	English Literature
11	Jenny Martin	302000	Business Administration
12	Jenny Martin	302000	English Literature

This is a strange requirement. Why should we have to add two rows of data simply to record the fact that a new SKU has been assigned to a buyer? Further, if we assign the product to Pete Hansen instead, we would only have to add one row, but if we assigned the product to a buyer who had four majors, we would have to add four new rows.

The more one thinks about the table in Figure 3-2, the more strange it becomes. What changes should we make if SKU 101100 is assigned to Pete Hansen? What changes should we make if SKU 100100 is assigned to Nancy Meyers? What should we do if all the SKU values in Figure 3-2 are deleted? Later in this chapter, you will learn that these problems arise because this table has a problem called a *multivalued dependency*. Even better, you will learn how to remove that problem.

Tables can have many different patterns; some patterns are susceptible to serious problems and other patterns are not. Before we can address this question, however, you need to learn some basic terms.

Relational Model Terminology

Figure 3-3 lists the most important terms used by the relational model. By the time you finish Chapters 3 and 4, you should be able to define each of these terms and explain how each pertains to the design of relational databases. Use this list of terms as a check on your comprehension.

Relations

So far, we have used the terms *table* and *relation* interchangeably. In fact, a relation is a special case of a table. This means that all relations are tables, but not all tables are relations. Codd defined the characteristics of a relation in his 1970 paper that laid the foundation for the relational model.[1] Those characteristics are summarized in Figure 3-4.

FIGURE 3-3

Important Relational Model Terms

Important Relational Terms
Relation
Functional dependency
Determinant
Candidate key
Composite key
Primary key
Surrogate key
Foreign key
Referential integrity constraint
Normal form
Multivalued dependency

---

[1]E. F. Codd, "A Relational Model of Data for Large Shared Databanks," *Communications of the ACM*, June 1970, pp. 377–387. A downloadable copy of this paper in PDF format is available at *http://dl.acm.org/citation.cfm?id=362685*.

FIGURE 3-4

Characteristics of Relations

Characteristics of Relations
Rows contain data about an entity.
Columns contain data about attributes of the entities.
All entries in a column are of the same kind.
Each column has a unique name.
Cells of the table hold a single value.
The order of the columns is unimportant.
The order of the rows is unimportant.
No two rows may be identical.

BY THE WAY In Figure 3-4 and in this discussion, we use the term **entity** to mean some identifiable thing. A customer, a salesperson, an order, a part, and a lease are all examples of what we mean by an entity. When we introduce the entity-relationship model in Chapter 5, we will make the definition of entity more precise. For now, just think of an entity as some identifiable thing that users want to track.

Characteristics of Relations

A **relation** has a specific definition, as shown in Figure 3-4, and for a table to be a relation, the criteria of this definition must be met. First, the rows of the table must store data about an entity and the columns of the table must store data about the characteristics of those entities. Next, the names of the columns are unique; no two columns in the same relation may have the same name.

Further, in a relation, all of the values in a column are of the same kind. If, for example, the second column of the first row of a relation has FirstName, then the second column of every row in the relation has FirstName. This is an important requirement that is known as the **domain integrity constraint**, where the term **domain** means a grouping of data that meets a specific type definition. For example, FirstName would have a domain of names such as *Albert, Bruce, Cathy, David, Edith*, and so forth, and all values of FirstName *must* come from the names in that domain. The EMPLOYEE table shown in Figure 3-5 meets these criteria and is a relation.

BY THE WAY Columns in different relations may have the same name. In Chapter 2, for example, two relations had a column named SKU. When there is risk of confusion, we precede the column name with the relation name followed by a period. Thus, the name of the SKU column in the SKU_DATA relation is SKU_DATA.SKU, and column C1 of relation R1 is named R1.C1. Because relation names are unique within a database and because column names are unique within a relation, the combination of relation name and column name uniquely identifies every column in the database.

Each cell of a relation has only a single value or item; multiple entries are not allowed. The table in Figure 3-6 is *not* a relation because the Phone values of employees Caruthers and Bandalone store multiple phone numbers.

EmployeeNumber	FirstName	LastName	Department	Email	Phone
100	Jerry	Johnson	Accounting	JJ@somewhere.com	834-1101
200	Mary	Abernathy	Finance	MA@somewhere.com	834-2101
300	Liz	Smathers	Finance	LS@somewhere.com	834-2102
400	Tom	Caruthers	Accounting	TC@somewhere.com	834-1102
500	Tom	Jackson	Production	TJ@somewhere.com	834-4101
600	Eleanore	Caldera	Legal	EC@somewhere.com	834-3101
700	Richard	Bandalone	Legal	RB@somewhere.com	834-3102

FIGURE 3-5

Sample EMPLOYEE Relation

In a relation, the order of the rows and the order of the columns are immaterial. No information can be carried by the ordering of rows or columns. The table in Figure 3-7 is not a relation because the entries for employees Caruthers and Caldera require a particular row arrangement. If the rows in this table were rearranged, we would not know which employee has the indicated Fax and Home numbers.

Finally, according to the last characteristic in Figure 3-4, for a table to be a relation, no two rows can be identical. As you learned in Chapter 2, some SQL statements do produce tables with duplicate rows. In such cases, you can use the DISTINCT keyword to force uniqueness. Such row duplication occurs only as a result of SQL manipulation. Tables that you design to be stored in the database should never contain duplicate rows.

> **BY THE WAY** Do not fall into a common trap. Even though every cell of a relation must have a single value, this does not mean that all values must have the same length. The table in Figure 3-8 is a relation even though the length of the Comment column varies from row to row. It is a relation because, even though the comments have different lengths, there is only *one* comment per cell.

FIGURE 3-6

Nonrelational Table—
Multiple Entries per Cell

EmployeeNumber	FirstName	LastName	Department	Email	Phone
100	Jerry	Johnson	Accounting	JJ@somewhere.com	834-1101
200	Mary	Abernathy	Finance	MA@somewhere.com	834-2101
300	Liz	Smathers	Finance	LS@somewhere.com	834-2102
400	Tom	Caruthers	Accounting	TC@somewhere.com	834-1102, 834-1191, 834-1192
500	Tom	Jackson	Production	TJ@somewhere.com	834-4101
600	Eleanore	Caldera	Legal	EC@somewhere.com	834-3101
700	Richard	Bandalone	Legal	RB@somewhere.com	834-3102, 834-3191

EmployeeNumber	FirstName	LastName	Department	Email	Phone
100	Jerry	Johnson	Accounting	JJ@somewhere.com	834-1101
200	Mary	Abernathy	Finance	MA@somewhere.com	834-2101
300	Liz	Smathers	Finance	LS@somewhere.com	834-2102
400	Tom	Caruthers	Accounting	TC@somewhere.com	834-1102
				Fax:	834-9911
				Home:	723-8795
500	Tom	Jackson	Production	TJ@somewhere.com	834-4101
600	Eleanore	Caldera	Legal	EC@somewhere.com	834-3101
				Fax:	834-9912
				Home:	723-7654
700	Richard	Bandalone	Legal	RB@somewhere.com	834-3102

FIGURE 3-7

Nonrelational Table—Order of Rows Matters and Kind of Column Entries Differs in Email

Alternative Terminology

As defined by Codd, the columns of a relation are called **attributes** and the rows of a relation are called **tuples** (rhymes with "couples"). Most practitioners, however, do not use these academic-sounding terms and instead use the terms *column* and *row*. Also, even though a table is not necessarily a relation, most practitioners mean *relation* when they say *table*. Thus, in most conversations the terms *relation* and *table* are synonymous. In fact, for the rest of this book *table* and *relation* will be used synonymously.

FIGURE 3-8

Relation with Variable-Length Column Values

EmployeeNumber	FirstName	LastName	Department	Email	Phone	Comment
100	Jerry	Johnson	Accounting	JJ@somewhere.com	834-1101	Joined the Accounting Department in March after completing his MBA. Will take the CPA exam this fall.
200	Mary	Abernathy	Finance	MA@somewhere.com	834-2101	
300	Liz	Smathers	Finance	LS@somewhere.com	834-2102	
400	Tom	Caruthers	Accounting	TC@somewhere.com	834-1102	
500	Tom	Jackson	Production	TJ@somewhere.com	834-4101	
600	Eleanore	Caldera	Legal	EC@somewhere.com	834-3101	
700	Richard	Bandalone	Legal	RB@somewhere.com	834-3102	Is a full-time consultant to Legal on a retainer basis.

FIGURE 3-9

Three Sets of Equivalent
Terms

Table	Column	Row
Relation	Attribute	Tuple
File	Field	Record

Additionally, a third set of terminology can be used. Some practitioners use the terms *file, field,* and *record* for the terms *table, column,* and *row,* respectively. These terms arose from traditional data processing and are common in connection with legacy systems. Sometimes people mix and match these terms. You might hear someone say, for example, that a relation has a certain column and contains 47 records. These three sets of terms are summarized in Figure 3-9.

To Key, or Not to Key—That Is the Question!

Again as defined by Codd, the rows of a relation must be unique (no two rows may be identical), but there is no requirement for a designated *primary key* in the relation. You will recall that in Chapter 1, we described a *primary key* as a column (or columns) with a set of values that uniquely identify each row.

However, the requirement that no two rows be identical *implies* that a primary key *can* be defined for the relation. Further, in the "real world" of databases, every relation (or table as they are more often referred to in daily use), *does* have a defined primary key.

To understand how to designate or assign a primary key for a relation, we need to learn about the different types of keys used in relational databases, and this means we need to learn about functional dependencies, which are the foundation upon which keys are built. We will then discuss specifically how to assign primary keys in relations.

Functional Dependencies

Functional dependencies are the heart of the database design process, and it is vital for you to understand them. We will first explain the concept in general terms and then examine two examples. We will then be able to define exactly what is a *functional dependency*.

We begin with a short excursion into the world of algebra. Suppose you are buying boxes of cookies and someone tells you that each box costs $5.00. With this fact, you can compute the cost of several boxes with the formula:

$$\text{CookieCost} = \text{NumberOfBoxes} \times \$5$$

A more general way to express the relationship between CookieCost and NumberOfBoxes is to say that CookieCost *depends on* NumberOfBoxes. Such a statement tells us the character of the relationship between CookieCost and NumberOfBoxes, even though it doesn't give us the formula. More formally, we can say that CookieCost is **functionally dependent** on NumberOfBoxes. Such a statement can be written as:

NumberOfBoxes → CookieCost

This expression can be read as "NumberOfBoxes *determines* CookieCost." The variable on the left, here NumberOfBoxes, is called the **determinant**.

Using another formula, we can compute the extended price of a part order by multiplying the quantity of the item times its unit price, or:

$$\text{ExtendedPrice} = \text{Quantity} \times \text{UnitPrice}$$

In this case, we say that ExtendedPrice is functionally dependent on Quantity and UnitPrice, or:

(Quantity, UnitPrice) → ExtendedPrice

Here the determinant is the composite (Quantity, UnitPrice).

Functional Dependencies That Are Not Equations

In general, a **functional dependency** exists when the value of one or more attributes determines the value of another attribute. Many functional dependencies exist that do not involve equations.

Consider an example. Suppose you know that a sack contains either red, blue, or yellow objects. Further, suppose you know that the red objects weigh 5 pounds, the blue objects weigh 5 pounds, and the yellow objects weigh 7 pounds. If a friend looks into the sack, sees an object, and tells you the color of the object, you can tell her the weight of the object. We can formalize this as:

ObjectColor → Weight

Thus, we can say that Weight is functionally dependent on ObjectColor and that ObjectColor determines Weight. The relationship here does not involve an equation, but the functional dependency holds. Given a value for ObjectColor, you can determine the object's weight.

If we also know that the red objects are balls, the blue objects are cubes, and the yellow objects are cubes, we can also say:

ObjectColor → Shape

Thus, ObjectColor determines Shape. We can put these two together to state:

ObjectColor → (Weight, Shape)

Thus, ObjectColor determines Weight and Shape.

Another way to represent these facts is to put them into a table:

Object Color	Weight	Shape
Red	5	Ball
Blue	5	Cube
Yellow	7	Cube

This table meets all of the conditions listed in Figure 3-4, and therefore it is a relation. You may be thinking that we performed a trick or sleight of hand to arrive at this relation, but, in truth, the only reason for having relations is *to store instances of functional dependencies.* If there were a formula by which we could take ObjectColor and somehow compute Weight and Shape, then we would not need the table. We would just make the computation. Similarly, if there were a formula by which we could take EmployeeNumber and compute EmployeeName and HireDate, then we would not need an EMPLOYEE relation. However, because there is no such formula, we must store the combinations of EmployeeNumber, EmployeeName, and HireDate in the rows of a relation.

BY THE WAY   Perhaps the easiest way to understand functional dependencies is:

If I tell you one specific fact, can you respond with a unique associated fact?

Using the table above, if I tell you that that the ObjectColor is Red, can you uniquely tell me the associated Shape? *Yes,* you can and it is Ball. Therefore, ObjectColor *determines* Shape, and a functional dependency exists with ObjectColor as the determinant.

Now, if I tell you that that the Shape is Cube, can you uniquely tell me the associated ObjectColor? *No,* you cannot because it could be either Blue or Yellow. Therefore, Shape *does not determine* ObjectColor, and ObjectColor is *not* functionally dependent on Shape.

Composite Functional Dependencies

The determinant of a functional dependency can consist of more than one attribute. For example, a grade in a class is determined by both the student and the class, or:

(StudentNumber, ClassNumber) → Grade

In this case, the determinant is called a **composite determinant**.

Notice that both the student and the class are needed to determine the grade. In general, if (A, B) → C, then neither A nor B will determine C by itself. However, if A → (B, C), then it is true that A → B and A → C (this is known as the **decomposition rule**). Work through examples of your own for both of these cases so that you understand why this is true. Also note that if A → B and A → C, then it is true that A → (B, C) (this is known as the **union rule**).

Finding Functional Dependencies

To fix the idea of functional dependency in your mind, consider what functional dependencies exist in the SKU_DATA and ORDER_ITEM tables in Figure 3-1.

Functional Dependencies in the SKU_DATA Table

To find functional dependencies in a table, we must ask "Does any column determine the value of another column?" For example, consider the values of the SKU_DATA table in Figure 3-1:

	SKU	SKU_Description	Department	Buyer
1	100100	Std. Scuba Tank, Yellow	Water Sports	Pete Hansen
2	100200	Std. Scuba Tank, Magenta	Water Sports	Pete Hansen
3	101100	Dive Mask, Small Clear	Water Sports	Nancy Meyers
4	101200	Dive Mask, Med Clear	Water Sports	Nancy Meyers
5	201000	Half-dome Tent	Camping	Cindy Lo
6	202000	Half-dome Tent Vestibule	Camping	Cindy Lo
7	301000	Light Fly Climbing Harness	Climbing	Jerry Martin
8	302000	Locking Carabiner, Oval	Climbing	Jerry Martin

Consider the last two columns. If we know the value of Department, can we determine a unique value of Buyer? No, we cannot, because a Department may have more than one Buyer. In these sample data, 'Water Sports' is associated with Pete Hansen and Nancy Meyers. Therefore, Department does not functionally determine Buyer.

What about the reverse? Does Buyer determine Department? In every row, for a given value of Buyer, do we find the same value of Department? Every time Jerry Martin appears, for example, is he paired with the same department? The answer is yes. Further, every time Cindy Lo appears, she is paired with the same department. The same is true for the other buyers. Therefore, assuming that these data are representative, Buyer does determine Department, and we can write:

Buyer → Department

Does Buyer determine any other column? If we know the value of Buyer, do we know the value of SKU? No, we do not, because a given buyer has many SKUs assigned to him or her.

Does Buyer determine SKU_Description? No, because a given value of Buyer occurs with many values of SKU_Description.

BY THE WAY   As stated, for the Buyer → Department functional dependency, a Buyer is paired with one and only one value of Department. Notice that a buyer can appear more than once in the table, but, if so, that buyer is always paired with the same department. This is true for all functional dependencies. If A → B, then each value of A will be paired with one and only one value of B. A particular value of A may appear more than once in the relation, but, if so, it is always paired with the same value of B. Note, too, that the reverse is not necessarily true. If A → B, then a value of B may be paired with many values of A.

What about the other columns? It turns out that if we know the value of SKU, we also know the values of all of the other columns. In other words:

SKU → SKU_Description

because a given value of SKU will have just one value of SKU_Description. Next,

SKU → Department

because a given value of SKU will have just one value of Department. And, finally,

SKU → Buyer

because a given value of SKU will have just one value of Buyer.

We can combine these three statements as:

SKU → (SKU_Description, Department, Buyer)

For the same reasons, SKU_Description determines all of the other columns, and we can write:

SKU_Description → (SKU, Department, Buyer)

In summary, the functional dependencies in the SKU_DATA table are:

SKU → (SKU_Description, Department, Buyer)
SKU_Description → (SKU, Department, Buyer)
Buyer → Department

BY THE WAY   You cannot always determine functional dependencies from sample data. You may not have any sample data, or you may have just a few rows that are not representative of all of the data conditions. In such cases, you must ask the users who are experts in the application that creates the data. For the SKU_DATA table, you would ask questions such as, "Is a Buyer always associated with the same Department?" and "Can a Department have more than one Buyer?" In most cases, answers to such questions are more reliable than sample data. When in doubt, trust the users.

Functional Dependencies in the ORDER_ITEM Table

Now consider the ORDER_ITEM table in Figure 3-1. For convenience, here is a copy of the data in that table:

	OrderNumber	SKU	Quantity	Price	ExtendedPrice
1	1000	201000	1	300.00	300.00
2	1000	202000	1	130.00	130.00
3	2000	101100	4	50.00	200.00
4	2000	101200	2	50.00	100.00
5	3000	100200	1	300.00	300.00
6	3000	101100	2	50.00	100.00
7	3000	101200	1	50.00	50.00

What are the functional dependencies in this table? Start on the left. Does OrderNumber determine another column? It does not determine SKU because several SKUs are associated with a given order. For the same reasons, it does not determine Quantity, Price, or ExtendedPrice.

What about SKU? SKU does not determine OrderNumber because several OrderNumbers are associated with a given SKU. It does not determine Quantity or ExtendedPrice for the same reason.

What about SKU and Price? From this data, it does appear that

SKU → Price

but that might not be true in general. In fact, we know that prices can change after an order has been processed. Further, an order might have special pricing due to a sale or promotion. To keep an accurate record of what the customer actually paid, we need to associate a particular SKU price with a particular order. Thus:

(OrderNumber, SKU) → Price

Considering the other columns, Quantity, Price, and ExtendedPrice do not determine anything else. You can decide this by looking at the sample data. You can reinforce this conclusion by thinking about the nature of sales. Would a Quantity of 2 ever determine an OrderNumber or an SKU? This makes no sense. At the grocery store, if I tell you I bought two of something, you have no reason to conclude that my OrderNumber was 1010022203466 or that I bought carrots. Quantity does not determine OrderNumber or SKU.

Similarly, if I tell you that the price of an item was $3.99, there is no logical way to conclude what my OrderNumber was or that I bought a jar of green olives. Thus, Price does not determine OrderNumber or SKU. Similar comments pertain to ExtendedPrice. It turns out that no single column is a determinant in the ORDER_ITEM table.

What about pairs of columns? We already know that

(OrderNumber, SKU) → Price

Examining the data, (OrderNumber, SKU) determines the other two columns as well. Thus:

(OrderNumber, SKU) → (Quantity, Price, ExtendedPrice)

This functional dependency makes sense. It means that given a particular order and a particular item on that order, there is only one quantity, one price, and one extended price.

Notice, too, that because ExtendedPrice is computed from the formula ExtendedPrice = (Quantity * Price) we have:

(Quantity, Price) → ExtendedPrice

In summary, the functional dependencies in ORDER_ITEM are:

(OrderNumber, SKU) → (Quantity, Price, ExtendedPrice)

(Quantity, Price) → ExtendedPrice

No single skill is more important for designing databases than the ability to identify functional dependencies. Make sure you understand the material in this section. Work through Review Questions 3.58 and 3.59, the Regional Labs case questions, and The Queen Anne Curiosity Shop and Morgan Importing project questions at the end of the chapter. Ask your instructor for help if necessary. You *must* understand functional dependencies and be able to work with them.

When Are Determinant Values Unique?

In the previous section, you may have noticed an irregularity. Sometimes the determinants of a functional dependency are unique in a relation, and sometimes they are not. Consider the SKU_DATA relation, with determinants SKU, SKU_Description, and Buyer. In SKU_DATA, the values of both SKU and SKU_Description are unique in the table. For example, the SKU value 100100 appears just once. Similarly, the SKU_Description value 'Half-dome Tent' occurs just once. From this, it is tempting to conclude that values of determinants are always unique in a relation. However, this is *not* true.

For example, Buyer is a determinant, but it is not unique in SKU_DATA. The buyer 'Cindy Lo' appears in two different rows. In fact, for these sample data all of the buyers occur in two different rows.

In truth, a determinant is unique in a relation only if it determines every other column in the relation. For the SKU_DATA relation, SKU determines all of the other columns. Similarly, SKU_Description determines all of the other columns. Hence, they both are unique. Buyer, however, only determines the Department column. It does not determine SKU or SKU_Description.

The determinants in ORDER_ITEM are (OrderNumber, SKU) and (Quantity, Price). Because (OrderNumber, SKU) determines all of the other columns, it will be unique in the relation. The composite (Quantity and Price) only determines ExtendedPrice. Therefore, it will not be unique in the relation.

This fact means that you cannot find the determinants of all functional dependencies simply by looking for unique values. Some of the determinants will be unique, but some will not be. Instead, to determine if column A determines column B, look at the data and ask, "Every time a value of column A appears, is it matched with the same value of Column B?" If so, it can be a determinant of B. Again, however, sample data can be incomplete, so the best strategies are to think about the nature of the business activity from which the data arise and to ask the users.

Keys

The relational model has more keys than a locksmith. There are candidate keys, composite keys, primary keys, surrogate keys, and foreign keys. In this section, we will define each of these types of keys. Because key definitions rely on the concept of functional dependency, make sure you understand that concept before reading on.

In general, a **key** is a combination of one or more columns that is used to identify particular rows in a relation. Keys that have two or more columns are called **composite keys**.

Candidate Keys

A **candidate key** is a determinant that determines all of the other columns in a relation. The SKU_DATA relation has two candidate keys: SKU and SKU_Description. Buyer is a determinant, but it is not a candidate key because it determines only Department.

The ORDER_ITEM table has just one candidate key: (OrderNumber, SKU). The other determinant in this table, (Quantity, Price), is not a candidate key because it determines only ExtendedPrice.

Candidate keys identify a unique row in a relation. Given the value of a candidate key, we can find one and only one row in the relation that has that value. For example, given the SKU value of 100100, we can find one and only one row in SKU_DATA.

Similarly, given the OrderNumber and SKU values (2000, 101100), we can find one and only one row in ORDER_ITEM.

Primary Keys

When designing a database, one of the candidate keys is selected to be the **primary key**. This term is used because this key will be defined to the DBMS, and the DBMS will use it as its primary means for finding rows in a table. A table has only one primary key. The primary key can have one column, or it can be a composite.

In this text, to clarify discussions we will sometimes indicate table structure by showing the name of a table followed by the names of the table's columns enclosed in parentheses. When we do this, we will underline the column(s) that comprise the primary key. For example, we can show the structure of SKU_DATA and ORDER_ITEM as follows:

SKU_DATA (<u>SKU</u>, SKU_Description, Department, Buyer)

ORDER_ITEM (<u>OrderNumber</u>, <u>SKU</u>, Quantity, Price, ExtendedPrice)

This notation indicates that SKU is the primary key of SKU_DATA and that (OrderNumber, SKU) is the primary key of ORDER_ITEM.

In order to function properly, a primary key, whether it is a single column or a composite key, *must* have unique data values inserted into every row of the table. While this fact may seem obvious, it is significant enough to be named the **entity integrity constraint** and is a fundamental requirement for the proper functioning of a relational database.

BY THE WAY   What do you do if a table has no candidate keys? In that case, define the primary key as the collection of all of the columns in the table. Because there are no duplicate rows in a stored relation, the combination of all of the columns of the table will always be unique. Again, although tables generated by SQL manipulation may have duplicate rows, the tables that you design to be stored should never be constructed to have data duplication. Thus, the combination of all columns is always a candidate key.

Surrogate Keys

A **surrogate key** is an artificial column that is added to a table to serve as the primary key. The DBMS assigns a unique value to a surrogate key when the row is created. The assigned value never changes. Surrogate keys are used when the primary key is large and unwieldy. For example, consider the relation RENTAL_PROPERTY:

RENTAL_PROPERTY (<u>Street</u>, <u>City</u>, <u>State/Province</u>, <u>Zip/PostalCode</u>, <u>Country</u>, Rental_Rate)

The primary key of this table is (Street, City, State/Province, Zip/PostalCode, Country). As we will dicuss further in Chapter 6, for good performance a primary key should be short and, if possible, numeric. The primary key of RENTAL_PROPERTY is neither.

In this case, the designers of the database would likely create a surrogate key. The structure of the table would then be:

RENTAL_PROPERTY (<u>PropertyID</u>, Street, City, State/Province, Zip/PostalCode, Country, Rental_Rate)

The DBMS can then be used to assign a numeric value to PropertyID when a row is created (exactly *how* this is done depends upon which DBMS product is being used). Using that key will result in better performance than using the original key. Note that surrogate key values are artificial and have no meaning to the users. In fact, surrogate key values are normally hidden in forms and reports.

Foreign Keys

A **foreign key** is a column or composite of columns that is the primary key of a table other than the one in which it appears. The term arises because it is a key of a table *foreign* to the one in which it appears. In the following two tables, DEPARTMENT.DepartmentName is the primary key of DEPARTMENT and EMPLOYEE.DepartmentName is a foreign key. In this text, we will show foreign keys in italics:

DEPARTMENT (<u>DepartmentName</u>, BudgetCode, ManagerName)

EMPLOYEE (<u>EmployeeNumber</u>, EmployeeLastName, EmployeeFirstName, *DepartmentName*)

Foreign keys express relationships between rows of tables. In this example, the foreign key EMPLOYEE.DepartmentName stores the relationship between an employee and his or her department.

Consider the SKU_DATA and ORDER_ITEM tables. SKU_DATA.SKU is the primary key of SKU_DATA, and ORDER_ITEM.SKU is a foreign key.

SKU_DATA (<u>SKU</u>, SKU_Description, Department, Buyer)

ORDER_ITEM (<u>OrderNumber</u>, *<u>SKU</u>*, Quantity, Price, ExtendedPrice)

Notice that ORDER_ITEM.SKU is both a foreign key and also part of the primary key of ORDER_ITEM. This condition sometimes occurs, but it is not required. In the example above, EMPLOYEE.DepartmentName is a foreign key, but it is not part of the EMPLOYEE primary key. You will see some uses for foreign keys later in this chapter and the next, and you will study them at length in Chapter 6.

In most cases, we need to ensure that the values of a foreign key match a valid value of a primary key. For the SKU_DATA and ORDER_ITEM tables, we need to ensure that all of the values of ORDER_ITEM.SKU match a value of SKU_DATA.SKU. To accomplish this, we create a **referential integrity constraint**, which is a statement that limits the values of the foreign key. In this case, we create the constraint:

SKU in ORDER_ITEM must exist in SKU in SKU_DATA

This constraint stipulates that every value of SKU in ORDER_ITEM must match a value of SKU in SKU_DATA.

BY THE WAY   While we have defined a *referential integrity constraint* to require a corresponding primary key value in the linked table, the technical definition of the referential integrity constraint allows for one other option—that the foreign key cell in the table is *empty* and *does not have a value*.[2] If a cell in a table does not have a value, it is said to have a **null value** (we will discuss null values in Chapter 4).

It is difficult to imagine a foreign key having null values in a real database when the referential integrity constraint is actually in use, and we will stick with our basic definition of the referential integrity constraint in this book. At the same time, be aware that the complete, formal definition of the referential integrity constraint does allow for null values in foreign key columns.

---

[2]For example, see the Wikipedia article on referential integrity at *http://en.wikipedia.org/wiki/Referential_integrity*.

> **BY THE WAY**   We have defined three constraints so far in our discussion:
>
> ■ The *domain integrity constraint*
> ■ The *entity integrity constraint*
> ■ The *referential integrity constraint*
>
> The purpose of these three constraints, taken as a whole, is to create **database integrity**, which means that the data in our database will be useful, meaningful data.[3]

Normal Forms

All relations are not equal. Some are easy to process, and others are problematic. Relations are categorized into **normal forms** based on the kinds of problems that they have. Knowledge of these normal forms will help you create appropriate database designs. To understand normal forms, we need first to define modification anomalies.

Modification Anomalies

Consider the EQUIPMENT_REPAIR relation in Figure 3-10, which stores data about manufacturing equipment and equipment repairs. Suppose we delete the data for repair number 2100. When we delete this row (the second one in Figure 3-10), we remove not only data about the repair but also data about the machine itself. We will no longer know, for example, that the machine was a Lathe and that its AcquisitionCost was 4750.00. When we delete one row, the structure of this table forces us to lose facts about two different things, a machine and a repair. This condition is called a **deletion anomaly**.

Now suppose we want to enter the first repair for a piece of equipment. To enter repair data, we need to know not just RepairNumber, RepairDate, and RepairCost but also ItemNumber, EquipmentType, and AcquisitionCost. If we work in the repair department, this is a problem because we are unlikely to know the value of AcquisitionCost. The structure of this table forces us to enter facts about two entities when we just want to enter facts about one. This condition is called an **insertion anomaly**.

Finally, suppose we want to change existing data. If we alter a value of RepairNumber, RepairDate, or RepairCost, there is no problem. But if we alter a value of ItemNumber, EquipmentType, or AcquisitionCost, we may create a data inconsistency. To see why, suppose we update the last row of the table in Figure 3-10 using the data (100, 'Drill Press', 5500, 2500, '08/17/15', 275).

Figure 3-11 shows the table after this erroneous update. The drill press has two different AcquisitionCosts. Clearly, this is an error. Equipment cannot be acquired at two different costs. If there were, say, 10,000 rows in the table, however, it might be very difficult to detect this error. This condition is called an **update anomaly**.

FIGURE 3-10

The EQUIPMENT_REPAIR Relation

	ItemNumber	EquipmentType	AcquisitionCost	RepairNumber	RepairDate	RepairCost
1	100	Drill Press	3500.00	2000	2015-05-05	375.00
2	200	Lathe	4750.00	2100	2015-05-07	255.00
3	100	Drill Press	3500.00	2200	2015-06-19	178.00
4	300	Mill	27300.00	2300	2015-06-19	1875.00
5	100	Drill Press	3500.00	2400	2015-07-05	0.00
6	100	Drill Press	3500.00	2500	2015-08-17	275.00

---

[3]For more information and discussion, see the Wikipedia article on database integrity at *http://en.wikipedia.org/wiki/Database_integrity* and the articles linked to that article.

> **BY THE WAY**   Notice that the EQUIPMENT_REPAIR table in Figures 3-10 and 3-11 duplicates data. For example, the AcquisitionCost of the same item of equipment appears several times. Any table that duplicates data is susceptible to update anomalies like the one in Figure 3-11. A table that has such inconsistencies is said to have **data integrity problems**.
>
> As we will discuss further in Chapter 4, to improve query speed we sometimes design a table to have duplicated data. Be aware, however, that any time we design a table this way, we open the door to data integrity problems.

A Short History of Normal Forms

When Codd defined the relational model, he noticed that some tables had modification anomalies. In his second paper,[4] he defined first normal form, second normal form, and third normal form. He defined **first normal form (1NF)** as the *set of conditions for a relation* shown in Figure 3-4. Any table meeting the conditions in Figure 3-4 is therefore a relation in 1NF.

This definition, however, brings us back to the "To Key or Not to Key" discussion. Codd's set of conditions for a relation does not require a primary key, but one is clearly implied by the condition that all rows must be unique. Thus, there are various opinions on whether or not a relation has to have a defined primary key to be in 1NF.[5]

For practical purposes, we will define 1NF as it is used in this book as a table that:

1. Meets the set of conditions for a relation, and
2. Has a defined primary key.[6]

Codd also noted that some tables (or, interchangeably in this book, relations) in 1NF had modification anomalies. He found that he could remove some of those anomalies by applying certain conditions. A relation that met those conditions, which we will discuss later in this chapter, was said to be in **second normal form (2NF)**. He also observed, however, that relations in 2NF could also have anomalies, and so he defined **third normal form (3NF)**, which is a set of conditions that removes even more anomalies and which we will also discuss later in this chapter. As time went by, other researchers found still other ways that anomalies can occur, and the conditions for **Boyce-Codd Normal Form (BCNF)** were defined.

These normal forms are defined so that a relation in BCNF is in 3NF, a relation in 3NF is in 2NF, and a relation in 2NF is in 1NF. Thus, if you put a relation into BCNF, it is automatically in the lesser normal forms.

Normal forms 2NF through BCNF concern anomalies that arise from functional dependencies. Other sources of anomalies were found later. They led to the definition of

FIGURE 3-11

The EQUIPMENT_REPAIR Relation After an Incorrect Update

	ItemNumber	EquipmentType	AcquisitionCost	RepairNumber	RepairDate	RepairCost
1	100	Drill Press	3500.00	2000	2015-05-05	375.00
2	200	Lathe	4750.00	2100	2015-05-07	255.00
3	100	Drill Press	3500.00	2200	2015-06-19	178.00
4	300	Mill	27300.00	2300	2015-06-19	1875.00
5	100	Drill Press	3500.00	2400	2015-07-05	0.00
6	100	Drill Press	5500.00	2500	2015-08-17	275.00

---

[4]E. F. Codd and A. L. Dean, "Proceedings of 1971 ACM-SIGFIDET Workshop on Data Description," *Access and Control*, San Diego, California, November 11–12, 1971 ACM 1971.

[5]For a review of some of the discussion, see the Wikipedia article **First normal form** at *http://en.wikipedia.org/wiki/First_normal_form*.

[6]Some definitions of 1NF also state that there can be "no repeating groups." This refers to the *multivalue, multicolumn problem* we discuss in Chapter 4, and also deal with in our discussion of *multivalued dependencies* later is this chapter.

fourth normal form (4NF) and **fifth normal form (5NF)**, both of which we will discuss later in this chapter. So it went, with researchers chipping away at modification anomalies, each one improving on the prior normal form.

In 1982, Ronald Fagin published a paper that took a different tack.[7] Instead of looking for just another normal form, Fagin asked, "What conditions need to exist for a relation to have no anomalies?" In that paper, he defined **domain/key normal form (DK/NF)**. Fagin ended the search for normal forms by showing that a relation in DK/NF has no modification anomalies and, further, that a relation that has no modification anomalies is in DK/NF. DK/NF is discussed in more detail later in this chapter.

Normalization Categories

As shown in Figure 3-12, normalization theory can be divided into three major categories. Some anomalies arise from functional dependencies, some arise from multivalued dependencies, and some arise from data constraints and odd conditions.

2NF, 3NF, and BCNF are all concerned with anomalies that are caused by functional dependencies. A relation that is in BCNF has no modification anomalies from functional dependencies. It is also automatically in 2NF and 3NF, and, therefore, we will focus on transforming relations into BCNF. However, it is instructive to work through the progression of normal forms from 1NF to BCNF in order to understand how each normal form deals with anomalies, and we will do this later in this chapter.[8]

As shown in the second row of Figure 3-12, some anomalies arise because of another kind of dependency called a multivalued dependency. Those anomalies can be eliminated by placing each multivalued dependency in a relation of its own, a condition known as 4NF. You will see how to do that in the last section of this chapter.

The third source of anomalies is esoteric. These problems involve specific, rare, and even strange data constraints. Accordingly, we will not discuss them in this text.

From First Normal Form to Boyce-Codd Normal Form Step by Step

As we discussed earlier in this chapter, a table is in 1NF if and only if (1) it meets the *definition of a relation* in Figure 3-4, and (2) it has a *defined primary key*. From Figure 3-4 this means that the following must hold: The cells of a table must be a single value, and neither repeating groups nor arrays are allowed as values; all entries in a column must be of the same data type; each column must have a unique name, but the order of the columns in the table is not significant; no two rows in a table may be identical, but the order of the rows is not significant. To this, we add the requirement of having a primary key defined for the table.

FIGURE 3-12

Summary of Normalization Theory

Source of Anomaly	Normal Forms	Design Principles
Functional dependencies	1NF, 2NF, 3NF, BCNF	BCNF: Design tables so that every determinant is a candidate key.
Multivalued dependencies	4NF	4NF: Move each multivalued dependency to a table of its own.
Data constraints and oddities	5NF, DK/NF	DK/NF: Make every constraint a logical consequence of candidate keys and domains.

---

[7] R. Fagin, "A Normal Form for Relational Databases That Is Based on Domains and Keys," *ACM Transactions on Database Systems*, September 1981, pp. 387–414.

[8] See C. J. Date, *An Introduction to Database Systems*, 8th ed. (New York: Addison-Wesley, 2003) for a complete discussion of normal forms.

Second Normal Form

When Codd discovered anomalies in 1NF tables, he defined 2NF to eliminate some of these anomalies. A relation is in 2NF if and only if *it is in 1NF* and *all non-key attributes are determined by the entire primary key*. This means that if the primary key is a composite primary key, then no non-key attribute can be determined by an attribute or set of attributes that make up only part of the key. Thus, if you have a relation **R (A, B, N, O, P)** with the composite key **(A, B)**, then none of the non-key attributes **N, O,** or **P** can be determined by just **A** or just **B**.

Note that the only way a non-key attribute can be dependent on part of the primary key is if there is a *composite primary key*. This means that relations with *single-attribute primary keys* are automatically in 2NF.

For example, consider the STUDENT_ACTIVITY relation:

STUDENT_ACTIVITY (**StudentID**, **Activity**, ActivityFee)

The STUDENT_ACTIVITY relation is in 1NF, and is shown with sample data in Figure 3-13. Note that STUDENT_ACTIVITY has the composite primary key (StudentID, Activity), which allows us to determine the fee a particular student will have to pay for a particular activity. However, because fees are determined by activities, Fee is also functionally dependent on just Activity itself, and we can say that ActivityFee is **partially dependent** on the key of the table. The set of functional dependencies is therefore:

(**StudentID, Activity**) → (**ActivityFee**)

(**Activity**) → (**ActivityFee**)

Thus, there is a non-key attribute determined by part of the composite primary key, and the STUDENT_ACTIVITY relation is *not* in 2NF. What do we do in this case? We will have to move the columns of the functional dependency based on the partial primary key attribute into a separate relation while leaving the determinant in the original relation as a foreign key. We will end up with two relations:

STUDENT_ACTIVITY (**StudentID**, *Activity*)

ACTIVITY_FEE (**Activity**, ActivityFee)

The Activity column in STUDENT_ACTIVITY becomes a foreign key. The new relations are shown in Figure 3-14. Now, are the two new relations in 2NF? Yes. STUDENT_ACTIVITY still has a composite primary key but now has no attributes that are dependent on only a part of this composite key. ACTIVITY_FEE has a set of attributes (just one each in this case) that are dependent on the entire primary key.

Third Normal Form

However, the conditions necessary for 2NF do not eliminate all anomalies. To deal with additional anomalies, Codd defined 3NF. A relation is in 3NF if and only if *it is in 2NF* and *there*

FIGURE 3-13

The 1NF STUDENT_ACTIVITY Relation

STUDENT_ACTIVITY

	StudentID	Activity	ActivityFee
1	100	Golf	65.00
2	100	Skiing	200.00
3	200	Skiing	200.00
4	200	Swimming	50.00
5	300	Skiing	200.00
6	300	Swimming	50.00
7	400	Golf	65.00
8	400	Swimming	50.00

FIGURE 3-14

The 2NF STUDENT_
ACTIVITY and ACTIVITY_FEE
Relations

STUDENT_ACTIVITY

	StudentID	Activity
1	100	Golf
2	100	Skiing
3	200	Skiing
4	200	Swimming
5	300	Skiing
6	300	Swimming
7	400	Golf
8	400	Swimming

ACTIVITY_FEE

	Activity	ActivityFee
1	Golf	65.00
2	Skiing	200.00
3	Swimming	50.00

are no non-key attributes determined by another non-key attribute. The technical name for a non-key attribute determined by another non-key attribute is **transitive dependency**.[9] We can therefore restate the definition of 3NF: A relation is in 3NF if and only if *it is in 2NF* and *it has no transitive dependencies*. Thus, in order for our relation **R (A, B, N, O, P)** to be in 3NF, none of the non-key attributes **N, O,** or **P** can be determined by **N, O,** or **P**.

For example, consider the relation STUDENT_HOUSING (StudentID, Building, Fee) shown in Figure 3-15. The STUDENT_HOUSING relation is in 2NF, and the table schema is:

STUDENT_HOUSING (StudentID, Building, HousingFee)

Here we have a single-attribute primary key, StudentID, so the relation is in 2NF because there is no possibility of a non-key attribute being dependent on only part of the primary key. Furthermore, if we know the student, we can determine the building where he or she is residing, so:

(StudentID) → Building

However, the building fee is independent of which student is housed in the building, and, in fact, the same fee is charged for every room in a building. Therefore, Building determines HousingFee:

(Building) → (HousingFee)

Thus, a non-key attribute (HousingFee) is functionally determined by another non-key attribute (Building), and the relation is *not* in 3NF.

FIGURE 3-15

The 2NF STUDENT_
HOUSING Relation

STUDENT_HOUSING

	StudentID	Building	BuildingFee
1	100	Randolph	3200.00
2	200	Ingersoll	3400.00
3	300	Randolph	3200.00
4	400	Randolph	3200.00
5	500	Pitkin	3500.00
6	600	Ingersoll	3400.00
7	700	Ingersoll	3400.00
8	800	Pitkin	3500.00

---

[9]In terms of functional dependencies, a transitive dependency is defined as: IF A → B and B → C, THEN A → C.

To put the relation into 3NF, we will have to move the columns of the functional dependency into a separate relation while leaving the determinant in the original relation as a foreign key. We will end up with two relations:

STUDENT_HOUSING (<u>StudentID</u>, *Building*)

BUILDING_FEE (<u>Building</u>, HousingFee)

The Building column in STUDENT_HOUSING becomes a foreign key. The two relations are now in 3NF (work through the logic yourself to make sure you understand 3NF) and are shown in Figure 3-16.

Boyce-Codd Normal Form

Some database designers normalize their relations to 3NF. Unfortunately, there are still anomalies due to functional dependences in 3NF. Together with Raymond Boyce, Codd defined BCNF to fix this situation. A relation is in BCNF if and only if *it is in 3NF* and *every determinant is a candidate key*.

For example, consider the relation STUDENT_ADVISOR shown in Figure 3-17, where a student (StudentID) can have one or more majors (Major), a major can have one or more faculty advisors (AdvisorName), and a faculty member advises in only one major area. Note that the figure shows two students (StudentIDs 700 and 800) with double majors (both students show Majors of Math and Psychology) and two Subjects (Math and Psychology) with two Advisors.

Because students can have several majors, StudentID does not determine Major. Moreover, because students can have several advisors, StudentID does not determine AdvisorName. Therefore, StudentID by itself cannot be a key. However, the composite key (StudentID, Major) determines AdvisorName, and the composite key (StudentID, AdvisorName) determines Major. This gives us (StudentID, Major) and (StudentId, AdvisorName) as two

FIGURE 3-16

The 3NF STUDENT_HOUSING and HOUSING_FEE Relations

STUDENT_HOUSING

	StudentID	Building
1	100	Randolph
2	200	Ingersoll
3	300	Randolph
4	400	Randolph
5	500	Pitkin
6	600	Ingersoll
7	700	Ingersoll
8	800	Pitkin

HOUSING_FEE

	Building	BuildingFee
1	Ingersoll	3400.00
2	Pitkin	3500.00
3	Randolph	3200.00

FIGURE 3-17

The 3NF STUDENT_ADVISOR Relation

STUDENT_ADVISOR

	StudentID	Major	AdvisorName
1	100	Math	Cauchy
2	200	Psychology	Jung
3	300	Math	Riemann
4	400	Math	Cauchy
5	500	Psychology	Perls
6	600	English	Austin
7	700	Psychology	Perls
8	700	Math	Riemann
9	800	Math	Cauchy
10	800	Psychology	Jung

candidate keys. We can select either of these as the primary key for the relation. Thus, two STUDENT_ADVISOR schemas with different candidate keys are possible:

STUDENT_ADVISOR (<u>StudentID</u>, <u>Major</u>, AdvisorName)

and

STUDENT_ADVISOR (<u>StudentID</u>, Major, <u>AdvisorName</u>)

Note that STUDENT_ADVISOR is in 2NF because it has no non-key attributes in the sense that every attribute is a part of *at least one* candidate key. This is a subtle condition, based on the fact that technically the definition of 2NF states that no *non-prime attribute* can be partially dependent on a candidate key, where a **non-prime attribute** is an attribute that is not contained in *any* candidate key. Furthermore, STUDENT_ADVISOR is in 3NF because there are no transitive dependencies in the relation.

The two candidate keys for this relation are **overlapping candidate keys** because they share the attribute StudentID. When a table in 3NF has overlapping candidate keys, it can still have modification anomalies based on functional dependencies. In the STUDENT_ADVISOR relation, there will be modification anomalies because there is one other functional dependency in the relation. Because a faculty member can be an advisor for only one major area, AdvisorName determines Major. Therefore, AdvisorName is a determinant but not a candidate key.

Suppose that we have a student (StudentID = 300) majoring in psychology (Major = Psychology) with faculty advisor Perls (AdvisorName = Perls). Further, assume that this row is the only one in the table with the AdvisorName value of Perls. If we delete this row, we will lose all data about Perls. This is a deletion anomaly. Similarly, we cannot insert the data to represent the Economics advisor Keynes until a student majors in Economics. This is an insertion anomaly. Situations like this led to the development of BCNF.

What do we do with the STUDENT_ADVISOR relation? As before, we move the functional dependency creating the problem to another relation while leaving the determinant in the original relation as a foreign key. In this case, we will create the relations:

STUDENT_ADVISOR (<u>StudentID</u>, *AdvisorName*)
ADVISOR_MAJOR (<u>AdvisorName</u>, Major)

The AdvisorName column in STUDENT_ADVISOR is the foreign key, and the two final relations are shown in Figure 3-18.

Note that a relation in 3NF *may also already be* in BCNF. The only way a relation in 3NF can have problems actually requiring further normalization work to get it into BCNF is if it has *overlapping composite candidate keys*. If the relation (1) does *not* have composite candidate keys, or (2) has *non-overlapping* composite candidate keys, then it is *already in BCNF* once it is in 3NF.

FIGURE 3-18

The BCNF STUDENT_ADVISOR and ADVISOR_MAJOR Relations

STUDENT_ADVISOR

	StudentID	AdvisorName
1	100	Cauchy
2	200	Jung
3	300	Riemann
4	400	Cauchy
5	500	Perls
6	600	Austin
7	700	Perls
8	700	Riemann
9	800	Cauchy
10	800	Jung

ADVISOR_MAJOR

	AdvisorName	Major
1	Austin	English
2	Cauchy	Math
3	Jung	Psychology
4	Perls	Psychology
5	Riemann	Math

Eliminating Anomalies from Functional Dependencies with BCNF

Most modification anomalies occur because of problems with functional dependencies. You can eliminate these problems by progressively testing a relation for 1NF, 2NF, 3NF, and BCNF using the definitions of these normal forms given previously. We will refer to this as the "Step-by-Step" method.

You can also eliminate such problems by simply designing (or redesigning) your tables so that every determinant is a candidate key. This condition, which, of course, is the definition of BCNF, will eliminate all anomalies due to functional dependencies. We will refer to this method as the "Straight-to-BCNF" or "general normalization" method.

We prefer the "Straight-to-BCNF" general normalization strategy and will use it extensively, but not exclusively, in this book. However, this is merely our preference—either method produces the same results, and you (or your professor) may prefer the "Step-by-Step" method.

The general normalization method is summarized in Figure 3-19. Identify every functional dependency in the relation, and then identify the candidate keys. If there are determinants that are not candidate keys, then the relation is not in BCNF and is subject to modification anomalies. To put the relation into BCNF, follow the procedure in step 3. To fix this procedure in your mind, we will illustrate it with five different examples. We will also compare it to the "Step-by-Step" approach.

BY THE WAY   Our process rule that a relation is in BCNF if and only if every determinant is a candidate key is summed up in a variation of a widely known phrase:

I swear to construct my tables so that all non-key columns are dependent on the key, the whole key and nothing but the key, so help me Codd!

This phrase actually is a very good way to remember the order of the normal forms:

I swear to construct my tables so that all non-key columns are dependent on

- *the key,*   [This is **1NF**]
- *the whole key,*   [This is **2NF**]
- *and nothing but the key,*   [This is **3NF** and **BCNF**]

so help me Codd!

FIGURE 3-19

Process for Putting a Relation into BCNF

Process for Putting a Relation into BCNF
1. Identify every functional dependency.
2. Identify every candidate key.
3. If there is a functional dependency that has a determinant that is not a candidate key:

A. Move the columns of that functional dependency into a new relation.
    B. Make the determinant of that functional dependency the primary key of the new relation.
    C. Leave a copy of the determinant as a foreign key in the original relation.
    D. Create a referential integrity constraint between the original relation and the new relation.

4. Repeat step 3 until every determinant of every relation is a candidate key.

Note: In step 3, if there is more than one such functional dependency, start with the one with the most columns.

> **BY THE WAY**   The goal of the normalization process is to create relations that are in BCNF. It is sometimes stated that the goal is to create relations that are in 3NF, but after the discussion in this chapter, you should understand why BCNF is preferred to 3NF.
>
> Note that there are some problems that are not resolved by even BCNF, and these will require relations in 4NF. We will explain when we need to use 4NF after we discuss our examples of normalizing to BCNF.

Normalization Example 1

Consider the SKU_DATA table:

SKU_DATA (SKU, SKU_Description, Department, Buyer)

As discussed earlier, this table has three functional dependencies:

SKU → (SKU_Description, Department, Buyer)

SKU_Description → (SKU, Department, Buyer)

Buyer → Department

Normalization Example 1: The "Step-by-Step" Method

Both SKU and SKU_Description are candidate keys. Logically, SKU makes more sense as the primary key because it is a surrogate key, so our relation, which is shown in Figure 3-20, is:

SKU_DATA (<u>SKU</u>, SKU_Description, Department, Buyer)

Checking the relation against Figure 3-4, and noting that it has a defined primary key, we find that SKU_DATA is in 1NF.

Is the SKU_DATA relation in 2NF? A relation is in 2NF if and only if *it is in 1NF* and *all non-key attributes are determined by the entire primary key.* Because the primary key SKU is a single attribute key, all the non-key attributes are therefore dependent on the entire primary key. Thus, the SKU_DATA relation is in 2NF.

Is the SKU_DATA relation in 3NF? A relation is in 3NF if and only if *it is in 2NF* and *there are no non-key attributes determined by another non-key attribute.* Because we seem to have two non-key attributes (SKU_Description and Buyer) that determine non-key attributes, the relation is *not* in 3NF!

However, this is where things get a bit tricky. A *non-key attribute* is an attribute that is neither (1) a candidate key itself nor (2) part of a candidate key. SKU_Description, therefore, is *not a non-key attribute* (sorry about the double negative). The only non-key attribute is Buyer! Therefore, we must remove only the functional dependency

Buyer → Department

FIGURE 3-20

The SKU_DATA Relation

SKU_DATA

	SKU	SKU_Description	Department	Buyer
1	100100	Std. Scuba Tank, Yellow	Water Sports	Pete Hansen
2	100200	Std. Scuba Tank, Magenta	Water Sports	Pete Hansen
3	101100	Dive Mask, Small Clear	Water Sports	Nancy Meyers
4	101200	Dive Mask, Med Clear	Water Sports	Nancy Meyers
5	201000	Half-dome Tent	Camping	Cindy Lo
6	202000	Half-dome Tent Vestibule	Camping	Cindy Lo
7	301000	Light Fly Climbing Harness	Climbing	Jerry Martin
8	302000	Locking carabiner, Oval	Climbing	Jerry Martin

We will now have two relations:

SKU_DATA_2 (<u>SKU</u>, SKU_Description, *Buyer*)

BUYER (<u>Buyer</u>, Department)

Is SKU_DATA_2 in 3NF? Yes, it is—there are no non-key attributes that determine another non-key attribute.

Is the SKU_DATA_2 relation in BCNF? A relation is in BCNF if and only if *it is in 3NF* and *every determinant is a candidate key*. The determinants in SKU_DATA_2 are SKU and SKU_Description:

SKU → (SKU_Description, Buyer)

SKU_Description → (SKU, Buyer)

Both determinants are candidate keys (they both determine all the other attributes in the relation). Thus, every determinant is a candidate key, and the relationship *is* in BCNF.

At this point, we need to check the BUYER relation to determine if it is in BCNF. Work through the steps yourself for BUYER to check your understanding of the "Step-by-Step" method. You will find that BUYER *is* in BCNF, and therefore our normalized relations, as shown with the sample data in Figure 3-21, are:

SKU_DATA_2 (<u>SKU</u>, SKU_Description, *Buyer*)

BUYER (<u>Buyer</u>, Department)

Both of these tables are now in BCNF and will have no anomalies due to functional dependencies. For the data in these tables to be consistent, however, we also need to define a referential integrity constraint (note that this is step 3D in Figure 3-19):

SKU_DATA_2.Buyer must exist in BUYER.Buyer

This statement means that every value in the Buyer column of SKU_DATA_2 must also exist as a value in the Buyer column of BUYER.

FIGURE 3-21

The Normalized SKU_DATA_2
and BUYER Relations

SKU_DATA_2

	SKU	SKU_Description	Buyer
1	100100	Std. Scuba Tank, Yellow	Pete Hansen
2	100200	Std. Scuba Tank, Magenta	Pete Hansen
3	101100	Dive Mask, Small Clear	Nancy Meyers
4	101200	Dive Mask, Med Clear	Nancy Meyers
5	201000	Half-dome Tent	Cindy Lo
6	202000	Half-dome Tent Vestibule	Cindy Lo
7	301000	Light Fly Climbing Harness	Jerry Martin
8	302000	Locking Carabiner, Oval	Jerry Martin

BUYER

	Buyer	Department
1	Cindy Lo	Camping
2	Jerry Martin	Climbing
3	Nancy Meyers	Water Sports
4	Pete Hansen	Water Sports

Normalization Example 1: The "Straight-to-BCNF" Method

Now let's rework this example using the "Straight-to-BCNF" method. SKU and SKU_ Description determine all of the columns in the table, so they are candidate keys. Buyer is a determinant, but it does not determine all of the other columns, and hence it is not a candidate key. Therefore, SKU_DATA has a determinant that is not a candidate key and is therefore not in BCNF. It will have modification anomalies.

To remove such anomalies, in step 3A in Figure 3-19, we move the columns of functional dependency whose determinant is not a candidate key into a new table. In this case, we place Buyer and Department into a new table:

BUYER (Buyer, Department)

Next, in step 3B in Figure 3-19, we make the determinant of the functional dependency the primary key of the new table. In this case, Buyer becomes the primary key:

BUYER (<u>Buyer</u>, Department)

Next, following step 3C in Figure 3-19, we leave a copy of the determinant as a foreign key in the original relation. Thus, SKU_DATA becomes SKU_DATA_2:

SKU_DATA_2 (<u>SKU</u>, SKU_Description, *Buyer*)

The resulting tables are thus:

SKU_DATA_2 (<u>SKU</u>, SKU_Description, *Buyer*)
BUYER (<u>Buyer</u>, Department)

where SKU_DATA_2.Buyer is a foreign key to the BUYER table.

Both of these tables are now in BCNF and will have no anomalies due to functional dependencies. For the data in these tables to be consistent, however, we also need to define the referential integrity constraint in step 3D in Figure 3-19:

SKU_DATA_2.Buyer must exist in BUYER.Buyer

This statement means that every value in the Buyer column of SKU_DATA_2 must also exist as a value in the Buyer column of BUYER. Sample data for the resulting tables is the same as shown in Figure 3-21.

Note that both the "Step-by-Step" method and the "Straight-to-BCNF" method produced exactly the same results. Use the method you prefer; the results will be the same. To keep this chapter reasonably short, we will use only the "Straight-to-BCNF" method for the rest of the normalization examples.

Normalization Example 2

Now consider the EQUIPMENT_REPAIR relation in Figure 3-10. The structure of the table is:

EQUIPMENT_REPAIR (ItemNumber, EquipmentType, AcquisitionCost, RepairNumber, RepairDate, RepairCost)

Examining the data in Figure 3-10, the functional dependencies are:

ItemNumber → (EquipmentType, AcquisitionCost)

RepairNumber → (ItemNumber, EquipmentType, AcquisitionCost, RepairDate, RepairCost)

Both ItemNumber and RepairNumber are determinants, but only RepairNumber is a candidate key. Accordingly, EQUIPMENT_REPAIR is not in BCNF and is subject to modification anomalies. Following the procedure in Figure 3-19, we place the columns of the problematic functional dependency into a separate table, as follows:

EQUIPMENT_ITEM (<u>ItemNumber</u>, EquipmentType, AcquisitionCost)

and remove all but ItemNumber from EQUIPMENT_REPAIR (and rearrange the columns so that the primary key RepairNumber is the first column in the relation) to create:

REPAIR (<u>RepairNumber</u>, *ItemNumber*, RepairDate, RepairCost)

We also need to create the referential integrity constraint:

REPAIR.ItemNumber must exist in EQUIPMENT_ITEM.ItemNumber

Data for these two new relations are shown in Figure 3-22.

BY THE WAY   There is another, more intuitive way to think about normalization. Do you remember your eighth-grade English teacher? She said that every paragraph should have a single theme. If you write a paragraph that has two themes, you should break it up into two paragraphs, each with a single theme.

The problem with the EQUIPMENT_REPAIR relation is that it has two themes: one about repairs and a second about items. We eliminated modification anomalies by breaking that single table with two themes into two tables, each with a single theme. Sometimes, it is helpful to look at a table and ask, "How many themes does it have?" If it has more than one, then redefine the table so that it has a single theme.

Normalization Example 3

Consider now the Cape Codd database ORDER_ITEM relation with the structure:

ORDER_ITEM (OrderNumber, SKU, Quantity, Price, ExtendedPrice)

with functional dependencies:

(OrderNumber, SKU) → (Quantity, Price, ExtendedPrice)
(Quantity, Price) → ExtendedPrice

FIGURE 3-22

The Normalized EQUIPMENT_ITEM and REPAIR Relations

EQUIPMENT_ITEM

	ItemNumber	Equipment Type	AcquisitionCost
1	100	Drill Press	3500.00
2	200	Lathe	4750.00
3	300	Mill	27300.00

REPAIR

	RepairNumber	ItemNumber	RepairDate	RepairCost
1	2000	100	2015-05-05	375.00
2	2100	200	2015-05-07	255.00
3	2200	100	2015-06-19	178.00
4	2300	300	2015-06-19	1875.00
5	2400	100	2015-07-05	0.00
6	2500	100	2015-08-17	275.00

This table is not in BCNF because the determinant (Quantity, Price) is not a candidate key. We can follow the same normalization practice as illustrated in examples 1 and 2, but in this case, because the second functional dependency arises from the formula ExtendedPrice = (Quantity * Price), we reach a silly result.

To see why, we follow the procedure in Figure 3-19 to create tables such that every determinant is a candidate key. This means that we move the columns Quantity, Price, and ExtendedPrice to tables of their own, as follows:

EXTENDED_PRICE (Quantity, Price, ExtendedPrice)

ORDER_ITEM_2 (OrderNumber, SKU, *Quantity*, *Price*)

Notice that we left both Quantity and Price in the original relation as a composite foreign key. These two tables are in BCNF, but the values in the EXTENDED_PRICE table are ridiculous. They are just the results of multiplying Quantity by Price. The simple fact is that we do not need to create a table to store these results. Instead, any time we need to know ExtendedPrice we will just compute it. In fact, we can define this formula to the DBMS and let the DBMS compute the value of ExtendedPrice when necessary. You will see how to do this with Microsoft SQL Server 2014, Oracle's Oracle Database, and MySQL 5.6 in Chapters 10A, 10B, and 10C, respectively.

Using the formula, we can remove ExtendedPrice from the table. The resulting table is in BCNF:

ORDER_ITEM_2 (OrderNumber, SKU, Quantity, Price)

Note that Quantity and Price are no longer foreign keys. The ORDER_ITEM_2 table with sample data now appears as shown in Figure 3-23.

Normalization Example 4

Consider the following table that stores data about student activities:

STUDENT_ACTIVITY (StudentID, StudentName, Activity, ActivityFee, AmountPaid)

where StudentID is a student identifier, StudentName is student name, Activity is the name of a club or other organized student activity, ActivityFee is the cost of joining the club or participating in the activity, and AmountPaid is the amount the student has paid toward the ActivityFee. Figure 3-24 shows sample data for this table.

StudentID is a unique student identifier, so we know that:

StudentID → StudentName

However, does the functional dependency exist?

StudentID → Activity

FIGURE 3-23

The Normalized ORDER_
ITEM_2 Relation

ORDER_ITEM_2

	OrderNumber	SKU	Quantity	Price
1	1000	201000	1	300.00
2	1000	202000	1	130.00
3	2000	101100	4	50.00
4	2000	101200	2	50.00
5	3000	100200	1	300.00
6	3000	101100	2	50.00
7	3000	101200	1	50.00

FIGURE 3-24

Sample Data for the
STUDENT_ACTIVITY
Relation

STUDENT_ACTIVITY

	StudentID	StudentName	Activity	ActivityFee	AmountPaid
1	100	Jones	Golf	65.00	65.00
2	100	Jones	Skiing	200.00	0.00
3	200	Davis	Skiing	200.00	0.00
4	200	Davis	Swimming	50.00	50.00
5	300	Garrett	Skiing	200.00	100.00
6	300	Garrett	Swimming	50.00	50.00
7	400	Jones	Golf	65.00	65.00
8	400	Jones	Swimming	50.00	50.00

It does if a student belongs to just one club or participates in just one activity, but it does not if a student belongs to more than one club or participates in more than one activity. Looking at the data, student Davis with StudentID 200 participates in both Skiing and Swimming, so StudentID does *not* determine Club. StudentID does not determine ActivityFee or AmountPaid, either.

Now consider the StudentName column. Does StudentName determine StudentID? Is, for example, the value 'Jones' always paired with the same value of StudentID? No, there are two students named 'Jones', and they have different StudentID values. StudentName does not determine any other column in this table, either.

Considering the next column, Activity, we know that many students can belong to a club. Therefore, Activity does not determine StudentID or StudentName. Does Activity determine ActivityFee? Is the value 'Skiing', for example, always paired with the same value of ActivityFee? From these data, it appears so, and using just this sample data, we can conclude that Activity determines ActivityFee.

However, this data is just a sample. Logically, it is possible for students to pay different costs, perhaps because they select different levels of activity participation. If that were the case, then we would say that

(StudentID, Activity) → ActivityFee

To find out, we need to check with the users. Here, assume that all students pay the same fee for a given activity. The last column is AmountPaid, and it does not determine anything.

So far, we have two functional dependencies:

StudentID → StudentName

Activity → ActivityFee

Are there other functional dependencies with composite determinants? No single column determines AmountPaid, so consider possible composite determinants for it. AmountPaid is dependent on both the student and the club the student has joined. Therefore, it is determined by the combination of the determinants StudentID and Activity. Thus, we can say

(StudentID, Activity) → AmountPaid

So far we have three determinants: StudentID, Activity, and (StudentID, Activity). Are any of these candidate keys? Do any of these determinants identify a unique row? From the data, it appears that (StudentID, Activity) identifies a unique row and is a candidate key. Again, in real situations, we would need to check this assumption out with the users.

STUDENT_ACTIVITY_PAYMENT is not in BCNF because columns StudentID and Activity are both determinants but neither is a candidate key. StudentID and Activity are only part of the candidate key (StudentID, Activity).

> **BY THE WAY**   Both StudentID and Activity are *part of* the candidate key (StudentID, Activity). This, however, is not good enough. A determinant must have *all* of the same columns to be the same as a candidate key.

To normalize this table, we need to construct tables so that every determinant is a candidate key. We can do this by creating a separate table for each functional dependency as we did before. The result is:

STUDENT (<u>StudentID</u>, StudentName)

ACTIVITY (<u>Activity</u>, ActivityFee)

PAYMENT (<u>*StudentID*</u>, <u>*Activity*</u>, AmountPaid)

with referential integrity constraints:

PAYMENT.StudentID must exist in STUDENT.StudentID

and

PAYMENT.Activity must exist in ACTIVITY.Activity

These tables are in BCNF and will have no anomalies from functional dependencies. The sample data for the normalized tables are shown in Figure 3-25.

Normalization Example 5

Now consider a normalization process that requires two iterations of step 3 in the procedure in Figure 3-19. To do this, we will extend the SKU_DATA relation by adding the budget code of each department. We call the revised relation SKU_DATA_3 and define it as follows:

SKU_DATA_3 (SKU, SKU_Description, Department, DeptBudgetCode, Buyer)

Sample data for this relation are shown in Figure 3-26. SKU_DATA_3 has the following functional dependencies:

SKU → (SKU_Description, Department, DeptBudgetCode, Buyer)

SKU_Description → (SKU, Department, DeptBudgetCode, Buyer)

Buyer → (Department, DeptBudgetCode)

Department → DeptBudgetCode

DeptBudgetCode → Department

FIGURE 3-25

The Normalized STUDENT, ACTIVITY, and PAYMENT Relations

STUDENT

	StudentID	StudentName
1	100	Jones
2	200	Davis
3	300	Garrett
4	400	Jones

ACTIVITY

	Activity	ActivityFee
1	Golf	65.00
2	Skiing	200.00
3	Swimming	50.00

PAYMENT

	StudentID	Activity	ActivityFee
1	100	Golf	65.00
2	100	Skiing	200.00
3	200	Skiing	200.00
4	200	Swimming	50.00
5	300	Skiing	200.00
6	300	Swimming	50.00
7	400	Golf	65.00
8	400	Swimming	50.00

FIGURE 3-26

Sample Data for the SKU_
DATA_3 Relation

SKU_DATA_3

	SKU	SKU_Description	Department	DeptBudgetCode	Buyer
1	100100	Std. Scuba Tank, Yellow	Water Sports	BC-100	Pete Hansen
2	100200	Std. Scuba Tank, Magenta	Water Sports	BC-100	Pete Hansen
3	101100	Dive Mask, Small Clear	Water Sports	BC-100	Nancy Meyers
4	101200	Dive Mask, Med Clear	Water Sports	BC-100	Nancy Meyers
5	201000	Half-dome Tent	Camping	BC-200	Cindy Lo
6	202000	Half-dome Tent Vestibule	Camping	BC-200	Cindy Lo
7	301000	Light Fly Climbing Harness	Climbing	BC-300	Jerry Martin
8	302000	Locking Carabiner, Oval	Climbing	BC-300	Jerry Martin

Of the five determinants, both SKU and SKU_Description are candidate keys, but Buyer, Department, and DeptBudgetCode are not candidate keys. Therefore, this relation is not in BCNF.

To normalize this table, we must transform this table into two or more tables that are in BCNF. In this case, there are two problematic functional dependencies. According to the note at the end of the procedure in Figure 3-19, we take the functional dependency whose determinant is not a candidate key and has the largest number of columns first. In this case, we take the columns of

Buyer → (Department, DeptBudgetCode)

and place them in a table of their own.

Next, we make the determinant the primary key of the new table, remove all columns except Buyer from SKU_DATA_3, and make Buyer a foreign key of the new version of SKU_DATA_3, which we will name SKU_DATA_4. We can also now assign SKU as the primary key of SKU_DATA_4. The results are:

BUYER (<u>Buyer</u>, Department, DeptBudgetCode)

SKU_DATA_4 (<u>SKU</u>, SKU_Description, *Buyer*)

We also create the referential integrity constraint:

SKU_DATA_4.Buyer must exist in BUYER.Buyer

The functional dependencies from SKU_DATA_4 are:

SKU → (SKU_Description, Buyer)

SKU_Description → (SKU, Buyer)

Because every determinant of SKU_DATA_4 is also a candidate key, the relationship is now in BCNF. Looking at the functional dependencies from BUYER we find:

Buyer → (Department, DeptBudgetCode)

Department → DeptBudgetCode

DeptBudgetCode → Department

BUYER is *not* in BCNF because neither of the determinants Department and DeptBudgetCode are candidate keys. In this case, we must move (Department, DeptBudgetCode) into a table of its own. Following the procedure in Figure 3-19 and breaking BUYER into two tables (DEPARTMENT and BUYER_2) gives us a set of three tables:

DEPARTMENT (<u>Department</u>, DeptBudgetCode)

BUYER_2 (<u>Buyer</u>, *Department*)

SKU_DATA_4 (<u>SKU</u>, SKU_Description, *Buyer*)

with referential integrity constraints:

SKU_DATA_4.Buyer must exist in BUYER_2.Buyer

BUYER_2.Department must exist in DEPARTMENT.Department

The functional dependencies from all three of these tables are:

Department → DeptBudgetCode

DeptBudgetCode → Department

Buyer → Department

SKU → (SKU_Description, Buyer)

SKU_Description → (SKU, Buyer)

At last, every determinant is a candidate key, and all three of the tables are in BCNF. The resulting relations from these operations are shown in Figure 3-27.

Eliminating Anomalies from Multivalued Dependencies

All of the anomalies in the last section were due to functional dependencies, and when we normalize relations to BCNF, we eliminate these anomalies. However, anomalies can also arise from another kind of dependency: the multivalued dependency. A **multivalued dependency** occurs when a determinant is matched with a particular *set* of values.

Examples of multivalued dependencies are:

EmployeeName → → EmployeeDegree

EmployeeName → → EmployeeSibling

PartKitName → → Part

In each case, the determinant is associated with a set of values, and example data for each of these multivalued dependencies are shown in Figure 3-28. Such expressions are read as "EmployeeName multidetermines EmployeeDegree" and "EmployeeName multidetermines EmployeeSibling" and "PartKitName multidetermines Part." Note that multideterminants are shown with a double arrow rather than a single arrow.

Employee Jones, for example, has degrees AA and BA. Employee Greene has degrees BS, MS, and PhD. Employee Chau has just one degree, BS. Similarly, employee Jones has siblings (brothers and sisters) Fred, Sally, and Frank. Employee Greene has sibling Nikki, and employee Chau has siblings Jonathan and Eileen. Finally, PartKitName Bike Repair has parts Wrench, Screwdriver, and Tube Fix. Other kits have parts as shown in Figure 3-28.

FIGURE 3-27

The Normalized DEPARTMENT, BUYER_2, and SKU_DATA_4 Relations

DEPARTMENT

	Department	DeptBudgetCode
1	Camping	BC-200
2	Climbing	BC-300
3	Water Sports	BC-100

BUYER_2

	Buyer	Department
1	Cindy Lo	Camping
2	Jerry Martin	Climbing
3	Nancy Meyers	Water Sports
4	Pete Hansen	Water Sports

SKU_DATA_4

	SKU	SKU_Description	Buyer
1	100100	Std. Scuba Tank, Yellow	Pete Hansen
2	100200	Std. Scuba Tank, Magenta	Pete Hansen
3	101100	Dive Mask, Small Clear	Nancy Meyers
4	101200	Dive Mask, Med Clear	Nancy Meyers
5	201000	Half-dome Tent	Cindy Lo
6	202000	Half-dome Tent Vestibule	Cindy Lo
7	301000	Light Fly Climbing Harness	Jerry Martin
8	302000	Locking Carabiner, Oval	Jerry Martin

FIGURE 3-28

Three Examples of
Multivalued Dependencies

EMPLOYEE_DEGREE

	EmployeeName	EmployeeDegree
1	Chau	BS
2	Green	BS
3	Green	MS
4	Green	PhD
5	Jones	AA
6	Jones	BA

EMPLOYEE_SIBLING

	EmployeeName	EmployeeSibling
1	Chau	Eileen
2	Chau	Jonathan
3	Green	Nikki
4	Jones	Frank
5	Jones	Fred
6	Jones	Sally

PARTKIT_PART

	PartKitName	Part
1	Bike Repair	Screwdriver
2	Bike Repair	Tube Fix
3	Bike Repair	Wrench
4	First Aid	Aspirin
5	First Aid	Bandaids
6	First Aid	Elastic Band
7	First Aid	Ibuprofin
8	Toolbox	Drill
9	Toolbox	Drill bits
10	Toolbox	Hammer
11	Toolbox	Saw
12	Toolbox	Screwdriver

Unlike functional dependencies, the determinant of a multivalued dependency can never be the primary key. In all three of the tables in Figure 3-28, the primary key consists of the composite of the two columns in each table. For example, the primary key of the EMPLOYEE_DEGREE table is the composite key (EmployeeName, EmployeeDegree).

Multivalued dependencies pose no problem as long as they exist in tables of their own. None of the tables in Figure 3-28 has modification anomalies. However, if $A \rightarrow \rightarrow B$, then any relation that contains A, B, and one or more additional columns will have modification anomalies.

For example, consider the situation if we combine the employee data in Figure 3-28 into a single EMPLOYEE_DEGREE_SIBLING table with three columns (EmployeeName, EmployeeDegree, EmployeeSibling), as shown in Figure 3-29.

Now, what actions need to be taken if employee Jones earns an MBA? We must add three rows to the table. If we do not, if we only add the row ('Jones', 'MBA', 'Fred'), it will appear as if Jones is an MBA with her brother Fred, but not with her sister Sally or her other brother Frank. However, suppose Greene earns an MBA. Then we need only add one row ('Greene',

EMPLOYEE_DEGREE_SIBLING

	EmployeeName	EmployeeDegree	EmployeeSibling
1	Chau	BS	Eileen
2	Chau	BS	Jonathan
3	Green	BS	Nikki
4	Green	MS	Nikki
5	Green	PhD	Nikki
6	Jones	AA	Frank
7	Jones	AA	Fred
8	Jones	AA	Sally
9	Jones	BA	Frank
10	Jones	BA	Fred
11	Jones	BA	Sally

FIGURE 3-30

PARTKIT_PART_PRICE
Relation with a Functional
Dependency and a
Multivalued Dependency

PARTKIT_PART_PRICE

	Part Kit Name	Part	Part Kit Price
1	Bike Repair	Screwdriver	14.95
2	Bike Repair	Tube Fix	14.95
3	Bike Repair	Wrench	14.95
4	First Aid	Aspirin	24.95
5	First Aid	Bandaids	24.95
6	First Aid	Elastic Band	24.95
7	First Aid	Ibuprofin	24.95
8	Toolbox	Drill	74.95
9	Toolbox	Drill bits	74.95
10	Toolbox	Hammer	74.95
11	Toolbox	Saw	74.95
12	Toolbox	Screwdriver	74.95

'MBA', 'Nikki'). But, if Chau earns an MBA, we need to add two rows. These are insertion anomalies. There are equivalent modification and deletion anomalies as well.

In Figure 3-29, we combined two multivalued dependencies into a single table and obtained modification anomalies. Unfortunately, we will also get anomalies if we combine a multivalued dependency with any other column, even if that other column has no multivalued dependency.

Figure 3-30 shows what happens when we combine the multivalued dependency

PartKitName → → Part

with the functional dependency

PartKitName → PartKitPrice

For the data to be consistent, we must repeat the value of price for as many rows as each kit has parts. For this example, we must add three rows for the Bike Repair kit and four rows for the First Aid kit. The result is duplicated data that can cause data integrity problems.

Now you also know the problem with the relation in Figure 3-2. Anomalies exist in that table because it contains two multivalued dependencies:

BuyerName → → SKU_Managed
BuyerName → → CollegeMajor

Fortunately, it is easy to deal with multivalued dependencies: Put them into a table of their own. None of the tables in Figure 3-28 has modification anomalies because each table consists of only the columns in a single, multivalued dependency. Thus, to fix the table in Figure 3-2, we must move BuyerName and SKU_Managed into one table and BuyerName and CollegeMajor into a second table:

PRODUCT_BUYER_SKU (BuyerName, SKU_Managed)
PRODUCT_BUYER_MAJOR (BuyerName, CollegeMajor)

The results are shown in Figure 3-31. If we want to maintain strict equivalence between these tables, we would also add the referential integrity constraint:

PRODUCT_BUYER_SKU.BuyerName must be identical to PRODUCT_BUYER_ MAJOR.BuyerName

FIGURE 3-31

Placing the Two Multivalued
Dependencies in Figure 3-2
into Separate Relations

PRODUCT_BUYER_SKU

	BuyerName	SKU_Managed
1	Cindy Lo	201000
2	Cindy Lo	202000
3	Jenny Martin	301000
4	Jenny Martin	302000
5	Nancy Meyers	101100
6	Nancy Meyers	101200
7	Pete Hansen	100100
8	Pete Hansen	100200

PRODUCT_BUYER_MAJOR

	BuyerName	College Major
1	Cindy Lo	History
2	Jenny Martin	Business Administration
3	Jenny Martin	English Literature
4	Nancy Meyers	Art
5	Nancy Meyers	Info Systems
6	Pete Hansen	Business Administration

This referential integrity constraint may not be necessary, depending on the requirements of the application.

Notice that when you put multivalued dependencies into a table of their own, they disappear. The result is just a table with two columns, and the primary key (and sole candidate key) is the composite of those two columns. When multivalued dependencies have been isolated in this way, the table is said to be in *fourth normal form (4NF)*.

The hardest part of multivalued dependencies is finding them. Once you know they exist in a table, just move them into a table of their own. Whenever you encounter tables with odd anomalies, especially anomalies that require you to insert, modify, or delete different numbers of rows to maintain integrity, check for multivalued dependencies.

> **BY THE WAY** You will sometimes hear people use the term *normalize* in phrases like, "that table has been normalized" or "check to see if those tables are normalized." Unfortunately, not everyone means the same thing with these words. Some people do not know about BCNF, and they will use it to mean tables in 3NF, which is a lesser form of normalization, one that allows for anomalies from functional dependencies that BCNF does not allow. Others use it to mean tables that are both BCNF and 4NF. Others may mean something else. The best choice is to use the term *normalize* to mean tables that are in both BCNF and 4NF.

Fifth Normal Form

There is a fifth normal form (5NF), also known as **Project-Join Normal Form (PJ/NF)**, which involves an anomaly where a table can be split apart but not correctly joined back together. However, the conditions under which this happens are complex, and generally if a relation is in 4NF it is in 5NF. We will not deal with 5NF in this book. For more information about 5NF, start with the works cited earlier in this chapter and the Wikipedia article at *http://en.wikipedia.org/wiki/Fifth_normal_form*.

Domain/Key Normal Form

As discussed earlier in this chapter, in 1982 Ronald Fagin published a paper that defined domain/key normal form (DK/NF). Fagin asked, "What conditions need to exist for a relation to have no anomalies?" He showed that a relation in DK/NF has no modification anomalies and, further, that a relation that has no modification anomalies is in DK/NF.

But what does this mean? Basically, DK/NF requires that all the constraints on the data values be logical implications of the definitions of domains and keys. To the level of detail in this text, and to the level of detail experienced by 99 percent of all database practitioners, this can be restated as follows: Every determinant of a functional dependency must be a candidate key. This, of course, is simply our definition of BCNF, and, for practical purposes, relations in BCNF are in DK/NF as well.

Summary

Databases arise from three sources: from existing data, from new systems development, and from the redesign of existing databases. This chapter and the next are concerned with databases that arise from existing data. Even though a table is a simple concept, certain tables can lead to surprisingly difficult processing problems. This chapter uses the concept of normalization to understand and possibly solve those problems. Figure 3-3 lists terms you should be familiar with.

A relation is a special case of a table; all relations are tables, but not all tables are relations. Relations are tables that have the properties listed in Figure 3-4. Three sets of terms are used to describe relation structure: (relation, attribute, tuple); (table, column, row); and (file, field, and record). Sometimes these terms are mixed and matched. In practice, the terms *table* and *relation* are commonly used synonymously, and we will do so for the balance of this text.

In a functional dependency, the value of one attribute, or attributes, determines the value of another. In the functional dependency A → B, attribute A is called the determinant. Some functional dependencies arise from equations, but many others do not. The purpose of a database is, in fact, to store instances of functional dependencies that do not arise from equations.

Determinants that have more than one attribute are called composite determinants. If A → (B, C), then A → B and A → C (decomposition rule). However, if (A, B) → C, then, in general, neither A → C nor B → C. It is true that if A → B and A → C, then A → (B, C) (union rule).

If A → B, the values of A may or may not be unique in a relation. However, every time a given value of A appears, it will be paired with the same value of B. A determinant is unique in a relation only if it determines every other attribute of the relation. You cannot always rely on determining functional dependencies from sample data. The best idea is to verify your conclusions with the users of the data.

A key is a combination of one or more columns used to identify one or more rows. A composite key is a key with two or more attributes. A determinant that determines every other attribute is called a candidate key. A relation may have more than one candidate key. One of them is selected to be used by the DBMS for finding rows and is called the primary key. A surrogate key is an artificial attribute used as a primary key. The value of a surrogate key is supplied by the DBMS and has no meaning to the user. A foreign key is a key in one table that references the primary key of a second table. A referential integrity constraint is a limitation on data values of a foreign key that ensures that every value of the foreign key has a match to a value of a primary key.

The three kinds of modification anomalies are insert, update, and delete. Codd and others defined normal forms for describing different table structures that lead to anomalies. A table that meets the conditions listed in Figure 3-4 is in 1NF. Some anomalies arise from functional dependencies. Three forms, 2NF, 3NF, and BCNF, are used to treat such anomalies.

In this text, we are only concerned with the best of these forms, BCNF. If a relation is in BCNF, then no anomalies from functional dependencies can occur. A relation is in BCNF if every determinant is a candidate key.

Relations can be normalized using either a "Step-by-Step" method or a "Straight-to-BCNF" method. Which method to use is a matter of personal preference, and both methods produce the same results.

Some anomalies arise from multivalued dependencies. A multidetermines B, or A → → B, if A determines a set of values. If A multidetermines B, then any relation that contains A, B, and one or more other columns will have modification anomalies. Anomalies due to multivalued dependencies can be eliminated by placing the multivalued dependency in a table of its own. Such tables are in 4NF.

There is a 5NF, but generally tables in 4NF are in 5NF. DK/NF has been defined, but in practical terms the definition of DK/NF is the same as the definition of BCNF.

Key Terms

attribute	determinant	fourth normal form (4NF)
Boyce-Codd Normal Form (BCNF)	domain	functional dependency
candidate key	domain integrity constraint	functionally dependent
composite determinant	domain/key normal form (DK/NF)	insertion anomaly
composite key	entity	key
data integrity problems	entity integrity constraint	multivalued dependency
database integrity	fifth normal form (5NF)	non-prime attribute
decomposition rule	first normal form (1NF)	normal forms
deletion anomaly	foreign key	null value

overlapping candidate key   relation   tuple
partially dependent   second normal form (2NF)   union rule
primary key   surrogate key   update anomaly
Project-Join Normal Form (PJ/NF) third normal form (3NF)
referential integrity constraint transitive dependency

Review Questions

3.1 Name three sources for databases.

3.2 What is the basic premise of this chapter?

3.3 Explain what is wrong with the table in Figure 3-2.

3.4 Define each of the terms listed in Figure 3-3.

3.5 Describe the characteristics of a table that make it a relation. Define the term *domain,* and explain the significance of the *domain integrity constraint* to a relation.

3.6 Give an example of two tables that are not relations.

3.7 Suppose that two columns in two different tables have the same column name. What convention is used to give each a unique name?

3.8 Must all the values in the same column of a relation have the same length?

3.9 Explain the three different sets of terms used to describe tables, columns, and rows.

3.10 Explain the difference between functional dependencies that arise from equations and those that do not.

3.11 Explain the intuitive meaning of the functional dependency

$$PartNumber \rightarrow PartWeight$$

3.12 Explain the following statement: "The only reason for having relations is to store instances of functional dependencies."

3.13 Explain the meaning of the expression

$$(FirstName, LastName) \rightarrow Phone$$

3.14 What is a composite determinant?

3.15 If $(A, B) \rightarrow C$, then can we also say that $A \rightarrow C$?

3.16 If $A \rightarrow (B, C)$, then can we also say that $A \rightarrow B$?

3.17 For the SKU_DATA table in Figure 3-1, explain why Buyer determines Department but Department does not determine Buyer.

3.18 For the SKU_DATA table in Figure 3-1, explain why

$$SKU\_Description \rightarrow (SKU, Department, Buyer)$$

3.19 If it is true that

$$PartNumber \rightarrow PartWeight$$

does that mean that PartNumber will be unique in a relation?

3.20 Under what conditions will a determinant be unique in a relation?

3.21 What is the best test for determining whether a determinant is unique?

3.22 What is a composite key?

3.23 What is a candidate key?

3.24 What is a primary key? Explain the significance of the *entity integrity constraint* to a primary key.

3.25 Explain the difference between a candidate key and a primary key.

3.26 What is a surrogate key?

3.27 Where does the value of a surrogate key come from?

3.28 When would you use a surrogate key?

3.29 What is a foreign key? Explain the significance of the *referential integrity constraint* to a foreign key.

3.30 The term *domestic key* is not used. If it were used, however, what do you think it would mean?

3.31 What is a normal form?

3.32 Illustrate deletion, modification, and insertion anomalies on the STUDENT_ ACTIVITY relation in Figure 3-24.

3.33 Explain why duplicated data lead to data integrity problems.

3.34 What relations are in 1NF?

3.35 Which normal forms are concerned with functional dependencies?

3.36 What conditions are required for a relation to be in 2NF?

3.37 What conditions are required for a relation to be in 3NF?

3.38 What conditions are required for a relation to be in BCNF?

3.39 If a relation is in BCNF, what can we say about it with regard to 2NF and 3NF?

3.40 What normal form is concerned with multivalued dependencies?

3.41 What is the premise of Fagin's work on DK/NF?

3.42 Summarize the three categories of normalization theory.

3.43 In general, how can you transform a relation not in BCNF into ones that are in BCNF?

3.44 What is a referential integrity constraint? Define the term, and give an example of its use. Are null values allowed in foreign key columns with a referential integrity constraint? How does the referential integrity constraint contribute to *database integrity*?

3.45 Explain the role of referential integrity constraints in normalization.

3.46 Why is an un-normalized relation like a paragraph with multiple themes?

3.47 In normalization example 3, why is the EXTENDED_PRICE relation "silly"?

3.48 In normalization example 4, under what conditions is the functional dependency

(StudentID, Activity) → ActivityFee

more accurate than

Activity → ActivityFee

3.49 If a determinant is part of a candidate key, is that good enough for BCNF?

3.50 In normalization example 5, why are the following two tables not correct?

DEPARTMENT (<u>Department</u>, DeptBudgetCode, Buyer)
SKU_DATA_4 (<u>SKU</u>, SKU_Description, *Department*)

3.51 How does a multivalued dependency differ from a functional dependency?

3.52 Consider the relation:

PERSON (Name, Sibling, ShoeSize)

Assume that the following functional dependencies exist:

Name → → Sibling
Name → ShoeSize

Describe deletion, modification, and insertion anomalies for this relation.

3.53 Place the PERSON relation in Review Question 3.52 into 4NF.

3.54 Consider the relation:

PERSON_2 (Name, Sibling, ShoeSize, Hobby)

Assume that the following functional dependencies exist:

Name → → Sibling
Name → ShoeSize
Name → → Hobby

Describe deletion, modification, and insertion anomalies for this relation.

3.55 Place the PERSON_2 relation in Review Question 3.54 into 4NF.

3.56 What is 5NF?

3.57 How do the conditions for DK/NF correspond to the conditions for BCNF?

Project Questions

3.58 Consider the table:

STAFF_MEETING (EmployeeName, ProjectName, Date)

The rows of this table record the fact that an employee from a particular project attended a meeting on a given date. Assume that a project meets at most once per day. Also, assume that only one employee represents a given project but that employees can be assigned to multiple projects.

A. State the functional dependencies in STAFF_MEETING.

B. Transform this table into one or more tables in BCNF. State the primary keys, candidate keys, foreign keys, and referential integrity constraints.

C. Is your design in part B an improvement over the original table? What advantages and disadvantages does it have?

3.59 Consider the table:

STUDENT (StudentNumber, StudentName, Dorm, RoomType, DormCost, Club, ClubCost, Sibling, Nickname)

Assume that students pay different dorm costs depending on the type of room they have but that all members of a club pay the same cost. Assume that students can have multiple nicknames.

A. State any multivalued dependencies in STUDENT.

B. State the functional dependencies in STUDENT.

C. Transform this table into two or more tables such that each table is in BCNF and in 4NF. State the primary keys, candidate keys, foreign keys, and referential integrity constraints.

Case Questions

Regional Labs Case Questions

Regional Labs is a company that conducts research and development work on a contract basis for other companies and organizations. Figure 3-32 shows data that Regional Labs collects about projects and the employees assigned to them. This data is stored in a relation (table) named PROJECT:

PROJECT (ProjectID, EmployeeName, EmployeeSalary)

A. Assuming that all functional dependencies are apparent in this data, which of the following are true?

1. ProjectID → EmployeeName

2. ProjectID → EmployeeSalary

3. (ProjectID, EmployeeName) → EmployeeSalary

4. EmployeeName → EmployeeSalary

5. EmployeeSalary → ProjectID

6. EmployeeSalary → (ProjectID, EmployeeName)

FIGURE 3-32

Sample Data for Regional Labs

ProjectID	EmployeeName	EmployeeSalary
100-A	Eric Jones	64,000.00
100-A	Donna Smith	70,000.00
100-B	Donna Smith	70,000.00
200-A	Eric Jones	64,000.00
200-B	Eric Jones	64,000.00
200-C	Eric Parks	58,000.00
200-C	Donna Smith	70,000.00
200-D	Eric Parks	58,000.00

B. What is the primary key of PROJECT?

C. Are all the non-key attributes (if any) dependent on the primary key?

D. In what normal form is PROJECT?

E. Describe two modification anomalies that affect PROJECT.

F. Is ProjectID a determinant? If so, based on which functional dependencies in part A?

G. Is EmployeeName a determinant? If so, based on which functional dependencies in part A?

H. Is (ProjectID, EmployeeName) a determinant? If so, based on which functional dependencies in part A?

I. Is EmployeeSalary a determinant? If so, based on which functional dependencies in part A?

J. Does this relation contain a transitive dependency? If so, what is it?

K. Redesign the relation to eliminate modification anomalies.

The Queen Anne Curiosity Shop

Figure 3-33 shows typical sales data for the Queen Anne Curiosity Shop, and Figure 3-34 shows typical purchase data.

A. Using these data, state assumptions about functional dependencies among the columns of data. Justify your assumptions on the basis of these sample data and also on the basis of what you know about retail sales.

B. Given your assumptions in part A, comment on the appropriateness of the following designs:

1. CUSTOMER (<u>LastName</u>, FirstName, Phone, Email, InvoiceDate, InvoiceItem, Price, Tax, Total)

2. CUSTOMER (<u>LastName</u>, <u>FirstName</u>, Phone, Email, InvoiceDate, InvoiceItem, Price, Tax, Total)

FIGURE 3-33

Sample Sales Data for the Queen Anne Curiosity Shop

LastName	FirstName	Phone	InvoiceDate	InvoiceItem	Price	Tax	Total
Shire	Robert	206-524-2433	14-Dec-15	Antique Desk	3,000.00	249.00	3,249.00
Shire	Robert	206-524-2433	14-Dec-15	Antique Desk Chair	500.00	41.50	541.50
Goodyear	Katherine	206-524-3544	15-Dec-15	Dining Table Linens	1,000.00	83.00	1,083.00
Bancroft	Chris	425-635-9788	15-Dec-15	Candles	50.00	4.15	54.15
Griffith	John	206-524-4655	23-Dec-15	Candles	45.00	3.74	48.74
Shire	Robert	206-524-2433	5-Jan-16	Desk Lamp	250.00	20.75	270.75
Tierney	Doris	425-635-8677	10-Jan-16	Dining Table Linens	750.00	62.25	812.25
Anderson	Donna	360-538-7566	12-Jan-16	Book Shelf	250.00	20.75	270.75
Goodyear	Katherine	206-524-3544	15-Jan-16	Antique Chair	1,250.00	103.75	1,353.75
Goodyear	Katherine	206-524-3544	15-Jan-16	Antique Chair	1,750.00	145.25	1,895.25
Tierney	Doris	425-635-8677	25-Jan-16	Antique Candle Holders	350.00	29.05	379.05

PurchaseItem	PurchasePrice	PurchaseDate	Vendor	Phone
Antique Desk	1,800.00	7-Nov-15	European Specialties	206-325-7866
Antique Desk	1,750.00	7-Nov-15	European Specialties	206-325-7866
Antique Candle Holders	210.00	7-Nov-15	European Specialties	206-325-7866
Antique Candle Holders	200.00	7-Nov-15	European Specialties	206-325-7866
Dining Table Linens	600.00	14-Nov-15	Linens and Things	206-325-6755
Candles	30.00	14-Nov-15	Linens and Things	206-325-6755
Desk Lamp	150.00	14-Nov-15	Lamps and Lighting	206-325-8977
Floor Lamp	300.00	14-Nov-15	Lamps and Lighting	206-325-8977
Dining Table Linens	450.00	21-Nov-15	Linens and Things	206-325-6755
Candles	27.00	21-Nov-15	Linens and Things	206-325-6755
Book Shelf	150.00	21-Nov-15	Harrison, Denise	425-746-4322
Antique Desk	1,000.00	28-Nov-15	Lee, Andrew	425-746-5433
Antique Desk Chair	300.00	28-Nov-15	Lee, Andrew	425-746-5433
Antique Chair	750.00	28-Nov-15	New York Brokerage	206-325-9088
Antique Chair	1,050.00	28-Nov-15	New York Brokerage	206-325-9088

FIGURE 3-34

Sample Purchase Data for the Queen Anne Curiosity Shop

3. CUSTOMER (LastName, FirstName, Phone, Email, InvoiceDate, InvoiceItem, Price, Tax, Total)

4. CUSTOMER (LastName, FirstName, Phone, Email, InvoiceDate, InvoiceItem, Price, Tax, Total)

5. CUSTOMER (LastName, FirstName, Phone, Email, InvoiceDate, InvoiceItem, Price, Tax, Total)

6. CUSTOMER (LastName, FirstName, Phone, Email)
   and
   SALE (InvoiceDate, InvoiceItem, Price, Tax, Total)

7. CUSTOMER (LastName, FirstName, Phone, Email, *InvoiceDate*)
   and
   SALE (InvoiceDate, InvoiceItem, Price, Tax, Total)

8. CUSTOMER (LastName, FirstName, Phone, Email, *InvoiceDate, InvoiceItem*)
   and
   SALE (InvoiceDate, Item, Price, Tax, Total)

C. Modify what you consider to be the best design in part B to include surrogate ID columns called CustomerID and SaleID. How does this improve the design?

D. Modify the design in part C by breaking SALE into two relations named SALE and SALE_ITEM. Modify columns and add additional columns as you think necessary. How does this improve the design?

E. Given your assumptions, comment on the appropriateness of the following designs:

1. PURCHASE (<u>PurchaseItem</u>, PurchasePrice, PurchaseDate, Vendor, Phone)

2. PURCHASE (<u>PurchaseItem</u>, <u>PurchasePrice</u>, PurchaseDate, Vendor, Phone)

3. PURCHASE (<u>PurchaseItem</u>, PurchasePrice, <u>PurchaseDate</u>, Vendor, Phone)

4. PURCHASE (<u>PurchaseItem</u>, PurchasePrice, PurchaseDate, <u>Vendor</u>, Phone)

5. PURCHASE (<u>PurchaseItem</u>, PurchasePrice, <u>PurchaseDate</u>)

   and

   VENDOR (<u>Vendor</u>, Phone)

6. PURCHASE (<u>PurchaseItem</u>, PurchasePrice, <u>PurchaseDate</u>,Vendor)

   and

   VENDOR (<u>Vendor</u>, Phone)

7. PURCHASE (<u>PurchaseItem</u>, PurchasePrice, <u>PurchaseDate</u>, *Vendor*)

   and

   VENDOR (<u>Vendor</u>, Phone)

F. Modify what you consider to be the best design in part E to include surrogate ID columns called PurchaseID and VendorID. How does this improve the design?

G. The relations in your design from part D and part F are not connected. Modify the database design so that sales data and purchase data are related.

Morgan Importing

A. James Morgan keeps a table of data about the stores from which he purchases. The stores are located in different countries and have different specialties. Consider the following relation:

STORE (StoreName, City, Country, OwnerName, Specialty)

Explain the conditions under which each of the following is true:

1. StoreName → City
2. City → StoreName
3. City → Country
4. (StoreName, Country) → (City, OwnerName)
5. (City, Specialty) → StoreName
6. OwnerName → → StoreName
7. StoreName → → Specialty

B. With regard to the relation in part A:

1. Specify which of the dependencies in part A seem most appropriate for a small import–export business.

2. Given your assumptions in B.1, transform the STORE table into a set of tables that are in both 4NF and BCNF. Indicate the primary keys, candidate keys, foreign keys, and referential integrity constraints.

C. Consider the relation:

SHIPMENT (ShipmentNumber, ShipperName, ShipperContact, ShipperFax, DepartureDate, ArrivalDate, CountryOfOrigin, Destination, ShipmentCost, InsuranceValue, Insurer)

1. Write a functional dependency that expresses the fact that the cost of a shipment between two cities is always the same.

2. Write a functional dependency that expresses the fact that the insurance value is always the same for a given shipper.

3. Write a functional dependency that expresses the fact that the insurance value is always the same for a given shipper and country of origin.

4. Describe two possible multivalued dependencies in SHIPMENT.

5. State what you believe are reasonable functional dependencies for the SHIPMENT relation for a small import-export business.

6. State what you believe are reasonable multivalued dependencies for the SHIPMENT relation.

7. Using your assumptions in 5 and 6, transform SHIPMENT into a set of tables in BCNF and 4NF. Indicate the primary keys, candidate keys, foreign keys, and referential integrity constraints.

4

Database Design Using Normalization

Chapter Objectives

- To design updatable databases to store data received from another source
- To use SQL to access table structure
- To understand the advantages and disadvantages of normalization
- To understand denormalization
- To design read-only databases to store data from updatable databases

- To recognize and be able to correct common design problems:
  - The multivalue, multicolumn problem
  - The inconsistent values problem
  - The missing values problem
  - The general-purpose remarks column problem

In Chapter 3, we defined the relational model, described modification anomalies, and discussed normalization using BCNF and 4NF. In this chapter, we apply those concepts to the design of databases that are created from existing data.

The premise of this chapter, as it was in Chapter 3, is that you have received, from some source, one or more tables of data that are to be stored in a new database. The question is, should that data be stored as is, or should it be transformed in some way before it is stored? Normalization theory plays an important role, as you will see.

Assess Table Structure

When someone gives you a set of tables and asks you to construct a database to store them, your first step should be to assess the tables' structure and content. General guidelines for assessing a table's structure are summarized in Figure 4-1.

As shown in Figure 4-1, you should examine the data and determine the functional dependencies, multivalued dependencies, candidate keys, and each table's primary key. Also, look for possible foreign keys. Again, you can base your conclusions on sample data, but that data might not have all of the possible data cases. Therefore, verify your assumptions and conclusions with the users.

For example, suppose you receive data for the following SKU_DATA and BUYER tables (with the primary keys logically determined at this point):

SKU_DATA (<u>SKU</u>, SKU_Description, Buyer)

BUYER (<u>Buyer</u>, Department)

Begin by counting the number of rows in each table using the **SQL COUNT(*) function**. Then, to determine the number and type of the table's columns, use an **SQL SELECT * statement**. If your table has thousands or millions of rows, however, a full query will take considerable time. One way to limit the results of this query is to use the **SQL TOP {NumberOfRows} function** as discussed in Chapter 2. For example, to obtain all columns for the first 5 rows of the SKU_DATA table, you would code:

```
/* *** SQL-Query-CH04-01 *** */
SELECT    TOP 5 *
FROM      SKU_DATA;
```

This query will show you all columns and data for 5 rows, as shown in the following results. If you want the top 50 rows, just use TOP 50 instead of TOP 5, and so on. At this point you should confirm the primary key and determine the data type of each of the columns in the table.

	SKU	SKU_Description	Buyer
1	100100	Std. Scuba Tank, Yellow	Pete Hansen
2	100200	Std. Scuba Tank, Magenta	Pete Hansen
3	101100	Dive Mask, Small Clear	Nancy Meyers
4	101200	Dive Mask, Med Clear	Nancy Meyers
5	201000	Half-dome Tent	Cindy Lo

With regard to foreign keys, it is risky to assume that referential integrity constraints have been enforced on the data. Instead, check it yourself. Suppose that, after investigation, you confirm that SKU is the primary key of SKU_DATA and that Buyer is the primary key of

FIGURE 4-1

Guidelines for Assessing Table Structure

Guidelines for Assessing Table Structure
• Count rows and examine columns
• Examine data values and interview users to determine:
Multivalued dependencies
Functional dependencies
Candidate keys
Primary keys
Foreign keys
• Assess validity of assumed referential integrity constraints

BUYER. You also think that SKU_DATA.Buyer is likely a foreign key to BUYER.Buyer. The question is whether the following referential integrity constraint holds:

SKU_DATA.Buyer must exist in BUYER.Buyer

You can use SQL to determine whether this is true. The following query will return any values of the foreign key that violate the constraint:

```
/* *** SQL-Query-CH04-02 *** */
SELECT      Buyer
FROM        SKU_DATA
WHERE       Buyer NOT IN
            (SELECT     BUYER.Buyer
             FROM       SKU_DATA JOIN BUYER
                ON      SKU_DATA.Buyer = BUYER.Buyer);
```

The subquery finds all values of Buyer for which there is a match between SKU_DATA.Buyer and BUYER.Buyer. If there is any value of Buyer that is not in this subquery, then that value will be displayed in the results of the main query. All such values violate the referential integrity constraint. In the following actual results of the query on the data in our dataset as shown in Figure 3-21 (where SKU_DATA appears with the table name SKU_DATA_2), we get an **empty set**–there are *no* values returned in response to the query–which means that there are *no* foreign key values that violate the referential integrity constraint.

After you have assessed the input tables, your next steps depend on whether you are creating an updatable database or a read-only database. We will consider updatable databases first.

Designing Updatable Databases

Updatable databases are typically the operational databases of a company, such as the **online transaction processing (OLTP) system** discussed for Cape Codd Outdoor Sports at the beginning of Chapter 2. If you are constructing an updatable database, then you need to be concerned about modification anomalies and inconsistent data. Consequently, you must carefully consider normalization principles. Before we begin, let's first review the advantages and disadvantages of normalization.

Advantages and Disadvantages of Normalization

Figure 4-2 summarizes the advantages and disadvantages of normalization. On the positive side, normalization eliminates modification anomalies and reduces data duplication.

FIGURE 4-2

Advantages and
Disadvantages of
Normalization

Advantages and Disadvantages of Normalization
• Advantages
Eliminate modification anomalies
Reduce duplicated data
• Eliminate data integrity problems
• Save file space
Single table queries will run faster
• Disadvantages
More complicated SQL required for multitable subqueries and joins
Extra work for DBMS can mean slower applications

Reduced data duplication eliminates the possibility of data integrity problems due to inconsistent data values. It also saves file space.

BY THE WAY   Why do we say *reduce* data duplication rather than *eliminate* data duplication? The answer is that we cannot eliminate all duplicated data because we must duplicate data in foreign keys. We cannot eliminate Buyer, for example, from the SKU_DATA table because we would then not be able to relate BUYER and SKU_DATA rows. Values of Buyer are thus duplicated in the BUYER and SKU_DATA tables.

This observation leads to a second question: If we only *reduce* data duplication, how can we claim to *eliminate* inconsistent data values? Data duplication in foreign keys will not cause inconsistencies because referential integrity constraints prohibit them. As long as we enforce such constraints, the duplicate foreign key values will cause no inconsistencies.

On the negative side, normalization requires application programmers to write more complex SQL. To recover the original data, they must write subqueries and joins to connect data stored in separate tables. Also, with normalized data, the DBMS must read two or more tables, and this can mean slower application processing.

Functional Dependencies

As we discussed in Chapter 3, we can eliminate anomalies due to functional dependencies by placing all tables in BCNF. Most of the time, the problems of modification anomalies are so great that you should put your tables into BCNF. There are exceptions, however, as you will see.

Normalizing with SQL

As we explained in Chapter 3, a table is in BCNF if all determinants are candidate keys. If any determinant is not a candidate key, we must break the table into two or more tables. Consider an example. Suppose you are given the EQUIPMENT_REPAIR table in Figure 4-3 (the same table shown in Figure 3-10). In Chapter 3, we found that ItemNumber is a determinant but not a candidate key. Consequently, we created the EQUIPMENT_ITEM and REPAIR tables shown in Figure 4-4. In these tables, ItemNumber is a determinant and a candidate key of EQUIPMENT_ITEM, and RepairNumber is a determinant and primary key of REPAIR; thus both tables are in BCNF.

Now, as a practical matter, how do we transform the data in the format in Figure 4-3 to that in Figure 4-4? To answer that question, we need to use the **SQL INSERT statement**. You will learn the particulars of the INSERT statement in Chapter 7. For now, we will use one version of it to illustrate the practical side of normalization.

First, we need to create the structure for the two new tables in Figure 4-4. If you are using Microsoft Access, you can follow the procedure in Appendix A to create the tables. Later, in Chapter 7, you will learn how to create tables using SQL, a process that works for all DBMS products.

Once the tables are created, you can fill them using the SQL INSERT command. To fill the ITEM table, we use:

```
/* *** SQL-INSERT-CH04-01 *** */

INSERT INTO EQUIPMENT_ITEM

    SELECT      DISTINCT ItemNumber, EquipmentType, AcquisitionCost
    FROM        EQUIPMENT_REPAIR;
```

FIGURE 4-3

The EQUIPMENT_REPAIR Table

EQUIPMENT_REPAIR

	ItemNumber	Equipment Type	AcquisitionCost	RepairNumber	RepairDate	RepairCost
1	100	Drill Press	3500.00	2000	2015-05-05	375.00
2	200	Lathe	4750.00	2100	2015-05-07	255.00
3	100	Drill Press	3500.00	2200	2015-06-19	178.00
4	300	Mill	27300.00	2300	2015-06-19	1875.00
5	100	Drill Press	3500.00	2400	2015-07-05	0.00
6	100	Drill Press	3500.00	2500	2015-08-17	275.00

FIGURE 4-4

The Normalized
EQUIPMENT_ITEM and
REPAIR Relations

EQUIPMENT_ITEM

	ItemNumber	EquipmentType	AcquisitionCost
1	100	Drill Press	3500.00
2	200	Lathe	4750.00
3	300	Mill	27300.00

REPAIR

	RepairNumber	ItemNumber	RepairDate	RepairCost
1	2000	100	2015-05-05	375.00
2	2100	200	2015-05-07	255.00
3	2200	100	2015-06-19	178.00
4	2300	300	2015-06-19	1875.00
5	2400	100	2015-07-05	0.00
6	2500	100	2015-08-17	275.00

Notice that we must use the DISTINCT keyword because the combination (ItemNumber, EquipmentType, AcquisitionCost) is not unique in the EQUIPMENT_REPAIR table. Once we have created the rows in EQUIPMENT_ITEM, we can then use the following INSERT command to fill the rows of REPAIR:

```
/* *** SQL-INSERT-CH04-02 *** */
INSERT INTO REPAIR
    SELECT    RepairNumber, ItemNumber, RepairDate, RepairCost
    FROM      EQUIPMENT_REPAIR;
```

As you can see, the SQL statements for normalizing tables are relatively simple. After this transformation, we should probably remove the EQUIPMENT_REPAIR table. For now, you can do this using the graphical tools in Microsoft Access, Microsoft SQL Server, Oracle Database, or MySQL. In Chapter 7, you will learn how to remove tables using the **SQL DROP TABLE statement**. You will also learn how to use SQL to create the referential integrity constraint:

REPAIR.ItemNumber must exist in ITEM.ItemNumber

If you want to try out this example, download the Microsoft Access 2013 database Equipment-Repair-Database.accdb from the text's Web site at *www.pearsonhighered.com/ kroenke*. This database has the EQUIPMENT_REPAIR table with data. Create the new tables (see Appendix A) and then do the normalization by executing the SQL INSERT statements illustrated.

This process can be extended to any number of tables. We will consider richer examples of it in Chapter 7. For now, however, you should have the gist of the process.

Choosing Not to Use BCNF

Although in most cases the tables in an updatable database should be placed in BCNF, in some situations BCNF is just too pure. The classic example of unneeded normalization involves U.S. ZIP codes and similar postal codes in other countries (although, in fact, ZIP codes *do not* always determine city and state). Consider the following table for customers in the United States:

CUSTOMER (CustomerID, LastName, FirstName, Street, City, State, ZIP)

The functional dependencies of this table are:

CustomerID → (LastName, FirstName, Street, City, State, ZIP)

ZIP → (City, State)

This table is not in BCNF because ZIP is a determinant that is not a candidate key. We can normalize this table as follows:

CUSTOMER_2 (<u>CustomerID</u>, LastName, FirstName, Street, ZIP)

ZIP_CODE (<u>ZIP</u>, City, State)

with referential integrity constraint:

CUSTOMER_2.ZIP must exist in ZIP_CODE.ZIP

The tables CUSTOMER_2 and ZIP_CODE are in BCNF, but consider these tables in light of the advantages and disadvantages of normalization listed in Figure 4-2. Normalization eliminates modification anomalies, but how often does ZIP code data change? How often does the post office change the city and state assigned to a ZIP code value? Almost never. The consequences on every business and person would be too severe. So, even though the design allows anomalies to occur, in practice, they will not occur because the data never change. Consider the second advantage: Normalization reduces data duplication and hence improves data integrity. In fact, data integrity problems can happen in the single-table example if someone enters the wrong value for City, State, or ZIP. In that case, the database will have inconsistent ZIP values. But normal business processes will cause ZIP code errors to be noticed, and they will be corrected without a problem.

Now consider the disadvantages of normalization. Two separate tables will require application programs to use more complex SQL. They also require the DBMS to process two tables, which may make the applications slow. Weighing the advantages and disadvantages, most practitioners would say that the normalized data are just too pure. ZIP code data would therefore be left in the original table.

In summary, when you design an updatable database from existing tables, examine every table to determine if it is in BCNF. If it is not, then the table is susceptible to modification anomalies and inconsistent data. In almost all cases, transform the table into tables that are in BCNF. However, if the data are never modified and if data inconsistencies will be easily corrected via the normal operation of business activity, then you may choose not to place the table into BCNF.

Multivalued Dependencies

Unlike functional dependencies, the anomalies from multivalued dependencies are so serious that multivalued dependencies should always be eliminated. Unlike BCNF, there is no gray area. Just place the columns of a multivalued dependency in tables of their own.

As shown in the last section, using SQL statements to create and populate normalized tables is not difficult. It does mean that application programmers will have to write subqueries and joins to re-create the original data. Writing subqueries and joins, however, is *nothing* compared with the complexity of code that must be written to handle the anomalies due to multivalued dependencies.

Some experts might object to such a hard and fast rule, but it is justifiable. Although there may be a few rare, obscure, and weird cases in which multivalued dependencies are not problematic, such cases are not worth remembering. Until you have years of database design experience, always eliminate multivalued dependencies from any updatable table.

Designing Read-Only Databases

Read-only databases are used in **business intelligence (BI) systems** for producing information for assessment, analysis, planning, and control, as we discussed for Cape Codd Outdoor Sports in Chapter 2, and will return to again when we discuss BI in depth in Chapter 12 and Appendix J. Read-only databases are commonly used in a **data warehouse**, which we also introduced in Chapter 2. The extracted sales data that we used for Cape Codd Outdoor Sports in Chapter 2 is a small, but typical example of a read-only database. Because such databases are updated by carefully controlled and timed procedures, the design guidelines and design priorities are different than those for operational databases that are frequently updated.

In the course of your career, you will likely be given tables of data and asked to create a read-only database. In fact, this task is commonly assigned to beginning database administrators.

For several reasons, normalization is seldom an advantage for a read-only database. For one, if a database is never updated, then no modification anomalies can occur. Hence, considering Figure 4-2, the only reason to normalize a read-only database is to reduce data duplication. However, with no update activity, there is no risk of data integrity problems, so the only remaining reason to avoid duplicated data is to save file space.

Today, however, file space is exceedingly cheap, nearly free. So unless the database is enormous, the cost of storage is minimal. It is true that the DBMS will take longer to find and process data in large tables, so data might be normalized to speed up processing. But even that advantage is not clear-cut. If data are normalized, then data from two or more tables may need to be read, and the time required for the join may overwhelm the time savings of searching in small tables. In almost all cases, normalization of the tables in a read-only database is a bad idea.

Denormalization

Often the data for a read-only database are extracted from operational databases. Because such databases are updatable, they are probably normalized. Hence, you will likely receive the extracted data in normalized form. In fact, if you have a choice, ask for normalized data. For one, normalized data are smaller in size and can be transmitted to you more quickly. Also, if the data are normalized, it will be easier for you to reformat the data for your particular needs.

According to the last section, you probably do not want to leave the data in normalized form for a read-only database. If that is the case, you will need to **denormalize**, or join, the data prior to storage.

Consider the example in Figure 4-5. This is a copy of the normalized STUDENT, ACTIVITY, and PAYMENT data in Figure 3-25. Suppose that you are creating a read-only database that will be used to report amounts due for student activity payments. If you store the data in this three-table form, every time someone needs to compare AmountPaid with ActivityFee, he or she must join the three tables together. To do this, that person will need to know how to write a three-table join, and the DBMS will need to perform the join every time the report is prepared.

You can reduce the complexity of the SQL required to read these data and also reduce DBMS processing by joining the tables once and storing the joined result as a single table. First use the techniques discussed in Chapter 7 to create a new table named STUDENT_ ACTIVITY_PAYMENT_DATA that will hold the results. The following SQL statement will join the three tables together and store them in STUDENT_ACTIVITY_PAYMENT_DATA:

```
/* *** SQL-INSERT-CH04-03 *** */

INSERT INTO STUDENT_ACTIVITY_PAYMENT_DATA

    SELECT      STUDENT.StudentID, StudentName,

                ACTIVITY.Activity, ActivityFee,

                AmountPaid

    FROM        STUDENT, PAYMENT, ACTIVITY

    WHERE       STUDENT.StudentID = PAYMENT.StudentID

        AND     PAYMENT.Activity = ACTIVITY.Activity;
```

As shown in Figure 4-6, the STUDENT_ACTIVITY_PAYMENT_DATA table that results from this join has the same data as the original STUDENT_ACTIVITY table as shown in Figure 3-24.

As you can see, denormalization is simple. Just join the data together and store the joined result as a table. By doing this when you place the data into the read-only database, you save the application programmers from having to code joins for each application, and you also save the DBMS from having to perform joins and subqueries every time the users run a query or create a report.

Customized Duplicated Tables

Because there is no danger of data integrity problems in a read-only database and because the cost of storage today is miniscule, read-only databases are often designed with many copies of the same data, each copy customized for a particular application.

FIGURE 4-5

The Normalized STUDENT, ACTIVITY, and PAYMENT Relations

STUDENT

	StudentID	StudentName
1	100	Jones
2	200	Davis
3	300	Garrett
4	400	Jones

ACTIVITY

	Activity	ActivityFee
1	Golf	65.00
2	Skiing	200.00
3	Swimming	50.00

PAYMENT

	StudentID	Activity	ActivityFee
1	100	Golf	65.00
2	100	Skiing	200.00
3	200	Skiing	200.00
4	200	Swimming	50.00
5	300	Skiing	200.00
6	300	Swimming	50.00
7	400	Golf	65.00
8	400	Swimming	50.00

FIGURE 4-6

The Denormalized STUDENT_ACTIVITY_PAYMENT_DATA Relation

STUDENT_ACTIVITY_PAYMENT_DATA

	StudentID	StudentName	Activity	ActivityFee	AmountPaid
1	100	Jones	Golf	65.00	65.00
2	100	Jones	Skiing	200.00	0.00
3	200	Davis	Skiing	200.00	0.00
4	200	Davis	Swimming	50.00	50.00
5	300	Garrett	Skiing	200.00	100.00
6	300	Garrett	Swimming	50.00	50.00
7	400	Jones	Golf	65.00	65.00
8	400	Jones	Swimming	50.00	50.00

For example, suppose a company has a large PRODUCT table with the columns listed in Figure 4-7. The columns in this table are used by different business processes. Some are used for purchasing, some are used for sales analysis, some are used for displaying parts on a Web site, some are used for marketing, and some are used for inventory control.

The values of some of these columns, such as those for the picture images, are large. If the DBMS is required to read all of these data for every query, processing is likely to be slow. Accordingly, the organization might create several customized versions of this table for use by different applications. In an updatable database, so much duplicated data would risk severe data integrity problems, but for a read-only database, there is no such risk.

Suppose for this example that the organization designs the following tables:

PRODUCT_PURCHASING (SKU, SKU_Description, VendorNumber, VendorName, VendorContact_1, VendorContact_2, VendorStreet, VendorCity, VendorState, VendorZIP)

PRODUCT_USAGE (SKU, SKU_Description, QuantitySoldPastYear, QuantitySoldPastQuarter, QuantitySoldPastMonth)

PRODUCT_WEB (SKU, DetailPicture, ThumbnailPicture, MarketingShortDescription, MarketingLongDescription, PartColor)

PRODUCT_INVENTORY (SKU, PartNumber, SKU_Description, UnitsCode, BinNumber, ProductionKeyCode)

You can create these tables using the graphical design facilities of Access or another DBMS. Once the tables are created, they can be filled using INSERT commands similar to those already discussed. The only tricks are to watch for duplicated data and to use DISTINCT where necessary. See Review Question 4.10.

FIGURE 4-7

Columns in the PRODUCT
Table

FIGURE 4-7

Columns in the PRODUCT
Table

Product
• SKU (Primary Key)
• PartNumber (Candidate key)
• SKU_Description (Candidate key)
• VendorNumber
• VendorName
• VendorContact_1
• VendorContact_2
• VendorStreet
• VendorCity
• VendorState
• VendorZip
• QuantitySoldPastYear
• QuantitySoldPastQuarter
• QuantitySoldPastMonth
• DetailPicture
• ThumbNailPicture
• MarketingShortDescription
• MarketingLongDescription
• PartColor
• UnitsCode
• BinNumber
• ProductionKeyCode

FIGURE 4-8

Practical Problems in
Designing Databases from
Existing Data

Practical Problems in Designing Databases from Existing Data
The multivalue, multicolumn problem
Inconsistent values
Missing values
General-purpose remarks column

Common Design Problems

Although normalization and denormalization are the primary considerations when designing databases from existing data, there are four additional practical problems to consider. These are summarized in Figure 4-8.

The Multivalue, Multicolumn Problem

The table in Figure 4-7 illustrates the first common problem. Notice the columns VendorContact_1 and VendorContact_2. These columns store the names of two contacts at the part vendor. If the company wanted to store the names of three or four contacts using this strategy, it would add columns VendorContact_3, VendorContact_4, and so forth.

Consider another example for an employee parking application. Suppose the EMPLOYEE_AUTO table includes basic employee data plus columns for license numbers for up to three cars. The following is the typical table structure:

EMPLOYEE (<u>EmployeeNumber</u>, EmployeeLastName, EmployeeFirstName, Email, Auto1_LicenseNumber, Auto2_LicenseNumber, Auto3_LicenseNumber)

Other examples of this strategy are to store employees' children's names in columns such as Child_1, Child_2, Child_3, and so forth, for as many children as the designer of the table thinks appropriate, to store a picture of a house in a real estate application in columns labeled Picture_1, Picture_2, Picture_3, and so forth.

Storing multiple values in this way is convenient, but it has two serious disadvantages. The more obvious one is that the number of possible items is fixed. What if there are three contacts at a particular vendor? Where do we put the third name if only columns VendorContact_1 and VendorContact_2 are available? Or, if there are only three columns for child names, where do we put the name of the fourth child? And so forth.

The second disadvantage occurs when querying the data. Suppose we have the following EMPLOYEE table:

EMPLOYEE (<u>EmployeeNumber</u>, EmployeeLastName, EmployeeFirstName, Email, Child_1, Child_2, Child_3, . . . {other data})

Further, suppose we want to know the names of employees who have a child with the first name Gretchen. If there are three child name columns as shown in our EMPLOYEE table, we must write:

```
/* *** EXAMPLE CODE - DO NOT RUN *** */
/* *** SQL-Query-CH04-03 *** */
SELECT      *
FROM        EMPLOYEE
WHERE       Child_1 = 'Gretchen'
    OR      Child_2 = 'Gretchen'
    OR      Child_3 = 'Gretchen';
```

Of course, if there are seven child names . . . well, you get the picture.

These problems can be eliminated by using a second table to store the multivalued attribute. For the employee-child case, the tables are:

EMPLOYEE (<u>EmployeeNumber</u>, EmployeeLastName, EmployeeFirstName, Email, . . . {other data})

CHILD (<u>*EmployeeNumber*</u>, <u>ChildFirstName</u>, . . . {other data})

Using this second structure, employees can have an unlimited number of children, and storage space will be saved for employees who have no children at all. Additionally, to find all of the employees who have a child named Gretchen, we can code:

```
/* *** EXAMPLE CODE - DO NOT RUN *** */
/* *** SQL-Query-CH04-04 *** */
```

```
SELECT      *

FROM        EMPLOYEE

WHERE       EmployeeNumber IN

            (SELECT    EmployeeNumber

             FROM      CHILD

             WHERE     ChildFirstName = 'Gretchen');
```

This second query is easier to write and understand and will work regardless of the number of children that an employee has. Another advantage of the new design is that we avoid storing a large number of NULLs in the database. For example, if employees can have up to three cars, but 99% of employees only have one car, then a lot of space will be wasted storing NULLs for those employees' nonexistent second and third cars.

The alternate design does require the DBMS to process two tables, and if the tables are large and performance is a concern, one can argue that the original design is better. In such cases, storing multiple values in multiple columns may be preferred. Another, less valid objection to the two-table design is as follows: "We only need space for three cars because university policy restricts each employee to registering no more than three cars." The problem with this statement is that databases often outlive policies. Next year that policy may change, and, if it does, the database will need to be redesigned. As we will discuss in Chapter 8, database redesign is tricky, complex, and expensive. It is better to avoid the need for a database redesign.

> **BY THE WAY** A few years ago, people argued that only three phone number columns were needed per person: Home, Office, and Fax. Later they said, "Well, OK, maybe we need four: Home, Office, Fax, and Mobile." Today, who would want to guess the maximum number of phone numbers a person might have? Rather than guess, just store Phone in a separate table; such a design will allow each person to have from none to an unlimited number of phone numbers.

You are likely to encounter the multivalue, multicolumn problem when creating databases from nondatabase data. It is particularly common in spreadsheet and text data files. Fortunately, the preferred two-table design is easy to create, and the SQL for moving the data to the new design is easy to write.

> **BY THE WAY** The multivalue, multicolumn problem is just another form of a multivalued dependency. For the parking application, for example, rather than store multiple rows in EMPLOYEE for each auto, multiple named columns are created in the table. The underlying problem is the same, however.

Inconsistent Values

Inconsistent values are a serious problem when creating databases from existing data. Inconsistencies occur because different users or different data sources may use slightly different forms of the same data value. These slight differences may be hard to detect and will create inconsistent and erroneous information.

One of the hardest such problems occurs when different users have coded the same entries differently. One user may have coded a SKU_Description as *Corn, Large Can*; another may have coded the same item as *Can, Corn, Large*; and another may have coded the entry as *Large Can Corn*. Those three entries all refer to the same SKU, but they will be exceedingly difficult to reconcile. These examples are not contrived; such problems frequently occur, especially when combining data from different database, spreadsheet, and file sources.

A related, but simpler, problem occurs when entries are misspelled. One user may enter *Coffee*; another may enter *Coffeee*. They will appear as two separate products.

Inconsistent data values are particularly problematic for primary and foreign key columns. Relationships will be missing or wrong when foreign key data are coded inconsistently or misspelled.

Two techniques can be used to find such problems. One is the same as the check for referential integrity shown on page 179. This check will find values for which there is no match and will find misspellings and other inconsistencies.

Another technique is to use GROUP BY on the suspected column. For example, if we suspect that there are inconsistent values in the SKU_Description column in the SKU_DATA table (and note that here we are discussing and using the original SKU_DATA table with four columns as shown in Figure 2-6, not the three-column version discussed in this chapter on page 178, even though the query would actually run correctly on either version of the table), we can use the SQL query:

```
/* *** SQL-Query-CH04-05 *** */

SELECT    SKU_Description, COUNT(*) as SKU_Description_Count

FROM      SKU_DATA

GROUP BY  SKU_Description;
```

The result of this query for the SKU_DATA values we have been using is:

	SKU_Description	SKU_Description_Count
1	Dive Mask, Med Clear	1
2	Dive Mask, Small Clear	1
3	Half-dome Tent	1
4	Half-dome Tent Vestibule	1
5	Light Fly Climbing Harness	1
6	Locking Carabiner, Oval	1
7	Std. Scuba Tank, Magenta	1
8	Std. Scuba Tank, Yellow	1

In this case, there are no inconsistent values, but if there were, they would stand out. If the list resulting from the select is too long, groups can be selected that have just one or two elements using HAVING. Neither check is foolproof. Sometimes, you just have to read the data.

When working with such data, it is important to develop an error reporting and tracking system to ensure that inconsistencies that users do find are recorded and fixed. Users grow exceedingly impatient with data errors that persist after they have been reported.

Missing Values

Missing values are a third problem that occurs when creating databases from existing data. A missing value, or **null value** (which typically appears in a database table in all upper case letters as **NULL**), is a value that has never been provided. It is not the same as a blank value because a blank value is a value that is known to be blank. A null value is not known to be anything.

The problem with null values is ambiguity. A null value can indicate one of three conditions: The value is inappropriate; the value is appropriate but unknown; or the value is appropriate and known, but no one has entered it into the database. Unfortunately, we cannot tell from a null value which of these conditions is true.

Consider, for example, a null value for the column DateOfLastChildbirth in a PATIENT table. If a row represents a male patient, then the null occurs because the value is inappropriate; a male cannot give birth. Alternatively, if the patient is a female, but the patient has never been asked for the data, then the value is appropriate but unknown. Finally, the null value could also mean that a date value is appropriate and known, but no one has recorded it into the database.

You can use the SQL comparison operator IS NULL, as discussed in Chapter 2, to check for null values. For example, to find the number of null values of Quantity in the ORDER_ITEM table, you can code:

```
/* *** SQL-Query-CH04-06 *** */
SELECT    COUNT (*) as QuantityNullCount
FROM      ORDER_ITEM
WHERE     Quantity IS NULL;
```

The result of this query for the ORDER_ITEM values we have been using is:

	QuantityNullCount
1	0

In this case, there are no NULL values, but if there were, we would know how many, and then we could use a SELECT * statement to find the data of any row that has a NULL value.

When creating a database from existing data, if you try to define a column that has null values as the primary key, the DBMS will generate an error message. You will have to remove the nulls before creating the primary key. Also, you can tell the DBMS that a given column is not allowed to have null values, and when you import the data, if any row has a null value in that column, the DBMS will generate an error message. The particulars depend on the DBMS in use. See Chapter 10A for Microsoft SQL Server 2014, Chapter 10B for Oracle Corporation's Oracle Database, and Chapter 10C for MySQL 5.6. You should form the habit of checking for null values in all foreign keys. Any row with a null foreign key will not participate in the relationship. That may or may not be appropriate—you will need to ask the users to find out. Also, null values can be problematic when implementing referential integrity while creating and populating a new database. We will discuss the implications allowing null values in foreign keys in Chapter 7.

A final warning about null values: Users who provide you with data will have often used other terms or data values when they should have used NULLs. Search for column values such as "unknown," "NULL," the empty string, a string of blanks, or a nonsensical value (e.g., a negative number for a salary), and you may find additional places that should use NULL.

The General-Purpose Remarks Column

The general-purpose remarks column problem is common, serious, and very difficult to solve. Columns with names such as Remarks, Comments, and Notes often contain important data that are stored in an inconsistent, verbal, and verbose manner. Learn to be wary of columns with any such names.

To see why, consider customer data for a company that sells expensive items such as airplanes, rare cars, boats, or paintings. In a typical setting, someone has used a spreadsheet to track customer data. That person used a spreadsheet not because it was the best tool for such a problem, but rather because he or she had a spreadsheet program and knew how to use it (although perhaps "*thought* he or she knew how to use it" would be more accurate).

The typical spreadsheet has columns like LastName, FirstName, Email, Phone, Address, and so forth. It almost always includes a column titled Remarks, Comments, Notes, or something similar. The problem is that needed data are usually buried in such columns and nearly impossible to dig out. Suppose you want to create a database for a customer contact application for an airplane broker. Assume your design contains the two tables:

CONTACT (<u>ContactID</u>, ContactLastName, ContactFirstName, Address,...{other data}, Remarks, *AirplaneModelID*)

AIRPLANE_MODEL (<u>AirplaneModelID</u>, AirplaneModelName, AirplaneModelDescription,...{other airplane model data})

where CONTACT.AirplaneModelID is a foreign key to AIRPLANE_MODEL. AirplaneModelID. You want to use this relationship to determine who owns, has owned, or is interested in buying a particular model of airplane.

In the typical situation, the data for the foreign key have been recorded in the Remarks column. If you read the Remarks column data in CONTACT, you will find entries like: 'Wants to buy a Piper Seneca II', 'Owner of a Piper Seneca II', and 'Possible buyer for a turbo Seneca'. All three of these rows should have a value of AirplaneModelID (the foreign key in CONTACT) that equals the value of AIRPLANE_MODEL.AirplaneModelID for the AirplaneModelName of 'Piper Seneca II', but without the proper foreign key value, you would pull your hair out making that determination.

Another problem with general-purpose remarks columns is that they are used inconsistently and contain multiple data items. One user may have used the column to store the name of the spouse of the contact, another may have used it to store airplane models as just described, and a third may have used it to store the date the customer was last contacted. Or the same user may have used it for all three purposes at different times!

The best solution in this case is to identify all of the different purposes of the remarks column, create new columns for each of those purposes, and then extract the data and store it in the new columns as appropriate. However, this solution can seldom be automated.

In practice, all solutions require patience and hours of labor. Learn to be wary of such columns, and don't take such jobs on a fixed-price basis!

Summary

When constructing a database from existing data, the first step is to assess the structure and content of the input tables. Count the number of rows and use the SQL SELECT TOP {NumberOfRows} * phrase to learn the columns in the data. Then examine the data and determine functional dependencies, multivalued dependencies, candidate keys, each table's primary key, and foreign keys. Check out the validity of possible referential integrity constraints.

Design principles differ depending on whether an updatable or read-only database is being constructed. If the former, then modification anomalies and inconsistent data are concerns. The advantages of normalization are elimination of modification anomalies, reduced data duplication, and the elimination of data inconsistencies. The disadvantages are that more complex SQL will be required and application performance may be slower.

For updatable databases, most of the time the problems of modification anomalies are so great that all tables should be placed in BCNF. SQL for normalization is easy to write. In some cases, if the data will be updated infrequently and if inconsistencies are readily corrected by business processes, then BCNF may be too pure and the tables should not be normalized. The problems of multivalued dependencies are so great that they should always be removed.

Read-only databases are created for reporting, querying, and data mining applications. Creating such a database is a task commonly assigned to beginners. When designing read-only databases, normalization is less desired. If input data is normalized, it frequently needs to be denormalized by joining it together and storing the joined result. Also, sometimes many copies of the same data are stored in tables customized for particular applications.

Four common problems occur when creating databases from existing data. The multivalue, multicolumn design sets a fixed number of repeating values and stores each in a column of its own. Such a design limits the number of items allowed and results in awkward SQL query statements. A better design results from putting multiple values in a table of their own.

Inconsistent values result when data arise from different users and applications. Inconsistent foreign key values create incorrect relationships. Data inconsistencies can be detected using SQL statements, as illustrated in this chapter. A null value is not the same as a blank. A null value is not known to be anything. Null values are a problem because they are ambiguous. They can mean that a value is inappropriate, unknown, or known but not yet entered into the database.

The general-purpose remarks column is a column that is used for different purposes. It collects data items in an inconsistent and verbose manner. Such columns are especially problematic if they contain data needed for a foreign key. Even if they do not, they often contain data for several different columns. Automated solutions are not possible, and the correction requires patience and labor.

Key Terms

business intelligence (BI) system
comments column
data warehouse
denormalize
empty set
inconsistent values
multivalue/multicolumn problem
notes column
null value (NULL)
online transaction processing (OLTP) system
remarks column
SQL COUNT(*) function
SQL DROP TABLE statement
SQL INSERT statement
SQL SELECT * statement
SQL TOP {NumberOfRows} function

Review Questions

4.1 Summarize the premise of this chapter.

4.2 When you receive a set of tables, what steps should you take to assess their structure and content?

4.3 Show SQL statements to count the number of rows and to list the top 15 rows of the RETAIL_ORDER table.

4.4 Suppose you receive the following two tables:

DEPARTMENT (<u>DepartmentName</u>, BudgetCode)

EMPLOYEE (<u>EmployeeNumber</u>, EmployeeLastName, EmployeeFirstName, Email, DepartmentName)

and you conclude that EMPLOYEE.DepartmentName is a foreign key to DEPARTMENT.DepartmentName. Show SQL for determining whether the following referential integrity constraint has been enforced:

DepartmentName in EMPLOYEE must exist in DepartmentName in DEPARTMENT

4.5 Summarize how database design principles differ with regards to the design of updatable databases and the design of read-only databases. What types of systems typically use updatable and read-only databases?

4.6 Describe two advantages of normalized tables.

4.7 Why do we say that data duplication is only reduced? Why is it not eliminated?

4.8 If data duplication is only reduced, how can we say that the possibility of data inconsistencies has been eliminated?

4.9 Describe two disadvantages of normalized tables.

4.10 Suppose you are given the table:

EMPLOYEE_DEPARTMENT (<u>EmployeeNumber</u>, EmployeeLastName, EmployeeFirstName, Email, DepartmentName, BudgetCode)

and you wish to transform this table into the two tables:

DEPARTMENT (<u>DepartmentName</u>, BudgetCode)

EMPLOYEE (<u>EmployeeNumber</u>, EmployeeLastName, EmployeeFirstName, Email, *DepartmentName*)

Write the SQL statements needed for filling the EMPLOYEE and DEPARTMENT tables with data from EMPLOYEE_DEPARTMENT.

4.11 Summarize the reasons explained in this chapter for not placing ZIP code values into BCNF.

4.12 Describe a situation, other than the one for ZIP codes, in which one would choose not to place tables into BCNF. Justify your decision not to use BCNF.

4.13 According to this text, under what situations should you choose not to remove multi-valued dependencies from a relation?

4.14 Compare the difficulty of writing subqueries and joins with the difficulty of dealing with anomalies caused by multivalued dependencies.

4.15 Describe three uses for a read-only database.

4.16 How does the fact that a read-only database is never updated influence the reasons for normalization?

4.17 For read-only databases, how persuasive is the argument that normalization reduces file space?

4.18 What is denormalization?

4.19 Suppose you are given the DEPARTMENT and EMPLOYEE tables in Review Question 4.10 and asked to denormalize them into the EMPLOYEE_DEPARTMENT relation. Show the design of the EMPLOYEE_DEPARTMENT relation. Write an SQL statement to fill this table with data.

4.20 Summarize the reasons for creating customized duplicated tables.

4.21 Why are customized duplicated tables not used for updatable databases?

4.22 List four common design problems when creating databases from existing data.

4.23 Give an example of a multivalue, multicolumn table other than one discussed in this chapter.

4.24 Explain the problems caused by the multivalue, multicolumn table in your example in Review Question 4.23.

4.25 Show how to represent the relation in your answer to Review Question 4.23 with two tables.

4.26 Show how the tables in your answer to Review Question 4.25 solve the problems you identified in Review Question 4.24.

4.27 Explain the following statement: "The multivalue, multicolumn problem is just another form of multivalued dependency." Show how this is so.

4.28 Explain ways in which inconsistent values arise.

4.29 Why are inconsistent values in foreign keys particularly troublesome?

4.30 Describe two ways to identify inconsistent values. Are these techniques certain to find all inconsistent values? What other step can be taken?

4.31 What is a null value?

4.32 How does a null value differ from a blank value?

4.33 What are three interpretations of null values? Use an example in your answer that is different from the one in this book.

4.34 Show SQL for determining the number of null values in the column EmployeeFirstName of the table EMPLOYEE.

4.35 Describe the general-purpose remarks column problem.

4.36 Give an example in which the general-purpose remarks column makes it difficult to obtain values for a foreign key.

4.37 Give an example in which the general-purpose remarks column causes difficulties when multiple values are stored in the same column. How is this problem solved?

4.38 Why should one be wary of general-purpose remarks columns?

Project Questions

The Elliot Bay Sports Club owns and operates three sports club facilities in Houston, Texas. Each facility has a large selection of modern exercise equipment, weight rooms, and rooms for yoga and other exercise classes. Elliot Bay offers 3-month and 1-year memberships. Members can use the facilities at any of the three club locations.

Elliot Bay maintains a roster of personal trainers who operate as independent consultants. Approved trainers can schedule appointments with clients at Elliot Bay facilities as long as their client is a member of the club. Trainers also teach yoga, Pilates, and other classes. Answer the following questions, assuming you have been provided the following three tables of data (PT stands for personal trainer):

> PT_SESSION (Trainer, Phone, Email, Fee, ClientLastName, ClientFirstName, ClientPhone, ClientEmail, Date, Time)
>
> CLUB_MEMBERSHIP (ClientNumber, ClientLastName, ClientFirstName, ClientPhone, ClientEmail, MembershipType, EndingDate, Street, City, State, Zip)
>
> CLASS (ClassName, Trainer, StartDate, EndDate, Time, DayOfWeek, Cost)

4.39 Identify possible multivalued dependencies in these tables.

4.40 Identify possible functional dependencies in these tables.

4.41 Determine whether each table is either in BCNF or in 4NF. State your assumptions.

4.42 Modify each of these tables so that every table is in BCNF and 4NF. Use the assumptions you made in your answer to question 4.41.

4.43 Using these tables and your assumptions, recommend a design for an updatable database.

4.44 Add a table to your answer to question 4.43 that would allow Elliot Bay to assign members to particular classes. Include an AmountPaid column in your new table.

4.45 Recommend a design for a read-only database that would support the following needs:

A. Enable trainers to ensure that their clients are members of the club.

B. Enable the club to assess the popularity of various trainers.

C. Enable the trainers to determine if they are assisting the same client.

D. Enable class instructors to determine if the attendees to their classes have paid.

Case Questions

Marcia's Dry Cleaning Case Questions

Marcia Wilson, the owner of Marcia's Dry Cleaning, is in the process of creating databases to support the operation and management of her business. For the past year, she and her staff have been using a cash register system that collects the following data:

> SALE (<u>InvoiceNumber</u>, DateIn, DateOut, Total, Phone, FirstName, LastName)

Unfortunately, during rush times, not all of the data are entered, and there are many null values in Phone, FirstName, and LastName. In some cases, all three are null; in other cases, one or two are null. InvoiceNumber, DateIn, and Total are never null. DateOut has a few null values. Also, occasionally during a rush, phone number and name data have been entered incorrectly. To help create her database, Marcia purchased a mailing list from a local business bureau. The mailing list includes the following data:

> HOUSEHOLD (**Phone**, **FirstName**, **LastName**, Street, City, State, Zip, Apartment)

In some cases, a phone number has multiple names. The primary key is thus the composite (Phone, FirstName, LastName). There are no null values in Phone, FirstName, and LastName, but there are some null values in the address data.

There are many names in SALE that are not in HOUSEHOLD, and there are many names in HOUSEHOLD that are not in SALE.

- **A.** Design an updatable database for storing customer and sales data. Explain how to deal with the problems of missing data. Explain how to deal with the problems of incorrect phone and name data.

- **B.** Design a read-only database for storing customer and sales data. Explain how to deal with the problems of missing data. Explain how to deal with the problems of incorrect phone and name data.

The Queen Anne Curiosity Shop

The Queen Anne Curiosity Shop project questions in Chapter 3 asked you to create a set of relations to organize and link the Queen Anne Curiosity Shop typical sales data shown in Figure 3-33 and the typical purchase data shown in Figure 3-34. The set of relations may look like the following:

> CUSTOMER (CustomerID, LastName, FirstName, Phone, Email)
>
> SALE (SaleID, CustomerID, InvoiceDate, PreTaxTotal, Tax, Total)
>
> SALE_ITEM (SaleID, SaleItemID, PurchaseID, SalePrice)
>
> PURCHASE (PurchaseID, PurchaseItem, PurchasePrice, PurchaseDate, VendorID)
>
> VENDOR (VendorID, Vendor, Phone)

Use these relations and the data in Figures 3-33 and 3-34 to answer the following questions.

- **A.** Follow the procedure shown in Figure 4-1 to assess these data.
  - **1.** List all functional dependencies.
  - **2.** List any multivalued dependencies.
  - **3.** List all candidate keys.
  - **4.** List all primary keys
  - **5.** List all foreign keys.
  - **6.** State any assumptions you make as you list these components.

- **B.** List questions you would ask the owners of the Queen Anne Curiosity Shop to verify your assumptions.

- **C.** If there are any multivalued dependencies, create the tables needed to eliminate these dependencies.

- **D.** Do these data have the multivalue, multicolumn problem? If so, how will you deal with it?

- **E.** Do these data have the inconsistent data problem? If so, how will you deal with it?

- **F.** Do these data have a null value data problem? If so, how will you deal with it?

- **G.** Do these data have the general-purpose remarks problem? If so, how will you deal with it?

Morgan Importing

Phillip Morgan, the owner of Morgan Importing, makes periodic buying trips to various countries. During the trips, he keeps notes about the items he purchases and basic data about their shipments. He hired a college student as an intern, and she transformed his notes into the spreadsheets in Figure 4-9. These are just sample data. Phillip has purchased hundreds of items over the years, and they have been shipped in dozens of different shipments.

Phillip wants to enter the information age, so he has decided to develop a database of his inventory. He wants to keep track of the items he has purchased, their shipments, and eventually customers and sales. To get started, he has asked you to create a database for the data in Figure 4-9.

A. Follow the procedure shown in Figure 4-1 to assess these data.

    1. List all functional dependencies.

    2. List any multivalued dependencies.

    3. List all candidate keys.

    4. List all primary keys.

    5. List all foreign keys.

    6. State any assumptions you make as you list these components.

B. List questions you would ask Phillip to verify your assumptions.

C. If there are any multivalued dependencies, create the tables needed to eliminate these dependencies.

D. The relationship between shipment and item data could possibly be inferred by matching values in the From cells to values in the City cells. Describe two problems with that strategy.

E. Describe a change to this spreadsheet that does express the shipment–item relationship.

F. Assume that Phillip wishes to create an updatable database from these data. Design tables you think are appropriate. State all referential integrity constraints.

G. Assume that Phillip wishes to create a read-only database from these data. Design tables you think are appropriate. State all referential integrity constraints.

H. Do these data have the multivalue, multicolumn problem? If so, how will you deal with it?

I. Do these data have the inconsistent data problem? If so, how will you deal with it?

J. Do these data have a null value data problem? If so, how will you deal with it?

K. Do these data have the general-purpose remarks problem? If so, how will you deal with it?

FIGURE 4-9

Spreadsheet from Morgan Imports

	A	B	C	D	E	F	G	H	I
1	ShipmentNumber	Shipper	Phone	Contact	From	Departure	Arrival	Contents	InsuredValue
2	49100300	Wordwide	800-123-4567	Jose	Philippines	5/5/2015	6/17/1999	QE dining set, large bureau, porcelain lamps	$27,500
3	488955	Intenational	800-123-8898	Marilyn	Singapore	6/2/2015		Miscellaneous linen, large masks, 14 setting Willow design china	$7,500
4	84899440	Wordwide	800-123-4567	Jose	Peru	7/3/2015	7/28/2013	Woven goods, antique leather chairs	
5	399400	Intenational	800-123-8898	Marilyn	Singaporeee	8/5/2015	9/11/2013	Large bureau, brass lamps, willow design serving dishes	$18,000
6									
7									
8									

	A	B	C	D	E	F	
9	Item	Date	City	Store	Salesperson	Price	
10	QE Dining Set	4/7/2015	Manila	E. Treasures	Gracielle	$14,300	
11	Willow Serving Dishes	7/15/2015	Singapore	Jade Antiques	Swee Lai	$4,500	
12	Large bureau	7/17/2015	Singapore	Eastern Sales	Jeremey	$9,500	
13	Brass lamps	7/20/2015	Singapore	Jade Antiques	Mr. James	$1,200	
14							
15							

5

Data Modeling with the Entity-Relationship Model

Chapter Objectives

- To understand the two-phase data modeling/database design process
- To understand the purpose of the data modeling process
- To understand entity-relationship (E-R) diagrams
- To be able to determine entities, attributes, and relationships
- To be able to create entity identifiers
- To be able to determine minimum and maximum cardinalities
- To understand variations of the E-R model
- To understand and be able to use ID-dependent and other weak entities
- To understand and be able to use supertype/subtype entities

- To understand and be able to use strong entity patterns
- To understand and be able to use the ID-dependent association pattern
- To understand and be able to use the ID-dependent multivalued attribute pattern
- To understand and be able to use the ID-dependent archetype/instance pattern
- To understand and be able to use the line-item pattern
- To understand and be able to use the for-use-by pattern
- To understand and be able to use recursive patterns
- To understand the iterative nature of the data modeling process
- To be able to apply the data modeling process

In this chapter and the next, we consider the design of databases that arise from the development of new information systems. As you will learn, such databases are designed by analyzing requirements and creating a data model, or blueprint, of a database that will meet those requirements. The data model is then transformed into a database design.

This chapter addresses the creation of data models using the entity-relationship data model, the most popular modeling technique. This chapter consists of three major sections. First, we explain the major elements of the entity-relationship model and briefly describe several variations on that model. Next, we examine a number of patterns in forms, reports, and data models that you will encounter when data modeling. We then illustrate the data modeling process using the example of a small database at a university. Before starting, however, you need to understand the purpose of a data model.

Data modeling occurs in the **requirements analysis** step of the **systems development life cycle (SDLC)** in the **systems analysis and design** process. For an introduction to systems analysis and design and to the SDLC, see Appendix B.

The Purpose of a Data Model

A **data model** is a plan, or blueprint, for a database design—it is a *generalized, non-DBMS-specific* design. By analogy, consider the construction of your dorm or apartment building. The contractor did not just buy some lumber, call for the concrete trucks, and start work. Instead, an architect constructed plans and blueprints for that building long before construction began. If, during the planning stage, it was determined that a room was too small or too large, the blueprint could be changed simply by redrawing the lines. If, however, the need for change occurs after the building is constructed, the walls, electrical system, plumbing, and so on, will need to be rebuilt, at great expense and loss of time. It is easier, simpler, and faster to change the plan than it is to change a constructed building.

The same argument applies to data models and databases. Changing a relationship during the data modeling stage is just a matter of changing the diagram and related documentation. Changing a relationship after the database and applications have been constructed, however, is much more difficult. Data must be migrated to the new structure, SQL statements will need to be changed, forms and reports will need to be altered, and so forth.

> **BY THE WAY**   Books on systems analysis and design often identify three design stages:
>
> - Conceptual design (conceptual schema)
> - Logical design (logical schema)
> - Physical design (physical schema)
>
> The *data model* we are discussing is equivalent to the *conceptual design* as defined in these books.

The Entity-Relationship Model

Dozens of different tools and techniques for constructing data models have been defined over the years. They include the hierarchical data model, the network data model, the ANSI/SPARC data model, the entity-relationship data model, the semantic object model, and many others. Of these, the entity-relationship data model has emerged as the standard data model, and we will consider only that data model in this chapter.

The entity-relationship data model is commonly known as the **entity-relationship (E-R) model** and was first published by Peter Chen in 1976.[1] In this paper, Chen set out the basic elements of the model. Subtypes (discussed later) were added to the E-R model to create the **extended E-R model**,[2] and today it is the extended E-R model that most people mean when they use the term *E-R model*. In this text, we will use the extended E-R model.

Entities

An **entity** is something that users want to track. It is something that is readily identified in the users' work environment. Example entities are EMPLOYEE Mary Lai, CUSTOMER 12345, SALES-ORDER 1000, SALESPERSON Wally Smith, and PRODUCT A4200. Entities of a

---

[1] Peter P. Chen, "The Entity-Relationship Model—Towards a Unified View of Data," *ACM Transactions on Database Systems*, January 1976, pp. 9-36. For information on Peter Chen, see *http://en.wikipedia.org/wiki/Peter_Chen*, and for a copy of the article, see *http://www2.cis.gsu.edu/dmcdonald/cis8040/Chen.pdf*.

[2] T. J. Teorey, D. Yang, and J. P. Fry, "A Logical Design Methodology for Relational Databases Using the Extended Entity-Relationship Model," *ACM Computing Surveys*, June 1986, pp. 197-222.

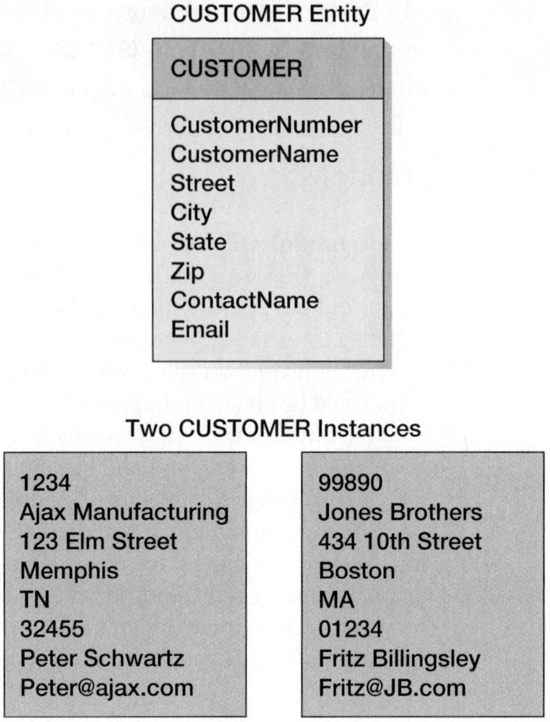

FIGURE 5-1

CUSTOMER Entity and Two
Entity Instances

CUSTOMER Entity

CUSTOMER
CustomerNumber CustomerName Street City State Zip ContactName Email

Two CUSTOMER Instances

1234 Ajax Manufacturing 123 Elm Street Memphis TN 32455 Peter Schwartz Peter@ajax.com

99890 Jones Brothers 434 10th Street Boston MA 01234 Fritz Billingsley Fritz@JB.com

given type are grouped into an **entity class**. Thus, the EMPLOYEE entity class is the collection of all EMPLOYEE entities. In this text, entity classes are shown in capital letters.

It is important to understand the differences between an entity class and an entity instance. An entity class is a collection of entities and is described by the structure of the entities in that class. An **entity instance** of an entity class is the occurrence of a particular entity, such as CUSTOMER 12345. An entity class usually has many instances of an entity. For example, the entity class CUSTOMER has many instances—one for each customer represented in the database. The CUSTOMER entity class and two of its instances are shown in Figure 5-1.

Attributes

Entities have **attributes** that describe their characteristics. Examples of attributes are EmployeeNumber, EmployeeName, Phone, and Email. In this text, attributes are written in both uppercase and lowercase letters. The E-R model assumes that all instances of a given entity class have the same attributes.

Figure 5-2 shows two different ways of displaying the attributes of an entity. Figure 5-2(a) shows attributes in ellipses that are connected to the entity. This style was used in the original E-R model, prior to the advent of data modeling software products. Figure 5-2(b) shows the rectangle style that is commonly used by data modeling software products today.

Identifiers

Entity instances have **identifiers**, which are attributes that name, or identify, entity instances. For example, EMPLOYEE instances can be identified by EmployeeNumber, SocialSecurityNumber, or EmployeeName. EMPLOYEE instances are not likely to be identified by attributes such as Salary or HireDate because these attributes are not normally used in a naming role. Similarly, customers can be identified by CustomerNumber or CustomerName, and sales orders can be identified by OrderNumber.

The identifier of an entity instance consists of one or more of the entity's attributes. Identifiers that consist of two or more attributes are called **composite identifiers**. Examples are (AreaCode, LocalNumber), (ProjectName, TaskName), and (FirstName, LastName, DateOfHire).

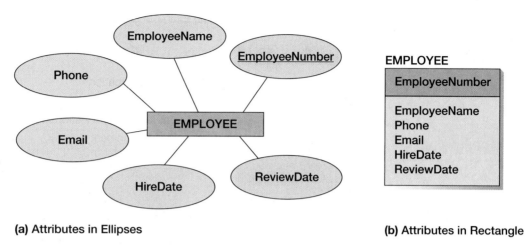

(a) Attributes in Ellipses   **(b) Attributes in Rectangle**

> **BY THE WAY** Notice the correspondence of identifiers and keys. The term *identifier* is
> used in a data model, and the term *key* (which we have already introduced
> in our discussion of relational databases in Chapter 3) is used in a database design.
> Thus, entities have identifiers, and tables (or relations) have keys. Identifiers serve the
> same role for entities that keys serve for tables.

As shown in Figure 5-3, entities are portrayed in three levels of detail in a data model. As shown in Figure 5-3(a), sometimes the entity and all of its attributes are displayed. In such cases, the identifier of the attribute is shown at the top of the entity and a horizontal line is drawn under the identifier. However, in a large data model, so much detail can make the data model diagrams unwieldy. In those cases, the entity diagram is abbreviated by showing just the identifier, as in Figure 5-3(b), or by showing just the name of the entity in a rectangle, as shown in Figure 5-3(c). All three techniques are used in practice; the more abbreviated form in Figure 5-3(c) is used to show the big picture and overall entity relationships. The more detailed view in Figure 5-3(a) is frequently used during database design. Most data modeling software products have the ability to show all three displays.

Relationships

Entities can be associated with one another in **relationships**. The E-R model contains both relationship classes and relationship instances.[3] **Relationship classes** are associations among entity classes, and **relationship instances** are associations among entity instances. In the original E-R model, relationships could have attributes. Today, that feature is less common, and we will not use it.

FIGURE 5-3

Variations on Level of Entity
Attribute Displays

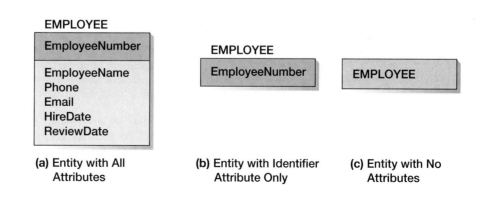

**(a) Entity with All
Attributes**   **(b) Entity with Identifier
Attribute Only**   **(c) Entity with No
Attributes**

---

[3]For brevity, we sometimes drop the word *instance* when the context makes it clear that an instance rather than a class is involved.

FIGURE 5-4

Binary Versus Ternary
Relationships

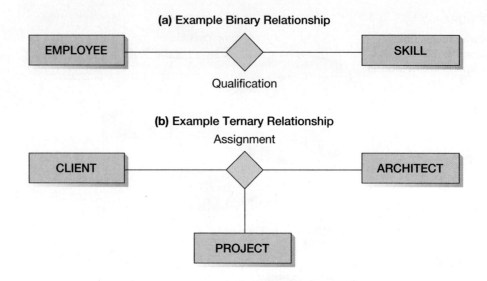

(a) Example Binary Relationship

EMPLOYEE — ◇ — SKILL

Qualification

(b) Example Ternary Relationship

Assignment

CLIENT — ◇ — ARCHITECT

PROJECT

Relationships are given names that describe the nature of the relationship, as shown in Figure 5-4. In Figure 5-4(a), the Qualification relationship shows which employees have which skills. In Figure 5-4(b), the Assignment relationship shows which combinations of clients, architects, and projects have been created. To avoid unnecessary complexity, in this chapter we will show the names of relationships only if there is a chance of ambiguity.

BY THE WAY   Your instructor may believe that it is important to always show the name of a relationship. If so, be aware that you can name a relationship from the perspective of either of the entities or both. For example, you can name the relationship between DEPARTMENT and EMPLOYEE as Department Consists Of; or you can name it as Employee Works In; or you can name it both ways, using a slash between the two names, Department Consists Of/Employee Works In. Relationship names are a necessity when there are two different relationships between the same two entities.

A relationship class can involve two or more entity classes. The number of entity classes in the relationship is the **degree** of the relationship. In Figure 5-4(a), the Qualification relationship is of degree two because it involves two entity classes: EMPLOYEE and SKILL. In Figure 5-4(b), the Assignment relationship is of degree three because it involves three entity classes: CLIENT, ARCHITECT, and PROJECT. Relationships of degree two are referred to as **binary relationships**. Similarly, relationships of degree three are called **ternary relationships**.

When transforming a data model into a relational database design, relationships of all degrees are treated as combinations of binary relationships. The Assignment relationship in Figure 5-4(b), for example, is decomposed into three binary relationships (can you spot them?). Most of the time, this strategy is not a problem. However, some nonbinary relationships need additional work, as you will learn in Chapter 6. All data modeling software products require you to express relationships as binary relationships.

BY THE WAY   At this point, you may be wondering, "What's the difference between an entity and a table?" So far, they seem like different terms for the same thing. *The principle difference between an entity and a table is that you can express a relationship between entities without using foreign keys.* In the E-R model, you can specify a relationship just by drawing a line connecting two entities. Because you are doing logical data modeling and not physical database design, you need not worry about primary and foreign keys, referential integrity constraints, and the like. Most data modeling products will allow you to consider such details if you choose to, but they do not require it.

This characteristic makes entities easier to work with than tables, especially early in a project when entities and relationships are fluid and uncertain. You can show relationships between entities before you even know what the identifiers are. For example, you can say that a DEPARTMENT relates to many EMPLOYEEs before you know any of the attributes of either EMPLOYEE or DEPARTMENT. This characteristic enables you to work from the general to the specific. First, identify the entities, then think about relationships, and, finally, determine the attributes.

In the entity-relationship model, relationships are classified by their **cardinality**, a word that means "count." The **maximum cardinality** is the maximum number of entity instances that can participate in a relationship instance. The **minimum cardinality** is the minimum number of entity instances that must participate in a relationship instance.

Maximum Cardinality

In Figure 5-5, the maximum cardinality is shown inside the diamond that represents the relationship. The three parts of this figure show the three basic maximum cardinalities in the E-R model.

Figure 5-5(a) shows a **one-to-one (abbreviated 1:1) relationship**. In a 1:1 relationship, an entity instance of one type is related to at most one entity instance of the other type. The Employee_Identity relationship in Figure 5-5(a) associates one EMPLOYEE instance with one BADGE instance. According to this diagram, no employee has more than one badge, and no badge is assigned to more than one employee.

The Computer_Assignment relationship in Figure 5-5(b) illustrates a **one-to-many (abbreviated 1:N) relationship**. Here a single instance of EMPLOYEE can be associated with many instances of COMPUTER, but a COMPUTER instance is associated with at most one instance of EMPLOYEE. According to this diagram, an employee can be associated with several computers, but a computer is assigned to just one employee.

The positions of the 1 and the N are significant. The 1 is close to the line connecting EMPLOYEE, which means that the 1 refers to the EMPLOYEE side of the relationship. The N is close to the line connecting COMPUTER, which means that the N refers to the COMPUTER side of the relationship. If the 1 and the N were reversed and the relationship was written N:1, an EMPLOYEE would have one COMPUTER, and a COMPUTER would be assigned to many EMPLOYEEs.

When discussing one-to-many relationships, the terms **parent** and **child** are sometimes used. The *parent* is the entity on the 1 side of the relationship, and the *child* is the entity on

FIGURE 5-5

Three Types of Maximum Cardinality

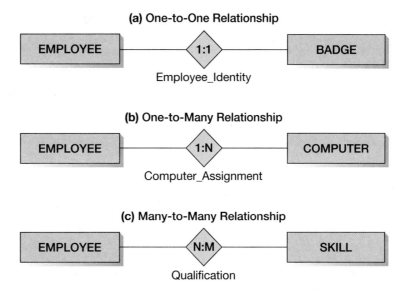

(a) One-to-One Relationship

EMPLOYEE — 1:1 — BADGE

Employee_Identity

(b) One-to-Many Relationship

EMPLOYEE — 1:N — COMPUTER

Computer_Assignment

(c) Many-to-Many Relationship

EMPLOYEE — N:M — SKILL

Qualification

the many side of the relationship. Thus, in a 1:N relationship between DEPARTMENT and EMPLOYEE, DEPARTMENT is the parent and EMPLOYEE is the child (one DEPARTMENT has many EMPLOYEEs).

Figure 5-5(c) shows a **many-to-many (abbreviated N:M) relationship**. According to the Qualification relationship, an EMPLOYEE instance can be associated with many SKILL instances, and a SKILL instance can be associated with many EMPLOYEE instances. This relationship documents the fact that an employee may have many skills and a skill may be held by many employees.

Sometimes students wonder why we do not write many-to-many relationships as N:N or M:M. The reason is that cardinality in one direction may be different than the cardinality in the other direction. In other words, in an N:M relationship, N need not equal M. An EMPLOYEE can have five skills, for example, but one of those skills can have three employees. Writing the relationship as N:M highlights the possibility that the cardinalities may be different.

Sometimes the maximum cardinality is an exact number. For example, for a sports team, the number of players on the roster is limited to some fixed number, say, 15. In that case, the maximum cardinality between TEAM and PLAYER would be set to 15 rather than to the more general N.

> **BY THE WAY**   Relationships like those in Figure 5-5 are sometimes called **HAS-A relationships**. This term is used because each entity instance has a relationship to a second entity instance. An employee has a badge, and a badge has an employee. If the maximum cardinality is greater than one, then each entity has a set of other entities. An employee has a set of skills, for example, and a skill has a set of employees who have that skill.

Minimum Cardinality

The minimum cardinality is the number of entity instances that *must* participate in a relationship. Generally, minimums are stated as either zero or one. If zero, then participation in the relationship is **optional**. If one, then at least one entity instance must participate in the relationship, which is called **mandatory** participation. In E-R diagrams, an optional relationship is represented by a small circle on the relationship line; a mandatory relationship is represented by a hash mark or line across the relationship line.

To better understand these terms, consider Figure 5-6. In the Employee_Identity relationship in Figure 5-6(a), the hash marks indicate that an EMPLOYEE is required to have a BADGE, and a BADGE must be allocated to an EMPLOYEE. Such a relationship is referred

FIGURE 5-6

Examples of Three Types of Minimum Cardinality

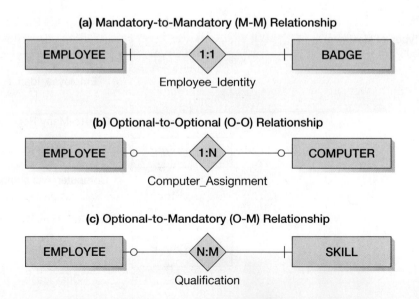

(a) Mandatory-to-Mandatory (M-M) Relationship

EMPLOYEE — 1:1 — BADGE

Employee_Identity

(b) Optional-to-Optional (O-O) Relationship

EMPLOYEE — 1:N — COMPUTER

Computer_Assignment

(c) Optional-to-Mandatory (O-M) Relationship

EMPLOYEE — N:M — SKILL

Qualification

to as a **mandatory-to-mandatory (M-M) relationship** because entities are required on both sides. The complete specification for the Employee_Identity relationship is that it is a 1:1, M-M relationship.

In Figure 5-6(b), the two small circles indicate that the Computer_Assignment relationship is an **optional-to-optional (O-O) relationship**. This means that an EMPLOYEE need not have a COMPUTER and a COMPUTER need not be assigned to an EMPLOYEE. The Computer_Assignment relationship is thus a 1:N, O-O relationship.

Finally, in Figure 5-6(c), the combination of a circle and a hash mark indicates an **optional-to-mandatory (O-M) relationship**. Here an EMPLOYEE must be assigned to at least one SKILL, but a SKILL may not necessarily be related to any EMPLOYEE. The complete specification for the Qualification relationship is thus an N:M, O-M relationship. The positions of the circle and the hash mark are important. Because the circle is next to EMPLOYEE, it means that the employee is optional in the relationship.

> **BY THE WAY**   Sometimes when interpreting diagrams like Figure 5-6(c) students become confused about which entity is optional and which is required. An easy way to clarify this situation is to imagine that you are standing in the diamond on the relationship line. Imagine looking toward one of the entities. If you see an oval in that direction, then that entity is optional; if you see a hash mark, then that entity is required. Thus, in Figure 5-6(c), if you stand on the diamond and look toward SKILL, you see a hash mark. This means that SKILL is required in the relationship. If you then turn around and look toward EMPLOYEE, you see a circle. This means that EMPLOYEE is optional in the relationship.

A fourth option, a **mandatory-to-optional (M-O) relationship**, is not shown in Figure 5-6. But if we exchange the circle and the hash mark in Figure 5-6(c), then Qualification becomes an M-O relationship. In that case, an EMPLOYEE need not have a SKILL, but a SKILL must have at least one EMPLOYEE.

As with maximum cardinalities, in rare cases the minimum cardinality is a specific number. To represent the relationship between PERSON and MARRIAGE, for example, the minimum cardinality would be 2:Optional.

Entity-Relationship Diagrams and Their Versions

The diagrams in Figures 5-5 and 5-6 are sometimes referred to as **entity-relationship (E-R) diagrams**. The original E-R model specified that such diagrams use diamonds for relationships, rectangles for entities, and connected ellipses for attributes, as shown in Figure 5-2. You may still see examples of such E-R diagrams, and it is important for you to be able to interpret them.

For two reasons, however, this original notation is seldom used today. First, there are a number of different versions of the E-R model, and these versions use different symbols. Second, data modeling software products use different techniques. For example, Computer Associates' ERwin product uses one set of symbols, and Microsoft Visio uses a second set.

Variations of the E-R Model

At least three different versions of the E-R model are in use today. One of them, the **Information Engineering (IE) model**, was developed by James Martin in 1990. This model uses crow's feet to show the many side of a relationship, and it is called the **IE Crow's Foot model**. It is easy to understand, and we will use it throughout this text. In 1993, the National Institute of Standards and Technology announced another version of the E-R model as a national standard. This version is called **Integrated Definition 1, Extended (IDEF1X)**.[4] This standard incorporates the basic ideas of the E-R model but

---

[4]*Integrated Definition for Information Modeling (IDEF1X)*, Federal Information Processing Standards Publication 184, 1993.

uses different graphical symbols. Although this model is a national standard, it is difficult to understand and use. As a national standard, however, it is used in government, and thus it may become important to you. Therefore, the fundamentals of the IDEF1X model are described in Appendix C.

Meanwhile, to add further complications, a new object-oriented development methodology called the **Unified Modeling Language (UML)** adopted the E-R model but introduced its own symbols while putting an object-oriented programming spin on it. UML notation is summarized in Appendix D.

> **BY THE WAY**   In addition to differences due to different versions of the E-R model, there also are differences due to software products. For example, two products that both implement the IE Crow's Foot model may do so in different ways. The result is a mess. When creating a data model diagram, you need to know not just the version of the E-R model you are using but also the idiosyncrasies of the data modeling product you use.

E-R Diagrams Using the IE Crow's Foot Model

Figure 5-7 shows two versions of a one-to-many, optional-to-mandatory relationship. Figure 5-7(a) shows the original E-R model version. Figure 5-7(b) shows the crow's foot model using common crow's foot symbols. Notice that the relationship is drawn as a dashed line. The reason for this will be explained later in this chapter. For now, notice the **crow's foot symbol** used to show the many side of the relationship.

The crow's foot model uses the notation shown in Figure 5-8 to indicate the relationship cardinality. The symbol closest to the entity shows the maximum cardinality, and the other symbol shows the minimum cardinality. A hash mark indicates one (and therefore also mandatory), a circle indicates zero (and thus optional), and the crow's foot symbol indicates many. Note that, as indicated in Figure 5-8, we can read the symbols in either purely numeric ("exactly one") or semi-numeric ("Mandatory-One") terms, and which reading is used is a matter of preference.

Thus, the diagram in Figure 5-7(b) means that a DEPARTMENT has one or more EMPLOYEEs (the symbol shows many and mandatory), and an EMPLOYEE belongs to zero or one DEPARTMENTs (the symbol shows one and optional).

A 1:1 relationship would be drawn in a similar manner, but the line connecting to each entity should be similar to the connection shown for the one side of the 1:N relationship in Figure 5-7(b).

Figure 5-9 shows two versions of an N:M, optional-to-mandatory relationship. Modeling N:M relationships presents some complications. According to the original E-R model diagram shown in Figure 5-9(a), an EMPLOYEE must have at least one SKILL and may have several. At the same time, although a SKILL may or may not be held by any EMPLOYEE, a SKILL may also be held by several EMPLOYEEs. The crow's foot version in Figure 5-9(b) shows the

FIGURE 5-7

Two Versions of a 1:N O-M Relationship

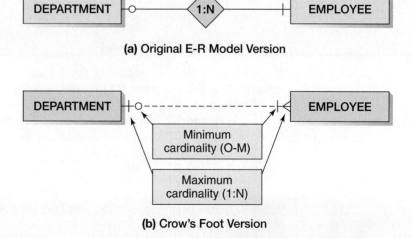

(a) Original E-R Model Version

(b) Crow's Foot Version

FIGURE 5-8

Crow's Foot Notation

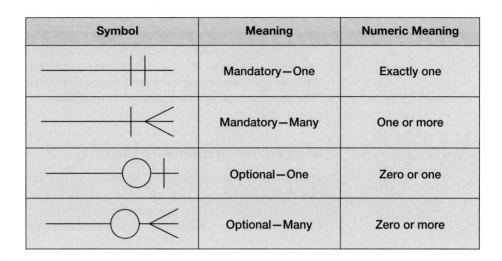

Symbol	Meaning	Numeric Meaning
	Mandatory—One	Exactly one
	Mandatory—Many	One or more
	Optional—One	Zero or one
	Optional—Many	Zero or more

FIGURE 5-9

Two Versions of an N:M O-M Relationship

(a) Original E-R Model Version

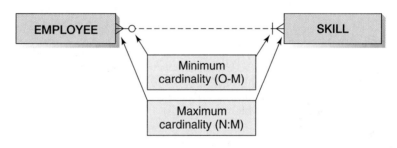

(b) Crow's Foot Version

N:M maximum cardinalities using the notation in Figure 5-8. The crow's foot symbols again indicate the minimum cardinalities for the N:M relationship.

Except for Appendices C and D, for the rest of this text, we will use the IE Crow's Foot model for E-R diagrams. There are no completely standard symbols for the crow's foot notation, and we explain our symbols and notation when we first use them. You can obtain various modeling products that will produce crow's foot models, and they are easily understood and related to the original E-R model. Be aware that those other products may use the oval, hash mark, crow's foot, and other symbols in slightly different ways. Further, your instructor may have a favorite modeling tool for you to use. If that tool does not support crow's feet, you will have to adapt the data models in this text to your tool.

> **BY THE WAY**   A number of modeling products are available, and each will have its own idiosyncrasies. CA Technologies produces ERwin, a commercial data modeling product that handles both data modeling and database design tasks. You can download the CA ERwin Data Modeler Community Edition, which is suitable for class use, from CA. You can use ERwin to produce either crow's foot or IDEF1X data models.
>
> You can also try ER-Assistant, which is free and downloadable from Software Informer.
>
> Microsoft Visio 2013 is also a possibility. A trial version is available from the Microsoft Web site. See Appendix F for a full discussion of using Microsoft Visio 2013 for data models.
>
> Finally, Oracle is continuing development of the MySQL Workbench, as described in this book in Chapters 2 and 10C, and a free (but somewhat limited) version is available

at the MySQL development Web site. (If you are using a Microsoft operating system, you should install the MySQL Workbench by downloading and running the MySQL Installer for Windows). Although it is better at database designs than data models, it is a very useful tool, and the database designs it produces can be used with any DBMS, not just MySQL. See Appendix E for a full discussion of using MySQL Workbench for database designs.

Strong Entities and Weak Entities

A **strong entity** is an entity that represents something that can exist on its own. For example, PERSON is a strong entity—we consider people to exist as individuals in their own right. Similarly, AUTOMOBILE is a strong entity. In addition to strong entities, the original version of the E-R model included the concept of a **weak entity**, which is defined as any entity whose existence depends on the presence of another entity.

ID-Dependent Entities

The E-R model includes a special type of weak entity called an **ID-dependent entity**. An ID-dependent entity is an entity whose identifier includes the identifier of another entity. Consider, for example, an entity for a student apartment in a building, as shown in Figure 5-10(a).

The identifier of such an entity is a composite (BuildingName, ApartmentNumber), where BuildingName is the identifier of the entity BUILDING. ApartmentNumber by itself is insufficient to tell someone where you live. If you say you live in apartment number 5, they must ask you, "In what building?" Therefore, APARTMENT is ID-dependent on BUILDING.

Figure 5-10 shows three different ID-dependent entities. In addition to APARTMENT (which is ID-dependent on BUILDING), the entity PRINT in Figure 5-10(b) is ID-dependent on PAINTING, and the entity EXAM in Figure 5-10(c) is ID-dependent on PATIENT.

In each of these cases, the ID-dependent entity cannot exist unless the parent (the entity on which it depends) also exists. Thus, the minimum cardinality from the ID-dependent entity to the parent is always one.

However, whether the parent is required to have an ID-dependent entity depends on the application requirements. In Figure 5-10, both APARTMENT and PRINT are optional,

FIGURE 5-10

Example ID-Dependent Entities

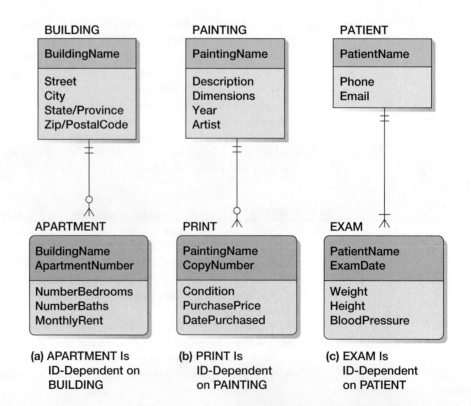

(a) APARTMENT Is ID-Dependent on BUILDING

(b) PRINT Is ID-Dependent on PAINTING

(c) EXAM Is ID-Dependent on PATIENT

but EXAM is required. These restrictions arise from the nature of the application and not from any logical requirement.

As shown in Figure 5-10, in our E-R models we use an entity with rounded corners to represent the ID-dependent entity. We also use a solid line to represent the relationship between the ID-dependent entity and its parent. This type of a relationship is called an **identifying relationship**. A relationship drawn with a dashed line (refer to Figure 5-7) is used between strong entities and is called a **nonidentifying relationship** because there are no ID-dependent entities in the relationship (ID-dependent entities may participate in other, nonidentifying relationships in addition to their identifying relationships—Figure 5-33 shows an example).

ID-dependent entities pose restrictions on the processing of the database that is constructed from them. Namely, the row that represents the parent entity must be created before any ID-dependent child row can be created. Further, when a parent row is deleted, all child rows must be deleted as well.

ID-dependent entities are common. Another example is the entity VERSION in the relationship between PRODUCT and VERSION, where PRODUCT is a software product and VERSION is a release of that software product. The identifier of PRODUCT is ProductName, and the identifier of VERSION is (ProductName, ReleaseNumber). Yet another example is EDITION in the relationship between TEXTBOOK and EDITION. The identifier of TEXTBOOK is Title, and the identifier of EDITION is (Title, EditionNumber).

BY THE WAY   The *parent entity* of a *child ID-dependent entity* is sometimes referred to as an **owner entity**. For example, a BUILDING is the *owner* of the APARTMENTs within it.

Non-ID-Dependent Weak Entities

All ID-dependent entities are weak entities. But, according to the original E-R model, some entities that are weak are not ID-dependent. Consider the AUTO_MODEL and VEHICLE entity classes in the database of a car manufacturer, such as Ford or Honda, as shown in Figure 5-11.

In Figure 5-11(a), each VEHICLE is assigned a sequential number as it is manufactured. So, for the manufacturer's "Super SUV" AUTO_MODEL, the first VEHICLE manufactured gets a ManufacturingSeqNumber of 1, the next gets a ManufacturingSeqNumber of 2, and so on. This is clearly an ID-dependent relationship because ManufacturingSeqNumber is based on the Manufacturer and Model.

Now let's assign VEHICLE an identifier that is independent of the Manufacturer and Model. We will use a VIN (vehicle identification number), as shown in Figure 5-11(b). Now the VEHICLE has a unique identifier of its own and does not need to be identified by its relation to AUTO_MODEL.

This is an interesting situation. VEHICLE has an identity of its own and therefore is not ID-dependent. Yet the VEHICLE is an AUTO_MODEL, and if that particular AUTO_MODEL did not exist, the VEHICLE itself would never have existed. Therefore, VEHICLE is now a *weak but non-ID-dependent entity*.

Consider *your* car—let's say it is a Ford Mustang just for the sake of this discussion. Your individual Mustang is a VEHICLE, and it exists as a physical object and is identified by the VIN that is required for each licensed automobile. It is *not* ID-dependent on AUTO_MODEL, which in this case is Ford Mustang, for its identity. However, if the Ford Mustang had never been created as an AUTO_MODEL—a logical concept that was first designed on paper—your car would never have been built because *no* Ford Mustangs would ever have been built! Therefore, your physical individual VEHICLE would not exist without a logical AUTO_MODEL of Ford Mustang, and in a data model (which *is* what we're talking about), a VEHICLE cannot exist without a related AUTO_MODEL. This makes VEHICLE a weak but non-ID-dependent entity. Most data modeling tools cannot model non-ID-dependent entities. So, to indicate such situations, we will use a nonidentifying relationship with a note added to the data model indicating that the entity is weak, as shown in Figure 5-11(b).

FIGURE 5-11

Non-ID-Dependent Weak
Entity Example

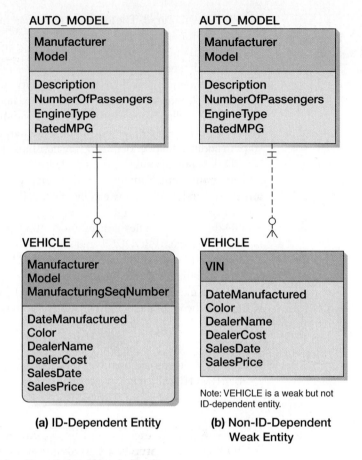

(a) ID-Dependent Entity

(b) Non-ID-Dependent Weak Entity

Note: VEHICLE is a weak but not ID-dependent entity.

The Ambiguity of the Weak Entity

Unfortunately, an ambiguity is hidden in the definition of a *weak entity*, and this ambiguity is interpreted differently by different database designers (as well as different textbook authors). The ambiguity is that in a strict sense, if a weak entity is defined as any entity whose presence in the database depends on another entity, then any entity that participates in a relationship having a minimum cardinality of one to a second entity is a weak entity. Thus, in an academic database, if a STUDENT must have an ADVISER, then STUDENT is a weak entity because a STUDENT entity cannot be stored without an ADVISER.

This interpretation seems too broad to some people. A STUDENT is not physically dependent on an ADVISER (unlike an APARTMENT to a BUILDING), and a STUDENT is not logically dependent on an ADVISER (despite how it might appear to either the student or the adviser), and, therefore, STUDENT should be considered a strong entity.

To avoid such situations, some people interpret the definition of weak entity more narrowly. They say that to be a weak entity an entity must logically depend on another entity. According to this definition, APARTMENT is a weak entity, but STUDENT is not. An APARTMENT cannot exist without a BUILDING in which it is located. However, a STUDENT can logically exist without an ADVISER, even if a business rule requires it.

We agree with the latter approach. Characteristics of ID-dependent and non-ID-dependent weak entities, as used in this book, are summarized in Figure 5-12.

Subtype Entities

The extended E-R model introduced the concept of *subtypes*. A **subtype** entity is a special case of another entity called its **supertype**. Students, for example, may be classified as undergraduate or graduate students. In this case, STUDENT is the supertype, and UNDERGRADUATE and GRADUATE are the subtypes.

Alternatively, a student could be classified as a freshman, sophomore, junior, or senior. In that case, STUDENT is the supertype, and FRESHMAN, SOPHOMORE, JUNIOR, and SENIOR are the subtypes.

Weak Entity Summary
A weak entity is an entity whose existence depends on another entity.
An ID-dependent entity is a weak entity whose identifier includes the identifier of another entity.
Identifying relationships are used to represent ID-dependent entities.
Some entities are weak but not ID-dependent. Using data modeling tools, they are shown with nonidentifying relationships, with separate documentation indicating they are weak.

As illustrated in Figure 5-13, in our E-R models we use a circle with a line under it as a subtype symbol to indicate a supertype–subtype relationship. Think of this as a symbol for an optional (the circle), 1:1 (the line) relationship. In addition, we use a solid line to represent an ID-dependent subtype entity because each subtype is ID-dependent on the supertype. Also note that none of the line end symbols shown in Figure 5-8 are used on the connecting lines.

In some cases, an attribute of the supertype indicates which of the subtypes is appropriate for a given instance. An attribute that determines which subtype is appropriate is called a **discriminator**. In Figure 5-13(a), the attribute named isGradStudent (which has only the values Yes and No) is the discriminator. In our E-R diagrams, the discriminator is shown next to the subtype symbol, as illustrated in Figure 5-13(a). Not all supertypes have a discriminator. Where a supertype does not have a discriminator, application code must be written to determine which subtype an entity belongs to.

Subtypes can be exclusive or inclusive (also referred to as *disjoint* and *partial*, respectively). With **exclusive subtypes**, a supertype instance is related to at most one subtype. With **inclusive subtypes**, a supertype instance can relate to one or more subtypes. In Figure 5-13(a), the X in the circle means that the UNDERGRADUATE and GRADUATE subtypes are exclusive. Thus, a STUDENT can be either an UNDERGRADUATE or a GRADUATE but not both. Figure 5-13(b) shows that a STUDENT can join either the HIKING_CLUB or the SAILING_CLUB or both. These subtypes are inclusive (note there is no X in the circle). Because a supertype may relate to more than one subtype, inclusive subtypes do not have a discriminator.

Some models include another dimension to subtypes, called the *total* or *partial* distinction: For example, in Figure 5-13(b), can there be students who are in *neither* club? If so, the subtype/supertype relationship is **partial**; if not, it is **total**. To indicate a total requirement, we would put a hash mark on the relationship line just below the supertype entity to indicate that the supertype is mandatory in the relationship.

FIGURE 5-13

Examples of Subtype
Entities

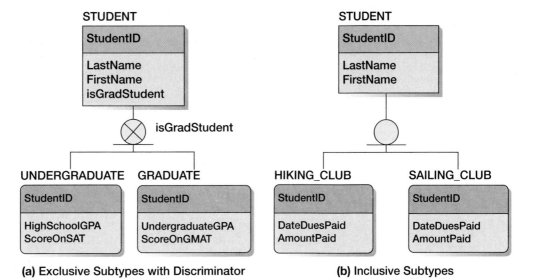

(a) Exclusive Subtypes with Discriminator   **(b) Inclusive Subtypes**

The most important (some would say the only) reason for creating subtypes in a data model is to avoid value-inappropriate nulls. Undergraduate students take the SAT exam and report that score, whereas graduate students take the GMAT and report their score on that exam. Thus, the SAT score would be NULL in all STUDENT entities for graduates, and the GMAT score would be NULL for all undergraduates. Such null values can be avoided by creating subtypes.

> **BY THE WAY**   The relationships that connect supertypes and subtypes are called **IS-A relationships** because a subtype is the same entity as the supertype. Because this is so, the identifier of a supertype and all its subtypes must be the same; they all represent different aspects of the same entity. Contrast this with HAS-A relationships, in which an entity has a relationship to another entity but the identifiers of the two entities are different.

The elements of the entity-relationship model and their IE Crow's Foot representation are summarized in Figure 5-14. The identifier and attributes are shown only in the first example. Note that, for 1:1 and 1:N nonidentifying relationships, a relationship to a parent entity may be optional. For identifying relationships, the parent is always required.

FIGURE 5-14

IE Crow's Foot Symbol Summary

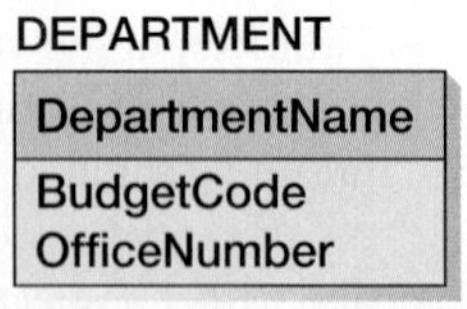 **DEPARTMENT** — DepartmentName / BudgetCode OfficeNumber	DEPARTMENT entity; DepartmentName is identifier; BudgetCode and OfficeNumber are attributes.
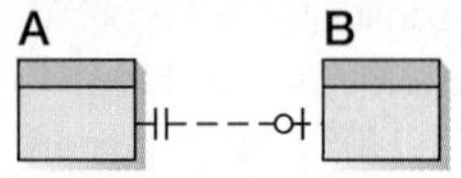 A — B	1:1, nonidentifying relationship. A relates to zero or one B; B relates to exactly one A. Identifier and attributes not shown.
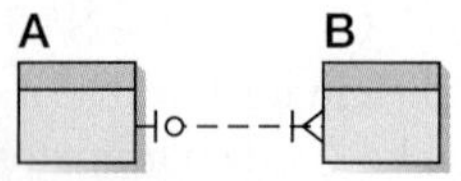 A — B	1:N, nonidentifying relationship. A relates to one or many Bs; B relates to zero or one A. Identifier and attributes not shown.
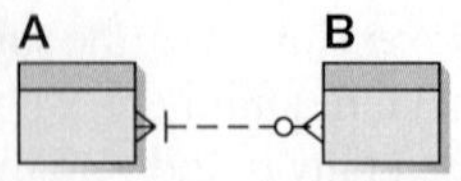 A — B	Many-to-many, nonidentifying relationship. A relates to zero or more Bs; B relates to one or more As. Identifier and attributes not shown.
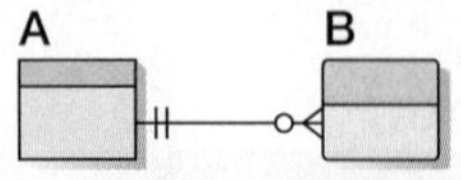 A — B	1:N identifying relationship. A relates to zero, one, or many Bs. B relates to exactly one A. Identifier and attributes not shown. For identifying relationships, the child must always relate to exactly one parent. The parent may relate to a combination of minimum and maximum cardinalities.
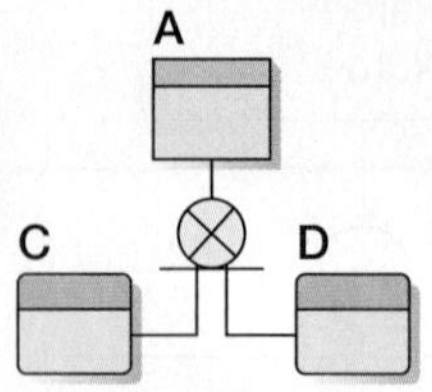 A — C / D	A is supertype, C and D are exclusive subtypes. Discriminator not shown. Identifier and attributes not shown.
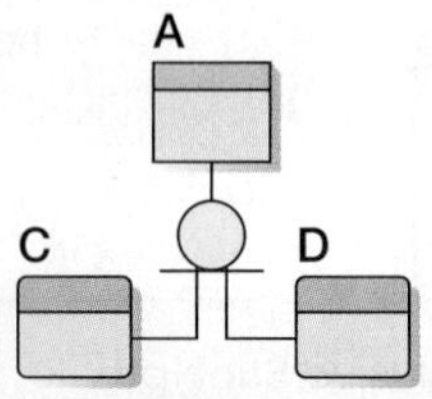 A — C / D	A is supertype, C and D are inclusive subtypes. Identifier and attributes not shown.

Patterns in Forms, Reports, and E-R Models

A data model is a representation of how users view their world. Unfortunately, you cannot walk up to most computer users and ask questions like, "What is the maximum cardinality between the EMPLOYEE and SKILL entities?" Few users would have any idea of what you mean. Instead, you must infer the data model indirectly from user documents and from users' conversations and behavior.

One of the best ways to infer a data model is to study the users' forms and reports. From such documents, you can learn about entities and their relationships. In fact, the structure of forms and reports determines the structure of the data model, and the structure of the data model determines the structure of forms and reports. This means that you can examine a form or report and determine the entities and relationships that underlie it.

You can also use forms and reports to validate the data model. Rather than showing the data model to the users for feedback, an alternative is to construct a form or report that reflects the structure of the data model and obtain user feedback on that form or report. For example, if you want to know if an ORDER has one or many SALESPERSONs, you can show the users a form that has a space for entering just one salesperson's name. If the user asks, "Where do I put the name of the second salesperson?" then you know that orders have at least two and possibly many salespeople. Sometimes, when no appropriate form or report exists, teams create a prototype form or report for the users to evaluate.

All of this means that you must understand how the structure of forms and reports determines the structure of the data model and the reverse. Fortunately, many forms and reports fall into common patterns. If you learn how to analyze these patterns, you will be well on your way to understanding the logical relationship between forms and reports and the data model. Accordingly, in the next sections, we will discuss the most common patterns in detail.

Strong Entity Patterns

Three relationships are possible between two strong entities: 1:1, 1:N, and N:M. When modeling such relationships, you must determine both the maximum and minimum cardinality. The maximum cardinality often can be determined from forms and reports. In most cases, to determine the minimum cardinality, you will have to ask the users.

1:1 Strong Entity Relationships

Figure 5-15 shows a data entry form and a report that indicate a one-to-one relationship between the entities CLUB_MEMBER and LOCKER. The Club Member Locker form in Figure 5-15(a) shows data for an athletic club member, and it lists just one locker for that member. This form indicates that a club member has at most one locker. The report in Figure 5-15(b) shows the lockers in the club and indicates the member who has been allocated that locker. Each locker is assigned to one club member.

The form and report in Figure 5-15 thus suggest that a CLUB_MEMBER has one LOCKER and a LOCKER is assigned to one CLUB_MEMBER. Hence, the relationship between them is 1:1. To model that relationship, we draw a nonidentifying relationship (meaning neither entity is ID-dependent) between the two entities, as shown in Figure 5-16. We then set the maximum cardinality to 1:1. You can tell that this is a nonidentifying relationship because the relationship line is dashed. Also, the absence of a crow's foot indicates that the relationship is 1:1.

Regarding minimum cardinality, every club member shown in the form has a locker and every locker shown in the report is assigned to a club member, so it appears that the relationship is mandatory to mandatory. However, this form and report are just instances; they may not show every possibility. If the club allows social, nonathletic memberships, then not every club member will have a locker. Furthermore, it is unlikely that every locker is occupied; there are likely some lockers that are unused and nonallocated. Accordingly, Figure 5-16 shows this relationship as optional to optional, as indicated by the small circles on the relationship lines.

BY THE WAY How do you recognize strong entities? You can use two major tests. First, does the entity have an identifier of its own? If it shares a part of its identifier with another entity, then it is an ID-dependent entity and is therefore weak. Second, does the entity seem to be logically different from and separate from the other entities? Does it stand alone, or is it part of something else? In this case, a CLUB_MEMBER and a LOCKER are two very different, separate things; they are not part of each other or of something else. Hence, they are strong.

Note also that a form or report shows only one side of a relationship. Given entities A and B, a form can show the relationship from A to B, but it cannot show the relationship from B to A at the same time. To learn the cardinality from B to A, you must examine a second form or report, ask the users, or take some other action.

Finally, it is seldom possible to infer minimum cardinality from a form or report. Generally, you must ask the users.

FIGURE 5-15

Form and Report Indicating a 1:1 Relationship

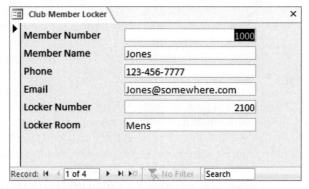

(a) Club Membership Data Entry Form

CLUB LOCKERS

Member Number	Member Name	Locker Number	Locker Room	Locker Size
1000	Jones	2100	Mens	Med
2000	Abernathy	2200	Womens	Large
3000	Wu	2115	Mens	Large
4000	Lai	2217	Womens	Small

(b) Club Locker Report

FIGURE 5-16

Data Model for the 1:1 Relationship in Figure 5-15

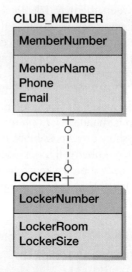

1:N Strong Entity Relationships

Figure 5-17 shows a form that lists the uniforms issued to the club members. A club member may have many uniforms, so the maximum cardinality from CLUB_MEMBER to CLUB_UNIFORM is N. But what about the opposite direction? To determine if a uniform relates to one or N club members, we need to examine a form or report that shows the relationship from a uniform to a club member. Alternatively, we can talk to the people at the club who manage the uniforms. We cannot ignore the issue because we need to know whether the relationship is 1:N or N:M.

In such a case, we must ask the users or at least make a determination by thinking about the nature of the business setting. Can a uniform be shared by more than one club member at one time? Because team uniforms have numbers on them to identify the team members, and because this number is generally issued for an entire season (think about your favorite baseball, basketball, or football team), this seems unlikely. Therefore, we can reasonably assume that a CLUB_UNIFORM relates to just one CLUB_MEMBER. Thus, we conclude the relationship is 1:N. Figure 5-18 shows the resulting data model. Note that the many side of the relationship is indicated by the crow's foot next to CLUB_UNIFORM.

Considering minimum cardinality, it seems reasonable that a CLUB_MEMBER may not be on a team and, therefore, is not required to have a uniform. Similarly, it seems reasonable that some uniforms may not be issued during a particular season. We will definitely need to confirm this by asking the users. Figure 5-18 depicts the situation in which a CLUB_MEMBER does not have to have a CLUB_UNIFORM and where a CLUB_UNIFORM does not have to be issued to a CLUB_MEMBER.

FIGURE 5-17

Form and Report Indicating a 1:N Relationship

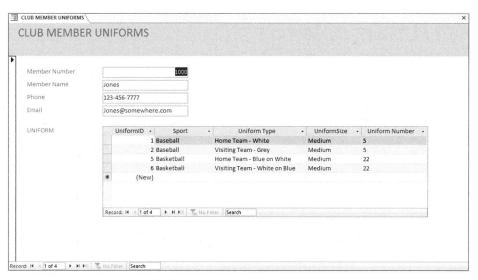

(a) CLUB MEMBER UNIFORM Form

(b) CLUB MEMBER UNIFORM Report

FIGURE 5-18

Data Model for the 1:N
Relationship in Figure 5-17

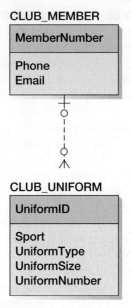

N:M Strong Entity Relationships

Figure 5-19(a) shows a form with data about a supplier and the parts it is prepared to supply. Figure 5-19(b) shows a report that summarizes parts and lists the companies that can supply those parts. In both cases, the relationship is many: A COMPANY supplies many PARTs, and a PART is supplied by many COMPANYs. Thus, the relationship is N:M.

FIGURE 5-19

Form and Report Indicating
an N:M Relationship

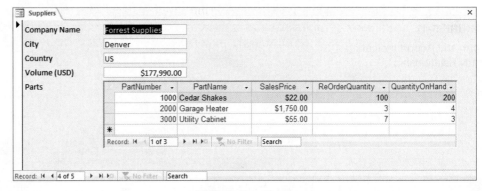

(a) Suppliers Form

Part Number	Part Name	Sales Price	ROQ	QOH	Company Name	City	Country
PART							
1000	Cedar Shakes	$22.00	100	200			
					Bristol Systems	Manchester	England
					ERS Systems	Vancouver	Canada
					Forrest Supplies	Denver	US
2000	Garage Heater	$1,750.00	3	4			
					Bristol Systems	Manchester	England
					ERS Systems	Vancouver	Canada
					Forrest Supplies	Denver	US
					Kyoto Importers	Kyoto	Japan
3000	Utility Cabinet	$55.00	7	3			
					Ajax Manufacturing	Sydney	Australia
					Forrest Supplies	Denver	US

(b) PART Report

FIGURE 5-20

Data Model for the N:M
Relationship in Figure 5-19

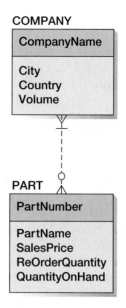

Figure 5-20 shows a data model that extends the data model in Figure 5-18 to include this new relationship. A supplier is a company, so we show the supplier entity as a COMPANY.

Because not all companies are suppliers, the relationship from COMPANY to PART must be optional. However, every part must be supplied from somewhere, so the relationship from PART to COMPANY is mandatory.

In summary, the three types of strong entity relationships are 1:1, 1:N, and N:M. You can infer the maximum cardinality in one direction from a form or report. You must examine a second form or report to determine the maximum cardinality in the other direction. If no form or report that shows the relationship is available, you must ask the users. Generally, it is not possible to determine minimum cardinality from forms and reports.

ID-Dependent Relationships

Three principal patterns use ID-dependent entities: multivalued attribute, archetype/ instance (also called *version/instance*), and association. Because the association pattern is often confused with the N:M strong entity relationships just discussed, we will look at that pattern first.

The Association Pattern and the Associative Entity

An **association pattern** is subtly and confusingly similar to an N:M strong relationship. To see why, examine the report in Figure 5-21 and compare it with the report in Figure 5-19(b).

FIGURE 5-21

Report Indicating an
Association Pattern

PART QUOTATIONS								
PartNumber	PartName	SalesPrice	ROQ	QOH	CompanyName	City	Country	Price
1000	Cedar Shakes	$22.00	100	200				
					Bristol Systems	Manchester	England	$14.00
					ERS Systems	Vancouver	Canada	$12.50
					Forrest Supplies	Denver	US	$15.50
2000	Garage Heater	$1,750.00	3	4				
					Bristol Systems	Manchester	England	$950.00
					ERS Systems	Vancouver	Canada	$875.00
					Forrest Supplies	Denver	US	$915.00
					Kyoto Importers	Kyoto	Japan	$1,100.00
3000	Utility Cabinet	$55.00	7	3				
					Ajax Manufacturing	Sydney	Australia	$37.50
					Forrest Supplies	Denver	US	$42.50

What is the difference? If you look closely, you'll see that the only difference is that the report in Figure 5-21 contains Price, which is the price quotation for a part from a particular supplier. The first line of this report indicates that the part Cedar Shakes is supplied by Bristol Systems for $14.00.

Price is neither an attribute of COMPANY nor an attribute of PART. It is an attribute of the combination of a COMPANY with a PART. Figure 5-22 shows the appropriate data model for such a case.

Here a third entity, QUOTATION, has been created to hold the Price attribute. This entity, which links the other two entities in the data model, is called an **associative entity** (or **association entity**). The identifier of QUOTATION is the combination of PartNumber and CompanyName. Note that PartNumber is the identifier of PART and CompanyName is the identifier of COMPANY. Hence, QUOTATION is ID-dependent on *both* PART and COMPANY.

In Figure 5-22, then, the relationships between PART and QUOTATION and between COMPANY and QUOTATION are both identifying. This fact is shown in Figure 5-22 by the solid, nondashed lines that represent these relationships.

As with all identifying relationships, the parent entities are required. Thus, the minimum cardinality from QUOTATION to PART is one, and the minimum cardinality from QUOTATION to COMPANY also is one. The minimum cardinality in the opposite direction is determined by business requirements. Here a PART must have a QUOTATION, but a COMPANY need not have a QUOTATION.

> **BY THE WAY**   Consider the differences between the data models in Figure 5-20 and Figure 5-22. The only difference between the two is that in the latter the relationship between COMPANY and PART has an attribute, Price. Remember this example whenever you model an N:M relationship. Is there a missing attribute that pertains to the combination and not just to one of the entities? If so, you are dealing with an association, ID-dependent pattern and not an N:M, strong entity pattern.

Associations can occur among more than two entity types. Figure 5-23, for example, shows a data model for the assignment of a particular client to a particular architect for a particular project. The attribute of the assignment is HoursWorked. This data model shows how the ternary relationship in Figure 5-4(b) can be modeled as a combination of three binary relationships.

FIGURE 5-22

Association Pattern Data Model for the Report in Figure 5-21

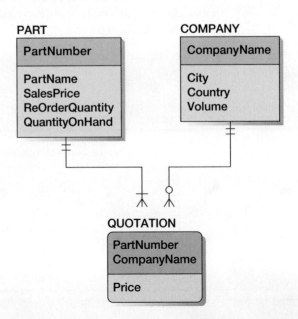

FIGURE 5-23

Association Pattern Data Model for the Ternary Relationship in Figure 5-4

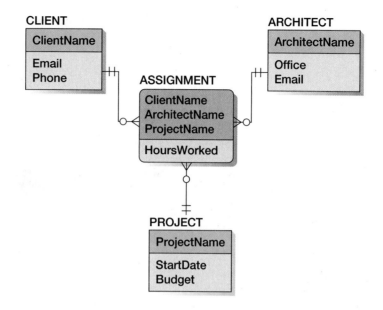

The Multivalued Attribute Pattern

In the E-R model as used today,[5] attributes must have a single value. If the COMPANY entity has PhoneNumber and Contact attributes, then a company can have at most one value for phone number and at most one value for contact.

In practice, however, companies can have more than one phone number and one contact. Consider, for example, the data entry form in Figure 5-24. This particular company has three phone numbers; other companies might have one or two or four or whatever. We need to create a data model that allows companies to have multiple phones, and placing the attribute PhoneNumber in COMPANY will not do it.

Figure 5-25 shows the solution. Instead of including PhoneNumber as an attribute of COMPANY, we create an ID-dependent entity, PHONE, that contains the attribute PhoneNumber. The relationship from COMPANY to PHONE is 1:N, so a company can have multiple phone numbers. Because PHONE is an ID-dependent entity, its identifier includes both CompanyName and PhoneNumber.

We can extend this strategy for as many multivalued attributes as necessary. The COMPANY data entry form in Figure 5-26 has multivalued Phone and multivalued Contact attributes. In this case, we just create a separate ID-dependent entity for each multivalued attribute, as shown in Figure 5-27.

FIGURE 5-24

Data Entry Form with a Multivalued Attribute

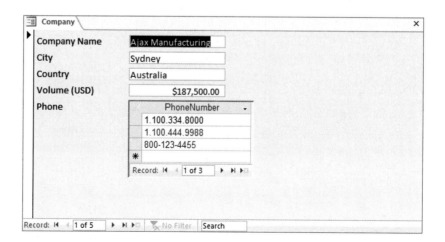

---

[5]The original E-R model allowed for multivalued attributes. Over time, that feature has been ignored, and today most people assume that the E-R model requires single-valued attributes. We will do so in this text.

FIGURE 5-25

Data Model for the Form
with a Multivalued Attribute
in Figure 5-24

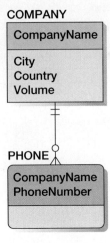

FIGURE 5-26

Data Entry Form with
Separate Multivalued
Attributes

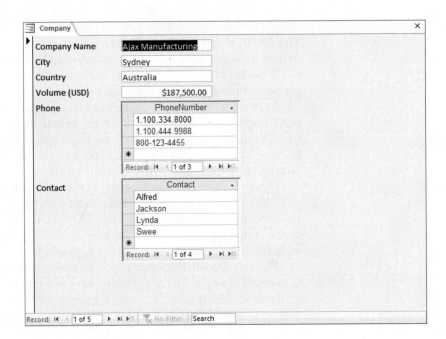

FIGURE 5-27

Data Model for the Form
with Separate Multivalued
Attributes in Figure 5-26

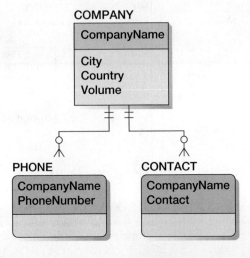

FIGURE 5-28

Data Entry Form with
Composite Multivalued
Attributes

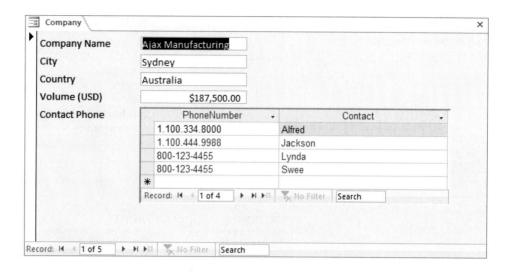

In Figure 5-27, PhoneNumber and Contact are independent. PhoneNumber is the phone number of the company and not necessarily the phone number of a contact. If PhoneNumber is not a general company phone number, but rather the phone number of a particular person at that company, then the data entry form would appear as in Figure 5-28. Here, for example, Alfred has one phone number and Jackson has another.

In this case, the attributes PhoneNumber and Contact belong together. Accordingly, we place them into a single ID-dependent entity, as shown in Figure 5-29. Notice that the identifier of PHONE_CONTACT is Contact and CompanyName. This arrangement means that a given Contact name can appear only once per company. Contacts can share phone numbers, however, as shown for employees Lynda and Swee. If the identifier of PHONE_CONTACT was PhoneNumber and CompanyName, then a phone number could occur only once per company, but contacts could have multiple numbers. Work through these examples to ensure that you understand them.

In all of these examples, the child requires a parent, which is always the case for ID-dependent entities. The parent may or may not require a child, depending on the application. A COMPANY may or may not require a PHONE or a CONTACT. You must ask the users to determine whether the ID-dependent entity is required.

Multivalued attributes are common, and you need to be able to model them effectively. Review the models in Figures 5-25, 5-27, and 5-29, and be certain that you understand their differences and what those differences imply.

FIGURE 5-29

Data Model for the Form
with Composite Multivalued
Attributes in Figure 5-28

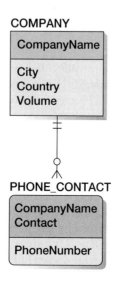

FIGURE 5-30

Three Archetype/Instance
Pattern Examples

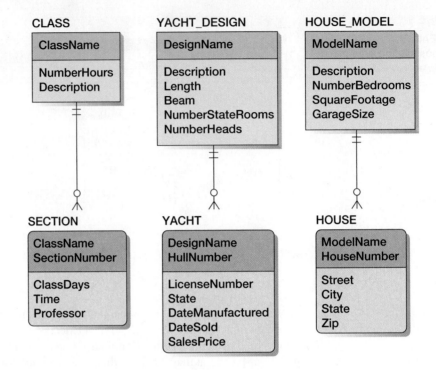

The Archetype/Instance Pattern

The archetype/instance pattern (also called *version/instance*) occurs when one entity represents a manifestation or an instance of another entity. You have already seen one example of archetype/instance in the example of PAINTING and PRINT in Figure 5-10. The painting is the archetype, and the prints made from the painting are the instances of that archetype.

Other examples of archetype/instances are shown in Figure 5-30. One familiar example concerns classes and sections of classes. The class is the archetype, and the sections of the class are instances of that archetype. Other examples involve designs and instances of designs. A yacht manufacturer has various yacht designs, and each yacht is an instance of a particular design archetype. In a housing development, a contractor offers several different house models, and a particular house is an instance of that house model archetype.

As with all ID-dependent entities, the parent entity is required. The child entities (here SECTION, YACHT, and HOUSE) may or may not be required, depending on application requirements.

Logically, the child entity of every archetype/instance pattern is an ID-dependent entity. All three of the examples in Figure 5-30 are accurate representations of the logical structure of the underlying data. However, sometimes users will add additional identifiers to the instance entity and in the process change the ID-dependent entity to a weak entity that is not ID-dependent (note that *ID-dependent* entities are drawn with *rounded corners*, while *non-ID-dependent* weak entities are drawn with *square corners* to distinguish them from each other).

For example, although you can identify a SECTION by class name and section, colleges and universities often will add a unique identifier to SECTION, such as ReferenceNumber. In that case, SECTION is no longer an ID-dependent entity, but it is still existence dependent on CLASS. Hence, as shown in Figure 5-31, SECTION is weak but not ID-dependent.

A similar change may occur to the YACHT entity. Although the manufacturer of a yacht may refer to it by specifying the hull number of a given design, the local tax authority may refer to it by State and LicenseNumber. If we change the identifier of YACHT from (HullNumber, DesignName) to (LicenseNumber, State), then YACHT is no longer ID-dependent; it becomes a weak, non-ID-dependent entity.

Similarly, although the home builder may think of a home as the third house constructed according to the Cape Codd design, everyone else will refer to it by its address. When we change the identifier of HOUSE from (HouseNumber, ModelName) to (Street, City, State, ZIP), then HOUSE becomes a weak, non-ID-dependent entity. All of these changes are shown in Figure 5-31.

FIGURE 5-31

Three Archetype/
Instance Patterns Using
Non-ID-Dependent
Relationships

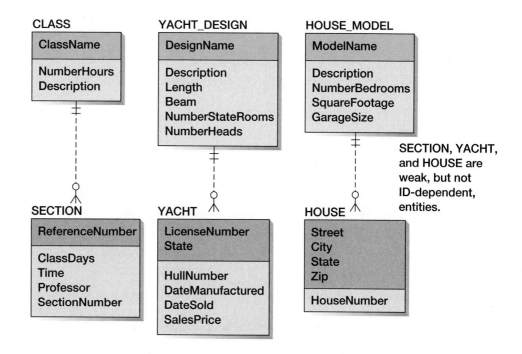

Mixed Identifying and Nonidentifying Patterns

Some patterns involve both identifying and nonidentifying relationships. The classic example is the line-item pattern, but there are other instances of mixed patterns as well. We begin with line items.

BY THE WAY   Data modelers continue to debate the importance of weak, non-ID-dependent entities. Everyone agrees that they exist, but not everyone agrees that they are important.

First, understand that existence dependence influences the way we write database applications. For the CLASS/SECTION example in Figure 5-31, we must insert a new CLASS before we can add a SECTION for that class. Additionally, when we delete a CLASS, we must delete all of the SECTIONs for that CLASS as well. This is one reason that some data modelers believe that weak, non-ID-dependent entities are important.

Skeptics say that although weak, non-ID-dependent entities may exist, they are not necessary. They say that we can obtain the same result by calling SECTION strong and making CLASS required. Because CLASS is required, the application will need to insert a CLASS before a SECTION is created and delete dependent SECTIONs when deleting a CLASS. So, according to that viewpoint, there is no practical difference between a weak, non-ID-dependent entity and a strong entity with a required relationship.

Others disagree. Their argument goes something like this: The requirement that a SECTION must have a CLASS comes from a logical necessity. It has to be that way—it comes from the nature of reality. The requirement that a strong entity must have a relationship to another strong entity arises from a business rule. Initially, we say that an ORDER must have a CUSTOMER (both strong entities), and then the application requirements change and we say that we can have cash sales, meaning that an ORDER no longer has to have a CUSTOMER. Business rules frequently change, but logical necessity never changes. We need to model weak, non-ID-dependent entities so that we know the strength of the required parent rule.

And so it goes. You, with the assistance of your instructor, can make up your own mind. Is there a difference between a weak, non-ID-dependent entity and a strong entity with a required relationship? In Figure 5-31, should we call the entities SECTION, YACHT, and HOUSE strong, as long as their relationships are required? We think not—we think there is a difference. Others think differently, however.

FIGURE 5-32

Data Entry Form for a
Sales Order

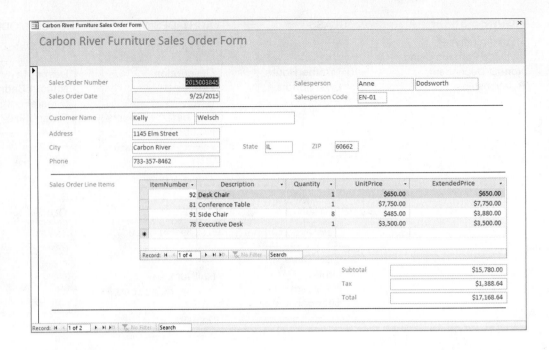

The Line-Item Pattern

Figure 5-32 shows a typical sales order, or invoice. Such forms usually have data about the order itself, such as the order number and order date, data about the customer, data about the salesperson, and then data about the items on the order. A data model for a typical sales order or invoice is shown in Figure 5-33.

In Figure 5-33, CUSTOMER, SALESPERSON, and SALES_ORDER are all strong entities, and they have the nonidentifying relationships you would expect. The relationship from CUSTOMER to SALES_ORDER is 1:N, and the relationship from SALESPERSON to SALES_ORDER also is 1:N. According to this model, a SALES_ORDER must have a CUSTOMER and may or may not have a SALESPERSON. All of this is readily understood.

The interesting relationships concern the line items on the order. Examine the data grid in the form in Figure 5-32. Some of the data values belong to the order itself, but other data values belong to items in general. In particular, Quantity and ExtendedPrice belong to the SALES_ORDER, but ItemNumber, Description, and UnitPrice belong to ITEM. The lines on an order do not have their own identifier. No one ever says, "Give me the data for line 12." Instead, they say, "Give me the data for line 12 of order 12345." Hence, the identifier of a line is a composite of the identifier of a particular line and the identifier of a particular order. Thus, entries for line items are always ID-dependent on the order in which they appear. In Figure 5-33, ORDER_LINE_ITEM is ID-dependent on SALES_ORDER. The identifier of the ORDER_LINE_ITEM entity is (SalesOrderNumber, LineNumber).

Now, and this is the part that is sometimes confusing for some students, ORDER_ LINE_ ITEM is not existence dependent on ITEM. It can exist even if no item has yet been assigned to it. Further, if an ITEM is deleted, we do not want the line item to be deleted with it. The deletion of an ITEM may make the value of ItemNumber and other data invalid, but it should not cause the line item itself to disappear.

Now consider what happens to a line item when an order is deleted. Unlike with the deletion of an item, which only causes data items to become invalid, the deletion of the order removes the existence of the line item. Logically, a line item cannot exist if its order is deleted. Hence, line items are existence dependent on orders.

Work through each of the relationships in Figure 5-33 and ensure that you understand their type and their maximum and minimum cardinalities. Also understand the implications of this data model. For example, do you see why this sales order data model is unlikely to be used by a company in which salespeople are on commission?

FIGURE 5-33

Data Model for the Sales
Order in Figure 5-32

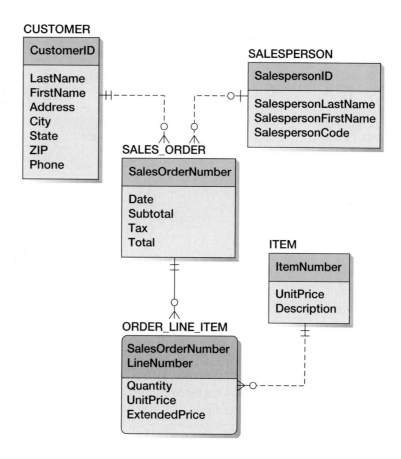

Other Mixed Patterns

Mixed identifying and nonidentifying relationships occur frequently. Learn to look for a mixed pattern when a strong entity has a multivalued composite group and when one of the elements in the composite group is an identifier of a second strong entity.

Consider, for example, baking recipes. Each recipe calls for a certain amount of a specific ingredient, such as flour, sugar, or butter. The ingredient list is a multivalued composite group, but one of the elements of that group, the name of the ingredient, is the identifier of a strong entity. As shown in Figure 5-34, the recipe and the ingredients are strong entities, but the amount and instructions for using each ingredient are ID-dependent on RECIPE.

FIGURE 5-34

Mixed Relationship Pattern
for Baking Recipes

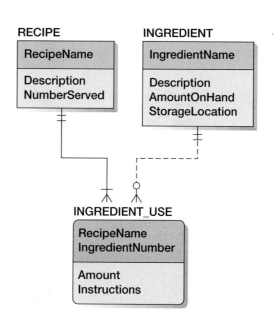

FIGURE 5-35

Mixed Relationship Pattern
for Employee Skills

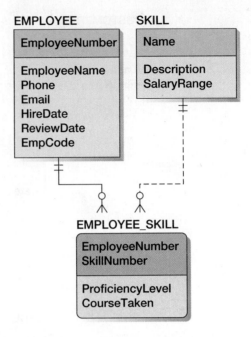

Or consider employees' skill proficiencies. The name of the skill (which is currently not listed in EMPLOYEE_SKILL, but will be added as a foreign key in the conversion to a database design in Chapter 6), the proficiency levels, and the courses taken by the employee are a multivalued group, but the skill itself is a strong entity, as shown in Figure 5-35. Dozens of other examples are possible.

Before continuing, compare the models in Figures 5-33, 5-34, and 5-35 with the association pattern in Figure 5-22. Make sure that you understand the differences and why the model in Figure 5-22 has two identifying relationships and the models in Figures 5-33, 5-34, and 5-35 have just one.

The For-Use-By Pattern

As stated earlier in this chapter, the major reason for using subtypes in a database design is to avoid value-inappropriate nulls. Some forms suggest the possibility of such nulls when they show blocks of data fields that are grayed out and labeled "For Use by *someone/something* Only." For example, Figure 5-36 shows two sections shaded in a darker color, one for commercial fishers and another for sport fishers. The presence of these shaded sections indicates the need for subtype entities.

FIGURE 5-36

Data Entry Form Suggesting
the Need for Subtypes

Resident Fishing License 2015 Season		License No: 03-1123432
Name:		
Street:		
City:	State:	Zip:
For Use by Commercial Fishers Only	For Use by Sport Fishers Only	
Vessel Number:	Number Years at This Address:	
Vessel Name:	Prior Year License Number:	
Vessel Type:		
Tax ID:		

FIGURE 5-37

Data Model for Form in
Figure 5-36

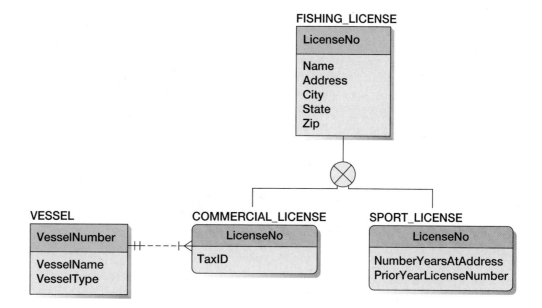

The data model for this form is shown in Figure 5-37. Observe that each grayed-out section has a subtype. Notice that the subtypes differ not only in their attributes, but that one has a relationship that the other does not have. Sometimes the only differences between subtypes are differences in the relationships they have.

The nonidentifying relationship from VESSEL to COMMERCIAL_LICENSE is shown as 1:N, mandatory to mandatory. In fact, this form does not have sufficient data for us to conclude that the maximum cardinality from VESSEL to COMMERCIAL_LICENSE is N. This fact was determined by interviewing users and learning that one boat is sometimes used by more than one commercial fisher. The minimum cardinalities indicate a commercial fisher must have a vessel and that only vessels that are used for licenses are to be stored in this database.

The point of this example is to illustrate how forms often suggest the need for subtypes. Whenever you see a grayed-out or otherwise distinguished section of a form with the words "For use by…," think "subtype."

Recursive Patterns

A **recursive relationship**, also called a **unary relationship**, occurs when an entity type has a relationship to itself. The classic examples of recursive relationships occur in manufacturing applications, but there are many other examples as well. As with strong entities, three types of recursive relationships are possible: 1:1, 1:N, and N:M. Let's consider each.

1:1 Recursive Relationships

Suppose you are asked to construct a database for a railroad, and you need to make a model of a freight train. You know that one of the entities is BOXCAR, but how are BOXCARs related? To answer that question, envision a train, as shown in Figure 5-38. Except for the first boxcar, each has one boxcar in front, and, except for the last boxcar, each boxcar has one boxcar in back. Thus, the relationship is 1:1 between boxcars, with an optional relationship for the first and last cars.

FIGURE 5-38

Freight Train Relationships

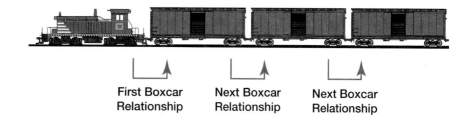

> **BY THE WAY**   If you are a casual observer of trains, you may be thinking that a freight train of all boxcars is unrealistic—what about the refrigerator cars, flat cars, tank cars, and so on? However, as any railfan or trainspotter (the British term) knows, *unit trains* consisting of only one type of freight car are common. Examples are unit trains of *grain cars* carrying wheat, *hopper cars* carrying coal, *tanker cars* carrying oil products, and *container cars* transporting the ubiquitous shipping containers.

Figure 5-39 shows a data model in which each BOXCAR has a 1:1 relationship to the BOXCAR behind. The BOXCAR entity at the head of the train has a 1:1 relationship to ENGINE. (This model assumes a train has just one engine. To model trains with multiple engines, create a second recursive relationship among engines. Construct that relationship just like the Boxcar behind relationship.)

Note that the 1:1 relationship between the ENGINE entity and the BOXCAR entity is optional–optional (O-O). This is because the BOXCAR entity represents *all* the BOXCARs in the train. While the first BOXCAR *must be* connected directly to the ENGINE, the second BOXCAR is *not* connected to the engine. Therefore, the relationship from ENGINE to BOXCAR is optional because the ENGINE does not have to be directly connected to each BOXCAR, and the relationship from BOXCAR to ENGINE is optional because *each* BOXCAR does *not* have to be connected to the ENGINE.

Also note that several years ago we would have also needed a CABOOSE entity to bring up the rear of the train. Today, railroads are permitted to use an *end-of-train marker light* on the last freight car, and there are few cabooses to be seen.

An alternative model is to use the relationship to represent the BOXCAR ahead. Either model works. Other examples of 1:1 recursive relationships are the succession of U.S. presidents, the succession of deans in a college of business, and the order of passengers on a waiting list.

1:N Recursive Relationships

The classic example of a 1:N recursive relationship occurs in organizational charts, in which an employee has a manager who may, in turn, manage several other employees. Figure 5-40 shows an example organizational chart. Note that the relationship between employees is 1:N. Figure 5-41 shows a data model for the managerial relationship. The crow's foot indicates that a manager may manage more than one employee. The relationship is

FIGURE 5-39

Data Model for a 1:1 Recursive Relationship

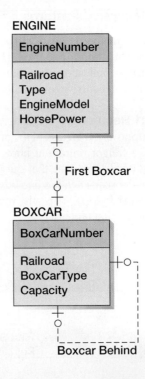

FIGURE 5-40

Organizational Chart
Relationships

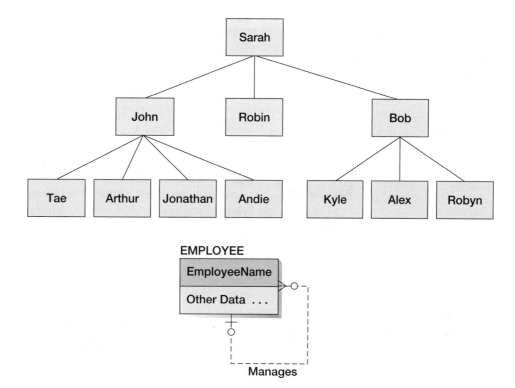

FIGURE 5-41

Data Model for the
Management Structure
in Figure 5-40 as a 1:N
Recursive Relationship

optional to optional because one manager (the president) has no manager and because some employees manage no one.

Another example of a 1:N recursive relationship concerns maps. For example, a world map has a relationship to many continent maps, each continent map has a relationship to many nation maps, and so forth. A third example concerns biological parents where the relationship from PERSON to PERSON is shown by tracing either mother or father (but not both).

N:M Recursive Relationships

N:M recursive relationships occur frequently in manufacturing applications, where they are used to represent bills of materials. Figure 5-42 shows an example.

The key idea of a bill of materials is that one part is composed of other parts. A child's red wagon, for example, consists of a handle assembly, a body, and a wheel assembly, each of which is a part. The handle assembly, in turn, consists of a handle, a bolt, a washer, and a nut. The wheel assembly consists of wheels, axles, washers, and nuts. The relationship among the parts is N:M because a part can be made up of many parts and because a part (such as washers and nuts) can be used in many parts.

The data model for a bill of materials is shown in Figure 5-43. Notice that each part has an N:M relationship to other parts. Because a part need not have any component parts and because a part need not have any parts that contain it, the minimum cardinality is optional to optional.

FIGURE 5-42

Bill of Materials

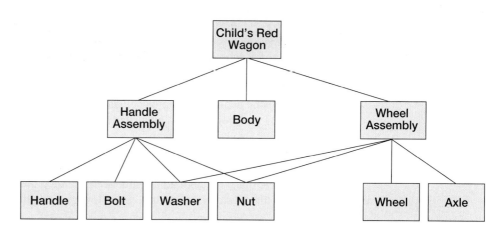

FIGURE 5-43

Data Model for the Bill of
Materials in Figure 5-42 as an
N:M Recursive Relationship

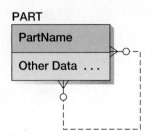

> **BY THE WAY** What would happen to the data model if the diagram showed how many
> of each part are used? Suppose, for example, that the wheel assembly
> requires four washers and the handle assembly requires just one. The data model in
> Figure 5-43 will not be correct for this circumstance. In fact, adding Quantity to this
> N:M relationship is analogous to adding Price to the N:M relationship in Figure 5-22.
> See Project Question 5.63.

N:M recursive relationships can be used to model directed networks, such as the flow of documents through organizational departments or the flow of gas through a pipeline. They also can be used to model the succession of parents, in which mothers, fathers, and stepparents are included.

If recursive structures seem hard to comprehend, don't fret. They may seem strange at first, but they are not difficult. Work through some data examples to gain confidence. Make up a train and see how the model in Figure 5-38 applies, or change the example in Figure 5-40 from employees to departments and see how the model in Figure 5-41 needs to be adjusted. Once you have learned to identify recursive patterns, you'll find it easy to create models for them.

The Data Modeling Process

During the data modeling process, the development team analyzes user requirements and constructs a data model from forms, reports, data sources, and user interviews. The process is always iterative; a model is constructed from one form or report and then supplemented and adjusted as more forms and reports are analyzed. Periodically, users are asked for additional information, such as that needed to assess minimum cardinality. Users also review and validate the data model. During that review, prototype databases evidencing data model constructs may need to be constructed to help users see how the database would work (Microsoft Access 2013 is often used for this purpose).

To give you an idea of the iterative nature of data modeling, we will consider the development of a simple data model for a university. As you read this example, strive to appreciate how the model evolves as more and more requirements are analyzed. For a more detailed version of this data modeling exercise, combined with an overview of the systems analysis and design process, see Appendix B.

> **BY THE WAY** One of the authors worked on a large data model for the U.S. Army's
> logistical system. The model contained more than 500 different entity
> types, and it took a team of seven people more than a year to develop, document,
> and validate it. On some occasions, the analysis of a new requirement indicated that
> the model had been conceived incorrectly, and days of work had to be redone. The
> most difficult aspect of the project was managing complexity. Knowing which entities
> related to which; whether an entity had already been defined; and whether a new entity
> was strong, weak, a supertype, or a subtype required a global understanding of the
> model. Memory was of poor help because an entity created in July could be a subtype
> of an entity created hundreds of entities earlier in February. To manage the model, the
> team used many different administrative tools. Keep this example in mind as you read
> through the development of the Highline University data model.

FIGURE 5-44

Highline University Sample
College Report

College of Business			
Mary B. Jefferson, Dean			
Phone: 232-1187		Campus Address:	
		Business Building, Room 100	
Department	Chairperson	Phone	Total Majors
Accounting	Jackson, Seymour P.	232-1841	318
Finance	HeuTeng, Susan	232-1414	211
Info Systems	Brammer, Nathaniel D.	236-0011	247
Management	Tuttle, Christine A.	236-9988	184
Production	Barnes, Jack T.	236-1184	212

Suppose the administration at a hypothetical university named Highline University wants to create a database to track colleges, departments, faculty, and students. To do this, a data modeling team has collected a series of reports as part of its requirements determination. In the next sections, we will analyze these reports to produce a data model.

The College Report

Figure 5-44 shows an example report from Highline University about one college within the university, the College of Business. This example is one instance of this report; Highline University has similar reports about other colleges, such as the College of Engineering and the College of Social Sciences. The data modeling team needs to gather enough examples to form a representative sample of all the college reports. Here assume that the report in Figure 5-44 is representative.

Examining the report, we find data specific to the college—such as the name, dean, telephone number, and campus address—and also facts about each department within the college. These data suggest that the data model should have COLLEGE and DEPARTMENT entities with a relationship between them, as shown in Figure 5-45.

The relationship in Figure 5-45 is nonidentifying. This relationship is used because DEPARTMENT is not ID-dependent and, logically, a DEPARTMENT is independent of a COLLEGE. We cannot tell from the report in Figure 5-44 whether a department can belong to many colleges. To answer this question, we need to ask the users or look at other forms and reports.

Assume that we know from the users that a department belongs to just one college, and the relationship is thus 1:N from COLLEGE to DEPARTMENT. The report in Figure 5-44 does not show us the minimum cardinalities. Again, we must ask the users. Assume we learn from the users that a college must have at least one department and a department must be assigned to exactly one college.

The Department Report

The Department Report shown in Figure 5-46 contains departmental data along with a list of the professors who are assigned to that department. This report contains data concerning the department's campus address. Because these data do not appear in the DEPARTMENT entity in Figure 5-45, we need to add them, as shown in Figure 5-47(a). This is typical of the data modeling process. That is, entities and relationships are adjusted as additional forms, reports, and other requirements are analyzed.

FIGURE 5-45

Data Model for the College
Report in Figure 5-44

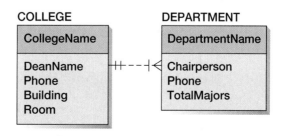

FIGURE 5-46

Highline University Sample
Department Report

Information Systems Department
College of Business

Chairperson: Brammer, Nathaniel D
Phone: 236-0011
Campus Address: Social Science Building, Room 213

Professor	Office	Phone
Jones, Paul D.	Social Science, 219	232-7713
Parks, Mary B	Social Science, 308	232-5791
Wu, Elizabeth	Social Science, 207	232-9112

Figure 5-47(a) also adds the relationship between DEPARTMENT and PROFESSOR. We initially model this as an N:M relationship because a professor might have a joint appointment. The data modeling team must further investigate the requirements to determine whether joint appointments are allowed. If not, the relationship can be redefined as a nonidentifying 1:N, as shown in Figure 5-47(b).

Another possibility regarding the N:M relationship is that some attribute about the combination of a professor and a department is missing. If so, then an association pattern is more appropriate. At Highline, suppose the team finds a report that describes the title and employment terms for each professor in each department. Figure 5-47(c) shows an entity for such a report, named APPOINTMENT. As you would expect from the association pattern, APPOINTMENT is ID-dependent on both DEPARTMENT and PROFESSOR.

A chairperson is a professor, so another improvement on the model is to remove the Chairperson data from DEPARTMENT and replace it with a chairperson relationship. This has been done in Figure 5-47(d). In the Chairs/Chaired By relationship, a professor can be the chair of zero or one departments, and a department must have exactly one professor as chair.

With the Chairs/Chaired By relationship, the attribute Chairperson is no longer needed in DEPARTMENT, so it is removed. Normally, a chairperson has his or her office in the department office; if this is the case, Phone, Building, and Room in DEPARTMENT duplicate Phone, Building, and OfficeNumber in PROFESSOR. Consequently, it might be possible to remove Phone, Building, and Room from DEPARTMENT. However, a professor may have a different phone from the official department phone, and the professor may also have an office outside of the department's office. Because of this possibility, we will leave Phone, Building, and Room in DEPARTMENT.

The Department/Major Report

Figure 5-48 shows a report of a department and the students who major in that department. This report indicates the need for a new entity called STUDENT. Because students are not ID-dependent on departments, the relationship between DEPARTMENT and STUDENT is nonidentifying, as shown in Figure 5-49. We cannot determine the minimum cardinality from Figure 5-48, but assume that interviews with users indicate that a STUDENT must have a MAJOR, but no MAJOR need have any students. Also, using the contents of this report as a guide, attributes StudentNumber, StudentName, and Phone are placed in STUDENT.

There are two subtleties in this interpretation of the report in Figure 5-48. First, observe that Major's Name was changed to StudentName when the attribute was placed in STUDENT. This was done because StudentName is more generic. Major's Name has no meaning outside the context of the Major relationship. Additionally, the report heading in Figure 5-48 has an ambiguity. Is the phone number for the department a value of DEPARTMENT.Phone or a value of PROFESSOR.Phone? The team needs to investigate this further with the users. Most likely, it is a value of DEPARTMENT.Phone.

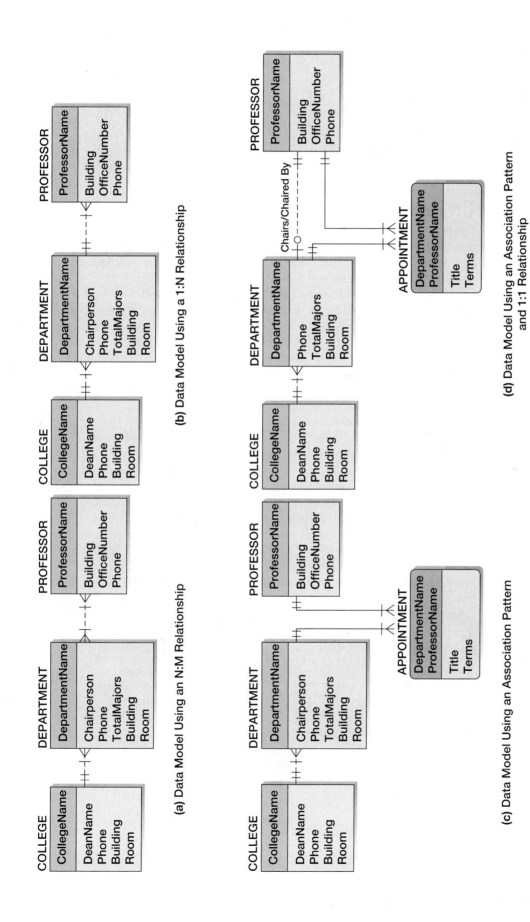

(a) Data Model Using an N:M Relationship

(b) Data Model Using a 1:N Relationship

(c) Data Model Using an Association Pattern

(d) Data Model Using an Association Pattern and 1:1 Relationship

FIGURE 5-47

Alternate Data Models for the DEPARTMENT-to-PROFESSOR Relationship

FIGURE 5-48

Highline University Sample
Department Student Report

Student Major List Information Systems Department		
Chairperson: Brammer, Nathaniel D Phone: 236-0011		
Major's Name	Student Number	Phone
Jackson, Robin R.	12345	237-8713
Lincoln, Fred J.	48127	237-8924
Madison, Janice A.	37512	237-9035

The Student Acceptance Letter

Figure 5-50 shows the acceptance letter that Highline sends to its incoming students. The data items in this letter that need to be represented in the data model are shown in boldface. In addition to data concerning the student, this letter also contains data regarding the student's major department as well as data about the student's adviser.

We can use this letter to add an Advises/Advised By relationship to the data model. However, which entity should be the parent of this relationship? Because an adviser is a professor, it is tempting to make PROFESSOR the parent. However, a professor acts as an adviser within the context of a particular department. Therefore, Figure 5-51 shows APPOINTMENT as the parent of STUDENT. To produce the report in Figure 5-50, the professor's data can be retrieved by accessing the related APPOINTMENT entity and then accessing that entity's PROFESSOR parent. This decision is not cut and dried, however. One can make a strong argument that the parent of the relationship should be PROFESSOR.

According to this data model, a student has at most one adviser. Also, a student must have an adviser, but no professor (via APPOINTMENT) need advise any students. These constraints cannot be determined from any of the reports shown and will need to be verified with the users. The acceptance letter uses the title *Mr.* in the salutation. Therefore, a new attribute called Title is added to STUDENT. Observe that this Title is different from the one in APPOINTMENT. This difference will need to be documented in the data model to avoid confusion. The acceptance letter also shows the need to add new home address attributes to STUDENT.

The acceptance letter reveals a problem. The name of the student is Fred Parks, but we have allocated only one attribute, StudentName, in STUDENT. It is difficult to reliably disentangle first and last names from a single attribute, so a better model is to have two attributes: StudentFirstName and StudentLastName. Similarly, note that the adviser in this letter is

FIGURE 5-49

Data Model with STUDENT Entity

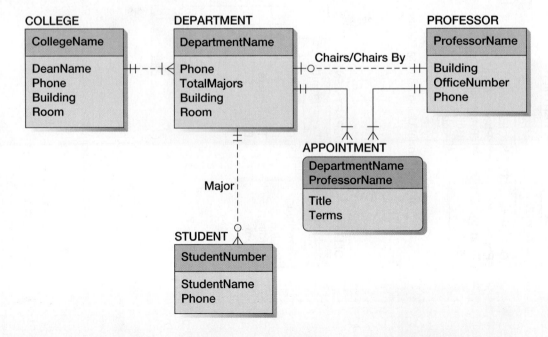

FIGURE 5-50

Highline University Sample
Student Acceptance Letter

> **Mr. Fred Parks**
> **123 Elm Street**
> **Los Angeles, CA 98002**
>
> Dear **Mr. Parks:**
>
> You have been admitted as a major in the **Accounting** Department at Highline
> University, starting in the Fall Semester, 2015. The office of the Accounting
> Department is located in the **Business** Building, Room **210.**
>
> Your adviser is professor **Elizabeth Johnson,** whose telephone number is **232-
> 8740** and whose office is located in the **Business** Building, Room **227.** Please
> schedule an appointment with your adviser as soon as you arrive on campus.
>
> Congratulations and welcome to Highline University!
>
> Sincerely,
>
>
>
> Jan P. Smathers
> President
>
> JPS/rkp

Elizabeth Johnson. So far, all professor names have been in the format Johnson, Elizabeth. To accommodate both forms of name, ProfessorName in PROFESSOR must be changed to the two attributes ProfessorFirstName and ProfessorLastName. A similar change is necessary for DeanName. These changes are shown in Figure 5-52, which is the final form of this data model.

This section should give you a feel for the nature of a data modeling project. Forms and reports are examined in sequence, and the data model is adjusted as necessary to accommodate the knowledge gained from each new form or report. It is very typical to revise the data model many, many times throughout the data modeling process. See Project Question 5.64 for yet another possible revision.

FIGURE 5-51

Data Model with
Advises Relationship

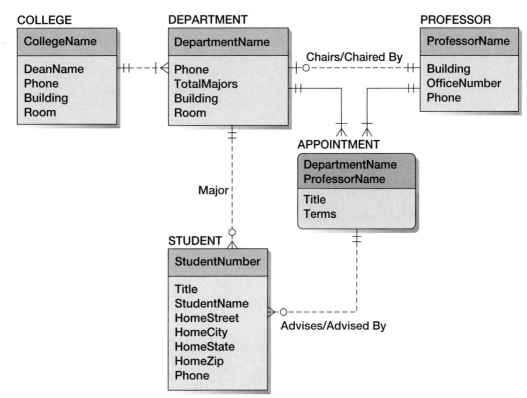

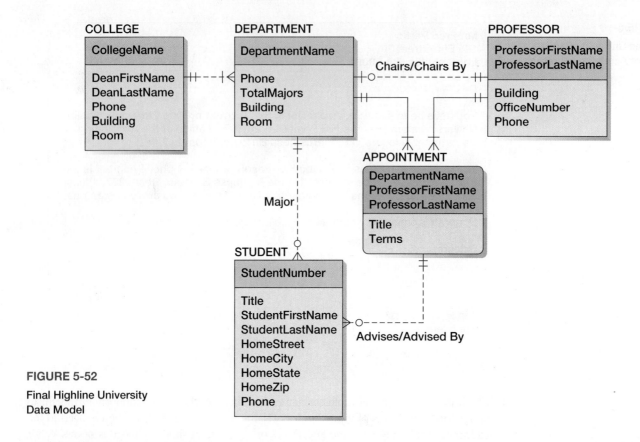

FIGURE 5-52

Final Highline University
Data Model

Summary

When databases are developed as part of a new information systems project, the database design is accomplished
in two phases. First, a data model is constructed from forms,
reports, data sources, and other requirements. The data
model is then transformed into a database design. A data
model is a blueprint for a database design. Like blueprints
for buildings, data models can be altered as necessary, with
little effort. Once the database is constructed, however, such
alterations are time consuming and very expensive.

The most prominent data model in use today is the
entity-relationship, or E-R, data model. It was invented by
Peter Chen and extended by others to include subtypes. An
entity is something that users want to track. An entity class is
a collection of entities of the same type and is described by
the structure of the entities in the class. An entity instance
is one entity of a given class. Entities have attributes that
describe their characteristics. Identifiers are attributes that
name entity instances. Composite identifiers consist of two
or more attributes.

The E-R model includes relationships, which are associations among entities. Relationship classes are associations
among entity classes, and relationship instances are associations among entity instances. Today, relationships are not
allowed to have attributes. Relationships can be given names
so that they can be identified.

The degree of a relationship is the number of entity
types that participate in the relationship. Binary relationships have only two entity types. In practice, relationships
of degrees greater than two are decomposed into multiple
binary relationships.

The main difference between an entity and a table is
that you can express an entity relationship without specifying
foreign keys. Working with entities reduces complexity and
makes it easier to revise the data model as work progresses.

Relationships are classified according to their cardinality. Maximum cardinality is the maximum number of
instances that can participate in a relationship instance.
Minimum cardinality is the least number of entities that
must participate in a relationship.

Relationships commonly have one of three maximum
cardinalities: 1:1, 1:N, or N:M. In rare instances, a maximum cardinality might be a specific number, such as 1:15.
Relationships commonly have one of four basic minimum
cardinalities: optional to optional, mandatory to optional,
optional to mandatory, or mandatory to mandatory. In rare
cases, the minimum cardinality is a specific number.

Unfortunately, many variations of the E-R model are in use. The original version represented relationships with diamonds. The Information Engineering version uses a line with a crow's foot, the IDEF1X version uses another set of symbols, and UML uses yet another set. To add further complication, many data modeling products have added their own symbols. In this text, we will use the IE Crow's Foot model with symbols, as summarized in Figure 5-14. Other models and techniques are summarized in Appendices B, C, D, and H.

An ID-dependent entity is an entity whose identifier includes the identifier of another entity. Such entities use an identifying relationship. In such relationships, the parent is always required, but the child (the ID-dependent entity) may or may not be required, depending on application requirements. Identifying relationships are shown with solid lines in E-R diagrams.

A weak entity is an entity whose existence depends on the presence of another entity. All ID-dependent entities are weak. Additionally, some entities are weak but not ID-dependent. Some people believe such entities are not important; others believe they are.

A subtype entity is a special case of another entity called its supertype. Subtypes may be exclusive or inclusive. Exclusive subtypes sometimes have discriminators, which are attributes that specify a supertype's subtype. The most important (and perhaps only) reason for creating subtypes in a data model is to avoid value-inappropriate nulls.

A relationship between an entity and itself is a recursive relationship. Recursive relationships can be 1:1, 1:N, or N:M.

Relationships among nonsubtype entities are called HAS-A relationships. Relationships among supertype/subtype entities are called IS-A relationships.

The elements of a data model are constructed by analyzing forms, reports, and data sources. Many forms and reports fall into common patterns. In this text, we discussed the 1:1, 1:N, and N:M strong entity patterns. We also discussed three patterns that use ID-dependent relationships: association, multivalued attribute, and version/instance. Some forms involve mixed identifying and nonidentifying patterns. Line items are the classic example of mixed forms, but there are other examples as well.

The for-use-by pattern indicates the need for subtypes. In some cases, subtypes differ because they have different attributes, but they also can differ because they have different relationships. The data modeling process is iterative. Forms and reports are analyzed, and the data model is created, modified, and adjusted as necessary. Sometimes the analysis of a form or report will require that earlier work be redone. *C'est la vie!*

Key Terms

association entity
association pattern
associative entity
attribute
binary relationship
cardinality
child
composite identifier
crow's foot symbol
data model
degree
discriminator
entity
entity class
entity instance
entity-relationship (E-R) diagrams
entity-relationship (E-R) model
exclusive subtype
extended E-R model
HAS-A relationship
ID-dependent entity

identifier
identifying relationship
IE Crow's Foot model
inclusive subtype
Information Engineering (IE) model
Integrated Definition 1, Extended (IDEF1X)
IS-A relationship
mandatory
mandatory-to-mandatory (M-M) relationship
mandatory-to-optional (M-O) relationship
many-to-many (N:M) relationship
maximum cardinality
minimum cardinality
nonidentifying relationship
one-to-many (1:N) relationship
one-to-one (1:1) relationship
optional

optional-to-mandatory (O-M) relationship
optional-to-optional (O-O) relationship
owner entity
parent
recursive relationship
relationship
relationship class
relationship instance
requirements analysis
strong entity
subtype
supertype
systems analysis and design
systems development life cycle (SDLC)
ternary relationship
unary relationship
Unified Modeling Language (UML)
weak entity

Review Questions

5.1 Describe the two phases in designing databases that arise from the development of new information systems.

5.2 In general terms, explain how a data model could be used to design a database for a small video rental store.

5.3 Explain how a data model is like a building blueprint. What is the advantage of making changes during the data modeling stage?

5.4 Who is the author of the entity-relationship data model?

5.5 Define *entity*. Give an example of an entity (other than one presented in this chapter).

5.6 Explain the difference between an entity class and an entity instance.

5.7 Define *attribute*. Give an example attribute for the entity in your answer to Review Question 5.5.

5.8 Define *identifier*. Give an example identifier for the entity in your answer to Review Question 5.5.

5.9 Give an example of a composite identifier.

5.10 Define *relationship*. Give an example of a relationship (other than one presented in this chapter). Name your relationship.

5.11 Explain the difference between a relationship class and a relationship instance.

5.12 What is the degree of a relationship? Give an example of a relationship of degree three (other than one presented in this chapter).

5.13 What is a binary relationship?

5.14 Explain the difference between an entity and a table. Why is this difference important?

5.15 What does cardinality mean?

5.16 Define the terms *maximum cardinality* and *minimum cardinality*.

5.17 Give examples of 1:1, 1:N, and N:M relationships (other than those presented in this chapter). Draw two E-R diagrams for each of your examples: one using the traditional diamond notation and one using IE Crow's Foot notation.

5.18 Give an example for which the maximum cardinality must be an exact number other than those presented in this chapter).

5.19 Give examples of M-M, M-O, O-M, and O-O relationships (other than those presented in this chapter). Draw two E-R diagrams for each of your examples: one using the traditional diamond notation and one using IE Crow's Foot notation.

5.20 Explain, in general terms, how the traditional E-R model, the IE Crow's Foot version, the IDEF1X version, and the UML version differ. Which version is used primarily in this text?

5.21 Explain how the notations shown in Figure 5-7 differ.

5.22 Explain how the notations shown in Figure 5-9 differ.

5.23 What is an ID-dependent entity? Give an example of an ID-dependent entity (other than one presented in this chapter).

5.24 Explain how to determine the minimum cardinality of both sides of an ID-dependent relationship.

5.25 What rules exist when creating an instance of an ID-dependent entity? What rules exist when deleting the parent of an ID-dependent entity?

5.26 What is an identifying relationship? How is it used?

5.27 Explain why the relationship between BUILDING and APARTMENT discussed on page 206 is an identifying relationship.

5.28 What is a weak entity? How do weak entities relate to ID-dependent entities?

5.29 What distinguishes a weak entity from a strong entity that has a required relationship to another entity?

5.30 Define *subtype* and *supertype*. Give an example of a subtype–supertype relationship (other than one presented in this chapter).

5.31 Explain the difference between exclusive subtypes and inclusive subtypes. Give an example of each.

5.32 What is a discriminator?

5.33 Explain the difference between IS-A and HAS-A relationships.

5.34 What is the most important reason for using subtypes in a data model?

5.35 Describe the relationship between the structure of forms and reports and the data model.

5.36 Explain two ways forms and reports are used for data modeling.

5.37 Explain why the form and report in Figure 5-15 indicate that the underlying relationship is 1:1.

5.38 Why is it not possible to infer minimum cardinality from the form and report in Figure 5-15?

5.39 Describe two tests for determining if an entity is a strong entity.

5.40 Why does the form in Figure 5-17 not indicate that the underlying relationship is 1:N? What additional information is required to make that assertion?

5.41 Explain why two forms or reports are usually needed to infer maximum cardinality.

5.42 How can you assess minimum cardinality for the entities in the form in Figure 5-17?

5.43 Explain why the form and report in Figure 5-19 indicate that the underlying relationship is N:M.

5.44 Name three patterns that use ID-dependent relationships.

5.45 Explain how the association pattern differs from the N:M strong entity pattern. What characteristic of the report in Figure 5-21 indicates that an association pattern is needed?

5.46 In general terms, explain how to differentiate an N:M strong entity pattern from an association pattern.

5.47 Explain why two entities are needed to model multivalued attributes.

5.48 How do the forms in Figures 5-26 and 5-28 differ? How does this difference affect the data model?

5.49 Describe, in general terms, the archetype/instance pattern. Why is an ID-dependent relationship needed for this pattern? Use the CLASS/SECTION example shown in Figure 5-30 in your answer.

5.50 Explain what caused the entities in Figure 5-31 to change from ID-dependent entities.

5.51 Summarize the two sides in the argument about the importance of weak but not ID-dependent entities.

5.52 Give an example of the line-item pattern as it could be used to describe the contents of a shipment. Assume that the shipment includes the names and quantities of various items as well as each item's insured value. Place the insurance value per item in an ITEM entity.

5.53 What entity type should come to mind when you see the words "For use by" in a form?

5.54 Give examples of 1:1, 1:N, and N:M recursive relationships (other than those presented in this chapter).

5.55 Explain why the data modeling process must be iterative. Use the Highline University example.

Project Questions

Answer the following questions using IE Crow's Foot notation.

5.56 Examine the subscription form shown in Figure 5-53. Using the structure of this form, do the following:

    A. Create a model with one entity. Specify the identifier and attributes.

    B. Create a model with two entities, one for customer and a second for subscription. Specify identifiers, attributes, relationship name, type, and cardinalities.

    C. Under what conditions do you prefer the model in A to that in B?

    D. Under what conditions do you prefer the model in B to that in A?

5.57 Examine the list of email messages in Figure 5-54. Using the structure and example data items in this list, do the following:

    A. Create a single-entity data model for this list. Specify the identifier and all entities.

    B. Modify your answer to A to include entities SENDER and SUBJECT. Specify the identifiers and attributes of entities and the types and cardinalities of the relationships. Explain which cardinalities can be inferred from Figure 5-54 and which need to be checked out with users.

    C. The email address in the From column in Figure 5-54 is in two different styles. One style has the true email address; the second style (e.g., Tom Cooper) is the name of an entry in the user's email directory. Create two categories of SENDER based on these two styles. Specify identifiers and attributes.

5.58 Examine the list of stock quotes in Figure 5-55. Using the structure and example data items in this list, do the following:

    A. Create a single-entity data model for this list. Specify the identifier and attributes.

FIGURE 5-53

Subscription Form

Subscription Form

☐ 1 year (6 issues) for just $18—20% off the newsstand price.
(Outside the U.S. $21/year—U.S. funds, please)

☐ 2 years (12 issues) for just $34—save 24%
(Outside the U.S. $40/2 years—U.S. funds, please)

Name _____

Address_____

City_____ State _____ Zip _____

☐ My payment is enclosed. ☐ Please bill me.

Please start my subscription with ☐ *current issue* ☐ *next issue .*

From	Subject	Date	Size
SailorBob256@somewhere.com	Big Wind	5/13/2015	3 KB
SailorBob256@somewhere.com	Update	5/12/2015	4 KB
SailorBob256@somewhere.com	Re: Saturday Am	5/11/2015	4 KB
SailorBob256@somewhere.com	Re: Weather window!	5/10/2015	4 KB
SailorBob256@somewhere.com	Re: Howdy!	5/10/2015	3 KB
SailorBob256@somewhere.com	Still here	5/9/2015	3 KB
SailorBob256@somewhere.com	Re: Turle Bay	5/8/2015	4 KB
SailorBob256@somewhere.com	Turle Bay	5/8/2015	4 KB
SailorBob256@somewhere.com	Re: Hi	5/6/2015	3 KB
SailorBob256@somewhere.com	Sunday, Santa Maria	5/5/2015	3 KB
MotorboatBobby314@elsewhere.com	Cabo, Thurs. Noon	5/2/2015	2 KB
SailorBob256@somewhere.com	turbo	5/1/2015	3 KB
SailorBob256@somewhere.com	on our way	4/28/2015	3 KB
TugboatAmanda756@anotherwhere.com	RE: Hola!	4/26/2015	3 KB
TugboatAmanda756@anotherwhere.com	RE: Hola!	4/24/2015	2 KB
TugboatAmanda756@anotherwhere.com	RE: Hola!	4/23/2015	3 KB

FIGURE 5-54
Email List

B. Modify your answer to A to include the entities COMPANY and INDEX. Specify the identifier and attributes of the entities and the types and cardinalities of the relationships. Explain which cardinalities can be inferred from Figure 5-55 and which need to be checked out with users.

C. The list in Figure 5-55 is for a quote on a particular day at a particular time of day. Suppose that the list were changed to show closing daily prices for each of these stocks and that it includes a new column: QuoteDate. Modify your model in B to reflect this change.

D. Change your model in C to include the tracking of a portfolio. Assume the portfolio has an owner name, a phone number, an email address, and a list of stocks held. The list includes the identity of the stock and the number of shares held. Specify all additional entities, their identifiers and attributes, and the type and cardinality of each relationship.

E. Change your answer to part D to keep track of portfolio stock purchases and sales in a portfolio. Specify entities, their identifiers and attributes, and the type and cardinality of each relationship.

FIGURE 5-55
Stock Quotations

Symbol	Name	Last	Change	% Chg
$COMPX	Nasdaq Combined Composite Index	1,400.74 ▼	-4.87	-0.35%
$INDU	Dow Jones Industrial Average Index	9,255.10 ▼	-19.80	-0.21%
$INX	S&P 500 INDEX	971.14 ▼	-5.84	-0.60%
ALTR	Altera Corporation	13.45 ▼	-0.450	-3.24%
AMZN	Amazon.com, Inc.	15.62 ▲	+0.680	+4.55%
CSCO	Cisco Systems, Inc.	13.39 ▼	-0.280	-2.05%
DELL	Dell Computer Corporation	24.58 ▼	-0.170	-0.69%
ENGCX	Enterprise Growth C	14.60 ▼	-0.210	-1.42%
INTC	Intel Corporation	18.12 ▼	-0.380	-2.05%
JNJ	Johnson & Johnson	53.29 ▼	-0.290	-0.54%
KO	Coca-Cola Company	56.70 ▼	-0.580	-1.01%
MSFT	Microsoft Corporation	53.96 ▲	+1.040	+1.97%
NKE	NIKE, Inc.	57.34 ▲	+0.580	+1.02%

FIGURE 5-56

Air Compressor
Specifications

Single Stage Air Compressors Set 95 to 150 PSI also available, substitute "C" for "A" in model number. i.e., S15A-30 make S15E-30												
			Air Performance								**Dimensions**	
HP	Model	Tank Gal	**A @ 125**			**C @ 150**			Approx Ship Weight			
			Pump RPM	CFM Disp	DEL'D Air	Pump RPM	CFM Disp	DEL'D Air		L	W	H
1/2	R12A-17	17	680	3.4	2.2	590	2.9	1.6	135	37	14	25
3/4	R34A-17	17	1080	5.3	3.1	950	4.7	2.3	140	37	14	25
3/4	R34A-30	30	1080	5.3	3.1	950	4.7	2.3	160	38	16	31
1	S1A-30	30	560	6.2	4.0	500	5.7	3.1	190	38	16	34
1 1/2	S15A-30	30	870	9.8	6.2	860	9.7	5.8	205	49	20	34
1 1/2	S15A-60	60	870	9.8	6.2	860	9.7	5.8	315	38	16	34
2	S2A-30	30	1140	13.1	8.0	1060	12.0	7.0	205	49	20	39
2	S2A-60	60	1140	13.1	8.0	1060	12.0	7.0	315	48	20	34
2	TD2A-30	30	480	13.1	9.1	460	12.4	7.9	270	38	16	36
2	TD2A-60	60	480	13.1	9.1	460	12.4	7.9	370	49	20	41
3	TD3A-60	60	770	21.0	14.0	740	19.9	12.3	288	38	16	36
5	TD5A-80	60	770	21.0	14.0	740	19.9	12.3	388	49	20	41
5	TD5A-60	60	1020	27.8	17.8	910	24.6	15.0	410	49	20	41
5	TD5A-80	80	1020	27.8	17.8	910	24.6	15.0	450	62	20	41
5	UE5A-80	60	780	28.7	19.0	770	28.6	18.0	570	49	23	43
5	UE5A-80	80	780	28.7	19.0	770	28.6	18.0	610	63	23	43

5.59 Figure 5-56 shows the specifications for single-stage air compressor products. Note that there are two product categories that are based on Air Performance: The A models are at 125 pounds per square inch of pressure, and the C models are at 150 pounds per square inch of pressure. Using the structure and example data items in this list, do the following:

A. Create a set of exclusive subtypes to represent these compressors. The supertype will have attributes for all single-stage compressors, and the subtypes will have attributes for products having the two different types of Air Performance. Assume that there might be additional products with different types of Air Performance. Specify the entities, identifiers, attributes, relationships, type of category cluster, and possible determinant.

B. Figure 5-57 shows a different model for the compressor data. Explain the entities, their types, the relationship, its type, and its cardinality. How well do you think this model fits the data shown in Figure 5-56?

C. Compare your answer in part A with the model in Figure 5-56. What are the essential differences between the two models? Which do you think is better?

FIGURE 5-57

Alternative Model for Air
Compressor Data

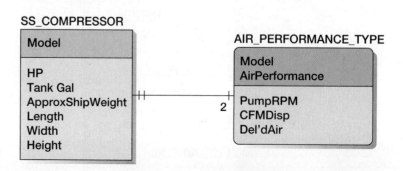

D. Suppose you had the job of explaining the differences in these two models to a highly motivated, intelligent end user. How would you accomplish this?

5.60 Figure 5-58 shows a listing of movie times at theaters in Seattle, Washington. Using the data in this figure as an example, do the following:

A. Create a model to represent this report using the entities MOVIE, THEATER, and SHOW_TIME. Assume that theaters may show multiple movies. Although this report is for a particular day, your data model should allow for movie times on different days as well. Specify the identifiers of the entities and their attributes. Name the relationships and the type and cardinality of each relationship. Explain which cardinalities you can logically deduce from Figure 5-58 and which need to be checked out with users. Assume that distance is an attribute of THEATER.

B. This report was prepared for a user who is located near downtown Seattle. Suppose that it is necessary to produce this same report for these theaters, but for a user located in a Seattle suburb, such as Bellevue, Renton, Redmond, or Tacoma. In this case, distance cannot be an attribute of THEATER. Change your answer in A for this situation. Specify the entity identifiers and attributes. Name the relationships and identify the type and cardinality of each relationship.

C. Suppose that you want to make this data model national. Change your answer to B so that it can be used for other metropolitan areas. Change your answer in

FIGURE 5-58

Movie Time Listing

Movie

The Hunger Games

Jennifer Lawrence, Josh Hutcherson, Liam Hemsworth, Woody Harrelson, and Elizabeth Banks lead a standout cast in this depiction of a dystopian future.

Local Theaters and Showtimes

40 miles from the center of Seattle, WA Change Area
Tue, Jul 9 Wed Thu Fri Sat

Displaying 1 - 32 results, sorted by distance.

AMC Pacific Place 11 (0.5 miles)
600 Pine St, Seattle (206) 652-2404
Showtimes: 11:00 am, 12:00 pm, 12:45 pm, 1:30 pm, 2:30 pm, 3:15 pm, 4:00 pm, 5:00 pm, 5:45 pm, 6:30 pm, 7:30 pm, 8:30 pm, 9:00 pm, 10:00 pm, 10:45 pm

Neptune Theatre (3.9 miles)
1303 NE 45th, Seattle (206) 633-5545
Showtimes: 11:20 am, 1:30 pm, 3:40 pm, 5:50 pm, 8:00 pm, 10:10 pm

Regal Bellevue Galleria 11 (6.2 miles)
500 106th Ave NE, Bellevue (425) 451-7161
Showtimes: 11:00 am, 11:30 am, 1:00 pm, 1:30 pm, 3:00 pm, 3:30 pm, 5:05 pm, 5:35 pm, 7:10 pm, 7:40 pm, 9:20 pm, 9:50 pm

LCE Oak Tree Cinema (6.6 miles)
10006 Aurora Ave N., Seattle (206) 527-1748
Showtimes: 11:45 am, 2:15 pm, 4:45 pm, 7:15 pm, 9:45 pm

LCE Factoria Cinemas 8 (7.8 miles)
3505 Factoria Blvd SE, Bellevue (425) 641-9206
Showtimes: 12:00 pm, 1:00 pm, 2:15 pm, 3:15 pm, 4:30 pm, 5:45 pm, 7:30 pm, 8:15 pm, 9:45 pm, 10:30 pm

Kirkland Parkplace Cinema (8 miles)
404 Parkplace Ctr, Kirkland (425) 827-9000
Showtimes: 12:15 pm, 2:30 pm, 4:45 pm, 7:20 pm, 9:35 pm

A for this situation. Specify the entity identifiers and attributes. Name the relationships and identify the type and cardinality of each relationship.

D. Modify your answer to C to include the leading cast members. Assume that the role of a cast member is not to be modeled. Specify the identifiers of new entities and their attributes. Name the relationships and identify the type and cardinality of each relationship.

E. Modify your answer to C to include the leading cast members. Assume that the role of a cast member is specified. Specify the identifiers of new entities and their attributes. Name the relationships and identify the type and cardinality of each relationship.

5.61 Consider the three reports in Figure 5-59. The data are samples of data that would appear in the reports like these.

A. Make a list of as many potential entities as these reports suggest.

FIGURE 5-59

Cereal Product Reports

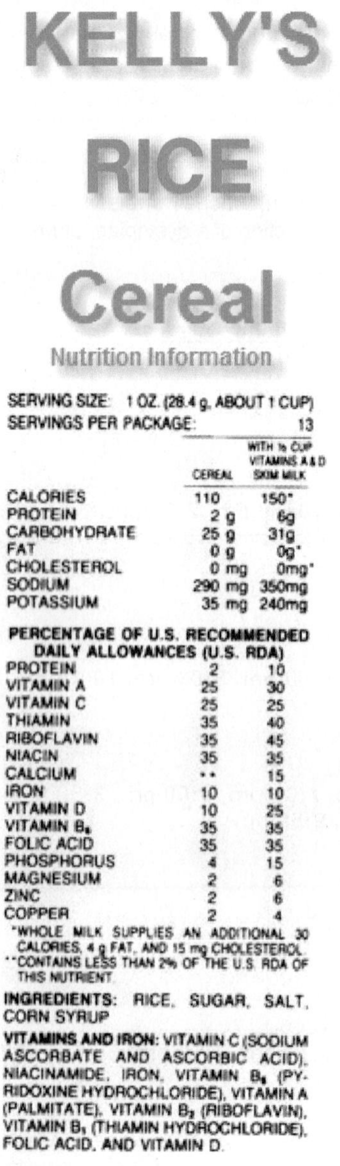

KELLY'S RICE Cereal

Nutrition Information

SERVING SIZE: 1 OZ. (28.4 g, ABOUT 1 CUP)
SERVINGS PER PACKAGE: 13

	CEREAL	WITH ½ CUP VITAMINS A & D SKIM MILK
CALORIES	110	150*
PROTEIN	2 g	6g
CARBOHYDRATE	25 g	31g
FAT	0 g	0g*
CHOLESTEROL	0 mg	0mg*
SODIUM	290 mg	350mg
POTASSIUM	35 mg	240mg

PERCENTAGE OF U.S. RECOMMENDED DAILY ALLOWANCES (U.S. RDA)

PROTEIN	2	10
VITAMIN A	25	30
VITAMIN C	25	25
THIAMIN	35	40
RIBOFLAVIN	35	45
NIACIN	35	35
CALCIUM	**	15
IRON	10	10
VITAMIN D	10	25
VITAMIN B₆	35	35
FOLIC ACID	35	35
PHOSPHORUS	4	15
MAGNESIUM	2	6
ZINC	2	6
COPPER	2	4

*WHOLE MILK SUPPLIES AN ADDITIONAL 30 CALORIES, 4 g FAT, AND 15 mg CHOLESTEROL.
**CONTAINS LESS THAN 2% OF THE U.S. RDA OF THIS NUTRIENT.

INGREDIENTS: RICE, SUGAR, SALT, CORN SYRUP

VITAMINS AND IRON: VITAMIN C (SODIUM ASCORBATE AND ASCORBIC ACID), NIACINAMIDE, IRON, VITAMIN B₆ (PYRIDOXINE HYDROCHLORIDE), VITAMIN A (PALMITATE), VITAMIN B₂ (RIBOFLAVIN), VITAMIN B₁ (THIAMIN HYDROCHLORIDE), FOLIC ACID, AND VITAMIN D.

FDA REPORT #6272
Date: June 30, 2011
Issuer: Kelly's Corporation
Report Title: Product Summary by Ingredient

Corn	Kelly's Corn Cereal
	Kelly's Multigrain Cereal
	Kelly's Crunchy Cereal
Corn syrup	Kelly's Corn Cereal
	Kelly's Rice Cereal
	Kelly's Crunchy Cereal
Malt	Kelly's Corn Cereal
	Kelly's Crunchy Cereal
Wheat	Kelly's Multigrain Cereal
	Kelly's Crunchy Cereal

SUPPLIERS LIST
Date: June 30, 2011

Ingredient	Supplier	Price
Corn	Wilson	2.80
	J. Perkins	2.72
	Pollack	2.83
	McKay	2.80
Wheat	Adams	1.19
	Kroner	1.19
	Schmidt	1.22
Barley	Wilson	0.85
	Pollack	0.84

B. Examine your list to determine whether any entities are synonyms. If so, consolidate your list.

C. Construct an IE Crow's Foot model showing relationships among your entities. Name each relationship and specify cardinalities. Indicate which cardinalities you can justify on the basis of these reports and which you will need to check out with the users.

5.62 Consider the CD cover in Figure 5-60.

A. Specify identifiers and attributes for the entities CD, ARTIST, ROLE, and SONG.

B. Construct a crow's foot model showing relationships among these four entities. Name each relationship and specify cardinalities. Indicate which cardinalities you can justify on the basis of the CD cover and which you will need to check out with the users.

C. Consider a CD that does not involve a musical, so there is no need for ROLE. However, the entity SONG_WRITER is needed. Create a crow's foot model for CD, ARTIST, SONG, and SONG_WRITER. Assume that an ARTIST can either be a group or an individual. Assume that some artists record individually and as part of a group.

D. Combine the models you developed in your answers to B and C. Create new entities if necessary, but strive to keep your model as simple as possible. Specify identifiers and attributes of new entities, name new relationships, and indicate their cardinalities.

5.63 Consider the data model in Figure 5-43. How should this model be altered if the users want to keep track of how many of each part are used? Suppose, for example, that the wheel assembly requires four washers and the handle assembly requires just one and the database must store these quantities. (Hint: Adding Quantity to this N:M relationship is analogous to adding Price to the N:M relationship in Figure 5-22.)

5.64 The data model in Figure 5-52 uses the attribute Room in COLLEGE and DEPARTMENT but uses OfficeNumber in PROFESSOR. These attributes have the same kind of data, even though they have different names. Examine Figure 5-46 and explain how this situation came to be. Do you think having different names for the same attribute types is rare? Do you think it is a problem? Why or why not?

FIGURE 5-60

CD Cover

West Side Story
Based on a conception of Jerome Robbins

Book by ARTHUR LAURENTS
Music by LEONARD BERNSTEIN
Lyrics by STEPHEN SONDHEIM

Entire Original Production Directed
and Choreographed by JEROME ROBBINS

Originally produced on Broadway by Robert E. Griffith and Harold S. Prince
by arrangement with Roger L. Stevens
Orchestration by Leonard Bernstein with Sid Ramin and Irwin Kostal

HIGHLIGHTS FROM THE COMPLETE RECORDING

Maria . . . . KIRI TE KANAWA	
Tony . . . . JOSE CARRERAS	
Anita . . . . TATIANA TROYANOS	
Riff . . . . KURT OLLMAN	
and MARILYN HORNE singing "Somewhere"	

Rosalia . . . . Louise Edeiken	Diesel . . . . Marty Nelson
Consuela. . . . . Stella Zambalis	Baby John . . . . . Stephen Bogardus
Fancisca. . . . . Angelina Reaux	A-rab . . . . Peter Thom
Action . . . . David Livingston	Snowboy . . . . Todd Lester
Bernardo. . . . Richard Harrell	

1	Jet Song (Riff, Action, Baby John, A-rab, Chorus)	[3'13]
2	Something's Coming (Tony)	[2'33]
3	Maria (Tony)	[2'56]
4	Tonight (Maria, Tony)	[5'27]
5	America (Anita, Rosalia, Chorus)	[4'47]
6	Cool (Riff, Chorus)	[4'37]
7	One Hand, One Heart (Tony, Maria)	[5'38]
8	Tonight (Ensemble) (Entire Cast)	[3'40]
9	I Feel Pretty (Maria, Chorus)	[3'22]
10	Somewhere (A Girl)	[2'34]
11	Gee Officer Krupke (Action, Snowboy, Diesel, A-rab, Baby John, Chorus)	[4'18]
12	A Boy Like That (Anita, Maria)	[2'05]
13	I Have a Love (Maria, Anita)	[3'30]
14	Taunting Scene (Orchestra)	[1'21]
15	Finale (Maria, Tony)	[2'40]

Case Questions

Writer's Patrol Case Questions

Consider the Writer's Patrol traffic citation shown in Figure 5-61. The rounded corners on this form provide graphical hints about the boundaries of the entities represented.

A. Draw an E-R data model based on the traffic citation form. Use five entities, and use the data items on the form to specify identifiers and attributes for those entities. Use the IE Crow's Foot E-R model for your diagram.

B. Specify relationships among the entities. Name the relationships and specifiy the relationship types and cardinalities. Justify the decisions you make regarding minimum and maximum cardinalities, indicating which cardinalities can be inferred from data on the form and which need to be checked out with systems users.

Highline University Mentor Program Case Questions

Highline University is a four-year undergraduate school located in the Puget Sound region of Washington State. A discussion of the design of a college information system for Highline University appears in this chapter on pages 228–234 as an example of creating data models, and a variant of that discussion is used in Appendix B.

In this set of case questions, we will consider a different information system for Highline University, one that will be used by the Highline University Mentor Program. The Highline University Mentor Program recruits business professionals as mentors for Highline University students. The mentors are unpaid volunteers who work together with the students' advisers to ensure that the students in the mentoring program learn needed and relevant management skills. In this case study, you will develop a data model for the Mentor Program Information System.

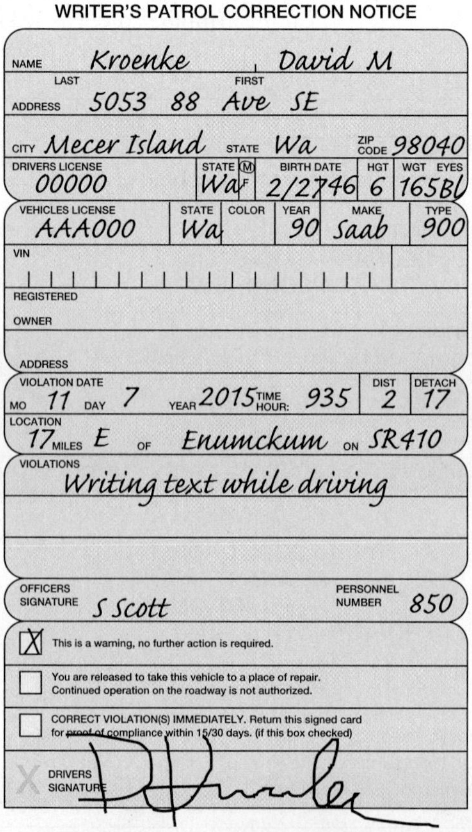
WRITER'S PATROL CORRECTION NOTICE

NAME Kroenke, David M
LAST FIRST
ADDRESS 5053 88 Ave SE
CITY Mecer Island STATE Wa ZIP CODE 98040
DRIVERS LICENSE 00000 STATE Wa M/F BIRTH DATE 2/27/46 HGT 6 WGT 165 EYES Bl
VEHICLES LICENSE AAA000 STATE Wa COLOR YEAR 90 MAKE Saab TYPE 900
VIN
REGISTERED
OWNER
ADDRESS
VIOLATION DATE MO 11 DAY 7 YEAR 2015 TIME HOUR: 935 DIST 2 DETACH 17
LOCATION 17 MILES E OF Enumckum ON SR410
VIOLATIONS Writing text while driving
OFFICERS SIGNATURE S Scott PERSONNEL NUMBER 850
[X] This is a warning, no further action is required.
[ ] You are released to take this vehicle to a place of repair. Continued operation on the roadway is not authorized.
[ ] CORRECT VIOLATION(S) IMMEDIATELY. Return this signed card for ~~proof of~~ compliance within 15/30 days. (if this box checked)
X DRIVERS SIGNATURE

FIGURE 5-61
Writer's Patrol Traffic Citation

Highline University, like many colleges and universities in the Pacific Northwest (see the Wikipedia article on *Pacific_Northwest*), is accredited by the Northwest Commission on Colleges and Universities (NWCCU–see the NWCCU Web site). Like all the colleges and universities accredited by the NWCCU, Highline University must be reaccredited at approximately five-year intervals. Additionally, the NWCCU requires annual status-update reports.

Highline University is made up of five colleges: the College of Business, the College of Social Sciences and Humanities, the College of Performing Arts, the College of Sciences and Technology, and the College of Environmental Sciences. Jan Smathers is the president of Highline University, and Dennis Endersby is the provost (a provost is a vice president of academics; the deans of the colleges report to the provost). Highline University is a fictional university and should not be confused with Highline Community College located in Des Moines, Washington. Any resemblance between Highline University and Highline Community College is unintentional and purely coincidental.

A. Draw an E-R data model for the Highline University Mentor Program Information System (MPIS). Use the IE Crow's Foot E-R model for your E-R diagrams. Justify the decisions you make regarding minimum and maximum cardinalities.

Your model should track students, advisers, and mentors. Additionally, Highline University needs to track alumni because the program administrators view alumni as potential mentors.

1. Create separate entities for students, alumni, faculty advisers, and mentors.

- At Highline University, all students are required to live on campus and are assigned Highline University ID numbers and email accounts in the format *FirstName.LastName@students.hu.edu.* The student entity should track student last name, student first name, student University ID number, student email address, dorm name, dorm room number, and dorm phone number.

- At Highline University, all faculty advisers have on-campus offices and are assigned Highline University ID numbers and email accounts in the format *FirstName.LastName@hu.edu.* The faculty entity should track faculty last name, faculty first name, faculty University ID number, faculty email address, department, office building name, office building room number, and office phone number.

- Highline University alumni live off campus and were previously assigned Highline University ID numbers. Alumni have private email accounts in the format *FirstName.LastName@somewhere.com.* The alumni entity should track alumnus last name, alumnus first name, alumnus former student number, email address, home address, home city, home state, home ZIP code, and phone number.

- Highline University mentors work for companies and use their company address, phone, and email address for contact information. They do not have Highline University ID numbers as mentors. Email addresses are in the format *FirstName.LastName@companyname.com.* The mentor entity should track mentor last name, mentor first name, mentor email address, company name, company address, company city, company state, company ZIP code, and company phone number.

2. Create relationships between entities based on the following facts:

- Each student is assigned one and only one faculty adviser and must have an adviser. One faculty member may advise several students, but faculty members are not required to advise students. Only the fact of this assignment is to be recorded in the data model–not possible related data (such as the date the adviser was assigned to the student).

- Each student may be assigned one and only one mentor, but students are not required to have a mentor. One mentor may mentor several students, and a person may be listed as a mentor before he or she is actually assigned students to mentor. Only the fact of this assignment is to be recorded in the data model–not possible related data (such as the date the mentor was assigned to the student).

■ Each mentor is assigned to work and coordinate with one and only one faculty member, and each mentor must work with a faculty member. One faculty member may work with several mentors, but faculty members are not required to work with mentors. Only the fact of this assignment is to be recorded in the data model—not possible related data (such as the date the faculty member was assigned to the mentor).

■ Each mentor may be an alumnus, but mentors are not required to be alumni. Alumni cannot, of course, be required to become mentors.

B. Revise the E-R data model you created in part A to create a new E-R data model based on the fact that students, faculty, alumni, and mentors are all a PERSON. Use the IE Crow's Foot E-R model for your E-R diagrams. Justify the decisions you make regarding minimum and maximum cardinalities. Note that:

■ A person may be a current student, an alumnus, or both because Highline University does have alumni return for further study.

■ A person may be a faculty member or a mentor but not both.

■ A person may be a faculty member and an alumnus.

■ A person may be a mentor and an alumnus.

■ A current student cannot be a mentor.

■ Each mentor may be an alumnus, but mentors are not required to be alumni.

■ Alumni cannot, of course, be required to become mentors.

C. Extend and modify the E-R data model you created in part B to allow more data to be recorded in the MPIS system. Use the IE Crow's Foot E-R model for your E-R diagrams. Justify the decisions you make regarding minimum and maximum cardinalities. The MPIS needs to record:

■ The date a student enrolled at Highline University, the date the student graduated, and the degree the student received.

■ The date an adviser was assigned to a student and the date the assignment ended.

■ The date an adviser was assigned to work with a mentor and the date the assignment ended.

■ The date a mentor was assigned to a student and the date the assignment ended.

D. Write a short discussion of the differences between the three data models you have created. How does data model B differ from data model A, and how does data model C differ from data model B? What additional features of the E-R data model were introduced when you created data models B and C?

The Queen Anne Curiosity Shop

The Queen Anne Curiosity Shop wants to expand its database applications beyond the current recording of sales. The company still wants to maintain data on customers, employees, vendors, sales, and items, but it wants to (a) modify the way it handles inventory and (b) simplify the storage of customer and employee data.

Currently, each item is considered unique, which means the item must be sold as a whole, and multiple units of the item in stock must be treated as separate items in the ITEM table. The Queen Anne Curiosity Shop management wants the database modified to include an inventory system that will allow multiple units of an item to be stored under one ItemID. The system should allow for a quantity on hand, a quantity on order, and an order due date. If the identical item is stocked by multiple vendors, the item should be orderable from any of these vendors. The SALE_ITEM table should then include Quantity and ExtendedPrice columns to allow for sales of multiple units of an item.

The Queen Anne Curiosity Shop management has noticed that some of the fields in CUSTOMER and EMPLOYEE store similar data. Under the current system, when an employee buys something at the store, his or her data has to be reentered into the

CUSTOMER table. The managers would like to have the CUSTOMER and EMPLOYEE tables redesigned using subtypes.

A. Draw an E-R data model for the Queen Anne Curiosity Shop database schema shown in Chapter 3's *The Queen Anne Curiosity Shop Project Questions*. Use the IE Crow's Foot E-R model for your E-R diagrams. Justify the decisions you make regarding minimum and maximum cardinalities.

B. Extend and modify the E-R data model by adding only the Queen Anne Curiosity Shop's inventory system requirements. Use the IE Crow's Foot E-R model for your E-R diagrams. Create appropriate identifiers and attributes for each entity. Justify the decisions you make regarding minimum and maximum cardinalities.

C. Extend and modify the E-R data model by adding only the Queen Anne Curiosity Shop's need for more efficient storage of CUSTOMER and EMPLOYEE data. Use the IE Crow's Foot E-R model for your E-R diagrams. Create appropriate identifiers and attributes for each entity. Justify the decisions you make regarding minimum and maximum cardinalities.

D. Combine the E-R data models from parts B and C to meet all of the Queen Anne Curiosity Shop's new requirements, making additional modifications as needed. Use the IE Crow's Foot E-R model for your E-R diagrams.

E. Describe how you would go about validating your data model in part D.

Morgan Importing

James Morgan of Morgan Importing has decided to expand his business and needs to staff and support a *procurement system*[6] to acquire the items sold at Morgan Importing. Suppose that you have been hired to create and implement a database application to support a procurement information system. Data in this procurement information system will include:

- The purchasing agents employed at Morgan Importing.
- The receiving clerks employed at Morgan Importing.
- The stores where the purchasing agents buy items.
- The purchases themselves at the store.
- The shippers used to ship the purchases to Morgan Importing.
- The shipments made by the shippers.
- The receipt of the shipments at Morgan Importing by the receiving clerks.

James Morgan and his wife Susan often make purchases themselves while traveling to various countries (and, therefore, even though they are not purchasing agents per se, they need to be listed as purchasing agents in the system when data is entered). Purchases may be made at the stores themselves or by Internet or phone. Sometimes several items are purchased from a store on a single visit, but do not assume that all of the items are placed on the same shipment. Shipping must track each item in a shipment and assign a separate insurance value to each item. Receiving must track the arrival date and time of a shipment, who accepted receipt of the shipment on behalf of Morgan Importing, and the condition of each item upon receipt.

A. Using your knowledge, create a data model for the Morgan Importing procurement information system. Name each entity, describe its type, and indicate all attributes and identifiers. Name each relationship, describe its type, and specify minimum and maximum cardinalities.

B. List any item in your answer to A that you believe should be checked out with James Morgan and/or his employees.

---

[6]If you are not familiar with the concept of a procurement system, see the Wikipedia article on *Procurement*.

6

Transforming Data Models into Database Designs

Chapter Objectives

- To understand how to transform data models into database designs
- To be able to identify primary keys and understand when to use a surrogate key
- To understand the use of referential integrity constraints
- To understand the use of referential integrity actions
- To be able to represent ID-dependent, 1:1, 1:N, and N:M relationships as tables

- To be able to represent weak entities as tables
- To be able to represent supertype/subtypes as tables
- To be able to represent recursive relationships as tables
- To be able to represent ternary relationships as tables
- To be able to implement referential integrity actions required by minimum cardinalities

This chapter explains the transformation of entity-relationship data models into relational database designs. This transformation consists of three primary tasks: (1) replacing entities and attributes with tables and columns; (2) representing relationships and maximum cardinalities by placing foreign keys; and (3) representing minimum cardinality by defining actions to constrain activities on values of primary and foreign keys. Steps 1 and 2 are relatively easy to understand and accomplish; step 3 may be easy or difficult, depending on the minimum cardinality type. In this chapter, we will create database designs, and we will implement a database design in Chapter 7 when we build a database using SQL DDL and DML.

Database design occurs in the **component design** step of the **systems development life cycle (SDLC)** in the **systems analysis and design** process. For an introduction to systems analysis and design and to the SDLC, see Appendix B.

The Purpose of a Database Design

A **database design** is a set of database specifications that can actually be implemented as a database in a DBMS. The *data model* we discussed in Chapter 5 is a *generalized, non-DBMS-specific* design. A database design, on the other hand, is a *DBMS-specific* design intended to be implemented in a DBMS product such as Microsoft SQL Server 2014 or Oracle Database.

Since each DBMS product has its own way of doing things, even if based on the same relational database model and the same SQL standards, each database design must be created for a particular DBMS product. The same data model will result in slightly different database designs depending upon the intended DBMS product.

> **BY THE WAY**   Books on systems analysis and design often identify three design stages:
>
> - Conceptual design (conceptual schema)
> - Logical design (logical schema)
> - Physical design (physical schema)
>
> The *database design* we are discussing is basically equivalent to the *logical design*, which is defined in these books as the conceptual design implemented in a specific DBMS product. The *physical design* deals with aspects of the database encountered when it is actually implemented in the DBMS (as we will discuss in Chapter 10A for Microsoft SQL Server 2014, in Chapter 10B for Oracle Database, and in Chapter 10C for MySQL 5.6), such as physical record and file structure and organization, indexing, and query optimization. However, our discussion of database design *will* include data type specifications, which is often considered a physical design issue in systems analysis and design.

Create a Table for Each Entity

We begin the database design by creating a table for each entity using the steps shown in Figure 6-1. In most cases, the table is assigned the same name as the entity. Each attribute of the entity becomes a column of the table. The identifier of the entity becomes the primary key of the table. The example in Figure 6-2 shows the creation of the EMPLOYEE table from the EMPLOYEE entity. In this text, to differentiate entities from tables, we will show entities with shadowed boxes and tables with nonshadowed boxes. This notation will help clarify our discussion, but be aware that it is not standard notation across the industry.

Be certain that you understand the difference between these similar-looking graphics. The shadowed rectangle in Figure 6-2(a) represents a logical structure that has no physical existence. It is a blueprint. The nonshadowed rectangle in Figure 6-2(b) represents a database table. It is the same as the following notation that we used in Chapters 3 and 4:

EMPLOYEE (**EmployeeNumber,** EmployeeName, Phone, Email, HireDate, ReviewDate, EmpCode)

Note, too, the key symbol next to EmployeeNumber. It documents the fact that EmployeeNumber is the table key, just as the underline does in the notation used in Chapters 3 and 4.

Selecting the Primary Key

The selection of the primary key is important. The DBMS will use the primary key to facilitate searching and sorting of table rows, and some DBMS products use it to organize table storage. DBMS products almost always create indexes and other data structures using the values of the primary key.

FIGURE 6-1

Steps for Transforming a
Data Model into a Database
Design

Transforming a Data Model into a Database Design
1. Create a table for each entity:
– Specify the primary key (consider surrogate keys, as appropriate)
– Specify alternate keys
– Specify properties for each column:
• Null status
• Data type
• Default value (if any)
• Data constraints (if any)
– Verify normalization
2. Create relationships by placing foreign keys
– Relationships between strong entities (1:1, 1:N, N:M)
– Identifying relationships with ID-dependent entities (intersection tables, association patterns, multivalued attributes, archetype/instance patterns)
– Relationships between a strong entity and a weak but non-ID-dependent entity (1:1, 1:N, N:M)
– Mixed relationships
– Relationships between supertype/subtype entities
– Recursive relationships (1:1, 1:N, N:M)
3. Specify logic for enforcing minimum cardinality:
– O-O relationships
– M-O relationships
– O-M relationships
– M-M relationships

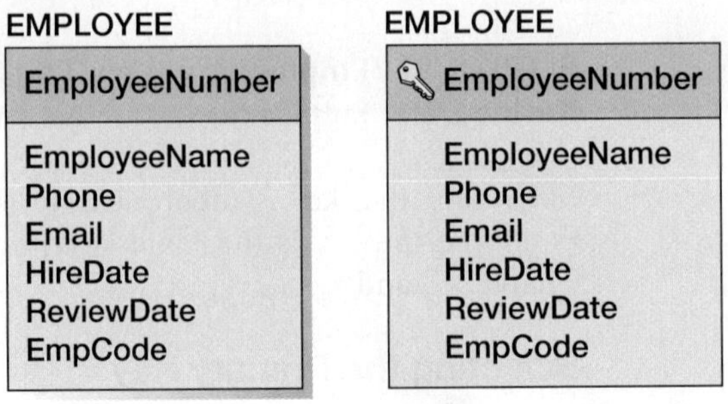

FIGURE 6-2

Transforming an Entity to
a Table

EMPLOYEE

EmployeeNumber
EmployeeName
Phone
Email
HireDate
ReviewDate
EmpCode

EMPLOYEE

🔑 EmployeeNumber
EmployeeName
Phone
Email
HireDate
ReviewDate
EmpCode

(a) EMPLOYEE Entity   **(b)** EMPLOYEE Table

The ideal primary key is short, numeric, and fixed. EmployeeNumber in Figure 6-2 meets all of these conditions and is acceptable. Beware of primary keys such as EmployeeName, Email, (AreaCode, PhoneNumber), (Street, City, State, ZIP), and other long character columns. In cases like these, when the identifier is not short, numeric, or fixed, consider using another candidate key as the primary key. If there are no additional candidate keys, or if none of them is any better, consider using a surrogate key.

A **surrogate key** is a DBMS-supplied identifier of each row of a table. Surrogate key values are unique within the table, and they never change. They are assigned when the row is created, and they are destroyed when the row is deleted. Surrogate key values are the best possible primary keys because they are designed to be short, numeric, and fixed. Because of these advantages, some organizations have gone so far as to require that surrogates be used for the primary key of every table.

Before endorsing such a policy, however, consider two disadvantages of surrogate keys. First, their values have no meaning to a user. Suppose you want to determine the department to which an employee is assigned. If DepartmentName is a foreign key in EMPLOYEE, then when you retrieve an employee row, you obtain a value such as 'Accounting' or 'Finance'. That value may be all that you need to know about department.

Alternatively, if you define the surrogate key DepartmentID as the primary key of DEPARTMENT, then DepartmentID will also be the foreign key in EMPLOYEE. When you retrieve a row of EMPLOYEE, you will get back a number such as 123499788 for the DepartmentID, a value that has no meaning to you at all. You have to perform a second query on DEPARTMENT to obtain DepartmentName.

The second disadvantage of surrogate keys arises when data are shared among different databases. Suppose, for example, that a company maintains three different SALES databases, one for each of three different product lines. Assume that each of these databases has a table called SALES_ORDER that has a surrogate key called ID. The DBMS assigns values to IDs so they are unique within a particular table within a database. It does not, however, assign ID values so they are unique across the three different databases. Thus, it is possible for two different SALES_ORDER rows, in two different databases, to have the same ID value.

This duplication is not a problem until data from the different databases are merged. When that happens, to prevent duplicates, ID values will need to be changed. However, if ID values are changed, then foreign key values may need to be changed as well, and the result is a mess, or at least a lot of work to prevent a mess.

It is, of course, possible to construct a scheme using different starting values for surrogate keys in different databases. Such a policy ensures that each database has its own range of surrogate key values. This requires careful management and procedures, however; and if the starting values are too close to one another, the ranges will overlap and duplicate surrogate key values will still result.

BY THE WAY   Some database designers take the position that, for consistency, if one table has a surrogate key, all of the tables in the database should have a surrogate key. Others think that such a policy is too rigid; after all, there are good data keys, such as ProductSKU (which would use SKU codes discussed in Chapter 2). If such a key exists, it should be used instead of a surrogate key. Your organization may have standards on this issue that you should follow.

Be aware that DBMS products vary in their support for surrogate keys. Microsoft Access 2013, Microsoft SQL Server 2014, and MySQL 5.6 provide them. Microsoft SQL Server 2014 allows the designer to pick the starting value and increment of the key, and MySQL 5.6 allows the designer to pick the starting value. Oracle's Oracle Database, however, does not provide direct support for surrogate keys, but you can obtain the essence of them in a rather backhanded way, as discussed in Chapter 10B.

We use surrogate keys unless there is some strong reason not to. In addition to the advantages described here, the fact that they are fixed simplifies the enforcement of minimum cardinality, as you will learn in the last section of this chapter.

FIGURE 6-3

Representing Alternate Keys

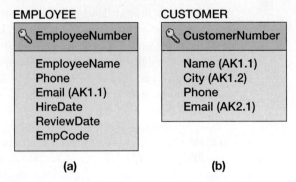

(a)   (b)

Specifying Alternate Keys

The next step in creating a table is to specify the alternate keys. As discussed in Chapter 3, a **candidate key** is an identifier of the unique rows in a table. There may be several candidate keys in a table, and we ultimately choose one of them to be the *primary key* of the table. Each of the *remaining* candidate keys then becomes an **alternate key (AK)** (note that they can still be also referred to as *candidate keys*, in the sense that they uniquely identify the rows in the tables and could be used as the primary key if we choose to). Figure 6-3 illustrates the use of alternate keys, using alternative key (AK) notation.

Figure 6-3(a) shows EMPLOYEE with a primary key of EmployeeNumber and a candidate, or alternate, key of Email. In Figure 6-3(b), CustomerNumber is the primary key of CUSTOMER, and both the composite (Name, City) and Email are candidate keys. In these diagrams, the symbol AK*n.m* means the *n*th alternate key and the *m*th column of that alternate key. In the EMPLOYEE table, Email is labeled AK1.1 because it is the first alternate key and the first column of that key. CUSTOMER has two alternate keys. The first is a composite of two columns, which are labeled AK1.1 and AK1.2. The nomenclature Name (AK1.1) means that Name is the first column of the first alternate key, and City (AK1.2) means that City is the second column of the first alternate key. In CUSTOMER, Email is marked as AK2.1 because it is the first (and only) column of the second alternate key.

Specifying Column Properties

The next step in the creation of a relation is to specify the column properties. Four properties are shown in Figure 6-1: null status, data type, default value, and data constraints.

Null Status

Null status refers to whether the column can have a null value. Typically, null status is specified by using the phrase NULL if nulls are allowed and NOT NULL if not. Thus, NULL does not mean that the column is always null; it means that null values are allowed. Because of this possible confusion, some people prefer the term NULL ALLOWED rather than NULL. Figure 6-4 shows the null status of each of the columns in the EMPLOYEE table.

FIGURE 6-4

Table Display Showing Null
Status

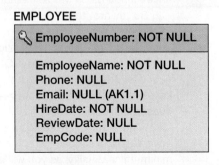

> **BY THE WAY**   The EMPLOYEE table in Figure 6-4 contains a subtlety. EmployeeNumber, the primary key, is marked NOT NULL, but Email, the alternate key, is marked NULL. It makes sense that EmployeeNumber should not be allowed to be null. If it were, and if more than one row had a null value, then EmployeeNumber would not identify a unique row. Why, however, if (1) an alternate key is a candidate key and (2) a candidate key must uniquely identify a row, should Email be allowed to have null values?
>
> The answer is that alternate keys often are used *just to ensure uniqueness*. Marking Email as a (possibly null) alternate key means that Email need not have a value, but, if it has one, then that value will be unique and different from all other values of Email in the EMPLOYEE table.
>
> This answer is dissatisfying because it means that alternate keys used in this manner are not truly alternate *primary* keys, and thus neither are they true *candidate* keys! Alas, that's the way it is. Just know that primary keys can never be null but that alternate keys can be.

Data Type

The next step is to define the data type for each column. For a database design, data types are *DBMS specific*. Unfortunately, each DBMS provides a different set of data types. For example, to record currency values, Microsoft Access has a data type called Currency and Microsoft SQL Server has a data type called Money, but Oracle Database has no data type for currency. Instead, with Oracle, you use the numeric data type for currency values.

Once you know which DBMS you will be using to create the database, use that DBMS product's data types in your design. Figure 6-5 illustrates the display of data types in a table using the data types for SQL Server (e.g., *Char, Varchar, and Date* are Microsoft SQL Server data types). A summary of data types for Microsoft SQL Server 2014, Oracle Database, and MySQL 5.6 is shown in Figure 6-6.

In fact, with many data modeling products, such as CA Technologies' ERwin, you can specify the DBMS you will use and the data modeling product will supply the appropriate set of data types. Other products are DBMS specific. For example, Oracle's MySQL Workbench is intended to design databases for MySQL and therefore uses MySQL-specific data types.

If you do not know which DBMS product you will be using or if you want to preserve independence from a particular DBMS, you can specify the data types in a generic way. The SQL standard defines many standard data types. Typical character string data types are *CHAR(n)* for a fixed-length character string of length *n*, *VARCHAR(n)* for a variable-length character string having a maximum length of *n*, and *NVARCHAR(n)* for a variable-length Unicode character string having a maximum length *n*. Date/Time data types include *DATE* and *TIME*, while numeric data types include *INTEGER (or INT)*, *FLOAT*, *NUMERIC(m,n)* and *DECIMAL(m,n)* [for NUMERIC and DECIMAL, the designation (m,n) means having a maximum length of *m* digits with *n* digits displayed to the right of the decimal place]. If you work for a larger organization, that company probably has its own generic data standards. If so, you should use those data standards.

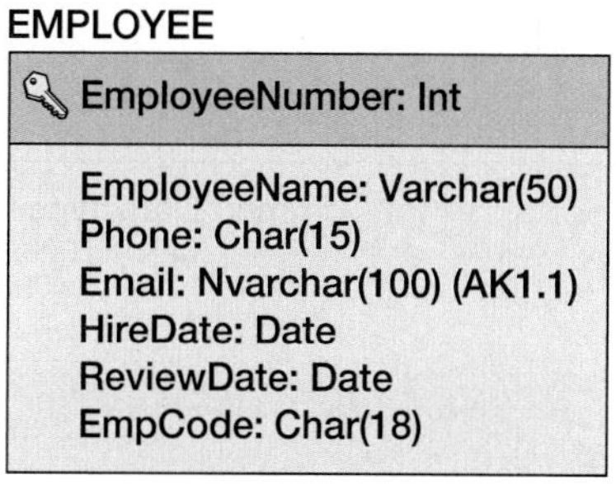

FIGURE 6-5

Table Display Showing Data Types

EMPLOYEE

🔑 **EmployeeNumber: Int**

EmployeeName: Varchar(50)
Phone: Char(15)
Email: Nvarchar(100) (AK1.1)
HireDate: Date
ReviewDate: Date
EmpCode: Char(18)

Numeric Data Types	Description
Bit	1-bit integer. Values of only **0, 1** or **NULL**.
Tinyint	1-byte integer. Range is from **0** to **255**.
Smallint	2-byte integer. Range is from $-2^{(15)}$ (**−32,768**) to $+2^{(15)}$ **−1** (**+32,767**).
Int	4-byte integer. Range is from $-2^{(31)}$ (**−2,147,483,468**) to $+2^{(31)}$ **−1** (**+2,147,483,467**).
Bigint	8-byte integer. Range is from $-2^{(63)}$ (**−9,223,372,036,854,775,808**) to $+2^{(63)}$ **−1** (**+9,223,372,036,854,775,807**).
Decimal (p[,s])	Fixed precision (p) and scale (s) numbers. Range is from -10^{38} **+1** to 10^{38} **−1** with maximum precision (p) of 38. Precision ranges from 1 through 38, and default precision is 18. Scale (s) indicates the number of digits to the right of the decimal place. Default scale value is 0, and scale values range from 0 to p, where 0 <= s <= p.
Numeric (p[,s])	Numeric works identically to Decimal.
Smallmoney	4-byte money. Range is from **−214,748.3646** to **+214,748.3647** with accuracy of one ten-thousandth of a monetary unit. Use decimal point to separate digits.
Money	9-byte money. Range is from **−922,337,203,685,477.5808** to **+922,337,203,685,477.5807** with accuracy of one ten-thousandth of a monetary unit. Use decimal point to separate digits.
Float (n)	n-bit storage of the mantissa in scientific floating point notation. The value of n ranges from 1 to 53, and the default is 53.
Real	Equivalent to Float (24).
Date and Time Data Types	**Description**
Date	3-bytes fixed. Default format YYYY-MM-DD. Range is from **January 1, 1** (0001-01-01) through **December 31, 9999** (9999-12-31).
Time	5-bytes fixed is default with 100 nanosecond precision (.0000000). Default format is HH:MM:SS.NNNNNNN. Range is from **00:00:00.0000000** through **23:59:59.9999999**.
Smalldatetime	4-bytes fixed. Restricted date range, and rounds time to nearest second. Range is from **January 1, 1900 00:00:00 AM** (1900-01-01 00:00:00) through **June 6, 2079 23:59.59 PM** (2079-06-06 23:59.59).
Datetime	8-bytes fixed. Basically combines Date and Time, but spans less dates and has less time precision (rounds to .000, .003 or .007 seconds). Use DATETIME2 for more precision. Date range is from **January 1, 1753** (1753-01-01) through **December 31, 9999** (9999-12-31).
Datetime2	8-bytes fixed. Combines Date and Time with full precision. Use instead of DATETIME. Range is from **January 1, 1 00:00:00.0000000 AM** (0001-01-01 00:00:00.0000000) through **December 31, 9999 23:59.59.9999999 PM** (9999-12-31 23:59.59.9999999).

(a) Common Data Types in SQL Server 2014

FIGURE 6-6

SQL Data Types in DBMS
Products

Date and Time Data Types	Description
Datetimeoffset	10-byte fixed-length default with 100 nanosecond precision (.0000000). Uses 24 hour clock, based on Coordinated Universal Time (UTC). UTC is a refinement of Greenwich Mean Time (GMT), based on the prime meridian at Greenwich, England, which defines when midnight (00:00:00.0000000) occurs. Offset is the time zone difference from the Greenwich time zone. Default format is YYYY-MM-DD HH:MM:SS.NNNNNNN (+|−)HH:MM. Range is from **January 1, 1 00:00:00.0000000 AM** (0001-01-01 00:00:00.0000000) through **December 31, 9999 23:59.59.9999999 PM** (9999-12-31 23:59.59.9999999) with an **offset of −14:59 to +14:59.** Use for 24 hour time.
Timestamp	See documentation.

String Data Types	Description
Char (n)	n-byte fixed-length string data (non-Unicode). Range of n is from **1** through **8000.**
Varchar (n | max)	n-byte variable-length string data (non-Unicode). Range of n is from **1** through **8000.** Max creates a maximum $+2^{(31)} -1$ bytes (2 GBytes).
Text	Use VARCHAR(max). See documentation.
Nchar (n)	(n x 2)-byte fixed-length **Unicode** string data. Range of n is from **1** through **4000.**
Nvarchar (n | max)	(n x 2)-byte variable-length **Unicode** string data. Range of n is from **1** through **4000.** Max creates a maximum $+2^{(31)} -1$ bytes (2 GBytes).
Ntext	Use NVARCHAR(max). See documentation.
Binary (n)	n-byte fixed-length binary data. Range of n is from **1** through **8000.**

Other Data Types	Description
Varbinary (n | max)	Variable-length binary data. Range of n is from **1** through **8000.** Max creates a maximum $+2^{(31)} -1$ bytes (2 GBytes).
Image	Use VARBINARY(max). See documentation.
Uniqueidentifier	16-byte Globally Unique Identifier (GUID). See documentation.
hierarchyid	See documentation.
Cursor	See documentation.
Table	See documentation.
XML	Use for storing XML data. See documentation.
Sql_variant	See documentation.

(a) continued - Common Data Types in SQL Server 2014

Numeric Data Types	Description
SMALLINT	Synonym for INTEGER, implemented as NUMBER(38,0).
INT	Synonym for INTEGER, implemented as NUMBER(38,0).
INTEGER	When specified as a data type, it is implemented as NUMBER(38,0).
NUMBER (p[,s])	1 to 22 bytes. Fixed precision (p) and scale (s) numbers. Range is from $-10^{38} +1$ to $10^{38} - 1$ with maximum precision (p) of 38. Precision ranges from 1 through 38, and default precision is 18. Scale (s) indicates the number of digits to the right of the decimal place. Default scale value is 0, and scale values range from −84 to 127, where s can be greater than p.

(b) Common Data Types in Oracle Database

FIGURE 6-6
Continued

(continued)

Numeric Data Types	Description
FLOAT (p)	1 to 22 bytes. Implemented as NUMBER(p). The value of p ranges from 1 to 126 bits.
BINARY_FLOAT	4-byte 32-bit floating point number.
BINARY_LONG	8-byte 64-bit floating point number.
RAW (n)	n-byte fixed-length raw binary data. Range of n is from 1 through 2000.
LONG RAW	Raw variable-length binary data. Maximum is 2 GBytes.
BLOB	Maximum [(4-GByte – 1)x(database block size)] binary large object.
BFILE	See documentation.
Date and Time Data Types	**Description**
DATE	7-bytes fixed. Default format is set explicitly with the NLS_DATE_FORMAT parameter. Range is from January 1, 4712 BC through December 31, 9999 AD. It contains the fields YEAR, MONTH, DAY, HOUR, MINUTE and SECOND (no fractional seconds). It does not include a time zone.
TIMESTAMP (p)	Includes fractional seconds base on a precision of p. Default of p is 6, and the range is 0 to 9. 7 to 11-bytes fixed, based on precision. Default format is set explicitly with the NLS_TIMESTAMP_FORMAT parameter. Range is from January 1, 4712 BC through December 31, 9999 AD. It contains the fields YEAR, MONTH, DAY, HOUR, MINUTE and SECOND. It contains fractional seconds. It does not include a time zone.
TIMESTAMP (p) WITH TIME ZONE	Includes fractional seconds base on a precision of p. Default of p is 6, and the range is 0 to 9. 13-bytes fixed. Default format is set explicitly with the NLS_TIMESTAMP_FORMAT parameter. Range is from January 1, 4712 BC through December 31, 9999 AD. It contains the fields YEAR, MONTH, DAY, TIMEZONE_HOUR, TIMEZONE_MINUTE and TIMEZONE_SECOND. It contains fractional seconds. It includes a time zone.
TIMESTAMP (p) WITH LOCAL TIME ZONE	Basically the same as TIMESTAMP WITH TIME ZONE, with the following modifications: (1) Data is stored with times based on the database time zone, and (2) Users view data in session time zone.
INTERVAL YEAR [p(year)] TO MONTH	See documentation.
INTERVAL DAY [p(day)] TO SECOND [p(seconds)]	See documentation.
String Data Types	**Description**
CHAR (n[BYTE | CHAR])	n-byte fixed-length string data (non-Unicode). Range of n is from 1 through **2000**. BYTE and CHAR refer to the semantic usage. See documentation.
VARCHAR2 (n[BYTE | CHAR])	n-byte variable-length string data (non-Unicode). Range of n is from 1 through **4000** BYTEs or CHARACTERs. BYTE and CHAR refer to the semantic usage. See documentation.
NCHAR (n)	(n x 2)-byte fixed-length **Unicode** string data. Up to (n x 3)-bytes for UTF8 encoding. Maximum size is from **2000** bytes.

(b) continued - Common Data Types in Oracle Database

FIGURE 6-6

Continued

String Data Types	Description
NVARCHAR2 (n)	Variable-length **Unicode** string data. Up to (n x 3)-bytes for UTF8 encoding. Maximum size is from **4000** bytes.
LONG	Variable-length string data (non-Unicode) with maximum a maximum $2^{(31-1)}$ bytes (2 GBytes). See documentation.
CLOB	Maximum [(4-GByte – 1)x(database block size)] character large object (non-Unicode). Supports fixed-length and variable length character sets.
NCLOB	Maximum [(4-GByte – 1)x(database block size)] **Unicode** character large object. Supports fixed-length and variable length character sets.
Other Data Types	**Description**
ROWID	See documentation.
UROWID	See documentation.
HTTPURIType	See documentation.
XMLType	Use for storing XML data. See documentation.
SDO_GEOMETRY	See documentation.

(b) continued - Common Data Types in Oracle Database

NumericData Type	Description
BIT (M)	M = 1 to 64.
TINYINT	Range is from –128 to 127.
TINYINT UNSIGNED	Range is from 0 to 255.
BOOLEAN	0 = FALSE; 1 = TRUE.
SMALLINT	Range is from –32,768 to 32,767.
SMALLINT UNSIGNED	Range is from 0 to 65,535.
MEDIUMINT	Range is from –8,388,608 to 8,388,607.
MEDIUMINT UNSIGNED	Range is from 0 to 16,777,215.
INT or INTEGER	Range is from –2,147,483,648 to 2,147,483,647.
INT UNSIGNED or INTEGER UNSIGNED	Range is from 0 to 4,294,967,295.
BIGINT	Range is from –9,223,372,036,854,775,808 to 9,223,372,036,854,775,807.
BIGINT UNSIGNED	Range is from 0 to 1,844,674,073,709,551,615.
FLOAT (P)	P = Precision; Range is from 0 to 24.
FLOAT (M, D)	Small (single-precision) floating-point number: M = Display width D = Number of significant digits
DOUBLE (M, P)	Normal (double-precision) floating-point number: M = Display width P = Precision; Range is from 25 to 53.
DEC (M[,D]) or DECIMAL (M[,D]) or FIXED (M[,D])	Fixed-point number: M = Total number of digits D = Number of decimals.

(c) Common Data Types in MySQL 5.6

FIGURE 6-6

Continued

(continued)

Date and Time Data Types	Description
DATE	YYYY-MM-DD : Range is from 1000-01-01 to 9999-12-31.
DATETIME	YYYY-MM-DD HH:MM:SS.
	Range is from 1000-01-01 00:00:00 to 9999-12-31 23:59:59.
TIMESTAMP	See documentation.
TIME	HH:MM:SS : Range is from 00:00:00 to 23:59:59.
YEAR (M)	M = 2 or 4 (default).
	IF M = 2, then range is from 1970 to 2069 (70 to 69).
	IF M = 4, then range is from 1901 to 2155.
String Data Types	**Description**
CHAR (M)	M = 0 to 255.
VARCHAR (M)	M = 1 to 255.
BLOB (M)	BLOB = Binary Large Object: maximum 65,535 characters.
TEXT (M)	Maximum 65,535 characters.
TINYBLOB MEDIUMBLOB LONGBLOB TINYTEXT MEDIUMTEXT LONGTEXT	See documentation.
ENUM ('value1', 'value2', . . .)	An enumeration. Only one value, but chosen from list. See documentation.
SET ('value1', 'value2', . . .)	A set. Zero or more values, all chosen from list. See documentation.

(c) continued - Common Data Types in MySQL 5.6

FIGURE 6-6

Continued

Figure 6-7 shows the EMPLOYEE table showing both data type and null status. The display becomes crowded, however, and from now on we will show tables with just column names. With most products, you can turn such displays on or off depending on the work you are doing.

> **BY THE WAY** The fact that a design tool is dedicated to one DBMS product does *not* mean that it cannot be used to design databases for other DBMSs. For example, an SQL Server database can be designed in MySQL Workbench, and most of the design will be correct. You will, however, have to understand the relevant differences in the DBMS products and make adjustments when creating the actual database.

Default Value

A **default value** is a value supplied by the DBMS when a new row is created. The value can be a constant, such as the string 'New Hire' for the EmpCode column in EMPLOYEE, or it can be the result of a function, such as the date value of the computer's clock for the HireDate column.

In some cases, default values are computed using more complicated logic. The default value for a price, for example, might be computed by applying a markup to a default cost and then reducing that marked-up price by a customer's discount. In such a case, an application component or a trigger (discussed in Chapter 7) will be written to supply such a value.

It is possible to use the data modeling tool to record default values, but such values often are shown in separate design documentation. Figure 6-8, for example, shows one way that default values are documented.

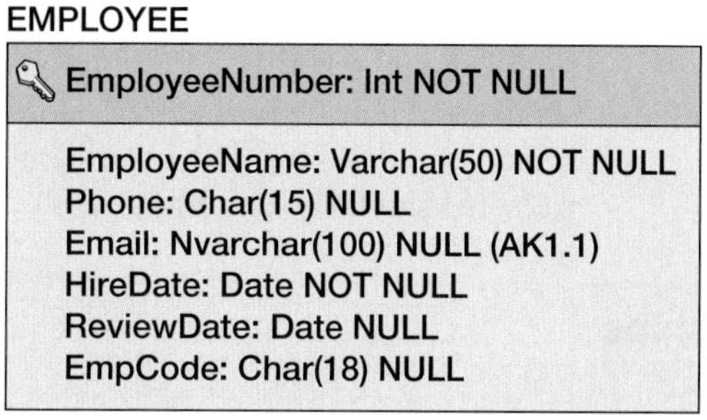

FIGURE 6-7

Table Display Showing Null
Status and Data Types

EMPLOYEE

🔑 EmployeeNumber: Int NOT NULL

EmployeeName: Varchar(50) NOT NULL
Phone: Char(15) NULL
Email: Nvarchar(100) NULL (AK1.1)
HireDate: Date NOT NULL
ReviewDate: Date NULL
EmpCode: Char(18) NULL

Data Constraints

Data constraints are limitations on data values. There are several different types. **Domain constraints** limit column values to a particular set of values. For example, EMPLOYEE.EmpCode could be limited to 'New Hire', 'Hourly', 'Salary', or 'Part Time'. **Range constraints** limit values to a particular interval of values. EMPLOYEE.HireDate, for example, could be limited to dates between January 1, 1990, and December 31, 2025.

An **intrarelation constraint** limits a column's values in comparison with other columns in the same table. The constraint that EMPLOYEE.ReviewDate be at least three months after EMPLOYEE.HireDate is an intrarelation constraint. An **interrelation constraint** limits a column's values in comparison with other columns in other tables. An example for the CUSTOMER table is that CUSTOMER.Name must not be equal to BAD_CUSTOMER.Name, where BAD_CUSTOMER is a table that contains a list of customers with credit and balance problems.

Referential integrity constraints, which we discussed in Chapter 3, are one type of interrelation constraint. Because they are so common, sometimes they are documented only when they are not enforced. For example, to save work, a design team might say that every foreign key is assumed to have a referential integrity constraint to the table that it references and that only exceptions to this rule are documented.

Verify Normalization

The last task in step 1 of Figure 6-1 is to verify table normalization. When data models are developed using forms and reports as guides, they generally result in normalized entities. This occurs because the structures of forms and reports usually reflect how users think about their data. Boundaries of a form, for example, often show the range of a functional dependency. If this is hard to understand, think of a functional dependency as a theme. A well-designed form or report will bracket themes using lines, colors, boxes, or other graphical elements. Those graphical hints will have been used by the data modeling team to develop entities, and the result will be normalized tables.

FIGURE 6-8

Sample Documentation for
Default Values

Table	Column	Default Value
ITEM	ItemNumber	Surrogate key
ITEM	Category	None
ITEM	ItemPrefix	If Category = 'Perishable' then 'P' If Category = 'Imported' then 'I' If Category = 'One-off' then 'O' Otherwise = 'N'
ITEM	ApprovingDept	If ItemPrefix = 'I' then 'SHIPPING/PURCHASING' Otherwise = 'PURCHASING'
ITEM	ShippingMethod	If ItemPrefix = 'P' then 'Next Day' Otherwise = 'Ground'

All of this, however, should be verified. You need to ask whether the resulting tables are in BCNF and whether all multivalued dependencies have been removed. If not, the tables should probably be normalized. However, as we discussed in Chapter 4, sometimes normalization is undesirable. Thus, you should also examine your tables to determine if any normalized ones should be denormalized.

Create Relationships

The result of step 1 is a set of complete, but independent, tables. The next step is to create relationships. In general, we create relationships by placing foreign keys into tables. The way in which this is done and the properties of the foreign key columns depend on the type of relationship. In this section, we consider each of the relationships described in Chapter 5: nonidentifying relationships between strong entities, identifying relationships between ID-dependent entities, relationships in mixed entity patterns, relationships between a supertype and its subtypes, and recursive relationships. We conclude this section with a discussion of special cases of ternary relationships.

Relationships Between Strong Entities

As you learned in Chapter 5, nonidentifying relationships between strong entities are characterized by their maximum cardinality. There are three types of these relationships: 1:1, 1:N, and N:M.

1:1 Relationships Between Strong Entities

After the tables corresponding to the strong entities have been designed, a 1:1 relationship between these entities can be represented in one of two ways. You can place the primary key of the first table in the second as a foreign key, or you can place the primary key of the second table in the first as a foreign key. Figure 6-9 shows the representation of the 1:1 nonidentifying relationship between CLUB_MEMBER and LOCKER. In Figure 6-9(a), MemberNumber is placed in LOCKER as a foreign key. In Figure 6-9(b), LockerNumber is placed in CLUB_MEMBER as a foreign key.

Either of these designs will work. If you have a club member's number and want his or her locker, then, using the design in Figure 6-9(a), you can query the LOCKER table for the given value of MemberNumber. But if you have the LockerNumber and want the club member's data, then, still using the design in Figure 6-9(a), you can query the LOCKER table for the LockerNumber, obtain the MemberNumber, and use that value to query the CLUB_MEMBER table for the rest of the club member's data.

Follow a similar procedure to verify that the design in Figure 6-8(b) works as well. However, one data constraint applies to both designs. Because the relationship is 1:1, a given value of a foreign key can appear only once in the table. For example, in the design in Figure 6-9(a), a given

FIGURE 6-9

The Two Alternatives for the Transformation of a 1:1 Relationship Between Strong Entities

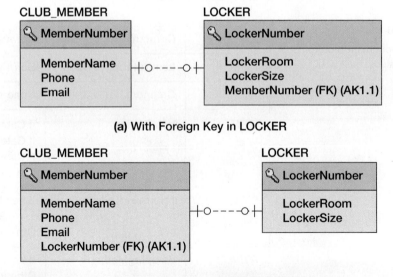

(a) With Foreign Key in LOCKER

(b) With Foreign Key in CLUB_MEMBER

value of MemberNumber can appear just once; each value must be unique in the LOCKER table. If a value of MemberNumber were to appear in two rows, then a member would be assigned to two lockers, and the relationship would not be 1:1.

To cause the DBMS to enforce the required uniqueness of the foreign key value, we define the foreign key column as unique. This can be done either directly in the column definition of the foreign key (in which case there is no designation in the table diagram) or by defining the foreign key as an alternate key. This latter technique, though common, is a bit confusing because, logically, MemberNumber is not an alternate key for LOCKER. We are just using the fact that alternate keys are unique to document the uniqueness of the foreign key in a 1:1 relationship. Depending on the database design software being used, the alternate key designation may appear in the database design of the tables and the relationship, and this is illustrated in Figure 6-9(a). A similar technique is used on the foreign key LockerNumber in Figure 6-9(b).

Figure 6-9 shows the minimum cardinalities of the relationship as optional-optional (O-O), and in this case either of the designs in Figure 6-9 will work, though the design team many prefer one over the other. However, if the minimum cardinalities of the relationship are either mandatory-optional (M-O) or optional-mandatory (O-M), then one design will be *greatly* preferred, as you will learn in the section on minimum cardinality design later in this chapter. Also, application requirements may mean that one design is faster than the other.

To summarize, to represent a 1:1 strong entity relationship, place the key of one table in the other table. Enforce the maximum cardinality by defining the foreign key as unique (or as an alternate key).

1:N Relationships Between Strong Entities

After the tables corresponding to the strong entities have been designed, a 1:N relationship between the entities is represented by placing the primary key of the table on the *one* side into the table on the *many* side as a foreign key. Recall from Chapter 5 that the term *parent* is used to refer to the table on the one side, and the term *child* is used to refer to the table on the many side. Using this terminology, you can summarize the design of 1:N relationships by saying, "Place the primary key of the parent in the child as a foreign key." This is illustrated in Figure 6-10.

Figure 6-10(a) shows an E-R diagram for the 1:N relationship between the CLUB_MEMBER and CLUB_UNIFORM entities. The relationship is represented in the database design in Figure 6-10(b) by placing the primary key of the parent (MemberNumber) in the child (CLUB_UNIFORM) as a foreign key. Because parents have many children (the relationship is 1:N), there is no need to make the foreign key unique.

For 1:N relationships between strong entities, that's all there is to it. Just remember: "Place the primary key of the parent in the child as a foreign key."

FIGURE 6-10

Transformation of a 1:N Relationship Between Strong Entities

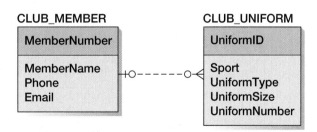

(a) 1:N Relationship Between Strong Entities

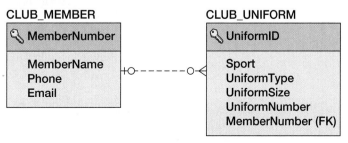

(b) Placing the Primary Key of the Parent in the Child as a Foreign Key

N:M Relationships Between Strong Entities

Again, we must first create the database design tables from the data model entities and then create the relationship. However, the situation for N:M relationships is more complicated. The problem is that there is no place in either table in an N:M relationship in which to place the foreign key. Consider the example in Figure 6-11(a), which shows a relationship between COMPANY and PART that specifies which companies can supply which parts. A COMPANY may supply many PARTs, and a PART may be supplied by many different COMPANY(ies).

Suppose we try to represent this relationship by placing the primary key of one table as a foreign key in the second table, as we did for 1:N relationships. Say we place the primary key of PART in COMPANY as follows:

COMPANY (<u>CompanyName</u>, City, Country, Volume, *PartNumber*)

PART (<u>PartNumber</u>, PartName, SalesPrice, ReOrderQuantity, QuantityOnHand)

With this design, a given PartNumber may appear in many rows of COMPANY so that many companies can supply the part. But how do we show that a company can supply many parts? There is only space to show one part. We do not want to duplicate the entire row for a company just to show a second part; such a strategy would result in unacceptable data duplication and data integrity problems. Therefore, this is not an acceptable solution, and a similar problem will occur if we try to place the primary key of COMPANY, CompanyName, into PART as a foreign key.

The solution is to create a third table, called an **intersection table**[1]. Such a table shows the correspondences of a given company and a given part. It holds only the primary keys of

FIGURE 6-11

Transformation of a N:M Relationship Between Strong Entities

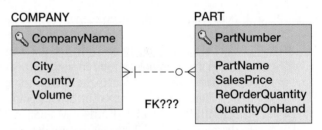

(a) The Foreign Key Has No Place in Either Table

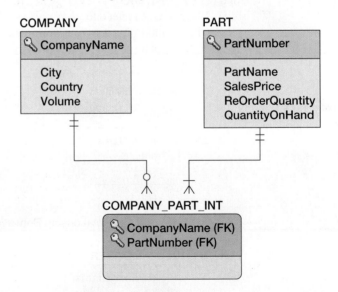

(b) Foreign Keys Placed in ID-Dependent Intersection Table

---

[1]While we use the term *intersection table* in this book, this table structure is known by many other names. In fact, Wikipedia lists 11 alternate names, including *intersection table, junction table, bridge table,* and *association table.* While we reserve the term *association table* for an *association relationship* (as explained later in this chapter), your instructor may prefer one of the other terms for this table structure. For more information, see the Wikipedia article *Junction table* at *http://en.wikipedia.org/wiki/Junction_table.*

the two tables as foreign keys, and this combination of keys serves as the composite primary key of the intersection table itself. The intersection holds only the key data; it contains no other user data. For the example in Figure 6-11(a) we create the following intersection table:

COMPANY_PART_INT (*CompanyName*, *PartNumber*)

The COMPANY_PART_INT table has one row for each company–part combination. Notice that both columns are part of the composite primary key (CompanyName, PartNumber), and that each column is also a foreign key to a different table. Because both columns are keys of other tables, intersection tables are always ID-dependent on both of their parent tables and the relationships with the parent tables are identifying relationships.

Thus, the database design in Figure 6-11(a) is drawn with an ID-dependent COMPANY_PART_INT intersection table and identifying relationship lines. Like all ID-dependent tables, the parent tables are required–COMPANY_PART_INT requires both a COMPANY and PART. The parents may or may not require an intersection table row, depending on application requirements. In Figure 6-11(b), a COMPANY need not supply a PART, but a PART must be supplied by at least one COMPANY.

BY THE WAY   The problem for the data models of N:M relationships between strong entities is that they have no direct representation. N:M relationships must *always* be decomposed into two 1:N relationships using an intersection table in the database design. This is why products like MySQL Workbench are unable to represent N:M relationships in a data model. These products force you to make the transformation to two 1:N relationships ahead of time, during modeling. As stated in Chapter 5, however, most data modelers consider this requirement to be a nuisance because it adds complexity to data modeling when the whole purpose of data modeling is to reduce complexity to the logical essentials.

Relationships Using ID-Dependent Entities

Figure 6-12 summarizes the four uses for ID-dependent entities. We have already described the first use shown in Figure 6-12: the representation of N:M relationships. As shown in Figure 6-11, an ID-dependent intersection table is created to hold the foreign keys of the two tables participating in the relationship, and identifying 1:N relationships are created between each table and the intersection table.

The other three uses shown in Figure 6-12 were discussed in Chapter 5, and here we will describe the creation of tables and relationships for each of these three uses.

Association Relationships

As we discussed in Chapter 5, an association relationship is subtly close to an N:M relationship between two strong entities. The only difference between the two types of relationships is that an association relationship has one or more attributes that pertain to the relationship *between the entities*, and not to either of the entities themselves. These attributes must be added to what would otherwise be the intersection table in the N:M relationship. In Chapter 5, we described this added entity as an **associative entity** (or **association entity**). (Figure 6-13(a) shows the

---

FIGURE 6-12

Four Uses for ID-Dependent Entities

Four Uses for ID-Dependent Entities
Representing N:M relationships
Representing association relationships
Storing multivalued attributes
Representing archetype/instance relationships

association relationship data model created in Figure 5-22. In this example, the association of a company and a part carries an attribute named Price, which is stored in an associative entity named QUOTATION.

The representation of such a relationship is straightforward: Start by creating an *intersection table* that is ID-dependent on both of its parents, and then convert it to an **association table** by adding the non-identifier attributes from the associative entity to that table. The result for the example in Figure 6-13(a) is the association table:

QUOTATION (*CompanyName*, *PartNumber*, Price)

This table appears in the database design in Figure 6-13(b). Like all ID-dependent relationships, the parents of an association table are required. The parents may or may not require the rows of the association table, depending on application requirements. In Figure 6-13(b), a COMPANY need not have any QUOTATION rows, but a PART must have at least one QUOTATION row.

FIGURE 6-13

Using ID-Dependent
Entities in an Association
Relationship

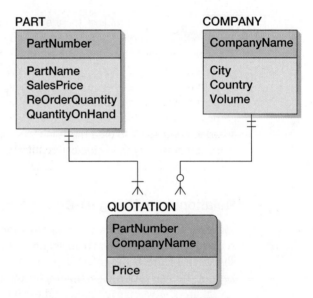

(a) Association Pattern Data Model from Figure 5-22

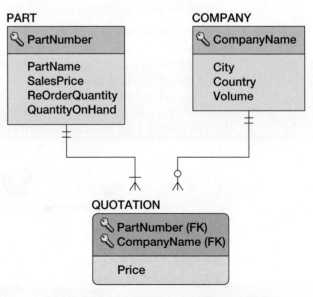

(b) Association Pattern Database Design

> **BY THE WAY** The table that represents the association entity looks very much like an intersection table; the only difference is the presence of the Price attribute. Because of the attribute, the need for association tables, such as QUOTATION, will appear in user requirements. Somewhere there will be a form or a report that has the attribute Price. However, the need for intersection tables never appears in the users' world. Such tables are an artifact of the relational model, and no form, report, or other user requirement will indicate the need for one.
>
> Intersection tables complicate the construction of applications. They must be processed to obtain related rows, but they never directly appear on a form or report. In Microsoft Access, they are frustratingly difficult to mangle into the form and report design tools. You will see more about this in later chapters. In any case, for now understand the key difference between association and intersection tables: Association tables have user data, but intersection tables do not.

As shown in Figure 6-14, associative entities sometimes connect more than two entity types. Figure 6-14(a) shows the association relationship among the CLIENT, ARCHITECT, and PROJECT entities from the data model we created in Figure 5-23. When there are several participants in the association, the strategy just shown is simply extended. The association table will have the key of each of its parents, as shown in Figure 6-14(b). In this case, the ASSIGNMENT table has three foreign keys and one nonkey attribute, HoursWorked.

In both of these examples, it is only coincidence that the association tables have only one nonkey attribute. In general, an association table can have as many nonkey attributes as necessary to meet user requirements.

Multivalued Attributes

The third use for ID-dependent entities is to represent multivalued entity attributes, as illustrated in Figure 6-15. Figure 6-15(a) is a copy of Figure 5-29. Here COMPANY has a multivalued composite, (Contact, PhoneNumber), that is represented by the ID-dependent entity PHONE_CONTACT.

As shown in Figure 6-15(b), representing the PHONE_CONTACT entity is straightforward. Just replace it with a table and replace each of its attributes with a column. In this example, the CompanyName attribute is both a part of the primary key and a foreign key.

Like all ID-dependent tables, PHONE_CONTACT must have a parent row in COMPANY. However, a COMPANY row may or may not have a required PHONE_CONTACT, depending on application requirements.

> **BY THE WAY** As you can see from these examples, it is not much work to transform an ID-dependent entity into a table. All that is necessary is to transform the entity into a table and copy the attributes into columns.
>
> Why is it so simple? There are two reasons. First, all identifying relationships are 1:N. If they were 1:1, there would be no need for the ID-dependent relationship. The attributes of the child entity could just be placed in the parent entity. Second, given that the relationship is 1:N, the design principle is to place the key of the parent into the child. However, the definition of an ID-dependent relationship is that part of its identifier is an identifier of its parent. Thus, by definition, the key of the parent is already in the child. Hence, it is not necessary to create a foreign key; that work has already been done during data modeling.

Archetype/Instance Pattern

As illustrated in Figure 6-16, the fourth use for ID-dependent entities and identifying relationships is the archetype/instance pattern (also referred to as the *version/instance* pattern). Figure 6-16(a), which is a copy of Figure 5-30, shows the CLASS/SECTION archetype/instance example from Chapter 5, and Figure 6-16(b) shows the relational design.

FIGURE 6-14

Transformation of
ID-Dependent Entities in an
Association Relationship
Among Three Entities

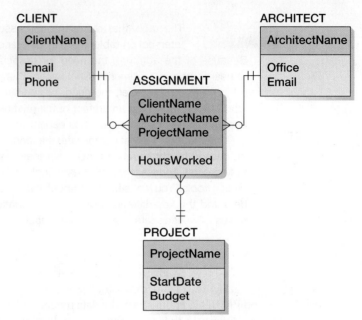

(a) Association Pattern Data Model from Figure 5-23

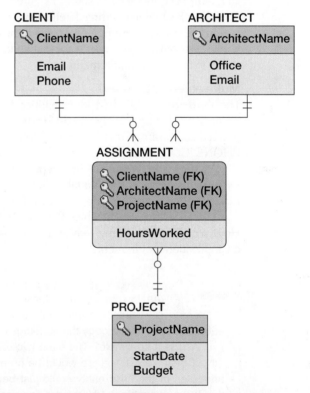

(b) Association Pattern Database Design

As noted in the previous chapter, however, sometimes the instances of an archetype/
instance pattern are given identifiers of their own. In that case, the instance entity becomes
a weak but not ID-dependent entity. When this occurs, the relationship must be transformed using the rules of a 1:N relationship between a strong entity and a weak but non-ID-
dependent entity. However, this transformation is the same as a 1:N relationship between
two strong entities. This just means that the primary key of the parent table should be placed
in the child table as a foreign key. Figure 6-17(a) shows a copy of the data model in Figure
5-31 in which SECTION has been given the identifier ReferenceNumber. In the relational
database design in Figure 6-17(b), ClassName (the primary key of the parent CLASS table)
has been placed in SECTION (the child table) as a foreign key.

FIGURE 6-15

Transformation of
ID-Dependent Entities that
Store Multivalued Attributes

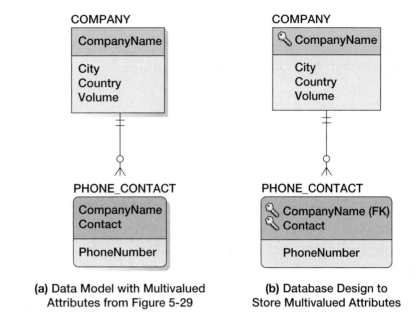

(a) Data Model with Multivalued
Attributes from Figure 5-29

(b) Database Design to
Store Multivalued Attributes

Keep in mind, however, that even though SECTION is no longer ID-dependent, it is still weak. SECTION requires a CLASS for its existence. This means that a SECTION must always have a CLASS as its parent, and this restriction arises from logical necessity, not just from application requirements. The fact that SECTION is weak should be recorded in design documentation.

Relationships with a Weak Non-ID-Dependent Entity

As you learned in Chapter 5, a relationship between a strong entity and a weak but non-ID-dependent entity behaves just the same as a relationship between two strong entities. The relationship is a nonidentifying relationship, and, again, these relationships are characterized by their maximum cardinality. The previous discussion of 1:1, 1:N, and N:M relationships between strong entities also applies to these types of relationships between a strong entity and a weak but non-ID-dependent entity.

For example, what happens when the identifier of the parent of an ID-dependent entity is replaced with a surrogate key? Consider the example of BUILDING and APARTMENT, in which the identifier of APARTMENT is the composite of an apartment number and a building identifier.

FIGURE 6-16

Transformation of
ID-Dependent Entities in an
Archetype/Instance Pattern

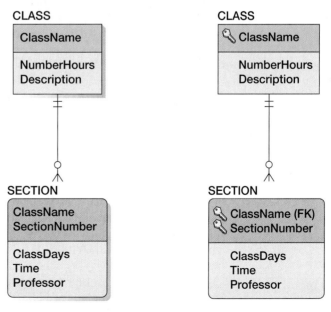

(a) Data Model with Archetype/Instance
Pattern from Figure 5-30

(b) Database Design for
Archetype/Instance Pattern

FIGURE 6-17

Transformation of the
Archetype/Instance Pattern
Using Non-ID-Dependent
Weak Entities

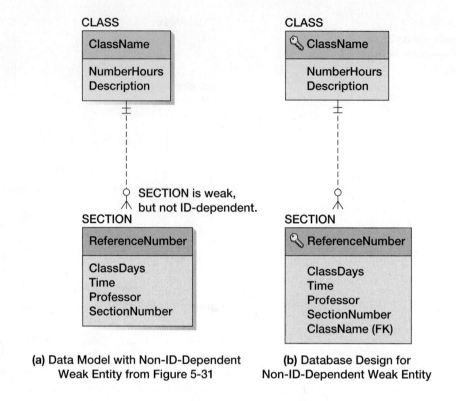

(a) Data Model with Non-ID-Dependent
Weak Entity from Figure 5-31

(b) Database Design for
Non-ID-Dependent Weak Entity

Suppose that the identifier of BUILDING is (Street, City, State/Province, Country). In this case, the identifier of APARTMENT is (Street, City, State/Province, Country, ApartmentNumber). This design can be improved by replacing the long BUILDING identifier with a surrogate key. Suppose that we replace the key of BUILDING with BuildingID, a surrogate.

Now, with a surrogate key for BUILDING, what is the key of APARTMENT? When we place the key of the parent in the child, we obtain (BuildingID, ApartmentNumber). But this combination has no meaning to the user. What does an identifier of (10045898, '5C') mean to a user? Nothing! The key became meaningless when Street, City, State/Province, and Country were replaced by BuildingID in BUILDING.

We can improve the design by using the following principle: When replacing the identifier of the parent of an ID-dependent entity with a surrogate key, replace the identifier of the ID-dependent entity with its own surrogate key. The resulting table will be weak but not ID-dependent (we will used this principle later in this chapter as we create a database design for the View Ridge Gallery–you can see the changes in Figures 6-38 and 6-39, where WORK becomes a weak but not ID-dependent table in the relationship with ARTIST).

Relationships in Mixed Entity Designs

As you might guess, the design of mixed entity patterns is a combination of strong entity and ID-dependent entity designs. Consider the example of employees and skills in Figure 6-18. Figure 6-18(a) is a copy of Figure 5-35. Here the entity EMPLOYEE_SKILL is ID dependent on EMPLOYEE, but it has a nonidentifying relationship to SKILL.

The database design of the E-R model for the data model in Figure 6-18(a) is shown in Figure 6-18(b). Notice that EmployeeNumber is both a part of the primary key of EMPLOYEE_SKILL and also a foreign key to EMPLOYEE. The 1:N nonidentifying relationship between SKILL and EMPLOYEE_SKILL is represented by placing the key of SKILL, which is Name, in EMPLOYEE_SKILL. Note that EMPLOYEE_SKILL.Name is a foreign key but not part of the primary key of EMPLOYEE_SKILL.

A similar strategy is used to transform the SALES_ORDER data model in Figure 6-19. Figure 6-19(a) is a copy of the SALES_ORDER data model originally shown in Figure 5-33. In Figure 6-19(b), the ID-dependent table, ORDER_LINE_ITEM, has SalesOrderNumber as part of its primary key and as a foreign key. It has ItemNumber as a foreign key only.

FIGURE 6-18

Transformation of the
Mixed Entity Pattern

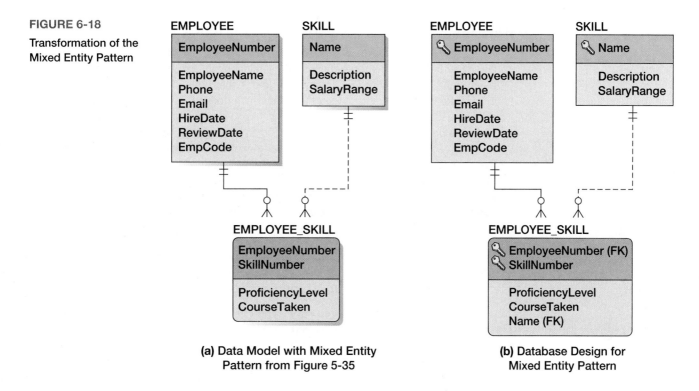

(a) Data Model with Mixed Entity
Pattern from Figure 5-35

(b) Database Design for
Mixed Entity Pattern

FIGURE 6-19

Transformation of the
SALES_ORDER Pattern

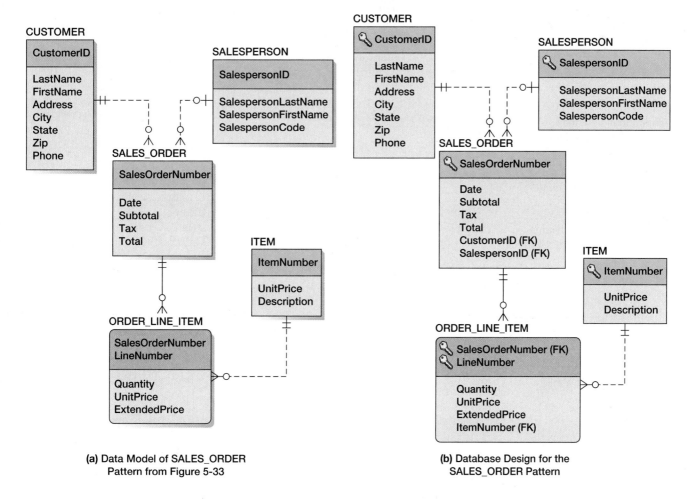

(a) Data Model of SALES_ORDER
Pattern from Figure 5-33

(b) Database Design for the
SALES_ORDER Pattern

> **BY THE WAY**   The design transformation process for all HAS-A relationships can be summarized by the phrase, "Place the primary key of the parent in the child as a foreign key." For strong entities, a 1:1 relationship can have either entity as the parent, and therefore the foreign key can go in either table. For 1:N relationships, the primary key of the parent goes in the child as the foreign key. For N:M relationships, decompose the model into two 1:N relationships by defining an intersection table and place the parent key of the parent in the child as a foreign key for each.
>
> For identifying relationships, the primary key of the parent is already in the child, so there is nothing more to do. For mixed relationships, on the identifying side, the primary key of the parent is already in the child. On the nonidentifying side, place the primary key of the parent in the child. In short, if you're going to memorize just a few rules for creating relationships, the first one is "HAS-A: Place the primary key of the parent in the child as the foreign key."

Relationships Between Supertype and Subtype Entities

Representing relationships between supertype entities and their subtypes is easy. Recall that these relationships are also called IS-A relationships because a subtype and its supertype are representations of the same underlying entity. A MANAGER (subtype) is an EMPLOYEE (supertype), and a SALESCLERK (subtype) is also an EMPLOYEE (supertype). Because of this equivalence, the keys of all subtype tables are identical to the key of the supertype table.

Figure 6-20(a) shows the data model in Figure 5-13(a), an example for two subtypes of STUDENT. Notice that the key of STUDENT is StudentID and that the key of each of the subtypes also is StudentID. UNDERGRADUATE.StudentID and GRADUATE.StudentID are both primary keys and foreign keys to their supertype.

While we are showing the transformation of a set of exclusive subtypes (with the discriminator attribute isGradStudent), the transformation of a set of inclusive subtypes is done exactly the same way. Note that discriminator attributes cannot be represented in relational designs. In Figure 6-20(b), we can do nothing with isGradStudent except note in the design documentation that isGradStudent determines subtype. Application programs will need to be written to use isGradStudent to determine which subtype pertains to a given STUDENT.

FIGURE 6-20

Transformation of the Supertype/Subtype Entities

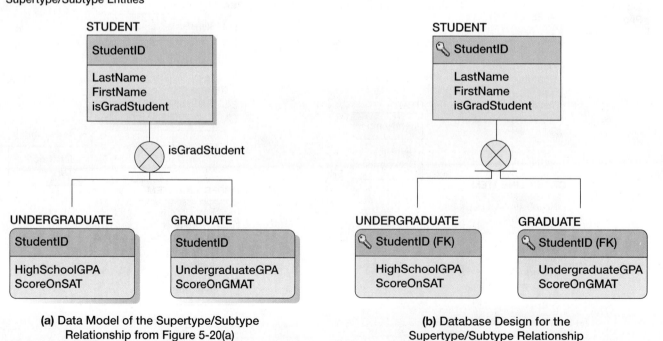

(a) Data Model of the Supertype/Subtype Relationship from Figure 5-20(a)

(b) Database Design for the Supertype/Subtype Relationship

Recursive Relationships

The representation of recursive relationships is just an extension of the techniques used for representing relationships between strong entities. These techniques may be a bit difficult to comprehend at first because they appear strange, but they involve principles that you have already learned.

1:1 Recursive Relationships

Consider the 1:1 recursive BOXCAR relationship in Figure 6-21(a), which is the same data model we developed in Figure 5-39. To represent the relationship, we create a foreign key in BOXCAR that contains the identifier of the boxcar behind, as shown in Figure 6-21(b). Because the relationship is 1:1, we make the foreign key unique by defining it as unique (shown here as an alternate key). This restriction enforces the fact that a boxcar can have at most one boxcar behind it.

Notice that both sides of the relationship are optional. This occurs because the last car on the train has no other car behind it and because the first car on the train is behind no other car. If the data structure were circular, this restriction would not be necessary. For example, if you wanted to represent the sequence of names of the calendar months and you wanted December to lead to January, then you could have a 1:1 recursive structure with required children.

BY THE WAY   If you find the concept of recursive relationships confusing, try this trick. Assume that you have two entities, BOXCAR_AHEAD and BOXCAR_BEHIND, each having the same attributes. Notice that there is a 1:1 relationship between these two entities. Replace each entity with its table. Like all 1:1 strong entity relationships, you can place the key of either table as a foreign key in the other table. For now, place the key of BOXCAR_BEHIND into BOXCAR_AHEAD.

Now realize that BOXCAR_BEHIND only duplicates data that reside in BOXCAR_AHEAD. The data are unnecessary. So, discard BOXCAR_BEHIND and you will have the same design as shown in Figure 6-21(b).

FIGURE 6-21

Transformation of 1:1 Recursive Relationships

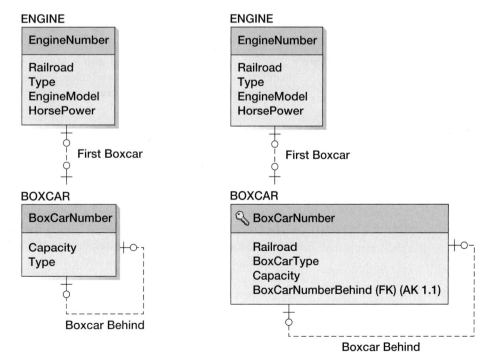

(a) Data Model for a 1:1 Recursive Relationship in Figure 5-38

(b) Database Design for a 1:1 Recursive Relationship

FIGURE 6-22

Transformation of 1:N
Recursive Relationships

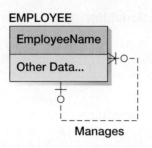

**(a) Data Model for a 1:N Recursive
Relationship in Figure 5-41**

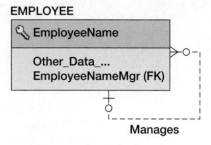

**(b) Database Design for a 1:N
Recursive Relationship**

1:N Recursive Relationships

As with all 1:N relationships, 1:N recursive relationships are represented by placing the primary key of the parent in the child as a foreign key. Consider the Manages relationship in Figure 6-22(a), which is the data model we developed in Figure 5-41. In this case, we place the name of the manager in each employee's row. Thus, in Figure 6-22(b), the EmployeeNameMgr has been added to the EMPLOYEE table.

Notice that both the parent and the child are optional. This is true because the lowest-level employees manage no one and because the highest-level person, the CEO or other most senior person, has no manager. If the data structure were circular, this would not be the case.

N:M Recursive Relationships

The trick for representing N:M recursive relationships is to decompose the N:M relationship into two 1:N relationships. We do this by creating an intersection table, just as we did for N:M relationships between strong entities.

Figure 6-23(a) is the data model we developed in Figure 5-43. It shows the solution to an example for a bill-of-materials problem. Each part has potentially many subordinate parts, and each part can be used as a component in potentially many other parts. To represent this relationship, create an intersection table that shows the correspondence of a part/part use. You can model upward or downward. If the former, the intersection table will carry the correspondence of a part and where that part is used. If the latter, the intersection table will carry the correspondence of a part and the parts that it contains. Figure 6-23(b) shows the intersection table for modeling downward in the bill of materials.

> **BY THE WAY** Again, if you find this to be confusing, assume that you have two different tables, one called PART and a second called CONTAINED_PART. Create the intersection table between the two tables. Note that CONTAINED_PART duplicates the attributes in PART and is thus unnecessary. Eliminate the table and you will have the design in Figure 6-23(b).

Representing Ternary and Higher-Order Relationships

As we discussed in Chapter 5, ternary and higher-order relationships can be represented by multiple binary relationships, and such a representation usually works without any problems. However, in some cases, there are constraints that add complexity to the situation. For example, consider the ternary relationship among the entities ORDER, CUSTOMER, and SALESPERSON. Assume that the relationship from CUSTOMER to ORDER is 1:N and that the relationship from SALESPERSON to ORDER also is 1:N. We can represent the three-part relationship among ORDER:CUSTOMER:SALESPERSON as two separate binary relationships: one between ORDER and CUSTOMER and a second between SALESPERSON and CUSTOMER. The design of the tables will be:

CUSTOMER (<u>CustomerNumber</u>, {nonkey data attributes})

SALESPERSON (<u>SalespersonNumber</u>, {nonkey data attributes})

ORDER (<u>OrderNumber</u>, {nonkey data attributes}, *CustomerNumber, SalespersonNumber*)

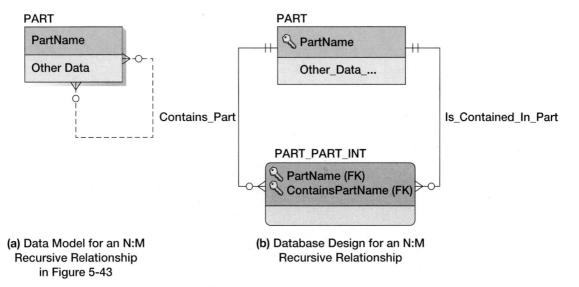

(a) Data Model for an N:M
Recursive Relationship
in Figure 5-43

(b) Database Design for an N:M
Recursive Relationship

FIGURE 6-23

Transformation of N:M
Recursive Relationships

Suppose, however, that the business has a rule that each CUSTOMER can place orders only with a particular SALESPERSON. In this case, the ternary relationship ORDER:CUSTOMER:SALESPERSON is constrained by an additional binary 1:N relationship between SALESPERSON and CUSTOMER. To represent the constraint, we need to add the key of SALESPERSON to CUSTOMER. The three tables will now be:

CUSTOMER (**<u>CustomerNumber</u>**, {nonkey data attributes}, *SalespersonNumber*)

SALESPERSON (**<u>SalespersonNumber</u>**, {nonkey data attributes})

ORDER (**<u>OrderNumber</u>**, {nonkey data attributes}, *CustomerNumber*, *SalespersonNumber*)

The constraint that a particular CUSTOMER is sold to by a particular SALESPERSON means that only certain combinations of CustomerNumber and SalespersonNumber can exist together in ORDER. Unfortunately, this constraint cannot be expressed in a relational model. It must be documented in the design, however, and enforced by program code, as shown in Figure 6-24.

A constraint that requires one entity to be combined with another entity is called a **MUST constraint**. Other similar constraints are the MUST NOT constraint and the MUST COVER

FIGURE 6-24

Ternary Relationship with
a MUST Constraint

SALESPERSON Table

SalespersonNumber	Other nonkey data
10	
20	
30	

CUSTOMER Table

<u>CustomerNumber</u>	Other nonkey data	*SalespersonNumber*
1000		10
2000		20
3000		30

Binary MUST Constraint

ORDER Table

<u>OrderNumber</u>	Other nonkey data	*SalespersonNumber*	*CustomerNumber*
100		10	1000
200		20	2000
300		10	1000
400		30	3000
500			2000

Only 20 is allowed here

FIGURE 6-25

Ternary Relationship with
a MUST NOT Constraint

DRUG Table

DrugNumber	Other nonkey data
10	
20	
30	
45	
70	
90	

ALLERGY Table

CustomerNumber	DrugNumber	Other nonkey data
1000	10	
1000	20	
2000	20	
2000	45	
3000	30	
3000	45	
3000	70	

Binary MUST NOT Constraint

PRESCRIPTION Table

PrescriptionNumber	Other nonkey data	DrugNumber	CustomerNumber
100		45	1000
200		10	2000
300		70	1000
400		20	3000
500			2000

Neither 20 nor 45 can appear here

constraint. In a **MUST NOT constraint**, the binary relationship indicates combinations that are not allowed to occur in the ternary relationship. For example, the ternary relationship PRESCRIPTION:DRUG:CUSTOMER shown in Figure 6-25 can be constrained by a binary relationship in the ALLERGY table that lists the drugs that a customer is not allowed to take.

In a **MUST COVER constraint**, the binary relationship indicates all combinations that must appear in the ternary relationship. For example, consider the relationship AUTO_REPAIR:REPAIR:TASK in Figure 6-26. Suppose that a given REPAIR consists of a number of TASKs, all of which must be performed for the REPAIR to be successful. In this case, in the table AUTO_REPAIR, when a given AUTO_REPAIR has a given REPAIR, then all of the TASKs for that REPAIR must appear as rows in that table.

None of the three types of binary constraints discussed here can be represented in the relational design. Instead, they are documented in the design and implemented in application code.

Relational Representation of the Highline University Data Model

Let's consider the data model we created for Highline University in Chapter 5. Our final data model for Highline University is shown in Figure 6-27.

Using the principles we have discussed in this chapter, we can turn this into a relational database design, and the resulting database design is a straightforward application of the principles described in this chapter. The database design for Highline University is shown in Figure 6-28.

You should review Figure 6-28 to ensure that you understand the representation of every relationship. Note that there are actually two foreign key references to a DepartmentName primary key column in STUDENT. The first is DepartmentName (FK), which is the foreign key linking to the DepartmentName primary key in DEPARTMENT. This relationship has the referential integrity constraint:

DepartmentName in STUDENT must exist in DepartmentName in DEPARTMENT

FIGURE 6-26

Ternary Relationship with a MUST COVER Constraint

REPAIR Table

RepairNumber	Other nonkey data
10	
20	
30	
40	

TASK Table

TaskNumber	Other nonkey data	RepairNumber
1001		10
1002		10
1003		10
2001		20
2002		20
3001		30
4001		40

Binary MUST COVER Constraint

AUTO_REPAIR Table

InvoiceNumber	RepairNumber	TaskNumber	Other nonkey data
100	10	1001	
100	10	1002	
100	10	1003	
200	20	2001	
200	20		

2002 must appear here

FIGURE 6-27

Data Model for Highline University in Figure 5-52

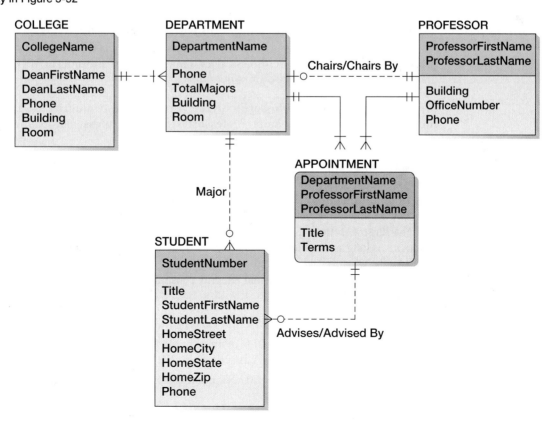

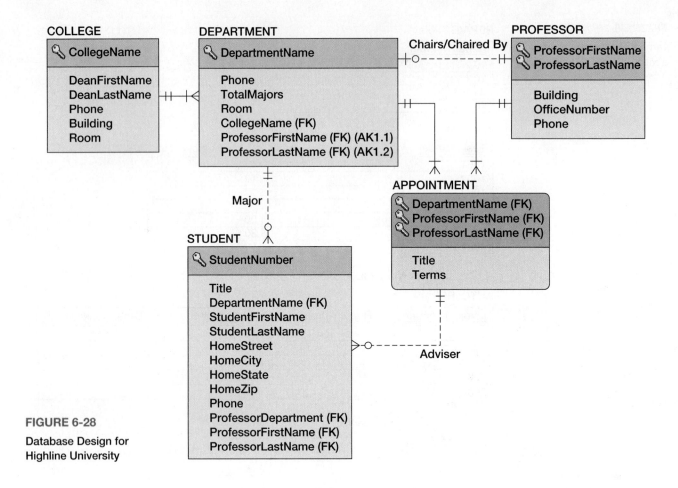

FIGURE 6-28

Database Design for
Highline University

The second is ProfessorDepartment (FK), which is part of the composite foreign key (ProfessorDepartment, ProfessorFirstName, ProfessorLastName). This foreign key links to the primary key (DepartmentName, ProfessorFirstName, ProfessorLastName) in APPOINTMENT and has the referential integrity constraint:

(ProfessorDepartment, ProfessorFirstName, ProfessorLastName) in STUDENT must exist in (DepartmentName, ProfessorFirstName, ProfessorLastName) in APPOINTMENT

Note that we had to change DepartmentName in APPOINTMENT to ProfessorDepartment in STUDENT because we cannot have two columns named DepartmentName in STUDENT and we had already used DepartmentName as the foreign key linking to DEPARTMENT.

This illustrates that a foreign key does not have to have the same name as the primary key it links to. As long as the referential integrity constraints are correctly specified, the foreign key name can be whatever we want it to be.

In addition to the two referential integrity constraints above our database design, we will also have the following:

CollegeName in DEPARTMENT must exist in CollegeName in COLLEGE

(ProfessorFirstName, ProfessorLastName) in DEPARTMENT must exist in (ProfessorFirstName, ProfessorLastName) in PROFESSOR

DepartmentName in APPOINTMENT must exist in DepartmentName in DEPARTMENT

(ProfessorFirstName, ProfessorLastName) in APPOINTMENT must exist in (ProfessorFirstName, ProfessorLastName) in PROFESSOR

Design for Minimum Cardinality

The third and last step of transforming data models into database designs is to create a plan for enforcing minimum cardinality. Unfortunately, this step can be considerably more complicated than the first two design steps. Relationships that have required children entities are particularly problematic because we cannot enforce such constraints with database structures. Instead, as you will see, we must design procedures for execution by the DBMS or by applications.

Relationships can have one of four minimum cardinalities: **parent optional and child optional (O-O)**, **parent mandatory and child optional (M-O)**, **parent optional and child mandatory (O-M)**, or **parent mandatory and child mandatory (M-M)**. As far as enforcing minimum cardinality is concerned, no action needs to be taken for O-O relationships, and we need not consider them further. The remaining three relationships pose restrictions on insert, update, and delete activities.

Figure 6-29 summarizes the actions needed to enforce minimum cardinality. Figure 6-29(a) shows needed actions when the parent row is required (M-O and M-M relationships), and Figure 6-29(b) shows needed actions when the child row is required (O-M and M-M relationships). In these figures and the accompanying discussion, the term **action** means **minimum cardinality enforcement action**. We use the shorter term *action* for ease of discussion.

To discuss these rules, we will use the database design for storing data on several companies shown in Figure 6-30. In this diagram, we have a 1:N, M-O relationship between COMPANY and DEPARTMENT and between DEPARTMENT and EMPLOYEE and a 1:N, M-M relationship between COMPANY and PHONE_CONTACT. In the COMPANY-to-DEPARTMENT relationship, COMPANY (on the 1 side of the relationship) is the parent entity and DEPARTMENT (on the N side of the relationship) is the child entity. In the DEPARMENT-to-EMPLOYEE relationship, DEPARTMENT (on the 1 side of the

FIGURE 6-29

Summary of Actions to Enforce Minimum Cardinality

Parent Required	Action on Parent	Action on Child
Insert	None.	Get a parent. Prohibit.
Modify key or foreign key	Change children's foreign key values to match new value (**cascade update**). Prohibit.	OK, if new foreign key value matches existing parent. Prohibit.
Delete	Delete children (**cascade delete**). Prohibit.	None.

(a) Actions When the Parent Is Required

Child Required	Action on Parent	Action on Child
Insert	Get a child. Prohibit.	None.
Modify key or foreign key	Update the foreign key of (at least one) child. Prohibit.	If not last child, OK. If last child, prohibit or find a replacement.
Delete	None.	If not last child, OK. If last child, prohibit or find a replacement.

(b) Actions When the Child Is Required

FIGURE 6-30

Database Design for Data on
Several Companies

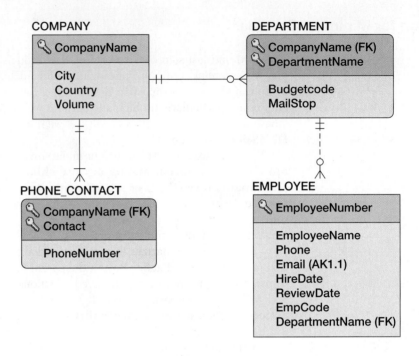

relationship) is the parent entity and EMPLOYEE (on the N side of the relationship) is the child entity. In the COMPANY-to-PHONE_CONTACT relationship, COMPANY (on the 1 side of the relationship) is the parent entity and PHONE_CONTACT (on the N side of the relationship) is the child entity.

Actions when the Parent Is Required

When the parent is required, we need to ensure that every row of the child table has a valid, non-null value of the foreign key. To accomplish this, we must restrict actions to update or delete the parent's primary key and actions to create or modify the child's foreign key. We will consider actions on the parent first.

Actions on the Parent Row when the Parent Is Required

According to Figure 6-29(a), when a new parent is created, nothing needs to be done. No child row can yet be dependent upon the new row. In our example, we can create a new DEPARTMENT and not worry about minimum cardinality enforcement in EMPLOYEE.

However, consider what happens if we attempt to change the value of an existing parent row's primary key. If that row has children, then those children have a foreign key value that matches the current primary key value. If the primary key of the parent changes, then any existing children will become orphans; their foreign key values will no longer match a parent row. To prevent the creation of orphans, either the foreign key values must be changed to match the new value of the parent's primary key or the modification to the parent's primary key must be prohibited.

In our example, if a DEPARTMENT attempts to change its DepartmentName from 'Info Sys' to 'Information Systems', then any child rows in EMPLOYEE that have a foreign key value of 'Info Sys' will no longer match a parent and will be orphans. To prevent orphans, either the values of the foreign key in EMPLOYEE must also be changed to 'Information Systems' or the update to the primary key in DEPARTMENT must be prohibited. The policy of propagating a change from the parent's primary key to the children's foreign key is called **cascading updates**.

Now consider what happens when there is an attempt to delete a parent. If that row has children and if the deletion is allowed, then the children will become orphans. Hence, when such a delete attempt is made, either the children must be deleted as well or the deletion must be prohibited. Deleting the children along with the parent is called **cascading deletions**. In our example, when an attempt is made to delete a DEPARTMENT, either all related rows in EMPLOYEE must be deleted as well or the deletion must be disallowed.

> **BY THE WAY**   Generally, cascading deletions are not chosen for relationships between strong entities. The deletion of a DEPARTMENT row should not force the deletion of EMPLOYEE rows. Instead, the deletion should be disallowed. To remove a DEPARTMENT row, the EMPLOYEE rows would be reassigned to a new DEPARTMENT and then the DEPARTMENT row would be deleted.
>
> However, cascading deletions are almost always chosen for weak child entities. For example, when you delete a COMPANY, you should always delete all of the weak PHONE_NUMBER rows that depend on that COMPANY.

Actions on the Child Row when the Parent Is Required

Now consider actions on the child row. If the parent is required, then when a new child row is created, the new row must have a valid foreign key value. When we create a new EMPLOYEE, for example, if DEPARTMENT is required, then the new EMPLOYEE row must have a valid value for DepartmentName. If not, the insert must be disallowed. Usually there is a default policy for assigning parents to a new row. In our example, when a new row is added to EMPLOYEE, the default policy could be to add the new employee to the department named 'Human Resources'.

With regards to modifications to the foreign key, the new value must match a value of the primary key in the parent. In EMPLOYEE, if we change DepartmentName from 'Accounting' to 'Finance', then there must already be a DEPARTMENT row with the primary key value of 'Finance'. If not, the modification must be prohibited.

If the parent row is required, there are no restrictions on the deletion of the child row. The child can go away without consequence on the parent.

> **BY THE WAY**   When the parent has a surrogate key, the enforcement actions for update are different between the parent and the child. On the parent side, the surrogate key will never change, and hence update actions can be ignored. On the child side, however, the foreign key can change if the child switches to a new parent. Hence, on the parent side, you can ignore actions when the key is a surrogate. On the child side, however, you must consider update actions even when the parent's key is a surrogate.

Actions when the Child Is Required

When the child is required, we need to ensure that there is at least one child row for the parent at all times. The last child cannot leave the parent. For example, in the DEPARTMENT-to-EMPLOYEE relationship, if a DEPARTMENT requires an EMPLOYEE, then the last EMPLOYEE cannot leave the DEPARTMENT. This has ramifications on actions on the child, as shown in Figure 6-29(b).

Enforcing required children is much more difficult than enforcing required parents. To enforce a required parent, we just need to check for a match between primary key and foreign key values. To enforce a required child, we must count the number of children that a parent has. This difference forces us to write code to enforce required children. To begin, consider the required child actions from the perspective of the parent.

Actions on the Parent Row when the Child Is Required

If the child is required, then we cannot create a new parent without also creating a relationship to a child. This means that either we must find an existing child row and change its foreign key to match that of the new parent or we must create a new child row at the same time the parent is created. If neither action can be taken, then the insertion of the new parent must be prohibited. These rules are summarized in the first row of Figure 6-29(b).

If the child is required, then to modify the parent's primary key, either the key of at least one child must also be changed or the update must be disallowed. This restriction never applies to parents with surrogate keys because their values never change.

Finally, if the child is required and the parent is deleted, no action need be taken. Because it is the child that is required, and not the parent, the parent can disappear without any consequence.

Actions on the Child Row when the Child Is Required

As shown in Figure 6-29(b), if the child is required, then no special action needs to be taken when inserting a new child. The child comes into existence without influencing any parent.

However, there are restrictions on updating the foreign key of a required child. In particular, if the child is the last child of its current parent, then the update cannot occur. If it were to occur, the current parent would be childless, and that is not allowed. Thus, a procedure must be written to determine the number of children of the current parent. If that number is two or greater, then the child foreign key value can be changed. Otherwise the update is prohibited.

A similar restriction pertains to the deletion of required children. If the child is the last child to the parent, then the deletion is not allowed. Otherwise, the child can be deleted without restriction.

Implementing Actions for M-O Relationships

Figure 6-31 summarizes the application of the actions in Figure 6-29 for each type of minimum cardinality. As stated earlier, O-O relationships pose no restrictions and need not be considered.

M-O relationships require that the actions in Figure 6-29(a) be enforced. We need to make sure that every child has a parent and that operations on either parent or child rows never create orphans.

Fortunately, these actions are easy to enforce using facilities available in most DBMS products. It turns out that we can enforce these actions with just two limitations. First, we need to define a referential integrity constraint that ensures that every foreign key value has a match in the parent table. Second, we make the foreign key column NOT NULL. With these two restrictions, all of the actions in Figure 6-29(a) will be enforced.

Consider the DEPARTMENT-to-EMPLOYEE example. If we define the referential integrity constraint

DepartmentName in EMPLOYEE must exist in DepartmentName in DEPARTMENT

then we know that every value of DepartmentName in EMPLOYEE will match a value in DEPARTMENT. If we then make DepartmentName required, we know that every row in EMPLOYEE will have a valid DEPARTMENT.

Almost every DBMS product has facilities for defining referential integrity constraints. You will learn how to write SQL statements for that purpose in the next chapter. In those statements, you will have the option of declaring whether updates and deletions are to cascade or are to be prohibited. Once you have defined the constraint and made the foreign key NOT NULL, the DBMS will take care of all of the actions in Figure 6-29(a) for you.

FIGURE 6-31

Actions to Apply to Enforce Minimum Cardinality

Relationship Minimum Cardinality	Action to Apply	Remarks
O-O	Nothing	
M-O	Parent-required actions [Figure 6-28(a)]	Easily enforced by DBMS; define referential integrity constraint and make foreign key NOT NULL.
O-M	Child-required actions [Figure 6-28(b)]	Difficult to enforce. Requires use of triggers or other application code.
M-M	Parent-required actions and child-required actions [Figures 6-28(a) and 6-28(b)]	Very difficult to enforce. Requires a combination of complex triggers. Triggers can lock each other out. Many problems!

> **BY THE WAY**   Recall that, in a 1:1 relationship between strong entities, the key of either table can be placed in the other table. If the minimum cardinality of such a relationship is either M-O or O-M, it is generally best to place the key in the optional table. This placement will make the parent required, which is easier to enforce. With a required parent, all you have to do is define the referential integrity constraint and set the foreign key to NOT NULL. However, if you place the foreign key so that the child is required, let the work begin! You will have your hands full, as you are about to see.

Implementing Actions for O-M Relationships

Unfortunately, if the child is required, the DBMS does not provide much help. No easy mechanism is available to ensure that appropriate child foreign keys exist nor is there any easy way to ensure that valid relationships stay valid when rows are inserted, updated, or deleted. You are on your own.

In most cases, required children constraints are enforced using **triggers**, which are modules of code that are invoked by the DBMS when specific events occur. Almost all DBMS products have triggers for insert, update, and delete actions. Triggers are defined for these actions on a particular table. Thus, you can create a trigger on *CUSTOMER INSERT* or a trigger on *EMPLOYEE UPDATE*, and so forth. You will learn more about triggers in Chapter 7.

To see how you would use triggers to enforce required children, consider Figure 6-29(b) again. On the parent side, we need to write a trigger on insert and update on the parent row. These triggers either create the required child or they steal an existing child from another parent. If they are unable to perform one of these actions, they must cancel the insert or update.

On the child side, a child can be inserted without problem. Once a child gets a parent, however, it cannot leave that parent if it is the last or only child. Hence, we need to write update and delete triggers on the child that have the following logic: If the foreign key is null, the row has no parent, and the update or delete can proceed. If the foreign key does have a value, however, check whether the row is the last child. If the row *is* the last child, then the trigger must do one of the following:

- Delete the parent.
- Find a substitute child.
- Disallow the update or delete.

None of these actions will be automatically enforced by the DBMS. Instead, you must write code to enforce these rules. You will see generic examples of such code in the next chapter and real examples for Microsoft SQL Server 2014 in Chapter 10A, Oracle Database in Chapter 10B, and MySQL 5.6 in Chapter 10C.

Implementing Actions for M-M Relationships

It is very difficult to enforce M-M relationships. All of the actions in both Figure 6-29(a) and Figure 6-29(b) must be enforced simultaneously. We have a needy parent and a needy child, and neither will let go of the other.

Consider, for example, what would happen if we change the relationship between DEPARTMENT and EMPLOYEE in Figure 6-30 to M-M, and the effect that would have on the creation of new rows in DEPARTMENT and EMPLOYEE. On the DEPARTMENT side, we must write an insert department trigger that tries to insert a new EMPLOYEE for the new DEPARTMENT. However, the EMPLOYEE table will have its own insert trigger. When we try to insert the new EMPLOYEE, the DBMS calls the insert employee trigger, which will prevent the insertion of an EMPLOYEE unless it has a DEPARTMENT row. But the new DEPARTMENT row does not yet exist because it is trying to create the new EMPLOYEE row, which does not exist because the new DEPARTMENT row does not yet exist, and 'round and 'round we go!

Now consider a deletion in this same M-M relationship. Suppose we want to delete a DEPARTMENT. We cannot delete a DEPARTMENT that has any EMPLOYEE children. So, before deleting the DEPARTMENT, we must first reassign (or delete) all of the employees in that department. However, when we try to reassign the last EMPLOYEE, an EMPLOYEE update trigger will be fired that will not allow the last employee to be reassigned. (The trigger is programmed to ensure that every DEPARTMENT has at least one EMPLOYEE.) We have a stalemate; the last employee cannot get out of the department, and the department cannot be deleted until all employees are gone!

This problem has several solutions, but none is particularly satisfying. In the next chapter, we will show one solution using SQL Views. That solution is complicated and requires careful programming that is difficult to test and fix. The best advice is to avoid M-M relationships if you can. If you cannot avoid them, budget your time with foreknowledge that a difficult task lies ahead.

Designing Special Case M-M Relationships

Not all M-M relationships are as bad as the last section indicates. Although M-M relationships between strong entities generally are as complicated as described, M-M relationships between strong and weak entities are often easier. For example, consider the relationship between COMPANY and PHONE_CONTACT in Figure 6-30. Because PHONE_CONTACT is an ID-dependent weak entity, it must have a COMPANY parent. In addition, assume that application requirements indicate that each COMPANY row must have at least one row in PHONE_CONTACT. Hence, the relationship is M-M.

However, transactions are almost always initiated from the side of the strong entity. A data entry form will begin with a COMPANY and then, somewhere in the body of the form, the data from the PHONE_CONTACT table will appear. Hence, all insert, update, and deletion activity on PHONE_CONTACT will come as a result of some action on COMPANY. Given this situation, we can ignore the Action on Child columns in Figure 6-29(a) and Figure 6-29(b) because no one will ever try to insert, modify, or delete a new PHONE_CONTACT except in the context of inserting, modifying, or deleting a COMPANY.

Because the relationship is M-M, however, we must take all of the actions in the Action on Parent columns of both Figure 6-29(a) and Figure 6-29(b). With regards to inserts on parents, we must always create a child. We can meet this need by writing a COMPANY INSERT trigger that automatically creates a new row of PHONE_CONTACT with null values for Contact and PhoneNumber.

With regard to updates and deletions, all we need to do is to cascade all of the remaining actions in Figure 6-29(a) and Figure 6-29(b). Changes to COMPANY.CompanyName will be propagated to PHONE_CONTACT.CompanyName. The deletion of a COMPANY will automatically delete that company's PHONE_CONTACT rows. This makes sense; if we no longer want data about a company, we certainly no longer want its contact and phone data.

BY THE WAY   Because of the difficulty of enforcing M-M relationships, developers look for special circumstances to ease the task. Such circumstances usually exist for relationships between strong and weak entities, as described. For relationships between strong entities, such special circumstances may not exist. In this case, the M-M cardinality is sometimes just ignored. Of course, this cannot be done for applications such as financial management or operations that require careful records management, but for an application such as airline reservations, where seats are overbooked anyway, it might be better to redefine the relationship as M-O.

Documenting the Minimum Cardinality Design

Because enforcing minimum cardinality can be complicated and because it often involves the creation of triggers or other procedures, clear documentation is essential. Because the design for the enforcement of required parents is easier than that for required children, we will use different techniques for each.

Documenting Required Parents

Database modeling and design tools such as CA Technologies ERwin and Oracle's MySQL Workbench allow you to define **referential integrity (RI) actions** on each table. These definitions are useful for documenting the actions necessary for a required parent. According to Figure 6-29(a), three design decisions are necessary for required parents: (1) determining whether updates to the parent's primary key should cascade or be prohibited; (2) determining whether deletions of the parent should cascade or be prohibited; and (3) identifying how a parent row is to be selected on the insert of a child.

> **BY THE WAY**   In theory, referential integrity actions can be used to document the actions to be taken to enforce required children as well as required parents. When they are used for both purposes, however, they become confusing and ambiguous. In an M-M relationship, for example, a child may have one set of rules for insert because of its required parent and another set of rules for insert because it is a required child. The insert referential integrity action will be overloaded with these two purposes, and its meaning will be ambiguous at best. Hence, in this text, we will use referential integrity actions only for documenting required parents. We will use another technique, described next, for documenting required children.

Documenting Required Children

One easy and unambiguous way for defining the actions to enforce a required child is to use Figure 6-29(b) as a boilerplate document. Create a copy of this figure for each relationship that has a required child and fill in the specific actions for insert, update, and delete operations.

For example, consider Figure 6-32, which shows the O-M relationship between DEPARTMENT and EMPLOYEE. A given department must have at least one employee, but an employee does not have to be assigned to a specific department. For example, the company may have an employee who is an expediter (whose job is to solve problems throughout the company and in whichever department is experiencing a problem) who is not formally assigned to a department. DEPARTMENT has a surrogate key, DepartmentID, and other columns as shown in Figure 6-32.

Because the DEPARTMENT-to-EMPLOYEE relationship has a required child, we will fill out the table in Figure 6-29(b). Figure 6-33 shows the result. Here triggers are described for DEPARTMENT insert, EMPLOYEE modification (update), and EMPLOYEE deletion. DEPARTMENT modification (update) actions are unneeded because DEPARTMENT has a surrogate key.

An Additional Complication

You should be aware of an additional complication that is beyond the scope of this text. A table can participate in many relationships. In fact, there can be multiple relationships between the

FIGURE 6-32

DEPARTMENT-to-EMPLOYEE O-M Relationship

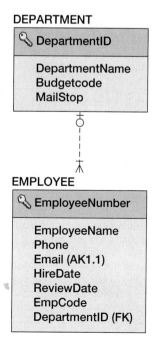

EMPLOYEE Is Required Child	Action on DEPARTMENT	Action on EMPLOYEE
Insert	Trigger to create row in EMPLOYEE when inserting DEPARTMENT. Disallow DEPARTMENT insert if EMPLOYEE data are not available.	None.
Modify key or foreign key	Not possible, surrogate key.	Trigger needed: If not last EMPLOYEE, OK. If last EMPLOYEE, prohibit or assign another EMPLOYEE
Delete	None.	Trigger needed: If not last EMPLOYEE, OK. If last EMPLOYEE, prohibit or assign another EMPLOYEE

same two tables. You need to specify a design for the minimum cardinality of every relationship. The minimum cardinality of each relationship will vary. Some will be O-M, some will be M-O, and some will be M-M. Some of the relationships will require triggers, which may mean that you have several sets of insert, update, and delete triggers per table. This array of triggers is not only complicated to write and test, the actions of different triggers may interfere with one another during execution. You will need more experience and knowledge to design, implement, and test such complex arrays of trigger code and DBMS constraints. For now, just be aware that these problems exist.

Summary of Minimum Cardinality Design

Figure 6-34 summarizes the design for relationship minimum cardinality. It shows each type of relationship, the design decisions that need to be made, and the documentation that should be created. Use this figure as a guide.

The View Ridge Gallery Database

We conclude this chapter with an example database design problem. This design will be used throughout the rest of the text, so take the time to understand it. This particular problem was chosen because it has typical relationships and moderate complexity. It has enough challenges to make it interesting, but not so many as to make it overwhelming.

Relationship Minimum Cardinality	Design Decisions to Be Made	Design Documentation
M-O	• Update cascade or prohibit? • Delete cascade or prohibit? • Policy for obtaining parent on insert of child	Referential integrity (RI) actions plus documentation for policy on obtaining parent for child insert.
O-M	• Policy for obtaining child on insert of parent • Primary key update cascade or prohibit? • Policy for update of child foreign key • Policy for deletion of child	Use Figure 6-28(b) as a boilerplate.
M-M	All decisions for M-O and O-M above, plus how to process trigger conflict on insertion of first instance of parent/child and deletion of last instance of parent/child.	For mandatory parent, RI actions plus documentation for policy on obtaining parent for child insert. For mandatory child, use Figure 6-28(b) as a boilerplate. Add documentation on how to process trigger conflict.

FIGURE 6-35

View Ridge Gallery Web Site
Home Page

View Ridge Gallery Database Summary of Requirements

The View Ridge Gallery (View Ridge or VRG) is a small art gallery that sells contemporary European and North American fine art, including lithographs, high-quality reproduction prints, original paintings and other artwork, and photographs. All of the lithographs, prints, and photos are signed and numbered, and the original art is usually signed. View Ridge also provides art framing services. It creates a custom frame for each artwork (rather than selling standardized, premade frames) and is known for its excellent collection of frame stock. The View Ridge Gallery Web site is shown in Figure 6-35.

View Ridge emphasizes reproduction artworks of European Impressionist, Abstractionist, and Modernist artists such as Wassily Kandinsky and Henri Matisse. For original art, View Ridge concentrates on Northwest School artists, such as Mark Tobey, Morris Graves, Guy Anderson, and Paul Horiuchi, and produces shows of contemporary artists who work in the Northwest School tradition or in Northwest Maritime art. The price of new reproduction prints ranges up to $1,000, and prices for contemporary artists range from $500 to $10,000. The price of art from the Northwest School artists varies considerably, depending on the artwork itself. Small pencil, charcoal, or watercolor sketches may sell for as little as $2,000, whereas major works can range from $10,000 to $100,000. Very occasionally, View Ridge may carry Northwest School art priced up to $500,000, but art priced above $250,000 is more likely to be sold at auction by a major art auction house.

View Ridge has been in business for 30 years and has one full-time owner, three salespeople, and two workers who make frames, hang art in the gallery, and prepare artwork for shipment. View Ridge holds openings and other gallery events to attract customers to the gallery. View Ridge owns all of the art that it acquires and sells—even the sale of contemporary artwork is treated as a purchase by View Ridge that then is resold to a customer. View Ridge does not take items on a consignment basis.

Note that this is *not* a sales order database as illustrated in Figure 6-19. Rather, it is an *art work acquisitions* database, designed to record each acquisition of a piece of art work by the View Ridge Gallery, and then to record the details of the sale of the piece of art. This system is necessary because a single piece of art may be acquired and resold more than once, and the View Ridge Gallery needs a database designed to meet these specialized data and information requirements.

The View Ridge Gallery does sell other products and services besides art work. For example, framing services, selected books on art and artists, and specialized post cards are all

FIGURE 6-36

Summary of View
Ridge Gallery Database
Requirements

Summary of View Ridge Gallery Database Requirements
Track customers and their interest in specific artists
Record the gallery's purchases
Record customer's purchases
Report how fast an artist's works have sold and at what margin
Show the artists represented by the gallery on a Web page
Show current inventory on a Web page
Show all the works of art that have appeared in the gallery on Web pages

available at the View Ridge Gallery. For these, products and services, however, there is a sale order system that interfaces will interface with the acquisition database.

The requirements for the View Ridge acquisition application are summarized in Figure 6-36. First, both the owner and the salespeople want to keep track of customers' names, addresses, phone numbers, and email addresses. They also want to know which artists have appeal to which customers. The salespeople use this information to determine whom to contact when new art arrives and to personalize verbal and email communications with their customers.

When the gallery purchases new art, data about the artist, the nature of the work, the acquisition date, and the acquisition price are recorded. Also, on occasion, the gallery repurchases art from a customer and resells it; thus, a work may appear in the gallery multiple times. When art is repurchased, the artist and work data are not reentered, but the most recent acquisition date and price are recorded. In addition, when art is sold, the purchase date, sales price, and identity of the purchasing customer are stored in the database.

Salespeople want to examine past purchase data so they can devote more time to the most active buyers. They also sometimes use the purchase records to identify the location of artworks they have sold in the past.

For marketing purposes, View Ridge wants its database application to provide a list of artists and works that have appeared in the gallery. The owner also would like to be able to determine how fast an artist's work sells and at what sales margin. The database application also should display current inventory on a Web page that customers can access via the Internet.

The View Ridge Data Model

Figure 6-37 shows a data model for the View Ridge database. This model has two strong entities: CUSTOMER and ARTIST. In addition, the entity WORK is ID-dependent on ARTIST, and the entity TRANS is ID-dependent on WORK. There is also a nonidentifying relationship from CUSTOMER to TRANS.

Note that we are using the entity name TRANS instead of TRANSACTION. We are doing this because *transaction* is a **DBMS reserved word** in most (if not all) DBMS products. Using DBMS reserved words such as *table*, *column*, or other names can create problems. Similarly, we cannot use the reserved word *tran*. The word *trans*, however, is not a DBMS reserved word, and we can use it without problems. We will discuss this problem more when we discuss Microsoft SQL Serve 201 in Chapter 10A, Oracle Database in Chapter 10B, and MySQL 5.6 in Chapter 10C.

In the View Ridge data model, an artist may be recorded in the database even if none of his or her works has appeared in the gallery. This is done to record customer preferences for artists whose works might appear in the future. Thus, an artist may have from zero to many works.

The identifier of WORK is the composite (Title, Copy) because, in the case of lithographs and photos, there may be many copies of a given title. Also, the requirements indicate that a work may appear in the gallery many times, so there is a need for potentially many TRANS

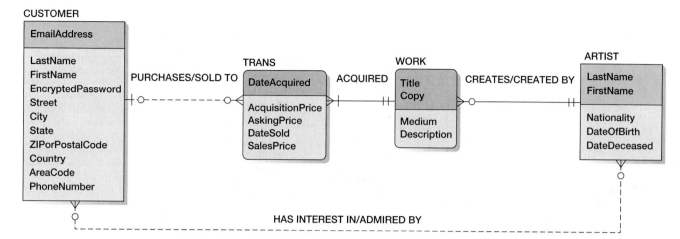

FIGURE 6-37

View Ridge Gallery Data
Model

entities for each WORK. Each time a work appears in the gallery, the acquisition date and price must be recorded. Thus, each WORK must have at least one TRANS row.

A customer may purchase many works; this is recorded in the 1:N relationship from CUSTOMER to TRANS. Note that this relationship is optional in both directions. Finally, there is an N:M relationship between CUSTOMERs and ARTISTs. This is an N:M relationship between strong entities—the team searched in vain for a missing attribute that would indicate an association pattern rather than an N:M relationship.

Database Design with Data Keys

A database design for the data model in Figure 6-37 is shown in Figure 6-38. This design uses data keys, and every primary key except the composite (ARTIST.LastName, ARTIST. FirstName) has problems. The keys for WORK and TRANS are huge, and the key for CUSTOMER is doubtful; many customers may not have an email address. Because of these problems, this design cries out for surrogate keys.

Surrogate Key Database Design

The database design for the View Ridge database using surrogate keys is shown in Figure 6-39. Notice that two identifying relationships (TRANS-to-WORK) and (WORK-to-ARTIST) have been changed to nonidentifying relationships represented by dashed lines. This was done because once ARTIST has a surrogate key, there is no need to keep ID-dependent keys in WORK and TRANS. Realize that WORK and TRANS are both weak entities even though they are no longer ID-dependent.

FIGURE 6-38

Initial View Ridge Gallery
Database Design

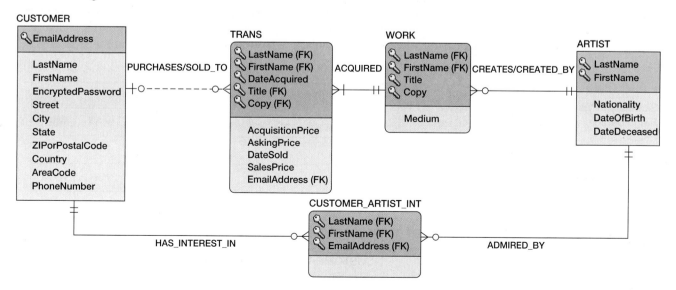

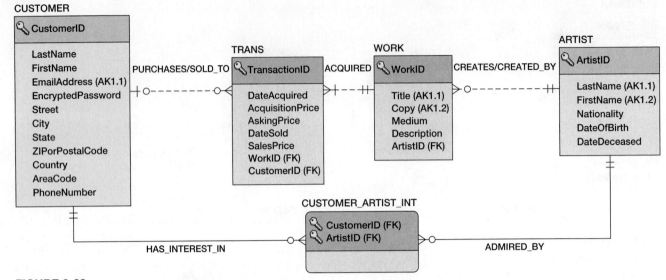

FIGURE 6-39

Final View Ridge Gallery Database Design

Notice that (LastName, FirstName) in ARTIST has been defined as an alternate key. This notation indicates that (LastName, FirstName) has a UNIQUE constraint, which ensures that artists are not duplicated in the database. Similarly, (Title, Copy) in WORK is defined as an alternate key so that a given work cannot appear more than once.

The foreign key placement is a straightforward application of the techniques described in this chapter, but note that the foreign key CustomerID in TRANS can have null values. This specification allows the creation of a TRANS row when a work is acquired, before any customer has purchased the work. All other foreign keys are required.

Minimum Cardinality Enforcement for Required Parents

According to Figure 6-29(a), for each relationship that involves a required parent, we need to decide:

- Whether to cascade or prohibit updates of the parent's primary key
- Whether to cascade or prohibit deletions of the parent
- How to obtain a parent when a new child is created

Because there is no consistent means of documenting these actions in commercial database design products, we will use the templates in Figure 6-29 to document our decisions. Figure 6-40 summarizes the relationships in the View Ridge database design.

Because all tables have surrogate keys, there is no need for any update cascade behavior for any parent. However, some update actions on child tables must be restricted. For example, once a WORK (child) is assigned to an ARTIST (parent), it is never to change to another parent. Because this database is used to record purchases and sales, View Ridge

FIGURE 6-40

Summary of View Ridge Database Design Relationships

Relationship		Cardinality		
Parent	**Child**	**Type**	**MAX**	**MIN**
ARTIST	WORK	Nonidentifying	1:N	M-O
WORK	TRANS	Nonidentifying	1:N	M-M
CUSTOMER	TRANS	Nonidentifying	1:N	O-O
CUSTOMER	CUSTOMER_ARTIST_INT	Identifying	1:N	M-O
ARTIST	CUSTOMER_ARTIST_INT	Identifying	1:N	M-O

management never wants to delete any data that are related to a transaction. From time to time, it may remove prior year's data in bulk, but it will do that using bulk data transfer and not as part of any application.

Hence, any CUSTOMER, WORK, or ARTIST row that is related to a TRANS row is never to be deleted. Note, however, that rows of CUSTOMERs who have never made a purchase and rows of ARTISTs whose works have never been carried in the gallery can be deleted. If either a CUSTOMER or ARTIST is deleted under these circumstances, the deletion will cascade to rows in the intersection table CUSTOMER_ARTIST_INT.

Finally, referential integrity actions are necessary for obtaining a parent WORK when a TRANS record is created and a parent ARTIST when a WORK record is created. In both cases, the policy will be for the application program to provide the ID of the required parent at the time the WORK or TRANS record is created.

All these actions are documented in Figure 6-41, where each part is based on the template for required children shown in Figure 6-29(a). Note that there is no diagram for the CUSTOMER-to-TRANS relationship because that is an O-O relationship without a required parent (or child).

Minimum Cardinality Enforcement for the Required Child

As shown in the summary in Figure 6-40, TRANS is the only required child in the database design in Figure 6-39. The actions to enforce that required child are documented in Figure 6-42, which is based on the template in Figure 6-29(b).

According to this document, an INSERT trigger on WORK will be written to create the required child. This trigger will be fired whenever a work is first introduced at the gallery. At that time, a new TRANS row will be created to store the values for DateAcquired and AcquisitionPrice.

FIGURE 6-41

Actions to Enforce Minimum Cardinality for Required Parents

ARTIST Is Required Parent	Action on ARTIST (Parent)	Action on WORK (Child)
Insert	None.	Get a parent.
Modify key or foreign key	Prohibit—ARTIST uses a surrogate key.	Prohibit—ARTIST uses a surrogate key.
Delete	Prohibit if WORK exists— data about a work and its related transaction is never deleted (business rule). Allow if no WORK exists (business rule).	None.

(a) For the ARTIST-to-WORK Relationship

WORK Is Required Parent	Action on WORK (Parent)	Action on TRANS (Child)
Insert	None.	Get a parent.
Modify key or foreign key	Prohibit—WORK uses a surrogate key.	Prohibit—WORK uses a surrogate key.
Delete	Prohibit—data about a work and its related transaction is never deleted (business rule).	None.

(b) For the WORK-to-TRANS Relationship

FIGURE 6-41

Continued

CUSTOMER Is Required Parent	Action on CUSTOMER (Parent)	Action on CUSTOMER_ARTIST_INT (Child)
Insert	None.	Get a parent.
Modify key or foreign key	Prohibit—CUSTOMER uses a surrogate key.	Prohibit—CUSTOMER uses a surrogate key.
Delete	Prohibit if a transaction related to this CUSTOMER exists—data related to a transaction is never deleted (business rule). Allow if no transaction related to this CUSTOMER exists—(business rule)—cascade delete children.	None.

(c) For the CUSTOMER-to-CUSTOMER_ARTIST_INT Relationship

ARTIST Is Required Parent	Action on ARTIST (Parent)	Action on CUSTOMER_ARTIST_INT (Child)
Insert	None.	Get a parent.
Modify key or foreign key	Prohibit—ARTIST uses a surrogate key.	Prohibit—ARTIST uses a surrogate key.
Delete	Prohibit if a transaction related to a work by this ARTIST exists—data related to a transaction is never deleted (business rule). Allow if no transaction related to a work by this ARTIST exists—(business rule)—cascade delete children.	None.

(d) For the ARTIST-to-CUSTOMER_ARTIST_INT Relationship

FIGURE 6-42

Actions to Enforce Minimum Cardinality for Required Children for the WORK-to-TRANS Relationship

TRANS Is Required Child	Action on WORK (Parent)	Action on TRANS (Child)
Insert	INSERT trigger on WORK to create row in TRANS. TRANS will be given data for DateAcquired and AcquisitionPrice. Other columns will be null.	Will be created by INSERT trigger on WORK.
Modify key or foreign key	Prohibit—surrogate key.	Prohibit—TRANS must always refer to the WORK associated with it.
Delete	Prohibit—data related to a transaction is never deleted (business rule).	Prohibit—data related to a transaction is never deleted (business rule).

Changes to the primary key in WORK will not occur because it has a surrogate key. Changes to the foreign key in TRANS will not be allowed because a TRANS never switches to another work. As stated earlier, the gallery has the policy that no transaction or related data will ever be deleted. Consequently, deletions of either WORK or TRANS are not allowed.

Column Properties for the View Ridge Database Design Tables

As we discussed at the beginning of this chapter, besides naming the columns in each table, we must specify the column properties summarized in Figure 6-1 for each column: null status, data type, default value (if any), and data constraints (if any). These are shown in Figure 6-43, where surrogate keys are shown using the **SQL Server IDENTITY({StartValue}, {Increment})**

FIGURE 6-43

Column Properties for the View Ridge Database Design

ARTIST

Column Name	Type	Key	NULL Status	Remarks
ArtistID	Int	Primary Key	NOT NULL	Surrogate Key IDENTITY (1,1)
LastName	Char (25)	Alternate Key	NOT NULL	Unique (AK1.1)
FirstName	Char (25)	Alternate Key	NOT NULL	Unique (AK1.2)
Nationality	Char (30)	No	NULL	IN ('Canadian', 'English', 'French', 'German', 'Mexican', 'Russian', 'Spanish', 'United States')
DateOfBirth	Numeric (4)	No	NULL	(DateOfBirth < DateDeceased) (BETWEEN 1900 and 2999)
DateDeceased	Numeric (4)	No	NULL	(BETWEEN 1900 and 2999)

(a) Column Characteristics for the ARTIST Table

WORK

Column Name	Type	Key	NULL Status	Remarks
WorkID	Int	Primary Key	NOT NULL	Surrogate Key IDENTITY (500,1)
Title	Char (35)	Alternate Key	NOT NULL	Unique (AK1.1)
Copy	Char (12)	Alternate Key	NOT NULL	Unique (AK1.2)
Medium	Char (35)	No	NULL	
Description	Varchar (1000)	No	NULL	DEFAULT value = 'Unknown provenance'
ArtistID	Int	Foreign Key	NOT NULL	

(b) Column Characteristics for the WORK Table

TRANS

Column Name	Type	Key	NULL Status	Remarks
TransactionID	Int	Primary Key	NOT NULL	Surrogate Key IDENTITY (100,1)
DateAcquired	Date	No	NOT NULL	
AcquisitionPrice	Numeric (8,2)	No	NOT NULL	
AskingPrice	Numeric (8,2)	No	NULL	
DateSold	Date	No	NULL	(DateAcquired <= DateSold)
SalesPrice	Numeric (8,2)	No	NULL	(SalesPrice > 0) AND (SalesPrice <= 500000)
CustomerID	Int	Foreign Key	NULL	
WorkID	Int	Foreign Key	NOT NULL	

(c) Column Characteristics for the TRANS Table

CUSTOMER

Column Name	Type	Key	NULL Status	Remarks
CustomerID	Int	Primary Key	NOT NULL	Surrogate Key IDENTITY (1000,1)
LastName	Char (25)	No	NOT NULL	
FirstName	Char (25)	No	NOT NULL	
EmailAddress	Varchar (100)	Alternate Key	NULL	Unique (AK 1.1)
EncryptedPassword	Varchar(50)	No	NULL	
Street	Char (30)	No	NULL	
City	Char (35)	No	NULL	
State	Char (2)	No	NULL	
ZIPorPostalCode	Char (9)	No	NULL	
Country	Char (50)	No	NULL	
AreaCode	Char (3)	No	NULL	
PhoneNumber	Char (8)	No	NULL	

(d) Column Characteristics for the CUSTOMER Table

CUSTOMER_ARTIST_INT

Column Name	Type	Key	NULL Status	Remarks
ArtistID	Int	Primary Key, Foreign Key	NOT NULL	
CustomerID	Int	Primary Key, Foreign Key	NOT NULL	

(e) Column Characteristics for the CUSTOMER_ARTIST_INT Table

FIGURE 6-43

Continued

property to specify the values the surrogate key will use. We will describe how to implement surrogate keys in our discussion of Microsoft SQL Server 2014 in Chapters 7 and 10A, for Oracle Database in Chapter 10B, and for MySQL 5.6 in Chapter 10C.

With this step, we have completed our database design for the View Ridge Gallery database, and now we are ready to create it as an actual, functioning database in a DBMS product. We will do so in many of the following chapters, so be certain that you understand the View Ridge Gallery database design we have built.

Summary

This chapter discusses the process of transforming a data model (as discussed in Chapter 5) into a database design. Figure 6-44 summarizes the various aspects of data models and database designs, how they relate to each other, and how they relate to the systems analysis and design process in general and to the systems development life cycle (SDLC) in particular. For more information about systems analysis and design and the SDLC, see Appendix B.

Transforming a data model into a database design requires three major tasks: replacing each entity with a table and each attribute with a column; representing relationships and maximum cardinality by placing foreign keys; and representing minimum cardinality by defining actions to constrain activities on values of primary and foreign keys.

During database design, each entity is replaced by a table. The attributes of the entity become columns of the table. The identifier of the entity becomes the primary key of the table, and candidate keys in the entity become candidate keys in the table. A good primary key is short, numeric, and fixed. If a good primary key is not available, a surrogate key may be used instead. Some organizations choose to use surrogate keys for all of their tables. An alternate key is the same as a candidate key and is used to ensure unique values in a column. The notation AK$n.m$ refers to the nth alternative key and the mth column in that key.

Four properties need to be specified for each table column: null status, data type, default value, and data constraints. A column can be NULL or NOT NULL. Primary keys are always NOT NULL; alternate keys can be NULL. Data types depend on the DBMS to be used. Generic data types include CHAR(n), VARCHAR(n), DATE, TIME, INTEGER, FLOAT, NUMERIC and DECIMAL. A default value is a value to be supplied by the DBMS when a new row is created. It can be a simple value or the result of a function. Sometimes triggers are needed to supply values of more complicated expressions.

Data constraints include domain constraints, range constraints, intrarelation constraints, and interrelation constraints. Domain constraints specify a set of values that a column may have; range constraints specify an interval of allowed values; intrarelation constraints involve comparisons among columns in the same table; and interrelation constraints involve comparisons among columns in different tables. A referential integrity constraint is an example of an interrelation constraint.

Once the tables, keys, and columns have been defined, they should be checked against normalization criteria. Usually the tables will already be normalized, but they should be checked in any case. Also, it may be necessary to denormalize some tables.

The second step in database design is to create relationships by placing foreign keys appropriately. For 1:1 strong relationships, the key of either table can go in the other table as a foreign key; for 1:N strong relationships, the key of the parent must go in the child; and for N:M strong relationships, a new table, called an intersection table, is constructed that has the keys of both tables. Intersection tables never have nonkey data.

Four uses for ID-dependent entities are N:M relationships, association relationships, multivalued attributes, and archetype/instance relationships. An association relationship differs from an intersection table because the ID-dependent entity has nonkey data. In all ID-dependent entities, the key of the parent is already in the child. Therefore, no foreign key needs to be created. When an instance entity of the archetype/instance pattern is given a non-ID-dependent identifier, it changes from an ID-dependent entity to a weak entity. The tables that represent such entities must have the key of the parent as a foreign key. They remain weak entities, however. When the parent of an ID-dependent entity is given a surrogate key, the ID-dependent entity is also given a surrogate key. It remains a weak entity, however.

Mixed entities are represented by placing the key of the parent of the nonidentifying relationship into the child. The key of the parent of the identifying relationship will already be in the child. Subtypes are represented by copying the key from the supertype into the subtype(s) as a foreign key. Recursive relationships are represented in the same ways that 1:1, 1:N, and N:M relationships are represented. The only difference is that the foreign key references rows in the table in which it resides.

Ternary relationships are decomposed into binary relationships. However, sometimes binary constraints must be documented. Three such constraints are MUST, MUST NOT, and MUST COVER.

	Data Model (Chapter 5)	Database Design (Chapter 6)
SDLC Stage	Requirements Analysis	Component Design
SA&D Reference	Conceptual Design/Schema	
		Logical Design/Schema
		Physical Design (Data Types)
Data Structure	Entity	Table (Relation)
Relationship Structure	Relationship	Relationship with Foreign Keys
Level of Generality	Generic	DBMS Specific
Relationships:		
1:1	Yes	Yes
1:N	Yes	Yes
1:N ID-Dependent	Yes	Yes
N:M	Yes	No - See Intersection Table
Intersection Table with two 1:N ID-Dependent Relationships	NO - See N:M Relationships	Yes
Association Table with two 1: N ID-Dependent Relationships	Yes (Associative Entity)	Yes
SuperType/SubType	Yes Depends on Data Modeling Software	Yes Depends on Data Modeling Software
Recursive	Yes	Yes
Software Tools: (used in this book)	Microsoft Visio 2013	MySQL Workbench

FIGURE 6-44

Summary of the Database
Design Process

The third step in database design is to create a plan for enforcing minimum cardinality. Figure 6-29 shows the actions that need to be taken to enforce minimum cardinality for required parents and required children. The actions in Figure 6-29(a) must be taken for M-O and M-M relationships; the actions in Figure 6-29(b) must be taken for O-M and M-M relationships.

Enforcing mandatory parents can be done by defining the appropriate referential integrity constraint and by setting the foreign key to NOT NULL. The designer must specify whether updates to the parent's primary key will cascade or be prohibited, whether deletions to the parent will cascade or be prohibited, and what policy will be used for finding a parent when a new child is created.

Enforcing mandatory children is difficult and requires the use of triggers or application code. The

particular actions that need to be taken are shown in Figure 6-29(b). Enforcing M-M relationships can be very difficult. Particular challenges concern the creation of the first parent/child rows and the deletion of the last parent/child rows. The triggers on the two tables interfere with one another. M-M relationships between strong and weak entities are not as problematic as those between strong entities.

In this text, the actions to enforce required parents are documented using referential integrity actions on the table design diagrams. The actions to enforce required children are documented by using Figure 6-29(b) as a boilerplate document. An additional complication is that a table can participate in many relationships. Triggers written to enforce the minimum cardinality on one relationship may interfere with triggers written to enforce the minimum cardinality on another relationship. This problem is beyond the scope of this text, but be aware that it exists. The principles for enforcing minimum cardinality are summarized in Figure 6-34.

A database design for the View Ridge Gallery is shown in Figures 6-39, 6-40, 6-41, 6-42, and 6-43. You should understand this design because it will be used throughout the remainder of this book.

Key Terms

action
alternate key (AK)
association entity
associative entity
association table
candidate key
cascading deletion
cascading update
component design
data constraint
database design
DBMS reserved word
default value

domain constraint
interrelation constraint
intersection table
intrarelation constraint
minimum cardinality enforcement
   action
MUST constraint
MUST COVER
   constraint
MUST NOT constraint
null status
parent mandatory and child
   mandatory (M-M)

parent mandatory and child
   optional (M-O)
parent optional and child mandatory
   (O-M)
parent optional and child optional (O-O)
range constraint
referential integrity (RI) action
SQL Server IDENTITY ({StartValue},
   {Increment}) property
surrogate key
systems analysis and design
systems development life cycle (SDLC)
trigger

Review Questions

6.1 Identify the three major tasks for transforming a data model into a database design.

6.2 What is the relationship between entities and tables? Between attributes and columns?

6.3 Why is the choice of the primary key important?

6.4 What are the three characteristics of an ideal primary key?

6.5 What is a surrogate key? What are its advantages?

6.6 When should you use a surrogate key?

6.7 Describe two disadvantages of surrogate keys.

6.8 What is the difference between an alternate key and a candidate key?

6.9 What does the notation LastName (AK2.2) mean?

6.10 Name four column properties.

6.11 Explain why primary keys may never be null but alternate keys can be null.

6.12 List five generic data types.

6.13 Describe three ways that a default value can be assigned.

6.14 What is a domain constraint? Give an example.

6.15 What is a range constraint? Give an example.

6.16 What is an intrarelation constraint? Give an example.

6.17 What is an interrelation constraint? Give an example.

6.18 What tasks should be accomplished when verifying normalization of a database design?

6.19 Describe two ways to represent a 1:1 strong entity relationship. Give an example other than one in this chapter.

6.20 Describe how to represent a 1:N strong entity relationship. Give an example other than one in this chapter.

6.21 Describe how to represent an N:M strong entity relationship. Give an example other than one in this chapter.

6.22 What is an intersection table? Why is it necessary?

6.23 What is the difference between the table that represents an ID-dependent association entity and an intersection table?

6.24 List four uses for ID-dependent entities.

6.25 Describe how to represent an association entity relationship. Give an example other than one in this chapter.

6.26 Describe how to represent a multivalued attribute entity relationship. Give an example other than one in this chapter.

6.27 Describe how to represent a archetype/instance entity relationship. Give an example other than one in this chapter.

6.28 What happens when an instance entity is given a non-ID-dependent identifier? How does this change affect relationship design?

6.29 What happens when the parent in an ID-dependent relationship is given a surrogate key? What should the key of the child become?

6.30 Describe how to represent a mixed entity relationship. Give an example other than one in this chapter.

6.31 Describe how to represent a supertype/subtype entity relationship. Give an example other than one in this chapter.

6.32 Describe two ways to represent a 1:1 recursive relationship. Give an example other than one in this chapter.

6.33 Describe how to represent a 1:N recursive relationship. Give an example other than one in this chapter.

6.34 Describe how to represent an N:M recursive relationship. Give an example other than one in this chapter.

6.35 In general, how are ternary relationships represented? Explain how a binary constraint may affect such a relationship.

6.36 Describe a MUST constraint. Give an example other than one in this chapter.

6.37 Describe a MUST NOT constraint. Give an example other than one in this chapter.

6.38 Describe a MUST COVER constraint. Give an example other than one in this chapter.

6.39 Explain, in general terms, what needs to be done to enforce minimum cardinality.

6.40 Explain the need for each of the actions in Figure 6-29(a).

6.41 Explain the need for each of the actions in Figure 6-29(b).

6.42 State which of the actions in Figure 6-29 must be applied for M-O relationships, O-M relationships, and M-M relationships.

6.43 Explain what must be done for the DBMS to enforce required parents.

6.44 What design decisions must be made to enforce required parents?

6.45 Explain why the DBMS cannot be used to enforce required children.

6.46 What is a trigger? How can triggers be used to enforce required children?

6.47 Explain why the enforcement of M-M relationships is particularly difficult.

6.48 Explain the need for each of the design decisions in Figure 6-34.

6.49 Explain the implications of each of the minimum cardinality specifications in Figure 6-40.

6.50 Explain the rationale for each of the entries in the table in Figure 6-42.

Project Questions

6.51 Answer Project Question 5.56 if you have not already done so. Design a database for your model in Project Question 5.56. Your design should include a specification of tables and attributes as well as primary, candidate, and foreign keys. Also specify how you will enforce minimum cardinality. Document your minimum cardinality enforcement using referential integrity actions for a required parent, if any, and the form in Figure 6-29(b) for a required child, if any.

6.52 Answer Project Question 5.57 if you have not already done so. Design a database for your model in Project Question 5.57(c). Your design should include a specification of tables and attributes as well as primary, candidate, and foreign keys. Also specify how you will enforce minimum cardinality. Document your minimum cardinality enforcement using referential integrity actions for required parents, if any, and the form in Figure 6-29(b) for required children, if any.

6.53 Answer Project Question 5.58 if you have not already done so. Design a database for your model in Project Question 5.58(d). Your design should include a specification of tables and attributes as well as primary, candidate, and foreign keys. Also specify how you will enforce minimum cardinality. Document your minimum cardinality enforcement using referential integrity actions for required parents, if any, and the form in Figure 6-29(b) for required children, if any.

6.54 Answer Project Question 5.59 if you have not already done so. Design databases for your model in Project Question 5.59(a) and for the model in Figure 5-57. Your designs should include a specification of tables and attributes as well as primary, candidate, and foreign keys. Also specify how you will enforce minimum cardinality. Document your minimum cardinality enforcement using referential integrity actions for required parents, if any, and the form in Figure 6-29(b) for required children, if any.

6.55 Answer Project Question 5.60 if you have not already done so. Design a database for your model in Project Question 5.60(e). Your design should include a specification of tables and attributes as well as primary, candidate, and foreign keys. Also specify how you will enforce minimum cardinality. Document your minimum cardinality enforcement using referential integrity actions for required parents, if any, and the form in Figure 6-29(b) for required children, if any.

6.56 Answer Project Question 5.61 if you have not already done so. Design a database for your model in Project Question 5.61(c). Your design should include a specification of tables and attributes as well as primary, candidate, and foreign keys. Also specify how you will enforce minimum cardinality. Document your minimum cardinality enforcement using referential integrity actions for required parents, if any, and the form in Figure 6-29(b) for required children, if any.

6.57 Answer Project Question 5.62 if you have not already done so. Design a database for your model in Project Question 5.62(d). Your design should include a specification of tables and attributes as well as primary, candidate, and foreign keys. Also specify how you will enforce minimum cardinality. Document your minimum cardinality enforcement using referential integrity actions for required parents, if any, and the form in Figure 6-29(b) for required children, if any.

Case Questions

Writer's State Patrol Case Questions

Answer the Writer's State Patrol Case Questions in Chapter 5 if you have not already done so. Design a database for your data model from Chapter 5.

A. Convert this data model to a database design. Specify tables, primary keys, and foreign keys. Using Figure 6-43 as a guide, specify column properties.

B. Describe how you have represented weak entities, if any exist.

C. Describe how you have represented supertype and subtype entities, if any exist.

D. Create a visual representation of your database design as a Crow's Foot E-R diagram similar to the one in Figure 6-39.

E. Document your minimum cardinality enforcement using referential integrity actions for required parents, if any, and the form in Figure 6-29(b) for required children, if any.

San Juan Sailboat Charters Case Questions

San Juan Sailboat Charters (SJSBC) is an agency that leases (charters) sailboats. SJSBC does not own the boats. Instead, SJSBC leases boats on behalf of boat owners who want to earn income from their boats when they are not using them, and SJSBC charges the owners a fee for this service. SJSBC specializes in boats that can be used for multiday or weekly charters. The smallest sailboat available is 28 feet in length, and the largest is 51 feet in length.

Each sailboat is fully equipped at the time it is leased. Most of the equipment is provided at the time of the charter. Most of the equipment is provided by the owners, but some is provided by SJSBC. The owner-provided equipment includes equipment that is attached to the boat, such as radios, compasses, depth indicators and other instrumentation, stoves, and refrigerators. Other owner-provided equipment, such as sails, lines, anchors, dinghies, life preservers, and equipment in the cabin (dishes, silverware, cooking utensils, bedding, and so on), is not physically attached to the boat. SJSBC provides consumable supplies, such as charts, navigation books, tide and current tables, soap, dish towels, toilet paper, and similar items. The consumable supplies are treated as equipment by SJSBC for tracking and accounting purposes.

Keeping track of equipment is an important part of SJSBC's responsibilities. Much of the equipment is expensive, and those items not physically attached to the boat can be easily damaged, lost, or stolen. SJSBC holds the customer responsible for all of the boat's equipment during the period of the charter.

SJSBC likes to keep accurate records of its customers and charters, and customers are required to keep a log during each charter. Some itineraries and weather conditions are more dangerous than others, and the data from these logs provide information about the customer experience. This information is useful for marketing purposes as well as for evaluating a customer's ability to handle a particular boat and itinerary.

Sailboats need maintenance. Note that two definitions of boat are (1) "break out another thousand" and (2) "a hole in the water into which one pours money." SJSBC is required by its contracts with the boat owners to keep accurate records of all maintenance activities and costs.

A data model of a proposed database to support an information system for SJSBC is shown in Figure 6-45. Note that, because the OWNER entity allows for owners to be companies are well as individuals, SJSBC can be included as an equipment owner (note that the

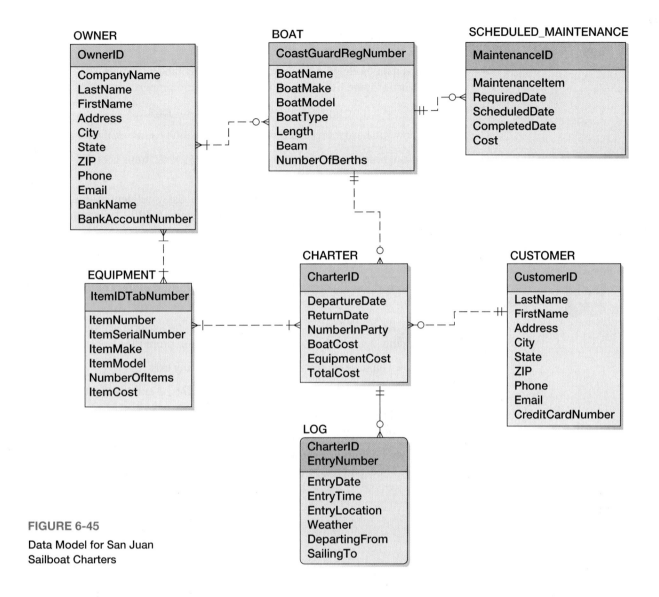

FIGURE 6-45

Data Model for San Juan
Sailboat Charters

cardinalities in the diagram allow SJSBC to own equipment while not owning any boats).
Also note that this model relates EQUIPMENT to CHARTER rather than BOAT even when
the equipment is physically attached to the boat. This is only one possible way to handle
EQUIPMENT, but it is satisfactory to the managers of SJSBC.

A. Convert this data model to a database design. Specify tables, primary keys, and foreign keys. Using Figure 6-43 as a guide, specify column properties.

B. Describe how you have represented weak entities, if any exist.

C. Describe how you have represented supertype and subtype entities, if any exist.

D. Create a visual representation of your database design as a Crow's Foot E-R diagram
similar to the one in Figure 6-39.

E. Document your minimum cardinality enforcement using referential integrity actions for required parents, if any, and the form in Figure 6-29(b) for required children, if any.

The Queen Anne Curiosity Shop

If you have not already done so, complete the Queen Anne Curiosity Shop project at the end of Chapter 5.

A. Convert this data model to a database design. Specify tables, primary keys, and foreign keys. Using Figure 6-43 as a guide, specify column properties.

B. Describe how you have represented weak entities, if any exist.

C. Describe how you have represented supertype and subtype entities, if any exist.

D. Create a visual representation of your database design as a Crow's Foot E-R diagram similar to the one in Figure 6-39.

E. Document your minimum cardinality enforcement using referential integrity actions for required parents, if any, and the form in Figure 6-29(b) for required children, if any.

Morgan Importing

If you have not already done so, complete the Morgan Importing project at the end of Chapter 5.

A. Convert this data model to a database design. Specify tables, primary keys, and foreign keys. Using Figure 6-43 as a guide, specify column properties.

B. Describe how you have represented weak entities, if any exist.

C. Describe how you have represented supertype and subtype entities, if any exist.

D. Create a visual representation of your database design as a Crow's Foot E-R diagram similar to the one in Figure 6-39.

E. Document your minimum cardinality enforcement using referential integrity actions for required parents, if any, and the form in Figure 6-29(b) for required children, if any.

Database Implementation

In Chapter 5, we discussed how to create a data model for a new database, and in Chapter 6, we demonstrated how to transform that data model into a database design that we can use to build an actual database in a relational DBMS. We used the View Ridge Gallery (VRG) database as our example in Chapter 6 and finished with a complete set of specifications for the VRG database. In Part 3, we will implement the VRG database design in Microsoft SQL Server 2014 (with versions for Oracle Database and MySQL 5.6 shown in Chapters 10B and 10C, respectively).

Part 3 consists of two chapters. Chapter 7 presents SQL data definition language statements for constructing database components and describes the SQL data manipulation statements for inserting, updating, and deleting data. You will also learn how to construct and use SQL views. The chapter concludes with an introduction to embedding SQL statements in application programs and SQL/Persistent Stored Modules (SQL/PSM), which leads to a discussion of SQL triggers and stored procedures.

Chapter 8 presents the use of SQL statements to redesign databases. It presents SQL correlated subqueries and then introduces SQL statements using the SQL EXISTS and NOT EXISTS keywords. Both of these advanced SQL statements are needed for database redesign. Chapter 8 also describes database reverse engineering, surveys common database redesign problems, and shows how to use SQL to solve database redesign problems.

PART

3

SQL for Database Construction and Application Processing

Chapter Objectives

- To create and manage table structures using SQL statements
- To understand how referential integrity actions are implemented in SQL statements
- To create and execute SQL constraints
- To understand several uses for SQL views
- To use SQL statements to create, use, and manage views

- To understand how SQL is used in application programming
- To understand SQL/Persistent Stored Modules (SQL/PSM)
- To understand how to create and use functions
- To understand how to create and use triggers
- To understand how to create and use stored procedures

In Chapter 2, we introduced SQL and classified SQL statements into five categories:

- **Data definition language (DDL)** statements, which are used for creating tables, relationships, and other database structures.
- **Data manipulation language (DML)** statements, which are used for querying, inserting, updating, and deleting data.
- **SQL/Persistent Stored Modules (SQL/PSM)** statements, which extend SQL by adding procedural programming capabilities, such as variables and flow-of-control statements, that provide some programmability within the SQL framework.
- **Transaction control language (TCL)** statements, which are used to mark transaction boundaries and control transaction behavior.
- **Data control language (DCL)** statements, which are used to grant database permissions (or to revoke those permissions) to users and groups so the users or groups can perform various operations on the data in the database

In Chapter 2, we discussed only DML query statements. This chapter describes and illustrates SQL DDL statements for constructing databases; SQL DML statements for inserting, modifying, and deleting data; and SQL statements to create and use SQL views. We also discuss how to embed SQL statements into application programs and

SQL/PSM and how to use SQL/PSM to create functions, triggers, and stored procedures. SQL TCL and SQL DCL statements are discussed in Chapter 9.

In this chapter, we use a DBMS product to create the database that we designed, by creating a **database design** based on a **data model**, in Chapter 6. We are now in the **implementation** step of the **systems development life cycle (SDLC)** in the **systems analysis and design** process. This is the SDLC step that we have been working toward all along—building and implementing the database and management information system application that uses that database. (For an introduction to systems analysis and design and to the SDLC, see Appendix B—Getting Started with Systems Analysis and Design.)

The knowledge in this chapter is important whether you become a database administrator or an application programmer. Even if you will not construct SQL user-defined functions, triggers, or stored procedures yourself, it is important that you know what they are, how they work, and how they influence database processing.

The Importance of Working with an Installed DBMS Product

In order to fully understand the DBMS concepts and features we discuss and illustrate in the chapter, you need to work with them in an installed DBMS product. This *hands-on* experience is necessary so that you move from an abstract understanding of these concepts and features to a practical knowledge of them and how they are used and implemented.

The topics in this chapter, as well as topics in Chapters 9 and 10 outline this material as it relates to the three major DBMS products discussed in this text.

The specific information you need to download, install, and use these DBMS products is found in three online chapters available at *www.pearsonhighered.com/kroenke/*. Microsoft SQL Server 2014 is discussed in online Chapter 10A, Oracle Database 12*c* and Oracle Database Express Edition 11*g* Release 2 are discussed in online Chapter 10B, and MySQL 5.6 is discussed in online Chapter 10C. As described in the introductory Chapter 10, portions of these chapters parallel the discussion in this chapter and illustrate the actual use of the concepts and features in each DBMS product.

To get the most out of this chapter, you should download and install the DBMS product(s) of your choice and then follow your work in each section of this chapter by working thorough the corresponding sections of the chapter for your DBMS product.

The View Ridge Gallery Database

In Chapter 6, we introduced the View Ridge Gallery, a small art gallery that sells contemporary North American and European fine art and provides art framing services. We also developed a data model and database design for a database for the View Ridge Gallery. Our final database design for the View Ridge Gallery is shown in Figure 7-1. You should review the database design, table column characteristics, and relationship specifications as described in Chapter 6. In this chapter, we will use SQL to build a database for the View Ridge Gallery named VRG based on that design. The SQL Scripts needed to create the VRG database are available at *www.pearsonhighered.com/kroenke*.

SQL DDL and DML

Figure 7-2 summarizes the new SQL DDL and DML statements described in this chapter. We begin with SQL DDL statements for managing table structures, including CREATE TABLE, ALTER TABLE, DROP TABLE, and TRUNCATE TABLE. Using these statements, we will build the table structure for the View Ridge database. Then we present the four SQL DML statements for managing data: INSERT, UPDATE, DELETE, and MERGE.

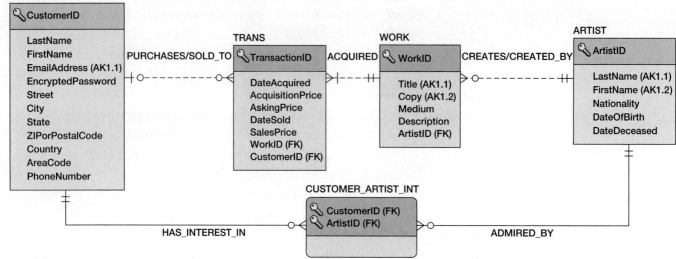

FIGURE 7-1

Final VRG Database Design
for the View Ridge Gallery

FIGURE 7-2

Chapter 7 SQL Elements

SQL Elements Discussed in Chapter 7
• SQL Data Definition Language (DDL)
— CREATE TABLE
— ALTER TABLE
— DROP TABLE
— TRUNCATE TABLE
• SQL Data Manipulation Language (DML)
— INSERT
— UPDATE
— DELETE
— MERGE
• SQL Views
— CREATE VIEW
— ALTER VIEW
— DROP VIEW
• SQL/Persistent Stored Modules (SQL/PSM)
— Functions
— Triggers
— Stored Procedures

Next, we will discuss the SQL statements used to create, use, and manage SQL views. We will end the chapter with a discussion of SQL/Persistent Stored Modules (SQL/PSM) and of functions, triggers, and stored procedures.

Managing Table Structure with SQL DDL

The **SQL CREATE TABLE statement** is used to construct tables, define columns and column constraints, and create relationships. Most DBMS products provide graphical tools for performing these tasks, and you may be wondering why you need to learn SQL to perform the same work. There are four reasons. First, creating tables and relationships with SQL is quicker than with graphical tools. Once you know how to use the SQL CREATE TABLE statement, you will be able to construct tables faster and more easily than by fussing around with buttons and graphical gimmickry. Second, some applications, particularly those for reporting, querying, and data mining, require you to create the same table repeatedly. You can do this efficiently if you create an SQL script text file with the necessary SQL CREATE TABLE statements. You then just execute the SQL script when you need to re-create a table. Third, some applications require you to create temporary tables during application work. The discussion of RFM reports in Appendix J shows one such application. The only way to create tables from program code is to use SQL. Finally, SQL DDL is standardized and DBMS independent. With the exception of some data types, the same CREATE TABLE statement will work with SQL Server, Oracle Database, DB2, or MySQL.

Creating the VRG Database

Of course, before you can create any tables, you have to create the database. The SQL-92 and subsequent standards include an SQL statement for creating databases, but it is seldom used. Instead, most developers use special commands or graphical tools for creating a database. These techniques are DBMS specific, and we describe them in context for SQL Server 2014 in Chapter 10A, for Oracle Database in Chapter 10B, for MySQL 5.6 in Chapter 10C, and for Microsoft Access 2013 in Appendix A.

At this point, we highly recommend that you read the section on creating a new database in the DBMS product you are using and use the appropriate steps to create a new database for the View Ridge Gallery named VRG. For illustrative purposes, we will use Microsoft SQL Server 2014 in this chapter, and our SQL code will be the correct code for Microsoft SQL Server 2014. The correct SQL statements for other DBMS products will be similar, but they will vary slightly. The correct SQL statements for Oracle Database and MySQL 5.6 can be found in Chapters 10B and 10C, respectively. Figure 7-3 shows the VRG database in the Microsoft SQL Server 2014 Management Studio.

Using SQL Scripts

Each DBMS product has a GUI utility program that is used to create, edit, and store SQL script files. An **SQL script file** or **SQL script** is a separately stored plain text file, and it usually uses a file name extension of *.sql*. An SQL script can be opened and run as an SQL command (or set of commands). SQL scripts are used to create and populate databases and to store a query or set of queries. They are also used to store the SQL statements to create SQL elements that we will discuss later in this chapter: SQL views and SQL/PSM functions, triggers, and stored procedures. We recommend that you use SQL scripts to edit and store any work you do in SQL in this chapter (as well as any SQL work in general).

The GUI utilities that we will use to create SQL scripts are:

- **Microsoft SQL Server 2014 Management Studio** for use with Microsoft SQL Server 2014 (see Chapter 10A for a discussion of Microsoft SQL Server 2014 Management Studio).
- **Oracle SQL Developer** for use with Oracle Database 12*c* and Oracle Database Express Edition 11*g* Release 2 (see Chapter 10B for a discussion of Oracle SQL Developer).

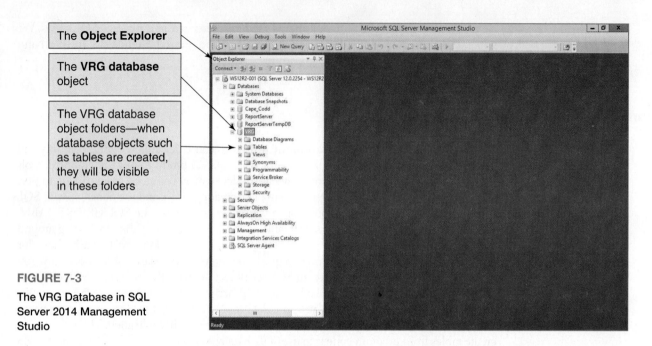

The **Object Explorer**

The **VRG database** object

The VRG database object folders—when database objects such as tables are created, they will be visible in these folders

FIGURE 7-3

The VRG Database in SQL Server 2014 Management Studio

- **Oracle MySQL Workbench** for use with Oracle MySQL 5.6 (see Chapter 10C for a discussion of Oracle MySQL Workbench).

When the Microsoft SQL Server 2014 Management Studio is installed, a new folder named *SQL Server Management Studio* is created in your Documents (or My Documents) folder. We recommend that you create a subfolder named *Projects* and use the Projects folder as the default location for SQL script files. Further, for each database, create a new folder in the Projects folder. For example, we will create a folder named *View-Ridge-Gallery-Database* to store the script files associated with the View Ridge Gallery database.

By default, Oracle SQL Developer stores **.sql* files in an obscure location within its own application files. We recommend that you create a subfolder in your Documents (or My Documents) folder named *SQL Developer* and then create a subfolder for each database in the SQL Developer folder. For example, we will create a folder named *View-Ridge-Gallery-Database* to store the script files associated with the View Ridge Gallery database.

By default, MySQL Workbench stores files in the user's Documents (or My Documents) folder. We recommend that you create a subfolder in your Documents (or My Documents) folder named *MySQL Workbench* and then create subfolders labeled *EER Models* and *Schemas*. Within each of these subfolders, create a sub-subfolder for each MySQL database. For example, we will create a folder named *View-Ridge-Gallery-Database* to store the script files associated with the View Ridge Gallery database.

Using the SQL CREATE TABLE Statement

The basic format of the SQL CREATE TABLE statement is:

```
CREATE TABLE NewTableName (

    three-part column definition,

    three-part column definition,

    . . .

    optional table constraints

    . . .

    );
```

The parts of the three-part column definition are the column name, the column data type, and, optionally, a constraint on column values. Thus, we can restate the CREATE TABLE format as:

```
CREATE TABLE NewTableName (

    ColumnName    DataType    OptionalConstraint,

    ColumnName    DataType    OptionalConstraint,

    . . .

    Optional table constraint

    . . .

    );
```

The column and table constraints we consider in this text are **PRIMARY KEY**, **FOREIGN KEY**, **NOT NULL**, **NULL**, **UNIQUE**, and **CHECK**. Additionally, the **DEFAULT keyword** (DEFAULT is not considered a column constraint) can be used to set initial values. Finally, most variants of SQL support a property to implement surrogate primary keys. For example, SQL Server 2014 uses the *IDENTITY({StartValue},{Increment})* property. Oracle Database, MySQL, and Microsoft Access use somewhat different techniques for creating surrogate keys.

If you are using those products, see the discussion of surrogate keys for Oracle Database in Chapter 10B, MySQL 5.6 in Chapter 10C, or Microsoft Access 2013 in Appendix A. We will explain each of these constraints, keywords, and properties as we meet them in the context of our discussion in this chapter.

Variations in SQL Data Types and SQL/PSM

Even though Microsoft Access reads standard SQL and the SQL used by SQL Server 2014, the results may be a bit different. For example, Microsoft Access ANSI-89 SQL converts both the Char and Varchar SQL data types to a fixed Text data type.

Each DBMS product also has its own variant of SQL and SQL **procedural programming language** extensions, which are additions that allow SQL to function similarly to a procedural programming language (e.g., IF...THEN...ELSE structures). In the ANSI/ISO SQL standard, these procedural programming language extensions are known as **SQL/Persistent Stored Modules (SQL/PSM)**. Some vendors have given their SQL variants specific names. Microsoft's SQL Server version of SQL is called **Transact-SQL (T-SQL)**, whereas Oracle's Oracle Database version of SQL is called **Procedural Language/SQL (PL/SQL)**. MySQL's variant, even though it, too, contains procedural extensions based on SQL/PSM, has no special name and is just called SQL in the MySQL documentation. We will point out specific SQL syntax differences as we encounter them in our discussion. For more on T-SQL, see the SQL Server 2014 Books Online section Transact-SQL Reference at *http://msdn.microsoft.com/en-us/library/bb510741.aspx*. For more on PL/SQL, see the Oracle Database PL/SQL User's Guide and Reference 12c at *http://docs.oracle.com/database/121/nav/portal_booklist.htm*. For more on SQL in MySQL, see the MySQL 5.6 Reference Manual Chapter 13 on SQL Statement Syntax at *http://dev.mysql.com/doc/refman/5.6/en/*.

One source of variation in DBMS SQL stems from the different data types implemented by each vendor. The SQL standard defines a set of data types, and the variations in DBMS data types was discussed in Figure 6-5.

Creating the VRG Database ARTIST Table

We will start by considering two of the tables in the VRG database design we developed at the end of Chapter 6, the ARTIST table and the WORK table. These tables are shown in Figure 7-1, and Figures 7-4 and 7-5 show the column properties for these tables. Three new features are shown in these figures.

ARTIST

Column Name	Type	Key	NULL Status	Remarks
ArtistID	Int	Primary Key	NOT NULL	Surrogate Key IDENTITY (1,1)
LastName	Char (25)	Alternate Key	NOT NULL	AK1.1
FirstName	Char (25)	Alternate Key	NOT NULL	AK1.2
Nationality	Char (30)	No	NULL	
DateOfBirth	Numeric (4,0)	No	NULL	
DateDeceased	Numeric (4,0)	No	NULL	

FIGURE 7-4

Column Characteristics for the VRG Database ARTIST Table

The first is the Microsoft SQL Server **IDENTITY ({StartValue}, {Increment}) property**, which is used to specify surrogate keys. In the ARTIST table, the expression IDENTITY (1, 1) means that ArtistID is to be a surrogate key with values starting at 1 and incremented by 1. Thus, the value of ArtistID for the second row in ARTIST will be $(1 + 1) = 2$. In the WORK table, the expression IDENTITY (500, 1) means that WorkID is to be a surrogate key with values starting at 500 and incremented by 1. Thus, the value of WorkID for the second row in WORK will be $(500 + 1) = 501$.

The second new feature is the designation of (LastName, FirstName) in ARTIST as an alternative key. This indicates that (LastName, FirstName) is a candidate key for the ARTIST table. Alternative keys are defined using the UNIQUE constraint.

The third new feature is the use of the DEFAULT column constraint in the Description column of the WORK table. The DEFAULT constraint is used to set a value that will be inserted into each row unless some other value is specified.

Figure 7-6 describes in tabular form the M-O relationship between ARTIST and WORK shown in Figure 7-1, and Figure 7-7 (based on the template in Figure 6-29(a)) details the referential integrity actions that will be needed to enforce the minimum cardinalities in the ARTIST-to-WORK relationship.

Figure 7-8 shows the SQL CREATE TABLE statement for constructing the ARTIST table. (All of the SQL in this chapter runs on SQL Server. If you are using a different DBMS, you may need to make adjustments, so consult the chapter or appendix for the DBMS you are using.) The format of the CREATE TABLE statement is the name of the table followed by a list of all column definitions and constraints enclosed in parentheses and ending with the ubiquitous SQL semicolon (;).

FIGURE 7-5

Column Characteristics for the VRG Database WORK Table

WORK

Column Name	Type	Key	NULL Status	Remarks
WorkID	Int	Primary Key	NOT NULL	Surrogate Key IDENTITY (500,1)
Title	Char (35)	No	NOT NULL	
Copy	Char (12)	No	NOT NULL	
Medium	Char (35)	No	NULL	
Description	Varchar (1000)	No	NULL	DEFAULT value = 'Unknown provenance'
ArtistID	Int	Foreign Key	NOT NULL	

FIGURE 7-6

The VRG Database ARTIST-to-WORK Relationship

Relationship		Cardinality		
Parent	**Child**	**Type**	**MAX**	**MIN**
ARTIST	WORK	Nonidentifying	1:N	M-O

FIGURE 7-7

Actions to Enforce Minimum Cardinality for the VRG Database ARTIST-to-WORK Relationship

ARTIST Is Required Parent	Action on ARTIST (Parent)	Action on WORK (Child)
Insert	None	Get a parent
Modify key or Foreign key	Prohibit—ARTIST uses a surrogate key	Allow foreign key updates if parent primary key exists
Delete	Prohibit if WORK exists— data related to a transaction is never deleted (business rule) Allow if no WORK exists (business rule)	None

As stated earlier, SQL has several column and table constraints: PRIMARY KEY, NULL, NOT NULL, UNIQUE, FOREIGN KEY, and CHECK. The PRIMARY KEY constraint is used to define the primary key of the table. Although it can be used as a column constraint, because it has to be used as a table constraint to define compound primary keys, we prefer to always use it as a table constraint, as shown in Figure 7-8. The NULL and NOT NULL column constraints are used to set the NULL status of a column, indicating whether data values are required in that column. The UNIQUE constraint is used to indicate that the values of a column or columns must not use repeated values. The FOREIGN KEY constraint is used to define referential integrity constraints, and the CHECK constraint is used to define data constraints.

In the first section of the CREATE TABLE statement for the ARTIST table, each column is defined by giving its name, data type, and null status. If you do not specify the null status using NULL or NOT NULL, then NULL is assumed.

In this database, DateOfBirth and DateDeceased are years. YearOfBirth and YearDeceased would have been better column names, but that is not how the gallery personnel refer to them. Because the gallery is not interested in the month and day of an artist's birth and death, those columns are defined as Numeric (4, 0), which means a four-digit number with zero places to the right of the decimal point.

The last two expressions in the SQL table definition statement in Figure 7-8 are constraints that define the primary key and a candidate, or alternate, key. As stated in Chapter 6, the primary purpose of an alternate key is to ensure uniqueness of column values. Thus, in SQL, alternate keys are defined using the UNIQUE constraint.

The format of such constraints is the word CONSTRAINT followed by a constraint name provided by the developer followed by a keyword indicating the type of constraint (PRIMARY

FIGURE 7-8

SQL Statements to Create the Initial Version of the VRG Database ARTIST Table

```
CREATE TABLE ARTIST (
    ArtistID        Int             NOT NULL IDENTITY(1,1),
    LastName        Char(25)        NOT NULL,
    FirstName       Char(25)        NOT NULL,
    Nationality     Char(30)        NULL,
    DateOfBirth     Numeric(4,0)    NULL,
    DateDeceased    Numeric(4,0)    NULL,
    CONSTRAINT      ArtistPK        PRIMARY KEY(ArtistID),
    CONSTRAINT      ArtistAK1       UNIQUE(LastName, FirstName)
    );
```

KEY or UNIQUE in this example) and then one or more columns in parentheses. For example, the following partial SQL statement defines a constraint named *MyExample* that ensures that the combination of first and last name is unique:

```
CONSTRAINT   MyExample   UNIQUE (FirstName, LastName),
```

As stated in Chapter 6, primary key columns must be NOT NULL, but alternate keys can be NULL or NOT NULL.

> **BY THE WAY**   SQL originated in the era of punched card data processing ("What is a punched card?" you ask? See the Wikipedia article *Punched card* for a full explanation). Punched cards had only uppercase letters, so there was no need to think about case sensitivity. When cards were replaced by regular keyboards, DBMS vendors chose to ignore the difference between uppercase and lowercase letters. Thus, CREATE TABLE, create table, and CReatE taBle are all the same in SQL. NULL, null, and Null are all the same as well.

Notice that the last line of the SQL statement in Figure 7-8 is a closed parenthesis followed by a semicolon. These characters could be placed on the line above, but dropping them to a new line is a style convention that makes it easy to determine the boundaries of CREATE TABLE statements. Also notice that column descriptions and constraints are separated by commas but that there is no comma after the last one.

> **BY THE WAY**   Many organizations have developed SQL coding standards of their own. Such standards specify not only the format of SQL statements but also conventions for naming constraints. For example, in the figures in this chapter, we use the suffix PK on the names of all primary key constraints and the suffix FK for all foreign key constraints. Most organizations have standards that are more comprehensive. You should follow your organization's standards, even if you disagree with them. Consistent SQL coding improves organizational efficiency and reduces errors.

Creating the VRG Database WORK Table and the 1:N ARTIST-to-WORK Relationship

Figure 7-9 shows SQL statements for creating the ARTIST and WORK tables and their relationship. Note that the column name Description is written as [Description] because Description is a Microsoft SQL Server 2014 reserved keyword (see Chapter 10A on Microsoft SQL Server 2014), and we must use the square brackets ([and]) to create a delimited identifier. This is the same reason that in Chapter 6 we decided to use the table name TRANS instead of TRANSACTION.

The only new syntax in Figure 7-9 is the FOREIGN KEY constraint at the end of WORK. Such constraints are used to define referential integrity constraints. The FOREIGN KEY constraint in Figure 7-9 is equivalent to the following referential integrity constraint:

```
ArtistID in WORK must exist in ArtistID in ARTIST
```

Note that the foreign key constraint contains two SQL clauses that implement the minimum cardinality enforcement requirements of Figure 7-7. The **SQL ON UPDATE clause** specifies whether updates should cascade form ARTIST to WORK, and the **SQL ON DELETE clause** specifies whether deletions in ARTIST should cascade to WORK.

The expression ON UPDATE NO ACTION indicates that updates to the primary key for a table that has children should be prohibited (this is the standard setting for surrogate keys that should never change). The expression ON UPDATE CASCADE would indicate that updates should cascade. ON UPDATE NO ACTION is the default.

```
CREATE TABLE ARTIST (
        ArtistID              Int                 NOT NULL IDENTITY(1,1),
        LastName              Char(25)            NOT NULL,
        FirstName             Char(25)            NOT NULL,
        Nationality           Char(30)            NULL,
        DateOfBirth           Numeric(4,0)        NULL,
        DateDeceased          Numeric(4,0)        NULL,
        CONSTRAINT      ArtistPK          PRIMARY KEY(ArtistID),
        CONSTRAINT      ArtistAK1         UNIQUE(LastName, FirstName)
        );


CREATE TABLE WORK (
        WorkID                Int                 NOT NULL IDENTITY(500,1),
        Title                 Char(35)            NOT NULL,
        Copy                  Char(12)            NOT NULL,
        Medium                Char(35)            NULL,
        [Description]         Varchar(1000)       NULL DEFAULT 'Unknown provenance',
        ArtistID              Int                 NOT NULL,
        CONSTRAINT      WorkPK            PRIMARY KEY(WorkID),
        CONSTRAINT      WorkAK1           UNIQUE(Title, Copy),
        CONSTRAINT      ArtistFK          FOREIGN KEY(ArtistID)
                        REFERENCES ARTIST(ArtistID)
                            ON UPDATE NO ACTION
                            ON DELETE NO ACTION
        );
```

FIGURE 7-9

SQL Statements to Create the VRG Database ARTIST-to-WORK 1:N Relationship

Similarly, the expression ON DELETE NO ACTION indicates that deletions of rows that have children should be prohibited. The expression ON DELETE CASCADE would indicate that deletions should cascade. ON DELETE NO ACTION is the default.

In the present case, the ON UPDATE NO ACTION is meaningless because the primary key of ARTIST is a surrogate and will never be changed. The ON UPDATE action would need to be specified for nonsurrogate data keys, however, and we show the option here so you will know how to code it.

> **BY THE WAY**   Note that you must define parent tables before child tables. In this case, you must define ARTIST before WORK. If you try to reverse the order of definition, the DBMS will generate an error message on the FOREIGN KEY constraint because it will not yet know about the ARTIST table.
>
> Similarly, you must delete tables in the opposite order. You must DROP (described later in this chapter) a child before a parent. Better SQL parsers would sort out all of this so that statement order would not matter, but, alas, that's not the way it's done! Just remember the following: *Parents are first in and last out.*

Implementing Required Parent Rows

In Chapter 6, you learned that to enforce a required parent constraint, you must define the referential integrity constraint and set the foreign key to NOT NULL in the child table. The SQL CREATE TABLE statement for the WORK table in Figure 7-9 does both. In this case, ARTIST is the required parent table, and WORK is the child. Thus, ArtistID in the WORK table is specified as NOT NULL (using the NOT NULL column constraint), and the ArtistFK FOREIGN KEY table constraint is used to define the referential integrity constraint. Together, these specifications thus cause the DBMS to enforce the required parent.

If the parent were not required, then we would specify ArtistID in WORK as NULL. In that case, WORK would not need to have a value for ArtistID and thus not need a parent. However, the FOREIGN KEY constraint would still ensure that all values of ArtistID in WORK would be present in the ArtistID in ARTIST.

Implementing 1:1 Relationships

SQL for implementing 1:1 relationships is almost identical to that for 1:N relationships, as just shown. The only difference is that the foreign key must be declared as unique. For example, if the relationship were 1:1 between ARTIST and WORK (i.e., each artist could have only one work at the View Ridge Gallery), then in Figure 7-9 we would add the following constraint to the WORK table:

```
CONSTRAINT  UniqueWork  UNIQUE (ArtistID)
```

Note that the ARTIST-to-WORK relationship in Figure 7-1 is of course *not* 1:1, so we will *not* specify this constraint to our current SQL statements. As before, if the parent is required, then the foreign key should be set to NOT NULL. Otherwise, it should be NULL.

Casual Relationships

Sometimes it is appropriate to create a foreign key column but not specify a FOREIGN KEY constraint. In that case, the foreign key value may or may not match a value of the primary key in the parent. If, for example, you define the column DepartmentName in EMPLOYEE but do not specify a FOREIGN KEY constraint, then a row may have a value of DepartmentName that does not match a value of DepartmentName in the DEPARTMENT table.

Such relationships, which we call **casual relationships**, occur frequently in applications that process tables with missing data. For example, you might buy consumer data that include names of consumers' employers. Assume that you have an EMPLOYER table that does not contain all of the possible companies for which the consumers might work. You want to use the relationship if you happen to have the values, but you do not want to require having those values. In that case, create a casual relationship by placing the key of EMPLOYER in the consumer data table but do *not* define a FOREIGN KEY constraint.

Figure 7-10 summarizes the techniques for creating relationships using FOREIGN KEY, NULL, NOT NULL, and UNIQUE constraints in 1:N, 1:1, and casual relationships.

Creating Default Values and Data Constraints with SQL

Figure 7-11 shows an example set of default value and example data constraints for the VRG database. The Description column in the WORK table is given the default value of 'Unknown provenance'. The ARTIST and TRANS tables are assigned various data constraints.

In the ARTIST table, Nationality is limited to the values in the domain constraint shown, and DateOfBirth is limited by the **intrarelation constraint** (within the same table) that DateOfBirth occurs before DateDeceased. Further, DateOfBirth and DateDeceased, which as

FIGURE 7-10

Summary of Relationship Definitions Using the SQL CREATE TABLE Statement

Relationship Type	CREATE TABLE Constraints
1:N relationship, parent optional	Specify FOREIGN KEY constraint. Set foreign key NULL.
1:N relationship, parent required	Specify FOREIGN KEY constraint. Set foreign key NOT NULL.
1:1 relationship, parent optional	Specify FOREIGN KEY constraint. Specify foreign key UNIQUE constraint. Set foreign key NULL.
1:1 relationship, parent required	Specify FOREIGN KEY constraint. Specify foreign key UNIQUE constraint. Set foreign key NOT NULL.
Casual relationship	Create a foreign key column, but do not specify FOREIGN KEY constraint. If relationship is 1:1, specify foreign key UNIQUE.

FIGURE 7-11

Default Values and Data
Constraints for the VRG
Database

Table	Column	Default Value	Constraint
WORK	Description	'Unknown provenance'	
ARTIST	Nationality		IN ('Candian', 'English', 'French', 'German', 'Mexican', 'Russian', 'Spainish', 'United States'.
ARTIST	DateOfBirth		Less than DateDeceased.
ARTIST	DateOfBirth		Four digits—1 or 2 is first digit, 0 to 9 for remaining three digits.
ARTIST	DateDeceased		Four digits—1 or 2 is first digit, 0 to 9 for remaining three digits.
TRANS	SalesPrice		Greater than 0 and less than or equal to 500,000.
TRANS	DateAcquired		Less than or equal to DateSold.

noted earlier are years, are limited to the domain defined by specifying that the first digit be a 1 or a 2 and the remaining three digits be any decimal numbers. Thus, they can have any value between 1000 and 2999. SalesPrice in the TRANS table is limited by a range constraint to a value greater than 0 but less than or equal to $500,000, and PurchaseDate is limited by an intrarelation constraint that the DateSold be no earlier than the DateAcquired (i.e., DateAcquired is less than or equal to DateSold).

Figure 7-11 shows no **interrelation constraints** between tables. Although the SQL-92 specification defined facilities for creating such constraints, no DBMS vendor has implemented those facilities. Such constraints must be implemented in triggers. An example of this is shown later in this chapter. Figure 7-12 shows the SQL statements to create the ARTIST and WORK tables modified with the appropriate default values and data constraints.

Implementing Default Values
Default values are created by specifying the DEFAULT keyword in the column definition just after the NULL/NOT NULL specification. Note how in Figure 7-12 the Description column in the WORK table is given the default value of 'Unknown provenance' using this technique.

Implementing Data Constraints
The data constraints are created using the SQL CHECK constraint. The format for the CHECK constraint is the word CONSTRAINT followed by a developer-provided constraint name followed by the word CHECK and then by the constraint specification in parentheses. Expressions in CHECK constraints are akin to those used in the WHERE clause of SQL statements. Thus, the SQL IN keyword is used to provide a list of valid values. The SQL NOT IN keyword also can be used for negatively expressed domain constraints (not shown in this example). The SQL LIKE keyword is used for the specification of decimal places. Range checks are specified using comparison operators such as the less than (<) and greater than (>) symbols. Because interrelation constraints are unsupported, comparisons can only be made as intrarelation constraints between columns in the same table.

BY THE WAY   DBMS products are inconsistent in their implementation of CHECK constraints. The *ValidBirthYear* and *ValidDeathYear* constraints in Figure 7-12, for example, will not work with Oracle Database. However, Oracle Database implements other types of constraints with or without the LIKE keyword. Unfortunately, you must learn the peculiarities of the DBMS you use to know how best to implement constraints.

```
CREATE TABLE ARTIST (
        ArtistID                Int                 NOT NULL IDENTITY(1,1),
        LastName                Char(25)            NOT NULL,
        FirstName               Char(25)            NOT NULL,
        Nationality             Char(30)            NULL,
        DateOfBirth             Numeric(4,0)        NULL,
        DateDeceased            Numeric(4,0)        NULL,
        CONSTRAINT              ArtistPK            PRIMARY KEY(ArtistID),
        CONSTRAINT              ArtistAK1           UNIQUE(LastName, FirstName),
        CONSTRAINT              NationalityValues   CHECK
                        (Nationality IN ('Canadian', 'English', 'French',
                         'German', 'Mexican', 'Russian', 'Spanish',
                         'United States')),
        CONSTRAINT              BirthValuesCheck    CHECK (DateOfBirth < DateDeceased),
        CONSTRAINT              ValidBirthYear      CHECK
                        (DateOfBirth LIKE '[1-2][0-9][0-9][0-9]'),
        CONSTRAINT              ValidDeathYear      CHECK
                        (DateDeceased LIKE '[1-2][0-9][0-9][0-9]')
        );

CREATE TABLE WORK (
        WorkID                  Int                 NOT NULL IDENTITY(500,1),
        Title                   Char(35)            NOT NULL,
        Copy                    Char(12)            NOT NULL,
        Medium                  Char(35)            NULL,
        [Description]           Varchar(1000)       NULL DEFAULT 'Unknown provenance',
        ArtistID                Int                 NOT NULL,
        CONSTRAINT              WorkPK              PRIMARY KEY(WorkID),
        CONSTRAINT              WorkAK1             UNIQUE(Title, Copy),
        CONSTRAINT              ArtistFK            FOREIGN KEY(ArtistID)
                            REFERENCES ARTIST(ArtistID)
                                ON UPDATE NO ACTION
                                ON DELETE NO ACTION
        );
```

FIGURE 7-12

SQL Statements to Create
the ARTIST and WORK
Tables with Default Values
and Data Constraints

Creating the VRG Database Tables

Figure 7-13 shows SQL for creating all of the tables in the VRG database documented at the end of Chapter 6. Read each line and be certain that you understand its function and purpose. Notice that deletions cascade for the relationships between CUSTOMER and CUSTOMER_ARTIST_INT and between ARTIST and CUSTOMER_ARTIST_INT.

Any DBMS reserved words used as table or column names need to be enclosed in square brackets ([and]) and thus converted to delimited identifiers. We have already decided to use the table name TRANS instead of TRANSACTION so we do not use the *transaction* reserved word. The table name WORK is also a potential problem; the word *work* is a reserved word in most DBMS products, as are the column names *Description* in the WORK table and *State* in the TRANS table. Enclosing such terms in brackets signifies to the SQL parser that these terms have been provided by the developer and are not to be used in the standard way. Ironically, SQL Server can process the word WORK without problem, but Oracle Database cannot, whereas SQL Server chokes on the word TRANSACTION, but Oracle Database has no problem with it. Because Figure 7-13 shows Microsoft SQL Server 2014 T-SQL statements, we use WORK (no brackets), [Description], and [State].

You can find a list of reserved words in the documentation for the DBMS product that you use, and we deal with some specific cases in the chapters dedicated to Microsoft SQL Server 2014, Oracle Database, and MySQL 5.6. Be assured that if you use any keyword from the SQL syntax, such as SELECT, FROM, WHERE, LIKE, ORDER, ASC, or DESC, for

```
CREATE TABLE ARTIST (
        ArtistID                Int                 NOT NULL IDENTITY(1,1),
        LastName                Char(25)            NOT NULL,
        FirstName               Char(25)            NOT NULL,
        Nationality             Char(30)            NULL,
        DateOfBirth             Numeric(4,0)        NULL,
        DateDeceased            Numeric(4,0)        NULL,
        CONSTRAINT      ArtistPK            PRIMARY KEY(ArtistID),
        CONSTRAINT      ArtistAK1           UNIQUE(LastName, FirstName),
        CONSTRAINT      NationalityValues   CHECK
                        (Nationality IN ('Canadian', 'English', 'French',
                         'German', 'Mexican', 'Russian', 'Spanish',
                         'United States')),
        CONSTRAINT      BirthValuesCheck    CHECK (DateOfBirth < DateDeceased),
        CONSTRAINT      ValidBirthYear      CHECK
                        (DateOfBirth LIKE '[1-2][0-9][0-9][0-9]'),
        CONSTRAINT      ValidDeathYear      CHECK
                        (DateDeceased LIKE '[1-2][0-9][0-9][0-9]')
        );

CREATE TABLE WORK (
        WorkID                  Int                 NOT NULL IDENTITY(500,1),
        Title                   Char(35)            NOT NULL,
        Copy                    Char(12)            NOT NULL,
        Medium                  Char(35)            NULL,
        [Description]           Varchar(1000)       NULL DEFAULT 'Unknown provenance',
        ArtistID                Int                 NOT NULL,
        CONSTRAINT      WorkPK              PRIMARY KEY(WorkID),
        CONSTRAINT      WorkAK1             UNIQUE(Title, Copy),
        CONSTRAINT      ArtistFK            FOREIGN KEY(ArtistID)
                        REFERENCES ARTIST(ArtistID)
                            ON UPDATE NO ACTION
                            ON DELETE NO ACTION
        );

CREATE TABLE CUSTOMER (
        CustomerID              Int                 NOT NULL IDENTITY(1000,1),
        LastName                Char(25)            NOT NULL,
        FirstName               Char(25)            NOT NULL,
        Street                  Char(30)            NULL,
        City                    Char(35)            NULL,
        [State]                 Char(2)             NULL,
        ZIPorPostalCode         Char(9)             NULL,
        Country                 Char(50)            NULL,
        AreaCode                Char(3)             NULL,
        PhoneNumber             Char(8)             NULL,
        EmailAddress            Varchar(100)        NULL,
        CONSTRAINT      CustomerPK          PRIMARY KEY(CustomerID),
        CONSTRAINT      EmailAK1            UNIQUE(EmailAddress)
        );

CREATE TABLE TRANS (
        TransactionID           Int                 NOT NULL IDENTITY(100,1),
        DateAcquired            Date                NOT NULL,
        AcquisitionPrice        Numeric(8,2)        NOT NULL,
        AskingPrice             Numeric(8,2)        NULL,
        DateSold                Date                NULL,
        SalesPrice              Numeric(8,2)        NULL,
        CustomerID              Int                 NULL,
        WorkID                  Int                 NOT NULL,
```

FIGURE 7-13

**SQL Statements to
Create the VRG
Database Table Structure**

```
        CONSTRAINT        TransPK           PRIMARY KEY(TransactionID),
        CONSTRAINT        TransWorkFK       FOREIGN KEY(WorkID)
                        REFERENCES WORK(WorkID)
                            ON UPDATE NO ACTION
                            ON DELETE NO ACTION,
        CONSTRAINT        TransCustomerFK FOREIGN KEY(CustomerID)
                        REFERENCES CUSTOMER(CustomerID)
                                ON UPDATE NO ACTION
                                ON DELETE NO ACTION,
        CONSTRAINT        SalesPriceRange      CHECK
                        ((SalesPrice > 0) AND (SalesPrice <=500000)),
        CONSTRAINT        ValidTransDate       CHECK (DateAcquired <= DateSold)
        );

CREATE TABLE CUSTOMER_ARTIST_INT(
        ArtistID          Int              NOT NULL,
        CustomerID        Int              NOT NULL,
        CONSTRAINT        CAIntPK          PRIMARY KEY(ArtistID, CustomerID),
        CONSTRAINT        CAInt_ArtistFK   FOREIGN KEY(ArtistID)
                        REFERENCES ARTIST(ArtistID)
                            ON UPDATE NO ACTION
                            ON DELETE CASCADE,
        CONSTRAINT        CAInt_CustomerFK FOREIGN KEY(CustomerID)
                        REFERENCES CUSTOMER(CustomerID)
                            ON UPDATE NO ACTION
                            ON DELETE CASCADE
        );
```

FIGURE 7-13

Continued

table or column names, you will have problems. Enclose such words in square brackets. And, of course, your life will be easier if you can avoid using such terms for tables or columns altogether.

BY THE WAY   Every now and then, the DBMS might generate bizarre syntax-error messages. For example, suppose you define a table with the name ORDER. When you submit the statement SELECT * FROM ORDER;, you will get very strange messages back from the DBMS because ORDER is an SQL reserved word.

If you do receive odd messages back from statements that you know are coded correctly, think about reserved words. If a term might be reserved, enclose it in brackets and see what happens when you submit it to the DBMS. No harm is done by enclosing SQL terms in brackets.

If you want to torture your DBMS, you can submit queries like:

```
SELECT [SELECT] FROM [FROM] WHERE [WHERE] < [NOT FIVE];
```

Most likely, you have better ways to spend your time, however. Without a doubt, the DBMS has better ways to spend its time!

Running the SQL statements in Figure 7-13 (or the specific variant for Oracle Database in Chapter 10B or for MySQL 5.6 in Chapter 10C) with your DBMS will generate all of the tables, relationships, and constraints for the VRG database. Figure 7-14 shows the completed table structure in SQL Server 2014 as a database diagram. It is far easier to create these tables and relationships using SQL code than by using GUI displays, which are discussed for Microsoft SQL Server in Chapter 10A, for Oracle Database in Chapter 10B, and for MySQL 5.6 in Chapter 10C.

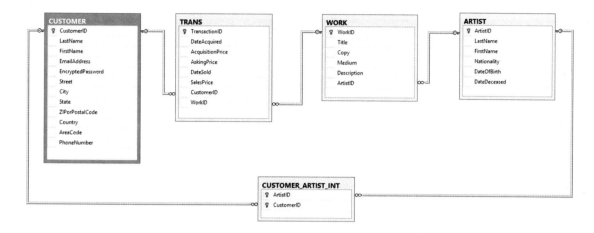

FIGURE 7-14

Microsoft SQL Server 2014
VRG Database Diagram

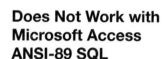

Does Not Work with Microsoft Access ANSI-89 SQL

Microsoft Access 2013 ANSI-89 SQL, unfortunately, does not support a number of standard SQL features we have examined in this discussion. However, you *can* run a basic SQL CREATE TABLE statement in ANSI-89 SQL and then use the Microsoft Access GUI display to finish building the tables and relationships. Specifically:

1. Although Microsoft Access supports a Number data type, it does not support the (*m, n*) extension to specify the number of digits and the number of digits to the right of the decimal place.

   Solution: You can set these values in the table Design view after the column is created.

2. Although Microsoft Access does support an AutoNumber data type, it *always* starts at 1 and increments by 1. Further, AutoNumber *cannot* be used as an SQL data type.

   Solution: Set AutoNumber data type manually after the table is created. Any other numbering system must be supported manually or by application code.

3. Microsoft Access ANSI-89 SQL does not support the UNIQUE and CHECK column constraints nor the DEFAULT keyword.

   Solution: Equivalent constraints and initial values can be set in the GUI table Design view.

4. Microsoft Access does completely support foreign key CONSTRAINT phrases. Although the basic referential integrity constraint can be created using SQL, the ON UPDATE and ON DELETE clauses are not supported.

   Solution: ON UPDATE and ON DELETE actions can be set manually after the relationship is created.

5. Unlike SQL Server, Oracle Database, and MySQL, Microsoft Access does not support SQL scripts.

   Solution: You can still create tables by using the SQL CREATE command and insert data by using the SQL INSERT command (discussed later in this chapter), but you must do so one command at a time.

The SQL ALTER TABLE Statement

The **SQL ALTER TABLE statement** is an SQL DDL statement that is used to change the structure of an existing table. It can be used to add, remove, or change columns. It also can be used to add or remove constraints.

Adding and Dropping Columns

The following statement will add a column named MyColumn to the CUSTOMER table by using the **SQL ADD clause** in the SQL ALTER TABLE statement:

```
/* *** SQL-ALTER-TABLE-CH07-01 *** */

ALTER TABLE CUSTOMER

    ADD MyColumn Char(5) NULL;
```

You can drop an existing column by using the **SQL DROP COLUMN clause** in the SQL ALTER TABLE statement:

```
/* *** SQL-ALTER-TABLE-CH07-02 *** */

ALTER TABLE CUSTOMER

    DROP COLUMN MyColumn;
```

Note the asymmetry in syntax; the keyword COLUMN is used in the DROP COLUMN clause but not in the ADD clause. You can also use the ALTER TABLE statement to change column properties, as you will see in the next three chapters.

Adding and Dropping Constraints

The ALTER TABLE statement can be used with an **SQL ADD CONSTRAINT clause** to add a constraint as follows:

```
/* *** SQL-ALTER-TABLE-CH07-03 *** */

ALTER TABLE CUSTOMER

    ADD CONSTRAINT MyConstraint CHECK

        (LastName NOT IN ('RobertsNoPay'));
```

You can also use the ALTER TABLE statement with an **SQL DROP CONSTRAINT clause** to DROP a constraint:

```
/* *** SQL-ALTER-TABLE-CH07-04 *** */

ALTER TABLE CUSTOMER

    DROP CONSTRAINT MyConstraint;
```

> **BY THE WAY**   The SQL ALTER TABLE statement can be used to add or drop any of the SQL constraints. You can use it to create primary keys and alternate keys, to set null status, to create referential integrity constraints, and to create data constraints. In fact, another SQL coding style uses CREATE TABLE only to declare the table's columns; all constraints are added using ALTER TABLE. We do not use that style in this text, but be aware that it does exist and that your employer might require it.

The SQL DROP TABLE Statement

It is very easy to remove a table in SQL. In fact, it is far too easy. The following **SQL DROP TABLE statement** will drop the TRANS table *and all of its data:*

```
/* *** EXAMPLE CODE - DO NOT RUN *** */

/* *** SQL-DROP-TABLE-CH07-01 *** */

DROP TABLE TRANS;
```

Because this simple statement drops the table and all of its data, be very careful when using it. Do not code this statement on the wrong table!

The DBMS will not drop a table that is the parent in a FOREIGN KEY constraint. It will not do so even if there are no children or even if you have coded DELETE CASCADE. Instead, to drop such a table, you must first either drop the foreign key constraint or drop the child table. Then you can delete the parent table. As mentioned earlier, parent tables must be first in and last out.

The following statements are needed to drop the CUSTOMER table:

```
/* *** EXAMPLE CODE - DO NOT RUN *** */
/* *** SQL-DROP-TABLE-CH07-02 *** */
DROP TABLE CUSTOMER_ARTIST_INT;
DROP TABLE TRANS;
DROP TABLE CUSTOMER;
```

Alternatively, you could drop CUSTOMER with:

```
/* *** EXAMPLE CODE - DO NOT RUN *** */
/* *** SQL-ALTER-TABLE-CH07-05 *** */
ALTER TABLE CUSTOMER_ARTIST_INT
    DROP CONSTRAINT Customer_Artist_Int_CustomerFK;
ALTER TABLE TRANS
    DROP CONSTRAINT TransactionCustomerFK;
/* *** SQL-DROP-TABLE-CH07-03 *** */
DROP TABLE CUSTOMER;
```

The SQL TRUNCATE TABLE Statement

The **SQL TRUNCATE TABLE statement** was officially added in the SQL:2008 standard, so it is one of the latest additions to SQL. It is used to remove all data from a table while leaving the table structure itself in the database. The SQL TRUNCATE TABLE statement does not use an SQL WHERE clause to specify conditions for the data deletion—*all* the data in the table is *always* removed when TRUNCATE is used. Although similar to the SQL DELETE statement discussed later in this chapter, there are two important differences between the two commands. First, the DELETE statement *does* allow the use of the SQL WHERE CLAUSE. Second, the TRUNCATE resets any surrogate key values back to the *initial value*, while the DELETE statement does not.

The following statement could be used to remove all the data in the CUSTOMER_ ARTIST_INT table:

```
/* *** EXAMPLE CODE - DO NOT RUN *** */
/* *** SQL-TRUNCATE-TABLE-CH07-01 *** */
TRUNCATE TABLE CUSTOMER_ARTIST_INT;
```

The TRUNCATE TABLE statement *cannot* be used with a table that is referenced by a foreign key constraint because this could create foreign key values that have no corresponding primary key value. Thus, while we can use TRUNCATE TABLE with the CUSTOMER_ ARTIST_INT table, we *cannot* use it with the CUSTOMER table.

The SQL CREATE INDEX Statement

An **index** is a special data structure that is created to improve database performance. SQL Server automatically creates an index on all primary and foreign keys. A developer can also direct SQL Server to create an index on other columns that are frequently used in WHERE clauses or on columns that are used for sorting data when sequentially processing a table for queries and reports. Indexing concepts are discussed in Appendix G.

SQL DDL includes an **SQL CREATE INDEX statement** to create indexes, an **SQL ALTER INDEX statement** to modify existing database indexes, and an **SQL DROP INDEX statement** to remove indexes from the database. Because each DBMS product implements indexing in different ways, we discuss the specific implementation of indexing in each DMBS as part of our detailed discussions of each DBMS product:

- Microsoft SQL Server 2014 in Chapter 10A
- Oracle Database in Chapter 10B
- MySQL 5.6 in Chapter 10C

BY THE WAY Books on systems analysis and design often identify three design stages:

- Conceptual design (conceptual schema)
- Logical design (logical schema)
- Physical design (physical schema)

The creation and use of indexes is a part of the *physical design*, which is defined in these books as the aspects of the database that are actually implemented in the DBMS. Besides indexes, this includes physical record and file structure and organization and query optimization. We discuss some of these issues for Microsoft SQL Server 2104 in Chapter 10A, for Oracle Database in Chapter 10B, and for MySQL 5.6 in Chapter 10C.

SQL DML Statements

At this point, you have learned how to query tables using SQL SELECT statements (in Chapter 2), and you should know how to create, alter, and drop tables, columns, and constraints. You do not yet know, however, how to use SQL statements to insert, modify, and delete data. We consider those statements next.

The SQL INSERT Statement

The **SQL INSERT statement** is used to add rows of data to a table. The statement has a number of different options.

The SQL INSERT Statement Using Column Names
The standard version of the INSERT statement is to name the table, name the columns for which you have data, and then list the data in the following format:

```
/* *** EXAMPLE CODE - DO NOT RUN *** */
/* *** SQL-INSERT-CH07-01 *** */
INSERT INTO ARTIST
    (LastName, FirstName, Nationality, DateOfBirth, DateDeceased)
    VALUES ('Miro', 'Joan', 'Spanish', 1893, 1983);
```

Note that both column names and values are enclosed in parentheses and that DBMS populated surrogate keys are not included in the statement. If you are providing data for all of the columns, if that data is in the same order as the columns in the table, and if you have no surrogate keys, then you can omit the column list.

```
/* *** EXAMPLE CODE - DO NOT RUN *** */
/* *** SQL-INSERT-CH07-02 *** */
INSERT INTO ARTIST VALUES
    ('Miro', 'Joan', 'Spanish', 1893, 1983);
```

Further, you need not provide the values in the same order as the columns in the table. If for some reason you want to provide Nationality first, you can revise the column names and the data value, as shown in the following example:

```
/* *** EXAMPLE CODE - DO NOT RUN *** */
/* *** SQL-INSERT-CH07-03 *** */
INSERT INTO ARTIST
     (Nationality, LastName, FirstName, DateOfBirth, DateDeceased)
     VALUES ('Spanish', 'Miro', 'Joan', 1893, 1983);
```

If you have partial values, just code the names of the columns for which you have data. For example, if you have only LastName, FirstName, and Nationality for an artist, you would use the SQL statement:

```
/* *** EXAMPLE CODE - DO NOT RUN *** */
/* *** SQL-INSERT-CH07-04 *** */
INSERT INTO ARTIST
     (LastName, FirstName, Nationality)
     VALUES ('Miro'; 'Joan', 'Spanish');
```

You must, of course, have values for all NOT NULL columns.

Bulk INSERT

One of the most often used forms of INSERT uses an SQL SELECT statement to provide values. Suppose you have the names, nationalities, birth dates, and dates deceased of a number of artists in a table named IMPORTED_ARTIST. In this case, you can add those data to the ARTIST table with the following statement:

```
/* *** EXAMPLE CODE - DO NOT RUN *** */
/* *** SQL-INSERT-CH07-05 *** */
INSERT INTO ARTIST
     (LastName, FirstName, Nationality, DateOfBirth, DateDeceased)
     SELECT     LastName, FirstName, Nationality,
                DateOfBirth, DateDeceased
     FROM       IMPORTED_ARTIST;
```

Note that the SQL keyword VALUES is not used with this form of insert. This syntax should seem familiar. We used it for normalization and denormalization examples in Chapters 3 and 4.

Populating the VRG Database Tables

Now that we know how to use the SQL INSERT statement to add rows of data to a table, we can put data into the VRG database. Sample data for the VRG database is shown in Figure 7-15 (note that the rows of the CUSTOMER table have been split apart in Figure 7-15(a) for ease of presentation on the page—they are not split in the database).

However, we need to be careful about exactly how we enter these data into the VRG database. Notice that in the SQL CREATE TABLE statements in Figure 7-13 CustomerID, ArtistID, WorkID, and TransactionID are all surrogate keys with values automatically inserted by the DBMS. This will produce sequential numbers. For example, if we insert the ARTIST table data shown in Figure 7-15(b) using the automatic ArtistID numbering from IDENTITY(1, 1), the ArtistID numbers for the nine artists will be (1, 2, 3, 4, 5, 6, 7, 8, 9). But in Figure 7-11(b), the ArtistID numbers are (1, 2, 3, 4, 5, 11, 17, 18, 19).

This happens because the View Ridge Gallery data shown in Figure 7-15 is *sample data*, not the complete data for the VRG database. Therefore, the primary key numbers for CustomerID, ArtistID, WorkID, and TransactionID in the data set are *not* sequential.

This, of course, raises the question of how to override DBMS mechanisms that provide automatic surrogate key numbering. The answer to this question varies among DBMS products (as does the method for generating the surrogate values). A discussion of this topic

CustomerID	LastName	FirstName	EmailAddress	EncryptedPassword
1000	Janes	Jeffrey	Jeffrey.Janes@somewhere.com	ng76tG9E
1001	Smith	David	David.Smith@somewhere.com	ttr67i23
1015	Twilight	Tiffany	Tiffany.Twilight@somewhere.com	gr44t5uz
1033	Smathers	Fred	Fred.Smathers@somewhere.com	mnF3D00Q
1034	Frederickson	Mary Beth	MaryBeth.Frederickson@somewhere.com	Nd5qr4Tv
1036	Warning	Selma	Selma.Warning@somewhere.com	CAe3Gh98
1037	Wu	Susan	Susan.Wu@somewhere.com	Ues3thQ2
1040	Gray	Donald	Donald.Gray@somewhere.com	NULL
1041	Johnson	Lynda	NULL	NULL
1051	Wilkens	Chris	Chris.Wilkens@somewhere.com	45QZjx59

CustomerID	LastName	FirstName	Street	City	State	ZIPorPostalCode
1000	Janes	Jeffrey	123 W. Elm St	Renton	WA	98055
1001	Smith	David	813 Tumbleweed Lane	Loveland	CO	81201
1015	Twilight	Tiffany	88 1st Avenue	Langley	WA	98260
1033	Smathers	Fred	10899 88th Ave	Bainbridge Island	WA	98110
1034	Frederickson	Mary Beth	25 South Lafayette	Denver	CO	80201
1036	Warning	Selma	205 Burnaby	Vancouver	BC	V6Z 1W2
1037	Wu	Susan	105 Locust Ave	Atlanta	GA	30322
1040	Gray	Donald	55 Bodega Ave	Bodega Bay	CA	94923
1041	Johnson	Lynda	117 C Street	Washington	DC	20003
1051	Wilkens	Chris	87 Highland Drive	Olympia	WA	98508

CustomerID	LastName	FirstName	Country	AreaCode	PhoneNumber
1000	Janes	Jeffrey	USA	425	543-2345
1001	Smith	David	USA	970	654-9876
1015	Twilight	Tiffany	USA	360	765-5566
1033	Smathers	Fred	USA	206	876-9911
1034	Frederickson	Mary Beth	USA	303	513-8822
1036	Warning	Selma	Canada	604	988-0512
1037	Wu	Susan	USA	404	653-3465
1040	Gray	Donald	USA	707	568-4839
1041	Johnson	Lynda	USA	202	438-5498
1051	Wilkens	Chris	USA	360	876-8822

FIGURE 7-15

Sample Data for
the VRG Database

(a) CUSTOMER Table Data

ArtistID	LastName	FirstName	Nationality	DateOfBirth	DateDeceased
1	Miro	Joan	Spanish	1893	1983
2	Kandinsky	Wassily	Russian	1866	1944
3	Klee	Paul	German	1879	1940
4	Matisse	Henri	French	1869	1954
5	Chagall	Marc	French	1887	1985
11	Sargent	John Singer	United States	1856	1925
17	Tobey	Mark	United States	1890	1976
18	Horiuchi	Paul	United States	1906	1999
19	Graves	Morris	United States	1920	2001

(b) ARTIST Table Data

ArtistID	CustomerID
1	1001
1	1034
2	1001
2	1034
4	1001
4	1034
5	1001
5	1034
5	1036
11	1001
11	1015
11	1036
17	1000
17	1015

ArtistID	CustomerID
17	1033
17	1040
17	1051
18	1000
18	1015
18	1033
18	1040
18	1051
19	1000
19	1015
19	1033
19	1036
19	1040
19	1051

(c) CUSTOMER_ARTIST_INT Table Data

FIGURE 7-15

Continued

(continued)

WorkID	Title	Medium	Description	Copy	ArtistID
500	Memories IV	Casein rice paper collage	31 × 24.8 in.	Unique	18
511	Surf and Bird	High Quality Limited Print	Northwest School Expressionist style	142/500	19
521	The Tilled Field	High Quality Limited Print	Early Surrealist style	788/1000	1
522	La Lecon de Ski	High Quality Limited Print	Surrealist style	353/500	1
523	On White II	High Quality Limited Print	Bauhaus style of Kandinsky	435/500	2
524	Woman with a Hat	High Quality Limited Print	A very colorful Impressionist piece	596/750	4
537	The Woven World	Color lithograph	Signed	17/750	17
548	Night Bird	Watercolor on Paper	50 × 72.5 cm. — Signed	Unique	19
551	Der Blaue Reiter	High Quality Limited Print	"The Blue Rider" — Early Pointilism influence	236/1000	2
552	Angelus Novus	High Quality Limited Print	Bauhaus style of Klee	659/750	3
553	The Dance	High Quality Limited Print	An Impressionist masterpiece	734/1000	4
554	I and the Village	High Quality Limited Print	Shows Belarusian folk-life themes and symbology	834/1000	5
555	Claude Monet Painting	High Quality Limited Print	Shows French Impressionist influence of Monet	684/1000	11
561	Sunflower	Watercolor and ink	33.3 × 16.1 cm. — Signed	Unique	19
562	The Fiddler	High Quality Limited Print	Shows Belarusian folk-life themes and symbology	251/1000	5
563	Spanish Dancer	High Quality Limited Print	American realist style — From work in Spain	583/750	11
564	Farmer's Market #2	High Quality Limited Print	Northwest School Abstract Expressionist style	267/500	17

(d) WORK Table Data

FIGURE 7-15
Continued

WorkID	Title	Medium	Description	Copy	ArtistID
565	Farmer's Market #2	High Quality Limited Print	Northwest School Abstract Expressionist style	268/500	17
566	Into Time	High Quality Limited Print	Northwest School Abstract Expressionist style	323/500	18
570	Untitled Number 1	Monotype with tempera	4.3 × 6.1 in. — Signed	Unique	17
571	Yellow covers blue	Oil and collage	71 × 78 in. — Signed	Unique	18
578	Mid Century Hibernation	High Quality Limited Print	Northwest School Expressionist style	362/500	19
580	Forms in Progress I	Color aquatint	19.3 × 24.4 in. — Signed	Unique	17
581	Forms in Progress II	Color aquatint	19.3 × 24.4 in. — Signed	Unique	17
585	The Fiddler	High Quality Limited Print	Shows Belarusian folk-life themes and symbology	252/1000	5
586	Spanish Dancer	High Quality Limited Print	American Realist style — From work in Spain	588/750	11
587	Broadway Boggie	High Quality Limited Print	Northwest School Abstract Expressionist style	433/500	17
588	Universal Field	High Quality Limited Print	Northwest School Abstract Expressionist style	114/500	17
589	Color Floating in Time	High Quality Limited Print	Northwest School Abstract Expressionist style	487/500	18
590	Blue Interior	Tempera on card	43.9 × 28 in.	Unique	17
593	Surf and Bird	Gouache	26.5 × 29.75 in. — Signed	Unique	19
594	Surf and Bird	High Quality Limited Print	Northwest School Expressionist style	366/500	19
595	Surf and Bird	High Quality Limited Print	Northwest School Expressionist style	366/500	19
596	Surf and Bird	High Quality Limited Print	Northwest School Expressionist style	366/500	19

(d) continued - WORK Table Data

FIGURE 7-15
Continued

(continued)

TransactionID	DateAcquired	AcquisitionPrice	AskingPrice	DateSoldID	SalesPrice	CustomerID	WorkID
100	11/4/2011	$30,000.00	$45,000.00	12/14/2011	$42,500.00	1000	500
101	11/7/2011	$250.00	$500.00	12/19/2011	$500.00	1015	511
102	11/17/2011	$125.00	$250.00	1/18/2012	$200.00	1001	521
103	11/17/2011	$250.00	$500.00	12/12/2012	$400.00	1034	522
104	11/17/2011	$250.00	$250.00	1/18/2012	$200.00	1001	523
105	11/17/2011	$200.00	$500.00	12/12/2012	$400.00	1034	524
115	3/3/2012	$1,500.00	$3,000.00	6/7/2012	$2,750.00	1033	537
121	9/21/2012	$15,000.00	$30,000.00	11/28/2012	$27,500.00	1015	548
125	11/21/2012	$125.00	$250.00	12/18/2012	$200.00	1001	551
126	11/21/2012	$200.00	$400.00	NULL	NULL	NULL	552
127	11/21/2012	$125.00	$500.00	12/22/2012	$400.00	1034	553
128	11/21/2012	$125.00	$250.00	3/16/2013	$225.00	1036	554
129	11/21/2012	$125.00	$250.00	3/16/2013	$225.00	1036	555
151	5/7/2013	$10,000.00	$20,000.00	6/28/2013	$17,500.00	1036	561
152	5/18/2013	$125.00	$250.00	8/15/2013	$225.00	1001	562
153	5/18/2013	$200.00	$400.00	8/15/2013	$350.00	1001	563
154	5/18/2013	$250.00	$500.00	9/28/2013	$400.00	1040	564
155	5/18/2013	$250.00	$500.00	NULL	NULL	NULL	565
156	5/18/2013	$250.00	$500.00	9/27/2013	$400.00	1040	566
161	6/28/2013	$7,500.00	$15,000.00	9/29/2013	$13,750.00	1033	570
171	8/23/2013	$35,000.00	$60,000.00	9/29/2013	$55,000.00	1000	571
175	9/29/2013	$40,000.00	$75,000.00	12/18/2013	$72,500.00	1036	500
181	10/11/2013	$250.00	$500.00	NULL	NULL	NULL	578
201	2/28/2014	$2,000.00	$3,500.00	4/26/2014	$3,250.00	1040	580
202	2/28/2014	$2,000.00	$3,500.00	4/26/2014	$3,250.00	1040	581
225	6/8/2014	$125.00	$250.00	9/27/2014	$225.00	1051	585
226	6/8/2014	$200.00	$400.00	NULL	NULL	NULL	586
227	6/8/2014	$250.00	$500.00	9/27/2014	$475.00	1051	587
228	6/8/2014	$250.00	$500.00	NULL	NULL	NULL	588
229	6/8/2014	$250.00	$500.00	NULL	NULL	NULL	589
241	8/29/2014	$2,500.00	$5,000.00	9/27/2014	$4,750.00	1015	590
251	10/25/2014	$25,000.00	$50,000.00	NULL	NULL	NULL	593
252	10/27/2014	$250.00	$500.00	NULL	NULL	NULL	594
253	10/27/2014	$250.00	$500.00	NULL	NULL	NULL	595
254	10/27/2014	$250.00	$500.00	NULL	NULL	NULL	596

FIGURE 7-15   (e) TRANS Table Data

Continued

specific to each DBMS product used in this book, and the complete set of SQL INSERT statements needed to enter the VRG data, can be found for SQL Server 2014 in Chapter 10A, for Oracle Database in Chapter 10B, and for MySQL 5.6 in Chapter 10C. At this point, we recommend that you read the appropriate section for the DBMS product you are using and populate the VRG database in your DBMS.

The SQL UPDATE Statement

The **SQL UPDATE statement** is used to change values of existing rows. For example, the following statement will change the value of City to 'New York City' for the View Ridge Gallery customer whose CustomerID is 1000 (Jeffrey Janes):

```
/* *** EXAMPLE CODE - DO NOT RUN *** */
/* *** SQL-UPDATE-CH07-01 *** */

UPDATE          CUSTOMER
    SET         City = 'New York City'
    WHERE       CustomerID = 1000;
```

To change the value of both City and State, we would use the SQL statement:

```
/* *** EXAMPLE CODE - DO NOT RUN *** */
/* *** SQL-UPDATE-CH07-02 *** */

UPDATE          CUSTOMER
    SET         City = 'New York City', State = 'NY'
    WHERE       CustomerID = 1000;
```

The DBMS will enforce all referential integrity constraints when processing UPDATE commands. For the VRG database, all keys are surrogate keys, but for tables with data keys, the DBMS will cascade or disallow (NO ACTION) updates according to the specification in the FOREIGN KEY constraint. Also, if there is a FOREIGN KEY constraint, the DBMS will enforce the referential integrity constraint on updates to a foreign key.

Bulk Updates

It is quite easy to make bulk updates with the UPDATE statement. It is so easy, in fact, that it is dangerous. Consider the SQL UPDATE statement:

```
/* *** EXAMPLE CODE - DO NOT RUN *** */
/* *** SQL-UPDATE-CH07-03 *** */

UPDATE          CUSTOMER
    SET         City = 'New York City';
```

This statement will change the value of City for every row of the CUSTOMER table. If we had intended to change just the value for customer 1000, we would have an unhappy result—every customer would have the value 'New York City' (data recovery methods are discussed in Chapter 9).

You can also perform bulk updates using an SQL WHERE clause that finds multiple rows. If, for example, we wanted to change the AreaCode for every customer who lives in Denver, we would code:

```
/* *** EXAMPLE CODE - DO NOT RUN *** */
/* *** SQL-UPDATE-CH07-04 *** */

UPDATE          CUSTOMER
    SET         AreaCode = '303'
    WHERE       City = 'Denver';
```

Updating Using Values from Other Tables

The SQL UPDATE statement can set a column equal to the value of a column in a different table. The VRG database has no appropriate example for this operation, so suppose instead that we have a table named TAX_TABLE with columns (Tax, City), where Tax is the appropriate tax rate for the City.

Now suppose we have a table named PURCHASE_ORDER that includes the columns TaxRate and City. We can update all rows for purchase orders in the city of Bodega Bay with the following SQL statement:

```
/* *** EXAMPLE CODE - DO NOT RUN *** */
/* *** SQL-UPDATE-CH07-05 *** */
UPDATE              PURCHASE_ORDER
    SET         TaxRate =
                (SELECT   Tax
                 FROM     TAX_TABLE
                 WHERE    TAX_TABLE.City = 'Bodega Bay')
        WHERE       PURCHASE_ORDER.City = 'Bodega Bay';
```

More likely, we want to update the value of the tax rate for a purchase order without specifying the city. Say we want to update the TaxRate for purchase order number 1000. In that case, we use the slightly more complex SQL statement:

```
/* *** EXAMPLE CODE - DO NOT RUN *** */
/* *** SQL-UPDATE-CH07-06 *** */
UPDATE              PURCHASE_ORDER
    SET         TaxRate =
                (SELECT   Tax
                 From     TAX_TABLE
                 WHERE    TAX_TABLE.City = PURCHASE_ORDER.City)
        WHERE       PURCHASE_ORDER.Number = 1000;
```

SQL SELECT statements can be combined with UPDATE statements in many different ways. We need to move on to other topics, but try these and other variations of UPDATE on your own.

The SQL MERGE Statement

The **SQL MERGE statement** (not available in Microsoft Access 2013) was introduced in SQL:2003 and, like the previously discussed SQL TRUNCATE TABLE statement, is one of the newest additions to SQL. The SQL MERGE statement essentially combines the SQL INSERT and SQL UPDATE statements into one statement that can either insert or update data depending upon whether some condition is met.

For example, suppose that before VRG staff insert data into the ARTIST table, they carefully research data about each artist and store it in a table named ARTIST_DATA_RESEARCH. Data on new artists is initially stored in ARTIST_DATA_RESEARCH, along with corrections to data on artists already in ARTIST. The VRG business rule is that ARTIST names are never changed after they have been entered, but if errors in Nationality, DateOfBirth, or DateDeceased are discovered, these errors will be corrected. In this case, new ARTIST data can be inserted and ARTIST data updated by using the following SQL MERGE statement:

```
/* *** EXAMPLE CODE - DO NOT RUN *** */
/* *** SQL-MERGE-CH07-01 *** */
MERGE INTO ARTIST AS A USING ARTIST_DATA_RESEARCH AS ADR
    ON  (A.LastName = ADR.LastName
        AND
        A.FirstName = ADR.FirstName)
```

```
WHEN MATCHED THEN
    UPDATE SET
         A.Nationality = ADR.Nationality,
         A.DateOfBirth = ADR.DateOfBirth,
         A.DateDeceased = ADR.DateDeceased
WHEN NOT MATCHED THEN
    INSERT (LastName, FirstName, Nationality,
            DateOfBirth, DateDeceased);
```

The SQL DELETE Statement

The **SQL DELETE statement** is also quite easy to use. The following SQL statement will delete the row for a customer with a CustomerID of 1000:

```
/* *** EXAMPLE CODE - DO NOT RUN *** */
/* *** SQL-DELETE-CH07-01 *** */
DELETE      FROM CUSTOMER
WHERE       CustomerID = 1000;
```

Of course, if you omit the WHERE clause, you will delete *every* customer row, so be careful with this command as well. Note that the DELETE statement without the WHERE clause is the logical equivalent of the SQL TRUNCATE TABLE statement previously discussed. However, the two statements use different methods to remove the data from the table and are *not* identical. For example, the DELETE statement *may* fire a trigger (as discussed later in this chapter), but the TRUNCATE TABLE statement never fires triggers. Further, the TRUNCATE resets any surrogate key values back to the *initial value*, while the DELETE statement does not.

The DBMS will enforce all referential integrity constraints when processing DELETE commands. For example, in the VRG database, you will be unable to delete a CUSTOMER row if that row has any TRANS children. Further, if a row with no TRANS children is deleted, any existing CUSTOMER_ARTIST_INT children will be deleted as well. This latter action occurs because of the CASCADE DELETE specification on the relationship between CUSTOMER and CUSTOMER_ARTIST_INT.

Using SQL Views

An **SQL view** is a virtual table that is constructed from other tables or views. A view has no data of its own but obtains data from tables or other views. Views are constructed from SQL SELECT statements using the **SQL CREATE VIEW statement**, and view names are then used just as table names would be in the FROM clause of other SQL SELECT statements.

SQL views are a very important part of application development for both Web client-based applications and smartphone apps, as shown in Figure 7-16. The design principle is that when an application requests information from a server to be displayed in the user's client program, the request should be as simple as possible. In Appendix B, we define **data** as recorded facts and numbers. Based on this definition, we can now define **information**[1] as:

- Knowledge derived from data.
- Data presented in a meaningful context.
- Data processed by summing, ordering, averaging, grouping, comparing, or other similar operations.

---

[1]These definitions are from David M. Kroenke and Randall J. Boyle's books *Using MIS* (8th ed., Upper Saddle River, NJ: Prentice-Hall, 2016) and *Experiencing MIS* (6th ed., Upper Saddle River: Prentice-Hall, 2016). See these books for a full discussion of these definitions, as well as a discussion of a fourth definition, "a difference that makes a difference."

FIGURE 7-16

SQL Views as the Basis
for Application Data

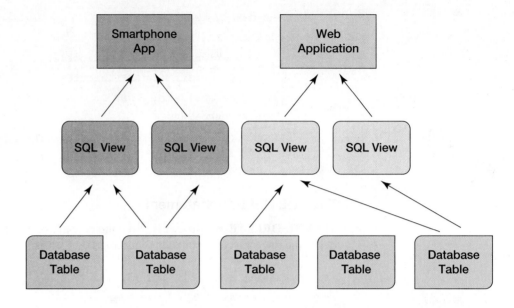

In general, application programmers prefer that the work of transforming *database data* into the *information* that will be used in and presented by the application be done by the DBMS itself. SQL views are the main DBMS tool for this work. The basic principle is that all *summing, averaging, grouping, comparing, and similar operations* should be done in SQL views and that it is the final result as it appears in the SQL view that is passed to the application program for use. This is the process illustrated in Figure 7-16.

In the SQL-92 standard, the only limitation on the SQL statements that are used to create views was that they could not contain an ORDER BY clause. In this case, the sort order must be provided by the SELECT statement that processes the view.

However, the methodology for how views are actually implemented varies by DBMS product. For example, Oracle Database and MySQL allow views to include ORDER BY, whereas SQL Server will only allow ORDER BY if the SQL phrase TOP 100 PERCENT is included in the SELECT clause of an SQL query statement. In this case, the included ORDER BY clause determines a default sorting order, which may be modified by including another ORDER BY clause in the SELECT statement that processes the view.

BY THE WAY   Views are a standard and popular SQL construct. Microsoft Access, however, does not support them. Instead, in Microsoft Access, you can create a view-equivalent *query*, name it, and then save it. You can then process the query in the same ways that we process views in the following discussion. SQL Server, Oracle Database, and MySQL all support views, and they are an important structure with many uses. Do not conclude from Microsoft Access's lack of support that views are unimportant. Read on, and, if possible, use SQL Server, Oracle Database, or MySQL to process the statements in this section.

We will begin our discussion of SQL views by defining a view named CustomerNameView on the CUSTOMER table that displays the customer's LastName and FirstName data, but re-labeling as CustomerLastName and CustomerFirstName:

```
/* *** SQL-CREATE-VIEW-CH07-01 *** */
CREATE VIEW CustomerNameView AS
    SELECT      LastName AS CustomerLastName,
                FirstName AS CustomerFirstName
    FROM        CUSTOMER;
```

Note that the results from executing this statement will be only a system message stating the action completed. With GUI utilities such as SQL Server Management Studio, an appropriately named object will also be created.[2]

Once the view is created, it can be used in the FROM clause of SELECT statements just like a table. The following obtains a list of customer names in sorted order:

```
/* *** SQL-Query-View-CH07-01 *** */

SELECT        *
FROM          CustomerNameView
ORDER BY      CustomerLastName, CustomerFirstName;
```

The result for the sample data in Figure 7-15 is:

	CustomerLastName	CustomerFirstName
1	Frederickson	Mary Beth
2	Gray	Donald
3	Janes	Jeffrey
4	Johnson	Lynda
5	Smathers	Fred
6	Smith	David
7	Twilight	Tiffany
8	Warning	Selma
9	Wilkens	Chris
10	Wu	Susan

Note that the number of columns returned in the result depends on the number of columns in the view, not on the number of columns in the underlying table. In this example, the SELECT clause produces just two columns because CustomerNameView itself has just two columns.

Also notice that the columns LastName and FirstName in the CUSTOMER table have been renamed to CustomerLastName and CustomerFirstName in the view. Because of this, the ORDER BY phrase in the SELECT statement uses CustomerLastName and CustomerFirstName, not LastName and FirstName. Also, the DBMS uses the labels CustomerLastName and CustomerFirstName when producing results.

BY THE WAY   If you need to change an SQL view after you have created it, use the **SQL ALTER VIEW statement**. For example, if you wanted to reverse the order of LastName and FirstName in the CustomerNameView, you would use the SQL statement:

```
/* *** EXAMPLE CODE - DO NOT RUN *** */
/* *** SQL-ALTER-VIEW-CH07-01 *** */
ALTER VIEW CustomerNameView AS
    SELECT        FirstName AS CustomerFirstName,
                  LastName AS CustomerLastName,
    FROM          CUSTOMER;
```

---

[2]The current versions of SQL Server, Oracle Database, and MySQL all process the CREATE VIEW statements as written here without difficulty. However, an earlier version of SQL Server, SQL Server 2000, has a quirk: To create views, you have to remove the semicolon from the CREATE VIEW statement. We have no idea why SQL Server 2000 accepts a semicolon for all other SQL statements but will not accept one for SQL statements that create views. If by chance you are still using SQL Server 2000, be aware that you must remove the semicolon when writing CREATE VIEW statements. Even better, upgrade your version of SQL Server—Microsoft stopped supporting SQL Server 2000 in April 2013, and important security updates are no longer being provided.

If you are using Oracle Database or MySQL 5.6, you can also use the **SQL CREATE OR REPLACE VIEW statement** in place of the SQL CREATE VIEW syntax. This allows you to modify the stored view without using the SQL ALTER VIEW syntax.

Figure 7-17 lists the uses for SQL views. SQL views can hide columns or rows. They also can be used to display the results of computed columns, to hide complicated SQL syntax, and to layer the use of built-in functions to create results that are not possible with a single SQL statement. Additionally, SQL views can provide an alias for table names and thus hide the true table names from applications and users. SQL views also are used to assign different processing permissions and different triggers to different views of the same table. We will show examples for each of these.

Using SQL Views to Hide Columns and Rows

SQL views can be used to hide columns to simplify results or to prevent the display of sensitive data. For example, suppose the users at the View Ridge Gallery want a simplified list of customers that has just names and phone numbers. The following SQL statement defines a view, BasicCustomerDataView, which will produce that list:

```
/* *** SQL-CREATE-VIEW-CH07-02 *** */
CREATE VIEW CustomerBasicDataView AS
    SELECT        LastName AS CustomerLastName,
                  FirstName AS CustomerFirstName,
                  AreaCode, PhoneNumber
    FROM          CUSTOMER;
```

To use this view, we can run the SQL statement:

```
/* *** SQL-Query-View-CH07-02 *** */
SELECT          *
FROM            CustomerBasicDataView
ORDER BY        CustomerLastName, CustomerFirstName;
```

FIGURE 7-17

Uses of SQL Views

Uses of SQL Views
Hide columns or rows.
Display results of computations.
Hide complicated SQL syntax.
Layer built-in functions.
Provide level of isolation between table data and users' view of data.
Assign different processing permissions to different views of the same table.
Assign different triggers to different views of the same table.

The result is:

	CustomerLastName	CustomerFirstName	AreaCode	PhoneNumber
1	Frederickson	Mary Beth	303	513-8822
2	Gray	Donald	707	568-4839
3	Janes	Jeffrey	425	543-2345
4	Johnson	Lynda	202	438-5498
5	Smathers	Fred	206	876-9911
6	Smith	David	970	654-9876
7	Twilight	Tiffany	360	765-5566
8	Warning	Selma	604	988-0512
9	Wilkens	Chris	360	876-8822
10	Wu	Susan	404	653-3465

If the management of the View Ridge Gallery wants to hide the columns AcquisitionPrice and SalesPrice in TRANS, it can define a view that does not include those columns. One use for such a view is to populate a Web page.

SQL views also can hide rows by providing a WHERE clause in the view definition. The next SQL statement defines a view of customer name and phone data for all customers with an address in Washington State:

```
/* *** SQL-CREATE-VIEW-CH07-03 *** */
CREATE VIEW CustomerBasicDataWAView AS
    SELECT        LastName AS CustomerLastName,
                  FirstName AS CustomerFirstName,
                  AreaCode, PhoneNumber
    FROM          CUSTOMER
    WHERE         State='WA';
```

To use this view, we can run the SQL statement:

```
/* *** SQL-Query-View-CH07-03 *** */
SELECT          *
FROM            CustomerBasicDataWAView
ORDER BY        CustomerLastName, CustomerFirstName;
```

The result is:

	CustomerLastName	CustomerFirstName	AreaCode	PhoneNumber
1	Janes	Jeffrey	425	543-2345
2	Smathers	Fred	206	876-9911
3	Twilight	Tiffany	360	765-5566
4	Wilkens	Chris	360	876-8822

As desired, only customers who live in Washington are shown in this view. This limitation is not obvious from the results because State is not included in the view. This characteristic is good or bad, depending on the use of the view. It is good if this view is used in a setting in which only Washington customers matter; it is bad if the view miscommunicates that these customers are the only View Ridge Gallery customers.

Using SQL Views to Display Results of Computed Columns

Another purpose of views is to show the results of computed columns without requiring the user to enter the computation expression. For example, the following view combines the AreaCode and PhoneNumber columns and formats the result:

```
/* *** SQL-CREATE-VIEW-CH07-04 *** */
CREATE VIEW CustomerPhoneView AS
    SELECT    LastName AS CustomerLastName,
              FirstName AS CustomerFirstName,
              ('(' + AreaCode + ')' + PhoneNumber) AS CustomerPhone
    FROM      CUSTOMER;
```

When the view user executes the SQL statement:

```
/* *** SQL-Query-View-CH07-04 *** */
SELECT       *
FROM         CustomerPhoneView
ORDER BY     CustomerLastName, CustomerFirstName;
```

the results[3] will be:

	CustomerLastName	CustomerFirstName	CustomerPhone
1	Frederickson	Mary Beth	(303) 513-8822
2	Gray	Donald	(707) 568-4839
3	Janes	Jeffrey	(425) 543-2345
4	Johnson	Lynda	(202) 438-5498
5	Smathers	Fred	(206) 876-9911
6	Smith	David	(970) 654-9876
7	Twilight	Tiffany	(360) 765-5566
8	Warning	Selma	(604) 988-0512
9	Wilkens	Chris	(360) 876-8822
10	Wu	Susan	(404) 653-3465

Placing computations in views has two major advantages. First, it saves users from having to know or remember how to write an expression to get the results they want. Second, it ensures consistent results. If each developer who uses a computation writes his or her own SQL expression, that developer may write it differently and obtain inconsistent results.

Using SQL Views to Hide Complicated SQL Syntax

Another use of SQL views is to hide complicated SQL syntax. Using a view, developers need not enter a complex SQL statement when they want a particular result. Also, such views give the benefits of complicated SQL statements to developers who do not know how to write such statements. This use of views also ensures consistency.

For example, suppose that the View Ridge Gallery salespeople want to see which customers are interested in which artists. To display these interests, two joins are necessary: one to join CUSTOMER to CUSTOMER_ARTIST_INT and another to join that result to ARTIST.

---

[3]As you might expect, different DBMS products use different operators for the concatenation operation in the CustomerPhoneView definition. For example, in Oracle Database, the plus sign (+) must be replaced by double vertical bars (||) for string concatenation, while MySQL uses the CONCAT() string function. See the example in Chapter 2 and the documentation for your DBMS for more details.

We can code an SQL statement that constructs these joins and define it as an SQL view to create the CustomerInterestsView:

```
/* *** SQL-CREATE-VIEW-CH07-05 *** */
CREATE VIEW CustomerInterestsView AS
    SELECT      C.LastName AS CustomerLastName,
                C.FirstName AS CustomerFirstName,
                A.LastName AS ArtistName
    FROM        CUSTOMER AS C JOIN CUSTOMER_ARTIST_INT AS CAI
      ON        C.CustomerID = CAI.CustomerID
        JOIN        ARTIST AS A
            ON    CAI.ArtistID = A.ArtistID;
```

Notice the aliasing of C.LastName to CustomerLastName and A.LastName to ArtistLastName. We *must* use at least one of these column aliases, for without them the resulting table has two columns named LastName. The DBMS would not be able to distinguish one LastName from the other and would generate an error when an attempt is made to create such a view.

This is a complicated SQL statement to write, but once the view is created, the result of this statement can be obtained with a simple SELECT statement. For example, the following statement shows the results sorted by CustomerLastName and CustomerFirstName:

```
/* *** SQL-Query-View-CH07-05 *** */
SELECT          *
FROM            CustomerInterestsView
ORDER BY        CustomerLastName, CustomerFirstName;
```

Figure 7-18 displays the fairly large result set. Clearly, using the view is much simpler than constructing the join syntax. Even developers who know SQL well will appreciate having a simpler SQL view with which to work.

Layering Built-in Functions

Recall from Chapter 2 that you cannot use a computation or a built-in function as part of an SQL WHERE clause. You can, however, construct a view that computes a variable and then write an SQL statement on that view that uses the computed variable in a WHERE clause. To understand this, consider the SQL view definition for the ArtistWorkNetView:

```
/* *** SQL-CREATE-VIEW-CH07-06 *** */
CREATE VIEW ArtistWorkNetView AS
    SELECT      LastName AS ArtistLastName,
                FirstName AS ArtistFirstName,
                W.WorkID, Title, Copy, DateSold,
                AcquisitionPrice, SalesPrice,
                (SalesPrice - AcquisitionPrice) AS NetProfit
    FROM        TRANS AS T JOIN WORK AS W
      ON        T.WorkID = W.WorkID
        JOIN        ARTIST AS A
            ON    W.ArtistID = A.ArtistID;
```

FIGURE 7-18

Result of SELECT on
CustomerInterestsView

	CustomerLastName	CustomerFirstName	ArtistName
1	Frederickson	Mary Beth	Chagall
2	Frederickson	Mary Beth	Kandinsky
3	Frederickson	Mary Beth	Miro
4	Frederickson	Mary Beth	Matisse
5	Gray	Donald	Tobey
6	Gray	Donald	Horiuchi
7	Gray	Donald	Graves
8	Janes	Jeffrey	Graves
9	Janes	Jeffrey	Horiuchi
10	Janes	Jeffrey	Tobey
11	Smathers	Fred	Tobey
12	Smathers	Fred	Horiuchi
13	Smathers	Fred	Graves
14	Smith	David	Chagall
15	Smith	David	Matisse
16	Smith	David	Kandinsky
17	Smith	David	Miro
18	Smith	David	Sargent
19	Twilight	Tiffany	Sargent
20	Twilight	Tiffany	Tobey
21	Twilight	Tiffany	Horiuchi
22	Twilight	Tiffany	Graves
23	Warning	Selma	Chagall
24	Warning	Selma	Graves
25	Warning	Selma	Sargent
26	Wilkens	Chris	Tobey
27	Wilkens	Chris	Graves
28	Wilkens	Chris	Horiuchi

This SQL view joins TRANS, WORK, and ARTIST and creates the computed column NetProfit. We can now use NetProfit in an SQL WHERE clause in a query as follows:

```
/* *** SQL-Query-View-CH07-06 *** */
SELECT          ArtistLastName, ArtistFirstName,
                WorkID, Title, Copy, DateSold, NetProfit
FROM            ArtistWorkNetView
WHERE           NetProfit > 5000
ORDER BY        DateSold;
```

Here we are using the named result of a computation in a WHERE clause, something that is not allowed in a single SQL statement (the *results* of a computation can be used in a WHERE clause, but *not by name*). The result of the SQL SELECT statement is:

	ArtistLastName	ArtistFirstName	WorkID	Title	Copy	DateSold	NetProfit
1	Horiuchi	Paul	500	Memories IV	Unique	2011-12-14	12500.00
2	Graves	Morris	548	Night Bird	Unique	2012-11-28	12500.00
3	Graves	Morris	561	Sunflower	Unique	2013-06-28	7500.00
4	Tobey	Mark	570	Untitled Number 1	Unique	2013-09-29	6250.00
5	Horiuchi	Paul	571	Yellow Covers Blue	Unique	2013-09-29	20000.00
6	Horiuchi	Paul	500	Memories IV	Unique	2013-12-18	32500.00

Such layering can be continued over many levels. We can define another view with another computation on the computation in the first view. For example, note that in the results above, the Horiuchi work *Memories IV* has been acquired and sold more than once by the View Ridge Gallery, and then consider the SQL view ArtistWorkTotalNetView, which will calculate the total net profit from *all* sales of each work:

```
/* *** SQL-CREATE-VIEW-CH07-07 *** */
CREATE VIEW ArtistWorkTotalNetView AS
    SELECT        ArtistLastName, ArtistFirstName,
                  WorkID,Title, Copy,
                  SUM(NetProfit) AS TotalNetProfit
    FROM          ArtistWorkNetView
    GROUP BY      ArtistLastName, ArtistFirstName,
                  WorkID, Title, Copy;
```

Now we can use TotalNetProfit in an SQL WHERE clause on the ArtistWorkTotalNet view as follows:

```
/* *** SQL-Query-View-CH07-07 *** */
SELECT        *
FROM          ArtistWorkTotalNetView
WHERE         TotalNetProfit > 5000
ORDER BY      TotalNetProfit;
```

In this SELECT, we are using an SQL view on an SQL view and a built-in function on a computed variable in the WHERE clause. The results are as follows:

	Artist Last Name	Artist First Name	Work ID	Title	Copy	Total Net Profit
1	Tobey	Mark	570	Untitled Number 1	Unique	6250.00
2	Graves	Morris	561	Sunflower	Unique	7500.00
3	Graves	Morris	548	Night Bird	Unique	12500.00
4	Horiuchi	Paul	571	Yellow Covers Blue	Unique	20000.00
5	Horiuchi	Paul	500	Memories IV	Unique	45000.00

Using SQL Views for Isolation, Multiple Permissions, and Multiple Triggers

SQL views have three other important uses. First, they can isolate source data tables from application code. To see how, suppose we define the view:

```
/* *** SQL-CREATE-VIEW-CH07-08 *** */
CREATE VIEW CustomerTableBasicDataView AS
    SELECT      *
    FROM        CUSTOMER;
```

This view assigns the alias CustomerTableBasicDataView to the CUSTOMER table, and when we query this view we can simply select all the data in the view:

```
/* *** SQL-Query-View-CH07-08 *** */
SELECT          *
FROM            CustomerTableBasicDataView;
```

The result, as expected, is the data in the CUSTOMER table itself. If all application code uses the CustomerTableBasicDataView as the data source in SQL statements, then the true source of the data is hidden from application programmers:

	CustomerID	LastName	FirstName	EmailAddress	EncryptedPassword	Street	City	State	ZIPorPostalCode	Country	AreaCode	PhoneNumber
1	1000	Janes	Jeffrey	Jeffrey.Janes@somewhere.com	ng76tG9E	123 W. Elm St	Renton	WA	98055	USA	425	543-2345
2	1001	Smith	David	David.Smith@somewhere.com	ttr67z23	813 Tumbleweed Lane	Loveland	CO	81201	USA	970	654-9876
3	1015	Twilight	Tiffany	Tiffany.Twilight@somewhere.com	gr44t5uz	88 1st Avenue	Langley	WA	98260	USA	360	765-5566
4	1033	Smathers	Fred	Fred.Smathers@somewhere.com	mnF3D00Q	10899 88th Ave	Bainbridge Island	WA	98110	USA	206	876-9911
5	1034	Frederickson	Mary Beth	MaryBeth.Frederickson@somewhere.com	Nd5qr4Tv	25 South Lafayette	Denver	CO	80201	USA	303	513-8822
6	1036	Warning	Selma	Selma.Warning@somewhere.com	CAe3Gh98	205 Burnaby	Vancouver	BC	V6Z 1W2	Canada	604	988-0512
7	1037	Wu	Susan	Susan.Wu@somewhere.com	Ues3thQ2	105 Locust Ave	Atlanta	GA	30322	USA	404	653-3465
8	1040	Gray	Donald	Donald.Gray@somewhere.com	NULL	55 Bodega Ave	Bodega Bay	CA	94923	USA	707	568-4839
9	1041	Johnson	Lynda	NULL	NULL	117 C Street	Washington	DC	20003	USA	202	438-5498
10	1051	Wilkens	Chris	Chris.Wilkens@somewhere.com	45QZjx59	87 Highland Drive	Olympia	WA	98508	USA	360	876-8822

Such table isolation provides flexibility to the database administration staff. For example, suppose that at some future date the source of customer data is changed to a different table (perhaps one that is imported from a different database) named NEW_CUSTOMER. In this situation, all the database administrator needs to do is redefine CustomerTableBasicDataView using the SQL ALTER VIEW statement as follows:

```
/* *** EXAMPLE CODE - DO NOT RUN *** */
/* *** SQL-ALTER-VIEW-CH07-08 *** */
ALTER VIEW CustomerTableBasicDataView AS
     SELECT        *
     FROM          NEW_CUSTOMER;
```

All of the application code that uses CustomerTableBasicDataView will now run on the new data source without any problem (assuming that the column names, data types, and other table characteristics have not been changed).

Another important use for SQL views is to give different sets of processing permissions to the same table. We will discuss security in more detail in Chapters 9, 10, 10A, 10B, and 10C, but for now understand that it is possible to limit insert, update, delete, and read permissions on tables and views.

For example, an organization might define a view of CUSTOMER called *CustomerTableReadView* with read-only permissions on CUSTOMER and a second view of CUSTOMER called *CustomerTableUpdateView* with both read and update permissions. Applications that need not update the customer data would work with CustomerTableReadView, whereas those that need to update these data would work with CustomerTableUpdateView.

The final use of SQL views is to enable the definition of multiple sets of triggers on the same data source. This technique is commonly used for enforcing O-M and M-M relationships. In this case, one view has a set of triggers that prohibits the deletion of a required child and another view has a set of triggers that deletes a required child as well as the parent. The views are assigned to different applications, depending on the authority of those applications.

Updating SQL Views

Some views can be updated; others cannot. The rules by which this is determined are both complicated and dependent on the DBMS in use. To understand why this is so, consider the following two update requests on views previously defined in our discussion of SQL views:

```
/* *** EXAMPLE CODE - DO NOT RUN *** */
/* *** SQL-UPDATE-VIEW-CH07-01 *** */
UPDATE            CustomerTableBasicDataView
     SET          Phone = '543-3456'
     WHERE        CustomerID = 1000;
```

and

```
/* *** EXAMPLE CODE - DO NOT RUN *** */
/* *** SQL-UPDATE-VIEW-CH07-02 *** */
```

FIGURE 7-19

Guidelines for Updating SQL
Views

Updatable Views
View based on a single table with no computed columns and all non-null columns present in the view.
View based on any number of tables, with or without computed columns, and INSTEAD OF trigger defined for the view.

Possibly Updatable Views
Based on a single table, primary key in view, some required columns missing from view, update and delete may be allowed. Insert is not allowed.
Based on multiple tables, updates may be allowed on the most subordinate table in the view if rows of that table can be uniquely identified.

```
UPDATE          ArtistWorkTotalNetView
   SET          TotalNetProfit = 23000
   WHERE        ArtistLastName = 'Tobey';
```

The first request can be processed without a problem because CustomerTableBasicDataView is just an alias for the CUSTOMER table. The second update, however, makes no sense at all. TotalNetProfit is a sum of a computed column. Nowhere in the actual tables in the database is there any such column to be updated, nor is it possible for the DBMS to decide how to divide up the total profit among the various sales.

Figure 7-19 shows general guidelines to determine if a view is updatable. Again, the specifics depend on the DBMS product in use. In general, the DBMS must be able to associate the column(s) to be updated with a particular row in a particular table. A way to approach this question is to ask yourself, "What would I do if I were the DBMS and I were asked to update this view? Would the request make sense, and, if so, do I have sufficient data to make the update?" Clearly, if the entire table is present and there are no computed columns, the view is updatable. Also, the DBMS will mark the view as updatable if it has an INSTEAD OF trigger defined for it, as described later.

However, if any of the required columns are missing, the view clearly cannot be used for inserts. It may be used for updates and deletes, however, as long as the primary key (or, for some DBMS products, a candidate key) is present in the view. Multi-table views may be updatable on the most subordinate table. Again, this can be done only if the primary key or candidate key for that table is in the view. We will revisit this topic for Microsoft SQL Server 2014 in Chapter 10A, Oracle Database in Chapter 10B, and MySQL 5.6 in Chapter 10C.

Embedding SQL in Program Code

SQL statements can be embedded in application programs, user-defined functions, triggers, and stored procedures. Before we discuss those subjects, however, we need to explain the placement of SQL statements in program code.

In order to embed SQL statements in program code, two problems must be solved. The first problem is that some means of assigning the results of SQL statements to program variables must be available. Many different techniques are used. Some involve object-oriented programs, whereas others are simpler. For example, in Oracle's PL/SQL the following statement (part of a larger program that has declared variables to be used within the program) assigns the count of the number of rows in the CUSTOMER table to the user-defined variable named *rowCount*:

```
/* *** EXAMPLE CODE - DO NOT RUN *** */

/* *** SQL-Code-Example-CH07-01 *** */

SELECT      Count(*) INTO rowCount

FROM        CUSTOMER;
```

MySQL SQL uses the same syntax. In SQL Server T-SQL, all user-defined variables must use the @ ("at" symbol) as the first character, and therefore the code in T-SQL uses the user-defined variable named *@rowCount*:

```
/* *** EXAMPLE CODE - DO NOT RUN *** */
/* *** SQL-Code-Example-CH07-02 *** */
SELECT      @rowCount = Count(*)
FROM        CUSTOMER;
```

In either case, the execution of this code will place the number of rows in CUSTOMER into the program variable rowCount or @rowCount.

The second problem to solve concerns a paradigm mismatch between SQL and application programming languages. SQL is table oriented; SQL SELECT statements start with one or more tables and produce a table as output. Programs, however, start with one or more variables, manipulate them, and store the result in a variable. Because of this difference, an SQL statement like the following makes no sense:

```
/* *** EXAMPLE CODE - DO NOT RUN *** */
/* *** SQL-Code-Example-CH07-03 *** */
SELECT      LastName INTO CustomerLastName
FROM        CUSTOMER;
```

If there are 100 rows in the CUSTOMER table, there will be 100 values of LastName. The program variable CustomerLastName, however, is expecting to receive just one value.

To avoid this problem, the results of SQL statements are treated as **pseudofiles**. When an SQL statement returns a set of rows, a **cursor**, which is a pointer to a particular row, is established. The application program can then place the cursor on the first, last, or some other row of the SQL statement output table. With the cursor placed, values of columns for that row can be assigned to program variables. When the application is finished with a particular row, it moves the cursor to the next, prior, or some other row and continues processing.

The typical pattern for using a cursor is as follows:

```
/* *** EXAMPLE CODE - DO NOT RUN *** */
/* *** SQL-Code-Example-CH07-04 *** */
DECLARE SQLCursor CURSOR FOR (SELECT * FROM CUSTOMER);
/* Opening SQLcursor executes (SELECT * FROM CUSTOMER) */
OPEN SQLcursor;
MOVE SQLcursor to first row of (SELECT * FROM CUSTOMER);
  WHILE (SQLcursor not past the last row) LOOP
    SET CustomerLastName = LastName;
    ...other statements...
    REPEAT LOOP UNTIL DONE;
CLOSE SQLcursor
...other processing...
```

In this way, the rows of an SQL SELECT are processed one at a time. You will see many examples of these techniques and others like them in the chapters that follow.

A typical and useful example of embedding SQL statements in an application is the use of SQL in Web database applications. We will discuss this topic in detail in Chapter 11, where we will provide several examples of SQL statements embedded in the PHP scripting language. For now, try to gain an intuitive understanding of how SQL is embedded in program code as we discuss how SQL application code is embedded within databases themselves.

SQL/Persistent Stored Modules (SQL/PSM)

As discussed previously in this chapter, each DBMS product has its own variant or extension of SQL, including features that allow SQL to function similarly to a procedural programming language. The ANSI/ISO standard refers to these as SQL/Persistent Stored Modules (SQL/PSM). Microsoft SQL Server calls its version of SQL *Transact-SQL (T-SQL)*, and Oracle Database calls its version of SQL *Procedural Language/SQL (PL/SQL)*. The MySQL variant also includes SQL/PSM components, but it has no special name and is just called *SQL* in the MySQL documentation.

SQL/PSM provides the program variables and cursor functionality previously discussed. It also includes control-of-flow language such as BEGIN...END blocks, IF...THEN...ELSE logic structures and LOOPs as well as the ability to provide usable output to users.

The most important feature of SQL/PSM, however, is that it allows the code that implements these features in a database to be contained in that database. The SQL code can be written as one of three module types: user-defined functions, triggers, and stored procedures. Thus the name: *Persistent*—the code remains available for use over time—*Stored*—the code is stored for reuse in the database—*Modules*—the code is written as a user-defined function, trigger, or stored procedure.

Using SQL User-Defined Functions

A **user-defined function** (also known as a **stored function**) is a stored set of SQL statements that:

- is *called by name* from another SQL statement,
- may have *input parameters* passed to it by the calling SQL statement, and
- *returns an output value* to the SQL statement that called the function.

The logical process flow of a user-defined function is illustrated in Figure 7-20. SQL/PSM user-defined functions are very similar to the SQL built-in aggregate functions (COUNT, SUM, AVG, MAX, and MIN) that we discussed and used in Chapter 2, except that, as the name implies, we create them ourselves to perform specific tasks that we need to do.

Depending upon DBMS product implementation, user-defined functions may be written as:

- a **scalar-valued function** which returns a *single value* based on a row,
- a **table-valued function** which returns a *table of values*, or
- an **aggregate function** which returns a *single value* based on a column grouping (similar to the SQL built-in aggregate functions such as SUM).

In this section, we will only discuss scalar-valued functions.

A common problem that can be solved using a scalar-valued user-defined function is needing a name in the format *LastName, FirstName* (including the comma!) in a report when the database stores the basic data in two fields named *FirstName* and *LastName*. Using the data in the VRG database, we could, of course, simply include the code to do this in an SQL statement (similar to SQL-Query-CH02-45 in Chapter 2—see the "By the Way" discussion on page 81 for a discussion of Oracle Database and MySQL concatenation methods) such as:

```
/* *** SQL-Query-CH07-01 *** */

SELECT      RTRIM(LastName)+', '+RTRIM(FirstName) AS CustomerName,
            AreaCode, PhoneNumber, EmailAddress
FROM        CUSTOMER
ORDER BY    CustomerName;
```

FIGURE 7-20

User-Defined Function Logical Process Flow

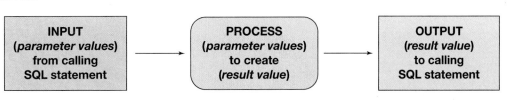

This produces the desired results, but at the expense of working out some cumbersome coding:

	CustomerName	AreaCode	PhoneNumber	EmailAddress
1	Frederickson, Mary Beth	303	513-8822	MaryBeth.Frederickson@somewhere.com
2	Gray, Donald	707	568-4839	Donald.Gray@somewhere.com
3	Janes, Jeffrey	425	543-2345	Jeffrey.Janes@somewhere.com
4	Johnson, Lynda	202	438-5498	NULL
5	Smathers, Fred	206	876-9911	Fred.Smathers@somewhere.com
6	Smith, David	970	654-9876	David.Smith@somewhere.com
7	Twilight, Tiffany	360	765-5566	Tiffany.Twilight@somewhere.com
8	Warning, Selma	604	988-0512	Selma.Warning@somewhere.com
9	Wilkens, Chris	360	876-8822	Chris.Wilkens@somewhere.com
10	Wu, Susan	404	653-3465	Susan.Wu@somewhere.com

The alternative is to create a user-defined function to store this code. Not only does this make it easier to use, but it also makes it available for use in other SQL statements. Figure 7-21 shows a user-defined function written in T-SQL for use with Microsoft SQL Server 2014, and the SQL code for the function uses, as we would expect, specific syntax requirements for Microsoft SQL Server's T-SQL 2014:

- The function is created and stored in the database by using the **SQL CREATE FUNCTION statement**.
- The function name starts with *dbo*, which is a Microsoft SQL Server *schema* name (SQL Server schemas are discussed in Chapter 10A). This use of a schema name appended to a database object name is common in Microsoft SQL Server.
- The variable names of both the input parameters and the returned output value start with @.
- The concatenation syntax is T-SQL syntax.

The Oracle Database version of this function, which uses Oracle's PL/SQL, is discussed in Chapter 10B, and the MySQL version, which uses the MySQL SQL/PSM standards, is discussed in Chapter 10C.

FIGURE 7-21

User-Defined Function to Concatenate FirstName and LastName

```
CREATE FUNCTION dbo.NameConcatenation

-- These are the input parameters
        (
        @FirstName      CHAR(25),
        @LastName       CHAR(25)
        )
RETURNS VARCHAR(60)
AS
BEGIN
     -- This is the variable that will hold the value to be returned
     DECLARE @FullName VARCHAR(60);

     -- SQL statements to concatenate the names in the proper order
     SELECT @FullName = RTRIM(@LastName) + ', ' + RTRIM(@FirstName);

     -- Return the concatentate name
     RETURN @FullName;
END;
```

Now that we have created and stored the user-defined function, we can use it in SQL-Query-CH07-02:

```
/* *** SQL-Query-CH07-02 *** */
SELECT      dbo.NameConcatenation(FirstName, LastName) AS CustomerName,
            AreaCode, PhoneNumber, EmailAddress
FROM        CUSTOMER
ORDER BY    CustomerName;
```

Now we have a function that produces the results we want, which of course are identical to the results for SQL-Query-CH07-01 above:

	CustomerName	AreaCode	PhoneNumber	EmailAddress
1	Frederickson, Mary Beth	303	513-8822	MaryBeth.Frederickson@somewhere.com
2	Gray, Donald	707	568-4839	Donald.Gray@somewhere.com
3	Janes, Jeffrey	425	543-2345	Jeffrey.Janes@somewhere.com
4	Johnson, Lynda	202	438-5498	NULL
5	Smathers, Fred	206	876-9911	Fred.Smathers@somewhere.com
6	Smith, David	970	654-9876	David.Smith@somewhere.com
7	Twilight, Tiffany	360	765-5566	Tiffany.Twilight@somewhere.com
8	Warning, Selma	604	988-0512	Selma.Warning@somewhere.com
9	Wilkens, Chris	360	876-8822	Chris.Wilkens@somewhere.com
10	Wu, Susan	404	653-3465	Susan.Wu@somewhere.com

The advantage of having a user-defined function is that we can now use it whenever we need to without having to re-create the code. For example, our previous query used data in the View Ridge Gallery CUSTOMER table, but we could just as easily use the function with the data in the ARTIST table:

```
/* *** SQL-Query-CH07-03 *** */
SELECT      dbo.NameConcatenation(FirstName, LastName) AS ArtistName,
            DateofBirth, DateDeceased
FROM        ARTIST
ORDER BY    ArtistName;
```

This query produces the expected result:

	ArtistName	DateOfBirth	DateDeceased
1	Chagall, Marc	1887	1985
2	Graves, Morris	1920	2001
3	Horiuchi, Paul	1906	1999
4	Kandinsky, Wassily	1866	1944
5	Klee, Paul	1879	1940
6	Matisse, Henri	1869	1954
7	Miro, Joan	1893	1983
8	Sargent, John Singer	1856	1925
9	Tobey, Mark	1890	1976

We can even use the function multiple times in the same SQL statement, as shown in SQL-Query-CH07-04, which is a variant on the SQL query we used to create the SQL view CustomerInterestView in our discussion of SQL views:

```
/* *** SQL-Query-CH07-04 *** */
SELECT    dbo.NameConcatenation(C.FirstName, C.LastName) AS CustomerName,
          dbo.NameConcatenation(A.FirstName, A.LastName) AS ArtistName
FROM      CUSTOMER AS C JOIN CUSTOMER_ARTIST_INT AS CAI
    ON    C.CustomerID = CAI.CustomerID
      JOIN    ARTIST AS A
        ON    CAI.ArtistID = A.ArtistID
ORDER BY  CustomerName, ArtistName;
```

This query produces the expected large result that is shown in Figure 7-22, where we see that both CustomerName and ArtistName display the names in the LastName, FirstName syntax produced by the *NameConcatenation* user-defined function. Compare the results in this figure to those in Figure 7-18, which presents essentially the same results, but without the formatting provided by the *NameConcatenation* function.

FIGURE 7-22

Result of SQL Query Using the NameConcatenation User-Defined Function

	CustomerName	ArtistName
1	Frederickson, Mary Beth	Chagall, Marc
2	Frederickson, Mary Beth	Kandinsky, Wassily
3	Frederickson, Mary Beth	Matisse, Henri
4	Frederickson, Mary Beth	Miro, Joan
5	Gray, Donald	Graves, Morris
6	Gray, Donald	Horiuchi, Paul
7	Gray, Donald	Tobey, Mark
8	Janes, Jeffrey	Graves, Morris
9	Janes, Jeffrey	Horiuchi, Paul
10	Janes, Jeffrey	Tobey, Mark
11	Smathers, Fred	Graves, Morris
12	Smathers, Fred	Horiuchi, Paul
13	Smathers, Fred	Tobey, Mark
14	Smith, David	Chagall, Marc
15	Smith, David	Kandinsky, Wassily
16	Smith, David	Matisse, Henri
17	Smith, David	Miro, Joan
18	Smith, David	Sargent, John Singer
19	Twilight, Tiffany	Graves, Morris
20	Twilight, Tiffany	Horiuchi, Paul
21	Twilight, Tiffany	Sargent, John Singer
22	Twilight, Tiffany	Tobey, Mark
23	Warning, Selma	Chagall, Marc
24	Warning, Selma	Graves, Morris
25	Warning, Selma	Sargent, John Singer
26	Wilkens, Chris	Graves, Morris
27	Wilkens, Chris	Horiuchi, Paul
28	Wilkens, Chris	Tobey, Mark

Using SQL Triggers

A **trigger** is a stored program that is executed by the DBMS whenever a specified event occurs. Triggers for Oracle Database are written in Java or in Oracle's PL/SQL. Microsoft SQL Server triggers are written in Microsoft .NET Common Language Runtime (CLR) languages, such as Visual Basic.NET, or Microsoft's T-SQL. MySQL triggers are written in MySQL's variant of SQL. In this chapter, we will discuss triggers in a generic manner without considering the particulars of those languages. We will discuss triggers written in DBMS-specific SQL variants for T-SQL in Chapter 10A, for PL/SQL in Chapter 10B, and for MySQL SQL in Chapter 10C.

A trigger is attached to a table or a view. A table or a view may have many triggers, but a trigger is associated with just one table or view. A trigger is invoked by an SQL DML INSERT, UPDATE, or DELETE request on the table or view to which it is attached. Figure 7-23 summarizes the triggers available for SQL Server 2014, Oracle Database, and MySQL 5.6.

Oracle Database 12*c* and Oracle Database Express Edition 11*g* Release 2 both support three kinds of triggers: BEFORE, INSTEAD OF, and AFTER. As you would expect, BEFORE triggers are executed before the DBMS processes the insert, update, or delete request. INSTEAD OF triggers are executed in place of any DBMS processing of the insert, update, or delete request. AFTER triggers are executed after the insert, update, or delete request has been processed. All together, nine trigger types are possible: BEFORE (INSERT, UPDATE, DELETE); INSTEAD OF (INSERT, UPDATE, DELETE); and AFTER (INSERT, UPDATE, DELETE).

Since SQL Server 2005, SQL Server supports DDL triggers (triggers on such SQL DDL statements as CREATE, ALTER, and DROP) as well as DML triggers. We will only deal with the DML triggers here, which for SQL Server 2014 are INSTEAD OF and AFTER triggers on INSERT, UPDATE, and DELETE. (Microsoft includes the FOR keyword, but this is a synonym for AFTER in Microsoft syntax.) Thus, we have six possible trigger types.

MySQL 5.6 supports only BEFORE and AFTER triggers–thus, like SQL Server 2014, it supports only six trigger types. Other DBMS products support triggers differently. See the documentation of your product to determine which trigger types it supports.

When a trigger is invoked, the DBMS makes the data involved in the requested action available to the trigger code. For an insert, the DBMS will supply the values of columns for the row that is being inserted. For deletions, the DBMS will supply the values of columns for the row that is being deleted. For updates, it will supply both the old and the new values.

The way in which this is done depends on the DBMS product. For now, assume that new values are supplied by prefixing a column name with the expression *new:*. Thus, during an insert on CUSTOMER, the variable new:LastName is the value of LastName for the row being inserted. For an update, new:LastName has the value of LastName after the update takes place. Similarly, assume that old values are supplied by prefixing a column name with the expression *old:*. Thus, for a deletion, the variable old:LastName has the value of LastName for the row being deleted. For an update, old:LastName has the value of Name prior to the requested update. This, in fact, is the strategy used by Oracle PL/SQL and MySQL SQL—you will see the equivalent SQL Server strategy in Chapter 10A.

FIGURE 7-23

Summary of SQL Triggers by DBMS Product

Trigger Type ╱ DML Action	BEFORE	INSTEAD OF	AFTER
INSERT	Oracle Database MySQL	Oracle Database SQL Server	Oracle Database SQL Server MySQL
UPDATE	Oracle Database MySQL	Oracle Database SQL Server	Oracle Database SQL Server MySQL
DELETE	Oracle Database MySQL	Oracle Database SQL Server	Oracle Database SQL Server MySQL

FIGURE 7-24
Uses for SQL Triggers

Uses of SQL Triggers
Provide default values.
Enforce data constraints.
Update views.
Perform referential integrity actions.

Triggers have many uses. In this chapter, we consider the four uses summarized in Figure 7-24:

- Providing default values
- Enforcing data constraints
- Updating SQL views
- Performing referential integrity actions

Using Triggers to Provide Default Values

Earlier in this chapter, you learned to use the SQL DEFAULT keyword to provide initial column values. DEFAULT works only for simple expressions, however. If the computation of a default value requires complicated logic, then an INSERT trigger must be used instead.

For example, suppose that there is a policy at View Ridge Gallery to set the value of AskingPrice equal either to twice the AcquisitionPrice or to the AcquisitionPrice plus the average net gain for sales of this art in the past, whichever is greater. The AFTER trigger in Figure 7-25 implements this policy. Note that the code in Figure 7-25, although resembling Oracle Database PL/SQL, is *generic pseudocode*. You will learn how to write specific code for SQL Server in Chapter 10A, for Oracle Database in Chapter 10B, and for MySQL in Chapter 10C.

After declaring program variables, the trigger reads the TRANS table to find out how many TRANS rows exist for this work. Because this is an AFTER trigger, the new TRANS row for the work will have already been inserted. Thus, the count will be one if this is the first time the work has been in the gallery. If so, the new value of SalesPrice is set to twice the AcquisitionPrice.

If the user variable *rowCount* is greater than one, then the work has been in the gallery before. To compute the average gain for this work, the trigger uses the ArtistWorkNetView described on page 335 to compute SUM(NetProfit) for this work. The sum is placed in the variable sum-NetProfit. Notice that the WHERE clause limits the rows to be used in the view to this particular work. The average is then computed by dividing this sum by *rowCount* minus one.

You may be wondering, why not use AVG(NetProfit) in the SQL statement? The answer is that the default SQL average function would have counted the new row in the computation of the average. We do not want that row to be included, so we subtract one from *rowCount* when the average is computed. Once the value of avgNetProfit has been computed, it is compared with twice the AcquisitionPrice; the larger result is used for the new value of AskingPrice.

Using Triggers to Enforce Data Constraints

A second purpose of triggers is to enforce data constraints. Although SQL CHECK constraints can be used to enforce domain, range, and intrarelation constraints, no DBMS vendor has implemented the SQL-92 features for interrelation CHECK constraints. Consequently, such constraints are implemented in triggers.

Suppose, for example, that the gallery has a special interest in Mexican painters and never discounts the price of their works. Thus, the SalesPrice of a work must always be at least the AskingPrice. To enforce this rule, the gallery database has an insert and update trigger on TRANS that checks to see if the work is by a Mexican painter. If so, the SalesPrice is checked against the AskingPrice. If it is less than the AskingPrice, the SalesPrice is reset to the AskingPrice. This, of course, must happen when the artwork is actually being sold, and the customer charged the full amount! This is *not* a postsale accounting adjustment.

```
/* *** EXAMPLE CODE - DO NOT RUN ***                                    */

CREATE TRIGGER TRANS_AskingPriceInitialValue
        AFTER INSERT ON TRANS

DECLARE
        rowCount          Int;
        sumNetProfit      Numeric(10,2);
        avgNetProfit      Numeric(10,2);
BEGIN
        /* First find if work has been here before                     */

        SELECT    Count(*) INTO rowCount
        FROM      TRANS AS T
        WHERE     new:WorkID = T.WorkID;

        IF (rowCount = 1)
        THEN
            /* This is first time work has been in gallery             */

            new:AskingPrice = 2 * new:AcquisitionPrice;

        ELSE
            IF rowCount > 1
            THEN
                /* Work has been here before                           */

                SELECT    SUM(NetProfit) into sumNetProfit
                FROM      ArtistWorkNetView AWNV
                WHERE     AWNV.WorkID = new.WorkID
                GROUP BY  AWNV.WorkID;

                avgNetProfit = sumNetProfit / (rowCount - 1);

                /* Now choose larger value for the new AskingPrice      */

                IF ((new:AcquisitionPrice + avgNetProfit)
                      > (2 * new:AcquisitionPrice))
                THEN
                    new:AskingPrice = (new:AcquisitionPrice + avgNetProfit);
                ELSE
                    new:AskingPrice = (2 * new:AcquisitionPrice);
                END IF;
            ELSE
                /* Error, rowCount cannot be less than 1               */
                /* Do something!                                        */
            END IF;
        END IF;
END;
```

FIGURE 7-25

Trigger Code to Insert a Default Value

Figure 7-26 shows *generic trigger code* that implements this rule. This trigger will be fired after any insert or update on a TRANS row. The trigger first checks to determine if the work is by a Mexican artist. If not, the trigger is exited. Otherwise, the SalesPrice is checked against the AskingPrice; if it is less than the AskingPrice, the SalesPrice is set equal to the AskingPrice.

This trigger will be called recursively; the update statement in the trigger will cause an update on TRANS, which will cause the trigger to be called again. The second time, however, the SalesPrice will be equal to the AskingPrice, no more updates will be made, and the recursion will stop.

Using Triggers to Update Views

As stated earlier, the DBMS can update some views but not others, depending on the way the view is constructed. Applications can sometimes update the views that the DBMS cannot update by applying logic that is particular to a given business setting. In this case, the application-specific logic for updating the view is placed in an INSTEAD OF trigger.

```
/* *** EXAMPLE CODE - DO NOT RUN ***                                    */

CREATE TRIGGER TRANS_CheckSalesPrice
       AFTER INSERT, UPDATE ON TRANS

DECLARE

       artistNationality   Char (30);

BEGIN
       /* First determine if work is by a Mexican artist */

       SELECT    Nationality into artistNationality
       FROM      ARTIST AS A JOIN WORK AS W
            ON A.ArtistID = W.ArtistID
       WHERE     W.WorkID = new:WorkID;

       IF (artistNationality <> 'Mexican')
       THEN
          Exit Trigger;
       ELSE

          /* Work is by a Mexican artist - enforce constraint         */

          IF (new:SalesPrice < new:AskingPrice)
          THEN

             /* Sales Price is too low, reset it                      */

             UPDATE    TRANS
             SET       SalesPrice = new:AskingPrice
             WHERE     TransactionID = new:TransactionID;

             /* Note:  The above update will cause a recursive call on this */
             /* trigger. The recursion will stop the second time through    */
             /* because SalesPrice will be = AskingPrice.                    */

             /* At this point send a message to the user saying what's been */
             /* done so that the customer has to pay the full amount         */

          ELSE
             /* new:SalesPrice >= new:AskingPrice                     */
          Exit Trigger;
          END IF;
       END IF;
END;
```

FIGURE 7-26

Trigger Code to Enforce an Interrelation Data Constraint

When an INSTEAD OF trigger is declared on a view, the DBMS performs no action other than to call the trigger. Everything else is up to the trigger. If you declare an INSTEAD OF INSERT trigger on view MyView and if your trigger does nothing but send an email message, then that email message becomes the result of an INSERT on the view. INSERT MyView means "send an email" and nothing more.

More realistically, consider the SQL view CustomerInterestsView on page 335 and the result of that view in Figure 7-18. This view is the result of two joins across the intersection table between CUSTOMER and ARTIST. Suppose that this view populates a grid on a user form, and further suppose that users want to make customer name corrections, when necessary, on this form. If such changes are not possible, the users will say something like, "But, hey, the name is right there. Why can't I change it?" Little do they know the trials and tribulations the DBMS went through to display those data!

In any case, if, for example, the customer LastName value happens to be unique within the database, the view has sufficient information to update the customer's last name. Figure 7-27 shows *generic trigger code* for such an update. The code just counts the number of customers that have the old value of LastName. If only one customer has that value, then the update is made; otherwise, an error message is generated. Notice that the update activity is on one of the tables that underlie the view. The view, of course, has no real data. Only actual tables can be updated.

```
/* *** EXAMPLE CODE - DO NOT RUN ***                                    */

CREATE TRIGGER CustomerInterestView_UpdateCustomerLastName
       INSTEAD OF UPDATE ON CustomerInterestView

DECLARE

       rowCount           Int;

BEGIN

       SELECT     COUNT(*) into rowCount
       FROM       CUSTOMER
       WHERE      CUSTOMER.LastName = old:LastName

       IF (rowCount = 1)
       THEN

           /* If get here, then only one customer has this last name.   */
           /* Make the name change.                                     */

           UPDATE     CUSTOMER
           SET        CUSTOMER.LastName = new:LastName
           WHERE      CUSTOMER.LastName = old:LastName;

       ELSE

           IF (rowCount > 1 )
           THEN

               /* Send a message to the user saying cannot update because */
               /* there are too many customers with this last name.       */

           ELSE
               /* Error, if rowcount <= 0 there is an error!              */
               /* Do something!                                          */
           END IF;
       END IF;
END;
```

FIGURE 7-27

Trigger Code to Update an SQL View

Using Triggers to Implement Referential Integrity Actions

The fourth use of triggers is to implement referential integrity actions. Consider, for example, the 1:N relationship between DEPARTMENT and EMPLOYEE. Assume that the relationship is M-M and that EMPLOYEE.DepartmentName is a foreign key to DEPARTMENT.

To enforce this constraint, we will construct two views, both based on EMPLOYEE. The first view, DeleteEmployeeView, will delete an EMPLOYEE row only if that row is not the last child in the DEPARTMENT. The second view, DeleteEmployeeDepartmentView, will delete an EMPLOYEE row, and if that row is the last EMPLOYEE in the DEPARTMENT, it will also delete the DEPARTMENT row.

An organization would make the view DeleteEmployeeView available to applications that do not have permission to delete a row in DEPARTMENT. The view DeleteEmployeeDepartmentView would be given to applications that have permission to delete both employees and departments that have no employees. At the same time, the organization would disallow all deletions directly on the EMPLOYEE and DEPARTMENT tables.

Both of the views DeleteEmployeeView and DeleteEmployeeDepartmentView have the identical structure:

```
/* *** EXAMPLE CODE - DO NOT RUN *** */

/* *** SQL-CREATE-VIEW-CH07-09 *** */

CREATE VIEW DeleteEmployeeView AS

       SELECT      *

       FROM        EMPLOYEE;
```

```
/* *** EXAMPLE CODE - DO NOT RUN *** */
/* *** SQL-CREATE-VIEW-CH07-10 *** */
CREATE VIEW DeleteEmployeeDepartmentView AS
    SELECT      *
    FROM        EMPLOYEE;
```

The trigger on DeleteEmployeeView, shown in Figure 7-28, determines if the employee is the last employee in the department. If not, the EMPLOYEE row is deleted. If, however, the employee *is* the last employee in the department, *nothing* is done. Note again that the DBMS does nothing when an INSTEAD OF trigger is declared on the deletion. All activity is up to the trigger. If the employee is the last employee, then this trigger does nothing, which means that no change will be made to the database because the DBMS left all processing tasks to the INSTEAD OF trigger.

The trigger on DeleteEmployeeDepartment, shown in Figure 7-29, treats the employee deletion a bit differently. First, the trigger checks to determine if the employee is the last employee in the department. If so, the EMPLOYEE is deleted, and then the DEPARTMENT itself is deleted. Notice that the row in EMPLOYEE is deleted in either case.

Triggers such as those in Figures 7-28 and 7-29 are used to enforce the referential integrity actions for O-M and M-M relationships, as described at the end of Chapter 6 (note that a full implementation of those actions would also have to deal with insertions of departments). You will learn how to write them for SQL Server 2014 in Chapter 10A, Oracle Database in Chapter 10B, and for MySQL 5.6 in Chapter 10C.

Using Stored Procedures

A **stored procedure** is a program that is stored within the database and compiled when used. In Oracle Database, stored procedures can be written in PL/SQL or in Java. With Microsoft SQL Server 2014, stored procedures are written in T-SQL or a .NET CLR language, such as Visual Basic.NET, C#.NET, or C++.NET. With MySQL, stored procedures are written in MySQL's variant of SQL.

FIGURE 7-28

Trigger Code to Delete All but Last Child

```
/* *** EXAMPLE CODE - DO NOT RUN ***                                    */
CREATE TRIGGER EMPLOYEE_DeleteCheck
    INSTEAD OF DELETE ON DeleteEmployeeView

DECLARE

    rowCount        Int;

BEGIN

    /*  First determine if this is the last employee in the department */

    SELECT    Count(*) into rowCount
    FROM      EMPLOYEE
    WHERE    ` EMPLOYEE.EmployeeNumber = old:EmployeeNumber;

    IF (rowCount > 1)
    THEN

        /* Not last employee, allow deletion                            */

        DELETE    EMPLOYEE
        WHERE     EMPLOYEE.EmployeeNumber = old:EmployeeNumber;

    ELSE

        /* Send a message to user saying that the last employee         */
        /* in a department cannot be deleted.                           */

    END IF;

END;
```

```
/* *** EXAMPLE CODE - DO NOT RUN ***                                          */

CREATE TRIGGER EMPLOYEE_DEPARTMENT_DeleteCheck
       INSTEAD OF DELETE ON DeleteEmployeeDepartmentView

DECLARE

       rowCount          Int;

BEGIN

     /*  First determine if this is the last employee in the department   */

     SELECT     Count(*) into rowCount
     FROM       EMPLOYEE
     WHERE      EMPLOYEE.EmployeeNumber = old:EmployeeNumber;

     /* Delete Employee row regardless of whether Department is deleted    */

     DELETE     EMPLOYEE
     WHERE      EMPLOYEE.EmployeeNumber = old:EmployeeNumber;

     IF (rowCount = 1)
     THEN

        /* Last employee in Department, delete Department                  */

        DELETE     DEPARTMENT
        WHERE      DEPARTMENT.DepartmentName = old:DepartmentName;

     END IF;

  END;
```

FIGURE 7-29

**Trigger Code to Delete
Last Child and Parent
When Necessary**

Stored procedures can receive input parameters and return results. Unlike triggers, which are attached to a given table or view, stored procedures are attached to the database. They can be executed by any process using the database that has permission to use the procedure. Differences between triggers and stored procedures are summarized in Figure 7-30.

Stored procedures are used for many purposes. Although database administrators use them to perform common administration tasks, their primary use is within database applications. They can be invoked from application programs written in languages such as COBOL, C, Java, C#, or C++. They also can be invoked from Web pages (as we will see in Chapter 11) using VBScript, JavaScript, or PHP. Ad hoc users can run them from DBMS management products such as SQL*Plus or SQL Developer in Oracle Database, SQL Server Management Studio in SQL Server, or the MySQLWorkbench in MySQL.

Advantages of Stored Procedures

The advantages of using stored procedures are listed in Figure 7-31. Unlike application code, stored procedures are never distributed to client computers. They always reside in the database and are processed by the DBMS on the database server. Thus, they are more secure than distributed application code, and they also reduce network traffic. Increasingly, stored procedures are the preferred mode of processing application logic over the Internet or corporate intranets. Another advantage of stored procedures is that their SQL statements can be optimized by the DBMS compiler.

When application logic is placed in a stored procedure, many different application programmers can use that code. This sharing results not only in less work but also in standardized processing. Further, the developers best suited for database work can create the stored procedures while other developers, say, those who specialize in Web-tier programming, can do other work. Because of these advantages, it is likely that stored procedures will see increased use in the future.

FIGURE 7-30

Triggers Versus Stored
Procedures

Triggers Versus Stored Procedures
Trigger
Module of code that is called by the DBMS when INSERT, UPDATE, or DELETE commands are issued.
Assigned to a table or view.
Depending on the DBMS, may have more than one trigger per table or view.
Triggers may issue INSERT, UPDATE, and DELETE commands and thereby may cause the invocation of other triggers.
Stored Procedure
Module of code that is called by a user or database administrator.
Assigned to a database, but not to a table or a view.
Can issue INSERT, UPDATE, DELETE, and MERGE commands.
Used for repetitive administration tasks or as part of an application.

The WORK_AddWorkTransaction Stored Procedure

Figure 7-32 shows a stored procedure that records the acquisition of a work in the VRG database. Again, this code is generic, but the code style in Figure 7-32 is closer to that used in Microsoft SQL Server T-SQL rather than the Oracle Database PL/SQL style that was used for the trigger examples in the prior section. If you compare the pseudocode examples in both sections, you can gain a sense of the differences between code written in PL/SQL and T-SQL.

The WORK_addWorkTransaction procedure receives five input parameters and returns none. In a more realistic example, a return parameter would be passed back to the caller to indicate the success or failure of the operation. That discussion takes us away from database concepts, however, and we will omit it here. This code does not assume that the value of ArtistID that is passed to it is a valid ID. Instead, the first step in the stored procedure is to check whether the ArtistID value is valid. To do this, the first block of statements counts the number of rows that have the given ArtistID value. If the count is zero, then the ArtistID value is invalid, and the procedure writes an error message and returns.

Otherwise,[4] the procedure then checks to determine if the work has been in the View Ridge Gallery before. If so, the WORK table will already contain a row for this ArtistID, Title, and Copy.

FIGURE 7-31

Advantages of Stored
Procedures

Advantages of Stored Procedures
Greater security.
Decreased network traffic.
SQL can be optimized.
Code sharing.
Less work.
Standardized processing.
Specialization among developers.

---

[4]This code does not check for more than one row having the given ArtistID because ArtistID is a surrogate key.

FIGURE 7-32

Stored Procedure to Record the Acquisition of a Work

```
/* *** EXAMPLE CODE - DO NOT RUN ***                                              */

CREATE PROCEDURE WORK_AddWorkTransaction
        (
        @ArtistID            Int,   /* Artist must already exist in database    */
        @Title               Char(25),
        @Copy                Char(8),
        @Description         Varchar(1000),
        @AcquisitionPrice    Numeric (6,2)
        )

/* Stored procedure to record the acquisition of a work.  If the work has        */
/* never been in the gallery before, add a new WORK row.  Otherwise, use         */
/* the existing WORK row.  Add a new TRANS row for the work and set              */
/* DateAcquired to the system date.                                              */

AS
BEGIN

        DECLARE @rowCount AS Int
        DECLARE @WorkID AS Int

        /* Check that the ArtistID is valid                                      */

        SELECT    @rowCount = COUNT(*)
        FROM      ARTIST AS A
        WHERE     A.ArtistID = @ArtistID

        IF (@rowCount = 0)
           /* The Artist does not exist in the database                          */
           BEGIN
              Print 'No artist with id of ' + Str(@artistID)
              Print 'Processing terminated.'
              RETURN
           END

        /* Check to see if the work is in the database                           */

        SELECT    @rowCount = COUNT(*)
        FROM      WORK AS W
        WHERE     W.ArtistID = @ArtistID and
                  W.Title = @Title and
                  W.Copy = @Copy

        IF (@rowCount = 0)
           /* The Work is not in database, so put it in.                         */
           BEGIN
              INSERT INTO WORK (Title, Copy, Description, ArtistID)
                 VALUES (@Title, @Copy, @Description, @ArtistID)
           END

        /* Get the work surrogate key WorkID value                               */

        SELECT    @WorkID = W.WorkID
        FROM      WORK AS W
        WHERE     W.ArtistID = @ArtistID
           AND    W.Title = @Title
           AND    W.Copy = @Copy

        /* Now put the new TRANS row into database.                              */

        INSERT INTO TRANS (DateAcquired, AcquisitionPrice, WorkID)
           VALUES (GetDate(), @AcquisitionPrice, @WorkID)

        RETURN
END
```

	User-Defined Functions	Triggers	Stored Procedures
Can accept parameters	Yes	No	Yes
Can return a result value or values	Yes	No	Yes
Can be used in SELECT statements	Yes	No	No
Can use SELECT statements	Yes	Yes	Yes
Can use INSERT statements	No	Yes	Yes
Can use UPDATE statements	No	Yes	Yes
Can use DELETE statements	No	Yes	Yes
Can call a User-Defined Function	Yes	Yes	Yes
Can invoke a Trigger	No	Yes (Indirectly via INSERT, UPDATE, or DELETE)	Yes (Indirectly via INSERT, UPDATE, or DELETE)
Can invoke a Stored Procedure	No	Yes	Yes
Is stored as a database-wide object	Yes	No	Yes
Is stored as a table-specific object	No	Yes	No

FIGURE 7-33

Comparison of User-Defined Functions, Triggers, and Stored Procedures

If no such row exists, the procedure creates a new WORK row. Once that has been done, it then uses a SELECT to obtain a value for the WorkID value. If the WORK row was just created, this statement is necessary to obtain the new value of the WorkID surrogate key. If the work was not created, the SELECT on WorkID is necessary to obtain the WorkID of the existing row. Once a value of WorkID has been obtained, the new row is inserted into TRANS. Notice that the system function GetDate() is used to supply a value for DateAcquired in the new row.

This procedure illustrates how SQL is embedded in stored procedures. It is not complete because we need to do something to ensure that either all updates originating in the stored procedures are made to the database or none of them are. You will learn how to do this in Chapter 9. For now, just concentrate on how SQL can be used as part of a database application.

Comparing User-Defined Functions, Triggers, and Stored Procedures

User-defined functions, triggers, and stored procedures are all modules of programming code that are stored and used with a database. They differ in their intended use and in their ability to perform specific actions within the database. Figure 7-33 summarizes these three components of SQL/PSM.

Summary

This chapter discusses the process of implementing a database in a DBMS product from a database design (as discussed in Chapter 6). Figure 7-34 summarizes the various aspects of data models, database designs, and how they relate to each other, as well as how they relate to the systems analysis and design process in general and to the systems development life cycle (SDLC) in particular. For more information about systems analysis and design and the SDLC, see Appendix B.

SQL DDL statements are used to manage the structure of tables. This chapter presented four SQL DDL statements: CREATE TABLE, ALTER TABLE, DROP TABLE, and TRUNCATE TABLE. SQL is preferred over graphical tools for creating tables because it is faster, it can be used to create the same table repeatedly, tables can be created from program code, and it is standardized and (mostly) DBMS independent.

	Data Model (Chapter 5)	Database Design (Chapter 6)	Database Implementation (Chapter 7)
SDLC Stage	**Requirements Analysis**	**Component Design**	**Implementation**
SA&D Reference	Conceptual Design/Schema		
		Logical Design/Schema	
		Physical Design (Data Types)	Physical Design (File and records, etc.)
Data Structure	Entity	Table (Relation)	Table
Relationship Structure	Relationship	Relationship with Foreign Keys	Foreign Keys
Level of Generality	Generic	DBMS Specific	DBMS and OS Specific
Relationships:			
1:1	Yes	Yes	Yes
1:N	Yes	Yes	Yes
1:N ID-Dependent	Yes	Yes	Yes
N:M	Yes	No - See Intersection Table	No - See Intersection Table
Intersection Table with two 1:N ID-Dependent Relationships	No - See N:M Relationships	Yes	Yes
Association Table with two 1:N ID-Dependent Relationships	Yes (Associative Entity)	Yes	Yes
SuperType/SubType	Yes Depends on Data Modeling Software	Yes Depends on Data Modeling Software	No Use 1:1 Relationships with Column Values
Recursive	Yes	Yes	Yes
Software Tools: (used in this book)	Microsoft Visio 2013	MySQL Workbench	Microsoft SQL Server Management Studio Oracle SQL Developer MySQL Workbench

FIGURE 7-34

Summary of the Database
Design and Implementation
Process

The IDENTITY (*N*, *M*) data type is used to create surrogate keys in Microsoft SQL Server 2014, where *N* is the starting value and *M* is the increment to be added. The SQL CREATE TABLE statement is used to define the name of the table, its columns, and constraints on columns. There are five types of constraints: PRIMARY KEY, UNIQUE, NULL/NOT NULL, FOREIGN KEY, and CHECK.

The purposes of the first three constraints are obvious. FOREIGN KEY is used to create referential integrity constraints; CHECK is used to create data constraints. Figure 7-10 summarizes techniques for creating relationships using SQL constraints.

Simple default values can be assigned using the DEFAULT keyword. Some data constraints are defined using CHECK constraints. Domain, range, and intratable constraints can be defined. Although SQL-92 defined facilities for interrelation CHECK constraints, those facilities were not implemented by DBMS vendors. Instead, interrelation constraints are enforced using triggers.

The ALTER statement is used to add and remove columns and constraints. The DROP statement is used to drop tables. In SQL DDL, parents need to be created first and dropped last.

The DML SQL statements are INSERT, UPDATE, DELETE, and MERGE. Each statement can be used on a single row, on a group of rows, or on the entire table. Because of their power, both UPDATE and DELETE need to be used with care.

An SQL view is a virtual table that is constructed from other tables and views. SQL SELECT statements are used to define views. The only restriction is that a view definition may not include an ORDER BY clause.

Views are used to hide columns or rows and to show the results of computed columns. They also can hide complicated SQL syntax, such as that used for joins and GROUP BY queries, and layer computations and built-in functions so that computations can be used in WHERE clauses. Some organizations use views to provide table aliases. Views also can be used to assign different sets of processing permissions to tables and to assign different sets of triggers as well. The rules for determining whether a view can be updated are both complicated and DBMS specific. Guidelines are shown in Figure 7-23.

SQL statements can be embedded in program code in functions, triggers, stored procedures, and application code. To do so, there must be a way to associate SQL table columns with program variables. Also, there is a paradigm mismatch between SQL and programs. Most SQL statements return sets of rows; an application expects to work on one row at a time. To resolve this mismatch, the results of SQL statements are processed as pseudofiles using a cursor. Web database applications are a good example of SQL statements embedded in application program code.

SQL/PSM is the portion of the SQL standard that provides for storing reusable modules of program code within a database. SQL/PSM specifies that SQL statements will be embedded in user-defined functions, triggers, and stored procedures in a database. It also specifies SQL variables, cursors, control-of-flow statements, and output procedures.

A user-defined function accepts input parameter values from an SQL statement, processes the parameter values, and returns a result value back to the calling statement. User-defined functions may be written to return a single value based on row values (a scalar-valued function), a table of values based on row values (a table-valued function), or a single value based on grouped column values (an aggregate function).

A trigger is a stored program that is executed by the DBMS whenever a specified event occurs on a specified table or view. In Oracle, triggers can be written in Java or in a proprietary Oracle language called PL/SQL. In SQL Server, triggers can be written in a propriety SQL Server language called TRANSACT-SQL, or T-SQL, and in Microsoft CLR languages, such as Visual Basic .NET, C# .NET, and C++ .NET. With MySQL, triggers can be written in MySQL's variant of SQL.

Possible triggers are BEFORE, INSTEAD OF, and AFTER. Each type of trigger can be declared for insert, update, and delete actions, so nine types of triggers are possible. Oracle supports all nine trigger types, SQL Server supports only INSTEAD OF and AFTER triggers, and MySQL supports the BEFORE and AFTER triggers. When a trigger is fired, the DBMS supplies old and new values for the update. New values are provided for inserts and updates, and old values are provided for updates and deletions. How these values are provided to the trigger depends on the DBMS in use.

Triggers have many uses. This chapter discussed four: setting default values, enforcing interrelation data constraints, updating views, and enforcing referential integrity actions.

A stored procedure is a program that is stored within the database and compiled when used. Stored procedures can receive input parameters and return results. Unlike triggers, their scope is database-wide; they can be used by any process that has permission to run the stored procedure.

Stored procedures can be called from programs written in the same languages used for triggers. They also can be called from DBMS SQL utilities. The advantages of using stored procedures are summarized in Figure 7-31.

A summary and comparison of user-defined functions, triggers, and stored procedures is shown in Figure 7-33.

Key Terms

aggregate function	intrarelation constraint	SQL ALTER INDEX statement
casual relationship	Microsoft SQL Server 2014	SQL ALTER TABLE statement
CHECK constraint	Management Studio	SQL ALTER VIEW statement
cursor	NOT NULL constraint	SQL CREATE FUNCTION statement
data control language (DCL)	NULL constraint	SQL CREATE INDEX statement
data definition language (DDL)	Oracle MySQL Workbench	SQL CREATE TABLE statement
data manipulation language (DML)	Oracle SQL Developer	SQL CREATE VIEW statement
data model	PRIMARY KEY constraint	SQL CREATE OR REPLACE VIEW
database design	procedural programming language	statement
DEFAULT keyword	Procedural Language/SQL (PL/SQL)	SQL DELETE statement
FOREIGN KEY constraint	psuedofile	SQL DROP COLUMN clause
IDENTITY({StartValue}, {Increment})	scalar-valued function	SQL DROP CONSTRAINT clause
property	SQL/Persistent Stored Modules	SQL DROP INDEX statement
implementation	(SQL/PSM)	SQL DROP TABLE statement
index	SQL ADD clause	SQL INSERT statement
interrelation constraint	SQL ADD CONSTRAINT clause	SQL MERGE statement

SQL ON DELETE clause

SQL ON UPDATE clause

SQL script

SQL script file

SQL TRUNCATE TABLE statement

SQL UPDATE statement

SQL view

stored procedure

systems analysis and design

systems development life cycle (SDLC)

table-valued function

transaction control language (TCL)

Transact-SQL (T-SQL)

trigger

UNIQUE constraint

user-defined function (stored function)

Review Questions

7.1 What does DDL stand for? List the SQL DDL statements.

7.2 What does DML stand for? List the SQL DML statements.

7.3 Explain the meaning of the following expression: IDENTITY (4000, 5).

For this set of Review Questions, we will create and use a database with a set of tables that will allow us to compare variations in SQL CREATE TABLE and SQL INSERT statements. The purpose of these questions is to illustrate different situations that call for specific uses of various SQL CREATE TABLE and SQL INSERT options.

The database will be named CH07_RQ_TABLES and will contain the following six tables:

> CUSTOMER_01 (<u>EmailAddress</u>, LastName, FirstName)
>
> CUSTOMER_02 (<u>CustomerID</u>, EmailAddress, LastName, FirstName)
>
> CUSTOMER_03 (<u>CustomerID</u>, EmailAddress, LastName, FirstName)
>
> CUSTOMER_04 (<u>CustomerID</u>, EmailAddress, LastName, FirstName)
>
> SALE_01 (<u>SaleID</u>, DateOfSale, *EmailAddress*, SaleAmount)
>
> SALE_02 (<u>SaleID</u>, DateOfSale, *CustomerID*, SaleAmount)

EmailAddress is a text column containing an email address, and is therefore not a surrogate key. CustomerID is a surrogate key that starts at 1 and increments by 1. SaleID is a surrogate key that starts at 20150001 and increases by 1.

The CH07_RQ_TABLES database has the following referential integrity constraints:

> EmailAddress in SALE_01 must exist in EmailAddress in CUSTOMER_01
>
> CustomerID in SALE_02 must exist in CustomerID in CUSTOMER_04

The relationship from SALE_01 to CUSTOMER_01 is N:1, O-M.
The relationship from SALE_02 to CUSTOMER_04 is N:1, O-M.
The column characteristics for these tables are shown in Figures 7-35 (CUSTOMER_01), 7-36 (CUSTOMER_02, CUSTOMER_03, and CUSTOMER_04), 7-37 (SALE_01), and 7-38 (SALE_02). The data for these tables are shown in Figures 7-39 (CUSTOMER_01), 7-40 (CUSTOMER_02), 7-41 (CUSTOMER_04), 7-42 (SALE_01), and 7-43 (SALE_02).

7.4 If you are using Microsoft SQL Server, Oracle Database, or MySQL, create a folder in your *Documents* folder to save and store the *.sql scripts containing the SQL

FIGURE 7-35

Column Characteristics for the CH07_RQ_TABLES Database CUSTOMER_01 Table

Column Name	Type	Key	Required	Remarks
EmailAddress	Varchar (100)	Primary Key	Yes	
LastName	Varchar (25)	No	Yes	
FirstName	Varchar (25)	No	Yes	

FIGURE 7-36

Column Characteristics
for the CH07_RQ_TABLES
Database CUSTOMER_02,
CUSTOMER_03, and
CUSTOMER_04 Tables

Column Name	Type	Key	Required	Remarks
CustomerID	Integer	Primary Key	Yes	Surrogate Key: Initial value=1 Increment=1
EmailAddress	Varchar (100)	No	Yes	
LastName	Varchar (25)	No	Yes	
FirstName	Varchar (25)	No	Yes	

FIGURE 7-37

Column Characteristics
for the CH07_RQ_TABLES
Database SALE_01 Table

Column Name	Type	Key	Required	Remarks
SaleID	Integer	Primary Key	Yes	Surrogate Key: Initial value=1 Increment=1
DateOfSale	Date	No	Yes	
EmailAddress	Varchar (100)	Foreign Key	Yes	REF: CUSTOMER_01
SaleAmount	Numeric (7,2)	No	Yes	

statements that you are asked to create in the following Review Questions about the CH07_RQ_TABLES database.

- For SQL Server Management Studio, create a folder named *CH07-RQ-TABLES-Database* in the *Projects* folder in your *SQL Server Management Studio* folder.
- For Oracle SQL Developer, create a folder named *CH07-RQ-TABLES-Database* in your *SQL Developer* folder.
- For SQL Workbench, create a folder named *CH07-RQ-TABLES-Database* in the *Schemas* folder in your *MySQL Workbench* folder.

If you are using Microsoft Access 2013, create a folder named *CH07-Databases* in your *DBP-e14-Access-2013-Databases* folder.

7.5 Create a database named CH07_RQ_TABLES.

FIGURE 7-38

Column Characteristics
for the CH07_RQ_TABLES
Database SALE_02 Table

Column Name	Type	Key	Required	Remarks
SaleID	Integer	Primary Key	Yes	Surrogate Key: Initial value=1 Increment=1
DateOfSale	Date	No	Yes	
CustomerID	Integer	Foreign Key	Yes	REF: CUSTOMER_04
SaleAmount	Numeric (7,2)	No	Yes	

FIGURE 7-39

Data for the CH07_RQ_
TABLES Database
CUSTOMER_01 Table

EmailAddress	LastName	FirstName
Robert.Shire@somewhere.com	Shire	Robert
Katherine.Goodyear@somewhere.com	Goodyear	Katherine
Chris.Bancroft@somewhere.com	Bancroft	Chris

FIGURE 7-40

Data for the CH07_RQ_ TABLES Database CUSTOMER_02 Table

CustomerID	EmailAddress	LastName	FirstName
1	Robert.Shire@somewhere.com	Shire	Robert
2	Katherine.Goodyear@somewhere.com	Goodyear	Katherine
3	Chris.Bancroft@somewhere.com	Bancroft	Chris

FIGURE 7-41

Data for the CH07_RQ_ TABLES Database CUSTOMER_04 Table

CustomerID	EmailAddress	LastName	FirstName
17	Robert.Shire@somewhere.com	Shire	Robert
23	Katherine.Goodyear@somewhere.com	Goodyear	Katherine
46	Chris.Bancroft@somewhere.com	Bancroft	Chris
47	John.Griffith@somewhere.com	Griffith	John
48	Doris.Tiemey@somewhere.com	Tiemey	Doris
49	Donna.Anderson@elsewhere.com	Anderson	Donna

7.6 If you are using Microsoft SQL Server, Oracle Database, or MySQL, create and save an SQL script named *CH07-RQ-TABLES-Tables-Data-and-Views.sql* to hold the answers to Review Questions 7.7–7.40. Use *SQL script commenting* (/* and */ symbols) to write your answers to Review Questions that require written answers as comments.

If you are running Microsoft Access 2013, create and save a Microsoft Notepad text file named *CH07-RQ-TABLES-Tables-Data-and-Views.txt* to hold the answers to Review Questions 7.7–7.40. After you run each SQL statement in Microsoft Access 2013, copy your SQL statement to this file.

7.7 Write and run an SQL CREATE TABLE statement to create the CUSTOMER_01 table.

FIGURE 7-42

Data for the CH07_RQ_ TABLES Database SALE_01 Table

SaleID	DateOfSale	EmailAddress	SaleAmount
20150001	2015-01-14	Robert.Shire@somewhere.com	234.00
20150002	2015-01-14	Chris.Bancroft@somewhere.com	56.50
20150003	2015-01-16	Robert.Shire@somewhere.com	123.00
20150004	2015-01-17	Katherine.Goodyear@somewhere.com	34.25

FIGURE 7-43

Data for the CH07_RQ_ TABLES Database SALE_02 Table

SaleID	DateOfSale	CustomerID	SaleAmount
20150001	2015-01-14	17	234.00
20150002	2015-01-14	46	56.50
20150003	2015-01-16	17	123.00
20150004	2015-01-17	23	34.25
20150005	2015-01-18	49	345.00
20150006	2015-01-21	46	567.35
20150007	2015-01-23	47	78.50

7.8 Write and run an SQL CREATE TABLE statement to create the CUSTOMER_02 table.

7.9 Are there any significant differences between the CUSTOMER_01 and CUSTOMER_02 tables? If so, what are they?

7.10 Write and run an SQL CREATE TABLE statement to create the CUSTOMER_03 table.

7.11 Are there any significant differences between the CUSTOMER_02 and CUSTOMER_03 tables? If so, what are they?

7.12 Write and run an SQL CREATE TABLE statement to create the CUSTOMER_04 table.

7.13 Are there any significant differences between the CUSTOMER_03 and CUSTOMER_04 tables? If so, what are they?

7.14 Write and run an SQL CREATE TABLE statement to create the SALE_01 table. Note that the foreign key is EmailAddress, which references CUSTOMER_01. EmailAddress. In this database, CUSTOMER_01 and SALE_01 records are never deleted, so that there will be no ON DELETE referential integrity action. However, you will need to decide how to implement the ON UPDATE referential integrity action.

7.15 In Review Question 7.14, how did you implement the ON UPDATE referential integrity action? Why?

7.16 Are there any significant differences between the CUSTOMER_01 and SALE_01 tables? If so, what are they?

7.17 Could we have created the SALE_01 table before creating the CUSTOMER_01 table? If not, why not?

7.18 Write and run an SQL CREATE TABLE statement to create the SALE_02 table. Note that the foreign key is CustomerID, which references CUSTOMER_04.CustomerID. In this database, CUSTOMER_04 and SALE_02 records are never deleted, so that there will be no ON DELETE referential integrity action. However, you will need to decide how to implement the ON UPDATE referential integrity action.

7.19 In Review Question 7.18, how did you implement the ON UPDATE referential integrity action? Why?

7.20 Are there any significant differences between the SALE_01 and SALE_02 tables? If so, what are they?

7.21 Could we have created the SALE_02 table before creating the CUSTOMER_04 table? If not, why not?

7.22 Write and run a set of SQL INSERT statements to populate the CUSTOMER_01 table.

7.23 Write and run a set of SQL INSERT statements to populate the CUSTOMER_02 table. Do *not* use a bulk INSERT command.

7.24 Are there any significant differences between the sets of SQL INSERT statements used to populate the CUSTOMER_01 and CUSTOMER_02 tables? If so, what are they?

7.25 Write and run an SQL INSERT statement to populate the CUSTOMER_03 table. Use a bulk INSERT command and the data in the CUSTOMER_01 table.

7.26 Are there any significant differences between the sets of SQL INSERT statements used to populate the CUSTOMER_02 and CUSTOMER_03 tables? If so, what are they?

7.27 Write and run a set of SQL INSERT statements to populate rows 1 thorugh 3 in the CUSTOMER_04 table. Note that this question involves non-sequential surrogate key values and is based on techniques for Microsoft SQL Server 2014 in Chapter 10A, for Oracle Database in Chapter 10B, or for MySQL 5.6 in Chapter 10C, depending upon which DBMS product you are using.

7.28 Are there any significant differences between the sets of SQL INSERT statements used to populate the CUSTOMER_02 table and rows 1-3 of the CUSTOMER_04 table? If so, what are they?

7.29 Write and run a set of SQL INSERT statements to populate rows 4 through 6 in the CUSTOMER_04 table. Note that this question involves sequential surrogate key values and is based on techniques for Microsoft SQL Server 2014 in Chapter 10A, for Oracle Database in Chapter 10B, or for MySQL 5.6 in Chapter 10C, depending upon which DBMS product you are using.

7.30 Are there any significant differences between the sets of SQL INSERT statements used to populate the CUSTOMER_02 table and rows 4-6 of the CUSTOMER_04 table? If so, what are they?

7.31 Write and run a set of SQL INSERT statements to populate the SALE_01 table.

7.32 Are there any significant differences between the sets of SQL INSERT statements used to populate the CUSTOMER_01 table and the SALE_01 table? If so, what are they?

7.33 Could we have populated the SALE_01 table before populating the CUSTOMER_01 table? If not, why not?

7.34 Write and run a set of SQL INSERT statements to populate the SALE_02 table.

7.35 Are there any significant differences between the sets of SQL INSERT statements used to populate the SALE_01 table and the SALE_02 table? If so, what are they?

7.36 Could we have populated the SALE_02 table before populating the CUSTOMER_04 table? If not, why not?

7.37 Write and run an SQL INSERT statement to insert the following record into the SALE_02 table:

SaleID	DateOfSale	CustomerID	SaleAmount
20150008	2015-01-25	50	890.15

What was the result of running this statement? Why did this result occur?

7.38 Write an SQL statement to create a view named Customer01DataView based on the CUSTOMER_01 table. In the view, include the values of EmailAddress, LastName as CustomerLastName, and FirstName as CustomerFirstName. Run this statement to create the view, and then test the view by writing and running an appropriate SQL SELECT statement.

7.39 Write an SQL statement to create a view named Customer04DataView based on the CUSTOMER_04 table. In the view, include the values of Customer ID, LastName as CustomerLastName, FirstName as CustomerFirstName, and EmailAddress in that order. Run this statement to create the view, and then test the view by writing and running an appropriate SQL SELECT statement.

7.40 Write an SQL statement to create a view named CustomerSalesView based on the the CUSTOMER_04 and SALE_02 tables. In this view, include the values of Customer ID, LastName as CustomerLastName, FirstName as CustomerFirstName, EmailAddress, SaleID, DateOfSale, and SaleAmount in that order. Run this statement to create the view, and then test the view by writing and running an appropriate SQL SELECT statement.

For this set of Review Questions, we will create and use a database for the Wedgewood Pacific Corporation (WPC) that is similar to the Microsoft Access database we created and used in Chapters 1 and 2. Founded in 1957 in Seattle, Washington, WPC has grown into an internationally recognized organization. The company is located in two buildings. One building houses the Administration, Accounting, Finance, and Human Resources departments, and the second houses the Production, Marketing, and Information Systems departments. The company database contains data about employees; departments; projects; assets, such as computer equipment; and other aspects of company operations.

The database will be named WPC and will contain the following four tables:

DEPARTMENT (<u>DepartmentName</u>, BudgetCode, OfficeNumber, Phone)

EMPLOYEE (<u>EmployeeNumber</u>, FirstName, LastName, *Department*, Phone, Email)

PROJECT (<u>ProjectID</u>, Name, *Department*, MaxHours, StartDate, EndDate)

ASSIGNMENT (<u>*ProjectID*</u>, <u>*EmployeeNumber*</u>, HoursWorked)

EmployeeNumber is a surrogate key that starts at 1 and increments by 1. ProjectID is a surrogate key that starts at 1000 and increases by 100. DepartmentName is the text name of the department and is therefore not a surrogate key.

The WPC database has the following referential integrity constraints:

Department in EMPLOYEE must exist in DepartmentName in DEPARTMENT

Department in PROJECT must exist in DepartmentName in DEPARTMENT

ProjectID in ASSIGNMENT must exist in ProjectID in PROJECT

EmployeeNumber in ASSIGNMENT must exist in EmployeeNumber in EMPLOYEE

The relationship from EMPLOYEE to ASSIGNMENT is 1:N, M-O and the relationship from PROJECT to ASSIGNMENT is 1:N, M-O.

The database also has the following business rules:

- If an EMPLOYEE row is to be deleted and that row is connected to any ASSIGNMENT, the EMPLOYEE row deletion will be disallowed.
- If a PROJECT row is deleted, then all the ASSIGNMENT rows that are connected to the deleted PROJECT row will also be deleted.

The business sense of these rules is as follows:

- If an EMPLOYEE row is deleted (e.g., if the employee is transferred), then someone must take over that employee's assignments. Thus, the application needs someone to reassign assignments before deleting the employee row.
- If a PROJECT row is deleted, then the project has been canceled, and it is unnecessary to maintain records of assignments to that project.

The column characteristics for these tables are shown in Figures 1-28 (DEPARTMENT), 1-30 (EMPLOYEE), 2-42 (PROJECT), and 2-44 (ASSIGNMENT). The data for these tables are shown in Figures 1-29 (DEPARTMENT), 1-31 (EMPLOYEE), 2-43 (PROJECT), and 2-45 (ASSIGNMENT).

If at all possible, you should run your SQL solutions to the following questions against an actual database. Because we have already created this database in Microsoft Access, you should use an SQL-oriented DBMS such as Microsoft SQL Server 2014, Oracle Database, or MySQL 5.6 in these exercises. Create a database named *WPC*, and create a folder in your *My Documents* folder to save and store the *.sql scripts containing the SQL statements that you are asked to create in the remaining questions pertaining to the WPC database in this section and the following Project Questions section.

- For the SQL Server Management Studio, create a folder named *WPC-Database* in the *Projects* folder structure in your *SQL Server Management Studio* folder.
- In the Oracle SQL Developer folder structure in your *SQL Developer* folder, create a folder named *WPC-Database*.
- For the MySQL Workbench, create a folder named *WPC-Database* in the *Schemas* folder in your *MySQL Workbench* folder.

If that is not possible, create a new Microsoft Access database named *WPC-CH07.accdb*, and use the SQL capabilities in these exercises. In all the exercises, use the data types appropriate for the DBMS you are using.

Write and save an SQL script named *WPC-Create-Tables.sql* that includes the answers to Review Questions 7.41–7.50. Use *SQL script commenting* (/* and */ symbols) to write your answers to Review Questions 7.45 and 7.46 as comments so that they cannot be run! Test and run your SQL statements for Review Questions 7.41, 7.42, 7.43, and 7.44 only. After the tables are created, run your answers to Review Questions 7.47–7.50. Note that after these four statements have been run the table structure is exactly the same as it was before you ran them.

7.41 Write a CREATE TABLE statement for the DEPARTMENT table.

7.42 Write a CREATE TABLE statement for the EMPLOYEE table. Email is required and is an alternate key, and the default value of Department is Human Resources. Cascade updates but not deletions from DEPARTMENT to EMPLOYEE.

7.43 Write a CREATE TABLE statement for PROJECT table. The default value for MaxHours is 100. Cascade updates but not deletions from DEPARTMENT to EMPLOYEE.

7.44 Write a CREATE TABLE statement for the ASSIGNMENT table. Cascade only deletions from PROJECT to ASSIGNMENT; do not cascade either deletions or updates from EMPLOYEE to ASSIGNMENT.

7.45 Modify your answer to Review Question 7.43 to include the constraint that StartDate be prior to EndDate.

7.46 Write an alternate SQL statement that modifies your answer to Review Question 7.44 to make the relationship between EMPLOYEE and ASSIGNMENT a 1:1 relationship.

7.47 Write an ALTER statement to add the column AreaCode to EMPLOYEE. Assume that AreaCode is not required.

7.48 Write an ALTER statement to remove the column AreaCode from EMPLOYEE.

7.49 Write an ALTER statement to make Phone an alternate key in EMPLOYEE.

7.50 Write an ALTER statement to drop the constraint that Phone is an alternate key in EMPLOYEE.

Create SQL scripts to answer Review Questions 7.51–7.56. Write the answer to Review Question 7.55 as an SQL text comment, but include it in your script. Write the answer to Review Question 7.56 as an SQL comment so that it *cannot* be run.

7.51 Write INSERT statements to add the data shown in Figure 1-29 to the DEPARTMENT table. Run these statements to populate the DEPARTMENT table. (Hint: Write and test an SQL script, and then run the script. Save the script as *WPC-Insert-DEPARTMENT-Data.sql* for future use.)

7.52 Write INSERT statements to add the data shown in Figure 1-31 to the EMPLOYEE table. Run these statements to populate the EMPLOYEE table. (Hint: Write and test an SQL script, and then run the script. Save the script as *WPC-Insert-EMPLOYEE-Data.sql* for future use.)

7.53 Write INSERT statements to add the data shown in Figure 2-43 to the PROJECT table. Run these statements to populate the PROJECT table. (Hint: Write and test an SQL script, and then run the script. Save the script as *WPC-Insert-PROJECT-Data.sql* for future use.)

7.54 Write INSERT statements to add the data shown in Figure 2-45 to the ASSIGNMENT table. Run these statements to populate the ASSIGNMENT table. (Hint: Write and test an SQL script, and then run the script. Save the script as *WPC-Insert-ASSIGNMENT-Data.sql* for future use.)

7.55 Why were the tables populated in the order shown in Review Questions 7.51–7.54?

7.56 Assume that you have a table named NEW_EMPLOYEE that has the columns Department, Email, FirstName, and LastName, in that order. Write an INSERT statement to add all of the rows from the table NEW_EMPLOYEE to EMPLOYEE. Do not attempt to run this statement!

Create and run an SQL script named *WPC-Update-Data.sql* to answer Review Questions 7.57–7.62. Write the answer to Review Question 7.62 as an SQL comment so that it *cannot* be run.

7.57 Write an UPDATE statement to change the phone number of the employee with EmployeeNumber 11 to 360-287-8810. Run this SQL statement.

7.58 Write an UPDATE statement to change the department of the employee with EmployeeNumber 5 to Finance. Run this SQL statement.

7.59 Write an UPDATE statement to change the phone number of the employee with EmployeeNumber 5 to 360-287-8420. Run this SQL statement.

7.60 Combine your answers to Review Questions 7.58 and 7.59 into one SQL statement. Run this statement.

7.61 Write an UPDATE statement to set the HoursWorked to 60 for every row in ASSIGNMENT having the value 10 for EmployeeNumber. Run this statement.

7.62 Assume that you have a table named NEW_EMAIL, which has new values of Email for some employees. NEW_EMAIL has two columns: EmployeeNumber and NewEmail. Write an UPDATE statement to change the values of Email in EMPLOYEE to those in the NEW_EMAIL table. Do *not* run this statement.

Create and run an SQL script named *WPC-Delete-Data.sql* to answer Review Questions 7.63 and 7.64. Write the answers to Review Questions 7.63 and 7.64 as SQL comments so that they *cannot* be run.

7.63 Write one DELETE statement that will delete all data for project '2015 Q3 Product Plan' and all of its rows in ASSIGNMENT. Do *not* run this statement.

7.64 Write a DELETE statement that will delete the rows for employees with last name 'Smith'. Do *not* run this statement. What happens if one of these employees has rows in ASSIGNMENT?

7.65 What is an SQL view? What purposes do views serve?

7.66 What is the limitation on SELECT statements used in SQL views?

Create and run an SQL script named *WPC-Create-Views.sql* to answer Review Questions 7.67–7.72.

7.67 Write an SQL statement to create a view named EmployeePhoneView that shows the values of EMPLOYEE.LastName as EmployeeLastName, EMPLOYEE.FirstName as EmployeeFirstName, and EMPLOYEE.Phone as EmployeePhone. Run this statement to create the view, and then test the view by writing and running an appropriate SQL SELECT statement.

7.68 Write an SQL statement to create a view named FinanceEmployeePhoneView that shows the values of EMPLOYEE.LastName as EmployeeLastName, EMPLOYEE.FirstName as EmployeeFirstName, and EMPLOYEE.Phone as EmployeePhone for employees who work in the Finance department. Run this statement to create the view, and then test the view by writing and running an appropriate SQL SELECT statement.

7.69 Write an SQL statement to create a view named CombinedNameEmployeePhoneView that shows the values of EMPLOYEE.LastName, EMPLOYEE.FirstName, and EMPLOYEE.Phone as EmployeePhone but that combines EMPLOYEE.LastName and EMPLOYEE.FirstName into one column named EmployeeName that displays the employee name first name first. Run this statement to create the view, and then test the view by writing and running an appropriate SQL SELECT statement.

7.70 Write an SQL statement to create a view named EmployeeProjectAssignmentView that shows the values of EMPLOYEE.LastName as EmployeeLastName, EMPLOYEE.FirstName as EmployeeFirstName, EMPLOYEE.Phone as EmployeePhone, and PROJECT.Name as ProjectName. Run this statement to create the view, and then test the view by writing and running an appropriate SQL SELECT statement.

7.71 Write an SQL statement to create a view named DepartmentEmployee-ProjectAssignmentView that shows the values of EMPLOYEE.LastName as EmployeeLastName, EMPLOYEE.FirstName as EmployeeFirstName, EMPLOYEE.Phone as EmployeePhone, DEPARTMENT.DepartmentName, Department.PHONE as DepartmentPhone, and PROJECT.Name as ProjectName. Run this statement to create the view, and then test the view by writing and running an appropriate SQL SELECT statement.

7.72   Write an SQL statement to create a view named ProjectHoursToDateView that shows the values of PROJECT.ProjectID, PROJECT.Name as ProjectName, PROJECT .MaxHours as ProjectMaxHours and the sum of ASSIGNMENT.HoursWorked as ProjectHoursWorkedToDate. Run this statement to create the view, and then test the view by writing and running an appropriate SQL SELECT statement.

7.73   Describe how views are used to provide aliases for tables. Why is this useful?

7.74   Explain how views can be used to improve data security.

7.75   Explain how views can be used to provide additional trigger functionality.

7.76   Give an example of a view that is clearly updatable.

7.77   Give an example of a view that is clearly not updatable.

7.78   Summarize the general idea for determining whether a view is updatable.

7.79   If a view is missing required items, what action on the view is definitely not allowed?

7.80   Explain the paradigm mismatch between SQL and programming languages.

7.81   How is the mismatch in your answer to Review Question 7.80 corrected?

7.82   Describe the SQL/PSM component of the SQL standard. What are PL/SQL and T-SQL? What is the MySQL equivalent?

7.83   What is a user-defined function?

Using the WPC database, create an SQL script named _WPC-Create-Function-and-View.sql_ to answer Review Questions 7.84 and 7.85.

7.84   Create and test a user-defined function named LastNameFirst that combines two parameters named FirstName and LastName into a concatenated name field formatted LastName, FirstName (including the comma and space).

7.85   Create and test a view called EmployeeDepartmentDataView that contains the employee name concatenated and formatted as LastName, FirstName in a field named _EmployeeName_, EMPLOYEE.Department, DEPARTMENT.OfficeNumber, DEPARTMENT.Phone as _DepartmentPhone_, and EMPLOYEE.Phone as _EmployeePhone_. Run this statement to create the view, and then test the view by writing and running an appropriate SQL SELECT statement.

7.86   What is a trigger?

7.87   What is the relationship between a trigger and a table or view?

7.88   Name nine possible trigger types.

7.89   Explain, in general terms, how new and old values are made available to a trigger.

7.90   Describe four uses for triggers.

7.91   Assume that the View Ridge Gallery will allow a row to be deleted from WORK if the work has never been sold. Explain, in general terms, how to use a trigger to accomplish such a deletion. (Hint: Check transactions.)

7.92   Assume that the Wedgewood Pacific Corporation will allow a row to be deleted from EMPLOYEE if the employee has no project assignments. Explain, in general terms, how to use a trigger to accomplish such a deletion. (Hint: Check assignments.)

7.93   What are stored procedures? How do they differ from triggers?

7.94   Summarize how to invoke a stored procedure.

7.95   Summarize the key advantages of stored procedures.

Project Questions

These Project Questions extend the Wedgewood Pacific Corporation database you created and used in the Review Questions with two new tables named COMPUTER and COMPUTER_ASSIGNMENT.

The data model for these modifications is shown in Figure 7-44. The column characteristics for the COMPUTER table are shown in Figure 7-45, and those for the COMPUTER_ASSIGNMENT table are shown in Figure 7-46. Data for the COMPUTER table are shown in Figure 7-47, and data for the COMPUTER_ASSIGNMENT table are shown in Figure 7-48.

7.96 Describe the relationships in terms of type (identifying or nonidentifying) and maximum and minimum cardinality.

7.97 Explain the need for each of the foreign keys.

7.98 Define referential integrity actions (such as ON UPDATE CASCADE) for the COMPUTER-to-COMPUTER_ASSIGNMENT relationship only. Explain the need for these actions.

FIGURE 7-44

WPC Database Design Extension

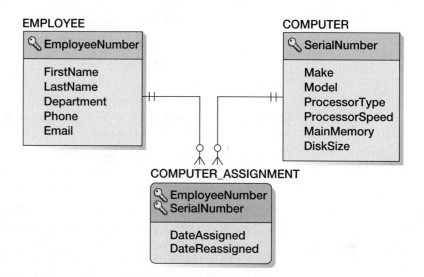

FIGURE 7-45

Column Characteristics for the WPC Database COMPUTER Table

COMPUTER

ColumnName	Type	Key	Required	Remarks
SerialNumber	Integer	Primary Key	Yes	
Make	Char (12)	No	Yes	Must be "Dell" or "HP" or "Other"
Model	Char (24)	No	Yes	
ProcessorType	Char (24)	No	No	
ProcessorSpeed	Numeric (3,2)	No	Yes	Between 2.0 and 5.0
MainMemory	Char (15)	No	Yes	
DiskSize	Char (15)	No	Yes	

FIGURE 7-46

Column Characteristics
for the WPC Database
COMPUTER_ASSIGNMENT
Table

COMPUTER_ASSIGNMENT

ColumnName	Type	Key	Required	Remarks
SerialNumber	Integer	Primary Key, Foreign Key	Yes	REF: COMPUTER
EmployeeNumber	Integer	Primary Key, Foreign Key	Yes	REF: EMPLOYEE
DateAssigned	Date	No	Yes	
DateReassigned	Date	No	No	

7.99 Assume that COMPUTER_ASSIGNMENT in the EMPLOYEE-to-COMPUTER_ ASSIGNMENT relationship is now mandatory (i.e., every employee must have at least one computer). Use Figure 6-29(b) as a boilerplate to define triggers for enforcing the required child between EMPLOYEE and COMPUTER_ASSIGNMENT. Define the purpose of any necessary triggers.

7.100 Explain the interaction between the trigger in your answer to Project Question 7.99 and the COMPUTER-to-COMPUTER_ASSIGNMENT relationship. What, if any, cascading behavior do you want to occur? Explain how you can test to find out if it works the way that you want it to.

Using the WPC database, create an SQL script named *WPC-Create-New-Tables.sql* to answer Project Question 7.101.

7.101 Write CREATE TABLE statements for the COMPUTER and COMPUTER_ ASSIGNMENT tables in Figure 7-44 using the column characteristics shown in Figures 7-45 and 7-46. Write CHECK constraints to ensure that Make is Dell, HP, or Other. Also, write constraints to ensure that ProcessorSpeed is between 2.0 and 5.0 (these are units of Gigahertz). Run these statements on your WPC database to extend the database structure.

FIGURE 7-47

WPC Database
COMPUTER Table Data

SerialNumber	Make	Model	ProcessorType	ProcessorSpeed	MainMemory	DiskSize
9871234	HP	Pavilion 500qe	Intel i5-4590	3.30	8.0 Gbytes	1.0 Tbytes
9871245	HP	Pavilion 500qe	Intel i5-4590	3.30	8.0 Gbytes	1.0 Tbytes
9871256	HP	Pavilion 500qe	Intel i5-4590	3.30	8.0 Gbytes	1.0 Tbytes
9871267	HP	Pavilion 500qe	Intel i5-4590	3.30	8.0 Gbytes	1.0 Tbytes
9871278	HP	Pavilion 500qe	Intel i5-4590	3.30	8.0 Gbytes	1.0 Tbytes
9871289	HP	Pavilion 500qe	Intel i5-4590	3.30	8.0 Gbytes	1.0 Tbytes
6541001	Dell	OptiPlex 9020	Intel i7-4790	3.60	8.0 Gbytes	1.0 Tbytes
6541002	Dell	OptiPlex 9020	Intel i7-4790	3.60	8.0 Gbytes	1.0 Tbytes
6541003	Dell	OptiPlex 9020	Intel i7-4790	3.60	8.0 Gbytes	1.0 Tbytes
6541004	Dell	OptiPlex 9020	Intel i7-4790	3.60	8.0 Gbytes	1.0 Tbytes
6541005	Dell	OptiPlex 9020	Intel i7-4790	3.60	8.0 Gbytes	1.0 Tbytes
6541006	Dell	OptiPlex 9020	Intel i7-4790	3.60	8.0 Gbytes	1.0 Tbytes

FIGURE 7-48

WPC Database
COMPUTER_ASSIGNMENT
Table Data

SerialNumber	EmployeeNumber	DateAssigned	DateReassigned
9871234	11	15-Sep-15	21-Oct-15
9871245	12	15-Sep-15	21-Oct-15
9871256	4	15-Sep-15	NULL
9871267	5	15-Sep-15	NULL
9871278	8	15-Sep-15	NULL
9871289	9	15-Sep-15	NULL
6541001	11	21-Oct-15	NULL
6541002	12	21-Oct-15	NULL
6541003	1	21-Oct-15	NULL
6541004	2	21-Oct-15	NULL
6541005	3	21-Oct-15	NULL
6541006	6	21-Oct-15	NULL
9871234	7	21-Oct-15	NULL
9871245	10	21-Oct-15	NULL

Using the WPC database, create an SQL script named *WPC-Insert-New-Data.sql* to answer Project Question 7.102.

7.102 Using the sample data for the COMPUTER table shown in Figure 7-47 and the COMPUTER_ASSIGNMENT table shown in Figure 7-48, write INSERT statements to add this data to these tables in the WPC database. Run these INSERT statements to populate the tables.

Using the WPC database, create an SQL script named *WPC-Create-New-Views-And-Functions.sql* to answer Project Questions 7.103–7.108.

7.103 Create a view of COMPUTER named ComputerView that displays SerialNumber and then Make and Model combined as one attribute named ComputerType. Place a colon and a space between Make and Model in the format: *Dell: OptiPlex 9020*. Do *not* create a user-defined function to perform this task. Run the statement to create the view, and then test the view with an appropriate SQL SELECT statement.

7.104 Create a view called ComputerMakeView that shows the Make and average Processor Speed for all computers. Run the statement to create the view, and then test the view with an appropriate SQL SELECT statement.

7.105 Create a view called ComputerUserView that has all of the data of COMPUTER and ASSIGNMENT. Run the statement to create the view, and then test the view with an appropriate SQL SELECT statement.

7.106 Create an SQL SELECT statement to use the view you created called ComputerView to show the computer SerialNumber, ComputerType, and Employee name. Run this statement.

7.107 Create and test a user-defined function named *ComputerMakeAndModel* to concatenate Make and Model to form the *{Make}: {Model}* character string as you did without a function in Project Question 7.103.

7.108 Create a view of COMPUTER named ComputerMakeAndModelView that displays SerialNumber and then uses the ComputerMakeAndModel function you created in

Project Question 7.107 to display an attribute named ComputerType. Test the view with an appropriate SQL SELECT statement.

7.109 Suppose you want to use a trigger to automatically place a DateReassigned value in an old row of the COMPUTER_ASSIGNMENT table whenever a new row is inserted into COMPUTER_ASSIGNMENT to record a new computer assignment of an existing computer. Describe, in general terms, the trigger logic.

7.110 Suppose you want to use a stored procedure to store a new row in COMPUTER. List the minimum list of parameters that need to be in the procedure. Describe, in general terms, the logic of the stored procedure.

Case Questions

Heather Sweeney Designs Case Questions

Heather Sweeney is an interior designer who specializes in home kitchen design. Her company is named Heather Sweeney Designs. Heather offers a variety of seminars at home shows, kitchen and appliance stores, and other public locations. The seminars are free; she offers them as a way of building her customer base. She earns revenue by selling books and videos that instruct people on kitchen design. She also offers custom-design consulting services.

After someone attends a seminar, Heather wants to leave no stone unturned in attempting to sell that person one of her products or services. She would therefore like to develop a database to keep track of customers, the seminars they have attended, the contacts she has made with them, and the purchases they have made. She wants to use this database to continue to contact her customers and offer them products and services.

The database will be named HSD. For reference, the SQL statements shown here are built from the HSD database design in Figure 7-49, the column characteristics specifications shown in Figure 7-50, and the referential integrity constraint specifications detailed in Figure 7-51.

FIGURE 7-49

Database Design for the HSD Database

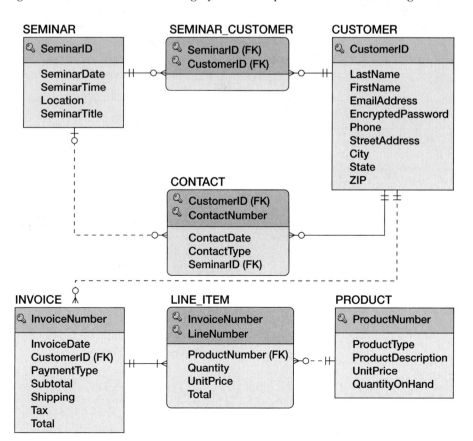

Column Name	Data Type (Length)	Key	Required	Default Value	Remarks
SeminarID	Integer	Primary Key	Yes	DBMS supplied	Surrogate Key: Initial Value=1 Increment=1
SeminarDate	Date	No	Yes	None	Format: yyyy-mm-dd
SeminarTime	Time	No	Yes	None	Format: 00:00:00.00
Location	Varchar (100)	No	Yes	None	
SeminarTitle	Varchar (100)	No	Yes	None	

(a) SEMINAR

Column Name	Data Type (Length)	Key	Required	Default Value	Remarks
CustomerID	Integer	Primary Key	Yes		DBMS Supplied Surrogate Key: Initial Value=1 Increment=1
LastName	Char (25)	No	Yes	None	
FirstName	Char (25)	No	Yes	None	
EmailAddress	Varchar (100)	Alternate Key	Yes	None	AK1.1
EncryptedPassword	Varchar (50)	No	No	None	
StreetAddress	Char(35)	No	No	None	
Phone	Char (12)	No	Yes	None	Format: ###-###-####
City	Char (35)	No	No	Dallas	
State	Char (2)	No	No	TX	Format: AA
ZIP	Char (10)	No	No	75201	Format: #####-####

(b) CUSTOMER

Column Name	Data Type (Length)	Key	Required	Default Value	Remarks
SeminarID	Integer	Primary Key, Foreign Key	Yes	None	REF: SEMINAR
CustomerID	Integer	Primary Key, Foreign Key	Yes	None	REF: CUSTOMER

(c) SEMINAR_CUSTOMER

FIGURE 7-50

Database Column Specifications for the HSD Database

Column Name	Data Type (Length)	Key	Required	Default Value	Remarks
CustomerID	Integer	Primary Key, Foreign Key	Yes	None	REF: CUSTOMER
ContactNumber	Integer	Primary Key	Yes	None	This is not quite a Surrogate Key—for *each* ContactNumber: Start=1 Increment=1 Application logic will be needed to supply the correct value
ContactDate	Date	No	Yes	None	Format: yyyy-mm-dd
ContactType	Char (30)	No	Yes	None	
SeminarID	Integer	Foreign Key	No	None	REF: SEMINAR

(d) CONTACT

Column Name	Data Type (Length)	Key	Required	Default Value	Remarks
InvoiceNumber	Integer	Primary Key	Yes	DBMS supplied	Surrogate Key: Initial Value=35000 Increment=1
InvoiceDate	Date	No	Yes	None	Format: yyyy-mm-dd
CustomerID	Integer	Foreign Key	Yes	None	REF: CUSTOMER
PaymentType	Char (25)	No	Yes	Cash	
Subtotal	Numeric (9,2)	No	No	None	
Shipping	Numeric (9,2)	No	No	None	
Tax	Numeric (9,2)	No	No	None	
Total	Numeric (9,2)	No	No	None	

(e) INVOICE

FIGURE 7-50
Continued

(continued)

Column Name	Data Type (Length)	Key	Required	Default Value	Remarks
InvoiceNumber	Integer	Primary Key, Foreign Key	Yes	None	REF: INVOICE
LineNumber	Integer	Primary Key	Yes	None	This is not quite a Surrogate Key—for *each* InvoiceNumber: Start=1 Increment=1 Application logic will be needed to supply the correct value
ProductNumber	Char (35)	Foreign Key	Yes	None	REF: PRODUCT
Quantity	Integer	No	No	None	
UnitPrice	Numeric (9,2)	No	No	None	
Total	Numeric (9,2)	No	No	None	

(f) LINE_ITEM

Column Name	Data Type (Length)	Key	Required	Default Value	Remarks
ProductNumber	Char (35)	Primary Key	Yes	None	
ProductType	Char (24)	No	Yes	None	
ProductDescription	Varchar (100)	No	Yes	None	
UnitPrice	Numeric (9,2)	No	Yes	None	
QuantityOnHand	Integer	No	Yes	None	

(g) PRODUCT

FIGURE 7-50

Continued

The SQL statements to create the HSD database for Heather Sweeney Designs are shown in Figure 7-52 in Microsoft SQL Server syntax. The SQL statements to populate the HSD database are shown in Figure 7-53, again in Microsoft SQL Server syntax.

Write SQL statements and answer questions for this database as follows:

A. Create a database named HSD in your DBMS.

B. Create a folder in your *My Documents* folder to save and store *.sql scripts containing the SQL statements that you are asked to create in the remaining questions in this section.

- For the SQL Server Management Studio, create a folder named *HSD-Database* in the *Projects* folder structure in your *SQL Server Management Studio* folder.
- In the Oracle SQL Developer folder structure in your *SQL Developer* folder, create a folder named *HSD-Database*.

Relationship		Referential Integrity Constraint	Cascading Behavior	
Parent	Child		On Update	On Delete
SEMINAR	SEMINAR_CUSTOMER	SeminarID in SEMINAR_ CUSTOMER must exist in SeminarID in SEMINAR	No	No
CUSTOMER	SEMINAR_CUSTOMER	CustomerID in SEMINAR_ CUSTOMER must exist in CustomerID in CUSTOMER	No	No
SEMINAR	CONTACT	SeminarID in CONTACT must exist in SeminarID in SEMINAR	No	No
CUSTOMER	CONTACT	CustomerID in CONTACT must exist in CustomerID in CUSTOMER	No	Yes
CUSTOMER	INVOICE	CustomerID in INVOICE must exist in CustomerID in CUSTOMER	No	No
INVOICE	LINE_ITEM	InvoiceNumber in LINE_ITEM must exist in InvoiceNumber in INVOICE	No	Yes
PRODUCT	LINE_ITEM	ProductNumber in LINE_ITEM must exist in ProductNumber in PRODUCT	Yes	No

FIGURE 7-51

Referential Integrity
Constraint Enforcement
for the HSD Database

    ▧ For the SQL Workbench, create a folder named *HSD-Database* in the *Schemas* folder in your *MySQL Workbench* folder.

C. Write an SQL script named *HSD-Create-Tables.sql* based on Figure 7-52 to create the tables and relationships for the HSD database. Save this script, and then execute the script to create the HSD tables.

D. Write an SQL script named *HSD-Insert-Data.sql* based on Figure 7-53 to insert the data for the HSD database. Save this script, and then execute the script to populate the HSD tables.

Using the HSD database, create an SQL script named *HSD-CQ-CH07.sql* to answer questions E–Q. Include your answer to part Q, but be sure to put it in comment marks so that it is interpreted as a comment by the DBMS and cannot actually be run!

E. Write SQL statements to list all columns for all tables.

F. Write an SQL statement to list LastName, FirstName, and Phone for all customers who live in Dallas.

G. Write an SQL statement to list LastName, FirstName, and Phone for all customers who live in Dallas and have a LastName that begins with the letter T.

```
CREATE  TABLE SEMINAR(
        SeminarID              Int                    NOT NULL IDENTITY (1, 1),
        SeminarDate            Date                   NOT NULL,
        SeminarTime            Time                   NOT NULL,
        Location               Varchar(100)           NOT NULL,
        SeminarTitle           Varchar(100)           NOT NULL,
        CONSTRAINT             SEMINAR_PK             PRIMARY KEY(SeminarID)
        );

CREATE  TABLE CUSTOMER(
        CustomerID             Int                    NOT NULL IDENTITY (1, 1),
        LastName               Char(25)               NOT NULL,
        FirstName              Char(25)               NOT NULL,
        EmailAddress           Varchar(100)           NOT NULL,
        EncryptedPassword      Varchar(50)            NULL,
        Phone                  Char(12)               NOT NULL,
        StreetAddress          Char(35)               NULL,
        City                   Char(35)               NULL DEFAULT 'Dallas',
        [State]                Char(2)                NULL DEFAULT 'TX',
        ZIP                    Char(10)               NULL DEFAULT '75201',
        CONSTRAINT             CUSTOMER_PK            PRIMARY KEY(CustomerID),
        CONSTRAINT             CUSTOMER_EMAIL         UNIQUE(EmailAddress)
        );

CREATE  TABLE SEMINAR_CUSTOMER(
        SeminarID              Int                    NOT NULL,
        CustomerID             Int                    NOT NULL,
        CONSTRAINT             S_C_PK                 PRIMARY KEY(SeminarID, CustomerID),
        CONSTRAINT             S_C_SEMINAR_FK         FOREIGN KEY(SeminarID)
                                    REFERENCES SEMINAR(SeminarID)
                                       ON UPDATE NO ACTION
                                       ON DELETE NO ACTION,
        CONSTRAINT             S_C_CUSTOMER_FK        FOREIGN KEY(CustomerID)
                                    REFERENCES CUSTOMER(CustomerID)
                                       ON UPDATE NO ACTION
                                       ON DELETE NO ACTION
        );

CREATE  TABLE CONTACT(
        CustomerID             Int                    NOT NULL,
        ContactNumber          Int                    NOT NULL,
        ContactDate            Date                   NOT NULL,
        ContactType            Varchar(30)            NOT NULL,
        SeminarID              Int                    NULL,
        CONSTRAINT             CONTACT_PK             PRIMARY KEY(CustomerID, ContactNumber),
        CONSTRAINT             CONTACT_ContactType CHECK (ContactType IN
                                    ('Seminar', 'FormLetterSeminar',
                                     'WebAccountCreation', 'WebPurchase',
                                     'EmailAccountMessage', 'EmailSeminarMessage',
                                     'EmailPurchaseMessage', 'EmailMessageExchange',
                                     'PhoneConversation')),
        CONSTRAINT             CONTACT_SEMINAR_FK  FOREIGN KEY(SeminarID)
                                    REFERENCES SEMINAR(SeminarID)
                                       ON UPDATE NO ACTION
                                       ON DELETE NO ACTION,
        CONSTRAINT             CONTACT_CUSTOMER_FK FOREIGN KEY(CustomerID)
                                    REFERENCES CUSTOMER(CustomerID)
                                       ON UPDATE NO ACTION
                                       ON DELETE CASCADE
        );
```

FIGURE 7-52

**SQL Statements to Create
the HSD Database**

```
CREATE   TABLE PRODUCT(
         ProductNumber        Char(35)              NOT NULL,
         ProductType          Char(24)              NOT NULL,
         ProductDescription   Varchar(100)          NOT NULL,
         UnitPrice            Numeric(9,2)          NOT NULL,
         QuantityOnHand       Int                   NULL,
         CONSTRAINT           PRODUCT_PK            PRIMARY KEY(ProductNumber),
         CONSTRAINT           PRODUCT_ProductType   CHECK (ProductType IN
                                   ('Video', 'Video Companion', 'Book'))
         );


CREATE   TABLE INVOICE(
         InvoiceNumber        Int                   NOT NULL IDENTITY (35000, 1),
         InvoiceDate          Date                  NOT NULL,
         CustomerID           Int                   NOT NULL,
         PaymentType          Char(25)              NOT NULL DEFAULT 'Cash',
         SubTotal             Numeric(9,2)          NULL,
         Shipping             Numeric(9,2)          NULL,
         Tax                  Numeric(9,2)          NULL,
         Total                Numeric(9,2)          NULL,
         CONSTRAINT           INVOICE_PK            PRIMARY KEY (InvoiceNumber),
         CONSTRAINT           INVOICE_PaymentType   CHECK (PaymentType IN
                                   ('VISA',  'MasterCard', 'American Express',
                                    'PayPal', 'Check', 'Cash')),
         CONSTRAINT           INVOICE_CUSTOMER_FK FOREIGN KEY(CustomerID)
                                   REFERENCES CUSTOMER(CustomerID)
                                       ON UPDATE NO ACTION
                                       ON DELETE NO ACTION
         );


CREATE   TABLE LINE_ITEM(
         InvoiceNumber        Int                   NOT NULL,
         LineNumber           Int                   NOT NULL,
         ProductNumber        Char(35)              NOT NULL,
         Quantity             Int                   NOT NULL,
         UnitPrice            Numeric(9,2)          NULL,
         Total                Numeric(9,2)          NULL,
         CONSTRAINT           LINE_ITEM_PK          PRIMARY KEY (InvoiceNumber, LineNumber),
         CONSTRAINT           L_I_INVOICE_FK        FOREIGN KEY(InvoiceNumber)
                                   REFERENCES INVOICE(InvoiceNumber)
                                       ON UPDATE NO ACTION
                                       ON DELETE CASCADE,
         CONSTRAINT           L_I_PRODUCT_FK        FOREIGN KEY(ProductNumber)
                                   REFERENCES PRODUCT (ProductNumber)
                                       ON UPDATE CASCADE
                                       ON DELETE NO ACTION
         );
```

FIGURE 7-52

Continued

```
/*****   CUSTOMER DATA   ***********************************************************/

INSERT INTO CUSTOMER VALUES(
      'Jacobs', 'Nancy', 'Nancy.Jacobs@somewhere.com', 'nf46tG9E', '817-871-8123',
      '1440 West Palm Drive', 'Fort Worth', 'TX', '76110');
INSERT INTO CUSTOMER VALUES(
      'Jacobs', 'Chantel', 'Chantel.Jacobs@somewhere.com', 'b65TG03f', '817-871-8234',
      '1550 East Palm Drive', 'Fort Worth', 'TX', '76112');
INSERT INTO CUSTOMER VALUES(
      'Able', 'Ralph', 'Ralph.Able@somewhere.com', 'm56fGH08', '210-281-7987',
      '123 Elm Street', 'San Antonio', 'TX', '78214');
INSERT INTO CUSTOMER VALUES(
      'Baker', 'Susan', 'Susan.Baker@elsewhere.com', 'PC93fEk9', '210-281-7876',
      '456 Oak Street', 'San Antonio', 'TX', '78216');
INSERT INTO CUSTOMER VALUES(
      'Eagleton', 'Sam', 'Sam.Eagleton@elsewhere.com', 'bnvR44W8', '210-281-7765',
      '789 Pine Street', 'San Antonio', 'TX', '78218');
INSERT INTO CUSTOMER VALUES(
      'Foxtrot', 'Kathy', 'Kathy.Foxtrot@somewhere.com', 'aa8tY4GL', '972-233-6234',
      '11023 Elm Street', 'Dallas', 'TX', '75220');
INSERT INTO CUSTOMER VALUES(
      'George', 'Sally', 'Sally.George@somewhere.com', 'LK8G2tyF', '972-233-6345',
      '12034 San Jacinto', 'Dallas', 'TX', '75223');
INSERT INTO CUSTOMER VALUES(
      'Hullett', 'Shawn', 'Shawn.Hullett@elsewhere.com', 'bu78WW3t', '972-233-6456',
      '13045 Flora', 'Dallas', 'TX', '75224');
INSERT INTO CUSTOMER VALUES(
      'Pearson', 'Bobbi', 'Bobbi.Pearson@elsewhere.com', 'kq6N2O0p', '512-974-3344',
      '43 West 23rd Street', 'Auston', 'TX', '78710');
INSERT INTO CUSTOMER VALUES(
      'Ranger', 'Terry', 'Terry.Ranger@somewhere.com', 'bv3F9Qc4', '512-974-4455',
      '56 East 18th Street', 'Auston', 'TX', '78712');
INSERT INTO CUSTOMER VALUES(
      'Tyler', 'Jenny', 'Jenny.Tyler@somewhere.com', 'Yu4be77Z', '972-233-6567',
      '14056 South Ervay Street', 'Dallas', 'TX', '75225');
INSERT INTO CUSTOMER VALUES(
      'Wayne', 'Joan', 'Joan.Wayne@elsewhere.com', 'JW4TX6g', '817-871-8245',
      '1660 South Aspen Drive', 'Fort Worth', 'TX', '76115');

/*****   SEMINAR   ***********************************************************/

INSERT INTO SEMINAR VALUES(
      '12-OCT-2014', '11:00 AM', 'San Antonio Convention Center',
      'Kitchen on a Budget');
INSERT INTO SEMINAR VALUES(
      '26-OCT-2014', '04:00 PM', 'Dallas Convention Center',
      'Kitchen on a Big D Budget');
INSERT INTO SEMINAR VALUES(
      '02-NOV-2014', '08:30 AM', 'Austin Convention Center',
      'Kitchen on a Budget');
INSERT INTO SEMINAR VALUES(
      '22-MAR-2015', '11:00 AM', 'Dallas Convention Center',
      'Kitchen on a Big D Budget');
INSERT INTO SEMINAR VALUES(
      '23-MAR-2015', '11:00 AM', 'Dallas Convention Center',
      'Kitchen on a Big D Budget');
INSERT INTO SEMINAR VALUES(
      '05-APR-2015', '08:30 AM', 'Austin Convention Center',
      'Kitchen on a Budget');
```

FIGURE 7-53

**SQL Statements to Populate
the HSD Database**

```
/*****    SEMINAR_CUSTOMER DATA   ************************************************/

INSERT INTO SEMINAR_CUSTOMER VALUES(1, 1);
INSERT INTO SEMINAR_CUSTOMER VALUES(1, 2);
INSERT INTO SEMINAR_CUSTOMER VALUES(1, 3);
INSERT INTO SEMINAR_CUSTOMER VALUES(1, 4);
INSERT INTO SEMINAR_CUSTOMER VALUES(1, 5);
INSERT INTO SEMINAR_CUSTOMER VALUES(2, 6);
INSERT INTO SEMINAR_CUSTOMER VALUES(2, 7);
INSERT INTO SEMINAR_CUSTOMER VALUES(2, 8);
INSERT INTO SEMINAR_CUSTOMER VALUES(3, 9);
INSERT INTO SEMINAR_CUSTOMER VALUES(3, 10);
INSERT INTO SEMINAR_CUSTOMER VALUES(4, 6);
INSERT INTO SEMINAR_CUSTOMER VALUES(4, 7);
INSERT INTO SEMINAR_CUSTOMER VALUES(4, 11);
INSERT INTO SEMINAR_CUSTOMER VALUES(4, 12);


/*****    CONTACT DATA   ************************************************/

-- 'Nancy.Jacobs@somewhere.com'
INSERT INTO CONTACT VALUES(1, 1, '12-OCT-2014', 'Seminar', 1);
-- 'Chantel.Jacobs@somewhere.com'
INSERT INTO CONTACT VALUES(2, 1, '12-OCT-2014', 'Seminar', 1);
-- 'Ralph.Able@somewhere.com'
INSERT INTO CONTACT VALUES(3, 1, '12-OCT-2014', 'Seminar', 1);
-- 'Susan.Baker@elsewhere.com'
INSERT INTO CONTACT VALUES(4, 1, '12-OCT-2014', 'Seminar', 1);
-- 'Sam.Eagleton@elsewhere.com'
INSERT INTO CONTACT VALUES(5, 1, '12-OCT-2014', 'Seminar', 1);

-- 'Nancy.Jacobs@somewhere.com',
INSERT INTO CONTACT (CustomerID, ContactNumber, ContactDate, ContactType)
     VALUES(1, 2, '15-OCT-2014', 'EmailSeminarMessage');
-- 'Chantel.Jacobs@somewhere.com'
INSERT INTO CONTACT (CustomerID, ContactNumber, ContactDate, ContactType)
     VALUES(2, 2, '15-OCT-2014', 'EmailSeminarMessage');
-- 'Ralph.Able@somewhere.com'
INSERT INTO CONTACT (CustomerID, ContactNumber, ContactDate, ContactType)
     VALUES(3, 2, '15-OCT-2014', 'EmailSeminarMessage');
-- 'Susan.Baker@elsewhere.com'
INSERT INTO CONTACT (CustomerID, ContactNumber, ContactDate, ContactType)
     VALUES(4, 2, '15-OCT-2014', 'EmailSeminarMessage');
-- 'Sam.Eagleton@elsewhere.com'
INSERT INTO CONTACT (CustomerID, ContactNumber, ContactDate, ContactType)
     VALUES(5, 2, '15-OCT-2014', 'EmailSeminarMessage');


-- 'Nancy.Jacobs@somewhere.com',
INSERT INTO CONTACT (CustomerID, ContactNumber, ContactDate, ContactType)
     VALUES(1, 3, '15-OCT-2014', 'FormLetterSeminar');
-- 'Chantel.Jacobs@somewhere.com'
INSERT INTO CONTACT (CustomerID, ContactNumber, ContactDate, ContactType)
     VALUES(2, 3, '15-OCT-2014', 'FormLetterSeminar');
-- 'Ralph.Able@somewhere.com'
INSERT INTO CONTACT (CustomerID, ContactNumber, ContactDate, ContactType)
     VALUES(3, 3, '15-OCT-2014', 'FormLetterSeminar');
```

FIGURE 7-53   (*continued*)

Continued

```
--  'Susan.Baker@elsewhere.com'
INSERT INTO CONTACT (CustomerID, ContactNumber, ContactDate,  ContactType)
     VALUES(4, 3, '15-OCT-2014', 'FormLetterSeminar');
--  'Sam.Eagleton@elsewhere.com'
INSERT INTO CONTACT (CustomerID, ContactNumber, ContactDate,  ContactType)
     VALUES(5, 3, '15-OCT-2014', 'FormLetterSeminar');


--  'Kathy.Foxtrot@somewhere.com'
INSERT INTO CONTACT VALUES(6, 1, '26-OCT-2014', 'Seminar', 2);
--  'Sally.George@somewhere.com'
INSERT INTO CONTACT VALUES(7, 1, '26-OCT-2014', 'Seminar', 2);
--  'Shawn.Hullett@elsewhere.com'
INSERT INTO CONTACT VALUES(8, 1, '26-OCT-2014', 'Seminar', 2);


--  'Kathy.Foxtrot@somewhere.com'
INSERT INTO CONTACT (CustomerID, ContactNumber, ContactDate,  ContactType)
     VALUES(6, 2, '30-OCT-2014', 'EmailSeminarMessage');
--  'Sally.George@somewhere.com'
INSERT INTO CONTACT (CustomerID, ContactNumber, ContactDate,  ContactType)
     VALUES(7, 2, '30-OCT-2014', 'EmailSeminarMessage');
--  'Shawn.Hullett@elsewhere.com'
INSERT INTO CONTACT (CustomerID, ContactNumber, ContactDate,  ContactType)
     VALUES(8, 2, '30-OCT-2014', 'EmailSeminarMessage');


--  'Kathy.Foxtrot@somewhere.com'
INSERT INTO CONTACT (CustomerID, ContactNumber, ContactDate,  ContactType)
     VALUES(6, 3, '30-OCT-2014', 'FormLetterSeminar');
--  'Sally.George@somewhere.com'
INSERT INTO CONTACT (CustomerID, ContactNumber, ContactDate,  ContactType)
     VALUES(7, 3, '30-OCT-2014', 'FormLetterSeminar');
--  'Shawn.Hullett@elsewhere.com'
INSERT INTO CONTACT (CustomerID, ContactNumber, ContactDate,  ContactType)
     VALUES(8, 3, '30-OCT-2014', 'FormLetterSeminar');


--  'Bobbi.Pearson@elsewhere.com'
INSERT INTO CONTACT VALUES(9, 1, '02-NOV-2014', 'Seminar', 3);
--  'Terry.Ranger@somewhere.com'
INSERT INTO CONTACT VALUES(10, 1, '02-NOV-2014', 'Seminar', 3);


--  'Bobbi.Pearson@elsewhere.com'
INSERT INTO CONTACT (CustomerID, ContactNumber, ContactDate,  ContactType)
     VALUES(9, 2, '06-NOV-2014', 'EmailSeminarMessage');
--  'Terry.Ranger@somewhere.com'
INSERT INTO CONTACT (CustomerID, ContactNumber, ContactDate,  ContactType)
     VALUES(10, 2, '06-NOV-2014', 'EmailSeminarMessage');


--  'Bobbi.Pearson@elsewhere.com'
INSERT INTO CONTACT (CustomerID, ContactNumber, ContactDate,  ContactType)
     VALUES(9, 3, '06-NOV-2014', 'FormLetterSeminar');
--  'Terry.Ranger@somewhere.com'
INSERT INTO CONTACT (CustomerID, ContactNumber, ContactDate,  ContactType)
     VALUES(10, 3, '06-NOV-2014', 'FormLetterSeminar');


--  'Ralph.Able@somewhere.com'
INSERT INTO CONTACT (CustomerID, ContactNumber, ContactDate,  ContactType)
     VALUES(3, 4, '20-FEB-2015', 'WebAccountCreation');
--  'Ralph.Able@somewhere.com'
INSERT INTO CONTACT (CustomerID, ContactNumber, ContactDate,  ContactType)
     VALUES(3, 5, '20-FEB-2015', 'EmailAccountMessage');
```

FIGURE 7-53

Continued

```
--  'Kathy.Foxtrot@somewhere.com'
INSERT INTO CONTACT (CustomerID, ContactNumber, ContactDate,  ContactType)
      VALUES(6, 4, '22-FEB-2015', 'WebAccountCreation');
--  'Kathy.Foxtrot@somewhere.com'
INSERT INTO CONTACT (CustomerID, ContactNumber, ContactDate,  ContactType)
      VALUES(6, 5, '22-FEB-2015', 'EmailAccountMessage');

--  'Sally.George@somewhere.com'
INSERT INTO CONTACT (CustomerID, ContactNumber, ContactDate,  ContactType)
      VALUES(7, 4, '25-FEB-2015', 'WebAccountCreation');
--  'Sally.George@somewhere.com'
INSERT INTO CONTACT (CustomerID, ContactNumber, ContactDate,  ContactType)
      VALUES(7, 5, '25-FEB-2015', 'EmailAccountMessage');
--  'Shawn.Hullett@elsewhere.com'
INSERT INTO CONTACT (CustomerID, ContactNumber, ContactDate,  ContactType)
      VALUES(8, 4, '07-MAR-2015', 'WebAccountCreation');
--  'Shawn.Hullett@elsewhere.com'
INSERT INTO CONTACT (CustomerID, ContactNumber, ContactDate,  ContactType)
      VALUES(8, 5, '07-MAR-2015', 'EmailAccountMessage');

--  'Kathy.Foxtrot@somewhere.com'
INSERT INTO CONTACT VALUES(6, 6, '22-MAR-2015', 'Seminar', 4);
--  'Sally.George@somewhere.com'
INSERT INTO CONTACT VALUES(7, 6, '22-MAR-2015', 'Seminar', 4);
--  'Jenny.Tyler@somewhere.com'
INSERT INTO CONTACT VALUES(11, 1, '22-MAR-2015', 'Seminar', 4);
--  'Joan.Wayne@elsewhere.com'
INSERT INTO CONTACT VALUES(12, 1, '22-MAR-2015', 'Seminar', 4);


/*****    PRODUCT DATA    ********************************************************/

INSERT INTO PRODUCT VALUES(
      'VK001', 'Video', 'Kitchen Remodeling Basics',14.95, 50);
INSERT INTO PRODUCT VALUES(
      'VK002', 'Video', 'Advanced Kitchen Remodeling',14.95, 35);
INSERT INTO PRODUCT VALUES(
      'VK003', 'Video', 'Kitchen Remodeling Dallas Style',19.95, 25);
INSERT INTO PRODUCT VALUES(
      'VK004', 'Video', 'Heather Sweeney Seminar Live in Dallas on 25-OCT-13', 24.95, 20);
INSERT INTO PRODUCT VALUES(
      'VB001', 'Video Companion', 'Kitchen Remodeling Basics',7.99, 50);
INSERT INTO PRODUCT VALUES(
      'VB002', 'Video Companion', 'Advanced Kitchen Remodeling I',7.99, 35);
INSERT INTO PRODUCT VALUES(
      'VB003', 'Video Companion', 'Kitchen Remodeling Dallas Style',9.99, 25);
INSERT INTO PRODUCT VALUES(
      'BK001', 'Book', 'Kitchen Remodeling Basics For Everyone',24.95, 75);
INSERT INTO PRODUCT VALUES(
      'BK002', 'Book', 'Advanced Kitchen Remodeling For Everyone',24.95, 75);
INSERT INTO PRODUCT VALUES(
      'BK003', 'Book', 'Kitchen Remodeling Dallas Style For Everyone',24.95, 75);
```

FIGURE 7-53

(continued)

Continued

```
/*****    INVOICE DATA    ********************************************************/

/*****    Invoice 35000    ****************************************************/
-- 'Ralph.Able@somewhere.com'
INSERT INTO INVOICE VALUES(
        '15-Oct-14', 3, 'VISA', 22.94, 5.95, 1.31, 30.20);
INSERT INTO LINE_ITEM VALUES(35000, 1, 'VK001', 1, 14.95, 14.95);
INSERT INTO LINE_ITEM VALUES(35000, 2, 'VB001', 1, 7.99, 7.99);


/*****    Invoice 35001    ****************************************************/
-- 'Susan.Baker@elsewhere.com'
INSERT INTO INVOICE VALUES(
        '25-Oct-14', 4, 'MasterCard', 47.89, 5.95, 2.73, 56.57);
INSERT INTO LINE_ITEM VALUES(35001, 1, 'VK001', 1, 14.95, 14.95);
INSERT INTO LINE_ITEM VALUES(35001, 2, 'VB001', 1, 7.99, 7.99);
INSERT INTO LINE_ITEM VALUES(35001, 3, 'BK001', 1, 24.95, 24.95);


/*****    Invoice 35002    ****************************************************/
-- 'Sally.George@somewhere.com'
INSERT INTO INVOICE VALUES(
        '20-Dec-14', 7, 'VISA', 24.95, 5.95, 1.42, 32.32);
INSERT INTO LINE_ITEM VALUES(35002, 1, 'VK004', 1, 24.95, 24.95);


/*****    Invoice 35003    ****************************************************/
-- 'Susan.Baker@elsewhere.com'
INSERT INTO INVOICE VALUES(
        '25-Mar-15', 4, 'MasterCard', 64.85, 5.95, 3.70, 74.50);
INSERT INTO LINE_ITEM VALUES(35003, 1, 'VK002', 1, 14.95, 14.95);
INSERT INTO LINE_ITEM VALUES(35003, 2, 'BK002', 1, 24.95, 24.95);
INSERT INTO LINE_ITEM VALUES(35003, 3, 'VK004', 1, 24.95, 24.95);


/*****    Invoice 35004    ****************************************************/
-- 'Kathy.Foxtrot@somewhere.com'
INSERT INTO INVOICE VALUES(
        '27-Mar-15', 6, 'MasterCard', 94.79, 5.95, 5.40, 106.14);
INSERT INTO LINE_ITEM VALUES(35004, 1, 'VK002', 1, 14.95, 14.95);
INSERT INTO LINE_ITEM VALUES(35004, 2, 'BK002', 1, 24.95, 24.95);
INSERT INTO LINE_ITEM VALUES(35004, 3, 'VK003', 1, 19.95, 19.95);
INSERT INTO LINE_ITEM VALUES(35004, 4, 'VB003', 1, 9.99, 9.99);
INSERT INTO LINE_ITEM VALUES(35004, 5, 'VK004', 1, 24.95, 24.95);


/*****    Invoice 35005    ****************************************************/
-- 'Sally.George@somewhere.com'
INSERT INTO INVOICE VALUES(
        '27-Mar-15', 7, 'MasterCard', 94.80, 5.95, 5.40, 106.15);
INSERT INTO LINE_ITEM VALUES(35005, 1, 'BK001', 1, 24.95, 24.95);
INSERT INTO LINE_ITEM VALUES(35005, 2, 'BK002', 1, 24.95, 24.95);
INSERT INTO LINE_ITEM VALUES(35005, 3, 'VK003', 1, 19.95, 19.95);
INSERT INTO LINE_ITEM VALUES(35005, 4, 'VK004', 1, 24.95, 24.95);


/*****    Invoice 35006    ****************************************************/
-- 'Bobbi.Pearson@elsewhere.com'
INSERT INTO INVOICE VALUES(
        '31-Mar-15', 9, 'VISA', 47.89, 5.95, 2.73, 56.57);
INSERT INTO LINE_ITEM VALUES(35006, 1, 'BK001', 1, 24.95, 24.95);
INSERT INTO LINE_ITEM VALUES(35006, 2, 'VK001', 1, 14.95, 14.95);
INSERT INTO LINE_ITEM VALUES(35006, 3, 'VB001', 1, 7.99, 7.99);
```

FIGURE 7-53

Continued

```
/*****    Invoice 35007    **************************************************/
-- 'Jenny.Tyler@somewhere.com'
INSERT INTO INVOICE VALUES(
       '03-Apr-15', 11, 'MasterCard', 109.78, 5.95, 6.26, 121.99);
INSERT INTO LINE_ITEM VALUES(35007, 1, 'VK003', 2, 19.95, 39.90);
INSERT INTO LINE_ITEM VALUES(35007, 2, 'VB003', 2, 9.99, 19.98);
INSERT INTO LINE_ITEM VALUES(35007, 3, 'VK004', 2, 24.95, 49.90);


/*****    Invoice 35008    **************************************************/
-- 'Sam.Eagleton@elsewhere.com'
INSERT INTO INVOICE VALUES(
       '08-Apr-15', 5, 'MasterCard', 47.89, 5.95, 2.73, 56.57);
INSERT INTO LINE_ITEM VALUES(35008, 1, 'BK001', 1, 24.95, 24.95);
INSERT INTO LINE_ITEM VALUES(35008, 2, 'VK001', 1, 14.95, 14.95);
INSERT INTO LINE_ITEM VALUES(35008, 3, 'VB001', 1, 7.99, 7.99);


/*****    Invoice 35009    **************************************************/
-- 'Nancy.Jacobs@somewhere.com'
INSERT INTO INVOICE VALUES(
       '08-Apr-15', 1, 'VISA', 47.89, 5.95, 2.73, 56.57);
INSERT INTO LINE_ITEM VALUES(35009, 1, 'BK001', 1, 24.95, 24.95);
INSERT INTO LINE_ITEM VALUES(35009, 2, 'VK001', 1, 14.95, 14.95);
INSERT INTO LINE_ITEM VALUES(35009, 3, 'VB001', 1, 7.99, 7.99);


/*****    Invoice 35010    **************************************************/
-- 'Ralph.Able@somewhere.com'
INSERT INTO INVOICE VALUES(
       '23-Apr-15', 3, 'VISA', 24.95, 5.95, 1.42, 32.32);
INSERT INTO LINE_ITEM VALUES(35010, 1, 'BK001', 1, 24.95, 24.95);


/*****    Invoice 35011    **************************************************/
-- 'Bobbi.Pearson@elsewhere.com'
INSERT INTO INVOICE VALUES(
       '07-May-15', 9, 'VISA', 22.94, 5.95, 1.31, 30.20);
INSERT INTO LINE_ITEM VALUES(35011, 1, 'VK002', 1, 14.95, 14.95);
INSERT INTO LINE_ITEM VALUES(35011, 2, 'VB002', 1, 7.99, 7.99);


/*****    Invoice 35012    **************************************************/
-- 'Shawn.Hullett@elsewhere.com'
INSERT INTO INVOICE VALUES(
       '21-May-15', 8, 'MasterCard', 54.89, 5.95, 3.13, 63.97);
INSERT INTO LINE_ITEM VALUES(35012, 1, 'VK003', 1, 19.95, 19.95);
INSERT INTO LINE_ITEM VALUES(35012, 2, 'VB003', 1, 9.99, 9.99);
INSERT INTO LINE_ITEM VALUES(35012, 3, 'VK004', 1, 24.95, 24.95);


/*****    Invoice 35013    **************************************************/
-- 'Ralph.Able@somewhere.com'
INSERT INTO INVOICE VALUES(
       '05-Jun-15', 3, 'VISA', 47.89, 5.95, 2.73, 56.57);
INSERT INTO LINE_ITEM VALUES(35013, 1, 'VK002', 1, 14.95, 14.95);
INSERT INTO LINE_ITEM VALUES(35013, 2, 'VB002', 1, 7.99, 7.99);
INSERT INTO LINE_ITEM VALUES(35013, 3, 'BK002', 1, 24.95, 24.95);
```

FIGURE 7-53

Continued

(*continued*)

```
/*****     Invoice 35014     **************************************************/
-- 'Jenny.Tyler@somewhere.com'
INSERT INTO INVOICE VALUES(
        '05-Jun-15', 11, 'MasterCard', 45.88, 5.95, 2.62, 54.45);
INSERT INTO LINE_ITEM VALUES(35014, 1, 'VK002', 2, 14.95, 29.90);
INSERT INTO LINE_ITEM VALUES(35014, 2, 'VB002', 2, 7.99, 15.98);


/*****     Invoice 35015     **************************************************/
-- 'Joan.Wayne@elsewhere.com'
INSERT INTO INVOICE VALUES(
        '05-Jun-15', 12, 'MasterCard', 94.79, 5.95, 5.40, 106.14);
INSERT INTO LINE_ITEM VALUES(35015, 1, 'VK002', 1, 14.95, 14.95);
INSERT INTO LINE_ITEM VALUES(35015, 2, 'BK002', 1, 24.95, 24.95);
INSERT INTO LINE_ITEM VALUES(35015, 3, 'VK003', 1, 19.95, 19.95);
INSERT INTO LINE_ITEM VALUES(35015, 4, 'VB003', 1, 9.99, 9.99);
INSERT INTO LINE_ITEM VALUES(35015, 5, 'VK004', 1, 24.95, 24.95);


/*****     Invoice 35016     **************************************************/
-- 'Ralph.Able@somewhere.com'
INSERT INTO INVOICE VALUES(
        '05-Jun-15', 3, 'VISA', 45.88, 5.95, 2.62, 54.45);
INSERT INTO LINE_ITEM VALUES(35016, 1, 'VK001', 1, 14.95, 14.95);
INSERT INTO LINE_ITEM VALUES(35016, 2, 'VB001', 1, 7.99, 7.99);
INSERT INTO LINE_ITEM VALUES(35016, 3, 'VK002', 1, 14.95, 14.95);
INSERT INTO LINE_ITEM VALUES(35016, 4, 'VB002', 1, 7.99, 7.99);


/****************************************************************************/
```

FIGURE 7-53

Continued

H. Write an SQL statement to list the INVOICE.InvoiceNumber for sales that include the *Heather Sweeney Seminar Live in Dallas on 25-OCT-13* video. Use a subquery. (Hint: The correct solution uses three tables in the query because the question asks for INVOICE.InvoiceNumber. Otherwise, there is a possible solution with only two tables in the query.)

I. Answer part H but use JOIN ON syntax. (Hint: The correct solution uses three tables in the query because the question asks for INVOICE.InvoiceNumber. Otherwise, there is a possible solution with only two tables in the query.)

J. Write an SQL statement to list the FirstName, LastName, and Phone of customers (list each name only once) who have attended the Kitchen on a Big D Budget seminar. Sort the results by LastName in descending order, and then by FirstName in descending order.

K. Write an SQL statement to list the FirstName, LastName, Phone, ProductNumber, and Description of customers (list each combination of name and video product only once) who have purchased a video product. Sort the results by LastName in descending order, then by FirstName in descending order, and then by ProductNumber in descending order. (Hint: Video products have a ProductNumber that starts with VK.)

L. Write an SQL statement to show the sum of SubTotal (this is the money earned by HSD on products sold exclusive of shipping costs and taxes) for INVOICE as SumOfSubTotal.

M. Write an SQL statement to show the average of Subtotal (this is the money earned by HSD on products sold exclusive of shipping costs and taxes) for INVOICE as AverageOfSubTotal.

N. Write an SQL statement to show both the sum and the average of Subtotal (this is the money earned by HSD on products sold exclusive of shipping costs and taxes) for INVOICE as SumOfSubTotal and AverageOfSubTotal respectively.

O. Write an SQL statement to modify PRODUCT UnitPrice for ProductNumber VK004 to $34.95 instead of the current UnitPrice of $24.95.

P. Write an SQL statement to undo the UnitPrice modification in part O.

Q. **Do not run your answer to the following question in your actual database!** Write the fewest number of DELETE statements possible to remove all the data in your database but leave the table structures intact.

Using the HSD database, create an SQL script named *HSD-Create-Views-and-Functions.sql* to answer questions R–T.

R. Write an SQL statement to create a view called InvoiceSummaryView that contains INVOICE.InvoiceNumber, INVOICE.InvoiceDate, LINE_ITEM.LineNumber, LINE_ITEM.ProductNumber, PRODUCT.ProductDescription and LINE_ITEM.UnitPrice. Run the statement to create the view, and then test the view with an appropriate SQL SELECT statement.

S. Create and test a user-defined function named *LastNameFirst* that combines two parameters named *FirstName* and *LastName* into a concatenated name field formatted *LastName, FirstName* (including the comma and space).

T. Write an SQL statement to create a view called CustomerInvoiceSummaryView that contains INVOICE.InvoiceNumber, INVOICE.InvoiceDate, the concatenated customer name using the *LastNameFirst* function, CUSTOMER.EmailAddress, and INVOICE.Total. Run the statement to create the view, and then test the view with an appropriate SQL SELECT statement.

The Queen Anne Curiosity Shop

Assume that the Queen Anne Curiosity Shop designs a database with the following tables:

CUSTOMER (CustomerID, LastName, FirstName, EmailAddress, EncryptedPassword, Address, City, State, ZIP, Phone)

EMPLOYEE (EmployeeID, LastName, FirstName, Phone, Email)

VENDOR (VendorID, CompanyName, ContactLastName, ContactFirstName, Address, City, State, ZIP, Phone, Fax, Email)

ITEM (ItemID, ItemDescription, PurchaseDate, ItemCost, ItemPrice, VendorID)

SALE (SaleID, CustomerID, EmployeeID, SaleDate, SubTotal, Tax, Total)

SALE_ITEM (SaleID, SaleItemID, ItemID, ItemPrice)

The referential integrity constraints are:

CustomerID in SALE must exist in CustomerID in CUSTOMER

VendorID in ITEM must exist in VendorID in VENDOR

EmployeeID in SALE must exist in EmployeeID in EMPLOYEE

SaleID in SALE_ITEM must exist in SaleID in SALE

ItemID in SALE_ITEM must exist in ItemID in ITEM

Assume that CustomerID of CUSTOMER, EmployeeID of EMPLOYEE, VendorID of VENDOR, ItemID of ITEM, and SaleID of SALE are all surrogate keys with values as follows:

CustomerID	Start at 1	Increment by 1
EmployeeID	Start at 1	Increment by 1
VendorID	Start at 1	Increment by 1
ItemID	Start at 1	Increment by 1
SaleID	Start at 1	Increment by 1

A vendor may be an individual or a company. If the vendor is an individual, the CompanyName field is left blank, while the ContactLastName and ContactFirstName fields must have data values. If the vendor is a company, the company name is recorded in the CompanyName field, and the name of the primary contact at the company is recorded in the ContactLastName and ContactFirstName fields.

A. Specify NULL/NOT NULL constraints for each table column.

B. Specify alternate keys, if any.

C. State relationships as implied by foreign keys, and specify the maximum and minimum cardinalities of each relationship. Justify your choices.

D. Explain how you will enforce the minimum cardinalities in your answer to part C. Use referential integrity actions for required parents, if any. Use Figure 6-29(b) as a boilerplate for required children, if any.

E. Create a database named QACS in your DBMS.

F. Create a folder in your *My Documents* folder to save and store *.sql scripts containing the SQL statements that you are asked to create in the remaining questions in this section.

- For the SQL Server Management Studio, create a folder named QACS-*Database* in the *Projects* folder structure in your *SQL Server Management Studio* folder.
- In the Oracle SQL Developer folder structure in your *SQL Developer* folder, create a folder named QACS-*Database*.
- For the SQL Workbench, create a folder named QACS-*Database* in the *Schemas* folder in your *MySQL Workbench* folder.

Using the QACS database, create an SQL script named *QACS-Create-Tables.sql* to answer parts G and H. Your answer to part H should be in the form of an SQL comment in the script.

G. Write CREATE TABLE statements for each of the tables using your answers to parts A–D, as necessary. Set the surrogate key values as shown above. Use FOREIGN KEY constraints to create appropriate referential integrity constraints. Set UPDATE and DELETE behavior in accordance with your referential integrity action design. Run these statements to create the QACS tables.

H. Explain how you would enforce the data constraint that SALE_ITEM.UnitPrice be equal to ITEM.ItemPrice, where SALE_ITEM.ItemID = ITEM.ItemID.

Using the QACS database, create an SQL script named *QACS-Insert-Data.sql* to answer part I.

I. Write INSERT statements to insert the data shown in Figures 7-54, 7-55, 7-56, 7-57, 7-58, and 7-59.

Using the QACS database, create an SQL script named *QACS-DML-CH07.sql* to answer parts J and K.

J. Write an UPDATE statement to change values of ITEM.ItemDescription from *Desk Lamp* to *Desk Lamps*.

K. Create and INSERT new data records to record a SALE and the SALE_ITEMs for that sale. Then write a DELETE statement(s) to delete that SALE and all of the items on that SALE. How many DELETE statements did you have to use? Why?

CustomerID	LastName	FirstName	Address	City	State	ZIP	Phone	Email
1	Shire	Robert	6225 Evanston Ave N	Seattle	WA	98103	206-524-2433	Robert.Shire@somewhere.com
2	Goodyear	Katherine	7335 11th Ave NE	Seattle	WA	98105	206-524-3544	Katherine.Goodyear@somewhere.com
3	Bancroft	Chris	12605 NE 6th Street	Bellevue	WA	98005	425-635-9788	Chris.Bancroft@somewhere.com
4	Griffith	John	335 Aloha Street	Seattle	WA	98109	206-524-4655	John.Griffith@somewhere.com
5	Tiemey	Doris	14510 NE 4th Street	Bellevue	WA	98005	425-635-8677	Doris.Tiemey@somewhere.com
6	Anderson	Donna	1410 Hillcrest Parkway	Mt. Vemon	WA	98273	360-538-7566	Donna.Anderson@elsewhere.com
7	Svane	Jack	3211 42nd Street	Seattle	WA	98115	206-524-5766	Jack.Svane@somewhere.com
8	Walsh	Denesha	6712 24th Avenue NE	Redmond	WA	98053	425-635-7566	Denesha.Walsh@somewhere.com
9	Enquist	Craig	534 15th Street	Bellingham	WA	98225	360-538-6455	Craig.Enquist@elsewhere.com
10	Anderson	Rose	6823 17th Ave NE	Seattle	WA	98105	206-524-6877	Rose.Anderson@elsewhere.com

FIGURE 7-54

Sample Data for the QACS
Database CUSTOMER Table

EmployeeID	LastName	FirstName	Phone	Email
1	Stuart	Anne	206-527-0010	Anne.Stuart@QACS.com
2	Stuart	George	206-527-0011	George.Stuart@QACS.com
3	Stuart	Mary	206-527-0012	Mary.Stuart@QACS.com
4	Orange	William	206-527-0013	William.Orange@QACS.com
5	Griffith	John	206-527-0014	John.Griffith@QACS.com

FIGURE 7-55

Sample Data for the QACS
Database EMPLOYEE Table

Using the **QACS database, create an SQL script named** *QACS-Create-Views-and-Functions.sql* **to answer parts L–Q.**

L. Write an SQL statement to create a view called SaleSummaryView that contains SALE.SaleID, SALE.SaleDate, SALE_ITEM.SaleItemID, SALE_ITEM.ItemID, ITEM.ItemDescription, and ITEM.ItemPrice. Run the statement to create the view, and then test the view with an appropriate SQL SELECT statement.

M. Create and test a user-defined function named *LastNameFirst* that combines two parameters named *FirstName* and *LastName* into a concatenated name field formatted *LastName, FirstName* (including the comma and space).

N. Write an SQL statement to create a view called CustomerSaleSummaryView that contains SALE.SaleID, SALE.SaleDate, CUSTOMER.LastName, CUSTOMER.FirstName, SALE_ITEM.SaleItemID, SALE_ITEM.ItemID, ITEM.ItemDescription, and ITEM.ItemPrice. Run the statement to create the view, and then test the view with an appropriate SQL SELECT statement.

O. Write an SQL statement to create a view called CustomerLastNameFirstSaleSummaryView that contains SALE.SaleID, SALE.SaleDate, the concatenated customer name using the *LastNameFirst* function, SALE_ITEM.SaleItemID, SALE_ITEM.ItemID, ITEM.ItemDescription, and ITEM.ItemPrice. Run the statement to create the view, and then test the view with an appropriate SQL SELECT statement.

P. Write an SQL statement to create a view called CustomerSaleHistoryView that:

(1) Includes all columns of CustomerSaleSummaryView *except* SALE_ITEM.SaleItemID, SALE_ITEM.ItemID, and ITEM.ItemDescription.

(2) Groups orders by SALE.SaleID, CUSTOMER.LastName, CUSTOMER.FirstName, and SALE.SaleDate in that order;

(3) Sums and averages SALE_ITEM.ItemPrice for each order for each customer. Run the statement to create the view, and then test the view with an appropriate SQL SELECT statement.

Q. Write an SQL statement to create a view called CustomerSaleCheckView that uses CustomerSaleHistoryView and that shows any customers and sales for which the sum of item prices for the sale is not equal to SALE.SubTotal. Run the statement to create the view, and then test the view with an appropriate SQL SELECT statement.

R. Explain, in general terms, how you would use triggers to enforce minimum cardinality actions as required by your design. You need not write the triggers; just specify which triggers you need and describe, in general terms, their logic.

VendorID	CompanyName	ContactLastName	ContactFirstName	Address	City	State	ZIP	Phone	Fax	Email
1	Linens and Things	Huntington	Anne	1515 NW Market Street	Seattle	WA	98107	206-325-6755	206-329-9675	LAT@business.com
2	European Specialties	Tadema	Ken	6123 15th Avenue NW	Seattle	WA	98107	206-325-7866	206-329-9786	ES@business.com
3	Lamps and Lighting	Swanson	Sally	506 Prospect Street	Seattle	WA	98109	206-325-8977	206-329-9897	LAL@business.com
4	NULL	Lee	Andrew	1102 3rd Street	Kirkland	WA	98033	425-746-5433	NULL	Andrew.Lee@somewhere.com
5	NULL	Hamison	Denise	533 10th Avenue	Kirkland	WA	98033	425-746-4322	NULL	Denise.Hamison@somewhere.com
6	New York Brokerage	Smith	Mark	621 Roy Street	Seattle	WA	98109	206-325-9088	206-329-9908	NYB@business.com
7	NULL	Walsh	Denesha	6712 24th Avenue NE	Redmond	WA	98053	425-635-7566	NULL	Denesha.Walsh@somewhere.com
8	NULL	Bancroft	Chris	12605 NE 6th Street	Bellevue	WA	98005	425-635-9788	425-639-9978	Chris.Bancroft@somewhere.com
9	Specialty Antiques	Nelson	Fred	2512 Lucky Street	San Francisco	CA	94110	415-422-2121	415-423-5212	SA@business.com
10	General Antiques	Gamer	Patty	2515 Lucky Street	San Francisco	CA	94110	415-422-3232	415-429-9323	GA@business.com

FIGURE 7-56

Sample Data for the QACS
Database VENDOR Table

FIGURE 7-57

Sample Data for the QACS
Database ITEM Table

ItemID	ItemDescription	PurchaseDate	ItemCost	ItemPrice	VendorID
1	Antique Desk	2014-11-07	$1,800.00	$3,000.00	2
2	Antique Desk Chair	2014-11-10	$300.00	$500.00	4
3	Dining Table Linens	2014-11-14	$600.00	$1,000.00	1
4	Candles	2014-11-14	$30.00	$50.00	1
5	Candles	2014-11-14	$27.00	$45.00	1
6	Desk Lamp	2014-11-14	$150.00	$250.00	3
7	Dining Table Linens	2014-11-14	$450.00	$750.00	1
8	Book Shelf	2014-11-21	$150.00	$250.00	5
9	Antique Chair	2014-11-21	$750.00	$1,250.00	6
10	Antique Chair	2014-11-21	$1,050.00	$1,750.00	6
11	Antique Candle Holders	2014-11-28	$210.00	$350.00	2
12	Antique Desk	2015-01-05	$1,920.00	$3,200.00	2
13	Antique Desk	2015-01-05	$2,100.00	$3,500.00	2
14	Antique Desk Chair	2015-01-06	$285.00	$475.00	9
15	Antique Desk Chair	2015-01-06	$339.00	$565.00	9
16	Desk Lamp	2015-01-06	$150.00	$250.00	10
17	Desk Lamp	2015-01-06	$150.00	$250.00	10
18	Desk Lamp	2015-01-06	$144.00	$240.00	3
19	Antique Dining Table	2015-01-10	$3,000.00	$5,000.00	7
20	Antique Sideboard	2015-01-11	$2,700.00	$4,500.00	8
21	Dining Table Chairs	2015-01-11	$5,100.00	$8,500.00	9
22	Dining Table Linens	2015-01-12	$450.00	$750.00	1
23	Dining Table Linens	2015-01-12	$480.00	$800.00	1
24	Candles	2015-01-17	$30.00	$50.00	1
25	Candles	2015-01-17	$36.00	$60.00	1

FIGURE 7-57

Sample Data for the QACS
Database ITEM Table

FIGURE 7-58

Sample Data
for the QACS
Database SALE
Table

SaleID	CustomerID	EmployeeID	SaleDate	SubTotal	Tax	Total
1	1	1	2014-12-14	$3,500.00	$290.50	$3,790.50
2	2	1	2014-12-15	$100.00	$83.00	$1,083.00
3	3	1	2014-12-15	$50.00	$4.15	$54.15
4	4	3	2014-12-23	$45.00	$3.74	$48.74
5	1	5	2015-01-05	$250.00	$20.75	$270.75
6	5	5	2015-01-10	$750.00	$62.25	$812.25
7	6	4	2015-01-12	$250.00	$20.75	$270.75
8	2	1	2015-01-15	$3,000.00	$249.00	$3,249.00
9	5	5	2015-01-25	$350.00	$29.05	$379.05
10	7	1	2015-02-04	$14,250.00	$1,182.75	$15,432.75
11	8	5	2015-02-04	$250.00	$20.75	$270.75
12	5	4	2015-02-07	$50.00	$4.15	$54.15
13	9	2	2015-02-07	$4,500.00	$373.50	$4,873.50
14	10	3	2015-02-11	$3,675.00	$305.03	$3,980.03
15	2	2	2015-02-11	$800.00	$66.40	$866.40

FIGURE 7-59

Sample Data for the QACS
Database SALE_ITEM Table

SaleID	SaleItemID	ItemID	ItemPrice
1	1	1	$3,000.00
1	2	2	$500.00
2	1	3	$1,000.00
3	1	4	$50.00
4	1	5	$45.00
5	1	6	$250.00
6	1	7	$750.00
7	1	8	$250.00
8	1	9	$1,250.00
8	2	10	$1,750.00
9	1	11	$350.00
10	1	19	$5,000.00
10	2	21	$8,500.00
10	3	22	$750.00
11	1	17	$250.00
12	1	24	$50.00
13	1	20	$4,500.00
14	1	12	$3,200.00
14	2	14	$475.00
15	1	23	$800.00

**Morgan
Importing**

Suppose that you have designed a database for Morgan Importing that has the following tables:

> EMPLOYEE (<u>EmployeeID</u>, LastName, FirstName, Department, Phone, Fax, EmailAddress)
>
> STORE (<u>StoreName</u>, City, Country, Phone, Fax, EmailAddress, Contact)
>
> ITEM (<u>ItemID</u>, *StoreName*, *PurchasingAgentID*, PurchaseDate, ItemDescription, Category, PriceUSD)
>
> SHIPPER (<u>ShipperID</u>, ShipperName, Phone, Fax, EmailAddress, Contact)
>
> SHIPMENT (<u>ShipmentID</u>, *ShipperID*, *PurchasingAgentID*, ShipperInvoiceNumber, Origin, Destination, ScheduledDepartureDate, ActualDepartureDate, EstimatedArrivalDate)
>
> SHIPMENT_ITEM (<u>*ShipmentID*</u>, <u>ShipmentItemID</u>, *ItemID*, InsuredValue)
>
> SHIPMENT_RECEIPT (<u>ReceiptNumber</u>, *ShipmentID*, *ItemID*, *ReceivingAgentID*, ReceiptDate, ReceiptTime, ReceiptQuantity, isReceivedUndamaged, DamageNotes)

A. Do you think STORE should have a surrogate key? If so, create it and make required adjustments in the design. If not, explain why not or make any other adjustments to STORE and other tables that you think are appropriate.

B. Specify NULL/NOT NULL constraints for each table column.

C. Specify alternate keys, if any.

D. State relationships as implied by foreign keys, and specify the maximum and minimum cardinality of each relationship. Justify your choices.

E. Explain how you will enforce the minimum cardinalities in your answer to part D. Use referential integrity actions for required parents, if any. Use Figure 6-29(b) as a boilerplate for required children, if any.

F. Create a database named MI in your DBMS.

G. Create a folder in your *My Documents* folder to save and store *.sql scripts containing the SQL statements that you are asked to create in the remaining questions in this section.

- For the SQL Server Management Studio, create a folder named *MI-Database* in the *Projects* folder structure in your *SQL Server Management Studio* folder.
- In the Oracle SQL Developer folder structure in your *SQL Developer* folder, create a folder named *MI-Database*.
- For the SQL Workbench, create a folder named *MI-Database* in the *Schemas* folder in your *MySQL Workbench* folder.

Using the MI database, create an SQL script named *MI-Create-Tables.sql* to answer parts H and I. Your answer to part I should be in the form of an SQL comment in the script.

H. Write CREATE TABLE statements for each of the tables using your answers to parts A–E, as necessary. If you decided to use a StoreID surrogate key, set the first value to 1000 and increment by 50. Set the first value of EmployeeID and ShipperID to 1 and increment it by 1. Set the first value of ItemID to 500 and increment it by 5. Set the first value of ShipmentID to 100 and increment it by 1. ReceiptNumber should start at 200001 and increment by 1. Use FOREIGN KEY constraints to create appropriate referential integrity constraints. Set UPDATE and DELETE behavior in accordance with your referential integrity action design. Set the default value of InsuredValue to 100. Write a constraint that STORE.Country be limited to seven countries (Hong Kong, India, Japan, Peru, Philippines, Singapore, United States).

EmployeeID	LastName	FirstName	Department	Phone	Fax	EmailAddress
101	Morgan	James	Executive	310-208-1401	310-208-1499	James.Morgan@morganimporting.com
102	Morgan	Jessica	Executive	310-208-1402	310-208-1499	Jessica.Morgan@morganimporting.com
103	Williams	David	Purchasing	310-208-1434	310-208-1498	David.Williams@morganimporting.com
104	Gilbertson	Teri	Purchasing	310-208-1435	310-208-1498	Teri.Gilbertson@morganimporting.com
105	Wright	James	Receiving	310-208-1456	310-208-1497	James.Wright@morganimporting.com
106	Douglas	Tom	Receiving	310-208-1457	310-208-1497	Tom.Douglas@morganimporting.com

FIGURE 7-60

Sample Data for the MI
Database EMPLOYEE Table

I. Explain how you would enforce the rule that SHIPMENT_ITEM.InsuredValue be at least as great as ITEM.PriceUSD.

Using the MI database, create an SQL script named *MI-Insert-Data.sql* to answer part J.

J. Write INSERT statements to insert the data shown in Figures 7-60, 7-61, 7-62, 7-63, 7-64, 7-65, and 7-66.

Using the MI database, create an SQL script named *MI-DML-CH07.sql* to answer parts K and L.

K. Write an UPDATE statement to change values of STORE.City from *New York City* to *NYC*.

L. Create and INSERT new data records to record a SHIPMENT and the SHIPMENT_ITEMs for that SHIPMENT. Then write a DELETE statement(s) to delete that SHIPMENT and all of the items on that SHIPMENT. How many DELETE statements did you have to use? Why?

Using the MI database, create an SQL script named *MI-Create-Views-and-Functions.sql* to answer parts M–R.

M. Write an SQL statement to create a view called PurchaseSummaryView that shows only ITEM.ItemID, ITEM.PurchaseDate, ITEM.ItemDescription, and ITEM.PriceUSD. Run the statement to create the view, and then test the view with an appropriate SQL SELECT statement.

N. Create and test a user-defined function named *StoreContactAndPhone* that combines two parameters named *StoreContact* and *ContactPhone* into a concatenated data field formatted *StoreContact: ContactPhone* (including the colon and space).

O. Write an SQL statement to create a view called StorePurchaseHistoryView that shows STORE.StoreName, STORE.Phone, STORE.Contact, ITEM.ItemID, ITEM.PurchaseDate, ITEM.ItemDescription, and ITEM.PriceUSD. Run the statement to create the view, and then test the view with an appropriate SQL SELECT statement.

P. Write an SQL statement to create a view called StoreContactPurchaseHistoryView that shows STORE.StoreName, the concatenated result of STORE.Phone and STORE.Contact from the *StoreContactAndPhone* function, ITEM.ItemID, ITEM.PurchaseDate, ITEM.ItemDescription, and ITEM.PriceUSD. Run the statement to create the view, and then test the view with an appropriate SQL SELECT statement.

StoreID	StoreName	City	Country	Phone	Fax	EmailAddress	Contact
1000	Eastern Sales	Singapore	Singapore	65-543-1233	65-543-1239	Sales@EasternSales.com.sg	Jeremy
1050	Eastern Treasures	Manila	Philippines	63-2-654-2344	63-2-654-2349	Sales@EasternTreasures.com.ph	Gracielle
1100	Jade Antiques	Singapore	Singapore	65-543-3455	65-543-3459	Sales@JadeAntiques.com.sg	Swee Lai
1150	Andes Treasures	Lima	Peru	51-14-765-4566	51-14-765-4569	Sales@AndesTreasures.com.pe	Juan Carlos
1200	Eastern Sales	Hong Kong	People's Republic of China	852-876-5677	852-876-5679	Sales@EasternSales.com.hk	Sam
1250	Eastern Treasures	New Delhi	India	91-11-987-6788	91-11-987-6789	Sales@EasternTreasures.com.in	Deepinder
1300	European Imports	New York City	United States	800-432-8766	800-432-8769	Sales@EuropeanImports.com.sg	Marcello

FIGURE 7-61

Sample Data for the MI
Database STORE Table

ItemID	StoreID	PurchasingAgentID	PurchaseDate	ItemDescription	Category	PriceUSD
500	1050	101	12/10/2014	Antique Large Bureaus	Furniture	$ 13,415.00
505	1050	102	12/12/2014	Porcelain Lamps	Lamps	$ 13,300.00
510	1200	104	12/15/2014	Gold Rim Design China	Tableware	$ 38,500.00
515	1200	104	12/16/2014	Gold Rim Design Serving Dishes	Tableware	$ 3,200.00
520	1050	102	4/7/2015	QE Dining Set	Furniture	$ 14,300.00
525	1100	103	5/18/2015	Misc Linen	Linens	$ 88,545.00
530	1000	103	5/19/2015	Large Masks	Decorations	$ 22,135.00
535	1100	104	5/20/2015	Willow Design China	Tableware	$ 147,575.00
540	1100	104	5/20/2015	Willow Design Serving Dishes	Tableware	$ 12,040.00
545	1150	102	6/14/2015	Woven Goods	Decorations	$ 1,200.00
550	1150	101	6/16/2015	Antique Leather Chairs	Furniture	$ 5,375.00
555	1100	104	7/15/2015	Willow Design Serving Dishes	Tableware	$ 4,500.00
560	1000	103	7/17/2015	Large Bureau	Furniture	$ 9,500.00
565	1100	104	7/20/2015	Brass Lamps	Lamps	$ 1,200.00

FIGURE 7-62

Sample Data for the MI
Database ITEM Table

Q. Write an SQL statement to create a view called StoreHistoryView that sums the PriceUSD column of StorePurchaseHistoryView for each store into a column named TotalPurchases. Run the statement to create the view, and then test the view with an appropriate SQL SELECT statement. (Hint: Assume unique store names.)

R. Write an SQL statement to create a view called MajorSources that uses StoreHistoryView and selects only those stores that have TotalPurchases greater than 100000. Run the statement to create the view, and then test the view with an appropriate SQL SELECT statement.

S. Explain, in general terms, how you would use triggers to enforce minimum cardinality actions as required by your design. You need not write the triggers; just specify which triggers you need and describe, in general terms, their logic.

FIGURE 7-63

Sample Data for the MI
Database SHIPPER Table

ShipperID	ShipperName	Phone	Fax	EmailAddress	Contact
1	ABC Trans-Oceanic	800-234-5656	800-234-5659	Sales@ABCTransOceanic.com	Jonathan
2	International	800-123-8898	800-123-8899	Sales@International.com	Marylin
3	Worldwide	800-123-4567	800-123-4569	Sales@worldwide.com	Jose

ShipmentID	ShipperID	PurchasingAgentID	ShipperInvoiceNumber	Origin	Destination	ScheduledDepartureDate	ActualDepartureDate	EstimatedArrivalDate
100	1	103	2010651	Manila	Los Angeles	10-Dec-14	10-Dec-14	15-Mar-15
101	1	104	2011012	Hong Kong	Seattle	10-Jan-15	12-Jan-15	20-Mar-15
102	3	103	49100300	Manila	Los Angeles	05-May-15	05-May-15	17-Jun-15
103	2	104	399400	Singapore	Portland	02-Jun-15	04-Jun-15	17-Jul-15
104	3	103	84899440	Lima	Los Angeles	10-Jul-15	10-Jul-15	28-Jul-15
105	2	104	488955	Singapore	Portland	05-Aug-15	09-Aug-15	11-Sep-15

FIGURE 7-64

Sample Data for the MI
Database SHIPMENT Table

FIGURE 7-65

Sample Data for the MI
Database SHIPMENT_ITEM
Table

ShipmentID	ShipmentItemID	PurchaseItemID	InsuredValue
100	1	500	$15,000.00
100	2	505	$15,000.00
101	1	510	$40,000.00
101	2	515	$3,500.00
102	1	520	$15,000.00
103	1	525	$90,000.00
103	2	530	$25,000.00
103	3	535	$150,000.00
103	4	540	$12,500.00
104	1	545	$12,500.00
104	2	550	$5,500.00
105	1	555	$4,500.00
105	2	560	$10,000.00
105	3	565	$1,500.00

FIGURE 7-66

Sample Data for the MI
Database SHIPMENT_
RECEIPT Table

ReceiptNumber	ShipmentID	ItemID	ReceivingAgentID	ReceiptDate	ReceiptTime	ReceiptQuantity	isReceivedUndamaged	DamageNotes
200001	100	500	105	17-Mar-15	10:00 AM	3	Yes	NULL
200002	100	505	105	17-Mar-15	10:00 AM	50	Yes	NULL
200003	101	510	105	23-Mar-15	3:30 PM	100	Yes	NULL
200004	101	515	105	23-Mar-15	3:30 PM	10	Yes	NULL
200005	102	520	106	19-Jun-15	10:15 AM	1	No	One leg on one chair broken.
200006	103	525	106	20-Jul-15	2:20 AM	1000	Yes	NULL
200007	103	530	106	20-Jul-15	2:20 AM	100	Yes	NULL
200008	103	535	106	20-Jul-15	2:20 AM	100	Yes	NULL
200009	103	540	106	20-Jul-15	2:20 AM	10	Yes	NULL
200010	104	545	105	29-Jul-15	9:00 PM	100	Yes	NULL
200011	104	550	105	29-Jul-15	9:00 PM	5	Yes	NULL
200012	105	555	106	14-Sep-15	2:45 PM	4	Yes	NULL
200013	105	560	106	14-Sep-15	2:45 PM	1	Yes	NULL
200014	105	565	106	14-Sep-15	2:45 PM	10	No	Base of one lamp scratched

8

Database Redesign

Chapter Objectives

- To understand the need for database redesign
- To be able to use correlated subqueries
- To be able to use the SQL EXISTS and NOT EXISTS comparison operators in correlated subqueries
- To understand reverse engineering
- To be able to use dependency graphs
- To be able to change table names
- To be able to change table columns
- To be able to change relationship cardinalities
- To be able to change relationship properties
- To be able to add and delete relationships

As stated in Chapter 1, database design and implementation is needed for three reasons. Databases can be created (1) from existing data (such as spreadsheets and databases tables), (2) for a new systems development project, or (3) for a database redesign. We have discussed the first two sources in Chapters 2 through 7. In this chapter, we will discuss the last source: database redesign.

We begin with a discussion of the need for database redesign, and then we will describe two important SQL statements: correlated subqueries and EXISTS. These statements play an important role when analyzing data prior to redesign. They also can be used for advanced queries and are important in their own right. After that discussion, we will turn to a variety of common database redesign tasks.

The Need for Database Redesign

You may be wondering, "Why do we have to redesign a database? If we build it correctly the first time, why would we ever need to redesign it?" This question has two answers. First, it is not easy to build a database correctly the first time, especially databases that arise from the development of new systems. Even if we obtain all of the users' requirements and build a correct data model, the transformation of that data model into a correct database design is difficult. For large databases, the tasks are daunting and may require several stages of development. During those stages, some aspects of the database will need to be redesigned. Also, inevitably, mistakes will be made that must be corrected.

The second answer to this question is the more important one. Reflect for a moment on the relationship between information systems and the organizations that use them. It is tempting to say that they influence each other; that is, that information systems influence organizations and that organizations influence information systems.

In truth, however, the relationship is much stronger than that. Information systems and organizations do not just influence each other; they *create* each other. When a new information system is installed, the users can behave in new ways. As the users behave in those new ways, they will want changes to the information system to accommodate their new behaviors. As those changes are made, the users will have more new behaviors, they will request more changes to the information system, and so forth, in a never-ending cycle.

We are now in the **system maintenance** step of the **systems development life cycle (SDLC)** in the **systems analysis and design** process. This is the SDLC step where we face the fact that revising an information system is a natural step in using and maintaining that information system. (For an introduction to systems analysis and design and to the SDLC, see Appendix B.) The system maintenance step may therefore result in the need for a redesigned and reimplemented system and thus start a new iteration of the SDLC. This circular process means that changes to an information system are not the sad consequence of a poor implementation, but rather a natural outcome of information system use. Therefore, the need for change to information systems never goes away; it neither can nor should be removed by better requirements definition, better initial design, better implementation, or anything else. Instead, change is part and parcel of information systems use. Thus, we need to plan for it. In the context of database processing, this means we need to know how to perform database redesign.

SQL Statements for Checking Functional Dependencies

Database redesign is not terribly difficult if the database has no data. The serious difficulties arise when we have to change a database that has data and when we want to make changes with minimum impact on existing data. Telling the users that the system now works the way they want but that all of their data were lost while making the change is not acceptable.

Often, we need to know whether certain conditions or assumptions are valid in the data before we can proceed with a change. For example, we may know from user requirements that Department functionally determines DeptPhone, but we may not know whether that functional dependency is correctly represented in all of the data.

Recall from Chapter 3 that if Department determines DeptPhone, every value of Department must be paired with the same value of DeptPhone. If, for example, Accounting has a DeptPhone value of 834-1100 in one row, it should have that value in every row in which it appears. Similarly, if Finance has a DeptPhone of 834-2100 in one row, it should have that value in all rows in which it appears. Figure 8-1 shows data that violate this assumption. In the third row, the DeptPhone for Finance is different than for the other rows; it has too many zeroes. Most likely, someone made a keying mistake when entering DeptPhone. Such errors are typical.

Now, before we make a database change, we need to find all such violations and correct them. For the small table shown in Figure 8-1, we can just look at the data, but what if the EMPLOYEE table has 4,000 rows? Two SQL statements are particularly helpful in this regard: correlated subqueries and their cousins, the SQL EXISTS and NOT EXISTS keywords. We will consider each of these in turn.

FIGURE 8-1

Table Showing Constraint
Assumption Violation

EmployeeNumber	LastName	EmailAddress	Department	DeptPhone
100	Johnson	JJ@somewhere.com	Accounting	834-1100
200	Abernathy	MA@somewhere.com	Finance	834-2100
300	Smathers	LS@somewhere.com	Finance	834-21000
400	Caruthers	TC@somewhere.com	Accounting	834-1100
500	Jackson	TJ@somewhere.com	Production	834-4100
600	Caldera	EC@somewhere.com	Legal	834-3100
700	Bandalone	RB@somewhere.com	Legal	834-3100

What Is a Correlated Subquery?

A **correlated subquery** looks very much like the noncorrelated subqueries we discussed in Chapter 2, but, in actuality, correlated subqueries are very different. To understand the difference, consider the following noncorrelated subquery, which is like those in Chapter 2:

```
/* *** SQL-Query-CH08-01 *** */
SELECT       A.FirstName, A.lastName
FROM         ARTIST AS A
WHERE        A.ArtistID IN
             (SELECT      W.ArtistID
              FROM        WORK AS W
              WHERE       W.Title = 'Blue Interior');
```

The DBMS can process such subqueries from the bottom up; that is, it can first find all of the values of ArtistID in WORK that have the title 'Blue Interior' and then process the upper query using that set of values. There is no need to move back and forth between the two SELECT statements. The result of this query is the artist Mark Tobey, as we would expect based on the data in Figure 7-15:

	First Name	Last Name
1	Mark	Tobey

Searching for Multiple Rows with a Given Title

Now, to introduce correlated subqueries, suppose that someone at View Ridge Gallery proposes that the Title column of WORK be an alternate key. If you look at the data in Figure 7-15(d), you can see that although there is only one copy of 'Blue Interior', there are two or more copies of other titles, such as 'Surf and Bird'. Therefore, Title cannot be an alternate key, and we can determine this by simply looking at the dataset.

However, if the WORK table had 10,000 or more rows, this would be difficult to determine. In that case, we need a query that examines the WORK table and displays the Title and Copy of any works that share the same title.

If we were asked to write a program to perform such a query, our logic would be as follows: Take the value of Title from the first row in WORK and examine all of the other rows in the table. If we find a row that has the same title as the one in the first row, we know there are duplicates, so we print the Title and Copy of the first work. We continue searching for duplicate title values until we come to the end of the WORK table.

Then we take the value of Title in the second row and compare it with all other rows in the WORK table, printing out the Title and Copy of any duplicate works. We proceed in this way until all rows of WORK have been examined.

A Correlated Subquery That Finds Rows with the Same Title
The following correlated subquery performs the action just described:

```
/* *** SQL-Query-CH08-02 *** */
SELECT      W1.Title, W1.Copy
FROM        WORK AS W1
WHERE       W1.Title IN
                (SELECT     W2.Title
                 FROM       WORK AS W2
                 WHERE      W1.Title = W2.Title
                   AND      W1.WorkID <> W2.WorkID);
```

The result of this query for the data in Figure 7-15(d) is:

	Title	Copy
1	Farmer's Market #2	267/500
2	Farmer's Market #2	268/500
3	Spanish Dancer	583/750
4	Spanish Dancer	588/750
5	Surf and Bird	142/500
6	Surf and Bird	362/500
7	Surf and Bird	365/500
8	Surf and Bird	366/500
9	Surf and Bird	Unique
10	The Fiddler	251/1000
11	The Fiddler	252/1000

Looking at these results, it is easy to see the nonunique, duplicated Title data that prevents Title from being used as an alternate key. When you are interpreting these results, note that a value of *Unique* in the Copy column indicates the original piece of art itself, which is by definition unique. Numbers such as *142/500* indicate one numbered print from a set of numbered reproduction prints of that artwork.

This subquery, which is a correlated subquery, looks deceptively similar to a regular, noncorrelated subquery. To the surprise of many students, this subquery and the one above are drastically different. Their similarity is only superficial.

Before learning why, first notice the notation in the correlated subquery. The WORK table is used in both the upper and the lower SELECT statements. In the upper statement, it is given the alias W1; in the lower SELECT statement, it is given the alias W2.

In essence, when we use this notation, it is as if we have made two copies of the WORK table. One copy is called W1, and the second copy is called W2. Therefore, in the last two lines of the correlated subquery, values in the W1 copy of WORK are compared with values in the W2 copy.

What Is the Difference Between Regular and Correlated Subqueries?
Now consider what makes this subquery so different. Unlike with a regular, noncorrelated subquery, the DBMS cannot run the bottom SELECT by itself, obtain a set of Titles, and then use that set to execute the upper query. The reason for this appears in the last two lines of the query:

```
WHERE     W1.Title = W2.Title
  AND     W1.WorkID <> W2.WorkID);
```

In these expressions, W1.Title (from the top SELECT statement) is being compared with W2.Title (from the bottom SELECT statement). The same is true for W1.WorkID and

W2.WorkID. Because of this fact, the DBMS cannot process the subquery portion independent of the upper SELECT.

Instead, the DBMS must process this statement as a subquery that is *nested* within the main query. The logic is as follows: Take the first row from W1. Using that row, evaluate the second query. To do that, for each row in W2, compare W1.Title with W2.Title and W1.WorkID with W2.WorkID. If the titles are equal and the values of WorkID are not equal, return the value of W2.Title to the upper query. Do this for every row in W2.

Once all of the rows in W2 have been evaluated for the first row in W1, move to the second row in W1 and evaluate it against all the rows in W2. Continue in this way until all rows of W1 have been compared with all of the rows of W2.

If this is not clear to you, write out two copies of the WORK data from Figure 7-15(d) on a piece of scratch paper. Label one of them W1 and the second W2, and then work through the logic as described. From this, you will see that correlated subqueries always require nested processing.

A Common Trap

By the way, do not fall into the following common trap:

```
/* *** SQL-Query-CH08-03 *** */
SELECT      W1.Title, W1.Copy
FROM        WORK AS W1
WHERE       W1.WorkID IN
            (SELECT       W2.WorkID
             FROM         WORK AS W2
             WHERE        W1.Title = W2.Title
                AND       W1.WorkID <> W2.WorkID);
```

The logic here seems correct, but it is not. Compare SQL-Query-CH08-03 to SQL-Query-CH08-02, and note the differences between the two SQL statements. The result of SQL-Query-CH08-03 when run on the View Ridge Gallery data in Figure 7-15(d) is an empty set:

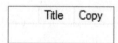

In fact, *no row will ever be displayed by this query*, regardless of the underlying data (see if you can figure out why this is so before continuing to the next paragraph).

The bottom query will indeed find all rows that have the same title and different WorkIDs. If one is found, it will produce the W2.WorkID of that row. But that value will then be compared with W1.WorkID. *These two values will always be different because of the condition*

```
W1.WorkID <> W2.WorkID
```

No rows are returned because the values of the two unequal WorkIDs are used in the IN instead of the values of the two equal Titles.

Using Correlated Subqueries to Check Functional Dependencies

Correlated subqueries can be used to your advantage during database redesign. As mentioned, one application of correlated subqueries is to verify functional dependencies. For example, suppose we have EMPLOYEE data like that in Figure 8-1 in a database and that we want to know whether the data conform to the functional dependency:

Department → DeptPhone

If so, every time a given value of Department occurs in the table, that value will be matched with the same value of DeptPhone.

The following correlated subquery will find any rows that violate this assumption:

```
/* *** SQL-Query-CH08-04 *** */
SELECT      E1.EmployeeNumber, E1.Department, E1.DeptPhone
FROM        EMPLOYEE AS E1
WHERE       E1.Department IN
            (SELECT      E2.Department
             FROM        EMPLOYEE AS E2
             WHERE       E1.Department = E2.Department
             AND         E1.DeptPhone <> E2.DeptPhone);
```

The results of this query for the data in Figure 8-1 are:

	EmployeeNumber	Department	DeptPhone
1	200	Finance	834-2100
2	300	Finance	834-21000

A listing like this can readily be used to find and fix any rows that violate the functional dependency.

SQL Correlated Subquiries Using the EXISTS and NOT EXISTS Comparison Operators

In Chapter 2, we discussed a set of SQL comparison operators, and these are summarized in Figure 2-23. To this set we will now add the **SQL EXISTS comparison operator** and the **SQL NOT EXISTS comparison operator**, as shown in Figure 8-2. When we use the EXIST or NOT EXISTS operator in a query, we are creating another form of correlated subquery.

These operators simply test whether or not there are *any* values returned by the subquery, which indicates there are values meeting the conditions of the subquery. If one or more values are returned, then values from the subquery are used to run the top-level query. If there are no values returned, the top-level query produces an empty set as the result.

For example, we can rewrite the SQL-Query-CH08-4 correlated subquery using the SQL EXISTS keyword as follows:

```
/* *** SQL-Query-CH08-05 *** */
SELECT      E1.EmployeeNumber, E1.Department, E1.DeptPhone
FROM        EMPLOYEE AS E1
WHERE       EXISTS
            (SELECT      E2.Department
             FROM        EMPLOYEE AS E2
             WHERE       E1.Department = E2.Department
             AND         E1.DeptPhone <> E2.DeptPhone);
```

Because using EXISTS creates a form of a correlated subquery, the processing of the SELECT statements is nested. The first row of E1 is input to the subquery. If the subquery

FIGURE 8-2

SQL Comparison Operators
EXISTS and NOT EXISTS

SQL Comparison Operators	
Operator	**Meaning**
EXISTS	Is a non-empty set of values
NOT EXISTS	Is an empty set

finds any row in E2 for which the department names are the same and the department phone numbers are different, then the EXISTS is *true* (returns a non-empty set of values) and the Department and DeptPhone for the first row are selected. Next, the second row of E1 is input to the subquery, the SELECT is processed, and the EXISTS is evaluated. If true, the Department and DeptPhone of the second row are selected. This process is repeated for all of the rows in E1.

The results of SQL-Query-CH08-05 are identical to the previous results from SQL-Query-CH08-04:

	EmployeeNumber	Department	DeptPhone
1	200	Finance	834-2100
2	300	Finance	834-21000

Using NOT EXISTS in a Double Negative

The SQL EXISTS operator will be true (will return a non-empty set of values) if *any* row in the subquery *meets the condition*. The SQL NOT EXISTS operator will be true (will return an empty set) only if *all* rows in the subquery *fail to meet the condition*. Consequently, the double use of NOT EXISTS can be used to find rows that do not *not match a condition*. And, yes, the word *not* is supposed to be there twice—this is a *double negative*.

Because of the logic of a double negative, if a row does not *not match any row*, then it *matches every row*! For example, suppose that at View Ridge the users want to know the name of any artist that *every* customer is interested in. We can proceed as follows:

- First, produce the set of all customers who are interested in a particular artist.
- Then take the complement of that set, which will be the customers who are *not* interested in that artist.
- If that complement is an empty set, then *all* customers are interested in the given artist.

> **BY THE WAY** The doubly nested NOT EXISTS pattern is famous in one guise or another among SQL practitioners. It is often used as a test of SQL knowledge in job interviews and in bragging sessions, and it can be used to your advantage when assessing the desirability of certain database redesign possibilities, as you will see in the last section of this chapter. Therefore, even though this example involves some serious study, it is worth your while to understand it.

The Double NOT EXISTS Query

The following SQL statement implements the strategy just described:

```
/* *** SQL-Query-CH08-06 *** */
SELECT      A.FirstName, A.LastName
FROM        ARTIST AS A
WHERE       NOT EXISTS
            (SELECT      C.CustomerID
             FROM        CUSTOMER AS C
             WHERE       NOT EXISTS
                         (SELECT      CAI.CustomerID
                          FROM        CUSTOMER_ARTIST_INT AS CAI
                          WHERE       C.CustomerID = CAI.CustomerID
                          AND         A.ArtistID = CAI.ArtistID));
```

The result of this query is an empty set, indicating that there is *no* artist that *every* customer is interested in:

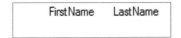

Let's see how this works. The bottom SELECT (the third SELECT in the SQL statement) finds all of the customers who are interested in a particular artist. As you read this SELECT (the last SELECT in the query), keep in mind that this is a correlated subquery; this SELECT is nested inside the query on CUSTOMER, which is nested inside the query on ARTIST. C.CustomerID is coming from the SELECT on CUSTOMER in the middle, and A.ArtistID is coming from the SELECT on ARTIST at the top.

Now the NOT EXISTS in the sixth line of the query will find the customers who are *not* interested in the given artist. If *all* customers are interested in the given artist, the result of the middle SELECT will be *null*. If the result of the middle SELECT is null, the NOT EXISTS in the third line of the query will be *true*, and the name of that artist will be produced, just as we want.

Consider what happens for artists who do not qualify in this query. Suppose that every customer except Tiffany Twilight is interested in the artist Joan Miro. (This is *not* the case for the data in Figure 7-15, but assume that it were true.) Now, for the preceding query, when Miro's row is considered, the bottom SELECT will retrieve every customer *except* Tiffany Twilight. In this case, because of the NOT EXISTS in the sixth line of the query, the middle SELECT will produce the CustomerID for Tiffany Twilight (because her row is the only one that does not appear in the bottom SELECT). Now, because there *is* a result from the middle SELECT, the NOT EXISTS in the top SELECT is *false*, and the name Joan Miro will *not* be included in the output of the query. This is correct because there is a customer who is not interested in Joan Miro.

Again, take some time to study this pattern. It is a famous one, and if you become a database professional, you will certainly see it again in one form or another. In fact, you will *not not* see it again!

How Do I Analyze an Existing Database?

Before we proceed with a discussion of database redesign, reflect for a moment on what this task means for a real company whose operations are dependent on the database. Suppose, for example, that you work for a company such as Amazon.com. Further suppose that you have been tasked with an important database redesign assignment, say to change the primary key of the vendor table.

To begin, you may wonder, why would Amazon want to do this? It could be that in the early days, when it only sold books, Amazon used company names for vendors. But, as Amazon began to sell more types of products, company name was no longer sufficient. Perhaps there are too many duplicates, and Amazon may have decided to switch to an Amazon-created VendorID.

Now, what does it mean to switch primary keys? Besides adding the new data to the correct rows, what else does it mean? Clearly, if the old primary key has been used as a foreign key, all of the foreign keys need to be changed as well. So we need to know all of the relationships in which the old primary key was used. But what about views? Do any views use the old primary key? If so, they will need to be changed. What about triggers and stored procedures? Do any of them use the old primary key? Not to mention any application code that may break when the old key is removed.

Now, to create a nightmare, what happens if you get partway through the change process and something fails? Suppose you encounter unexpected data and receive errors from the DBMS while trying to add the new primary key. Amazon cannot change its Web site to display, "Sorry, our database is broken—come back tomorrow (we hope)!"

This nightmare brings up many topics, most of which relate to systems analysis and design (see Appendix B for a brief introduction to systems analysis and design). But with regard to database processing, three principles become clear. First, as carpenters say, "Measure twice and cut once." Before we attempt any structural changes to a database, we must clearly understand the current structure and contents of the database, and we must know what depends on what. Second, before we make any structural changes to an operational database, we must test those changes on a realistically sized test database that has all of the important test data cases. Finally, if at all possible, we need to create a complete backup of the operational database prior to making any structural changes. If all goes awry, the backup can be used to restore the database while problems are corrected. We will consider each of these important topics next.

Reverse Engineering

Reverse engineering is the process of reading a database schema and producing a data model from that schema. The data model produced is not truly a logical model because entities will be generated for every table, including entities for intersection tables that have no non-key data and should not appear in a logical model at all. The model generated by reverse engineering is a thing unto itself, a table-relationship diagram that is dressed in entity-relationship clothes. In this text, we will call it the **reverse engineered (RE) data model**.

Figure 8-3 shows the RE data model of the View Ridge Gallery VRG database produced by the MySQL Workbench from a MySQL 5.6 version of the VRG database created in Chapter 7. Note that due to the limitations of the MySQL Workbench, this is a physical database design rather than a logical data model. Nonetheless, it illustrates the reverse engineering technique we are discussing.

We used the MySQL Workbench because of its general availability. The MySQL Workbench, as discussed in Appendix E, uses standard IE Crow's Foot database modeling notation. Figure 6-37 shows the VRG data model, and Figure 6-39 shows the VRG database design.

If you compare these to the VRG RE data model in Figure 8-3, you will see that the MySQL Workbench came close to duplicating the VRG database design rather than the VRG data model. The MySQL Workbench:

- Contains the final *primary keys* and *foreign keys*, rather than the data model entity indentifiers.
- Contains the *customer_artist_int* table, rather than the N:M relationship between CUSTOMER and ARTIST shown in the data model.
- Contains wrong *minimum cardinality* values. All of the many sides of the 1:N relationships should be optional except for the WORK-to-TRANS relationship, based on the VRG database design.

All in all, however, this is a reasonable representation of the View Ridge Gallery database design. For more information about using the MySQL Workbench, see Appendix E.

FIGURE 8-3

Reverse-Engineered VRG Data Model

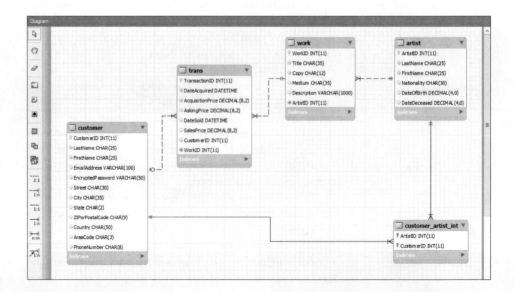

Although the MySQL Workbench produces only a database design and not a data model, some other design software, such as CA Technologies' ERwin, can create both logical (data model) and physical (database design) versions of the database structure. In addition to tables and views, some data modeling products will capture constraints, triggers, and stored procedures from the database (in fact, the MySQL Workbench can capture some of these, although we have not included them in Figure 8-3).

These constructs are not interpreted, but their text is imported into the data model. With some products, the relationship of the text to the items it references also is obtained. The redesign of constraints, triggers, and stored procedures is beyond the scope of our discussion here. You should realize that they, too, are part of the database, however, and are subject to redesign.

Dependency Graphs

Before making changes to database structures, it is vitally important to understand the dependencies of those structures. What changes will affect what? For example, consider changing the name of a table. Where is the table name used? In which triggers? In which stored procedures? In which relationships? Because of the need to know all of the dependencies, many database redesign projects begin by making a **dependency graph**.

The term *graph* arises from the mathematical topic of graph theory. Dependency graphs are not graphical displays like bar charts; rather, they are diagrams that consist of nodes and arcs (or lines) that connect those nodes.

Figure 8-4 shows a partial dependency graph that was drawn using the results of the RE model but manually interpreting views and triggers we developed in Chapter 7. For simplicity, this graph does not show the views and triggers of CUSTOMER, nor does it show CUSTOMER_ARTIST_INT and related structures. Also, the stored procedure WORK_AddWorkTransaction is not shown, nor are the constraints.

Even this partial diagram reveals the complexity of dependencies among database constructs. You can see that it would be wise to tread lightly, for example, when changing anything in the TRANS table. The consequences of such a change need to be assessed against two relationships, two triggers, and two views. Again, measure twice and cut once!

Database Backup and Test Databases

Because of the potential damage that can be done to a database during redesign, a complete backup of the operational database should be made prior to making any changes. Equally important, it is essential that any proposed changes be thoroughly tested. Not only must structural changes proceed successfully, but all triggers, stored procedures, and applications must also run correctly on the revised database.

FIGURE 8-4

Example Dependency
Graph (Partial)

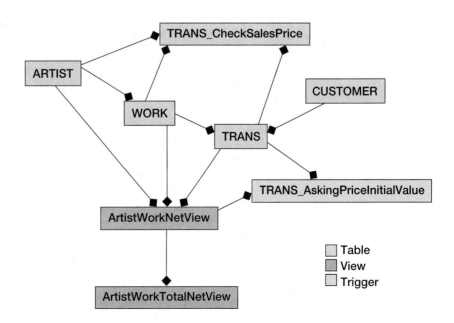

Typically, at least three different copies of the database schema are used in the redesign process. One is a small test database that can be used for initial testing. The second is a large test database, which may even be a full copy of the operational database. Sometimes, there are several large test databases. Finally, there is the operational database.

A means must be created to restore all test databases to their original state during the testing process. In that way, the test can be rerun as necessary against the same starting point. Depending on the facilities of the DBMS, backup and recovery or other means are used to restore the database after a test run.

Obviously, for enterprises with very large databases, it is not possible to have a test database that is a copy of the operational database. Instead, smaller test databases need to be created, but those test databases must have all the important data characteristics of the operational database; otherwise, they will not provide a realistic test environment. The construction of such test databases is in itself a difficult and challenging job. In fact, many interesting career opportunities are available for developing test databases and database test suites.

Finally, for organizations that have very large databases, it may not be possible to make a complete copy of the operational database prior to making structural changes. In this case, the database is backed up in pieces, and the changes are made in pieces as well. This task is very difficult and requires great knowledge and expertise. It also requires weeks or months of planning. You may participate as a junior member of a team to make such a change, but you should have years of database experience before you attempt to make structural changes to such large databases. Even then, it is a daunting task.

Changing Table Names and Table Columns

In this section, we will consider alterations to tables and their columns. To accomplish these changes, we will use only SQL statements. Many DBMS products have features to facilitate changing structures other than SQL. For example, some products have graphical design tools that simplify this process. But such features are not standardized, and you should not depend on them. The statements shown in this chapter will work with any enterprise-class DBMS product, and most will work with Microsoft Access as well.

Changing Table Names

At first glance, changing a table name seems like an innocent and easy operation. A review of Figure 8-3, however, shows that the consequences of such a change are greater than you would think. If, for example, we want to change the name of the table WORK to WORK_VERSION2, several tasks are necessary. The constraint that defines the relationship from WORK to TRANS must be altered, ArtistWorkNetView view must be redefined, and then the TRANS_CheckSalesPrice trigger must be rewritten to use the new name.

Oracle Database and MySQL have an SQL RENAME {Name01} TO {Name02} statement that can be used to rename tables, while Microsoft SQL Server uses the system stored procedure *sp_rename* to accomplish the same task. However, while the table name itself is changed, other objects that use that table name, such as triggers and stored procedures, will *not* be modified! Therefore, these methods of renaming a table are useful only in certain situations. Instead, we will use the following strategy for making table name changes. First, create the new table with all attendant structures and then drop the old one once everything is working with the new table. If the table to be renamed is too large to be copied, other strategies will have to be used, but they are beyond the scope of this discussion.

This strategy has one serious problem, however. WorkID is a surrogate key. When we create the new table, the DBMS will create new values of WorkID in the new table. The new values will not necessarily match the values in the old table, which means values of the foreign key TRANS. WorkID will be wrong. The easiest way to solve this problem is to first create the new version of the WORK table and not define WorkID as a surrogate key. Then fill the table with the current values of WORK, including the current values of WorkID. Then change WorkID to a surrogate key.

First, we create the table by submitting an SQL CREATE TABLE WORK_VERSION2 statement to the DBMS. We make WorkID an integer, but not a surrogate key. We also must give new names to the WORK constraints. The prior constraints still exist, and if new names are not used, the DBMS will issue a duplicate constraint error when processing the CREATE TABLE statements. Examples of new constraint names are:

```
/* *** EXAMPLE CODE - DO NOT RUN *** */

CONSTRAINT      WorkV2PK         PRIMARY KEY (WorkID),

CONSTRAINT      WorkV2AK1        UNIQUE (Title, Copy),

CONSTRAINT      ArtistV2FK        FOREIGN KEY (ArtistID)

                         REFERENCES ARTIST (ArtistID)

                              ON DELETE NO ACTION

                              ON UPDATE NO ACTION
```

Next, copy the data into the new table with the following SQL statement:

```
/* *** EXAMPLE CODE - DO NOT RUN *** */
/* *** SQL-INSERT-CH08-01 *** */
INSERT INTO WORK_VERSION2

        (WorkID, Copy, Title, Medium, Description, ArtistID)

    SELECT    WorkID, Copy, Title, Medium, Description, ArtistID

    FROM      WORK;
```

At this point, alter the WORK_VERSION2 table to make WorkID a surrogate key. In Microsoft SQL Server, the easiest way to do that is to open the graphical table designer and redefine WorkID as an IDENTITY column (there is no standard SQL for making this change). Set the Identity Seed value [this is the same as the {StartValue} value that we have used when discussing the Microsoft SQL Server 2014 *IDENTITY({StartValue}, {Increment})* property] to the original value of 500, and Microsoft SQL Server will set the next new value of WorkID to be the maximum largest value of WorkID plus one. A different strategy is used for surrogate keys with Oracle Database and MySQL, and these topics will be discussed in Chapters 10B and 10C, respectively.

Now all that remains is to define the two triggers. This can be done by copying the text of the old triggers and changing the name WORK to WORK_VERSION2.

At this point, tests should be run against the database to verify that all changes have been made correctly. After that, stored procedures and applications that use WORK can be changed to run against the new table name.[1] If all is correct, then the foreign key constraint TransWorkFK and the WORK table can be dropped with the following:

```
/* *** EXAMPLE CODE - DO NOT RUN *** */
/* *** SQL-ALTER-TABLE-CH08-01 *** */
ALTER TABLE TRANS

    DROP CONSTRAINT TransWorkFK;
/* *** SQL-DROP-TABLE-CH08-01 *** */
DROP TABLE WORK;
```

---

[1]The timing is important. The WORK_VERSION2 table was created from WORK. If triggers, stored procedures, and applications continue to run against WORK while the verification of WORK_VERSION2 is under way, then WORK_VERSION2 will be out of date. Some action will need to be taken to bring it up to date before switching the stored procedures and applications over to WORK_VERSION2.

The TransWorkFK constraint then can be added back to TRANS using the new name for the work table:

```
/* *** EXAMPLE CODE - DO NOT RUN *** */
/* *** SQL-ALTER-TABLE-CH08-02 *** */
ALTER TABLE TRANS
    ADD CONSTRAINT       TransWorkFK      FOREIGN KEY(WorkID)
                         REFERENCES WORK_VERSION2(WorkID)
                             ON UPDATE NO ACTION
                             ON DELETE NO ACTION;
```

Clearly, there is more to changing a table name than you would think. You now can see why some organizations do not allow programmers or users to employ the true name of a table. Instead, views are described that serve as table aliases, as explained in Chapter 7. If this were done here, only the views that define the aliases would need to be changed when the source table name is changed *as long as* the view references all the columns in the table using the asterisk (*) wild card. However, if the view references the columns by name and if any column name has been changed, then more work will be needed to revise the view.

Adding and Dropping Columns

Adding null columns to a table is straightforward. For example, to add the null column DateCreated to WORK, we simply use the ALTER TABLE statement as follows:

```
/* *** SQL-ALTER-TABLE-CH08-03 *** */
ALTER TABLE WORK
    ADD  DateCreated   Date    NULL;
```

If there are other column constraints, such as DEFAULT or UNIQUE, include them with the column definition, just as you would if the column definition were part of a CREATE TABLE statement. However, if you include a DEFAULT constraint, be aware that the default value will be applied to all new rows, but existing rows will have null values.

Suppose, for example, that you want to set the default value of DateCreated to 1/1/1900 to signify that the value has not yet been entered. In this case, you would use the ALTER TABLE statement:

```
/* *** SQL-ALTER-TABLE-CH08-04 *** */
ALTER TABLE WORK
    ADD  DateCreated   Date    NULL DEFAULT '01/01/1900';
```

This statement causes DateCreated for new rows in WORK to be set to 1/1/1900 by default. To set existing rows, you would need to execute the following query:

```
/* *** SQL-UPDATE-CH08-01 *** */
UPDATE WORK
    SET        DateCreated ='01/01/1900'
    WHERE      DateCreated IS NULL;
```

Adding NOT NULL Columns

To add a new NOT NULL column, first add the column as NULL. Then use an UPDATE statement like that just shown to give the column a value in all rows. After the update, the following SQL ALTER TABLE ALTER COLUMN statement can be executed to change DateCreated from NULL to NOT NULL.

```
/* *** SQL-ALTER-TABLE-CH08-05 *** */
ALTER TABLE WORK
    ALTER COLUMN  DateCreated   Date   NOT NULL;
```

Note that this statement will fail if DateCreated has not been given values in all rows.

Dropping Columns

Dropping non-key columns is easy. For example, eliminating the DateCreated column from WORK can be done with the following:

```
/* *** SQL-ALTER-TABLE-CH08-06 *** */
ALTER TABLE WORK
    DROP COLUMN DateCreated;
```

To drop a foreign key column, the constraint that defines the foreign key must first be dropped. Making such a change is equivalent to dropping a relationship, and that topic is discussed later in this chapter.

To drop the primary key, the primary key constraint first needs to be dropped. To drop that, however, all foreign keys that use the primary key must first be dropped. Thus, to drop the primary key of WORK and replace it with the composite primary key (Title, Copy, ArtistID), the following steps are necessary:

- Drop the constraint WorkFK from TRANS.
- Drop the constraint WorkPK from WORK.
- Create a new WorkPK constraint using (Title, Copy, ArtistID).
- Create a new WorkFK constraint referencing (Title, Copy, ArtistID) in TRANS.
- Drop the column WorkID.

It is important to verify that all changes have been made correctly before dropping WorkID. Once it is dropped, there is no way to recover it except by restoring the WORK table from a backup.

Changing a Column Data Type or Column Constraints

To change a column data type or to change column constraints, the column is redefined using the ALTER TABLE ALTER COLUMN command. However, if the column is being changed from NULL to NOT NULL, then all rows must have a value in that column for the change to succeed.

Also, some data type changes may cause data loss. Changing Char(50) to Date, for example, will cause loss of any text field that the DBMS cannot successfully transform into a date value. Or, alternatively, the DBMS may simply refuse to make the column change. The results depend on the DBMS product in use.

Generally, converting numeric to Char or Varchar will succeed. Also, converting Date or Money or other more specific data types to Char or Varchar will usually succeed. Converting Char or Varchar back to Date, Money, or Numeric is risky, and it may or may not be possible.

In the View Ridge schema, if DateOfBirth had been defined as Char(4), then a risky but sensible data type change would be to modify DateOfBirth in the ARTIST table to Numeric(4,0).

This would be a sensible change because all of the values in this column are numeric. Recall the check constraint that was used to define DateOfBirth (refer to Figure 7-13). The following makes that change and simplifies the CHECK constraint.

```
/* *** EXAMPLE CODE - DO NOT RUN *** */
/* *** SQL-ALTER-TABLE-CH08-07 *** */
ALTER TABLE ARTIST
    ALTER COLUMN   DateOfBirth   Numeric(4,0)   NULL;
ALTER TABLE ARTIST
    ADD CONSTRAINT NumericBirthYearCheck
        CHECK (DateOfBirth > 1900 AND DateOfBirth < 2100);
```

The prior check constraints on DateOfBirth should now be deleted.

Adding and Dropping Constraints

As already shown, constraints can be added and removed using the ALTER TABLE ADD CONSTRAINT and ALTER TABLE DROP CONSTRAINT statements.

Changing Relationship Cardinalities

Changing cardinalities is a common database redesign task. Sometimes, the need is to change minimum cardinalities from zero to one or from one to zero. Another common task is to change the maximum cardinality from 1:1 to 1:N or from 1:N to N:M. Another possibility, which is less common, is to decrease maximum cardinality from N:M to 1:N or from 1:N to 1:1. This latter change can be made only with data loss, as you will see.

Changing Minimum Cardinalities

The action to be taken in changing minimum cardinalities depends on whether the change is on the parent side or on the child side of the relationship.

Changing Minimum Cardinalities on the Parent Side

If the change is on the parent side, meaning that the child will or will not be required to have a parent, making the change is a matter of changing whether null values are allowed for the foreign key that represents the relationship. For example, suppose that in the 1:N relationship from DEPARTMENT to EMPLOYEE the foreign key DepartmentNumber appears in the EMPLOYEE table. Changing whether an employee is required to have a department is simply a matter of changing the null status of DepartmentNumber.

If the change is from a minimum cardinality of zero to one, then the foreign key, which would have been null, must be changed to NOT NULL. Changing a column to NOT NULL can be done only if all the rows in the table have a value. In the case of a foreign key, this means that every record must already be related. If not, all records must be changed so that all have a relationship before the foreign key can be made NOT NULL. In the previous example, every employee must be related to a department before DepartmentNumber can be changed to NOT NULL.

Depending on the DBMS product in use, the foreign key constraint that defines the relationship may have to be dropped before the change is made to the foreign key. Then the foreign key constraint can be re-added. The following SQL will work for the preceding example:

```
/* *** EXAMPLE CODE - DO NOT RUN *** */
/* *** SQL-ALTER-TABLE-CH08-08 *** */
ALTER TABLE EMPLOYEE
    DROP CONSTRAINT DepartmentFK;
ALTER TABLE EMPLOYEE
    ALTER COLUMN   DepartmentNumber    Int    NOT NULL;
ALTER TABLE EMPLOYEE
    ADD CONSTRAINT DepartmentFK FOREIGN KEY (DepartmentNumber)
        REFERENCES DEPARTMENT (DepartmentNumber)
            ON UPDATE CASCADE;
```

Also, cascade behavior for UPDATE and DELETE must be specified when changing the minimum cardinality from zero to one. In this example, updates are to cascade, but deletions will not (recall that the default behavior is NO ACTION).

Changing the minimum cardinality from one to zero is simple. Just change DepartmentNumber from NOT NULL to NULL. You also may want to change the cascade behavior on updates and deletions, if appropriate.

Changing Minimum Cardinalities on the Child Side

As noted in Chapter 6, the only way to enforce a minimum cardinality other than zero on the child side of a relationship is to write triggers or application code that enforce the constraint.

So, to change the minimum cardinality from zero to one, it is necessary to write the appropriate triggers. Design the trigger behavior using Figure 6-29, and then write the triggers. To change the minimum cardinality from one to zero, just drop the triggers that enforce that constraint.

In the DEPARTMENT-to-EMPLOYEE relationship example, to require each DEPARTMENT to have an EMPLOYEE means that triggers would need to be written on INSERT of DEPARTMENT and on UPDATE and DELETE of EMPLOYEE. The trigger code in DEPARTMENT ensures that an EMPLOYEE is assigned to the new DEPARTMENT, and the trigger code in EMPLOYEE ensures that the employee being moved to a new department or the employee being deleted is not the last employee in the relationship to its parent.

This discussion assumes that the required child constraint is enforced by triggers. If the required child constraint is enforced by application programs, then all of those programs also must be changed. Dozens of programs may need to be changed, which is one reason why it is better to enforce such constraints using triggers rather than application code.

Changing Maximum Cardinalities

The only difficulty when increasing cardinalities from 1:1 to 1:N or from 1:N to N:M is preserving existing relationships. This can be done, but it requires a bit of manipulation, as you will see. When reducing cardinalities, relationship data will be lost. In this case, a policy must be created for deciding which relationships to lose.

Changing a 1:1 Relationship to a 1:N Relationship

Figure 8-5 shows a 1:1 relationship between EMPLOYEE and PARKING_PERMIT. As we discussed in Chapter 6, the foreign key can be placed in either table for a 1:1 relationship. The action taken depends on whether EMPLOYEE is to be the parent entity in the 1:N relationship or whether PARKING_PERMIT is to be the parent.

If EMPLOYEE is to be the parent (employees are to have multiple parking permits), then the only change necessary is to drop the constraint that PARKING_PERMIT. EmployeeNumber be unique. The relationship will then be 1:N.

If PARKING_PERMIT is to be the parent (e.g., if parking permits are to be allocated to many employees, say, for a carpool), then the foreign key and appropriate values must be moved from PARKING_PERMIT to EMPLOYEE. The following SQL will accomplish this:

```
/* *** EXAMPLE CODE - DO NOT RUN *** */
/* *** SQL-ALTER-TABLE-CH08-09 *** */
ALTER TABLE EMPLOYEE
    ADD  PermitNumber   Int      NULL;
/* *** SQL-UPDATE-CH08-02 *** */
UPDATE EMPLOYEE
    SET EMPLOYEE.PermitNumber =
        (SELECT    PP.PermitNumber
         FROM      PARKING_PERMIT AS PP
         WHERE     PP.EmployeeNumber = EMPLOYEE.EmployeeNumber);
```

Once the foreign key has been moved over to EMPLOYEE, the EmployeeNumber column of PARKING_PERMIT should be dropped. Next, create a new foreign key constraint to define referential integrity. So multiple employees can relate to the same parking permit, the new foreign key must not have a UNIQUE constraint.

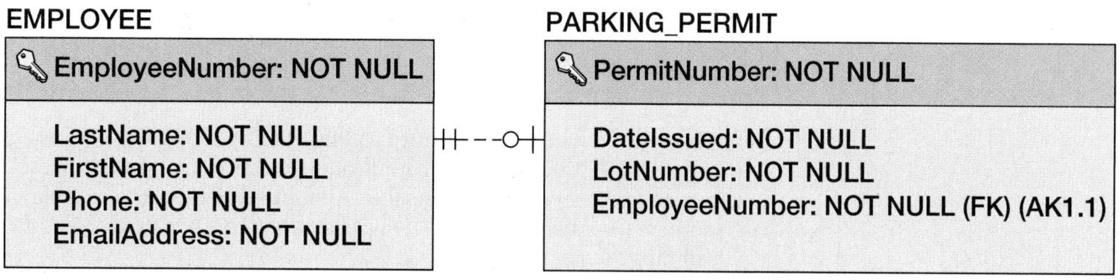

FIGURE 8-5

The Employee-to-Parking_Permit 1:1 Relationship

EMPLOYEE

🔑 **EmployeeNumber: NOT NULL**

LastName: NOT NULL
FirstName: NOT NULL
Phone: NOT NULL
EmailAddress: NOT NULL

PARKING_PERMIT

🔑 **PermitNumber: NOT NULL**

DateIssued: NOT NULL
LotNumber: NOT NULL
EmployeeNumber: NOT NULL (FK) (AK1.1)

Changing a 1:N Relationship to an N:M Relationship

Suppose that View Ridge Gallery decides that it wants to record multiple purchasers for a given transaction. It may be that some of its art is co-owned between a customer and a bank or trust account, for example; or perhaps it may want to record the names of both owners when a couple purchases art. For whatever reason, this change will require that the 1:N relationship between CUSTOMER and TRANS be changed to an N:M relationship.

Changing a 1:N relationship to an N:M relationship is surprisingly easy.[2] Just create the new intersection table with appropriate foreign key constraints, fill it with data, and drop the old foreign key column. Figure 8-6 shows the View Ridge database design with a new intersection table to support the N:M relationship.

We need to create this table and then copy the values of TransactionID and CustomerID from TRANS for rows in which CustomerID is not null. First, create the new intersection table using the following SQL:

```
/* *** EXAMPLE CODE - DO NOT RUN *** */
/* *** SQL-CREATE-TABLE-CH08-01 *** */
CREATE TABLE CUSTOMER_TRANSACTION_INT(
    CustomerID      Int  NOT NULL,
    TransactionID   Int  NOT NULL,
    CONSTRAINT      CustomerTransaction_PK
        PRIMARY KEY(CustomerID, TransactionID),
    CONSTRAINT      Customer_Transaction_Int_Trans_FK
        FOREIGN KEY (TransactionID) REFERENCES TRANS(TransactionID),
    CONSTRAINT          Customer_Transaction_Int_Customer_FK
        FOREIGN KEY (CustomerID) REFERENCES CUSTOMER(CustomerID)
    );
```

FIGURE 8-6

View Ridge Gallery Database Design with New N:M Relationship

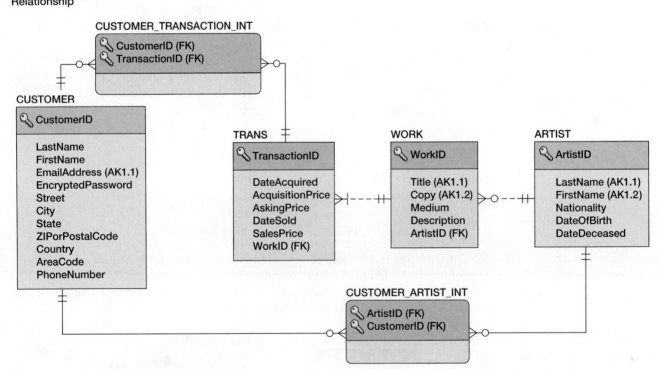

---

[2]Making the data change is easy. Dealing with the consequences of the data change with regard to views, triggers, stored procedures, and application code will be more difficult. All of these will need to be rewritten to join across a new intersection table. All forms and reports also will need to be changed to portray multiple customers for a transaction; this will mean changing text boxes to grids, for example. All of this work is time consuming and, hence, expensive.

Note that there is no cascade behavior for updates because CustomerID is a surrogate key. There is no cascade behavior for deletions because of the business policy never to delete data that involve transactions. The next task is to fill the table with data from the TRANS table using the following SQL statement:

```
/* *** EXAMPLE CODE - DO NOT RUN *** */
/* *** SQL-INSERT-CH08-02 *** */
INSERT INTO CUSTOMER_TRANSACTION_INT (CustomerID, TransactionID)
    SELECT      CustomerID, TransactionID
    FROM        TRANS
    WHERE       CustomerID IS NOT NULL;
```

Once all of these changes have been made, the CustomerID column of TRANS can be dropped.

Reducing Cardinalities (with Data Loss)

It is easy to make the structural changes to reduce cardinalities. To reduce an N:M relationship to 1:N, we just create a new foreign key in the relation that will be the child and fill it with data from the intersection table. To reduce a 1:N relationship to 1:1, we just make the values of the foreign key of the 1:N relationship unique and then define a unique constraint on the foreign key. In either case, the most difficult problem is deciding which data to lose.

Consider the reduction of N:M to 1:N. Suppose, for example, that the View Ridge Gallery decides to keep just one artist interest for each customer. Thus, the relationship will then be 1:N from ARTIST to CUSTOMER. Accordingly, we add a new foreign key column ArtistID to CUSTOMER and set up a foreign key constraint to ARTIST on that customer. The following SQL will accomplish this:

```
/* *** EXAMPLE CODE - DO NOT RUN *** */
/* *** SQL-ALTER-TABLE-CH08-10 *** */
ALTER TABLE CUSTOMER
    ADD ArtistID   Int   NULL;
ALTER TABLE CUSTOMER
    ADD CONSTRAINT ArtistInterestFK FOREIGN KEY (ArtistID)
        REFERENCES ARTIST(ArtistID);
```

Updates need not cascade because of the surrogate key, and deletions cannot cascade because the customer may have a valid transaction and ought not to be deleted just because an artist interest goes away.

Now, which of a customer's potentially many artist interests should be preserved in the new relationship? The answer depends on the business policy at the gallery. Here suppose we decide simply to take the first artist interest:

```
/* *** EXAMPLE CODE - DO NOT RUN *** */
/* *** SQL-UPDATE-CH08-03 *** */
UPDATE      CUSTOMER
    SET       ArtistID =
              (SELECT     TOP 1 ArtistID
               FROM       CUSTOMER_ARTIST_INT AS CAI
               WHERE      CUSTOMER.CustomerID = CAI.CustomerID);
```

The SQL Top 1 phrase is used to return the first qualifying row.

All views, triggers, stored procedures, and application code need to be changed to account for the new 1:N relationship. Then the constraints defined on CUSTOMER_ ARTIST_INT can be dropped. Finally, the table CUSTOMER_ARTIST_INT can be dropped.

To change a 1:N to a 1:1 relationship, we just need to remove any duplicate values of the foreign key of the relationship and then add a unique constraint on the foreign key. See Review Question 8.51.

Adding and Deleting Tables and Relationships

Adding new tables and relationships is straightforward. Just add the tables and relationships using CREATE TABLE statements with FOREIGN KEY constraints, as shown before. If an existing table has a child relationship to the new table, add a FOREIGN KEY constraint using the existing table.

For example, if a new table, COUNTRY, were added to the View Ridge database with the primary key Name and if CUSTOMER.Country is to be used as a foreign key in the new table, a new FOREIGN KEY constraint would be defined in CUSTOMER:

```
/* *** EXAMPLE CODE – DO NOT RUN *** */
/* *** SQL-ALTER-TABLE-CH08-11 *** */
ALTER TABLE CUSTOMER
    ADD CONSTRAINT CountryFK FOREIGN KEY (Country)
        REFERENCES COUNTRY(Name)
            ON UPDATE CASCADE;
```

Deleting relationships and tables is just a matter of dropping the foreign key constraints and then dropping the tables. Of course, before this is done, dependency graphs must be constructed and used to determine which views, triggers, stored procedures, and application programs will be affected by the deletions.

As described in Chapter 4, another reason to add new tables and relationships or to compress existing tables into fewer tables is for normalization and denormalization. We will not address that topic further in this chapter, except to say that normalization and denormalization are common tasks during database redesign.

Forward Engineering

You can use a variety of different data modeling products to make database changes on your behalf. To do so, you first reverse engineer the database, make changes to the RE data model, and then invoke the forward engineering functionality of the data modeling tool.

We will not consider forward engineering here because it hides the SQL that you need to learn. Also, the specifics of the forward engineering process are product dependent.

Because of the importance of making data model changes correctly, many professionals are skeptical about using an automated process for database redesign. Certainly, it is necessary to test the results thoroughly before using forward engineering on operational data. Some products will show the SQL they are about to execute for review before making the changes to the database.

Database redesign is one area in which automation may not be the best idea. Much depends on the nature of the changes to be made and the quality of the forward engineering features of the data modeling product. Given the knowledge you have gained in this chapter, you should be able to make most redesign changes by writing your own SQL. There is nothing wrong with that approach!

Summary

Database design and implementation is needed for three reasons. Databases can be created (1) from existing data (such as spreadsheets and databases tables), (2) for a new systems development project, or (3) for a database redesign. Database redesign is part of the system maintenance step of the SDLC and is necessary both to fix mistakes made during the initial database design and also to adapt the database to changes in system requirements. Such changes are common because information systems and organizations do not just influence each other—they create each other. Thus, new information systems cause changes in systems requirements.

Correlated subqueries and SQL EXISTS and NOT EXISTS comparison operators are important tools. They can be used to answer advanced queries. They also are useful during database redesign for determining whether specified data conditions exist. For example, they can be used to determine whether possible functional dependencies exist in the data.

A correlated subquery appears deceptively similar to a regular subquery. The difference is that a regular subquery can be processed from the bottom up. In a regular subquery, results from the lowest query can be determined and then used to evaluate the upper-level queries. In contrast, in a correlated subquery, the processing is nested; that is, a row from an upper-level query statement is compared with rows in a lower-level query. The key distinction of a correlated subquery is that the lower-level SELECT statements use columns from upper-level statements.

The SQL EXISTS and NOT EXISTS keywords create specialized forms of correlated subqueries. When these are used, the upper-level query produces results, depending on the existence or nonexistence of rows in lower-level queries. An EXISTS condition is true if any row in the subquery meets the specified conditions; a NOT EXISTS condition is true only if all rows in the subquery do not meet the specified condition. NOT EXISTS is useful for queries that involve conditions that must be true for all rows, such as a "customer who has purchased all products." The double use of NOT EXISTS is a famous SQL pattern that often is used to test a person's knowledge of SQL.

Before redesigning a database, the existing database needs to be carefully examined to avoid making the database unusable by partially processing a database change. The rule is to measure twice and cut once. Reverse engineering is used to create a data model of the existing database. This is done to better understand the database structure before proceeding with a change. The data model produced, called a reverse engineered (RE) data model, is not a true data model but is a thing unto itself. Most data modeling tools can perform reverse engineering. The RE data model almost always has missing information; such models should be carefully reviewed.

All of the elements of a database are interrelated. Dependency graphs are used to portray the dependency of one element on another. For example, a change in a table can potentially affect relationships, views, indexes, triggers, stored procedures, and application programs. These impacts need to be known and accounted for before making database changes.

A complete backup must be made to the operational database prior to any database redesign changes. Additionally, such changes must be thoroughly tested, initially on small test databases and later on larger test databases that may even be duplicates of the operational databases. The redesign changes are made only after such extensive testing has been completed.

Database redesign changes can be grouped into different types. One type involves changing table names and table columns. Changing a table name has a surprising number of potential consequences. A dependency graph should be used to understand these consequences before proceeding with the change. Non-key columns are readily added and deleted. Adding a NOT NULL column must be done in three steps: First, add the column as NULL; then add data to every row; and then alter the column constraint to NOT NULL. To drop a column used as a foreign key, the foreign key constraint must first be dropped.

Column data types and constraints can be changed using the ALTER TABLE ALTER COLUMN statement. Changing the data type to Char or Varchar from a more specific type, such as Date, is usually not a problem. Changing a data type from Char or Varchar to a more specific type can be a problem. In some cases, data will be lost or the DBMS may refuse the change.

Constraints can be added or dropped using the ADD CONSTRAINT and DROP CONSTRAINT with the SQL ALTER TABLE statement. Use of this statement is easier if the developers have provided their own names for all constraints.

Changing minimum cardinalities on the parent side of a relationship is simply a matter of altering the constraint on the foreign key from NULL to NOT NULL or from NOT NULL to NULL. Changing minimum cardinalities on the child side of a relationship can be accomplished only by adding or dropping triggers that enforce the constraint.

Changing maximum cardinality from 1:1 to 1:N is simple if the foreign key resides in the correct table. In that case, just remove the unique constraint on the foreign key column. If the foreign key resides in the wrong table for this change, move the foreign key to the other table and do not place a unique constraint on that table.

Changing a 1:N relationship to an N:M relationship requires building a new intersection table and moving the primary key and foreign key values to the intersection table. This aspect of the change is relatively simple. It is more difficult to change all of the views, triggers, stored procedures, application programs, and forms and reports to use the new intersection table.

Reducing cardinalities is easy, but such changes may result in data loss. Prior to making such reductions, a policy must be determined to decide which data to keep. Changing N:M to 1:N involves creating a foreign key in the child table and moving one value from the intersection table into that foreign key. Changing 1:N to 1:1 requires first eliminating duplicates in the foreign key and then setting a uniqueness constraint on that key. Adding and deleting relationships can be accomplished by defining new foreign key constraints or by dropping existing foreign key constraints.

Most data modeling tools have the capacity to perform forward engineering, which is the process of applying data model changes to an existing database. If forward engineering is used, the results should be thoroughly tested before using it on an operational database. Some tools will show the SQL that they will execute during the forward engineering process. Any SQL generated by such tools should be carefully reviewed. All in all, there is nothing wrong with writing database redesign SQL statements by hand rather than using forward engineering.

Key Terms

correlated subquery
dependency graph
reverse engineered (RE) data model

SQL EXISTS comparison operator
SQL NOT EXISTS comparison
 operator

systems analysis and design
systems development life cycle (SDLC)
system maintenance

Review Questions

8.1 Review the three sources of database design and implementation.

8.2 Describe why database redesign is necessary.

8.3 Explain the following statement in your own words: "Information systems and organizations create each other." How does this relate to database redesign?

8.4 Suppose that a table contains two non-key columns: AdviserName and AdviserPhone. Further suppose that you suspect that AdviserPhone → AdviserName. Explain how to examine the data to determine if this supposition is true.

8.5 Write a subquery, other than one in this chapter, that is not a correlated subquery.

8.6 Explain the following statement: "The processing of correlated subqueries is nested, whereas that of regular subqueries is not."

8.7 Write a correlated subquery, other than one in this chapter.

8.8 Explain how the query in your answer to Review Question 8.5 differs from the query in your answer to Review Question 8.7.

8.9 Explain what is wrong with the correlated subquery SQL-Query-CH08-03 on page 400.

8.10 Write a correlated subquery to determine whether the data support the supposition in Review Question 8.4.

8.11 Explain the meaning of the SQL EXISTS comparison operator.

8.12 Answer Review Question 8.10, but use the SQL EXISTS comparison operator.

8.13 Explain how the words *any* and *all* pertain to the SQL EXISTS and NOT EXISTS comparison operators.

8.14 Explain the processing of SQL-Query-CH08-06 on page 402.

8.15 Using the View Ridge Gallery database, write a query that will display the names of any customers who are interested in all artists.

8.16 Explain how the query in your answer to Review Question 8.15 works.

8.17 Why is it important to analyze the database before implementing database redesign tasks? What can happen if this is not done?

8.18 Explain the process of reverse engineering.

8.19 Why is it important to carefully evaluate the results of reverse engineering?

8.20 What is a dependency graph? What purpose does it serve?

8.21 Explain the dependencies for WORK in the graph in Figure 8-4.

8.22 What sources are used when creating a dependency graph?

8.23 Explain two different types of test databases that should be used when testing database redesign changes.

8.24 Explain the problems that can occur when changing the name of a table.

8.25 Describe the process of changing a table name.

8.26 Considering Figure 8-4, describe the tasks that need to be accomplished to change the name of the table WORK to WORK_VERSION2.

8.27 Explain how views can simplify the process of changing a table name.

8.28 Under what conditions is the following SQL statement valid?

```
INSERT    INTO T1 (A, B)
     SELECT   (C, D)
     FROM     T2;
```

8.29 Show an SQL statement to add an integer column C1 to the table T2. Assume that C1 is NULL.

8.30 Extend your answer to Review Question 8.29 to add C1 when C1 is to be NOT NULL.

8.31 Show an SQL statement to drop the column C1 from table T2.

8.32 Describe the process for dropping primary key C1 and making the new primary key C2.

8.33 Which data type changes are the least risky?

8.34 Which data type changes are the most risky?

8.35 Write an SQL statement to change a column C1 to Char(10) NOT NULL. What conditions must exist in the data for this change to be successful?

8.36 Explain how to change the minimum cardinality when a child that was required to have a parent is no longer required to have one.

8.37 Explain how to change the minimum cardinality when a child that was not required to have a parent is now required to have one. What condition must exist in the data for this change to work?

8.38 Explain how to change the minimum cardinality when a parent that was required to have a child is no longer required to have one.

8.39 Explain how to change the minimum cardinality when a parent that was not required to have a child is now required to have one.

8.40 Describe how to change the maximum cardinality from 1:1 to 1:N. Assume that the foreign key is on the side of the new child in the 1:N relationship.

8.41 Describe how to change the maximum cardinality from 1:1 to 1:N. Assume that the foreign key is on the side of the new parent in the 1:N relationship.

8.42 Assume that tables T1 and T2 have a 1:1 relationship. Assume that T2 has the foreign key. Show the SQL statements necessary to move the foreign key to T1. Make up your own names for the primary and foreign keys.

8.43 Explain how to transform a 1:N relationship into an N:M relationship.

8.44 Suppose that tables T1 and T2 have a 1:N relationship. Show the SQL statements necessary to fill an intersection T1_T2_INT. Make up your own names for the primary and foreign keys.

8.45 Explain how the reduction of maximum cardinalities causes data loss.

8.46 Using the tables in your answer to Review Question 8.44, show the SQL statements necessary to change the relationship back to 1:N. Assume that the first row in the qualifying rows of the intersection table is to provide the foreign key. Use the keys and foreign keys from your answer to Review Question 8.44.

8.47 Using the results of your answer to Review Question 8.46, explain what must be done to convert this relationship to 1:1. Use the keys and foreign keys from your answer to Review Question 8.46.

8.48 In general terms, what must be done to add a new relationship?

8.49 Suppose that tables T1 and T2 have a 1:N relationship, with T2 as the child. Show the SQL statements necessary to remove table T1. Make your own assumptions about the names of keys and foreign keys.

8.50 What are the risks and problems of forward engineering?

Project Questions

8.51 Suppose that the table EMPLOYEE has a 1:N relationship to the table PHONE_ NUMBER. Further suppose that the primary key of EMPLOYEE is EmployeeID and the columns of PHONE_NUMBER are PhoneNumberID (a surrogate key), AreaCode, LocalNumber, and EmployeeID (a foreign key to EMPLOYEE). Alter this design so that EMPLOYEE has a 1:1 relationship to PHONE_NUMBER. For employees having more than one phone number, keep only the first one.

8.52 Suppose that the table EMPLOYEE has a 1:N relationship to the table PHONE_ NUMBER. Further suppose that the key of EMPLOYEE is EmployeeID and the columns of PHONE_NUMBER are PhoneNumberID (a surrogate key), AreaCode, LocalNumber, and EmployeeID (a foreign key to EMPLOYEE). Write all SQL statements necessary to redesign this database so that it has just one table. Explain the difference between the result of Project Question 8.51 and the result of this question.

8.53 Consider the following table:

TASK (EmployeeID, EmpLastName, EmpFirstName, Phone, OfficeNumber, ProjectName, Sponsor, WorkDate, HoursWorked)

Also consider the following possible functional dependencies:

EmployeeID → (EmpLastName, EmpFirstName, Phone, OfficeNumber)
ProjectName → Sponsor

A. Write SQL statements to display the values of any rows that violate these functional dependencies.

B. If no data violate these functional dependencies, can we assume that they are valid? Why or why not?

C. Assume that these functional dependencies are true and that the data have been corrected, as necessary, to reflect them. Write all SQL statements necessary to redesign this table into a set of tables in BCNF and 4NF. Assume that the table has data values that must be appropriately transformed to the new design.

Case Questions

Marcia's Dry Cleaning Case Questions

Marcia Wilson owns and operates *Marcia's Dry Cleaning*, which is an upscale dry cleaner in a well-to-do suburban neighborhood. Marcia makes her business stand out from the competition by providing superior customer service. She wants to keep track of each of her customers and their orders. Ultimately, she wants to notify them that their clothes are ready via email. Suppose that you have designed a database for Marcia's Dry Cleaning that has the following tables:

> CUSTOMER (<u>CustomerID</u>, FirstName, LastName, Phone, Email)
>
> INVOICE (<u>InvoiceNumber</u>, *CustomerID*, DateIn, DateOut, Subtotal, Tax, TotalAmount)
>
> INVOICE_ITEM (<u>*InvoiceNumber*</u>, <u>ItemNumber</u>, *ServiceID*, Quantity, UnitPrice, ExtendedPrice)
>
> SERVICE (<u>ServiceID</u>, ServiceDescription, UnitPrice)

Assume that all relationships have been defined, as implied by the foreign keys in this table list, and that the appropriate referential integrity constraints are in place. If you want to run these solutions in a DBMS product, first create a version of the MDC database described in the Case Questions in Chapter 10A for Microsoft SQL Server 2014, Chapter 10B for Oracle Database, and Chapter 10C for MySQL 5.6. Name the database MDC_CH08.

A. Create a dependency graph that shows dependencies among these tables. Explain how you need to extend this graph for views and other database constructs, such as triggers and stored procedures.

B. Using your dependency graph, describe the tasks necessary to change the name of the INVOICE table to CUST_INVOICE.

C. Write all SQL statements to make the name change described in part B.

D. Suppose that Marcia decides to allow multiple customers per order (e.g., for customers' spouses). Modify the design of these tables to accommodate this change.

E. Code SQL statements necessary to redesign the database, as described in your answer to part D.

F. Suppose that Marcia considers changing the primary key of CUSTOMER to (FirstName, LastName). Write correlated subqueries to display any data that indicate that this change is not justifiable.

G. Suppose that (FirstName, LastName) can be made the primary key of CUSTOMER. Make appropriate changes to the table design with this new primary key.

H. Code all SQL statements necessary to implement the changes described in part G.

The Queen Anne Curiosity Shop

Assume that the Queen Anne Curiosity Shop designs a database with the tables described at the end of Chapter 7:

> CUSTOMER (<u>CustomerID</u>, LastName, FirstName, EmailAddress, EncryptedPassword, Address, City, State, ZIP, Phone)
>
> EMPLOYEE (<u>EmployeeID</u>, LastName, FirstName, Phone, Email)
>
> VENDOR (<u>VendorID</u>, CompanyName, ContactLastName, ContactFirstName, Address, City, State, ZIP, Phone, Fax, Email)
>
> ITEM (<u>ItemID</u>, ItemDescription, PurchaseDate, ItemCost, ItemPrice, *VendorID*)
>
> SALE (<u>SaleID</u>, *CustomerID*, *EmployeeID*, SaleDate, SubTotal, Tax, Total)
>
> SALE_ITEM (<u>*SaleID*</u>, <u>SaleItemID</u>, *ItemID*, ItemPrice)

The referential integrity constraints are:

> VendorID in ITEM must exist in VendorID in VENDOR
>
> CustomerID in SALE must exist in CustomerID in CUSTOMER
>
> EmployeeID in SALE must exist in EmployeeID in EMPLOYEE
>
> SaleID in SALE_ITEM must exist in SaleID in SALE
>
> ItemID in SALE_ITEM must exist in ItemID in ITEM

Assume that CustomerID of CUSTOMER, EmployeeID of EMPLOYEE, ItemID of ITEM, SaleID of SALE, and SaleItemID of SALE_ITEM are all surrogate keys with values as follows:

> | | | |
> |---|---|---|
> | CustomerID | Start at 1 | Increment by 1 |
> | EmployeeID | Start at 1 | Increment by 1 |
> | VendorID | Start at 1 | Increment by 1 |
> | ItemID | Start at 1 | Increment by 1 |
> | SaleID | Start at 1 | Increment by 1 |

A vendor may be an individual or a company. If the vendor is an individual, the CompanyName field is left blank, while the ContactLastName and ContactFirstName fields must have data values. If the vendor is a company, the company name is recorded in the CompanyName field, and the name of the primary contact at the company is recorded in the ContactLastName and ContactFirstName fields.

If you want to run these solutions in a DBMS product, first create a version of the of the QACS database described in Chapter 7 and name it QACS_CH08.

A. Create a dependency graph that shows dependencies among these tables. Explain how you need to extend this graph for views and other database constructs, such as triggers and stored procedures.

B. Using your dependency graph, describe the tasks necessary to change the name of the SALE table to CUSTOMER_SALE.

C. Write all SQL statements to make the name change described in part B.

D. Suppose that the Queen Anne Curiosity Shop owners decide to allow multiple customers per order (e.g., for customers' spouses). Modify the design of these tables to accommodate this change.

E. Code SQL statements necessary to redesign the database, as described in your answer to part D.

F. Suppose that the Queen Anne Curiosity Shop owners are considering changing the primary key of CUSTOMER to (FirstName, LastName). Write correlated subqueries to display any data that indicate that this change is not justifiable.

G. Suppose that (FirstName, LastName) can be made the primary key of CUSTOMER. Make appropriate changes to the table design with this new primary key.

H. Code all SQL statements necessary to implement the changes described in part G.

Morgan Importing

Assume that Morgan has created a database with the tables described at the end of Chapter 7 (note that STORE uses the surrogate key StoreID):

EMPLOYEE (<u>EmployeeID</u>, LastName, FirstName, Department, Phone, Fax, EmailAddress)

STORE (<u>StoreID</u>, StoreName, City, Country, Phone, Fax, EmailAddress, Contact)

PURCHASE_ITEM (<u>PurchaseItemID</u>, *StoreID*, *PurchasingAgentID*, PurchaseDate, ItemDescription, Category, PriceUSD)

SHIPMENT (<u>ShipmentID</u>, *ShipperID*, *PurchasingAgentID*, ShipperInvoiceNumber, Origin, Destination, ScheduledDepartureDate, ActualDepartureDate, EstimatedArrivalDate)

SHIPMENT_ITEM (<u>*ShipmentID*</u>, <u>ShipmentItemID</u>, *PurchaseItemID*, InsuredValue)

SHIPPER (<u>ShipperID</u>, ShipperName, Phone, Fax, Email, Contact)

SHIPMENT_RECEIPT (<u>ReceiptNumber</u>, *ShipmentID*, *PurchaseItemID*, *ReceivingAgent*, ReceiptDate, ReceiptTime, ReceiptQuantity, isReceivedUndamaged, DamageNotes)

Assume that all relationships have been defined as implied by the foreign keys in this table list.

James Morgan wants to modify the database design of the Morgan Importing procurement information system (MIPIS) to separate the items in PURCHASE_ITEM in a separate table named ITEM. This will allow each item to be tracked as a unique entity throughout its acquisition and sale. The schema for the ITEM table is:

ITEM (<u>ItemID</u>, ItemDescription, Category)

PURCHASE_ITEM will then be replaced by two tables named INVOICE and INVOICE_LINE_ITEM, linked in a modified sales order configuration as shown in Figure 8-7 (compare this figure to Figure 6-18(b)).

Similarly, the shipping part of the MIPIS will be modified by changes to the SHIPMENT_ITEM tables as follows:

SHIPMENT_LINE_ITEM (<u>*ShipmentID*</u>, <u>ShipmentLineNumber</u>, *ItemID*, InsuredValue)

If you want to run these solutions in a DBMS product, first create a version of the MI database described in Chapter 7 and name it MI_CH08.

A. Create a dependency graph that shows dependencies among the original set of tables. Explain how you need to extend this graph for views and other database constructs, such as stored procedures.

FIGURE 8-7

The Morgan Importing MIPIS Modified SALES_ORDER Configuration

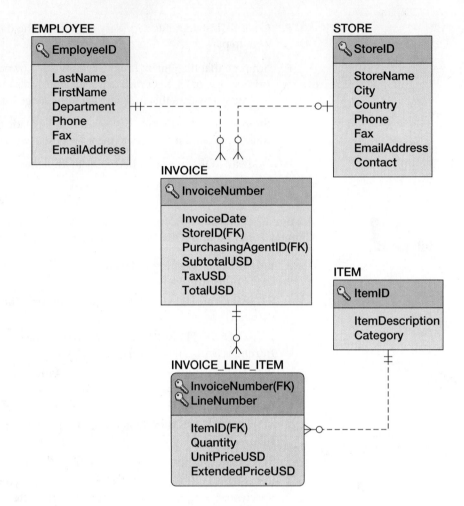

B. Using your dependency graph, describe the tasks necessary to create and populate the ITEM table.

C. Write all SQL statements to make the name change described in part B.

D. Using your dependency graph, describe the tasks necessary to change the name of the SHIPMENT_ITEM table to SHIPMENT_LINE_ITEM and the needed changes to column names.

E. Write all SQL statements to make the name change described in part B.

F. Using your dependency graph, describe the tasks necessary to convert the sales order component of the MIPIS to the new configuration.

G. Code SQL statements to implement your redesign recommendations in your answer to part D.

Multiuser Database Processing

The five chapters in Part 4 introduce and discuss the major problems of multiuser database processing and describe the features and functions for solving those problems offered by three important DBMS products. We begin in Chapter 9 with a description of database administration and the major tasks and techniques for multiuser database management. The next three chapters illustrate the implementation of these concepts using Microsoft SQL Server 2014 (Chapter 10A), Oracle Corporation's Oracle Database (Chapter 10B), and Oracle Corporation's MySQL 5.6 (Chapter 10C).

PART

4

9

Managing Multiuser Databases

Chapter Objectives

- To understand the need for and importance of database administration
- To understand the need for concurrency control, security, and backup and recovery
- To learn about typical problems that can occur when multiple users process a database concurrently
- To understand the use of locking and the problem of deadlock
- To learn the difference between optimistic and pessimistic locking
- To know the meaning of an ACID transaction

- To learn the four 1992 ANSI standard isolation levels
- To understand the need for security and specific tasks for improving database security
- To know the difference between recovery via reprocessing and recovery via rollback/rollforward
- To understand the nature of the tasks required for recovery using rollback/rollforward
- To know basic administrative and managerial DBA functions

Although multiuser databases offer great value to the organizations that create and use them, they also pose difficult problems for those same organizations. For one, multiuser databases are complicated to design and develop because they support many overlapping user views.

Additionally, as discussed in the last chapter, requirements change over time, and those changes necessitate other changes to the database structure. Such structural changes must be carefully planned and controlled so that a change made for one group does not cause problems for another. In addition, when users process a database concurrently, special controls are needed to ensure that the actions of one user do not inappropriately influence the results for another. This topic is both important and complicated, as you will see.

In large organizations, processing rights and responsibilities need to be defined and enforced. What happens, for example, when an employee leaves the firm? When can the employee's records be deleted? For the purposes of payroll processing, records can be deleted after the last pay period. For the purposes of quarterly reporting, they can be deleted at the end of the quarter. For the purposes of end-of-year tax record processing, they can be deleted at the end of the year. Clearly, no department can unilaterally decide when to delete that data. Similar comments pertain to the insertion and changing of data values. For these and other reasons, security systems need to be developed that enable only authorized users to take authorized actions at authorized times.

Databases have become key components of organizational operations and even key components of an organization's value. Unfortunately, database failures and disasters do occur. Thus, effective backup and recovery plans, techniques, and procedures are essential.

Finally, over time, the DBMS itself will need to be changed to improve performance by incorporating new features and releases and to conform to changes made in the underlying operating system. All of this requires attentive management.

To ensure that these problems are addressed and solved, most organizations have a database administration office. We begin with a description of the tasks of that office. We then describe the combination of software and manual practices and procedures that are used to perform those tasks. In Chapter 10, we introduce Chapter 10A, 10B, and 10C, which are the three chapters that discuss and illustrate the features and functions of Microsoft SQL Server 2014, Oracle Database, and MySQL 5.6, respectively, for dealing with these issues.

The Importance of Working with an Installed DBMS Product

In order to fully understand the DBMS concepts and features we discuss and illustrate in the chapter, you need to work with them in an installed DBMS product. This *hands-on* experience is necessary so that you move from an abstract understanding of these concepts and features to a practical knowledge of them and how they are used and implemented. The information you need to download, install, and use the DBMS products discussed in this book is in Chapter 10 (introduction to the DBMS products), Chapter 10A (Microsoft SQL Server 2014), Chapter 10B (Oracle Database) and Chapter 10C (MySQL 5.6). Portions of these chapters parallel the discussion in this chapter and illustrate the actual use of the concepts and features in each DBMS product.

To get the most out of this chapter, you should download and install the DBMS product(s) of your choice and then follow along as you work in each section of this chapter by working thorough the corresponding sections of the chapter for your DBMS product.

Database Administration

The terms **data administration** and **database administration** are both used in practice. In some cases, the terms are considered to be synonymous; in other cases, they have different meanings. Most commonly, the term *data administration* refers to a function that applies to an entire organization; it is a management-oriented function that concerns corporate data privacy and security issues. In contrast, the term *database administration* refers to a more technical function that is specific to a particular database, including the applications that process that database. This chapter addresses database administration.

Databases vary considerably in size and scope, ranging from single-user personal databases to large interorganizational databases, such as airline reservation systems. All of these databases have a need for database administration, though the tasks to be accomplished vary in complexity. For personal databases, individuals follow simple procedures for backing up their data, and they keep minimal records for documentation. In this case, the person who uses the database also performs the database administration functions, even though he or she is probably unaware of it.

For multiuser database applications, database administration becomes both more important and more difficult. Consequently, it generally has formal recognition. For some applications, one or two people are given this function on a part-time basis. For large Internet or intranet databases, database administration responsibilities are often too time consuming and too varied to be handled even by a single full-time person. Supporting a database with dozens or hundreds of users requires considerable time as well as both technical knowledge and diplomatic skills. Such support usually is handled by an office of database administration. The manager of the office is often known as the **database administrator**. In this case, the acronym **DBA** refers to either the office or the manager.

The overall responsibility of the DBA is to facilitate the development and use of the database. Usually, this means balancing the conflicting goals of protecting the database and maximizing its availability and benefit to users. Specific tasks are shown in Figure 9-1. We consider each of these tasks in the following sections.

Managing the Database Structure

Managing the database structure includes participating in the initial database design and implementation as well as controlling and managing changes to the database. Ideally, the DBA is involved early in the development of the database and its applications; participates in the requirements study; helps evaluate alternatives, including the DBMS to be used; and helps design the database structure. For large organizational applications, the DBA usually is a manager who supervises the work of technically oriented database design personnel.

Creating the database involves several different tasks. First, the database is created and disk space is allocated for database files and logs. Then tables are generated, indexes are created, and stored procedures and triggers are written. We will discuss examples of all of these tasks in the next three chapters. Once the database structures are created, the database is filled with data.

Configuration Control

After a database and its applications have been implemented, changes in requirements are inevitable, as described in Chapter 8. Such changes can arise from new needs, from changes in the business environment, from changes in policy, and from changes in business processes that evolve with system use. When changes to requirements necessitate changes to the database structure, great care must be used because changes to the database structure seldom involve just one application.

Hence, effective database administration includes procedures and policies by which users can register their needs for changes, the entire database community can discuss the impacts of the changes, and a global decision can be made whether to implement proposed changes. Because of the size and complexity of a database and its applications, changes sometimes have unexpected results. Thus, the DBA must be prepared to repair the database and to gather sufficient information to diagnose and correct the problem that caused the damage. The database is most vulnerable to failure after its structure has been changed.

FIGURE 9-1

Summary of Database
Administration Tasks

Summary of Database Administration Tasks
• Manage database structure
• Control concurrent processing
• Manage processing rights and responsibilities
• Develop database security
• Provide for database recovery
• Manage the DBMS
• Maintain the data repository

Documentation

The DBA's final responsibility in managing the database structure is documentation. It is extremely important to know what changes have been made, how they were made, and when they were made. A change in the database structure may cause an error that is not revealed for six months; without proper documentation of the change, diagnosing the problem is next to impossible. Considerable work may be required to identify the point at which certain symptoms first appeared. For this reason, it also is important to maintain a record of the test procedures and test runs made to verify a change. If standardized test procedures, test forms, and recordkeeping methods are used, recording the test results does not have to be time consuming.

Although maintaining documentation is tedious and unfulfilling, the effort pays off when disaster strikes and the documentation is the difference between a quick problem solution and a confused muddle of activity. Today, several products are emerging that ease the burden of documentation. Many CASE tools, for example, can be used to document logical database designs. Version-control software can be used to track changes. Data dictionaries provide reports and other outputs that present database data structures.

Another reason for carefully documenting changes in the database structure is so that historical data are used properly. If, for example, marketing wants to analyze three-year-old sales data that have been in the archives for two years, it will be necessary to know what structure was current at the time the data were last active. Records that show the changes in the structure can be used to answer that question. A similar situation arises when a six-month-old backup copy of data must be used to repair a damaged database (although this should not happen, it sometimes does). The backup copy can be used to reconstruct the database to the state it was in at the time of the backup. Then transactions and structural changes can be made in chronological order to restore the database to its current state. Figure 9-2 summarizes the DBA's responsibilities for managing the database structure.

Concurrency Control

Concurrency control measures are taken to ensure that one user's work does not inappropriately influence another user's work. In some cases, these measures ensure that a user gets the same result when processing with other users that he or she would have received if processing alone. In other cases, it means that the user's work is influenced by other users but in an anticipated way. For example, in an order entry system, a user should be able to enter an order and get the same result, regardless of whether there are no other users or hundreds of other

FIGURE 9-2

Summary of DBA's Responsibilities for Managing Database Structure

Participate in Database and Application Development
• Assist in the requirements analysis stage and data model creation
• Play an active role in database design and creation
Facilitate Changes to Database Structure
• Seek communitywide solutions
• Assess impact on all users
• Provide configuration control forum
• Be prepared for problems after changes are made
• Maintain documentation

users. In contrast, a user who is printing a report of the most current inventory status may want to obtain in-process data changes from other users, even if there is a danger that those changes may later be canceled.

Unfortunately, no concurrency control technique or mechanism is ideal for every circumstance. All involve trade-offs. For example, a program can obtain very strict concurrency control by locking the entire database, but no other programs will be able to do anything while it runs. This is strict protection, but at a high cost. As you will see, other measures are available that are more difficult to program or enforce but that allow more throughput. Still other measures are available that maximize throughput but have a low level of concurrency control. When designing multiuser database applications, you will need to choose among these trade-offs.

The Need for Atomic Transactions

In most database applications, users submit work in the form of **transactions**, which are also known as **logical units of work (LUWs)**. A transaction (or LUW) is a series of actions to be taken on the database so that either all of them are performed successfully or none of them is performed at all, in which case the database remains unchanged. Such a transaction is sometimes called *atomic* because it is performed as a unit.

Consider the following sequence of database actions that could occur when recording a new order:

1. Change a customer's row, increasing AmountDue.
2. Change a salesperson's row, increasing CommissionDue.
3. Insert a new order row into the database.

Suppose that the last step failed, perhaps because of insufficient file space. Imagine the confusion if the first two changes were made but the third one was not. The customer would be billed for an order never received, and a salesperson would receive a commission on an order that was never sent to the customer. Clearly, these three actions need to be taken as a unit—either all of them should be done or none of them should be done.

Figure 9-3 compares the results of performing these activities as a series of independent steps (Figure 9-3(a)) and as an atomic transaction (Figure 9-3(b)). Notice that when the steps are carried out atomically and one fails, no changes are made in the database. Also note that the commands Start Transaction, Commit Transaction, and Rollback Transaction are issued by the application program to mark the boundaries of the transaction logic. You will learn more about these commands later in this chapter and in Chapter 10A, 10B, and 10C.

Concurrent Transaction Processing

When two transactions are being processed against a database at the same time, they are termed **concurrent transactions**. Although it may appear to the users that concurrent transactions are being processed simultaneously, this cannot be true because the CPU of the machine processing the database can execute only one instruction at a time. Usually, transactions are interleaved, which means that the operating system switches CPU services among tasks so that some portion of each transaction is carried out in a given interval. This switching among tasks is done so quickly that two people seated at browsers side by side, processing the same database, may believe that their two transactions are completed simultaneously; in reality, however, the two transactions are interleaved.

Figure 9-4 shows two concurrent transactions. User A's transaction reads Item 100, changes it, and rewrites it in the database. User B's transaction takes the same actions but on Item 200. The CPU processes User A's transactions until it encounters an I/O interrupt or some other delay for User A. The operating system shifts control to User B. The CPU now processes User B's transactions until an interrupt, at which point the operating system passes control back to User A. To the users, the processing appears to be simultaneous, but it is interleaved, or concurrent.

The Lost Update Problem

The concurrent processing illustrated in Figure 9-4 poses no problems because the users are processing different data. But suppose that both users want to process Item 100. For example,

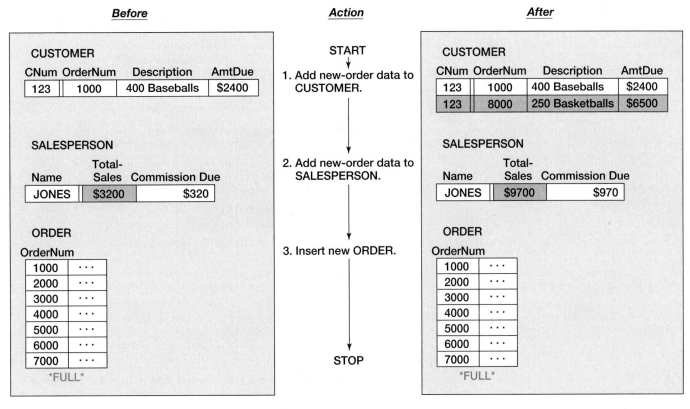

(a) Errors Introduced Without Transaction

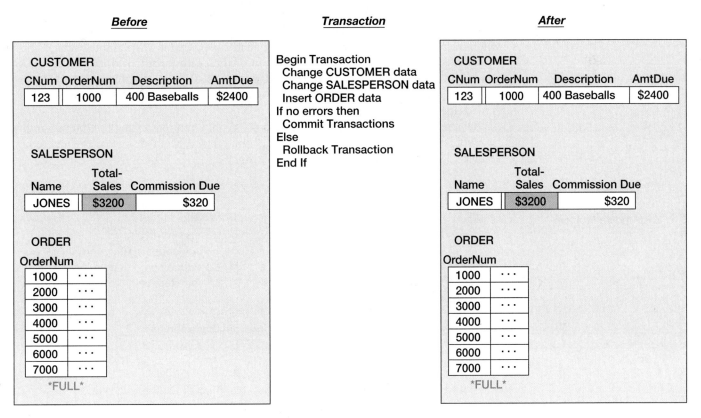

(b) Atomic Transaction Prevents Errors

FIGURE 9-3

Transaction Processing
Example

FIGURE 9-4

Concurrent-Processing
Example

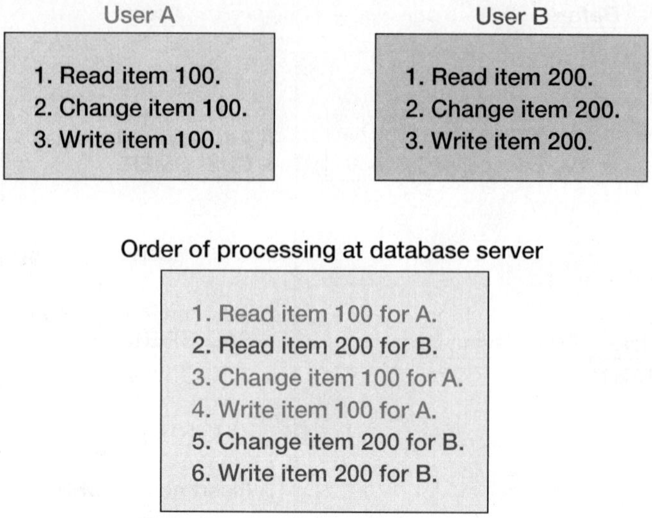

User A

1. Read item 100.
2. Change item 100.
3. Write item 100.

User B

1. Read item 200.
2. Change item 200.
3. Write item 200.

Order of processing at database server

1. Read item 100 for A.
2. Read item 200 for B.
3. Change item 100 for A.
4. Write item 100 for A.
5. Change item 200 for B.
6. Write item 200 for B.

User A wants to order five units of Item 100, and User B wants to order three units of the same item. Figure 9-5 illustrates the problem.

User A reads a copy of Item 100's record into memory. According to the record, there are 10 items in inventory. Then User B reads another copy of Item 100's record into a different section of memory. Again, according to the record, there are 10 items in inventory. Now User A takes five, decrements the count of items in its copy of the data to five, and rewrites the record for Item 100. Then User B takes three, decrements the count in its copy of the data to seven, and rewrites the record for Item 100. The database now shows, incorrectly, that there are seven Item 100s in inventory. To review: We started with 10 in inventory, User A took 5, User B took 3, and the database shows that 7 are in inventory. Clearly, this is a problem.

Both users obtained data that were correct at the time they obtained them. But when User B read the record, User A already had a copy that it was about to update. This situation is called the **lost update problem** or the **concurrent update problem**. A similar problem is the **inconsistent read problem**. With this problem, User A reads data that have been processed by a portion of a transaction from User B. As a result, User A reads incorrect data.

One remedy for the inconsistencies caused by concurrent processing is to prevent multiple applications from obtaining copies of the same record when the record is about to be changed. This remedy is called **resource locking**.

FIGURE 9-5

Lost Update Problem

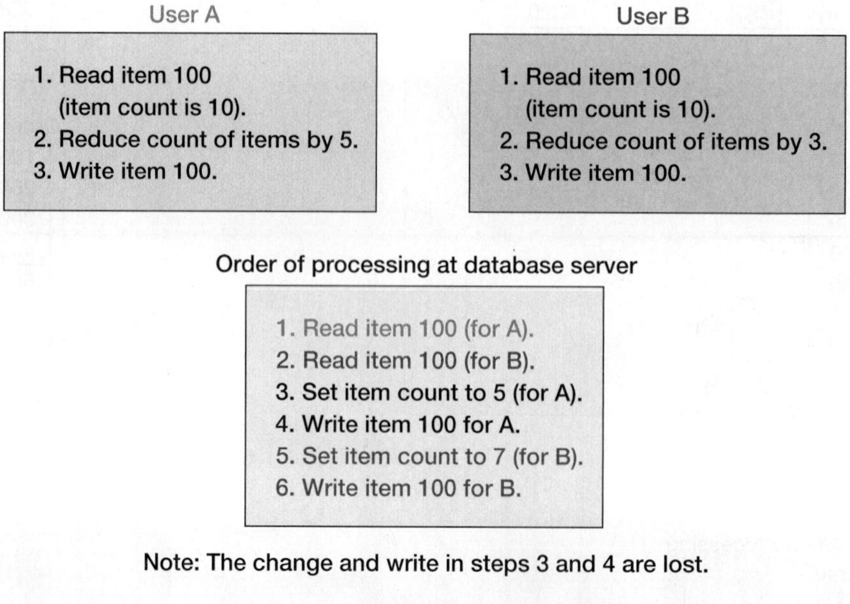

User A

1. Read item 100
   (item count is 10).
2. Reduce count of items by 5.
3. Write item 100.

User B

1. Read item 100
   (item count is 10).
2. Reduce count of items by 3.
3. Write item 100.

Order of processing at database server

1. Read item 100 (for A).
2. Read item 100 (for B).
3. Set item count to 5 (for A).
4. Write item 100 for A.
5. Set item count to 7 (for B).
6. Write item 100 for B.

Note: The change and write in steps 3 and 4 are lost.

Resource Locking

One way to prevent concurrent processing problems is to disallow sharing by locking data that are retrieved for update. Figure 9-6 shows the order of processing using a **lock** command.

Because of the lock, User B's transaction must wait until User A is finished with the Item 100 data. Using this strategy, User B can read Item 100's record only after User A has completed the modification. In this case, the final item count stored in the database is two, as it should be. (We started with 10, User A took 5, and User B took 3, leaving 2.)

Lock Terminology

Locks can be placed either automatically by the DBMS or by a command issued to the DBMS from the application program. Locks placed by the DBMS are called **implicit locks**; those placed by command are called **explicit locks**. Today, almost all locking is implicit. The program declares the behavior it wants, and the DBMS places locks accordingly. You will learn how to do that later in this chapter.

In the preceding example, the locks were applied to rows of data. Not all locks are applied at this level, however. Some DBMS products lock groups of rows within a table, some lock entire tables, and some lock the entire database. The size of a lock is referred to as **lock granularity**. Locks with large granularity are easy for the DBMS to administer but frequently cause conflicts. Locks with small granularity are difficult to administer (the DBMS has to track and check many more details), but conflicts are less common.

Locks also vary by type. An **exclusive lock** locks the item from any other access. No other transaction can read or change the data. A **shared lock** locks the item from change but not from read; that is, other transactions can read the item as long as they do not attempt to alter it.

Serializable Transactions

When two or more transactions are processed concurrently, the results in the database should be logically consistent with the results that would have been achieved had the transactions been processed in an arbitrary, serial fashion. A scheme for processing concurrent transactions in this way is said to be **serializable**.

Serializability can be achieved by a number of different means. One way is to process the transaction using **two-phase locking**. With this strategy, transactions are allowed to obtain locks as necessary, but once the first lock is released, no other lock can be obtained.

FIGURE 9-6

Concurrent Processing
with Explicit Locks

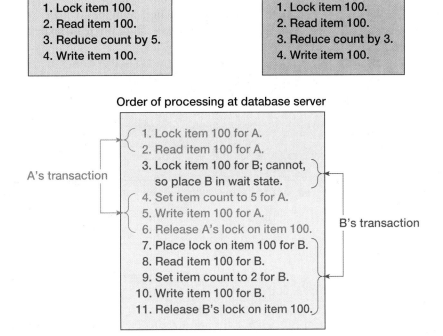

Transactions thus have a **growing phase**, during which the locks are obtained, and a **shrinking phase**, during which the locks are released.

A special case of two-phase locking is used with a number of DBMS products. With it, locks are obtained throughout the transaction, but no lock is released until the COMMIT or ROLLBACK command is issued. This strategy is more restrictive than two-phase locking requires, but it is easier to implement.

Consider an order-entry transaction that processes data in the CUSTOMER, SALESPERSON, and ORDER tables. To avoid concurrency problems, the order entry transaction issues locks on CUSTOMER, SALESPERSON, and ORDER as needed; makes all database changes; and then releases all locks.

Deadlock

Although locking solves one problem, it introduces another. Consider what can happen when two users want to order two items from inventory. Suppose that User A wants to order some paper, and if she can get the paper, she wants to order some pencils. Then suppose that User B wants to order some pencils, and if he can get the pencils, he wants to order some paper. The order of processing is shown in Figure 9-7.

In this figure, Users A and B are locked in a condition known as **deadlock** or sometimes as the **deadly embrace**. Each user is waiting for a resource that the other has locked. This problem can be solved either by preventing the deadlock from occurring or by allowing the deadlock to occur and then breaking it.

Deadlock can be prevented in several ways. One way is to require users to issue all lock requests at one time. In Figure 9-7, if User A had locked both the paper and the pencil records at the beginning, deadlock would not occur. A second way to prevent deadlock is to require all application programs to lock resources in the same order.

> **BY THE WAY** Even if all the applications do not lock resources in the same order, deadlock will be prevented for those that do. Sometimes this policy is implemented with an organizational programming standard such as "Whenever processing rows from tables in a parent–child relationship, lock the parent row before the child rows." This policy will at least reduce the likelihood of deadlock and thus save the DBMS from having to recover from some deadlocked transactions.

Almost every DBMS has algorithms for breaking deadlock, when it does occur. First, the DBMS must detect that it has occurred. Then the typical solution is to cancel one of the transactions and remove its changes from the database. You will see variants of this with Microsoft SQL Server, Oracle Database, and MySQL in the next three chapters.

FIGURE 9-7

Deadlock Example

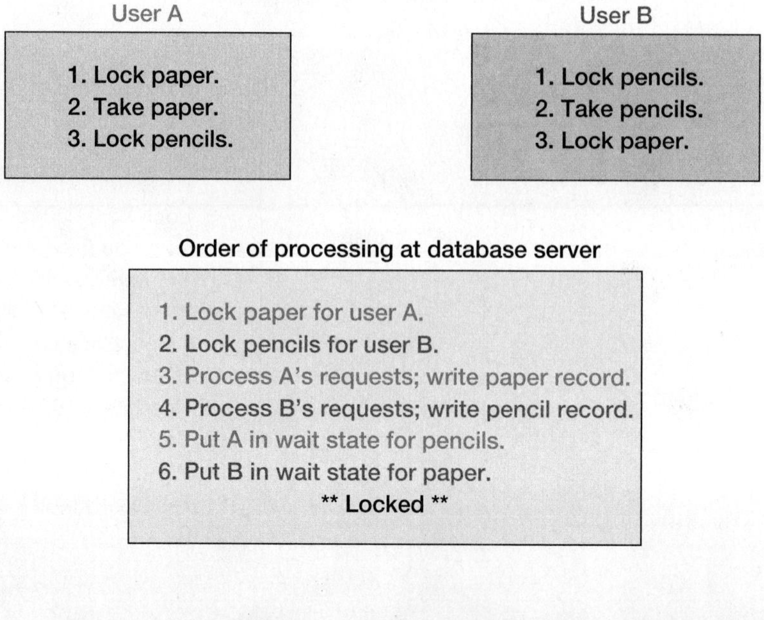

User A

1. Lock paper.
2. Take paper.
3. Lock pencils.

User B

1. Lock pencils.
2. Take pencils.
3. Lock paper.

Order of processing at database server

1. Lock paper for user A.
2. Lock pencils for user B.
3. Process A's requests; write paper record.
4. Process B's requests; write pencil record.
5. Put A in wait state for pencils.
6. Put B in wait state for paper.
   ** Locked **

Optimistic Versus Pessimistic Locking

Locks can be invoked in two basic styles. With **optimistic locking**, the assumption is made that no conflict will occur. Data are read, the transaction is processed, updates are issued, and then a check is made to see if conflict occurred. If not, the transaction is finished. If conflict did occur, the transaction is repeated until it processes with no conflict. With **pessimistic locking**, the assumption is made that conflict will occur. Locks are issued, the transaction is processed, and then the locks are freed.

Figures 9-8 and 9-9 show examples of each style for a transaction that is reducing the quantity of the pencil row in PRODUCT by 5. Figure 9-8 shows optimistic locking. First, the data are read and the current value of Quantity of pencils is saved in the variable OldQuantity. The transaction is then processed, and assuming that all is OK, a lock is obtained on PRODUCT. (In fact, the lock might be only for the pencil row or it might be at a larger level of granularity, but the principle is the same.) After obtaining the lock, an SQL statement is issued to update the pencil row with a WHERE condition that the current value of Quantity equals OldQuantity. If no other transaction has changed the Quantity of the pencil row, then this UPDATE will be successful. If another transaction has changed the Quantity of the pencil row, the UPDATE will fail. In either case, the lock is released. If the transaction failed, the process is repeated until the transaction finishes with no conflict.

Figure 9-9 shows the logic for the same transaction using pessimistic locking. Here a lock is obtained on PRODUCT before any work is begun. Then values are read, the transaction is processed, the UPDATE occurs, and PRODUCT is unlocked.

The advantage of optimistic locking is that locks are held for much less time than with pessimistic locking because locks are obtained only after the transaction has finished. If the transaction is complicated or if the client is slow (due to transmission delays, the client doing other work, or the user getting a cup of coffee or shutting down without exiting the browser), optimistic locking can dramatically improve throughput. This advantage will be especially true if the lock granularity is large—say, the entire PRODUCT table.

The disadvantage of optimistic locking is that if there is a lot of activity on the pencil row, the transaction may have to be repeated many times. Thus, transactions that involve a lot of activity on a given row (purchasing a popular stock, for example) are poorly suited for optimistic locking.

In general, the Internet is a wild and woolly place, and users are likely to take unexpected actions, such as abandoning transactions in the middle. So, unless Internet users have been prequalified (by enrolling in an online brokerage stock purchase plan, for example),

FIGURE 9-8

Optimistic Locking

```
/* *** EXAMPLE CODE - DO NOT RUN *** */
/* *** SQL-Code-Example-CH09-01 *** */

SELECT    PRODUCT.Name, PRODUCT.Quantity
FROM      PRODUCT
WHERE     PRODUCT.Name = 'Pencil';

Set NewQuantity = PRODUCT.Quantity - 5;

{process transaction - take exception action if NewQuantity < 0, etc.

Assuming all is OK: }

LOCK      PRODUCT;

UPDATE    PRODUCT
SET       PRODUCT.Quantity = NewQuantity
WHERE     PRODUCT.Name = 'Pencil'
    AND PRODUCT.Quantity = OldQuantity;

UNLOCK    PRODUCT;

{check to see if update was successful;
if not, repeat transaction}
```

FIGURE 9-9

Pessimistic Locking

```
/* *** EXAMPLE CODE - DO NOT RUN *** */
/* *** SQL-Code-Example-CH09-02 *** */

LOCK      PRODUCT;

SELECT    PRODUCT.Name, PRODUCT.Quantity
FROM      PRODUCT
WHERE     PRODUCT.Name = 'Pencil';

Set NewQuantity = PRODUCT.Quantity - 5;

{process transaction - take exception action if NewQuantity < 0, etc.

Assuming all is OK: }

UPDATE    PRODUCT
SET       PRODUCT.Quantity = NewQuantity
WHERE     PRODUCT.Name = 'Pencil';

UNLOCK    PRODUCT;

{no need to check if update was successful}
```

optimistic locking is the better choice in that environment. On intranets, however, the decision is more difficult. Optimistic locking is probably still preferred unless some characteristic of the application causes substantial activity on particular rows or if application requirements make reprocessing transactions particularly undesirable.

SQL Transaction Control Language and Declaring Lock Characteristics

As you can see, concurrency control is a complicated subject; determining the level, type, and placement of the lock is difficult. Sometimes, too, the optimum locking strategy depends on which transactions are active and what they are doing. For these and other reasons, database application programs do not generally explicitly issue locks as shown in Figures 9-8 and 9-9. Instead, they mark transaction boundaries using **SQL Transaction Control Language (TCL)** and then declare the type of locking behavior they want the DBMS to use. In this way, the DBMS can place and remove locks and even change the level and type of locks dynamically.

Figure 9-10 shows the pencil transaction with transaction boundaries marked with the SQL TCL standard commands for controlling transactions:

- The **SQL BEGIN TRANSACTION statement**,
- The **SQL COMMIT TRANSACTION statement**, and
- The **SQL ROLLBACK TRANSACTION statement**.

The SQL BEGIN TRANSACTION statement explicitly marks the start of a new transaction, while the SQL COMMIT TRANSACTION statement makes any database changes made by the transaction permanent and marks the end of the transaction. If there is a need to undo the changes made during the transaction due to an error in the process, the SQL ROLLBACK TRANSACTION statement is used to undo all transaction changes and return the database to the state it was in before the transaction was attempted. Thus, the SQL ROLLBACK TRANSACTION statement also marks the end of the transaction, but with a very different outcome.

These boundaries are the essential information that the DBMS needs to enforce the different locking strategies. If the developer now declares via a system parameter that he or she wants optimistic locking, the DBMS will implicitly set locks for that locking style. If, however, the developer declares pessimistic locking, the DBMS will set the locks differently.

FIGURE 9-10

Marking Transaction
Boundaries

```
/* *** EXAMPLE CODE - DO NOT RUN *** */
/* *** SQL-Code-Example-CH09-03 *** */

BEGIN TRANSACTION;

SELECT      PRODUCT.Name, PRODUCT.Quantity
FROM        PRODUCT
WHERE       PRODUCT.Name = 'Pencil';

Set NewQuantity = PRODUCT.Quantity - 5;

{process transaction - take exception action if NewQuantity < 0, etc.}

UPDATE      PRODUCT
SET         PRODUCT.Quantity = NewQuantity
WHERE       PRODUCT.Name = 'Pencil';

{continue processing transaction} . . .



IF {transaction has completed normally} THEN

     COMMIT TRANSACTION;

ELSE

     ROLLBACK TRANSACTION;

END IF;

Continue processing other actions not part of this transaction . . .
```

> **BY THE WAY** As usual, each DBMS product implements these SQL statements in a
> slightly different way. Microsoft SQL Server does not require the SQL
> keyword TRANSACTION, allows the abbreviation TRANS, and also allows the use
> of the **SQL WORK keyword** with COMMIT and ROLLBACK. Oracle Database uses
> SET TRANSACTION with COMMIT and ROLLBACK. MySQL does not use the SQL
> keyword TRANSACTION, while it allows (but does not require) use of the SQL WORK
> keyword in its place.
>
> Also note that the SQL BEGIN TRANSACTION statement is *not* the same as the
> SQL BEGIN statement used in SQL/PSM control-of-flow statements (as discussed
> in Chapters 7, 10A, 10B, and 10C). Thus, you may have to use a different syntax
> for marking transactions within a trigger or stored procedure. For example, MySQL
> marks the beginning of transactions in a BEGIN…END block with the **SQL START
> TRANSACTION statement**. As usual, be sure to consult the documentation for the
> DBMS product you are using.

Implicit and Explicit COMMIT TRANSACTION

Some DBMS products allow and implement an implicit COMMIT TRANSACTION whenever a SQL DML statement is run. For example, suppose we run a transaction using the SQL UPDATE command:

```
/* *** EXAMPLE CODE - DO NOT RUN *** */
/* *** SQL-UPDATE-CH09-01 *** */
UPDATE         CUSTOMER
   SET         AreaCode = '425'
   WHERE       ZIPCode = '98050';
```

Microsoft SQL Server 2014 and MySQL 5.6 will, by default, automatically commit the changes to the database after the transaction is complete. You do not have to use a COMMIT statement to make the database changes permanent. This is an *implicit* COMMIT setting.

On the other hand, Oracle Database does *not* provide a mechanism for implicit COMMITs, and an *explicit* COMMIT statement *must* be run to make the changes to the database permanent (Oracle Database uses COMMIT instead of COMMIT TRANSACTION). Thus, we would have to run the SQL UPDATE as:

```
/* *** EXAMPLE CODE - DO NOT RUN *** */
/* *** SQL-UPDATE-CH09-02 *** */
UPDATE          CUSTOMER
    SET         AreaCode = '425'
    WHERE       ZIPCode = '98050';
COMMIT;
```

Note that this statement applies *only* to the Oracle Database DBMS itself. Some Oracle Database utilities *do* implement the ability to automatically issue COMMIT statements, and thus it can appear to the user that there is an implicit COMMIT. We will discuss this in detail when we work with Oracle Database in Chapter 10B.

Consistent Transactions

Sometimes, you will see the acronym ACID applied to transactions. An **ACID transaction** is one that is **a**tomic, **c**onsistent, **i**solated, and **d**urable. Atomic and durable are easy to define. As you just learned, an **atomic** transaction is one in which either all of the database actions occur or none of them does. A **durable** transaction is one in which all committed changes are permanent. Once a durable change is committed, the DBMS takes responsibility for ensuring that the change will survive system failures.

The terms **consistent** and **isolated** are not as definitive as the terms *atomic* and *durable*. Consider a transaction with just one SQL UPDATE statement:

```
/* *** EXAMPLE CODE - DO NOT RUN *** */
/* *** SQL-UPDATE-CH09-03 *** */
BEGIN TRANSACTION;
UPDATE          CUSTOMER
    SET         AreaCode = '425'
    WHERE       ZIPCode = '98050';
COMMIT TRANSACTION;
```

Suppose that there are 500,000 rows in the CUSTOMER table and that 500 of them have ZIPCode equal to '98050'. It will take some time for the DBMS to find those 500 rows. During that time, other transactions may attempt to update the AreaCode or ZIPCode fields of CUSTOMER. If the SQL statement is consistent, such update requests will be disallowed. Hence, the update shown in SQL-UPDATE-CH09-03 will apply to the set of rows as they existed at the time the SQL statement started. Such consistency is called **statement-level consistency**.

Now, consider a transaction (SQL-Code-Example-CH09-01) that contains two SQL UPDATE statements as part (with possible other transaction actions) of a transaction marked by SQL transaction boundaries:

```
/* *** EXAMPLE CODE - DO NOT RUN *** */
/* *** SQL-Code-Example-CH09-04 *** */
BEGIN TRANSACTION;
```

```
/* *** SQL-UPDATE-CH09-03 *** */
UPDATE    CUSTOMER
    SET       AreaCode = '425'
    WHERE     ZIPCode = '98050';
— Other transaction work
/* *** SQL-UPDATE-CH09-04 *** */
UPDATE    CUSTOMER
    SET       Discount = 0.05
    WHERE     AreaCode = '425';
— Other transaction work
COMMIT TRANSACTION;
```

In this context, what does *consistent* mean? Statement-level consistency means that each statement independently processes rows consistently, but that changes from other users to these rows might be allowed during the interval between the two SQL statements. **Transaction-level consistency** means that all rows affected by either of the SQL statements are protected from changes during the entire transaction.

Observe that transaction-level consistency is so strong that, for some implementations of it, a transaction will not see its own changes. In this example, the SQL statement SQL-Update-CH09-04 may not see rows changed by the SQL statement SQL-Update-CH09-03.

Thus, when you hear the term *consistent,* look further to determine which type of consistency is meant. Be aware as well of the potential trap of transaction-level consistency.

Transaction Isolation Level

The term *isolated* has several different meanings. To understand those meanings, we need first to define several new terms that describe various problems that can occur when we read data from a database, which are summarized in Figure 9-11.

- A **dirty read** occurs when a transaction reads a row that has been changed but for which the change has not yet been committed to the database. The danger of a dirty read is that the uncommitted change can be rolled back. If so, the transaction that made the dirty read will be processing incorrect data.
- A **nonrepeatable read** occurs when a transaction rereads data it has previously read and finds modifications or deletions caused by a committed transaction.
- A **phantom read** occurs when a transaction rereads data and finds new rows that were inserted by a committed transaction since the prior read.

In order to deal with these potential data read problems, the SQL standard defines four **transaction isolation levels** or **isolation levels** that control which of these problems are allowed to occur. Using these SQL defined isolation levels, the application programmer can

FIGURE 9-11

Summary of Data Read Problems

Data Read Problem Type	Definition
Dirty Read	The transaction reads a row that has been changed, but the change has *not* been committed. If the change is rolled back, the transaction has incorrect data.
Nonrepeatable Read	The transaction rereads data that has been changed, and finds updates or deletions due to committed transactions.
Phantom Read	The transaction rereads data and finds new rows inserted by a committed transaction.

		Isolation Level			
		Read Uncommitted	**Read Committed**	**Repeatable Read**	**Serializable**
Problem Type	**Dirty Read**	Possible	Not Possible	Not Possible	Not Possible
	Nonrepeatable Read	Possible	Possible	Not Possible	Not Possible
	Phantom Read	Possible	Possible	Possible	Not Possible

FIGURE 9-12

Summary of Transaction
Isolation Levels

declare the type of isolation level he or she wants, and the DBMS will create and manage locks to achieve that level of isolation.

These transaction isolation levels are summarized in Figure 9-12 and can be defined as:

■ The **read-uncommitted isolation level** allows dirty reads, nonrepeatable reads, and phantom reads to occur.
■ The **read-committed isolation level** allows nonrepeatable reads and phantom reads but disallows dirty reads.
■ The **repeatable-read isolation level** allows phantom reads but disallows both dirty reads and nonrepeatable reads.
■ The **serializable isolation level** will not allow any of these three data read problems to occur.

Generally, the more restrictive the level, the less the throughput, though much depends on the workload and how the application programs are written. Moreover, not all DBMS products support all of these levels. As usual, the support of SQL transaction isolation levels varies between DBMS products, and you will learn how Microsoft SQL Server 2014, Oracle Database, and MySQL 5.6 support isolation levels in Chapter 10A, Chapter 10B, and Chapter 10C, respectively.

SQL Cursors

An **SQL cursor** or **cursor** is a pointer into a set of rows. SQL cursors are usually defined in an **SQL DECLARE CURSOR statement** that defines the cursor by using an SQL SELECT statement. For example, the following DECLARE CURSOR statement defines a cursor named TransCursor that operates over the set of rows indicated by the included SELECT statement:

```
/* *** EXAMPLE CODE - DO NOT RUN *** */
/* *** SQL-Code-Example-CH09-05 *** */
DECLARE CURSOR TransCursor AS
    SELECT        *
    FROM          TRANS
    WHERE         PurchasePrice > 10000;
```

As was explained in Chapter 7, after an application program opens a cursor, it can place the cursor somewhere in the result set. Most commonly, the cursor is placed on the first or last row, but other possibilities exist.

A transaction can open several cursors—either sequentially or simultaneously. Additionally, two or more cursors may be open on the same table; either directly on the table or through an SQL view on that table. Because cursors require considerable memory, having many cursors open at the same time for, say, a thousand concurrent transactions will consume exorbitant memory. One way to reduce cursor burden is to define reduced-capability cursors and use them when a full-capability cursor is not needed.

Figure 9-13 lists four SQL cursor types used in the Microsoft SQL Server 2014 environment (cursor types for other systems are similar). The simplest cursor is the **forward only cursor**.

FIGURE 9-13

Summary of SQL
Cursor Types

CursorType	Description	Comments
Forward only	Application can only move forward through the recordset.	Changes made by other cursors in this transaction or in other transactions will be visible only if they occur on rows ahead of the cursor.
Static	Application sees the data as they were at the time the cursor was opened.	Changes made by this cursor are visible. Changes from other sources are not visible. Backward and forward scrolling allowed.
Keyset	When the cursor is opened, a primary key value is saved for each row in the recordset. When the application accesses a row, the key is used to fetch the current values for the row.	Updates from any source are visible. Inserts from sources outside this cursor are not visible (there is no key for them in the keyset). Inserts from this cursor appear at the bottom of the recordset. Deletions from any source are visible. Changes in row order are not visible. If the isolation level is read-uncommitted, then uncommitted updates and deletions are visible; otherwise only committed updates and deletions are visible.
Dynamic	Changes of any type and from any source are visible.	All inserts, updates, deletions, and changes in recordset order are visible. If the isolation level is dirty read, then uncommitted changes are visible. Otherwise, only committed changes are visible.

With it, the application can move only forward through the records. Changes made by other cursors in this transaction and by other transactions will be visible only if they occur to rows ahead of the cursor.

The next three types of cursors are called **scrollable cursors** because the application can scroll forward and backward through the records. A **static cursor** takes a snapshot of a relation and processes that snapshot. Changes made using this cursor are visible; changes from other sources are not visible.

A **keyset cursor** combines some of the features of static cursors with some of the features of dynamic cursors. When the cursor is opened, a primary key value is saved for each row. When the application positions the cursor on a row, the DBMS uses the key value to read the current value of the row. Inserts of new rows by other cursors (in this transaction or in other transactions) are not visible. If the application issues an update on a row that has been deleted by a different cursor, the DBMS creates a new row with the old key value and places the updated values in the new row (assuming that all required fields are present). Unless the isolation level of the transaction is a dirty read, only committed updates and deletions are visible to the cursor.

A **dynamic cursor** is a fully featured cursor. All inserts, updates, deletions, and changes in row order are visible to a dynamic cursor. As with keyset cursors, unless the isolation level of the transaction is a dirty read, only committed changes are visible.

The amount of overhead and processing required to support a cursor is different for each type of cursor. In general, the cost goes up as we move down the cursor types shown in Figure 9-13. To improve DBMS performance, the application developer should create cursors that are just powerful enough to do the job. It is also very important to understand how a particular DBMS implements cursors and whether cursors are located on the server or on the client. In some cases, it might be better to place a dynamic cursor on the client than to have a static cursor on the server. No general rule can be stated because performance depends on the implementation used by the DBMS product and the application requirements.

A word of caution: If you do not specify the isolation level of a transaction or do not specify the type of cursors you open, the DBMS will use a default level and default types. These defaults may be perfect for your application, but they also may be terrible. Thus, even though these issues can be ignored, their consequences cannot be avoided. You must learn the capabilities of your DBMS product.

Database Security

The goal of database security is to ensure that only authorized users can perform authorized activities at authorized times. This goal is difficult to achieve, and to make any progress at all, the database development team must determine the processing rights and responsibilities of all users during the project's requirements specification phase. These security requirements can then be enforced using the security features of the DBMS and additions to those features written into the application programs.

Processing Rights and Responsibilities

Consider, for example, the needs of View Ridge Gallery. The View Ridge database has three types of users: sales personnel, management personnel, and system administrators. View Ridge designed processing rights for each as follows: Sales personnel are allowed to enter new customer and transaction data, to change customer data, and to query any of the data. They are not allowed to enter new artist or work data. They are never allowed to delete data.

Management personnel are allowed all of the permissions of sales personnel, plus they are allowed to enter new artist and work data and to modify transaction data. Even though management personnel have the authority to delete data, they are not given that permission in this application. This restriction is made to prevent the possibility of accidental data loss.

The system administrator can grant processing rights to other users, and he or she can change the structure of the database elements such as tables, indexes, stored procedures, and the like. The system administrator is not given rights to process the data. Figure 9-14 summarizes these processing rights.

> **BY THE WAY**   You may be wondering what good it does to say that the system administrator cannot process the data when that person has the ability to grant processing rights. He or she can just grant the right to change data to himself or herself. Although this is true, the granting of those rights will leave an audit trail in the database log. Clearly, this limitation is not foolproof, but it is better than just allowing the system administrator (or DBA) full access to all rights in the database.

FIGURE 9-14

Processing Rights at View Ridge Gallery

	CUSTOMER	TRANSACTION	WORK	ARTIST
Sales personnel	Insert, change, query	Insert, query	Query	Query
Management personnel	Insert, change, query	Insert, change, query	Insert, change, query	Insert, change, query
System administrator	Grant rights, modify structure	Grant rights, modify structure	Grant rights, modify structure	Grant rights, modify structure

The permissions in this table are not given to particular people, but rather are given to groups of people. Sometimes these groups are termed **roles** because they describe people acting in a particular capacity. The term **user groups** is also used. Assigning permission to roles (or user groups) is typical but not required. It would be possible to say, for example, that the user identified as "Benjamin Franklin" has certain processing rights. Note, too, that when roles are used, it is necessary to have a way to allocate users to roles. When "Mary Smith" signs on to the computer, there must be some way to determine which role or roles she has. We will discuss this further in the next section.

In this discussion, we have used the phrase **processing rights and responsibilities**. As this phrase implies, responsibilities go with processing rights. If, for example, the manager modifies transaction data, the manager has the responsibility to ensure that these modifications do not adversely affect the gallery's operation, accounting, and so forth.

Processing responsibilities cannot be enforced by the DBMS or by the database applications. Instead, they are encoded in manual procedures and explained to users during systems training. These are topics for a systems development text, and we will not consider them further here–except to reiterate that *responsibilities* go with *rights*. Such responsibilities must be documented and enforced.

According to Figure 9-1, the DBA has the task of managing processing rights and responsibilities. As this implies, these rights and responsibilities will change over time. As the database is used and as changes are made to the applications and to the structure of the DBMS, the need for new or different rights and responsibilities will arise. The DBA is a focal point for the discussion of such changes and for their implementation.

Once processing rights have been defined, they can be implemented at many levels: operating system, network, Web server, DBMS, and application. In the next two sections, we will consider DBMS and application implementation. The other levels are beyond the scope of this text.

DBMS Security

The terminology, features, and functions of DBMS security depend on the DBMS product in use. Basically, all such products provide facilities that limit certain actions on certain objects to certain users. A general model of DBMS security is shown in Figure 9-15.

A USER can be assigned to one or more ROLEs (or USER GROUPs), and a ROLE can have one or more USERs. An OBJECT is an element of a database, such as a table, view, or stored procedure. PERMISSION is an association entity among USER, ROLE, and OBJECT. Hence, the relationships from USER to PERMISSION, ROLE to PERMISSION, and OBJECT to PERMISSION are all 1:N, O-M.

Permissions can be managed using **SQL Data Control Language (DCL)** statements:

- The **SQL GRANT statement** is used to assign permissions to users and groups so that the users or groups can perform various operations on the data in the database.
- The **SQL REVOKE statement** is used to take existing permissions away from users and groups.

FIGURE 9-15

A Model of DBMS Security

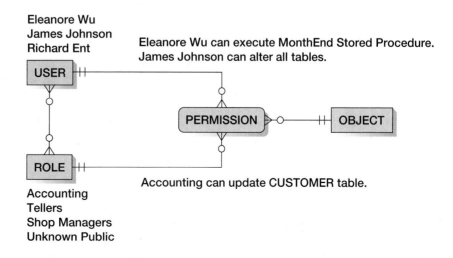

While these statements can be used in SQL scripts and with SQL command line utilities, we will find it much easier to use the GUI DBMS administration utilities provided for use with each of the major DBMS products and will illustrate how to use these utilities for Microsoft SQL Server 2014 in Chapter 10A, Oracle Database in Chapter 10B, and for MySQL 5.6 in Chapter 10C.

When a user signs on to the database, the DBMS limits the user's actions to the permissions defined for that user and to the permissions for roles to which that user has been assigned. Determining whether someone actually is who he or she claims to be is a difficult task in general. All commercial DBMS products use some version of username and password verification, even though such security is readily circumvented if users are careless with their identities.

Users can enter their **username** (also called the **login name**) and password, or, in some applications, the name and password is entered on the user's behalf. For example, the Windows username and password can be passed directly to the DBMS. In other cases, an application program provides the username and password. Internet applications usually define a group such as "Unknown Public" and assign anonymous users to that group when they sign on. In this way, companies, such as Dell, need not enter every potential customer into their security system by username and password.

Microsoft SQL Server 2014, Oracle Database, and MySQL 5.6 security systems are variations of the model in Figure 9-15. You will learn about them in Chapters 10A, 10B, and 10C, respectively.

DBMS Security Guidelines

Guidelines for improving security in database systems are listed in Figure 9-16. First, the DBMS must always be run behind a firewall. However, the DBA should plan security with the assumption that the firewall has been breached. The DBMS, the database, and all applications should be secure even if the firewall fails.

DBMS vendors, including IBM, Oracle, and Microsoft, are constantly adding product features to improve security and reduce vulnerability. Consequently, organizations using

FIGURE 9-16

Summary of DBMS
Security Guidelines

- Run DBMS behind a firewall, but plan as though the firewall has been breached

- Apply the latest operating system and DBMS service packs and fixes

- Use the least functionality possible
  - Support the fewest network protocols possible
  - Delete unnecessary or unused system stored procedures
  - Disable default logins and guest users, if possible
  - Unless required, never allow users to log on to the DBMS interactively

- Protect the computer that runs the DBMS
  - No user allowed to work at the computer that runs the DBMS
  - DBMS computer physically secured behind locked doors
  - Visits to the room containing the DBMS computer should be recorded in a log

- Manage accounts and passwords
  - Use a low privilege user account for the DBMS service
  - Protect database accounts with strong passwords
  - Monitor failed login attempts
  - Frequently check group and role memberships
  - Audit accounts with null passwords
  - Assign accounts the lowest privileges possible
  - Limit DBA account privileges

- Planning
  - Develop a security plan for preventing and detecting security problems
  - Create procedures for security emergencies and practice them

DBMS products should continually check the vendors' Web sites for service packs and fixes; any service packs or fixes that involve security features, functions, and processing should be installed as soon as possible.

The installation of new service packs and fixes is not quite as simple as described here. The installation of a service pack or fix can break some applications, particularly some licensed software that requires specific service packs and fixes to be installed (or not installed). It may be necessary to delay installation of DBMS service packs until vendors of licensed software have upgraded their products to work with the new versions. Sometimes just the possibility that a licensed application *might* fail after a DBMS service pack or fix is applied is sufficient reason to delay the fix. However, the DBMS is still vulnerable during this period. Pick your regret!

Additionally, database features and functions that are not required by the applications should be removed or disabled from the DBMS. For example, if TCP/IP is used to connect to the DBMS, other communications protocols should be removed. This action reduces the pathways by which unauthorized activity can reach the DBMS. Further, all DBMS products are installed with system-stored procedures that provide services such as starting a command file, modifying the system registry, initiating email, and the like. Any of these stored procedures that are not needed should be removed. If all users are known to the DBMS, default logins and guest user accounts should be removed as well. Finally, unless otherwise required, users should never be allowed to log on to the DBMS in interactive mode. They should always access the database via an application.

In addition, the computer(s) that runs the DBMS must be protected. No one other than authorized DBA personnel should be allowed to work at the keyboard of the computer that runs the DBMS. The computer running the DBMS should be physically secured behind locked doors, and access to the facility housing the computer should be controlled. Visits to the DBMS computer room should be recorded in a log.

Accounts and passwords should be assigned carefully and continually managed. The DBMS itself should run on an account that has the lowest possible operating system privileges. In that way, if an intruder were to gain control of the DBMS, the intruder would have limited authority on that local computer or network. Additionally, all accounts within the DBMS should be protected by **strong passwords**. Such passwords have at least 15 characters and contain upper- and lowercase letters; numbers; special characters, such as +, @, #, ***; and unprintable key combinations (certain Alt + key combinations).

The DBA should frequently check the accounts that have been assigned to groups and roles to ensure that all accounts and roles are known, are authorized, and have the correct permissions. Further, the DBA should audit accounts with null passwords. The users of such accounts should be required to protect those accounts with strong passwords. Also, as a general rule, accounts should be granted the lowest privileges possible.

As stated, the privileges for the DBA should normally not include the right to process the users' data. If the DBA grants himself or herself that privilege, the unauthorized grant operation will be visible in the database log.

In the spring of 2003, the Slammer worm invaded thousands of sites running Microsoft SQL Server. Microsoft had previously released a patch to SQL Server that prevented this attack. Sites that had installed the patch had no problems. The moral: Install security patches to your DBMS as promptly as possible. Create a procedure for regularly checking for such patches.

Finally, the DBA should participate in security planning. Procedures for both preventing and detecting security problems should be developed. Furthermore, procedures should be developed for actions to be taken in case of a security breach. Such procedures should be practiced. The importance of security in information systems has increased dramatically in recent years. DBA personnel should regularly search for security information on the Web in general and at the DBMS vendor's Web site.

Application Security

Although DBMS products such as Oracle Database, Microsoft SQL Server, and MySQL do provide substantial database security capabilities, those capabilities are generic. If the application requires specific security measures, such as "No user can view a row of a table or of a join of a table that has an employee name other than his or her own," the DBMS facilities will not be adequate. In these cases, the security system must be augmented by features in database applications.

For example, as you will learn in Chapter 11, application security in Internet applications is often provided on the Web server. Executing application security on this server means that sensitive security data need not be transmitted over the network.

To understand this better, suppose that an application is written so that when users click a particular button on a browser page, the following query is sent to the Web server and then to the DBMS:

```
/* *** EXAMPLE CODE - DO NOT RUN *** */
/* *** SQL-Code-Example-CH09-06 *** */
SELECT        *
FROM          EMPLOYEE;
```

This statement will, of course, return all EMPLOYEE rows. If the application security policy permits employees to access only their own data, then a Web server could add the following WHERE clause to this query:

```
/* *** EXAMPLE CODE - DO NOT RUN *** */
/* *** SQL-Code-Example-CH09-07 *** */
SELECT        *
FROM          EMPLOYEE
WHERE         EMPLOYEE.Name = '<% = SESSION(("EmployeeName"))%>';
```

An expression like this one will cause the Web server to fill the employee's name into the WHERE clause. For a user signed in under the name 'Benjamin Franklin', the statement that results from this expression is:

```
/* *** EXAMPLE CODE - DO NOT RUN *** */
/* *** SQL-Code-Example-CH09-08 *** */
SELECT        *
FROM          EMPLOYEE
WHERE         EMPLOYEE.Name = 'Benjamin Franklin';
```

Because the name is inserted by a program on the Web server, the browser user does not know that it is occurring and cannot interfere with it even if he or she did.

Such security processing can be done as shown here on a Web server, but it also can be done within the application programs themselves or written as stored procedures or triggers to be executed by the DBMS at the appropriate times.

This idea can be extended by storing additional data in a security database that is accessed by the Web server or by stored procedures and triggers. That security database could contain, for example, the identities of users paired with additional values of WHERE clauses. For example, suppose that the users in the personnel department can access more than just their own data. The predicates for appropriate WHERE clauses could be stored in the security database, read by the application program, and appended to SQL SELECT statements as necessary.

Many other possibilities exist for extending DBMS security with application processing. In general, however, you should use the DBMS security features first. Only if they are inadequate for the requirements should you add to them with application code. The closer the security enforcement is to the data, the less chance there is for infiltration. Also, using the DBMS security features is faster and cheaper and probably results in higher-quality results than developing your own.

The SQL Injection Attack

Whenever data from the user are used to modify an SQL statement, an **SQL injection attack** is possible. For example, in the prior section, if the value of EmployeeName used in the SELECT statement is not obtained via a secure means, such as from the operating system rather than from a Web form, there is the chance that the user can inject SQL into the statement.

For example, suppose that users are asked to enter their names into a Web form textbox. Suppose that a user enters the value *'Benjamin Franklin' OR TRUE* for his or her name. The SQL statement generated by the application will then be the following:

```
/* *** EXAMPLE CODE - DO NOT RUN *** */
/* *** SQL-Code-Example-CH09-09 *** */
SELECT      *
FROM        EMPLOYEE
WHERE       EMPLOYEE.Name = 'Benjamin Franklin' OR TRUE;
```

Of course, the value TRUE is true for every row, so every row of the EMPLOYEE table will be returned! Thus, any time user input is used to modify an SQL statement, that input must be carefully edited to ensure that only valid input has been received and that no additional SQL syntax has been entered.

Despite being a well-known hacker attack, the SQL injection attack can still be very effective if not defended against. On March 29, 2011, the LizaMoon[1] attack struck and affected more than 1.5 million URLs!

Database Backup and Recovery

Computer systems fail. Hardware breaks. Programs have bugs. Human procedures contain errors, and people make mistakes. All of these failures can and do occur in database applications. Because a database is shared by many people and because it often is a key element of an organization's operations, it is important to recover it as soon as possible.

Several problems must be addressed. First, from a business standpoint, business functions must continue. During the failure, customer orders, financial transactions, and packing lists must be completed somehow, even manually. Later, when the database application is operational again, the data from those activities must be entered into the database. Second, computer operations personnel must restore the system to a usable state as quickly as possible and as close as possible to what it was when the system crashed. Third, users must know what to do when the system becomes available again. Some work may need to be reentered, and users must know how far back they need to go.

When failures occur, it is impossible simply to fix the problem and resume processing. Even if no data are lost during a failure (which assumes that all types of memory are nonvolatile—an unrealistic assumption), the timing and scheduling of computer processing are too complex to be accurately re-created. Enormous amounts of overhead data and processing would be required for the operating system to be able to restart processing precisely where it was interrupted. It is simply not possible to roll back the clock and put all of the electrons in the same configuration they were in at the time of the failure. Two other approaches are possible: **recovery via reprocessing** and **recovery via rollback/rollforward**.

Recovery via Reprocessing

Because processing cannot be resumed at a precise point, the next best alternative is to go back to a known point and reprocess the workload from there. The simplest form of this type of recovery is to periodically make a copy of the database (called a **database save**) and to keep a record of all transactions that have been processed since the save. Then, when there is a failure, the operations staff can restore the database from the save and then reprocess all the transactions. Unfortunately, this simple strategy is normally not feasible. First, reprocessing transactions takes the same amount of time as processing them in the first place did. If the computer is heavily scheduled, the system may never catch up.

Second, when transactions are processed concurrently, events are asynchronous. Slight variations in human activity, such as a user reading an email before responding to an

---

[1] For more information, see *http://en.wikipedia.org/wiki/LizaMoon.*

application prompt, can change the order of the execution of concurrent transactions. Therefore, whereas Customer A got the last seat on a flight during the original processing, Customer B may get the last seat during reprocessing. For these reasons, reprocessing is normally not a viable form of recovery from failure in concurrent processing systems.

Recovery via Rollback/Rollforward

A second approach is to periodically make a copy of the database (the database save) and to keep a log of the changes made by transactions against the database since the save. Then, when there is a failure, one of two methods can be used. Using the first method, called **rollforward**, the database is restored using the saved data, and all valid transactions since the save are reapplied. (We are not reprocessing the transactions because the application programs are not involved in the rollforward. Instead, the processed changes, as recorded in the log, are reapplied.)

The second method is **rollback**. With this method, we undo changes made by erroneous or partially processed transactions by undoing the changes they have made in the database. Then the valid transactions that were in process at the time of the failure are restarted.

Both of these methods require that a **log** of the transaction results be kept. This log contains records of the data changes in chronological order. Transactions must be written to the log before they are applied to the database. That way, if the system crashes between the time a transaction is logged and the time it is applied, at worst there is a record of an unapplied transaction. If, however, the transactions were to be applied before they were logged, it would be possible (as well as undesirable) to change the database but have no record of the change. If this happened, an unwary user might reenter an already completed transaction. In the event of a failure, the log is used both to undo and to redo transactions, as shown in Figure 9-17.

To undo a transaction, the log must contain a copy of every database record (or page) before it was changed. Such records are called **before images**. A transaction is undone by applying before images of all of its changes to the database.

To redo a transaction, the log must contain a copy of every database record (or page) after it was changed. These records are called **after images**. A transaction is redone by applying

FIGURE 9-17

Undo and Redo Transactions

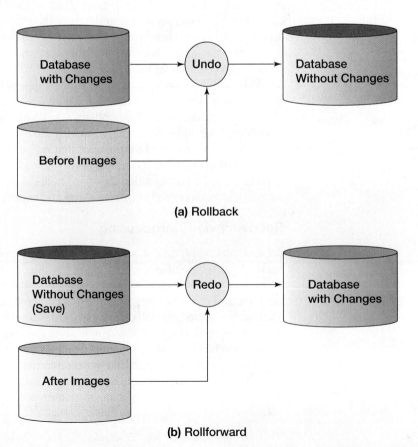

(a) Rollback

(b) Rollforward

FIGURE 9-18

Example Transaction Log

Relative Record Number	Transaction ID	Reverse Pointer	Forward Pointer	Time	Type of Operation	Object	Before Image	After Image
1	OT1	0	2	11:42	START			
2	OT1	1	4	11:43	MODIFY	CUST 100	(old value)	(new value)
3	OT2	0	8	11:46	START			
4	OT1	2	5	11:47	MODIFY	SP AA	(old value)	(new value)
5	OT1	4	7	11:47	INSERT	ORDER 11		(value)
6	CT1	0	9	11:48	START			
7	OT1	5	0	11:49	COMMIT			
8	OT2	3	0	11:50	COMMIT			
9	CT1	6	10	11:51	MODIFY	SP BB	(old value)	(new value)
10	CT1	9	0	11:51	COMMIT			

after images of all of its changes to the database. Possible data items in a transaction log are shown in Figure 9-18.

In this example log, each transaction has a unique name for identification purposes. Furthermore, all of the images for a given transaction are linked together with pointers. One pointer points to the previous change made by this transaction (the reverse pointer), and the other points to the next change made by this transaction (the forward pointer). A zero in the pointer field means that this is the end of the list. The DBMS recovery subsystem uses these pointers to locate all of the records for a particular transaction. Figure 9-18 shows an example of the linking of log records.

Other data items in the log are the time of the action; the type of operation (START marks the beginning of a transaction and COMMIT terminates a transaction, releasing all locks that were in place); the object acted on, such as record type and identifier; and, finally, the before images and the after images.

Given a log with before images and after images, the undo and redo actions are straightforward. To undo the transaction in Figure 9-19, the recovery processor simply replaces each changed record with its before image. For *rollforward*, the *after images* are applied in *forward* time order; for *rollback*, the *before images* are applied in *reverse* time order.

When all of the before images have been restored, the transaction is undone. To redo a transaction, the recovery processor starts with the version of the database at the time the transaction started and applies all of the after images. As stated, this action assumes that an earlier version of the database is available from a database save.

Restoring a database to its most recent save and reapplying all transactions may require considerable processing. To reduce the delay, DBMS products sometimes use checkpoints. A **checkpoint** is a point of synchronization between the database and the transaction log. To perform a checkpoint, the DBMS refuses new requests, finishes processing outstanding requests, and writes its buffers to disk. The DBMS then waits until the operating system notifies it that all outstanding write requests to the database and to the log have been successfully completed. At this point, the log and the database are synchronized. A checkpoint record is then written to the log. Later, the database can be recovered from the checkpoint and only after images for transactions that started after the checkpoint need be applied.

Checkpoints are inexpensive operations, and it is feasible to take three or four (or more) per hour. In this way, no more than 15 or 20 minutes of processing need to be recovered. Most DBMS products perform automatic checkpoints, making human intervention unnecessary.

FIGURE 9-19

Recovery Example

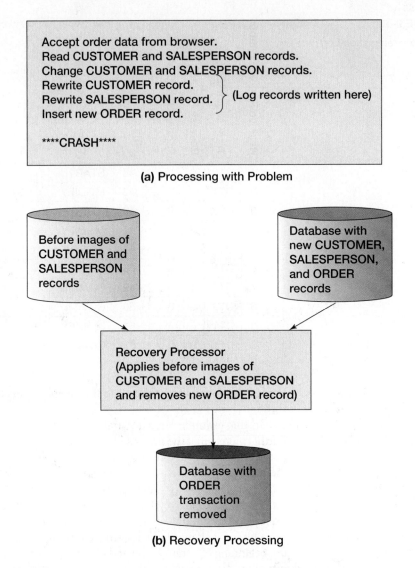

Accept order data from browser.
Read CUSTOMER and SALESPERSON records.
Change CUSTOMER and SALESPERSON records.
Rewrite CUSTOMER record.
Rewrite SALESPERSON record. } (Log records written here)
Insert new ORDER record.

****CRASH****

(a) Processing with Problem

Before images of CUSTOMER and SALESPERSON records

Database with new CUSTOMER, SALESPERSON, and ORDER records

Recovery Processor
(Applies before images of CUSTOMER and SALESPERSON and removes new ORDER record)

Database with ORDER transaction removed

(b) Recovery Processing

You will see specific examples of backup and recovery techniques for Microsoft SQL Server, Oracle Database, and MySQL in the next three chapters. For now, you only need to understand the basic ideas and to realize that it is the responsibility of the DBA to ensure that adequate backup and recovery plans have been developed and that database saves and logs are generated as required.

Managing the DBMS

In addition to managing data activity and the database structure, the DBA must manage the DBMS itself. The DBA should compile and analyze statistics concerning the system's performance and identify potential problem areas. Keep in mind that the database is serving many user groups. The DBA needs to investigate all complaints about the system's response time, accuracy, ease of use, and so forth. If changes are needed, the DBA must plan and implement them.

The DBA must periodically monitor the users' activity on the database. DBMS products include features that collect and report statistics. For example, some of these reports may indicate which users have been active, which files—and perhaps which data items—have been used, and which access methods have been employed. Error rates and types also can be captured and reported. The DBA analyzes these data to determine whether a change to the database design is needed to improve performance or to ease the users' tasks. If change is necessary, the DBA will ensure that it is accomplished.

The DBA should analyze run-time statistics on database activity and performance. When a performance problem is identified (by either a report or a user's complaint), the DBA must determine whether a modification of the database structure or system is appropriate. Examples of possible structural modifications are establishing new keys, purging data, deleting keys, and establishing new relationships among objects.

When the vendor of the DBMS being used announces new product features, the DBA must consider them in light of the overall needs of the user community. If the DBA decides to incorporate the new DBMS features, the developers must be notified and trained in their use. Accordingly, the DBA must manage and control changes in the DBMS as well as in the database structure.

Other changes in the system for which the DBA is responsible vary widely, depending on the DBMS product as well as on other software and hardware in use. For example, changes in other software (such as the operating system or the Web server) may mean that some DBMS features, functions, or parameters must be changed. The DBA must therefore also tune the DBMS product with other software in use.

The DBMS options (such as transaction isolation levels) are initially chosen when little is known about how the system will perform in the particular user environment. Consequently, operational experience and performance analysis over a period of time may reveal that changes are necessary. Even if the performance seems acceptable, the DBA may want to alter the options and observe the effect on performance. This process is referred to as *tuning*, or *optimizing*, the system. Figure 9-20 summarizes the DBA's responsibilities for managing the DBMS product.

Maintaining the Data Repository

Consider a large and active Internet database application, such as those used by e-commerce companies—for instance, an application that is used by a company that sells clothing over the Internet. Such a system may involve data from several different databases, dozens of different Web pages, and hundreds, or even thousands, of users.

Suppose that the company using this application decides to expand its product line to include the sale of sporting goods. Senior management of this company might ask the DBA to develop an estimate of the time and other resources required to modify the database application to support this new product line.

To respond to this request, the DBA needs accurate metadata about the database, about the database applications and application components, about the users and their rights and privileges, and about other system elements. The database does carry some of this metadata in system tables, but this metadata is inadequate to answer the questions posed by senior management. The DBA needs additional metadata about COM and ActiveX objects, script procedures and functions, Active Server Pages (ASPs), style sheets, document type definitions, and the like. Furthermore, although DBMS security mechanisms document users, groups, and privileges, they do so in a highly structured, and often inconvenient, form.

For all of these reasons, many organizations develop and maintain **data repositories**, which are collections of metadata about databases, database applications, Web pages, users, and other application components. The repository may be virtual in that it is composed of metadata from many different sources: the DBMS, version-control software, code libraries,

FIGURE 9-20

Summary of the DBA's Responsibilities for Managing the DMBS

• Generate database application performance reports
• Investigate user performance complaints
• Assess need for changes in database structure or application design
• Modify database structure
• Evaluate and implement new DBMS features
• Tune the DBMS

Web page generation and editing tools, and so forth. Or the data repository may be an integrated product from a CASE tool vendor or from a company such as Microsoft or Oracle.

Either way, the time for the DBA to think about constructing such a facility is long before senior management asks questions. In fact, the repository should be constructed as the system is developed and should be considered an important part of the system deliverables. If such a facility is not constructed, the DBA will always be playing catch-up—trying to maintain the existing applications, adapting them to new needs, and somehow gathering together the metadata to form a repository.

The best repositories are **active repositories**—they are part of the systems development process in that metadata is created automatically as the system components are created. Less desirable, but still effective, are **passive repositories**, which are filled only when someone takes the time to generate the needed metadata and place it in the repository.

The Internet has created enormous opportunities for businesses to expand their customer bases and increase their sales and profitability. The databases and database applications that support these companies are an essential element of that success. Unfortunately, the growth of some organizations will be stymied by their inability to grow their applications or adapt them to changing needs. Often, building a new system is easier than adapting an existing one. Building a new system that integrates with an old one while it replaces that old one can be very difficult.

Summary

Multiuser databases pose difficult problems for the organizations that create and use them, and most organizations have created an office of database administration to ensure that such problems are solved. In this text, the term *database administrator* refers to the person or office that is concerned with a single database. The term *data administrator* is used to describe a management function that is concerned with the organization's data policy and security. Major functions of the database administrator are listed in Figure 9-1.

The database administrator (DBA) participates in the initial development of database structures and in providing configuration control when requests for changes arise. Keeping accurate documentation of the structure and changes to the databases is an important DBA function.

The goal of concurrency control is to ensure that one user's work does not inappropriately influence another user's work. No single concurrency control technique is ideal for all circumstances. Trade-offs need to be made between the level of protection and throughput. A transaction, or logical unit of work (LUW), is a series of actions taken against the database that occurs as an atomic unit; either all of them occur or none of them does. The activity of concurrent transactions is interleaved on the database server. In some cases, updates can be lost if concurrent transactions are not controlled. Another concurrency problem concerns inconsistent reads.

To avoid concurrency problems, database elements are locked. Implicit locks are placed by the DBMS; explicit locks are issued by the application program. The size of the locked resource is called lock granularity. An exclusive lock prohibits other users from reading the locked resource; a shared lock allows other users to read the locked resource but not update it. Two transactions that run concurrently and generate results that are consistent with the results that would have occurred if they had run separately are referred to as serializable transactions. Two-phase locking, in which locks are acquired in a growing phase and released in a shrinking phase, is one scheme for serializability. A special case of two-phase locking is to acquire locks throughout the transaction but to not free any lock until the transaction is finished.

Deadlock, or the deadly embrace, occurs when two transactions are each waiting on a resource that the other transaction holds. Deadlock can be prevented by requiring transactions to acquire all locks at the same time. Once deadlock occurs, the only way to cure it is to abort one of the transactions (and back out of partially completed work). Optimistic locking assumes that no transaction conflict will occur and deals with the consequences if it does. Pessimistic locking assumes that conflict will occur and so prevents it ahead of time with locks. In general, optimistic locking is preferred for the Internet and for many intranet applications.

Most application programs do not explicitly declare locks. Instead, they use SQL Transaction Control Language (TCL) to mark transaction boundaries with BEGIN, COMMIT, and ROLLBACK transaction statements and declare the concurrent behavior they want. The DBMS then places locks for the application that will result in the desired behavior.

An ACID transaction is one that is atomic, consistent, isolated, and durable. *Durable* means that database changes are permanent. *Consistency* can mean either statement-level or transaction-level consistency. With transaction-level consistency, a transaction may not see its own changes. The SQL standard defines four SQL transaction isolation levels: read uncommitted, read committed, repeatable read, and serializable. The characteristics of each are summarized in Figure 9-12.

An SQL cursor is a pointer into a set of records. Four cursor types are prevalent: forward only, static, keyset, and dynamic. Developers should select isolation levels and cursor types that are appropriate for their application workload and for the DBMS product in use.

The goal of database security is to ensure that only authorized users can perform authorized activities at authorized times. To develop effective database security, the processing rights and responsibilities of all users must be determined.

DBMS products provide security facilities. Most involve the declaration of users, groups, objects to be protected, and permissions or privileges on those objects. Almost all DBMS products use some form of username and password security. Security guidelines are listed in Figure 9-16. DBMS security can be augmented by application security.

In the event of system failure, the database must be restored to a usable state as soon as possible. Transactions in process at the time of the failure must be reapplied or restarted. Although in some cases recovery can be done by reprocessing, the use of logs and rollback and rollforward is almost always preferred. Checkpoints can be taken to reduce the amount of work that needs to be done after a failure.

In addition to these tasks, the DBA manages the DBMS product itself, measuring database application performance and assessing the need for changes in database structure or DBMS performance tuning. The DBA also ensures that new DBMS features are evaluated and used as appropriate. Finally, the DBA is responsible for maintaining the data repository.

Key Terms

ACID transaction
active repository
after image
atomic
before image
checkpoint
concurrent transaction
concurrent update problem
consistent
cursor
data administration
data repository
database administration
database administrator
database save
DBA
deadlock
deadly embrace
dirty read
durable
dynamic cursor
exclusive lock
explicit lock
forward only cursor
growing phase
implicit lock
inconsistent read problem
isolated

isolation level
keyset cursor
lock
lock granularity
log
logical unit of work (LUW)
login name
lost update problem
nonrepeatable read
optimistic locking
passive repository
pessimistic locking
phantom read
processing rights and
    responsibilities
read-committed isolation level
read-uncommitted isolation level
recovery via reprocessing
recovery via rollback/rollforward
repeatable-read isolation level
resource locking
role
rollback
rollforward
scrollable cursor
serializable
serializable isolation level
shared lock

shrinking phase
SQL BEGIN TRANSACTION
    statement
SQL COMMIT TRANSACTION
    statement
SQL cursor
SQL Data Control Language (DCL)
SQL DECLARE CURSOR
    statement
SQL GRANT statement
SQL REVOKE statement
SQL ROLLBACK TRANSACTION
    statement
SQL START TRANSACTION
    statement
SQL Transaction Control Language
    (TCL)
SQL WORK keyword
SQL injection attack
statement-level consistency
static cursor
strong password
transaction
transaction isolation level
transaction-level consistency
two-phase locking
user group
username

Review Questions

9.1 Briefly describe five difficult problems for organizations that create and use multiuser databases.

9.2 Explain the difference between a database administrator and a data administrator.

9.3 List seven important DBA tasks.

9.4 Summarize the DBA's responsibilities for managing database structure.

9.5 What is configuration control? Why is it necessary?

9.6 Explain the meaning of the word *inappropriately* in the phrase "one user's work does not inappropriately influence another user's work."

9.7 Explain the trade-off that exists in concurrency control.

9.8 Define an atomic transaction, and explain why atomicity is important.

9.9 Explain the difference between concurrent transactions and simultaneous transactions. How many CPUs are required for simultaneous transactions?

9.10 Give an example, other than the one in this text, of the lost update problem.

9.11 Explain the difference between an explicit and an implicit lock.

9.12 What is lock granularity?

9.13 Explain the difference between an exclusive lock and a shared lock.

9.14 Explain two-phase locking.

9.15 How does releasing all locks at the end of the transaction relate to two-phase locking?

9.16 In general, how should the boundaries of a transaction be defined?

9.17 What is deadlock? How can it be avoided? How can it be resolved once it occurs?

9.18 Explain the difference between optimistic and pessimistic locking.

9.19 Explain the benefits of marking transaction boundaries, declaring lock characteristics, and letting the DBMS place locks.

9.20 What is SQL Transaction Control Language (TCL)? Explain the use of the SQL BEGIN TRANSACTION, COMMIT TRANSACTION, and ROLLBACK TRANSACTION statements. Why does MySQL also use the SQL START TRANSACTION statement?

9.21 Explain the meaning of the expression *ACID transaction*.

9.22 Describe statement-level consistency.

9.23 Describe transaction-level consistency. What disadvantage can exist with it?

9.24 What is the purpose of transaction isolation levels?

9.25 Explain the read-uncommitted isolation level. Give an example of its use.

9.26 Explain the read-committed isolation level. Give an example of its use.

9.27 Explain the repeatable-read isolation level. Give an example of its use.

9.28 Explain the serializable isolation level. Give an example of its use.

9.29 Explain the term *SQL cursor*.

9.30 Explain why a transaction may have many cursors. Also, how is it possible that a transaction may have more than one cursor on a given table?

9.31 What is the advantage of using different types of cursors?

9.32 Explain forward-only cursors. Give an example of their use.

9.33 Explain static cursors. Give an example of their use.

9.34 Explain keyset cursors. Give an example of their use.

9.35 Explain dynamic cursors. Give an example of their use.

9.36 What happens if you do not declare the transaction isolation level and the cursor type to the DBMS? Is this good or bad?

9.37 What is SQL Data Control Language (DCL)? Explain the necessity of defining processing rights and responsibilities. How are such responsibilities enforced, and what is the role of SQL DCL in enforcing them?

9.38 Explain the relationships among USER, ROLE, PERMISSION, and OBJECT for a generic database security system.

9.39 Should the DBA assume a firewall when planning security?

9.40 What should be done with unused DBMS features and functions?

9.41 Explain how to protect the computer that runs the DBMS.

9.42 With regard to security, what actions should the DBA take on user accounts and passwords?

9.43 List two elements of a database security plan.

9.44 Describe the advantages and disadvantages of DBMS-provided and application-provided security.

9.45 What is an SQL injection attack, and how can it be prevented?

9.46 Explain how a database could be recovered via reprocessing. Why is this generally not feasible?

9.47 Define *rollback* and *rollforward*.

9.48 Why is it important to write to the log before changing the database values?

9.49 Describe the rollback process. Under what conditions should it be used?

9.50 Describe the rollforward process. Under what conditions should it be used?

9.51 What is the advantage of taking frequent checkpoints of a database?

9.52 Summarize the DBA's responsibilities for managing the DBMS.

9.53 What is a data repository? A passive data repository? An active data repository?

9.54 Explain why a data repository is important. What is likely to happen if one is not available?

Project Questions

9.56 Visit *www.oracle.com*, and search for "Oracle Security Guidelines." Read articles at three of the links you find, and summarize them. How does the information you find compare with that in Figure 9-15?

9.57 Visit *www.msdn.microsoft.com*, and search for "SQL Server Security Guidelines." Read articles at three of the links you find, and summarize them. How does the information you find compare with that in Figure 9-15?

9.58 Visit *www.mysql.com*, and search for "MySQL Security Guidelines." Read articles at three of the links you find, and summarize them. How does the information you find compare with that in Figure 9-15?

9.59 Use Google (*www.google.com*) or another search engine, and search the Web for "Database Security Guidelines." Read articles at three of the links you find, and summarize them. How does the information you find compare with that in Figure 9-15?

9.60 Search the Web for "distributed two-phase locking." Find a tutorial on that topic, and explain, in general terms, how this locking algorithm works.

9.61 Answer the following questions for the View Ridge Gallery VRG database discussed in Chapter 7 with the tables shown in Figures 7-13 and 7-14 and the data shown in Figure 7-15.

    A. Suppose that you are developing a stored procedure to record an artist who has never been in the gallery before, a work for that artist, and a row in the TRANS table to record the date acquired and the acquisition price. How will you declare the boundaries of the transaction? What transaction isolation level will you use?

    B. Suppose that you are writing a stored procedure to change values in the CUSTOMER table. What transaction isolation level will you use?

    C. Suppose that you are writing a stored procedure to record a customer's purchase. Assume that the customer's data are new. How will you declare the boundaries of the transaction? What isolation level will you use?

    D. Suppose that you are writing a stored procedure to check the validity of the intersection table. Specifically, for each customer, your procedure should read the customer's transaction and determine the artist of that work. Given the artist, your procedure should then check to ensure that an interest has been declared for that artist in the intersection table. If there is no such intersection row, your procedure should create one. How will you set the boundaries of your transaction? What isolation level will you use? What cursor types (if any) will you use?

Case Questions

Marcia's Dry Cleaning Case Questions

Marcia Wilson owns and operates *Marcia's Dry Cleaning*, which is an upscale dry cleaner in a well-to-do suburban neighborhood. Marcia makes her business stand out from the competition by providing superior customer service. She wants to keep track of each of her customers and their orders. Ultimately, she wants to notify them that their clothes are ready via email. Suppose that Marcia has hired you as a database consultant to develop a database for Marcia's Dry Cleaning that has the following tables:

    CUSTOMER (<u>CustomerID</u>, FirstName, LastName, Phone, EmailAddress)

    INVOICE (<u>InvoiceNumber</u>, *CustomerID*, DateIn, DateOut, Subtotal, Tax, TotalAmount)

    INVOICE_ITEM (*<u>InvoiceNumber</u>*, <u>ItemNumber</u>, *ServiceID*, Quantity, UnitPrice, ExtendedPrice)

    SERVICE (<u>ServiceID</u>, ServiceDescription, UnitPrice)

Assume that all relationships have been defined, as implied by the foreign keys in this table list, and that the appropriate referential integrity constraints are in place.

    A. Assume that Marcia's has the following personnel: two owners, a shift manager, a part-time seamstress, and two salesclerks. Prepare a two- to three-page memo that addresses the following points:

        1. The need for database administration.

        2. Your recommendation as to who should serve as database administrator. Assume that Marcia's is not sufficiently large to need or afford a full-time database administrator.

3. Using Figure 9-1 as a guide, describe the nature of database administration activities at Marcia's. As an aggressive consultant, keep in mind that you can recommend yourself for performing some of the DBA functions.

B. For the employees described in part A, define users, groups, and permissions on data in these four tables. Use the security scheme shown in Figure 9-15 as an example. Create a table like that in Figure 9-14. Don't forget to include yourself.

C. Suppose that you are writing a stored procedure to create new records in SERVICE for new services that Marcia's will perform. Suppose that you know that while your procedure is running, another stored procedure that records new or modifies existing customer orders and order line items can also be running. Additionally, suppose that a third stored procedure that records new customer data also can be running.

1. Give an example of a dirty read, a nonrepeatable read, and a phantom read among this group of stored procedures.

2. What concurrency control measures are appropriate for the stored procedure that you are creating?

3. What concurrency control measures are appropriate for the two other stored procedures?

The Queen Anne Curiosity Shop

Assume that the owners of the Queen Anne Curiosity Shop have hired you as a database consultant to develop an operational database having the same tables described at the end of Chapter 7:

CUSTOMER (<u>CustomerID</u>, LastName, FirstName, Address, EmailAddress, EncryptedPassword, City, State, ZIP, Phone)

EMPLOYEE (<u>EmployeeID</u>, LastName, FirstName, Phone, Email)

VENDOR (<u>VendorID</u>, CompanyName, ContactLastName, ContactFirstName, Address, City, State, ZIP, Phone, Fax, Email)

ITEM (<u>ItemID</u>, ItemDescription, PurchaseDate, ItemCost, ItemPrice, *VendorID*)

SALE (<u>SaleID</u>, *CustomerID*, *EmployeeID*, SaleDate, SubTotal, Tax, Total)

SALE_ITEM (<u>*SaleID*</u>, <u>SaleItemID</u>, *ItemID*, ItemPrice)

The referential integrity constraints are:

CustomerID in SALE must exist in CustomerID in CUSTOMER

EmployeeID in SALE must exist in EmployeeID in EMPLOYEE

SaleID in SALE_ITEM must exist in SaleID in SALE

ItemID in SALE_ITEM must exist in ItemID in ITEM

VendorID in ITEM must exist in VendorID in VENDOR

Assume that CustomerID of CUSTOMER, EmployeeID of EMPLOYEE, ItemID of ITEM, SaleID of SALE, and SaleItemID of SALE_ITEM are all surrogate keys with values as follows:

CustomerID	Start at 1	Increment by 1
EmployeeID	Start at 1	Increment by 1
VendorID	Start at 1	Increment by 1
ItemID	Start at 1	Increment by 1
SaleID	Start at 1	Increment by 1

A vendor may be an individual or a company. If the vendor is an individual, the CompanyName field is left blank, while the ContactLastName and ContactFirstName fields must have data values. If the vendor is a company, the company name is recorded in the CompanyName field, and the name of the primary contact at the company is recorded in the ContactLastName and ContactFirstName fields.

A. Assume that the Queen Anne Curiosity Shop personnel are the two owners, an office administrator, one full-time salesperson, and two part-time salespeople. The two owners and the office administrator want to process data in all tables. Additionally, the full-time salesperson can enter purchase and sales data. The part-time employees can only read sales data. Prepare a three- to five-page memo for the owner that addresses the following issues:

   1. The need for database administration at the Queen Anne Curiosity Shop.

   2. Your recommendation as to who should serve as database administrator. Assume that the Queen Anne Curiosity Shop is not sufficiently large that it needs or can afford a full-time database administrator.

   3. Using Figure 9-1 as a guide, describe the nature of database administration activities at the Queen Anne Curiosity Shop. As an aggressive consultant, keep in mind that you can recommend yourself for performing some of the DBA functions.

B. For the employees described in part A, define users, groups, and permissions on data in these six tables. Use the security scheme shown in Figure 9-15 as an example. Create a table like that in Figure 9-14. Don't forget to include yourself.

C. Suppose that you are writing a stored procedure to record new purchases. Suppose that you know that while your procedure is running, another stored procedure that records new customer sales and sale line items can also be running. Additionally, suppose that a third stored procedure that records new customer data also can be running.

   1. Give an example of a dirty read, a nonrepeatable read, and a phantom read among this group of stored procedures.

   2. What concurrency control measures are appropriate for the stored procedure that you are creating?

   3. What concurrency control measures are appropriate for the two other stored procedures?

Morgan Importing

Assume that Morgan has hired you as a database consultant to develop an operational database having the same tables described at the end of Chapter 7 (note that STORE uses the surrogate key StoreID):

EMPLOYEE (<u>EmployeeID</u>, LastName, FirstName, Department, Phone, Fax, EmailAddress)

STORE (<u>StoreID</u>, StoreName, City, Country, Phone, Fax, EmailAddress, Contact)

ITEM (<u>ItemID</u>, *StoreName*, *PurchasingAgentID*, PurchaseDate, ItemDescription, Category, PriceUSD)

SHIPPER (<u>ShipperID</u>, ShipperName, Phone, Fax, EmailAddress, Contact)

SHIPMENT (<u>ShipmentID</u>, *ShipperID*, *PurchasingAgentID*, ShipperInvoiceNumber, Origin, Destination, ScheduledDepartureDate, ActualDepartureDate, EstimatedArrivalDate)

SHIPMENT_ITEM (<u>*ShipmentID*</u>, <u>ShipmentItemID</u>, *ItemID*, InsuredValue)

SHIPMENT_RECEIPT (<u>ReceiptNumber</u>, *ShipmentID*, *ItemID*, *ReceivingAgentID*, ReceiptDate, ReceiptTime, ReceiptQuantity, isReceivedUndamaged, DamageNotes)

A. Assume that Morgan personnel are the owner (Morgan), an office administrator, one full-time salesperson, and two part-time salespeople. Morgan and the office administrator want to process data in all tables. Additionally, the full-time salesperson can enter purchase and shipment data. The part-time employees can read only shipment data; they are not allowed to see InsuredValue, however. Prepare a three- to five-page memo for the owner that addresses the following issues:

 1. The need for database administration at Morgan.

 2. Your recommendation as to who should serve as database administrator. Assume that Morgan is not sufficiently large that it needs or can afford a full-time database administrator.

 3. Using Figure 9-1 as a guide, describe the nature of database administration activities at Morgan. As an aggressive consultant, keep in mind that you can recommend yourself for performing some of the DBA functions.

B. For the employees described in part A, define users, groups, and permissions on data in these five tables. Use the security scheme shown in Figure 9-15 as an example. Create a table like that in Figure 9-14. Don't forget to include yourself.

C. Suppose that you are writing a stored procedure to record new purchases. Suppose that you know that while your procedure is running, another stored procedure that records shipment data can be running, and a third stored procedure that updates shipper data can also be running.

 1. Give an example of a dirty read, a nonrepeatable read, and a phantom read among this group of stored procedures.

 2. What concurrency control measures are appropriate for the stored procedure that you are creating?

 3. What concurrency control measures are appropriate for the two other stored procedures?

10

Managing Databases with Microsoft SQL Server 2014, Oracle Database, and MySQL 5.6

Chapter Objectives

- To install the DBMS software
- To use the DBMS database administration and database development graphical utilities
- To create a database in the DBMS
- To submit both SQL DDL and DML via the DBMS utilities
- To understand the implementation and use of SQL/ Persistent Stored Modules (SQL/PSM) in the DBMS
- To understand the purpose and role of user-defined functions and to create simple user-defined functions

- To understand the purpose and role of stored procedures and to create simple stored procedures
- To understand the purpose and role of triggers and to create simple triggers
- To understand how the DBMS implements concurrency control
- To understand how the DBMS implements server and database security
- To understand the fundamental features of the DBMS backup and recovery facilities

This chapter is an overview of the material that is covered in depth for three enterprise-class DBMS products in three separate online chapters:

- **Microsoft SQL Server 2014** in online Chapter 10A
- Oracle's **Oracle Database** in online Chapter 10B
- Oracle's **MySQL 5.6** in online Chapter 10C

These chapters have been placed online to allow us to include more material relevant to each separate DBMS product than the length of this book would otherwise allow. The online chapters are available at the *Database Processing: Fundamentals, Design, and Implementation (14th edition)* companion Web site, accessible at *www.pearsonhighered.com/kroenke*.

The online material (which also includes all the Appendices to this book) is in PDF format and requires that you have a PDF reader installed. If you need a PDF reader, we suggest you download and install the current version of the free Adobe Reader from *https://acrobat.adobe.com/us/en/products/pdf-reader.html*.

The material in these chapters describes the basic features and functions of Microsoft SQL Server 2014 in Chapter 10A, Oracle Database 12c (and Oracle Database Express Edition 11g Release 2) in Chapter 10B, and MySQL 5.6 in Chapter 10C. The discussion in these chapters uses the View Ridge Gallery database from Chapter 7, and it parallels the discussion of SQL DDL, DML, and SQL/PSM in Chapter 7 and the discussion of database administration tasks in Chapter 9.

These DBMS products are large and complicated systems. In these chapters, we will only be able to scratch the surface of what each is capable of. Your goal should be to learn sufficient basics so you can continue learning on your own or in other classes.

The topics and techniques discussed in these chapters will usually also apply to earlier versions of each software product. For example, the material on Microsoft SQL Server 2014 will also apply to SQL Server 2012, to SQL Server 2008 R2, and even to the earlier SQL Server 2005, though the exact functions of the earlier versions vary a bit from SQL Server 2014. Similarly, the material on Oracle Database 12c will usually work with Oracle Database 11g Release 2, and the material on MySQL 5.6 will work with MySQL 5.5.

Installing the DBMS

In this section of each online chapter, we will discuss the various versions of each DBMS available, recommend which version you should use, and cover important points about DBMS installation and setup. Each of these DBMS products has a freely available version that is easy to download and install and that can be used with most of the material in this book (the exception being some of the business intelligence (BI) topics in Appendix J).

For example, Microsoft SQL Server 2014 is available in the **Microsoft SQL Server 2014 Express Advanced** package (downloadable from *http://msdn.microsoft.com/en-us/evalcenter/dn434042.aspx*), and MySQL 5.6 is available in the **MySQL Community Server 5.6** (downloadable from *http://dev.mysql.com/downloads/mysql/.html*, but if you are using a Windows operating system, you should download and use the **MySQL Installer 5.6 for Windows** from *http://dev.mysql.com/downloads/windows/installer/5.6.html*).

Oracle Database presents a more complex situation. The current version of Oracle Database is Oracle Database 12c. If you have Oracle Database 12c available to you in a computer lab or other situation where it has been installed for your use in a class or work setting, you will be able to use it for the work in this book. Otherwise, you should download and use the current version of Oracle Database Express Edition, which is the **Oracle Database Express Edition 11g Release 2** package (downloadable from *www.oracle.com/technetwork/database/database-technologies/express-edition/downloads/index.html*). The Oracle SQL Developer GUI utility discussed later in this chapter will work well with both versions of Oracle Database and will allow you to complete nearly all the exercises in this book.

Installing and using one of these DBMS products (or, at a minimum, having **Microsoft Access 2013**) is a necessity for getting the most out of your study of the material in this book—using the material in a real DBMS is an important part of your learning process.

Of course, in order to use a DBMS product, you first have to install it and configure it on your computer. Therefore, we discuss what you need to know to be able to successfully install and use each DBMS product in the relevant online chapter.

Using the DBMS Database Administration and Database Development Utilities

Each of these DBMS products has one or more utility programs that you will use for database administration tasks and for database development. Examples of these utilities are:

- Microsoft SQL Server 2014 uses the **Microsoft SQL Server 2014 Management Studio**.
- Oracle Database 12*c* and Oracle Database Express Edition 11*g* Release 2 use **Oracle SQL Developer**.
- MySQL 5.6 uses the **MySQL Workbench**.

In each online chapter, we discuss the appropriate utility programs for each DBMS product and show you how to use them.

Creating a Database

The first step in working with a specific database in a DBMS is to actually create that database. However, this step is a bit more complicated than it might seem because each DBMS product has different terminology for what we just called a *database*!

- In Microsoft SQL Server 2014, we create a *database* (that was easy!).
- In Oracle Database 12*c* and Oracle Database Express Edition 11*g* Release 2 we may (but it is not required that we) create a **tablespace** to store the tables and other objects that make up what we are referring to as a database.
- In MySQL 5.6, we create a **schema**.

In each online chapter for the specific DBMS product, we tell you exactly what in that DBMS product constitutes what we have been calling a *database* and the steps to create and name it. In each case, we end up with a usable database named *Cape_Codd* for use with the Chapter 2 SQL queries, and a second usable database named *VRG* for the View Ridge Gallery database project.

Creating and Running SQL Scripts

Now that we have created the Cape_Codd and VRG databases, we need to create the table and relationship structure of the database and then populate the tables with data. We prefer to do this with SQL scripts, as we have discussed in Chapter 2 on SQL queries and in Chapter 7 on SQL DDL. Therefore, we discuss how to create, store, retrieve, and run SQL scripts using one of the DBMS utilities:

- For Microsoft SQL Server 2014, we use the Microsoft SQL Server 2014 Management Studio.
- For Oracle Database 12*c* and Oracle Database Express Edition 11*g* Release 2, we use Oracle SQL Developer.
- For MySQL 5.6, we use the MySQL Workbench.

Further, each DBMS product has its own variant of SQL and SQL/Persistent Stored Modules (SQL/PSM):

- For Microsoft SQL Server 2014, we have **Transact-SQL (T-SQL)**.
- For Oracle Database 12*c* and Oracle Database Express Edition 11*g* Release 2, we have **Procedural Language/SQL (PL/SQL)**.
- For MySQL 5.6, there is no separate variant name and we just use SQL and SQL/PSM.

We discuss each of these in the context of its parent DBMS product in the separate online chapters.

Reviewing the Database Structure in the DBMS GUI Utility

Besides giving us a good SQL editor to create and run SQL scripts, each DBMS product has also built its GUI utilities with the capability to work with database objects such as tables in a GUI mode (similar to what we do in Microsoft Access 2013). We discuss how to use specific GUI utilities to do this:

- For Microsoft SQL Server 2014, we use the Microsoft SQL Server 2014 Management Studio.
- For Oracle Database 12c and Oracle Database Express Edition 11g Release 2 we use Oracle SQL Developer.
- For MySQL 5.6, we use the MySQL Workbench.

Creating and Populating the View Ridge Gallery VRG Database Tables

Having created the VRG database and knowing how to use SQL scripts, we turn to actually creating the VRG tables, referential integrity constraints, and indexes that form the basic structure of the database itself. As you might expect, each DBMS product has its own variation on exactly how this should be done. A good example of these differences is how each DBMS product handles surrogate keys:

- In Microsoft SQL Server 2014, we use the **T-SQL IDENTITY property**.
- For Oracle Database 12c and Oracle Database Express Edition 11g Release 2, we use the **PL/SQL SEQUENCE object**.
- For MySQL 5.6, we use the **MySQL AUTO_INCREMENT property**.

Once the database structure is created, we discuss how to populate the tables with data. Because the VRG data as provided in Figure 7-15 contains noncontinuous surrogate key values, we discuss how to handle this situation when inputting data into tables.

Creating SQL Views for the View Ridge Gallery VRG Database

In Chapter 7, we discussed the use of SQL views in a database. We now show how to create and use them in each specific DBMS.

Database Application Logic and SQL/Persistent Stored Modules (SQL/PSM)

In order to be used in an application (such as a Web site application), a database must be accessible from that application, and several application-related problems (such as creating and storing application variables) must be overcome. While this can be done within an application programming language such as Java; a Microsoft .NET language such as C#.NET, C++.NET, or VB.NET; or the PHP Web scripting language (discussed in Chapter 11), we base our main discussion on how application logic can be embedded in SQL/Persistent Stored Modules (SQL/PSM)–**user-defined functions**, **triggers**, and **stored procedures**.

For each specific DBMS product, we examine and explain various SQL/PSM constructs and features:

- Variables
- Parameters
- Control-of-flow statements
  - BEGIN…END blocks
  - IF…THEN…ELSE structures
  - WHILE (looping) structures
  - RETURN {value} statements

■ Cursor structures and statements
■ SQL transaction control statements
■ Output statements

We then use these elements to build DBMS SQL/PSM-specific user-defined functions, stored procedures, and triggers, and we cover these topics in a depth far beyond our coverage in Chapter 7. We build and run several stored procedures and triggers, explaining both the application use of the trigger or stored procedure and additional programming elements that are useful when creating user-defined functions, stored procedures, and triggers.

DBMS Concurrency Control

We discussed the concept of concurrency control in Chapter 9. As you would expect, each DBMS product implements concurrency **transaction isolation level** and **locking behavior** in its own way, which we examine for each specific DBMS product in the appropriate online chapter.

DBMS Security

We discussed security in general terms in Chapter 9. For each specific DBMS product, we summarize how those general ideas pertain to that product, examine the specific server and database security options available, and create users with specific security privileges. We cover these topics in a depth far beyond our coverage in Chapter 7, and when we are done creating the needed database users for the VRG database, we are ready to use these users to provide the needed database security for our Web database applications in Chapter 11.

DBMS Database Backup and Recovery

As explained in Chapter 9, databases and associated log files should be backed up periodically. When backups are available, it is possible to recover a failed database by restoring it from a prior database save and applying changes in the log. Again, we cover these topics in a depth far beyond our coverage in Chapter 7, and we examine and discuss the specific backup and recovery features and methods of the specific DBMS.

Other DBMS Topics Not Discussed

Each online chapter covers essential topics for a specific DBMS product, but we cannot possibly cover everything about each DBMS in this book and online chapters. Therefore, we briefly discuss some of the important topics *not* covered in the chapter and point you toward information about those topics.

Choose Your DBMS Product(s)!

Please see the online chapter for the DBMS product(s) you want to install and use. Download the appropriate online chapter, and study it, as it will be your guide to implementing the concepts discussed in this book in a DBMS, and to really learn these concepts, you need to actually use them in a DBMS.

**CHAPTER 10A: MANAGING DATABASES WITH
MICROSOFT SQL SERVER 2014**

**CHAPTER 10B: MANAGING DATABASES WITH
ORACLE DATABASE**

AND

CHAPTER 10C: MANAGING DATABASES WITH MySQL 5.6

ARE AVAILABLE ONLINE ON THE

DATABASE PROCESSING:

FUNDAMENTALS, DESIGN, AND IMPLEMENTATION (14th EDITION)

COMPANION WEBSITE AT

www.pearsonhighered.com/kroenke

Summary

There are online chapters available at the *Database Processing: Fundamentals, Design, and Implementation (14th Edition)* Companion Web site, accessible at *www.pearsonhighered.com/ kroenke.*

These chapters have been placed online to allow us to include more material relevant to each separate DBMS product than the length of this book would otherwise allow. The online materials are in PDF format and require that you have a PDF reader installed. If you need a PDF reader, we suggest you download and install the current version of the free Adobe Reader from *https://acrobat.adobe.com/us/en/ products/pdf-reader.html.*

The material in these chapters describes the basic features and functions of Microsoft SQL Server 2014 in Chapter 10A, Oracle Database 12c and Oracle Database Express Edition 11g Release 2 in Chapter 10B, and Oracle MySQL 5.6 in Chapter 10C. The discussion in these chapters uses the Cape_Codd database for Chapter 2 and the View Ridge Gallery VRG database from Chapter 7, and it parallels the discussion of SQL DDL, DML, and SQL/PSM in Chapter 7 and the discussion of database administration tasks in Chapter 9.

Topics in each online chapter written to cover each specific DBMS product include:

- Installing the DBMS
- Using the DBMS Database Administration and Database Development Utilities
- Creating a Database
- Creating and Running SQL Scripts
- Reviewing the Database Structure in the DBMS GUI Utility
- Creating and Populating the View Ridge Gallery VRG Database Tables
- Creating SQL Views for the View Ridge Gallery VRG Database
- Database Application Logic and SQL/Persistent Stored Modules (SQL/PSM)
- DBMS Concurrency Control
- DBMS Security
- DBMS Database Backup and Recovery
- Other DBMS Topics Not Discussed

These chapters build on the material presented in Chapter 7, but coverage of these topics is at a depth far beyond the Chapter 7 coverage. Please see the online chapter for the DBMS product you want to install and use.

Key Terms

locking behavior
Microsoft Access 2013
Microsoft SQL Server 2014
Microsoft SQL Server 2014 Express
 Advanced
Microsoft SQL Server 2014
 Management Studio
MySQL 5.6
MySQL AUTO_INCREMENT property

MySQL Community Server 5.6
MySQL Installer 5.6 for Windows
MySQL Workbench
Oracle Database Express Edition 11*g*
 Release 2
Oracle Database 12*c*
Oracle SQL Developer
PL/SQL SEQUENCE object
Procedural Language/SQL (PL/SQL)

schema
stored procedures
tablespace
Transact-SQL (T-SQL)
transaction isolation level
triggers
T-SQL IDENTITY property
user-defined functions

Project Questions

10.1 Determine which DBMS product or products you will be using while working through the material in this book.

10.2 Based on your answer to Project Question 10.1, download Chapter 10A, Chapter 10B, and/or Chapter 10C as appropriate from the *Database Processing: Fundamentals, Design, and Implementation (14th Edition)* Companion Website at *www.pearsonhighered.com/kroenke*.

10.3 Based on your answer to Project Question 10.1 and the discussions in Chapter 10A, Chapter 10B, and/or Chapter 10C, download and install the DBMS software that you will be using while working through the material in this book. When you have completed this Project Question, you should have available for your use a working installation of the DBMS product or products you want to use.

Database Access Standards

The two chapters in this section examine standards for database application processing. We begin in Chapter 11 by discussing database access standards, including ODBC, ADO.NET, and ASP.NET in Microsoft's .NET Framework and the Java-based JDBC and Java Server Pages (JSP) technologies. Even though some of these standards are no longer on the leading edge of database processing, many applications still use them, and you will likely encounter them in your career. In fact, ODBC is making a comeback as relational DBMS products need to interconnect to BigData structured storage products (discussed in Chapter 12), and ODBC is an established standard that can handle the task. Chapter 11 then describes the use of the popular PHP scripting language to create Web pages that access the View Ridge Gallery database. This is followed by a discussion of the confluence of database processing and document processing in an introduction to XML.

Chapter 12 discusses business intelligence (BI) systems, the data warehouse and data mart databases that support BI systems, and BigData structured storage.

PART

5

11

The Web Server Environment

Chapter Objectives

- To understand the nature and characteristics of the data environment that surrounds Internet technology database applications
- To learn the purpose, features, and facilities of ODBC
- To understand the characteristics of the Microsoft .NET Framework
- To understand the nature and goals of OLE DB
- To learn the characteristics and object model of ADO.NET
- To understand the characteristics of JDBC and the four types of JDBC drivers

- To understand the nature of JSP and know the differences between JSP and ASP.NET
- To understand HTML and PHP
- To be able to construct Web database applications pages using PHP
- To understand the importance of XML
- To learn the basic concepts involved in using the SQL SELECT...FOR XML statement

We have now learned how to design and implement databases. Specifically, we have used the VRG database we have designed and implemented for the View Ridge Gallery as our example throughout most of this book. We started by creating the VRG data model and the VRG database design in Chapter 6 and then implemented that database design in SQL Server 2014 in Chapter 7. We used it as the basis of our discussion of database redesign in Chapter 8 and of database administration in Chapter 9.

Databases, however, do not exist in isolation. Rather, they are created as part of an information system and are used to store the data that the system processes to provide information to the people who use it, as discussed at the beginning of our work in Chapter 1.

In one way or another, today we are usually working with the **World Wide Web (WWW or W3 or Web)**, which is now so ubiquitous and commonly used that everyone takes it for granted. Application clients running in a **Web browser** such as **Microsoft Internet Explorer**, **Google Chrome**, or **Mozilla Firefox** are the norm, and allow users to shop online and communicate with their friends by posts on Facebook or tweets on Twitter.

The WWW is not a communications network itself. Instead, the WWW runs on the **Internet**, a system of interconnected smaller networks that now spans the Earth and allows computer communication worldwide.

We no longer need a computer to use the Web. In addition to using the Web on their computers, people are using a **mobile phone** (or **cell phone**) over a **cellular network** provided by vendors such as Verizon, T-Mobile, AT&T, and Sprint. The emerging **smartphone** makes use of the data packages available from cellular providers to access the WWW, making smartphones very portable computers.

Another emerging form factor is the **tablet**, of which the **Apple iPad** is the best example (although many other tablets running the **Google Android operating system (OS)** are also available). Tablets connecting to the Internet provide another link in the interconnected life style we are living today.

Figure 11-1 illustrates how people use these devices today, in what is technically known as **client server architecture**. Users actually want some sort of **service**, such as shopping online or communicating on Facebook. To get this service, a user has a hardware **device** (computer, smartphone, or tablet) that runs a software **client** application that provides the user with an interface for a desired service. A Web browser is often the client for a service such as Facebook or Twitter (a smartphone **app** is also a client for these services). A service is provided by a special computer called a **server** (because it provide the service). For example, Twitter uses servers to receive, store, and broadcast tweets. The client and the server communicate over the Internet or a cellular data network (which itself will connect to the Internet at some point). Internet hardware such as **routers** running networking software are responsible for the connections between the client and the server.

FIGURE 11-1
Client Server Architecture

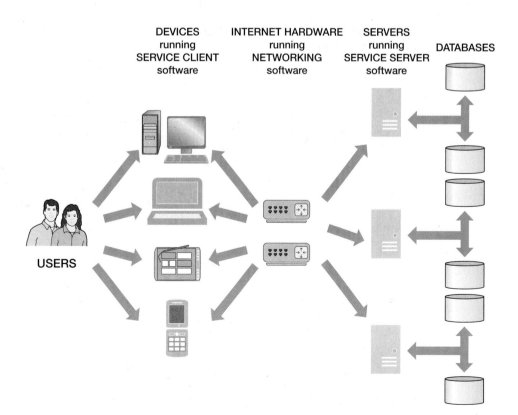

DEVICES	INTERNET HARDWARE	SERVERS	
running	running	running	DATABASES
SERVICE CLIENT	NETWORKING	SERVICE SERVER	
software	software	software	

USERS

And supporting all the client server applications are databases. Every application needs to store, update, read, and delete data, and, as we have learned, that is the purpose of a database. Databases do not exist for their own sake—they exist to be used by applications needing the data they hold and maintain.

In this chapter, we will discuss and demonstrate exactly how databases are used to support the services that users want. This chapter begins by discussing some traditional standard interfaces and some current tools for accessing database servers. *ODBC*, or the Open Database Connectivity standard, was developed in the early 1990s to provide a product-independent interface to relational and other tabular data. Today, it is finding new life because of the new nonrelational databases being developed to deal with the *Big Data* environment (which we will discuss in detail in Chapter 12 and Appendix K—*Big Data*). In the mid-1990s, Microsoft announced *OLE DB*, which is an object-oriented interface that encapsulates data-server functionality. Microsoft then developed *Active Data Objects (ADO)*, which is a set of objects for utilizing OLE DB that is designed for use by any language, including VBScript and JScript/JavaScript. This technology was used in *Active Server Pages (ASP)*, which were the basis of Web database applications. In 2002, Microsoft introduced the .NET Framework, which included *ADO.NET* (the successor to ADO) and *ASP.NET* (the successor to ASP) components. Today, the .NET Framework is the basis for all application development using Microsoft technology.

As an alternative to the Microsoft technologies, Sun Microsystems developed the Java platform, which includes the Java programming language, *Java Database Connectivity (JDBC)*, and *Java Server Pages (JSP)*, in the 1990s. Sun Microsystems was purchased by Oracle Corporation in 2010, and the Java platform is now part of the Oracle family.

Although the .NET and Java technologies are important development platforms, additional technologies have been developed by other companies and open source projects. We will use two of these independently developed tools in this chapter: the NetBeans integrated development environment (IDE) and the PHP scripting language.

This chapter also considers one of the most important recent developments in information systems technology. It discusses the confluence of two information technology subject areas: database processing and document processing. For more than 20 years, these two subject areas developed independently of one another. With the advent of the Internet, however, they crashed together in what some industry pundits called a technology train wreck. The result is still being sorted out, with new products, product features, technology standards, and development practices emerging every month.

A Web Database Application for the View Ridge Gallery

Now that we have created the VRG database, we will use it in this chapter as the basis for developing a Web database application for the View Ridge Gallery. We will call this Web database application the View Ridge Gallery Information System (VRGIS), and the VRGIS will provide both reporting and data input capabilities for the gallery. A screen shot of the VRGIS was used in Figure 6-35 to illustrate our introduction of the View Ridge Gallery. But before we build the VRGIS, we need to understand the underlying basis and process for developing Web database applications.

The Web Database Processing Environment

The environment in which today's Web database applications reside is rich and complicated. As shown in Figure 11-2, users use Web browsers on their computers to request Web pages from Web servers, which in turn request information from database servers, which use a DBMS to obtain the data from their databases. Various programming languages are used in the process of creating the Web page code that is returned to the Web browser, which formats the Web page and displays it for the user. The final Web page coded may include:

- Scripting language code, such as **JavaScript**, which runs on the user's computer.
- Code generated by Web server programming languages, such as **PHP**, which controls the code content returned to the Web browser.
- Output from databases generated by Web servers sending requests for DBMS operations using SQL and SQL/PSM.

While we will not discuss scripting languages in this text, you are undoubtedly familiar with their actions. A very familiar example is the "Does not match" message you see every time a Web form requires you to reenter some data such as an email address or new password for validation and you don't retype it exactly. This type of error checking is performed locally on your computer by a Web page scripting language such as JavaScript.

We will discuss the interaction between the Web server and the DBMS, In a Web-based database processing environment, if the Web server and the DBMS can run on the same computer, the system has **two-tier architecture**. (One tier is for the Web browsers, and one is for the Web server/DBMS computer.) Alternatively, the Web server and DBMS can run on different computers, in which case the system has **three-tier architecture**, as illustrated in Figure 11-2. High-performance applications might use many Web server computers, and in some systems several computers can run the DBMS as well. In the latter case, if the DBMS computers are processing the same databases, the system is referred to as a *distributed database*. Distributed databases are discussed later in this chapter.

As shown in Figure 11-3, a typical Web server needs to create Web pages that involve data from dozens of different sources, each with different data types. So far in this text, we have considered only relational databases, but as you can see from this figure, there are many other data types as well.

Consider the problems that the developer of Web server applications has when integrating these data. The developer may need to connect to:

- A relational database created in Microsoft SQL Server or Oracle Database.
- A nonrelational database, such as *Apache Cassandra* or Neo Technology's *Neo4j*.
- File-based data, such as found in spreadsheets such as Microsoft Excel.
- Email directories.

Each one of these products has a different programming interface that the developer must learn. Further, these products evolve; thus, new features and functions will be added over time that will increase the developer's challenge.

FIGURE 11-2

Three-Tier Architecture

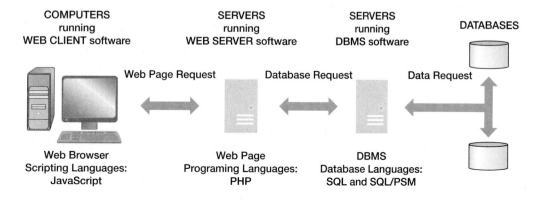

COMPUTERS running WEB CLIENT software	SERVERS running WEB SERVER software	SERVERS running DBMS software	DATABASES

Web Page Request — Database Request — Data Request

| Web Browser Scripting Languages: JavaScript | Web Page Programing Languages: PHP | DBMS Database Languages: SQL and SQL/PSM | |

FIGURE 11-3

The Variety of Data Types in
Web Database Applications

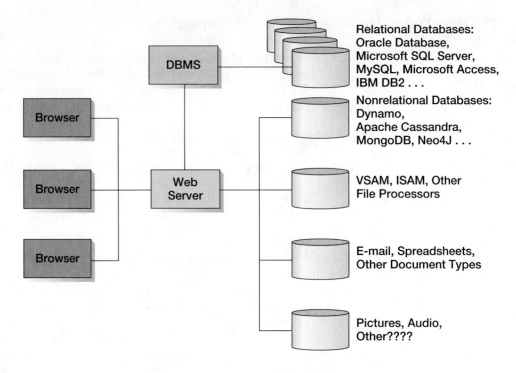

Database Server Access Standards

To solve the problem of communicating with different products, several standard interfaces have been developed for accessing database servers. Every DBMS product has an **application programming interface (API)**. An API is a collection of objects, methods, and properties for executing DBMS functions from program code. Unfortunately, each DBMS has its own API, and APIs vary from one DBMS product to another. To save programmers from having to learn to use many different interfaces, the computer industry has developed standards for database access.

The **Open Database Connectivity (ODBC)** standard was developed in the early 1990s to provide a DBMS-independent means for processing relational database data. In the mid-1990s, Microsoft announced **OLE DB**, which is an object-oriented interface that encapsulates data-server functionality. OLE DB was designed not just for access to relational databases, but also for accessing many other types of data as well. As a **Component Object Model (COM)** interface, OLE DB is readily accessible to programmers through the use of programming languages such as C, C#, and Java. However, OLE DB is not as accessible to users of Visual Basic (VB) and scripting languages. Therefore, Microsoft developed **Active Data Objects (ADO)**, which is a set of objects for utilizing OLE DB that is designed for use by any language, including Visual Basic (VB), VBScript, and JScript. ADO has now been followed by **ADO.NET** (pronounced "A-D-O-dot-NET"), which is an improved version of ADO developed as part of Microsoft's .NET (pronounced "dot-NET") initiative and a component of the .NET Framework.

ADO technology is used to build Web pages as part of Microsoft's **Active Server Pages (ASP)**, which are then used to create Web-based database applications. ASP is a combination of Hypertext Markup Language (HTML) and VBScript or JScript that can read and write database data and transmit it over public and private networks using Internet protocols. ASP runs on Microsoft's Web server product, **Internet Information Services (IIS)**. When ADO.NET was introduced, Microsoft also introduced **ASP.NET**. ASP.NET is the successor to ASP and is the preferred Web page technology in the .NET Framework.

Of course, there are other connectivity methods and standards besides those propagated by Microsoft. The main alternatives to ADO.NET technology are based on or associated with Oracle Corporation's **Java platform** and include the **Java programming language**, **Java Database Connectivity (JBDC)**, **Java Data Objects (JDO)**, and **JavaServer Pages (JSP)**.

JSP technology is a combination of HTML and Java that accomplishes the same function as ASP.NET by compiling pages into Java servlets. JSP may connect to databases using JDBC. JSP is often used with Apache Tomcat, which implements JSP in an open source Web server (and is often used in conjunction with the open source **Apache Web server**).

However, the defining characteristic of the Java-related technology is that you must use Java as the programming language. You cannot even use JavaScript, Java's somewhat-related scripting language cousin. If you know (or want to learn) Java, this is fine.

Although the Microsoft .NET Framework and the Oracle Corporation's Java platform are the two major players in Web database application development, other options are available. One such product is PHP, which is an open source Web page programming language, and another favorite combination of Web developers is the Apache Web server with the MySQL DBMS and the PHP language. This combination is called **AMP** (Apache-MySQL-PHP). When running on the Linux operating system, it is referred to as **LAMP**; when running on the Windows operating system, it is referred to as **WAMP**. And because PHP works with all DBMS products, we will use it in this book. Other possibilities include the Perl and Python languages (both of which can be the "P" in AMP, LAMP, or WAMP) and the Ruby language with its Web development framework called Ruby on Rails.

The ODBC Standard

The ODBC standard was created to address the data access problem that concerns relational databases and data sources that are table-like, such as spreadsheets. As shown in Figure 11-4, ODBC is an interface between the Web server (or other database application) and the DBMS. It consists of a set of standards by which SQL statements can be issued and results and error messages can be returned. As shown in Figure 11-4, developers can call the DBMS using native DBMS interfaces (which are APIs) if they want to (sometimes they do this to improve performance), but the developer who does not have the time or desire to learn many different DBMS native libraries can use the ODBC instead.

The ODBC standard is an interface by which application programs can access and process databases and tabular data in a DBMS-independent manner. This means, for example, that an application that uses the ODBC interface could process an Oracle Database database, an SQL Server database, a spreadsheet, or any other ODBC-compliant database without

FIGURE 11-4

Role of the ODBC Standard

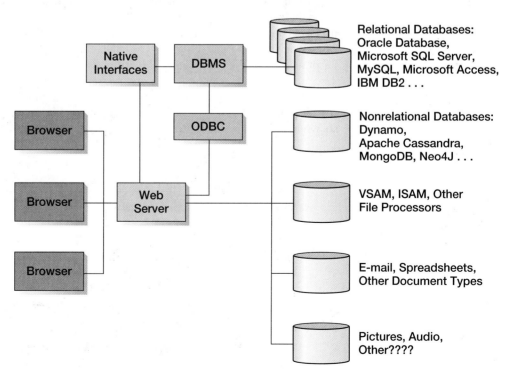

making any coding changes. The goal is to allow a developer to create a single application that can access databases supported by different DBMS products without needing to be changed or even recompiled.

ODBC was developed by a committee of industry experts from the X/Open and SQL Access Group committees. Several such standards were proposed, but ODBC emerged as the winner, primarily because it had been implemented by Microsoft and is an important part of Windows. Microsoft's initial interest in support of such a standard was to allow products such as Microsoft Excel to access database data from a variety of DBMS products without having to be recompiled. Of course, Microsoft's interests have changed since the introduction of OLE DB and ADO.NET.

ODBC Architecture

Figure 11-5 shows the components of the ODBC standard. The application program, driver manager, and DBMS drivers all reside on the application server computer. The drivers send requests to data sources, which reside on the database server. According to the standard, an **ODBC data source** is the database and its associated DBMS, operating system, and network platform. An ODBC data source can be a relational database; it can also be a file server, such as BTrieve, or even a spreadsheet.

The application issues requests to create a connection with a data source; to issue SQL statements and receive results; to process errors; and to start, commit, and roll back transactions. ODBC provides a standard means for each of these requests, and it defines a standard set of error codes and messages.

The **ODBC driver manager** serves as an intermediary between the application and the DBMS drivers. When the application requests a connection, the driver manager determines the type of DBMS that processes a given ODBC data source and loads that driver into memory (if it is not already loaded). The driver manager also processes certain initialization requests and validates the format and order of ODBC requests that it receives from the application. For Windows, the driver manager is provided by Microsoft.

An **ODBC driver** processes ODBC requests and submits specific SQL statements to a given type of data source. Each data source type has a different driver. For example, there are drivers for SQL Server, for Oracle Database, for MySQL, for Microsoft Access, and for all of the other products whose vendors have chosen to participate in the ODBC standard. Drivers are supplied by DBMS vendors and by independent software companies.

It is the responsibility of the driver to ensure that standard ODBC commands execute correctly. In some cases, if the data source is itself not SQL compliant, the driver may need to perform considerable processing to fill in for a lack of capability at the data source. In other cases, when the data source supports full SQL, the driver need only pass the request through for processing by the data source. The driver also converts data source error codes and messages into the ODBC standard codes and messages.

ODBC identifies two types of drivers: single tier and multiple tier. An **ODBC single-tier driver** processes both ODBC calls and SQL statements. An example of a single-tier driver is shown in Figure 11-6(a). In this example, the data are stored in Xbase files (the format used

FIGURE 11-5

ODBC Architecture

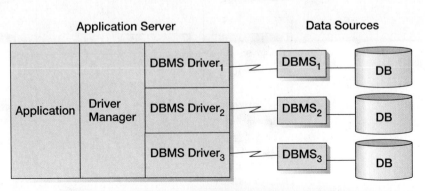

Application can process a database using any of the three DBMS products.

FIGURE 11-6

ODBC Driver Types

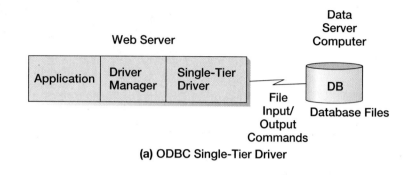

(a) ODBC Single-Tier Driver

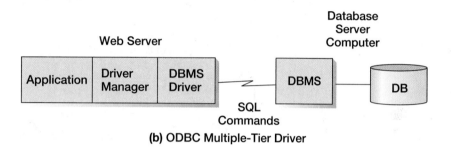

(b) ODBC Multiple-Tier Driver

by FoxPro, dBase, and others). Because Xbase file managers do not process SQL, it is the job of the driver to translate the SQL request into Xbase file-manipulation commands and to transform the results back into SQL form.

An **ODBC multiple-tier driver** processes ODBC calls but passes the SQL requests directly to the database server. Although it may reformat an SQL request to conform to the dialect of a particular data source, it does not process the SQL. An example of the use of a multiple-tier driver is shown in Figure 11-6(b).

Conformance Levels

The creators of the ODBC standard faced a dilemma. If they chose to describe a standard for a minimal level of capability, many vendors would be able to comply. But if they did so, the standard would represent only a small portion of the complete power and expressiveness of ODBC and SQL. However, if the standard addressed a very high level of capability, only a few vendors would be able to comply with the standard, and it would become unimportant. To deal with this dilemma, the committee wisely chose to define levels of conformance to the standard. The committee defined two types of conformance: ODBC conformance and SQL conformance.

ODBC Conformance Level

ODBC conformance levels are concerned with the features and functions that are made available through the driver's API. As previously discussed, a driver API is a set of functions that the application can call to receive services. Figure 11-7 summarizes the three levels of ODBC conformance that are addressed in the standard. In practice, almost all drivers provide at least Level 1 API conformance, so the core API level is not too important.

An application can call a driver to determine which level of ODBC conformance it provides. If the application requires a level of conformance that is not present, it can terminate the session in an orderly fashion and generate appropriate messages to the user. Or the application can be written to use higher-level conformance features if they are available and to work around the missing functions if a higher level is not available.

For example, drivers at the Level 2 API must provide a scrollable cursor. Using conformance levels, an application could be written to use cursors if they are available; but if they are not, to work around the missing feature, the application would select needed data using very restrictive WHERE clauses. Doing this would ensure that only a few rows were returned at a time to the application, and it would process those rows using a cursor that it maintained itself. Performance would likely be slower in the second case, but at least the application would be able to successfully execute.

FIGURE 11-7

Summary of ODBC
Conformance Levels

Core API
Connect to data sources
Prepare and execute SQL statements
Retrieve data from a result set
Commit or roll back transactions
Retrieve error information

Level 1 API
Core API
Connect to data sources with driver-specific information
Send and receive partial results
Retrieve catalog information
Retrieve information about driver options, capabilities, and functions

Level 2 API
Core and Level 1 API
Browse possible connections and data sources
Retrieve native form of SQL
Call a translation library
Process a scrollable cursor

SQL Conformance Level

ODBC SQL conformance levels specify which SQL statements, expressions, and data types a driver can process. Three SQL conformance levels are defined, as summarized in Figure 11-8. The capability of the minimum SQL grammar is very limited, and most drivers support at least the core SQL grammar.

As with ODBC conformance levels, an application can call the driver to determine what level of SQL conformance it supports. With that information, the application can then determine which SQL statements can be issued. If necessary, the application can then terminate the session or use alternative, less-powerful means of obtaining the data.

Creating an ODBC Data Source Name

An ODBC data source is an ODBC data structure that identifies a database and the DBMS that processes it. Data sources identify other types of data, such as spreadsheets and other nondatabase tabular data stores, but we are not concerned with that use here.

The three types of data sources are file, system, and user. A **file data source** is a file that can be shared among database users. The only requirement is that the users have the same DBMS driver and privilege to access the database. The data source file can be emailed or otherwise distributed to possible users. A **system data source** is one that is local to a single computer. The operating system and any user on that system (with proper privileges) can use a system data source. A **user data source** is available only to the user who created it.

In general, the best choice for Internet applications is to create a system data source on the Web server. Browser users then access the Web server, which, in turn, uses the system data source to set up a connection with the DBMS and the database.

FIGURE 11-8

Summary of SQL
Conformance Levels

Minimum SQL Grammar
CREATE TABLE, DROP TABLE
Simple SELECT (does not include subqueries)
INSERT, UPDATE, DELETE
Simple expressions (A > B + C)
CHAR, VARCHAR, LONGVARCHAR data types

Core SQL Grammar
Minimum SQL Grammar
ALTER TABLE, CREATE INDEX, DROP INDEX
CREATE VIEW, DROP VIEW
GRANT, REVOKE
Full SELECT (includes subqueries)
Aggregate functions such as SUM, COUNT, MAX, MIN, AVG
DECIMAL, NUMERIC, SMALLINT, INTEGER, REAL, FLOAT, DOUBLE PRECISION data types

Extended SQL Grammar
Core SQL Grammar
Outer joins
UPDATE and DELETE using cursor positions
Scalar functions such as SUBSTRING, ABS
Literals for date, time, and timestamp
Batch SQL statements
Stored procedures

As our first step in developing the VRGIS, we need to create a system data source for the VRG database so that we can use it in the Web database processing application. We created the VRG database in SQL Server 2014, and the system data source will provide a connection to the SQL Server 2014 DBMS. To create a system data source in a Windows operating system, you use the **ODBC Data Source Administrator**.[1]

---

[1]**Important:** If you are using a 64-bit Windows operating system, be aware that there are two different ODBC Data Source Administrator programs provided—one for 32-bit applications and one for 64-bit applications. The ODBC Data Source Administrator used if you follow the steps in the text is the 64-bit version. However, if you are running a 32-bit program in the Web application set (e.g., a 32-bit DBMS such as the 32-bit version of SQL Server 2014 Express Advanced), then you must use the 32-bit version of the ODBC Data Source Administrator. In the 64-bit version of Windows 7, this is the odbcad32.exe program located at C:\Windows\sysWOW64\ odbcad32.exe. In Windows 8, Windows 8.1, Windows Server 2012, and Windows Server 2012 R2, the programs are, fortunately, clearly labeled as either 32-bit or 64-bit. Nonetheless, if everything seems to be set up correctly yet the Web pages are not displaying properly, then this is likely to be the problem.

Opening the ODBC Data Source Administrator in Windows Server 2012 R2

1. Click the **Start** button, and then click the **All Programs** button.
2. Click the **Administrative Tools** folder to open it.
3. Click the **Data Sources (ODBC)** program.

We can now use the ODBC Data Source Administrator to create a system data source named VRG for use with SQL Server 2014:

Creating the VRG System Data Source

1. In the ODBC Data Source Administrator, click the **System DSN** tab, and then click the **Add** button.
2. In the Create New Data Source dialog box, we need to connect to SQL Server 2014, so we select the **SQL Server Native Client 11.0**, as shown in Figure 11-9.
3. Click the **Finish** button. The Create New Data Source to SQL Server dialog box appears.
4. In the Create New Data Source to SQL Server dialog box, enter the information shown for the VRG in Figure 11-10(a) (note that the database server is selected from the Server drop-down list), and then click the **Next** button.
   - **NOTE:** If the name of the installed SQL server instance, preceded by the name of the computer on which it is installed, does not appear in the Server drop-down list, enter it manually as **ComputerName\SQLServerName**. If the SQL Server instance is the *default installation* (always named MSSQLSERVER) of SQL Server on the computer, enter *only* **ComputerName**.
5. As shown in Figure 11-10(b), in the next page of the Create a New Data Source to SQL Server dialog box, click the radio button that selects SQL Server authentication, and then enter the Login ID of **VRG-User** and the Password of **VRG-User+password** that we created in Chapter 9. After these data have been entered, click the **Next** button.
   - **NOTE:** If the Login ID and Password are not correct, an error message will appear. Make sure you have correctly created the SQL Server login as discussed in Chapter 9 and have entered the correct data here.

FIGURE 11-9

The Create New Data Source Dialog Box

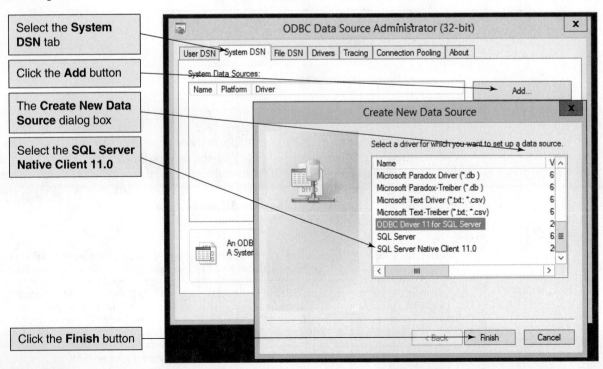

Select the **System DSN** tab

Click the **Add** button

The **Create New Data Source** dialog box

Select the **SQL Server Native Client 11.0**

Click the **Finish** button

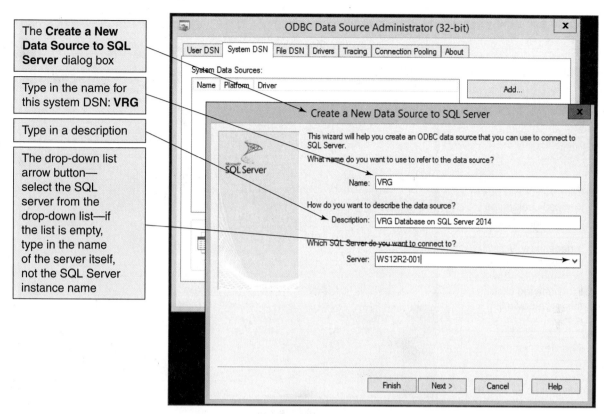

The Create a New Data Source to SQL Server dialog box

Type in the name for this system DSN: **VRG**

Type in a description

The drop-down list arrow button— select the SQL server from the drop-down list—if the list is empty, type in the name of the server itself, not the SQL Server instance name

(a) Naming the ODBC Data Source

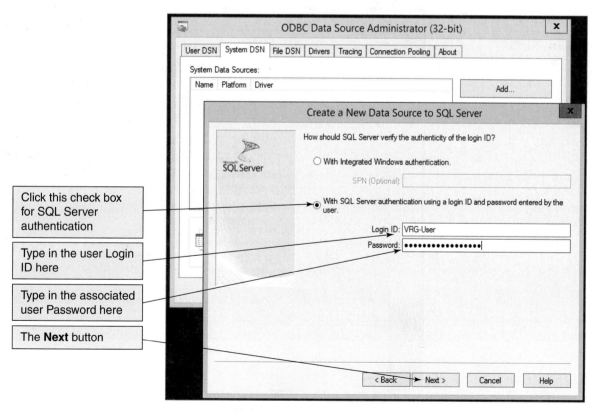

Click this check box for SQL Server authentication

Type in the user Login ID here

Type in the associated user Password here

The **Next** button

(b) Selecting the User Login ID Authentication Method

FIGURE 11-10

The Create New Data Source to SQL Server Dialog Box

(continued)

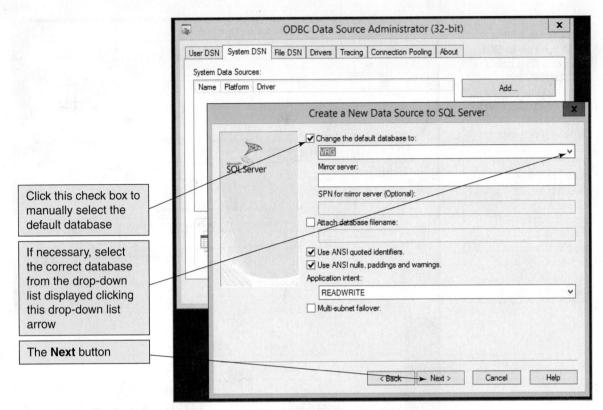

Click this check box to manually select the default database

If necessary, select the correct database from the drop-down list displayed clicking this drop-down list arrow

The **Next** button

(c) Selecting the Default Database

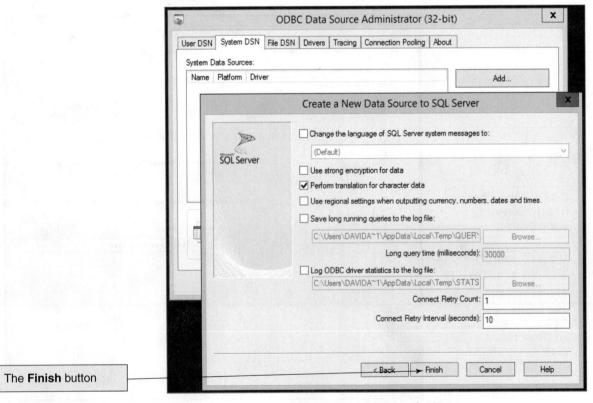

The **Finish** button

(d) Additional Setting Options

FIGURE 11-10

Continued

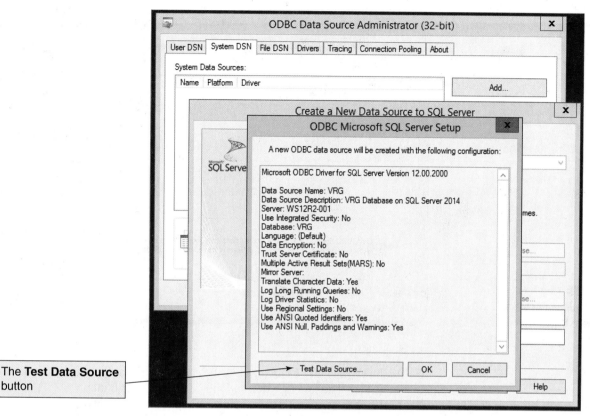

(e) Testing the Data Source

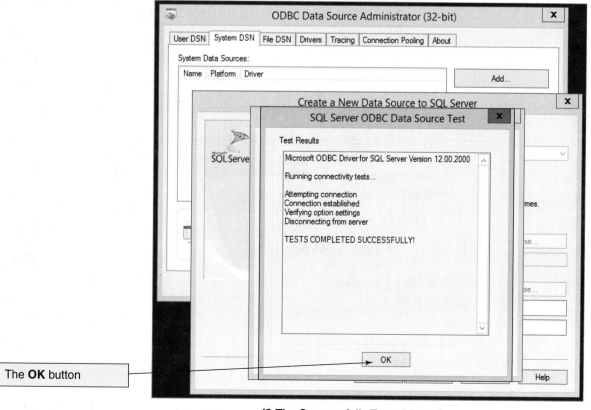

(f) The Successfully Tested Data Source

FIGURE 11-10

Continued

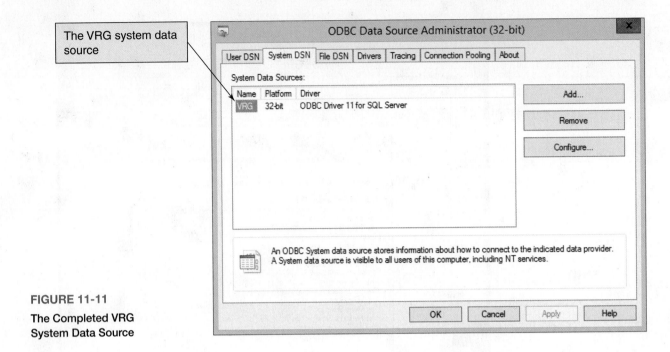

The VRG system data source

FIGURE 11-11

The Completed VRG System Data Source

6. As shown in Figure 11-10(c), click the check box to change the default database, set the default database to **VRG**, and then click the **Next** button.

7. As shown in Figure 11-10(d), another group of settings is displayed. There is no need to change any of these settings, so click the **Finish** button to close the Create a New Data Source to SQL Server dialog box.

8. The ODBC Microsoft SQL Server Setup dialog box is displayed, as shown in Figure 11-10(e). This dialog box is used to summarize the settings to be created for the new ODBC data source. Click the **Test Data Source...** button to test the settings.

9. As shown in Figure 11-10(f), the SQL Server ODBC Data Source Test dialog box appears, showing that the tests completed successfully. Click the **OK** button to exit the dialog box and create the ODBC data source.

10. The completed VRG system data source is shown in Figure 11-11. Click the **OK** button to close the ODBC Data Source Administrator.

We will use the VRG DSN later in this chapter to process the SQL Server database created in Chapter 10. Similarly, if you are using either the Oracle or MySQL DBMS, you should create an appropriate system data source for use with your Oracle or MySQL version of the View Ridge Gallery database.

The Microsoft .NET Framework and ADO.NET

The **.NET Framework** is Microsoft's comprehensive application development platform. Web database applications tools are included in the .NET Framework. Originally released as the .NET Framework 1.0 in January 2002, the current version is the .NET Framework 4.5, which itself has been updated to .NET Framework 4.5.1 to support Windows 8.1 and Windows Server 2012 R2.

As shown in Figure 11-12, the .NET Framework can best be visualized as a set of building blocks stacked on top of each other. Each additional block adds additional functionality to the components already existing in previous blocks, and if earlier components need to be updated, this is done by service packs to the older blocks. Thus, .NET Framework 2.0 SP2 and .NET Framework SP2 were included as part of .NET Framework 3.5 SP1, and upgrades to all portions of the .NET Framework are included in .NET Framework 4.0, .NET Framework 4.5, and .NET Framework 4.5.1.

FIGURE 11-12

The Microsoft .NET Framework Structure

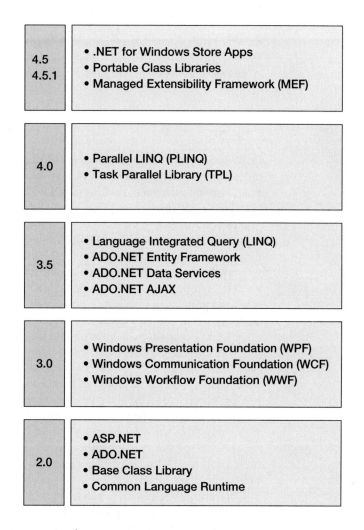

Although Figure 11-12 does not show every feature of the .NET Framework 3.5 SP1, the basic structure is easy to see. The .NET Framework 2.0 is now the basic layer and contains the most basic features. These include the **Common Language Runtime (CLT)** and the **Base Class Library**, which support all of the programming languages (e.g., VB.NET and Visual C#.NET) used with the .NET Framework. This layer also includes the ADO.NET and ASP.NET components, which are needed for Web database applications.

The .NET Framework 3.0 added a set of components that are not of interest to us here. We are more concerned with the features added in .NET Framework 3.5 and 3.5 SP1, noting that these features were upgraded, but not replaced, by .NET Framework 4.0. Note that several extensions to ADO.NET were included in .NET Framework 3.5 and 3.5 SP1, such as the **ADO.NET Entity Framework**, which supports Microsoft's emerging **Entity Data Model (EDM)** data modeling technology, as well as the **Language Integrated Query (LINQ)** component, which allows SQL queries to be programmed directly into application programs in a simple manner.

Besides updating existing features, the .NET Framework 4.0 added features needed for parallel processing on clustered servers. These include **Parallel LINQ (PLINQ)** and **Task Parallel Library (TPL)**, but these parallel processing features are beyond the scope of this book. The .NET Framework 4.5 again updated many existing features and added functionality for Windows 8 Apps, including **.NET for Windows Store Apps**, **Portable Class Libraries**, and the **Managed Extensibility Framework (MEF)**. For more information on .NET Framework 4.5, see the Microsoft MSDN Web page *What's New in the .NET Framework 4.5* at *http://msdn.microsoft.com/en-us/library/ms171868.aspx*. .Net Framework 4.5.1 is a minor update and is distributed with Windows 8.1 and Windows Server 2012 R2.

Now that we understand the basic structure of the .NET Framework, we can look at some of the pieces in detail.

> **BY THE WAY**   The Microsoft Entity Data Model (EDM) is similar in concept to the Semantic Object Model discussed in Appendix H of this book. A discussion of the EDM can be found at *http://msdn.microsoft.com/en-us/library/aa697428(VS.80).aspx*.

OLE DB

ODBC has been a tremendous success and has greatly simplified some database development tasks. However, it does have some disadvantages, and in particular one substantial disadvantage that Microsoft addressed by creating OLE DB. Figure 11-13 shows the relationship among OLE DB, ODBC, and other data types. OLE DB is one of the foundations of data access in the Microsoft world. As such, it is important to understand the fundamental ideas of OLE DB, even if you will only work with the ADO.NET interface that lies on top of it because, as you will see, OLE DB remains as a data provider to ADO.NET. In this section, we present essential OLE DB concepts and use them to introduce some important object-oriented programming topics.

OLE DB provides an object-oriented interface to data of almost any type. DBMS vendors can wrap portions of their native libraries in OLE DB objects to expose their product's functionality through this interface. OLE DB can also be used as an interface to ODBC data sources. Finally, OLE DB was developed to support the processing of nonrelational data as well.

OLE DB is an implementation of the Microsoft **Object Linking and Embedding (OLE)** object standard. OLE DB objects are Component Object Model (COM) objects and support all required interfaces for such objects. Fundamentally, OLE DB breaks the features and functions of a DBMS up into COM objects. Some objects support query operations; others perform updates; others support the creation of database schema constructs, such as tables, indexes, and views; and still others perform transaction management, such as optimistic locking.

This characteristic overcomes a major disadvantage of ODBC. With ODBC, a vendor must create an ODBC driver for almost all DBMS features and functions in order to participate in ODBC at all. This is a large task that requires a substantial investment. With OLE DB, however, a DBMS vendor can implement portions of a product. One could, for example, implement only the query processor, participate in OLE DB, and hence be accessible to customers using ADO.NET. Later, the vendor could add more objects and interfaces to increase OLE DB functionality.

FIGURE 11-13

The Role of OLE DB

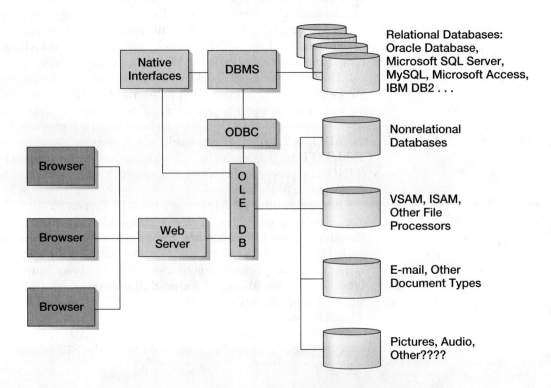

This text does not assume that you are an object-oriented programmer, so we need to develop a few concepts. In particular, you need to understand objects, abstractions, methods, properties, and collections. An **abstraction** is a generalization of something. ODBC interfaces are abstractions of native DBMS access methods. When we abstract something, we lose detail, but we gain the ability to work with a broader range of types.

For example, a **recordset** is an abstraction of a relation. In this abstraction, a recordset is defined to have certain characteristics that will be common to all recordsets. Every recordset, for instance, has a set of columns, which in this abstraction is called Fields. Now, the goal of abstraction is to capture everything important but to omit details that are not needed by users of the abstraction. Thus, Oracle relations may have some characteristics that are not represented in a recordset; the same might be true for relations in SQL Server, in DB2, and in other DBMS products. These unique characteristics will be lost in the abstraction, but if the abstraction is a good one, no one will care.

Moving up a level, a **rowset** is the OLE DB abstraction of a recordset. Now, why does OLE DB need to define another abstraction? Because OLE DB addresses data sources that are not tables but that do have *some* of the characteristics of tables. Consider all of the email addresses in your personal email file. Are those addresses the same as a relation? No, but they do share some of the characteristics that relations have. Each address is a semantically related group of data items. Like rows of a table, it is sensible to go to the first one, move to the next one, and so forth. But, unlike relations, they are not all of the same type. Some addresses are for individuals; others are for mailing lists. Thus, any action on a recordset that depends on everything in the recordset being the same kind of thing cannot be used on a rowset.

Working from the top down, OLE DB defines a set of data properties and behaviors for rowsets. Every rowset has those properties and behaviors. Furthermore, OLE DB defines a recordset as a subtype of a rowset. Recordsets have all of the properties and behaviors that rowsets have, plus they have some that are uniquely characteristic of recordsets.

Abstraction is both common and useful. You will hear of abstractions of transaction management or abstractions of querying or abstractions of interfaces. This simply means that certain characteristics of a set of things are formally defined as a type.

An object-oriented programming **object** is an abstraction that is defined by its properties and methods. For example, a recordset object has an AllowEdits property and a RecordsetType property and an EOF property. These **properties** represent characteristics of the recordset abstraction. An object also has actions that it can perform that are called **methods**. A recordset has methods such as Open, MoveFirst, MoveNext, and Close. Strictly speaking, the definition of an object abstraction is called an **object class** or just a *class*. An instance of an object class, such as a particular recordset, is called an *object*. All objects of a class have the same methods and the same properties, but the values of the properties vary from object to object.

The last term we need to address is *collection*. A **collection** is an object that contains a group of other objects. A recordset has a collection of other objects called Fields. The collection has properties and methods. One of the properties of all collections is Count, which is the number of objects in the collection. Thus, recordset.Fields.Count is the number of fields in the collection. In OLE DB, collections are named as the plural of the objects they collect. Thus, there is a Fields collection of Field objects, an Errors collection of Error objects, a Parameters collection of Parameters, and so forth. An important method of a collection is an iterator, which is a method that can be used to process each member of the collection or otherwise identify the items in the collection.

Goals of OLE DB

The major goals for OLE DB are listed in Figure 11-14. First, as mentioned, OLE DB breaks DBMS functionality and services into object pieces. This partitioning means great flexibility for both **data consumers** (users of OLE DB functionality) and **data providers** (vendors of products that deliver OLE DB functionality). Data consumers take only the objects and functionality they need; a wireless device for reading a database can have a very slim footprint. Unlike with ODBC, data providers need only implement a portion of DBMS functionality. This partitioning also means that data providers can deliver capabilities in multiple interfaces.

This last point needs expansion. An object interface is a packaging of objects. An **interface** is specified by a set of objects and the properties and methods that they expose. An object need not expose all of its properties and methods in a given interface. Thus, a recordset

FIGURE 11-14

The Goals of OLE DB

Create object interfaces for DBMS functionality pieces
Query
Update
Transaction management
Other DBMS functionality
Increase flexibility
Allow data consumers to use only the objects they need
Allow data providers to expose pieces of DBMS functionality
Providers can deliver functionality in multiple interfaces
Interfaces are standardized and extensible
Object interface over any type of data
Relational database
ODBC or native
Nonrelational database
VSAM and other files
E-mail
Other
Do not force data to be converted or moved from where they are

object would expose only read methods in a query interface but would expose create, update, and delete methods in a modification interface.

How the object supports the interface, or the **implementation**, is completely hidden from the user. In fact, the developers of an object are free to change the implementation whenever they want. Who will know? But they may not ever change the interface without incurring the justifiable disdain of their users!

OLE DB defines standardized interfaces. Data providers, however, are free to add interfaces on top of the basic standards. Such extensibility is essential for the next goal, which is to provide an object interface to any data type. Relational databases can be processed through OLE DB objects that use ODBC or that use the native DBMS drivers. OLE DB includes support for the other types as indicated in Figure 11-13.

The net result of these design goals is that data need not be converted from one form to another, nor need they be moved from one data source to another. The Web server shown in Figure 11-13 can utilize OLE DB to process data in any of the formats, right where the data reside. This means that transactions may span multiple data sources and may be distributed on different computers. The OLE DB provision for this is the **Microsoft Transaction Server (MTS)**; however, discussion of the MTS is beyond the scope of this text.

OLE DB Terminology

As shown in Figure 11-15, OLE DB has two types of data providers. **Tabular data providers** present their data via rowsets. Examples are DBMS products, spreadsheets, and ISAM file processors, such as dBase and FoxPro. Additionally, other types of data, such as email, can also be presented in rowsets. Tabular data providers bring data of some type into the OLE DB world.

A **service provider**, in contrast, is a transformer of data. Service providers accept OLE DB data from an OLE DB tabular data provider and transform it in some way. Service providers

Tabular data provider
Exposes data via rowsets
Examples: DBMS, spreadsheets, ISAMs, e-mail
Service provider
Transforms data through OLE DB interfaces
Both a consumer and a provider of data
Examples: query processors, XML document creator

are both consumers and providers of transformed data. An example of a service provider is one that obtains data from a relational DBMS and then transforms them into XML documents. Both data and service providers process rowset objects. A rowset is equivalent to what we called a **cursor** in Chapter 9, and in fact the two terms are frequently used synonymously.

For database applications, rowsets are created by processing SQL statements. The results of a query, for example, are stored in a rowset. OLE DB rowsets have dozens of different methods, which are exposed via the interfaces listed in Figure 11-16.

IRowSet provides object methods for forward-only sequential movement through a rowset. When you declare a forward-only cursor in OLE DB, you are invoking the IRowSet interface. The IAccessor interface is used to bind program variables to rowset fields.

The IColumnsInfo interface has methods for obtaining information about the columns in a rowset. IRowSet, IAccessor, and IColumnsInfo are the basic rowset interfaces. Other interfaces are defined for more advanced operations such as scrollable cursors, update operations, direct access to particular rows, explicit locks, and so forth.

ADO and ADO.NET

Because OLE DB is an object-oriented interface, it is particularly suited to object-oriented languages such as VB.NET and Visual C#.NET. Many database application developers, however, program in scripting languages such as VBScript or JScript (Microsoft's version of JavaScript). To meet the needs of these programmers, Microsoft developed Active Data Objects (ADO) as a cover over OLE DB objects, as shown in Figure 11-17. ADO has enabled programmers to use almost any language to access OLE DB functionality.

IRowSet
Methods for sequential iteration through a rowset
IAccessor
Methods for setting and determining bindings between rowset and client program variables
IColumnsInfo
Methods for determining information about the columns in the rowset
Other interfaces
Scrollable cursors
Create, update, delete rows
Directly access particular rows (bookmarks)
Explicitly set locks
Additional capabilities

FIGURE 11-17

The Role of ADO

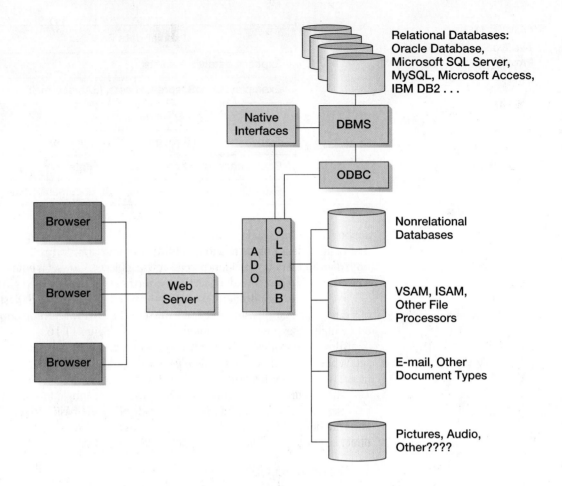

ADO is a simple object model that overlies the more complex OLE DB object model. ADO can be called from scripting languages, such as JScript and VBScript, and it can also be called from more powerful languages, such as Visual Basic .NET, Visual C#.NET, Visual C++. NET, and even Java. Because ADO is easier to understand and use than OLE DB, ADO was (and still is) often used for database applications.

ADO.NET is a new, improved, and greatly expanded version of ADO that was developed as part of Microsoft's .NET initiative. It incorporates the functionality of ADO and OLE DB but adds much more. In particular, ADO.NET facilitates the transformation of XML documents (discussed later in this chapter) to and from relational database constructs. ADO.NET also provides the ability to create and process in-memory databases called *datasets*. Figure 11-18 shows the role of ADO.NET.

The ADO.NET Object Model

Now we need to look at ADO.NET in more detail. As shown in Figure 11-19, an **ADO.NET Data Provider** is a class library that provides ADO.NET services. Microsoft supplied ADO.NET Data Providers are available for ODBC, OLE DB, SQL Server, Oracle Database, and

FIGURE 11-18

The Role of ADO.NET

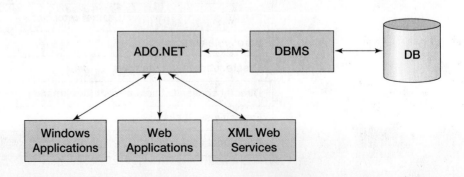

FIGURE 11-19

Components of an
ADO.NET Data Provider

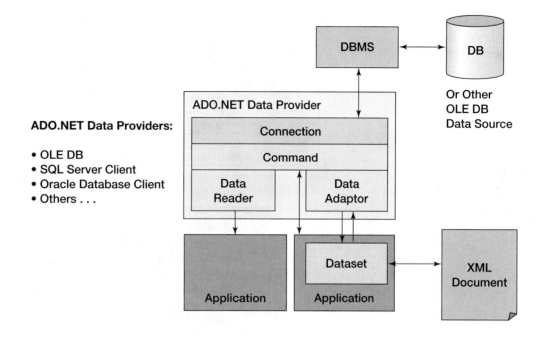

EDM applications, which means that ADO.NET works not only with the ODBC and OLE DB data access methods we have discussed in this chapter but directly with SQL Server, Oracle Database, and .NET language applications that use EDM as well. ADO Data Providers from other vendors are available through *http://msdn.microsoft.com/en-us/data/dd363565*.

A simplified version of the ADO.NET object model is shown in Figure 11-20. The ADO.NET object classes are grouped into Data Providers and DataSets.

The **ADO.NET Connection object** is responsible for connecting to the data source. It is basically the same as the ADO Connection object, except that ODBC is not used as a data source.

FIGURE 11-20

The ADO.NET Object
Model

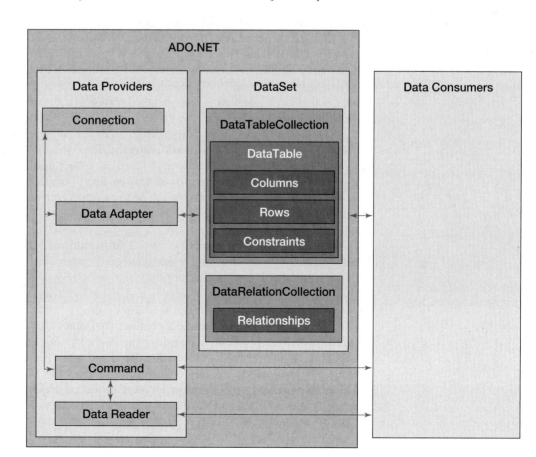

FIGURE 11-21

The ADO.NET DataSet
Object Model

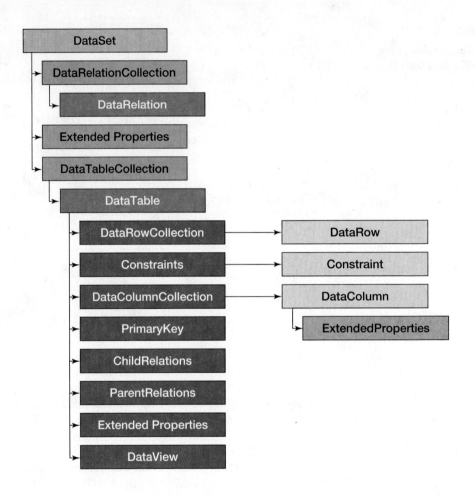

The **ADO.NET DataSet** is a representation of the data stored in the computer memory as a set of data separate from the one in the DBMS. The DataSet is distinct and disconnected from the DBMS data. This allows commands to be run against the DataSet instead of the actual data. DataSet data can be constructed from data in multiple databases, and they can be managed by different DBMS products. The DataSet contains the DataTableCollection and the DataRelationCollection. A more detailed version of the ADO.NET dataset object model is shown in Figure 11-21.

The **DataTableCollection** mimics DBMS tables with **DataTable objects**. DataTable objects include a **DataColumnCollection**, a **DataRowCollection**, and **Constraints**. Data values are stored in DataRow collections in three forms: **original values**, **current values**, and **proposed values**. Each DataTable object has a **PrimaryKey property** to enforce row uniqueness. The Constraints collection uses two constraints. The **ForeignKeyConstraint** supports referential integrity, and the **UniqueConstraint** supports data integrity.

The **DataRelationCollection** stores **DataRelations**, which act as the relational links between tables. Note again that referential integrity is maintained by the ForeignKeyConstraint in the Constraints collection. Relationships among DataSet tables can be processed just as relationships in a database can be processed. A relationship can be used to compute the values of a column, and DataSet tables can also have views.

The **ADO.NET Command object** shown in Figures 11-19 and 11-20 is used as an SQL statement or stored procedure and is run on data in the DataSet. The **ADO.NET DataAdapter object** is the link between a Connection object and a DataSet object. The DataAdapter uses four Command objects: the **SelectCommand object**, the **InsertCommand object**, the **UpdateCommand object**, and the **DeleteCommand object**. The SelectCommand object gets data from a DBMS and places it in a DataSet. The other commands send changes in the DataSet back to the DBMS data.

The **ADO.NET DataReader** is similar to a cursor that provides read-only, forward-only data transfers from a data source and can be used only through an Execute method of a Command.

Looking ahead to our discussion of XML later in this chapter, we see some advantages of ADO.NET over ADO. Once a DataSet is constructed, its contents can be formatted as an XML document with a single command. Similarly, an XML Schema document for the DataSet can also be produced with a single command. This process works in reverse as well. An XML Schema document can be used to create the structure of a DataSet, and the DataSet data can then be filled by reading an XML document.

BY THE WAY   As Microsoft developed .NET technology, it became clear that a generalized means was needed to define and process database views and related structures. Microsoft could have defined a new proprietary technology for this purpose, but thankfully it did not. Instead, it recognized that the concepts, techniques, and facilities used to manage regular databases can be used to manage in-memory databases as well. The benefit to you is that all of the concepts and techniques that you have learned to this point for processing regular databases can also be used to process datasets.

You may be wondering, "Why is all of this necessary? Why do we need an in-memory database?" The answer lies in database views like that shown in the XML discussion in Appendix K and, specifically, in Figure K-19. There is no standardized way to describe and process such data structures. Because it involves two multivalued paths through the data, SQL cannot be used to describe the data. Instead, we must execute two SQL statements and somehow patch the results to obtain the view.

Views like that shown in Figure K-19 have been processed for many years, but only by private, proprietary means. Every time such a structure needs to be processed, a developer designs programs for creating and manipulating the data in memory and for saving them to the database. Object-oriented programmers define a class for this data structure and create methods to serialize (transfer from memory representation to persistent disk storage) objects of this class into the database. Other programmers use other means. The problem is that every time a different view is designed, a different scheme must be designed and developed to process the new view.

DataSets do have a downside, and a serious one for some applications. Because DataSet data are disconnected from the regular database, only optimistic locking can be used. The data are read from the database, placed into the DataSet, and processed there. No attempt is made to propagate changes in the DataSet back to the database. If, after processing, the application later wants to save all of the DataSet data into a regular database, it needs to use optimistic locking. If some other application has changed the data, either the DataSet will need to be reprocessed or the data change will be forced onto the database, causing the lost update problem.

Thus, DataSets cannot be used for applications in which optimistic locking is problematic. For such applications, the ADO.NET Command object should be used instead. But for applications in which conflict is rare or for those in which reprocessing after conflict can be accommodated, DataSets provide significant value.

BY THE WAY   Combining Oracle Database with ASP.NET applications is somewhat complex and beyond the scope of this discussion. A good starting point is the Oracle Database 2 Day + .NET Developer's Guide for Oracle Database 11*g* R2 at *http://docs.oracle.com/cd/E11882_01/appdev.112/e10767/toc.htm*. In particular, see Chapter 7: Using ASP.NET with Oracle Database at *http://docs.oracle.com/cd/E11882_01/appdev.112/e10767/using_aspnt.htm*.

The only way to use Oracle Database XML facilities is to write in Java, an object-oriented programming language. Further, the only way to process ADO.NET is from one of the .NET languages, all of which, like Visual Basic .NET, are object-oriented languages. Thus, if you do not yet know object-oriented design and programming and if you want to work in the emerging world of database processing, you should run, not walk, to your nearest object-oriented design and programming class!

The Java Platform

Having looked at the Microsoft .NET Framework in some detail, we will now turn our attention to the Java platform and look at its components.

JDBC

Originally, and contrary to many sources, JDBC did *not* stand for Java Database Connectivity. According to Sun Microsystems—the inventor of Java and the original source of many Java-oriented products—JDBC was not an acronym; it just stood for JDBC. At this point in time, however, we can even find the name Java Database Connectivity (JDBC) on Oracle's Web site (Oracle Corporation purchased Sun Microsystems in January of 2010—see *www.oracle.com/ technetwork/java/javase/tech/index-jsp-136101.html*)! Still, because we use acronyms in this book after introducing the full term, we will use *JDBC*.

A JDBC driver is available for almost every conceivable DBMS product. Oracle maintains a directory of them available through *www.oracle.com/technetwork/java/javase/jdbc/index.html*—click on the *Industry Support* link at the bottom of the page. Some of the drivers are free, and almost all of them have an evaluation edition that can be used for free for a limited period of time. The JDBC driver for MySQL is the MySQL Connector/J, which is available at *http://dev.mysql.com/ downloads/connector/j/*.

Driver Types

As summarized in Figure 11-22, there are four defined JDBC driver types. Type 1 drivers are JDBC-ODBC bridge drivers, which provide an interface between Java and regular ODBC drivers. Most ODBC drivers are written in C or C++. For reasons unimportant to us here, there are incompatibilities between Java and C/C++. Bridge drivers resolve these incompatibilities and allow access to ODBC data sources from Java. Because we use ODBC in the chapter, if you are using MySQL, you will want to download the MySQL Connector/ODBC driver. The MySQL Connector/ODBC is available from *http://dev.mysql.com/downloads/connector/odbc/*. Note that the

FIGURE 11-22

Summary of JDBC Driver Types

Summary of JDBC Driver Types	
Driver Type	**Characteristics**
1	JDBC–ODBC bridge. Provides a Java API that interfaces to an ODBC driver. Enables processing of ODBC data sources from Java.
2	A Java API that connects to the native-library of a DBMS product. The Java program and the DBMS must reside on the same machine, or the DBMS must handle the intermachine communication, if not.
3	A Java API that connects to a DBMS-independent network protocol. Can be used for servlets and applets.
4	A Java API that connects to a DBMS-dependent network protocol. Can be used for servlets and applets.

MySQL connector for Windows operating systems is included in the MySQL Installer for Windows discussed in Chapter 10C.

Drivers of Types 2 through 4 are written entirely in Java; they differ only in how they connect to the DBMS. Type 2 drivers connect to the native API of the DBMS. For example, they call Oracle Database using the standard (non-ODBC) programming interface to Oracle Database. Drivers of Types 3 and 4 are intended for use over communications networks. A Type 3 driver translates JDBC calls into a DBMS-independent network protocol. This protocol is then translated into the network protocol used by a particular DBMS. Finally, Type 4 drivers translate JDBC calls into DBMS-specific network protocols.

To understand how drivers Types 2 through 4 differ, you must first understand the difference between a *servlet* and an *applet*. As you probably know, Java was designed to be portable. To accomplish portability, Java programs are not compiled into a particular machine language, but instead are compiled into machine-independent bytecode. Oracle, Microsoft, and others have written **bytecode interpreters** for each machine environment (Intel Pentium, Intel Core, Alpha, and so on). These interpreters are referred to as **Java virtual machines**.

To run a compiled Java program, the machine-independent bytecode is interpreted by the virtual machine at run time. The cost of this, of course, is that bytecode interpretation constitutes an extra step, so such programs can never be as fast as programs that are compiled directly into machine code. This may or may not be a problem, depending on the application's workload.

An **applet** is a Java bytecode program that runs on the application user's computer. Applet bytecode is sent to the user via HTTP and is invoked using the HTTP protocol on the user's computer. The bytecode is interpreted by a virtual machine, which is usually part of the browser. Because of portability, the same bytecode can be sent to a Windows, a UNIX, or an Apple computer.

A **servlet** is a Java program that is invoked via HTTP on the Web server computer. It responds to requests from browsers. Servlets are interpreted and executed by a Java virtual machine running on the server.

Because they have a connection to a communications protocol, Type 3 and Type 4 drivers can be used in either applet or servlet code. Type 2 drivers can be used only in situations where the Java program and the DBMS reside on the same machine or where the Type 2 driver connects to a DBMS program that handles the communications between the computer running the Java program and the computer running the DBMS.

Thus, if you write code that connects to a database from an applet (two-tier architecture), only a Type 3 or Type 4 driver can be used. In these situations, if your DBMS product has a Type 4 driver, use it; it will be faster than a Type 3 driver.

In three-tier or *n*-tier architecture, if the Web server and the DBMS are running on the same machine, you can use any of the four types of drivers. If the Web server and the DBMS are running on different machines, Type 3 and Type 4 drivers can be used without a problem. Type 2 drivers can also be used if the DBMS vendor handles the communications between the Web server and the DBMS. The MySQL Connector/J is a Type 4 driver.

Using JDBC

Unlike ODBC, JDBC does not have a separate utility for creating a JDBC data source. Instead, all of the work to define a connection is done in Java code via the JDBC driver. The coding pattern for using a JDBC driver is as follows:

1. Load the driver.
2. Establish a connection to the database.
3. Create a statement.
4. Do something with the statement.

To load the driver, you must first obtain the driver library and install it in a directory. You need to ensure that the directory is named in the CLASSPATH both for the Java compiler and for the Java virtual machine. The name of the DBMS product to be used and the name of the database are provided at step 2. Figure 11-23 summarizes the JDBC components.

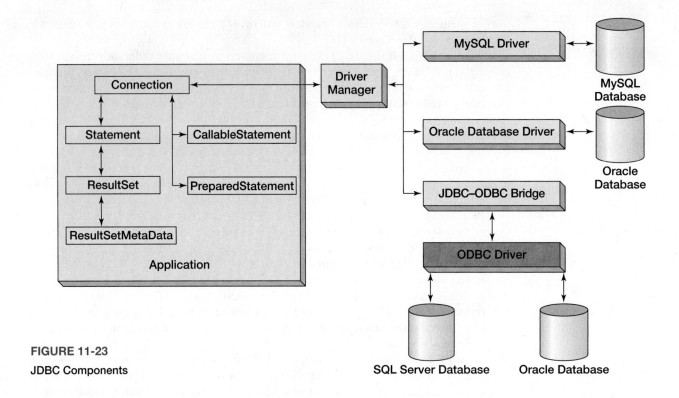

FIGURE 11-23

JDBC Components

Note that Java is used to create the application shown in the figure, and because Java is an object-oriented programming language, we see a set of objects in the application that are similar to those we have discussed for ADO.NET. The application creates a **JDBC Connection object**, **JDBC Statement objects**, a **JDBC ResultSet object**, and a **JDBC ResultSetMetaData object**. Calls from these objects are routed via the **JDBC DriverManager** to the proper driver. Drivers then process their databases. Notice that the Oracle database in this figure could be processed either via a JDBC-ODBC bridge or via a pure JDBC driver.

> **BY THE WAY**   Most of this technology arose in the UNIX operating system world (see the Wikipedia article *UNIX*). UNIX is case sensitive, and almost everything you enter here also is case sensitive. Thus, *jdbc* and *JDBC* are *not* the same.

Prepared Statement objects and **Callable Statement objects** can be used to invoke compiled queries and stored procedures in the database. Their use is similar to the use of ADO.NET Command objects discussed previously in this chapter. It is possible to receive values back from procedures as well. Start at *www.oracle.com/technetwork/java/javase/documentation/index.html* for more information.

Java Server Pages (JSP) and Servlets

Java Server Pages (JSP) technology provides a means to create dynamic Web pages using HTML (and XML) and the Java programming language. With Java, the capabilities of a complete object-oriented language are directly available to the Web page developer. This is similar to what can be done using ASP.NET using the Microsoft .NET languages.

Because Java is machine independent, JSP is also machine independent. With JSP, you are not locked into using Windows and IIS. You can run the same JSP page on a Linux server, on a Windows server, and on others as well. The official specification for JSP can be found at *www.oracle.com/technetwork/java/javaee/jsp/index.html*.

JSP pages are transformed into standard Java language and then compiled just like a regular program. In particular, they are transformed into Java servlets, which means that JSP pages are transformed into subclasses of the HTTPServlet class behind the scenes. JSP code thus has access to the HTTP request and response objects and also to their methods and to other HTTP functionality.

Apache Tomcat

The Apache Web server does not support servlets. However, the Apache Foundation and Sun cosponsored the Jakarta Project that developed a servlet processor named **Apache Tomcat** (now in version 8.0.23). You can obtain the source and binary code of Tomcat from the Apache Tomcat Web site at *http://tomcat.apache.org/*.

Tomcat is a servlet processor that can work in conjunction with Apache or as a stand-alone Web server. Tomcat has limited Web server facilities, however, so it is normally used in stand-alone mode only for testing servlets and JSP pages. For commercial production applications, Tomcat should be used in conjunction with Apache. If you are running Tomcat and Apache separately on the same Web server, they need to use different ports. The default port for a Web server is 80, and Apache normally uses it. When used in stand-alone mode, Tomcat is usually configured to listen to port 8080, though this, of course, can be changed.

Figure 11-24 shows the process by which JSP pages are compiled. When a request for a JSP page is received, a Tomcat (or other) servlet processor finds the compiled version of the page and checks to determine whether it is current. It does this by looking for an uncompiled version of the page having a creation date and time later than the compiled page's creation date and time. If the page is not current, the new page is parsed and transformed into a Java source file, and that source file is then compiled. The servlet is then loaded and executed. If the compiled JSP page is current, then it is loaded into memory, if not already there, and then executed. If it is in memory, it is simply executed.

FIGURE 11-24

JSP Compilation Process

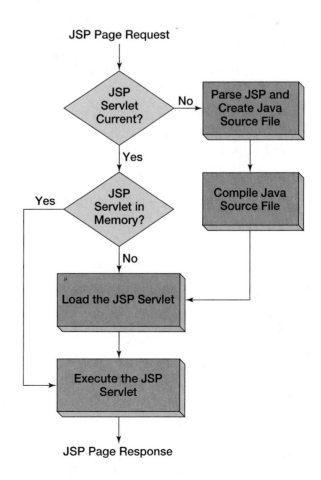

> **BY THE WAY**   The downside of such automatic compilation is that if you make syntax errors and forget to test your pages, the first user to access your page will receive the compiler errors!
>
>   Unlike common gateway interface (CGI) files (see the Wikipedia article *Common_Gateway_Interface*) and some other Web server programs, only one copy of a JSP page can be in memory at a time. Further, pages are executed by one of Tomcat's threads, not by an independent process. This means that much less memory and processor time are required to execute a JSP page than to execute a comparable CGI script.

Web Database Processing with PHP

At this point in our discussion, it is time to build an actual Web database application and apply both some of the knowledge from this chapter and some new techniques yet to be discussed. We have already created an ODBC data source for the View Ridge Gallery database, and now we will use it to look at Web database processing. Although we have introduced technologies such as ADO.NET, ASP.NET, Java, and JSP, these technologies are complex subjects and beyond the scope of this book. Further, these technologies tend to become vendor specific—you are either working in a Microsoft-centric world with .NET technologies and ASPs or an Oracle Corporation-centic world with Java and JSPs.

> **BY THE WAY**   Before working your way through this chapter, you should install and set up the software we will be using—the Microsoft IIS Web server, the Java JRE, PHP, and the NetBeans IDE—on your computer if you do not have the software available for your use in a computer lab or similar facility. Installing and setting up this software correctly, which is complex but straightforward, is described in detail in Appendix I. We strongly suggest that you read Appendix I now and make sure your computer is completely set up before continuing with the material in this chapter. Then try out each of our examples on your computer to get the most out of this discussion.

In this book, we will take a vendor-neutral approach and use technologies that can be used with any operating system or DBMS. We will use the **PHP** language. PHP, which is an abbreviation for **PHP: Hypertext Processor** (and which was previously known as the *Personal Hypertext Processor*), is a scripting language that can be embedded in Web pages. Although PHP started as purely a scripting language, it now also has object-oriented programming elements, but we will not cover those in this book.

PHP is extremely popular. In January 2013, there were about 244 million PHP Web sites,[2] and the February 2015 TIOBE Programming Community Index ranked PHP as the seventh most popular programming language (following, in order, C, Java, C++, Objective C, C#, and JavaScript).[3] PHP is easy to learn and can be used in most Web server environments and with most databases. As an added bonus, it is an open source product available for free download from the PHP Web site (*www.php.net* and *http://windows.php.net/download/* for the Windows versions).

Although Microsoft would probably prefer that you use ASP.NET for Web applications, there is still good information on using PHP in a Microsoft environment on the Microsoft Web site (e.g., see Running PHP on IIS at *http://php.iis.net*). Both Oracle DBMS products—Oracle Database and MySQL—enthusiastically support PHP. Oracle publishes the *Oracle Database 2 Day + PHP Developer's Guide* (available in both HTML and PDF

---

[2]See *www.php.net/usage.php*.
[3]See *www.tiobe.com/index.php/content/paperinfo/tpci/index.html*.

format at *https://docs.oracle.com/database/121/nav/portal_5.htm*), which is an excellent reference for using PHP with Oracle Database 11*g* Release 2. Because PHP is often the P in AMP, LAMP, and WAMP, many books are available that discuss the combination of PHP and MySQL, and the MySQL Web site contains basic documentation on using PHP with MySQL (e.g., see *http://dev.mysql.com/doc/refman/5.6/en/apis-php-info.html*).

Web Database Processing with PHP and the NetBeans IDE

To start, we need a Web server to store the Web pages that we will build and use. We could use the Apache HTTP Server (available from the Apache Software Foundation at *www.apache.org*). This is the most widely used Web server, and there is a version that will run on just about every operating system in existence. However, because we have been using the Windows operating system for the DBMS products shown in this book, we will build a Web site using the Microsoft IIS Web server. One advantage of using this Web server for users of the Windows 8 and the Windows Server 2012 R2 operating systems is that IIS is included with the operating system: IIS version 8.5 is included with both Windows 8 and Windows Server 2012 R2. IIS is installed but not operational by default, but it can easily be made operational at any time. This means that any user can practice creating and using Web pages on his or her own workstation as well as working on a networked Web server. See Appendix I for a detailed discussion of setting up IIS.

> **BY THE WAY** This discussion of Web database processing has been written to be as widely applicable as possible. With minor adjustments to the following steps, you should be able to use the Apache Web server if you have it available. Whenever possible, we have chosen to use products and technologies that are available for many operating systems.

When IIS is installed, it creates an **inetpub folder** on the C: drive as C:\inetpub. Within the inetpub folder is the **wwwroot folder**, which is where IIS stores the most basic Web pages used by the Web server. Figure 11-25 shows this directory structure in Windows Server 2012 R2 after IIS has been installed, with the files in the wwwroot folder displayed in the file pane.

FIGURE 11-25

The IIS wwwroot Folder in Windows Server 2012 R2

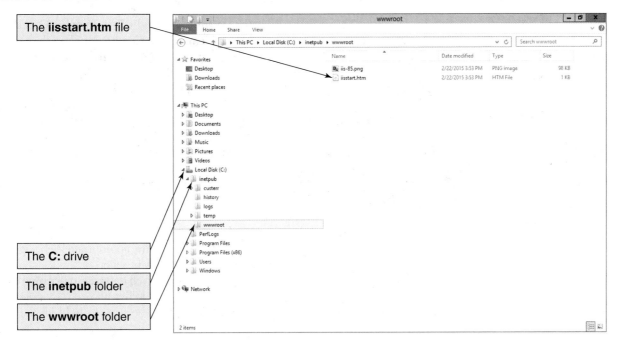

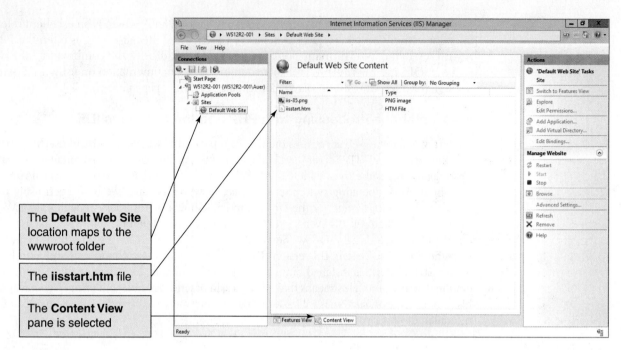

The **Default Web Site** location maps to the wwwroot folder

The **iisstart.htm** file

The **Content View** pane is selected

FIGURE 11-26

Managing IIS with the Internet Information Services Manager in Windows Server 2012 R2

IIS is managed using a program called **Internet Information Services Manager** as shown in Figure 11-26 for Windows Server 2012 R2. The location of the program icon varies depending on the operating system.

- For Windows 7, open **Control Panel**, then open **System and Security,** and then open **Administrative Tools**. The shortcut icon for Internet Information Services Manager is located in Administrative Tools.
- For Windows Server 2008 R2, use **Start | Administrative Tools | Internet Information Services (IIS) Manager**.
- For Windows 8.1, click **[Windows Key]+X** to open the Quick Access Menu, then click **Control Panel** to open the Control Panel. In the Control Panel, open **System and Security**, and then open **Administrative Tools**. The shortcut icon for Internet Information Services Manager is located in Administrative Tools.
- For Windows Server 2012 R2, click **[Windows Key]+X** to open the Quick Access Menu, then click **Control Panel** to open the Control Panel. In the Control Panel, open **System and Security**, and then open **Administrative Tools**. The shortcut icon for Internet Information Services Manager is located in Administrative Tools.

Note that the files shown in the **Default Web Site folder** in Figure 11-26 are the same files that are in the wwwroot folder in Figure 11-25—they are the default files created by IIS when it is installed. In Windows 7, Windows 8, Windows Server 2008 R2, and Windows Server 2012 R2, the file **iisstart.htm** generates the Web page that Internet Explorer (or any other Web browser) contacting this Web server over the Internet will display.

To test the Web server installation, open your Web browser, type in the URL **http://localhost**, and press the **Enter** key. For Windows Server 2012 R2, the Web page shown in Figure 11-27 (in the Microsoft IE 10 Web browser) appears. If the appropriate Web page isn't displayed in your Web browser, your Web server is not properly installed.

Now we will set up a small Web site that can be used for Web database processing of the View Ridge Gallery VRG database. First, we will create a new folder named *DBP* (Database Processing) under the wwwroot folder. This new folder will be used to hold all the Web

This Web page is generated by the iisstart.htm file

FIGURE 11-27

The Default IIS Web Page for IIS 8 in Windows Server 2012 R2

pages developed in discussions and exercises in this book. Second, we will create a subfolder of DBC named *VRG*. This folder will hold the VRG Web site. You create these folders using Windows Explorer.

Getting Started with HTML Web Pages

The most basic Web pages are created using **Hypertext Markup Language (HTML)**. The term *hypertext* refers to the fact that you can include links to other objects, such as Web pages, maps, pictures, and even audio and video files in a Web page, and when you click the link, you are immediately taken to that other object and it is displayed in your Web browser. HTML itself is a standard set of **HTML syntax rules** and **HTML document tags** that can be interpreted by Web browsers to create specific onscreen displays.

Tags are usually paired, with a specific beginning tag and a matching ending tag that includes the slash character (/). Thus, a paragraph of text is tagged as <p>*{paragraph text here}*</p>, and a main heading is tagged as <h1>*{heading text here}*</h1>. Some tags do not need a separate end tag because they are essentially self-contained. For example, to insert a horizontal line on a Web page, you use the horizontal rule tag <hr />. Note that such single, self-contained tags must include the slash character as part of the tag (in HTML 5 these tags can optionally be written without the slash [the horizontal rule tag is just <hr>], but we prefer to use the older form in this book).

The rules of HTML are defined as standards by the **World Wide Web Consortium (W3C)**, and the details of current and proposed standards can be found at *www.w3c.org* (this site also has several excellent tutorials on HTML[4]). The W3C Web site has current standards for HTML and **Extensible Markup Language (XML)** (which we will discuss later in this chapter). A full discussion of these standards is beyond the scope of this text; this chapter uses the current HTML 5.0 standard.

In this chapter, we will create a simple HTML home page for the View Ridge Gallery Web site and place it in the VRG folder. We will discuss some of the numerous available Web page editors shortly, but all you really need to create Web pages is a

---

[4]To learn more about HTML, go to the Web site of the World Wide Web Consortium (W3C) at *www.w3.org*. For good HTML tutorials, see David Raggett's "Getting Started with HTML" tutorial at *www.w3.org/MarkUp/ Guide*, his "More Advanced Features" tutorial at *www.w3.org/MarkUp/Guide/Advanced.html*, and his "Adding a Touch of Style" tutorial at *www.w3.org/MarkUp/Guide/Style.html*.

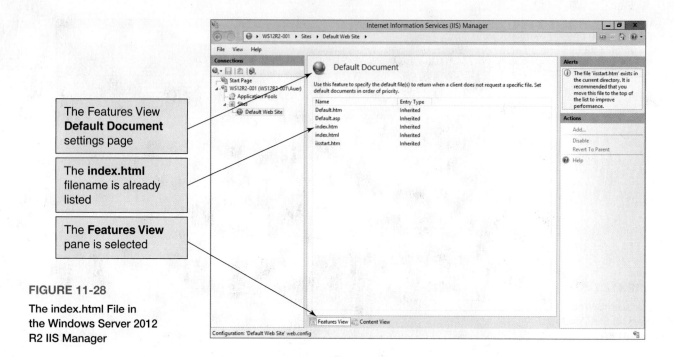

The Features View **Default Document** settings page

The **index.html** filename is already listed

The **Features View** pane is selected

FIGURE 11-28

The index.html File in the Windows Server 2012 R2 IIS Manager

simple text editor. For this first Web page, we will use the Microsoft Notepad ASCII text editor, which has the advantage of being supplied with every version of the Windows operating system.

The index.html Web Page

The name for the file we are going to create is **index.html**. We need to use the name *index.html* because it is a special name as far as Web servers are concerned. The file name index.html is one of only a few file names that *most* Web servers automatically display when a URL request is made without a specific file reference, and thus it will become the new default display page for our Web database application. However, note the phrase "*most* Web servers" in the last sentence. Although Apache, IIS 7.0, IIS 7.5, and IIS 8 (as shown in Figure 11-28) are configured to recognize index.html, IIS 5.1 is not. If you are using Windows XP and IIS 5.1, you need to add index.html to the list of recognized files using the Internet Information Services management program.

Creating the index.html Web Page

Now we can create the index.html Web page, which consists of the basic HTML statements shown in Figure 11-29. Figure 11-30 shows the HTML code in Microsoft Notepad.

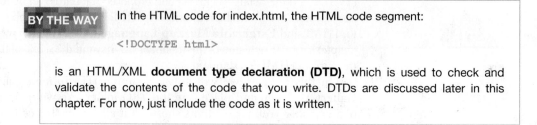

BY THE WAY   In the HTML code for index.html, the HTML code segment:

```
<!DOCTYPE html>
```

is an HTML/XML **document type declaration (DTD)**, which is used to check and validate the contents of the code that you write. DTDs are discussed later in this chapter. For now, just include the code as it is written.

If we now use either the URL *http://localhost/DBP/VRG* (if the Web server is on the same computer we are working on) or the URL *http://{Web server DNS Name or IP Number}/DBP/VRG* (if the Web server is on another computer), we get the Web page shown in Figure 11-31.

```html
<!DOCTYPE html>
<html>
    <head>
        <meta http-equiv="Content-Type" content="text/html; charset=utf-8" />
        <title>View Ridge Gallery Demonstration Pages Home Page</title>
    </head>
    <body>
        <h1 style="text-align: center; color: blue">
            Database Processing (14th Edition)
        </h1>
        <h2 style="text-align: center; font-weight: bold">
            David M. Kroenke
        </h2>
        <h2 style="text-align: center; font-weight: bold">
            David J. Auer
        </h2>
        <hr />
        <h2 style="text-align: center; color: blue">
            Welcome to the View Ridge Gallery Home Page
        </h2>
        <hr />
        <p>Chapter 11 Demonstration Pages From Figures in the Text:</p>
        <p>Example 1:   
            <a href="ReadArtist.php">
                Display the ARTIST Table (LastName, FirstName, Nationality)
            </a>
        </p>
        <hr />
    </body>
</html>
```

FIGURE 11-29

**The HTML Code for the
index.html File in the *VRG*
Folder**

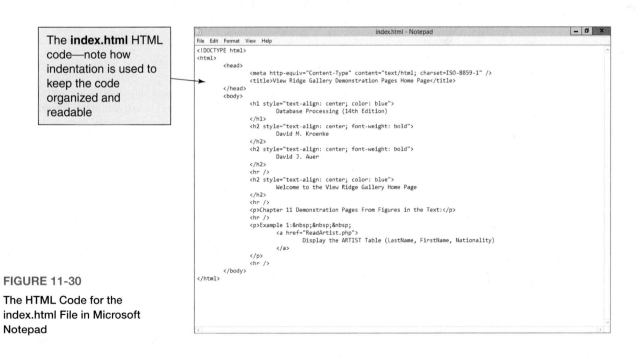

The **index.html** HTML
code—note how
indentation is used to
keep the code
organized and
readable

FIGURE 11-30

**The HTML Code for the
index.html File in Microsoft
Notepad**

This URL of *http://localhost/DBP/VRG* indicates that the Web server is on your computer itself.

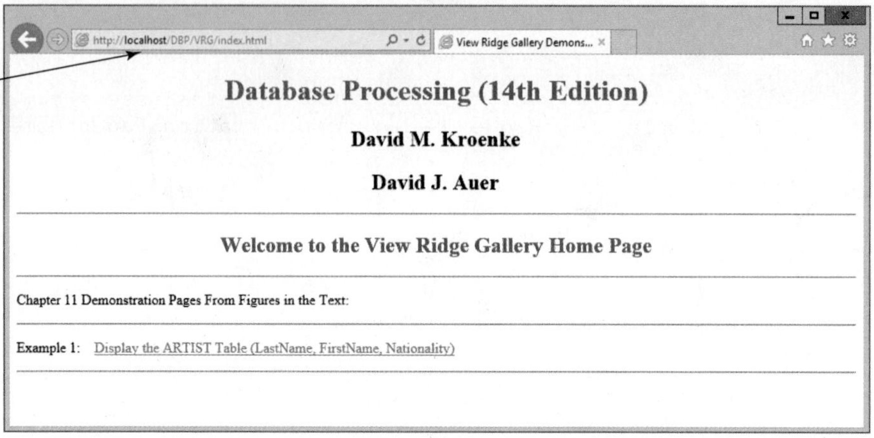

FIGURE 11-31

The VRG index.html Web Page

BY THE WAY If you are working on a single computer, with the DBMS, Web server, and development tools all installed together, you will see a consistent user interface. It may be Windows XP, Windows Vista, or a version of Linux. This is, in fact, typical of small development platforms and allows you to easily test each application component as you create it.

In a larger production environment, however, the Web server and database server (which may or may not be the same physical server) are separate from the developer's workstation. In this case you, as the developer, will see different user interfaces depending on which computer you are using.

We are illustrating this latter setup in this chapter. Our Web server (IIS) and DBMS server (SQL Server 2014) are on one server running Windows Server 2012 R2. Our development tools (the IE 8 Web browser and the NetBeans IDE) are on a separate workstation running Windows 8.1. Thus, you will see the differences in the user interface depending on whether the work is being done on the server (e.g., in Figures 11-25, 11-26, and 11-28) or on the workstation (e.g., Figure 11-31).

Using PHP

Now that we have our basic Web site set up, we will expand its capabilities with a Web development environment that allows us to connect Web pages to our database. Several technologies allow us to do this. Developers using Microsoft products usually work with the .NET framework and use ASP.NET technology. Developers who use the Apache Web server may prefer creating JSP files in the JavaScript scripting language or using the Java programming language in the Java Enterprise Edition (Java EE) environment.

The PHP Scripting Language

In this chapter, we will use PHP, which is available as this is being written in several versions, including 5.4.41, 5.525, and 5.6.9 (we are using a version of 5.6), and available for free download from the PHP Web site (*www.php.net*). See Appendix I for a complete discussion of installing and testing PHP on your computer. You should download the latest version of PHP available for your operating system and install it on your computer. In addition to Appendix I, documentation is available on the PHP Web site, and good discussion can also be found by searching the Web for "PHP installation." Setting up PHP usually requires several steps (not just running an installation routine), so take some time and be sure you have PHP running correctly. Also be sure to enable PHP Data Objects (PDO)—this is not done automatically.

The NetBeans Integrated Development Environment (IDE)

Although a simple text editor such as Microsoft Notepad is fine for simple Web pages, as we start creating more complex pages, we will move to an **integrated development**

environment (IDE). An IDE is intended to be a complete development framework, with all the tools you need in one place. An IDE gives you the most robust and user-friendly means of creating and maintaining your Web pages.

If you are working with Microsoft products, you will most likely use Visual Studio (or the Visual Studio Community 2013 edition, available for free from *www.visualstudio.com/en-us/products/visual-studio-community-vs.aspx*). In fact, if you have installed SQL Server 2014 Express Advanced or any non-Express version of the product, you have already installed some Visual Studio components. These are installed to support SQL Server Reporting Services, and they are sufficient for creating basic Web pages. If you are working with JavaScript or Java, you might prefer the Eclipse IDE (downloadable from *www.netbeans.org*).

For this chapter, we will again turn to the open source development community and use the **NetBeans IDE**. NetBeans provides a framework that can be modified by add-in modules for many purposes. For PHP, we can use NetBeans with the **PHP plugin**, which is specifically intended to provide a PHP development environment within the NetBean IDE. For more information on installing and using PHP and the NetBeans IDE, see Appendix I.

Figure 11-32 shows the index.html file as created in the NetBeans IDE. Compare this version with the Notepad version in Figure 11-30.

The ReadArtist.php File

Now that we have our basic Web site set up, we will start to integrate PHP into the Web pages. First, we will create a page to read data from a database table and display the results in a Web page. Specifically, we will create a Web page in the VRG folder named ReadArtist. php to run the SQL query:

```
SELECT LastName, FirstName, Nationality FROM ARTIST;
```

This page displays the result of the query, without the table's surrogate key of ArtistID, in a Web page. The HTML and PHP code for ReadArtist.php is shown in Figure 11-33, and the same code is shown in NetBeans in Figure 11-34.

Now if you use the URL *http://localhost/DBP/VRG* in your Web browser and then click the **Example 1: Display the ARTIST Table (No surrogate key)** link on that page, the Web page shown in Figure 11-35 is displayed.

The ReadArtist.php code blends HTML (executed on the user's workstation) and PHP statements (executed on the Web server). In Figure 11-33, the statements included between the **?php and ?** tags are program code that is to be executed on the Web server

FIGURE 11-32

The HTML Code for the index.html File in the NetBean's IDE

The **DBP-e14-VRG** project—Eclipse organizes work into projects

The **index.html** HTML code—note how color coding has been added to indentation to keep the code organized and readable

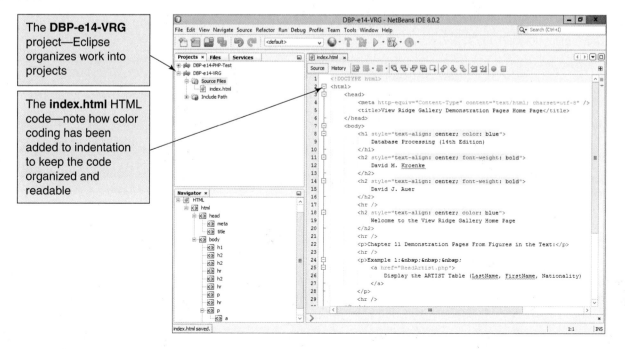

```html
<!DOCTYPE html>
<html>
    <head>
        <meta http-equiv="Content-Type" content="text/html; charset=UTF-8">
        <title>ReadArtist</title>
        <style type="text/css">
            h1 {text-align: center; color: blue}
            h2 {font-family: Ariel, sans-serif; text-align: left; color: blue}
            p.footer {text-align: center}
            table.output {font-family: Ariel, sans-serif}
        </style>
    </head>
    <body>
<?php
    // Get connection
    $DSN = "VRG";
    $User = "VRG-User";
    $Password = "VRG-User+password";

    $Conn = odbc_connect($DSN, $User, $Password);

    // Test connection
    if (!$Conn)
    {
        exit ("ODBC Connection Failed: " . $Conn);
    }
    // Create SQL statement
    $SQL = "SELECT LastName, FirstName, Nationality FROM ARTIST";

    // Execute SQL statement
    $RecordSet = odbc_exec($Conn,$SQL);

    // Test existence of recordset
    if (!$RecordSet)
        {
            exit ("SQL Statement Error: " . $SQL);
        }
?>
    <!-- Page Headers -->
    <h1>
        The View Ridge Gallery ARTIST Table
    </h1>
    <hr />
    <h2>
        ARTIST
    </h2>
<?php

    // Table headers
    echo "<table class='output' border='1'>
        <tr>
            <th>LastName</th>
            <th>FirstName</th>
            <th>Nationality</th>
        </tr>";

    // Table data
    while($RecordSetRow = odbc_fetch_array($RecordSet))
        {
        echo "<tr>";
        echo "<td>" . $RecordSetRow['LastName'] . "</td>";
        echo "<td>" . $RecordSetRow['FirstName'] . "</td>";
        echo "<td>" . $RecordSetRow['Nationality'] . "</td>";
        echo "</tr>";
        }
    echo "</table>";
```

FIGURE 11-33

The HTML and PHP
Code for ReadArtist
.php

FIGURE 11-33

Continued

```
                        // Close connection
                        odbc_close($Conn);
            ?>

            <br />
            <hr />
            <p class="footer">
                    <a href="../VRG/index.html">
                            Return to View Ridge Gallery Home Page
                    </a>
            </p>
            <hr />
        </body>
    </html>
```

The **ReadArtist.php** code—PHP code is enclosed in the **<?php** and **?>** symbols, which are displayed in red in Eclipse

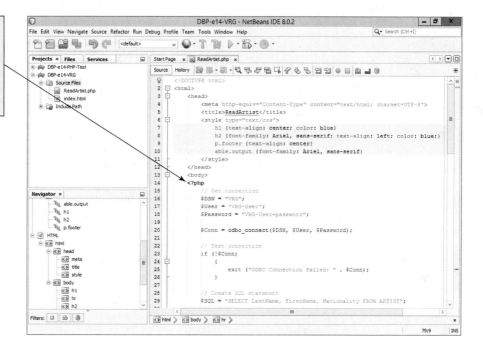

FIGURE 11-34

The HTML and PHP Code for ReadArtist.php in the Netbeans IDE

This URL of *http:// localhost/DBP/VRG* indicates that the Web server is on your computer itself.

Click to return to the View Ridge Gallery Home Page

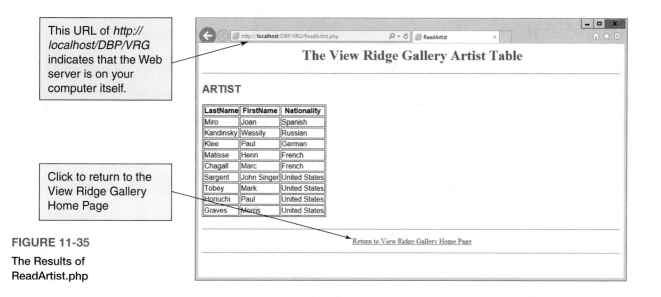

FIGURE 11-35

The Results of ReadArtist.php

computer. All the rest of the code is HTML that is generated and sent to the browser client. In Figure 11-33, the statements:

```
<!DOCTYPE HTML PUBLIC "-//W3C//DTD HTML 4.01 Frameset//EN">
<html>

    <head>

        <meta http-equiv="Content-Type" content="text/html;
        charset=UTF-8">
        <title>ReadArtist</title>
        <style type="text/css">
            h1 {text-align: center; color: blue}
            h2 {font-family: Ariel, sans-serif; text-align:
            left; color: blue}
            p.footer {text-align: center}
            table.output {font-family: Ariel, sans-serif}
        </style>
    </head>
  <body>
```

are normal HTML code. When sent to the browser, these statements set the title of the browser window to ReadArtist PHP Page; define styles to be used by the headings,[5] the results table, and the footer; and cause other HTML-related actions. The next group of statements are included between and, thus, are PHP code that will be executed on the Web server. Also note that all PHP statements, like SQL statements, must end with a semicolon (;).

Creating a Connection to the Database

In the HTML and PHP code in Figure 11-33, the following PHP code is embedded in the HTML code to create and test a connection to the database:

```
<?php
    // Get connection
    $DSN = "VRG";
    $User = "VRG-User";
    $Password = "VRG-User+password";

    $Conn = odbc_connect($DSN, $User, $Password);

    // Test connection
    if (!$Conn)
        {
            exit ("ODBC Connection Failed: " . $Conn);
        }
```

After it runs, the variable $Conn can be used to connect to the ODBC data source VRG. Note that all PHP variables start with the dollar sign symbol ($).

---

[5]Styles are used to control the visual presentation of the Web page and are defined in the HTML section between the <style> and </style> tags. For more information about styles, see David Raggett's "Adding a Touch of Style" tutorial at *www.w3.org/MarkUp/Guide/Style.html*.

> **BY THE WAY**   Be sure to use comments to document your Web pages. PHP code segments with two forward slashes (//) in front of them are comments. This symbol is used to define single-line comments. In PHP, comments can also be inserted in blocks between the symbols /* and */, whereas in HTML comments *must* be inserted between the symbols <!-- and -->.

The connection is used to open the VRG ODBC data source. Here the user ID of *VRG-User* and the password of *VRG-User+password* that we created in Chapter 10A for Microsoft SQL Server 2014 are being used to authenticate to the DBMS. If you are using Oracle Database or MySQL, use the ODBC data source name, username, and user password as you created it for your database. Note that the user ID and password are sent to the database server *only* to get data and are never seen in either (1) the resulting Web page as displayed in the user's Web browser or (2) the underlying HTML code. There is *no* security problem here!

The test of the connection is contained in the code segment:

```
// Test connection
if (!$Conn)
    {
            exit ("ODBC Connection Failed: " . $Conn);
    }
```

In English, this statement says, "IF the connection Conn does not exist, THEN print the error message 'ODBC Connection Failed' followed by the contents of the variable $Conn." Note that the code (!$Conn) means NOT $Conn—in PHP the exclamation point symbol (!) means NOT.

At this point, a connection has been established to the DBMS via the ODBC data source, and the database is open. The $Conn variable can be used whenever a connection to the database is needed.

Creating a RecordSet

Given the connection with an open database, the following code segment from Figure 11-33 will store an SQL statement in the variable $SQL and then use the PHP odbc_exec command to run that SQL statement against the database to retrieve the query results and store them in the variable $RecordSet:

```
// Create SQL statement
$SQL = "SELECT LastName, FirstName, Nationality FROM ARTIST";

// Execute SQL statement
$RecordSet = odbc_exec($Conn,$SQL);

// Test existence of recordset
if (!$RecordSet)
    {
            exit ("SQL Statement Error: " . $SQL);
    }
?>
```

Note that you need to test the results to be sure the PHP command executed correctly.

Displaying the Results

Now that the RecordSet name $RecordSet has been created and populated, we can process the $RecordSet collection with the following code:

```
<!-- Page Headers -->

<H1>
     The View Ridge Gallery ARTIST Table
</H1>
<hr />
<H2>
     ARTIST
</H2>
<?php

// Table headers
echo "<table class='output' border='1'>
     <tr>
          <th>LastName</th>
          <th>FirstName</th>
          <th>Nationality</th>
     </tr>";

// Table data
while($RecordSetRow = odbc_fetch_array($RecordSet))
     {
          echo "<tr>";
               echo "<td>".$RecordSetRow['LastName']."</td>";
               echo "<td>".$RecordSetRow['FirstName']."</td>";
               echo "<td>".$RecordSetRow['Nationality']."</td>";
          echo "</tr>";
     }
echo "</table>";
```

The HTML section defines the page headers, and the PHP section defines how to display the SQL results in a table format. Note the use of the PHP command *echo* to allow PHP to use HTML syntax within the PHP code section. Also note that a loop is executed to iterate through the rows of the RecordSet using the PHP variable $RecordSetRow.

Disconnecting from the Database

Now that we have finished running the SQL statement and displaying the results, we can end our ODBC connection to the database with the code:

```
// Close connection
odbc_close($Conn);

?>
```

The basic page we have created here illustrates the basic concepts of using ODBC and PHP to connect to a database and process data from that database in a Web database processing application. We can now build on this foundation by studying PHP command syntax and incorporating additional PHP features into our Web pages.[6]

Web Page Examples with PHP

The following three examples extend our discussion of using PHP Web pages in Web database applications. These examples focus mainly on the use of PHP and not as much on the graphics, presentation, or workflow. If you want a flashy, better-behaving application, you should be able to modify these examples to obtain that result. Here, just learn how PHP is used.

All of these examples process the View Ridge Gallery database. In all of them we use the VRG database in each DBMS as we constructed it for SQL Server 2014 in Chapter 10A, Oracle Database in Chapter 10B, and MySQL 5.6 in Chapter10C. For simplicity, we connect to each using an ODBC system data source–VRG for SQL Server, VRG-Oracle for Oracle, and VRG-MySQL for MySQL. And if we use the same username and password in each DBMS, we need to only change the ODBC data source name to switch between DBMSs! That is amazing, and exactly what the originators of ODBC hoped for when they created the ODBC specification.

Note, however, that although we are using ODBC functions, PHP actually provides a specific set for most DBMS products. These sets are generally more efficient than ODBC, and if you are working with a specific DBMS, you will want to explore the PHP function set for it.[7] As an example of this, note that we connected to the database using:

```
// Get connection
$DSN = "VRG";
$User = "VRG-User";
$Password = "VRG-User+password";
$Conn = odbc_connect($DSN, $User, $Password);
```

If we are using MySQL, however, we can use:

```
// Get connection
$Host = "localhost";
$User = "VRG-User";
$Password = "VRG-User+password";
$Database = "VRG";
$Conn = mysqli_connect($Host, $User, $Password, $Database);
```

Similarly, SQL Server uses the *sqlsrv_connect* function (using the Microsoft PHP driver described in footnote 7), and Oracle uses the *oci_connect* function.

PHP 5.3.*x* and later versions also support object-oriented programming and a new data abstraction layer called **PHP Data Objects (PDO)** that provides a common syntax for accessing DBMS products. There is a lot of power in PHP, and we will barely scratch the surface here.

---

[6]For more information on PHP, see the PHP documentation at *www.php.net/docs.php*.

[7]Microsoft has created an updated set of functions for SQL Server. If you are going to use the SQL Server-specific functions, you should download the Microsoft Drivers for PHP for SQL Server version 3.1 from the Microsoft SQL 2012 Feature Pack Web page at *www.microsoft.com/en-us/download/details.aspx?id=20098*, which also includes the documentation.

```
<p>Chapter 10 Demonstration Pages From Figures in the Text:</p>
        <p>Example 1:   
            <a href="ReadArtist.php">
                Display the ARTIST Table (LastName, FirstName, Nationality)
            </a>
        </p>
    <!-- *********** New text starts here ***********  -->
        <p>Example 2:   
            <a href="NewArtistForm.html">
                Add a New Artist to the ARTIST Table
            </a>
        </p>
        <p>Example 3:   
            <a href="NewCustomerWithInterestsForm.html">
                Add a New Customer to the CUSTOMER Table
            </a>
        </p>
        <p>Example 4:   
            <a href="ReadArtistPDO.php">
                Display the ARTIST Table Using PHP PDO
            </a>
        </p>
    <!-- *********** New text ends here ***********  -->
        <hr />
```

FIGURE 11-36

Modifications to the VRG index.html Home Page

However, before proceeding with our examples, we need to add some links to our VRG home page. The necessary code is shown in Figure 11-36. If you are working through these examples (and you should be), be sure to make these changes.

Example 1: Updating a Table

The previous example of a PHP Web page just read data. This next example shows how to update table data by adding a row to a table with PHP. Figure 11-37 shows a data entry form that will capture artist name and nationality and create a new row. This form has three data entry fields: the First Name and Last Name fields are text boxes where the user types in the artist's name, and the Nationality field has been implemented as a drop-down list to control

FIGURE 11-37

The Add New Artist Form

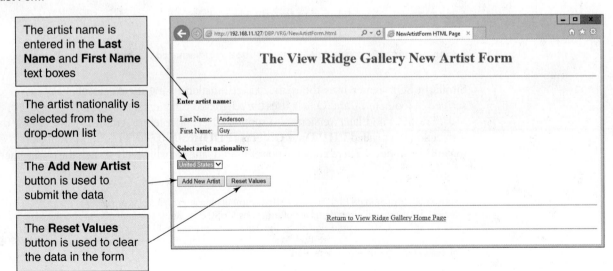

The artist name is entered in the **Last Name** and **First Name** text boxes

The artist nationality is selected from the drop-down list

The **Add New Artist** button is used to submit the data

The **Reset Values** button is used to clear the data in the form

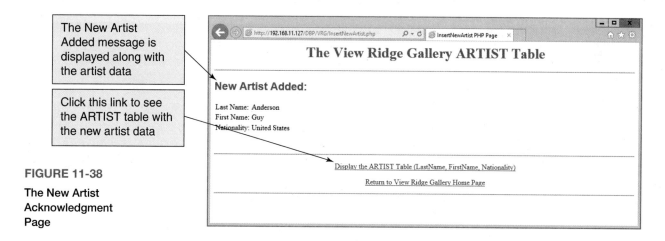

The New Artist Added message is displayed along with the artist data

Click this link to see the ARTIST table with the new artist data

FIGURE 11-38

The New Artist Acknowledgment Page

the possible values and to make sure they are spelled correctly. When the user clicks the **Add New Artist** button, the artist is added to the database; and if the results are successful, the acknowledgment Web page in Figure 11-38 is displayed. The *Display the ARTIST Table (LastName, FirstName, Nationality)* link will invoke the ReadArtist.php page, which will display the ARTIST table with the new row, as shown in Figure 11-39. We have tested these pages by adding the American artist Guy Anderson (born 1906, deceased 1998), who is a member of the Northwest School.

This processing necessitates two PHP pages. The first, shown in Figure 11-40, is the data entry form with three fields: artist last name, artist first name, and artist nationality.

It also contains the form tag:

```
<form action="InsertNewArtist.php" method="POST">
```

This tag defines a form section on the page, and the section will be set up to obtain data entry values. This form has only one data entry value: the table name. The **POST method** refers to a process that causes the data in the form (here the last name, the first name, and the selected nationality) to be delivered to the PHP server so they can be used in an array variable named $_POST. Note that $_POST is an array and thus can have multiple values. An alternative method is GET, but POST can carry more data, and this distinction

FIGURE 11-39

The Artist Table with the New Artist

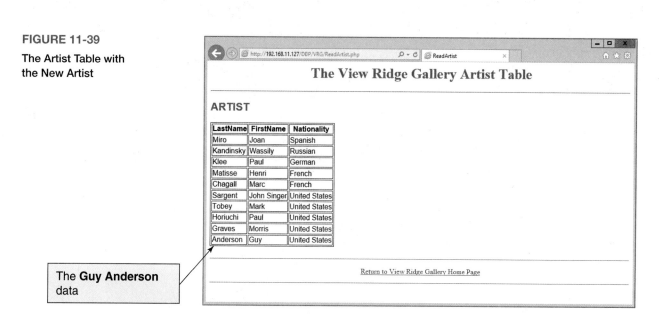

The **Guy Anderson** data

FIGURE 11-40

The HTML Code
for NewArtistForm
.html

```html
<!DOCTYPE html>
<html>
    <head>
        <meta http-equiv="Content-Type" content="text/html; charset=UTF-8">
        <title>NewArtistForm</title>
        <style type="text/css">
            h1 {text-align: center; color: blue}
            h2 {font-family: Ariel, sans-serif; text-align: left; color: blue}
            p.footer {text-align: center}
            table.output {font-family: Ariel, sans-serif}
        </style>
    </head>
    <body>
        <form action="InsertNewArtist.php" method="POST">
            <!--  Page Headers -->
            <h1>
                The View Ridge Gallery New Artist Form
            </h1>
            <hr />
            <br />
            <p>
                <b>Enter artist name:</b>
            </p>
            <table>
                <tr>
                    <td> Last Name:  </td>
                    <td>
                        <input type="text" name="LastName" size="25" />
                    </td>
                </tr>
                <tr>
                    <td> First Name:  </td>
                    <td>
                        <input type="text" name="FirstName" size="25" />
                    </td>
                </tr>
            </table>
            <p>
                <b>Select artist nationality:</b>
            </p>
            <select name="Nationality">
                <option value="Canadian">Canadian</option>
                <option value="English">English</option>
                <option value="French">French</option>
                <option value="German">German</option>
                <option value="Mexican">Mexican</option>
                <option value="Russian">Russian</option>
                <option value="Spanish">Spanish</option>
                <option value="United States">United States</option>
            </select>
            <br />
            <p>
                <input type="submit" value="Add New Artist" />
                <input type="reset" value="Reset Values" />
            </p>
        </form>
        <br />
        <hr />
        <p class="footer">
            <a href="../VRG/index.html">
                Return to View Ridge Gallery Home Page
            </a>
        </p>
        <hr />
    </body>
</html>
```

is not too important to us here. The second parameter of the form tag is *action*, which is set to InsertNewArtist.php. This parameter tells the Web server that when it receives the response from this form it should store the data values in the $_POST array and pass control to the InsertNewArtist.php page.

The rest of the page is standard HTML, with the addition of the <select>…</select> structure for creating a drop-down list in the form. Note that the name for the selected value is Nationality.

When the user clicks the Add New Artist button, these data are to be processed by the InsertNewArtist.php page. Figure 11-41 shows the InsertNewArtist.php, the page that will be invoked when the response is received from the form. Note that the variable values for the INSERT statement are obtained from the $_POST[] array. First, we create short variable

FIGURE 11-41

The HTML and PHP Code for InsertNewArtist .php

```
<!DOCTYPE html>
<html>
    <head>
        <meta http-equiv="Content-Type" content="text/html; charset=UTF-8">
        <title>InsertNewArtist</title>
        <style type="text/css">
            h1 {text-align: center; color: blue}
            h2 {font-family: Ariel, sans-serif; text-align: left; color: blue}
            p.footer {text-align: center}
            table.output {font-family: Ariel, sans-serif}
        </style>
    </head>
    <body>
<?php
    // Get connection
        $DSN = "VRG";
        $User = "VRG-User";
        $Password = "VRG-User+password";

        $Conn = odbc_connect($DSN, $User, $Password);

    // Test connection
    if (!$Conn)
        {
            exit ("ODBC Connection Failed: " . $Conn);
        }
    // Create short variable names
    $LastName = $_POST["LastName"];
    $FirstName = $_POST["FirstName"];
    $Nationality = $_POST["Nationality"];

    // Create SQL statement
    $SQL = "INSERT INTO ARTIST(LastName, FirstName, Nationality) ";
    $SQL .= "VALUES('$LastName', '$FirstName', '$Nationality')";

    // Execute SQL statement
    $Result = odbc_exec($Conn, $SQL);

    // Test existence of result
    echo "<h1>
        The View Ridge Gallery ARTIST Table
        </h1>
        <hr />";
    if ($Result){
        echo "<h2>
            New Artist Added:
        </h2>
```

(continued)

```
            <table>
                <tr>";
                echo "<td>Last Name:</td>";
                echo "<td>" . $LastName . "</td>";
                echo "</tr>";
                echo "<tr>";
                echo "<td>First Name:</td>";
                echo "<td>" . $FirstName . "</td>";
                echo "</tr>";
                echo "<tr>";
                echo "<td>Nationality:</td>";
                echo "<td>" . $Nationality . "</td>";
                echo "</tr>";
            echo "</table><br />";
            }
            else {
                exit ("SQL Statement Error: " . $SQL);
            }

        // Close connection
        odbc_close($Conn);
    ?>
        <br />
        <hr />
        <p class="footer">
            <a href="../VRG/ReadArtist.php">
                Display the ARTIST Table (LastName, FirstName, Nationality)
            </a>
        </p>
        <p class="footer">
            <a href="../VRG/index.html">
                Return to View Ridge Gallery Home Page
            </a>
        </p>
        <hr />
    </body>
</html>
```

FIGURE 11-41

Continued

names for the $_POST version of the name, and then we use these short variable names to create the SQL INSERT statement. Thus:

```
// Create short variable names
$LastName = $_POST["LastName"];

$FirstName = $_POST["FirstName"];

$Nationality = $_POST["Nationality"];

// Create SQL statement
$SQL = "INSERT INTO ARTIST(LastName, FirstName, Nationality) ";

$SQL .= "VALUES('$LastName', '$FirstName', '$Nationality')";
```

Note the use of the **PHP concatenation operator (.=)** (a combination of a period and an equal sign) to combine the two sections of the SQL INSERT statement. As another example, to create a variable named $AllOfUs with the value *me, myself, and I*, we would use:

```
$AllOfUs = "me, ";

$AllOfUs .= "myself, ";

$AllOfUs .= "and I";
```

Most of the code is self-explanatory, but make sure you understand how it works.

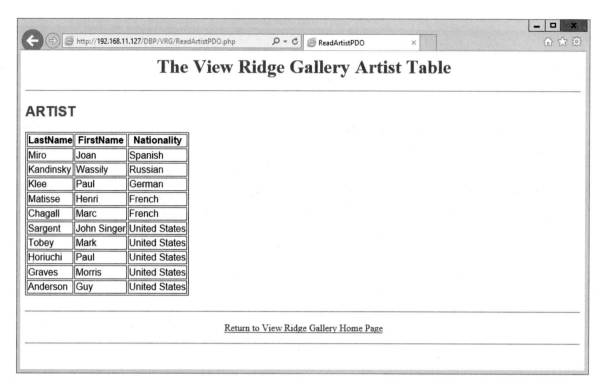

FIGURE 11-42

The Results of
ReadArtistPDO.php

Example 2: Using PHP Data Objects (PDO)

Our next example is an exercise in using PHP Data Objects (PDO). Here we are re-creating the
ReadArtist.php page but using PDO to do it. We call the new Web page ReadArtistPDO.php,
and it is shown in Figure 11-42. The PHP code to create the page is shown in Figure 11-43,
and you should compare this PHP code to the PHP code for ReadArtist.php in Figure 11-33.

PHP PDO will become important as newer versions of PHP are released. The power
of PHP PDO is that the only line of PHP code that needs to be changed when using a
different DBMS product is the one that establishes the connection to the database. In
Figure 11-43, this is the line:

```
$PDOconnection = new PDO("odbc:$DSN", $User, $Password);
```

Example 3: Invoking a Stored Procedure

We created a stored procedure named InsertCustomerAndInterest for the SQL Server 2014,
Oracle Database, and MySQL 5.6 versions of the VRG database in Chapters 10A, 10B, and
10C, respectively. In all cases, the stored procedure accepts a new customer's last name, first
name, area code, local number, and email and the nationality of all artists in whom the customer is interested. It then creates a new row in CUSTOMER and adds appropriate rows to
the CUSTOMER_ARTIST_INT table.

To invoke the stored procedure using a PHP page using PDO, we create a Web form
page to collect the necessary data, as shown in Figure 11-44. Then, when the user clicks
the **Add New Customer** button, we want to invoke a PHP page that uses PDO to call the
stored procedure with the form data as the input parameters. So that the user can verify
that the new data have been entered correctly, the PHP code then queries a view that joins
customer names with artist names and nationalities. The result is shown in Figure 11-45. In
this case, we are adding Richard Baxendale, with phone number 206-876-7733 and email
address Richard.Baxendale@elsewhere.com. Richard is interested in United States artists.

Figure 11-46 shows the code for the NewCustomerAndInterestsForm.html page used to
generate the data-gathering form. The form invokes the InsertNewCustomerAndInterestsPDO.
php page code shown in Figure 11-47.

FIGURE 11-43

The HTML and
PHP Code for
ReadArtistPDO
.php

```html
<!DOCTYPE html>
<html>
    <head>
        <meta http-equiv="Content-Type" content="text/html; charset=UTF-8">
        <title>ReadArtistPDO</title>
        <style type="text/css">
            h1 {text-align: center; color: blue}
            h2 {font-family: Ariel, sans-serif; text-align: left; color: blue;}
            p.footer {text-align: center}
            table.output {font-family: Ariel, sans-serif}
        </style>
    </head>
    <body>
    <?php
        // Get connection
        $DSN = "VRG";
        $User = "VRG-User";
        $Password = "VRG-User+password";

        $PDOconnection = new PDO("odbc:$DSN", $User, $Password);

        // Test connection
        if (!$PDOconnection)
            {
                exit ("ODBC Connection Failed: " . $PDOconnection);
            }

        // Create SQL statement
        $SQL = "SELECT LastName, FirstName, Nationality FROM ARTIST";

        // Execute SQL statement
        $RecordSet = $PDOconnection->query($SQL);

        // Test existence of recordset
        if (!$RecordSet)
            {
                exit ("SQL Statement Error: " . $SQL);
            }
    ?>
        <!-- Page Headers -->
        <h1>
            The View Ridge Gallery Artist Table
        </h1>
        <hr />
        <h2>
            ARTIST
        </h2>
    <?php

        // Table headers
        echo "<table class='output' border='1'
            <tr>
                <th>LastName</th>
                <th>FirstName</th>
                <th>Nationality</th>
            </tr>";

        //Table data
        while($RecordSetRow = $RecordSet->fetch())
            {
                echo "<tr>";
                    echo "<td>" . $RecordSetRow['LastName'] . "</td>";
                    echo "<td>" . $RecordSetRow['FirstName'] . "</td>";
                    echo "<td>" . $RecordSetRow['Nationality'] . "</td>";
                echo "</tr>";
            }
        echo "</table>";
```

FIGURE 11-43

Continued

```
                              // Close connection
                              $PDOconnection = null;
                          ?>
                              <br />
                              <hr />
                              <p class="footer">
                                 <a href="../VRG/index.html">
                                     Return to View Ridge Gallery Home Page
                                 </a>
                              </p>
                              <hr />
                          </body>
                      </html>
```

FIGURE 11-44

The New Customer
and Interests Form

The customer data is
entered in the **Last
Name, First Name,
Email Address,
Area Code,** and
Phone text boxes

The artist nationality is
selected from the
drop-down list

The **Add New
Customer** button is
used to submit
the data

The **Reset Values**
button is used to clear
the data in the form

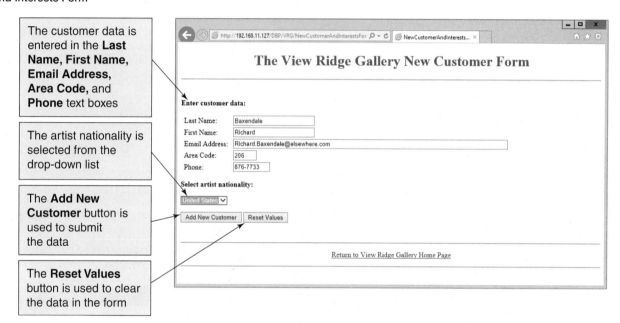

The New Customer
and Artist Interests
Added message is
displayed along with
the customer and
artist interest data

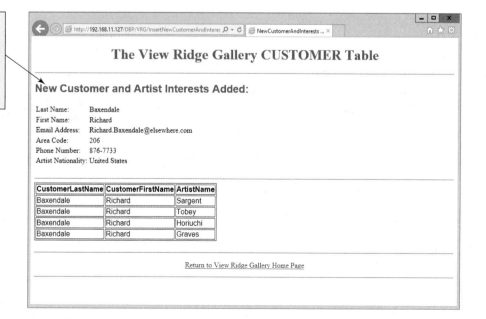

FIGURE 11-45

The Added New Customer
and Artist Interests
Acknowledgment Page

In Figure 11-47, note that the PDO statements take the form of:

```
$Variable01 = $Variable02->{PDO command}($Variable03)
```

For example, in the PDO statement

```
$RecordSet = $PDOconnection->query($SQL)
```

we are using the PDO command query to send the contents of the variable $SQL to the database through the connection named $PDOconnection and then storing the results in the variable $RecordSet. Note that although PDO standardizes the PDO command set itself, the exact SQL statements used by various DBMS products will vary, and even PHP code using PDO has to be modified for those differences. For example, SQL Server uses EXEC to call a stored procedure, whereas MySQL uses CALL.

FIGURE 11-46

The HTML Code for NewCustomer AndInterestsForm .html

```html
<!DOCTYPE html>
<html>
    <head>
        <meta http-equiv="Content-Type" content="text/html; charset=UTF-8">
        <title>NewCustomerAndInterestsForm</title>
        <style type="text/css">
            h1 {text-align: center; color: blue}
            h2 {font-family: Ariel, sans-serif; text-align: left; color: blue}
            p.footer {text-align: center}
            table.output {font-family: Ariel, sans-serif}
        </style>
    </head>
    <body>
        <form action="InsertNewCustomerAndInterestsPDO.php" method="POST">
            <!-- Page Headers -->
            <h1>
                The View Ridge Gallery New Customer Form
            </h1>
            <hr />
            <br />
            <p>
                <b>Enter customer data:</b>
            </p>
            <table>
                <tr>
                    <td> Last Name:  </td>
                    <td>
                        <input type="text" name="LastName" size="25" />
                    </td>
                </tr>
                <tr>
                    <td> First Name:  </td>
                    <td>
                        <input type="text" name="FirstName" size="25" />
                    </td>
                </tr>
                <tr>
                    <td> Email Address:  </td>
                    <td>
                        <input type="text" name="EmailAddress" size="100" />
                    </td>
                </tr>
                <tr>
                    <td> Area Code:  </td>
                    <td>
                        <input type="text" name="AreaCode" size="3" />
                    </td>
                </tr>
```

FIGURE 11-46

Continued

```html
      <tr>
         <td> Phone:  </td>
         <td>
            <input type="text" name="PhoneNumber" size="8" />
         </td>
      </tr>
   </table>
   <p>
      <b>Select artist nationality:</b>
   </p>
   <select name="Nationality">
      <option value="Canadian">Canadian</option>
      <option value="English">English</option>
      <option value="French">French</option>
      <option value="German">German</option>
      <option value="Mexican">Mexican</option>
      <option value="Russian">Russian</option>
      <option value="Spanish">Spanish</option>
      <option value="United States">United States</option>
   </select>
   <br />
   <p>
      <input type="submit" value="Add New Customer" />
      <input type="reset" value="Reset Values" />
   </p>
</form>
<br />
<hr />
<p class="footer">
   <a href="../VRG/index.html">
      Return to View Ridge Gallery Home Page
   </a>
</p>
<hr />
</body>
</html>
```

FIGURE 11-47

The HTML and
PHP Code for
InsertNewCustomer
AndInterestsPDO
.php

```php
<!DOCTYPE html>
<html>
   <head>
      <meta http-equiv="Content-Type" content="text/html; charset=UTF-8">
      <title>NewCustomerAndInterestsPDO</title>
      <style type="text/css">
         h1 {text-align: center; color: blue}
         h2 {font-family: Ariel, sans-serif; text-align: left; color: blue}
         p.footer {text-align: center}
         table.output {font-family: Ariel, sans-serif}
      </style>
   </head>
   <body>
   <?php
      // Get connection
         $DSN = "VRG";
         $User = "VRG-User";
         $Password = "VRG-User+password";

         $PDOConnection = new PDO("odbc:$DSN", $User, $Password);

      // Test connection
      if (!$PDOConnection)
      {
         exit ("ODBC Connection Failed: " . $PDOConnection);
      }
```

(continued)

FIGURE 11-47

Continued

```php
// Create short variable names
$LastName = $_POST["LastName"];
$FirstName = $_POST["FirstName"];
$EmailAddress = $_POST["EmailAddress"];
$AreaCode = $_POST["AreaCode"];
$PhoneNumber = $_POST["PhoneNumber"];
$Nationality = $_POST["Nationality"];

// Create SQL statement to call the Stored Procedure
$SQLSP  = "EXEC InsertCustomerAndInterests ";
$SQLSP .= "'$LastName', '$FirstName', '$EmailAddress',
$SQLSP .= "'$AreaCode','$PhoneNumber', ";
$SQLSP .= "'$Nationality'";

// Create SQL statement to retrieve additions to
// CUSTOMER_ARTIST_INT table
$SQL  = "SELECT * FROM CustomerInterestsView ";
$SQL .= "WHERE CustomerLastName = '$LastName' ";
$SQL .= "AND CustomerFirstName = '$FirstName'";

// Execute SQL Stored Procedure statement
$Result = $PDOConnection->exec($SQLSP);

// Test existence of $Result
if (!$Result)
    {
        exit ("SQL Statement Error: " . $SQL);
    }

// Execute SQL statement
$RecordSet = $PDOConnection->exec($SQL);

// Test existence of $ResultSet
if (!$RecordSet)
    {
        exit ("SQL Statement Error: " . $SQL);
    }


echo "<h1>
    The View Ridge Gallery CUSTOMER Table
    </h1>
    <hr />";

echo "<h2>
    New Customer and Artist Interests Added:
    </h2>
    <table>
        <tr>";
        echo "<td>Last Name:</td>";
        echo "<td>" . $LastName . "</td>";
        echo "</tr>";
        echo "<tr>";
        echo "<td>First Name:</td>";
        echo "<td>" . $FirstName . "</td>";
        echo "</tr>";
        echo "<tr>";
        echo "<td>Email Address:</td>";
        echo "<td>" . $EmailAddress . "</td>";
        echo "</tr>";
        echo "<tr>";
        echo "<td>Area Code:</td>";
        echo "<td>" . $AreaCode . "</td>";
        echo "</tr>";
        echo "<tr>";
        echo "<td>Phone Number:</td>";
        echo "<td>" . $PhoneNumber . "</td>";
        echo "</tr>";
```

FIGURE 11-47

Continued

```
            echo "<tr>";
            echo "<td>Artist Nationality:</td>";
            echo "<td>" . $Nationality . "</td>";
            echo "</tr>";
        echo "</table><br /><hr />";

    // Table headers
    echo "<table class='output' border='1'>
        <tr>
            <th>CustomerLastName</th>
            <th>CustomerFirstName</th>
            <th>ArtistName</th>
        </tr>";

    // Table data
    while($RecordSetRow = odbc_fetch_array($RecordSet))
        {
        echo "<tr>";
        echo "<td>" . $RecordSetRow['CustomerLastName'] . "</td>";
        echo "<td>" . $RecordSetRow['CustomerFirstName'] . "</td>";
        echo "<td>" . $RecordSetRow['ArtistName'] . "</td>";
        echo "</tr>";
        }
    echo "</table>";

    // Close connection
    $PDOConnection = null;
?>
    <br />
    <hr />
    <p class="footer">
        <a href="../VRG/index.html">
            Return to View Ridge Gallery Home Page
        </a>
    </p>
    <hr />
</body>
</html>
```

This PHP page is very straightforward, but it is interesting because it includes two SQL statements. First, we use an SQL CALL statement to invoke the stored procedure and pass the necessary parameters to it. Then we use an SQL SELECT statement to retrieve the values we need for the construction of our Web page acknowledging the addition of a new customer. The rest of the page reuses the same elements we have used in the previous examples.

It is also interesting that in this page we have made use of both an SQL view (CustomerInterestsView) and an SQL stored procedure (InsertCustomerAndInterests). This page illustrates the power of both these SQL structures and how we can use them in a Web database processing environment.

These examples give you an idea of the uses of PHP. The best way to learn more is to write some pages yourself. This chapter has shown all the basic techniques that you will need. You have worked hard to get to this point, and if you are able to understand enough to create some of your own pages, you have come very far indeed since Chapter 1.

Challenges for Web Database Processing

Web database application processing is complicated by an important characteristic of HTTP. Specifically, HTTP is stateless; it has no provision for maintaining sessions between requests. Using HTTP, a client at a browser makes a request of a Web server. The server services the client request, sends results back to the browser, and forgets about the interaction with that client. A second request from that same client is treated as a new request from a new client. No data are kept to maintain a session or connection with the client.

This characteristic poses no problem for serving content, either static Web pages or responses to queries of a database. However, it is not acceptable for applications that require multiple database actions in an atomic transaction. Recall from Chapter 9 that in some cases, a group of database actions needs to be grouped into a transaction, with all of them committed to the database or none of them committed to the database. In this case, the Web server or other program must augment the base capabilities of HTTP.

For example, IIS provides features and functions for maintaining data about sessions between multiple HTTP requests and responses. Using these features and functions, the application program on the Web server can save data to and from the browser. A particular session will be associated with a particular set of data. In this way, the application program can start a transaction, conduct multiple interactions with the user at the browser, make intermediate changes to the database, and commit or roll back all changes when ending the transaction. Other means are used to provide for sessions and session data with Apache.

In some cases, the application programs must create their own methods for tracking session data. PHP does include support for sessions—see the PHP documentation for more information.

The particulars of session management are beyond the scope of this chapter. However, you should be aware that HTTP is stateless, and, regardless of the Web server, additional code must be added to database applications to enable transaction processing.

SQL Injection Attacks

When we create Web pages that allow data inserts, updates, or deletes on a database, we may create a vulnerability that allows an *SQL injection attack*. An **SQL injection attack** attempts to issue hacker-modified SQL commands to the DBMS. For example, suppose that a Web page is used to update a user's phone number and thus requires the user to input the new phone number. The Web application would then use PHP code to create and run an SQL statement such as:

```
// Create SQL statement
$varSQL = "UPDATE CUSTOMER SET PHONE = '$NewPhone' ";
$varSQL .= "WHERE CustomerID = '$CustomerID'";
// Execute SQL statement
$RecordSet = odbc_exec($Conn, $varSQL);
```

If the input value of NewPhone is not carefully checked, it may be possible for an attacker to use an input value such as:

```
678-345-1234; DELETE FROM CUSTOMER;
```

If this input value is accepted and the SQL statement is run, we may lose all data in the CUSTOMER table if the Web application has DELETE permissions on the CUSTOMER table. Therefore, Web database applications must be very carefully constructed to provide for data checking and to ensure that only necessary database permissions are granted.

Extensible Markup Language (XML)

XML is a standard means for defining the structure of documents and for transmitting documents from one computer to another. XML is important for database processing because it provides a standardized means of submitting data to a database and for receiving results back from the database. XML is a large, complicated subject that requires several books to explain fully. Here we touch on the fundamentals and further explain why XML is important for database processing.

The Importance of XML

Database processing and document processing need each other. Database processing needs document processing for transmitting database views; document processing needs database processing for storing and manipulating data. However, even though these technologies need each other, it took the popularity of the Internet to make that need obvious. As Web sites evolved, organizations wanted to use Internet technology to display and update data from organizational databases. Web developers began to take a serious interest in SQL, database performance, database security, and other aspects of database processing.

As the Web developers invaded the database community, database practitioners wondered, "Who are these people, and what do they want?" Database practitioners began to learn about Hypertext Markup Language (HTML), the language used to mark up documents for display by Web browsers. At first, the database community scoffed at HTML because of its limitations, but it soon learned that HTML was the output of a more robust document markup language called **Standard Generalized Markup Language (SGML)**. SGML was clearly important, just as important to document processing as the relational model was to database processing. Obviously, this powerful language had some role to play in the display of database data, but what role?

In the early 1990s, the two communities began to meet, and the result of their work is a series of standards that concerns a language called **Extensible Markup Language (XML)**. XML is a subset of SGML, but additional standards and capabilities have been added to XML, and today XML technology is a hybrid of document processing and database processing. In fact, as XML standards evolved, it became clear that the communities had been working on different aspects of the same problem for many years. They even used the same terms but with different meanings. You will see later in this chapter how the term *schema* is used in XML for a concept that is completely different from the use of *schema* in the database world.

XML provides a standardized yet customizable way to describe the content of documents. As such, it can be used to describe any database view but in a standardized way. As you will learn in Appendix K, SQL views have certain limitations, which can be overcome by using XML views.

In addition, when used with the XML Schema standard, XML documents can automatically be generated from database data. Further, database data can automatically be extracted from XML documents. Even more, there are standardized ways of defining how document components are mapped to database schema components, and vice versa.

Meanwhile, the rest of the computing community began to take notice of XML. **SOAP**, which originally meant **Simple Object Access Protocol**, was defined as an XML-based standard for providing remote procedure calls over the Internet. Initially, SOAP assumed the use of HTTP as a transport mechanism. When Microsoft, IBM, Oracle Corporation, and other large companies joined forces in support of the SOAP standard, this assumption was removed, and SOAP was generalized to become a standard protocol for sending messages of any type using any protocol. With this change, SOAP no longer meant Simple Object Access Protocol, so now SOAP is just a name and not an acronym.

Today, XML is used for many purposes. One of the most important is its use as a standardized means to define and communicate documents for processing over the Internet. XML plays a key role in Microsoft's .NET initiative, and in 2001, Bill Gates called XML the "*lingua franca* of the Internet age."

As you read the rest of this chapter and more information on XML in Appendix K, keep in mind that this area is an important part of database processing. Standards, products, and product capabilities are frequently changing. You can keep abreast of these changes by checking the following Web sites: *www.w3c.org*, *www.xml.org*, *http://msdn.microsoft.com*, *www.oracle.com*, *www.ibm.com*, and *www.mysql.com*. Learning as much as you can about XML and database processing is one of the best ways you can prepare yourself for a successful career in database processing.

XML as a Markup Language

As a markup language, XML is significantly better than HTML in several ways. For one, XML provides a clean separation between document structure, content, and materialization. XML has facilities for dealing with each, and they cannot be confounded, as they are with HTML.

Additionally, XML is standardized, but as its name implies, the standards allow for extension by developers. With XML, you are not limited to a fixed set of elements such as <title>, <H1>, and <p>; you can create your own.

Third, XML eliminates the inconsistent tag use that is possible (and popular) with HTML. For example, consider the following HTML:

```
<H2>Hello World</H2>
```

Although the tag can be used to mark a level-two heading in an outline, it can be used for other purposes, too, such as causing "Hello World" to be displayed in a particular font size, weight, and color. Because a tag has potentially many uses, we cannot rely on tags to discern the structure of an HTML page. Tag use is too arbitrary; it may mean a heading, or it may mean nothing at all.

As you will see, the structure of an XML document can be formally defined. Tags are defined in relationship to one another. In XML, if we find the tag <street>, we know exactly what data we have, where those data belong in the document, and how that tag relates to other tags.

Creating XML Documents from Database Data

SQL Server, Oracle Database, and MySQL have facilities for generating XML documents from database data. The Oracle Database XML features require the use of Java. Because we do not assume that you are a Java programmer, we will not discuss those features further in this chapter. If you are a Java programmer, you can learn more about Oracle Database's XML features at *www.oracle.com*.

The facilities in SQL Server, Oracle Database, and MySQL are undergoing rapid development. In the case of SQL Server, version 7.0 added the expression FOR XML to SQL SELECT syntax. That expression was carried forward to SQL Server 2000. In 2002, the SQL Server group extended the SQL Server capabilities with the SQLXML class library. SQLXML, which was produced by the SQL Server group, is different from ADO.NET. All of these features and functions were merged together in SQL Server 2005 and are carried forward in SQL Server 2008, 2008 R2, 2012, and now 2012 R2.

Using the SQL SELECT...FOR XML Statement

SQL Server 2014 uses the **SQL SELECT...FOR XML statement** to work with XML. Consider the following SQL statement:

```
/* *** SQL-Query-CH11-01 *** */

SELECT    *

FROM      ARTIST

    FOR   XML RAW;
```

FIGURE 11-48

FOR XML RAW Examples

Figure 11-48(a) shows an example of a FOR XML RAW query in the Microsoft SQL Server Management Studio. The results of the query are displayed in a single cell.

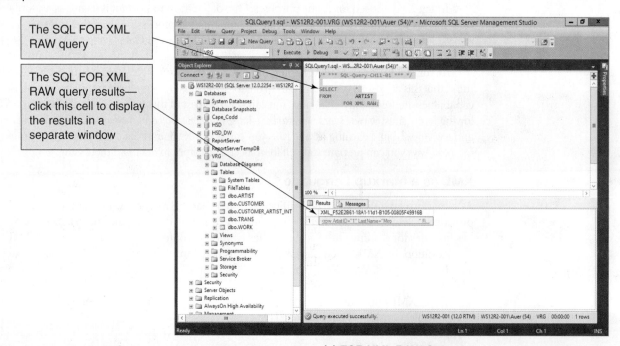

(a) FOR XML RAW Query

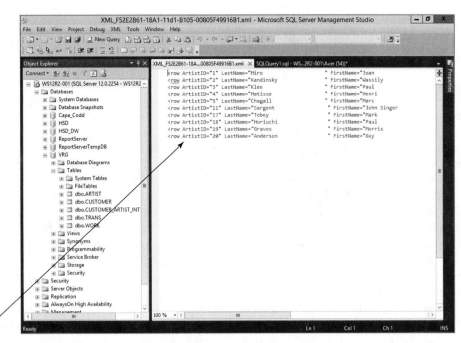

(b) FOR XML RAW Results in the Microsoft SQL Server Management Studio

```
<row ArtistID="1" LastName="Miro" FirstName="Joan"
     Nationality="Spanish" DateOfBirth= "1893" DateDeceased="1983" />
<row ArtistID="2" LastName="Kandinsky" FirstName="Wassily"
     Nationality="Russian" DateOfBirth="1866" DateDeceased="1944" />
<row ArtistID="3" LastName="Klee" FirstName="Paul"
     Nationality="German" DateOfBirth="1879" DateDeceased="1940" />
<row ArtistID="4" LastName="Matisse" FirstName="Henri"
     Nationality="French" DateOfBirth="1869" DateDeceased="1954" />
<row ArtistID="5" LastName="Chagall" FirstName="Marc"
     Nationality="French" DateOfBirth="1887" DateDeceased="1985" />
<row ArtistID="11" LastName="Sargent" FirstName="John Singer"
     Nationality="United States" DateOfBirth="1856" DateDeceased="1925" />
<row ArtistID="17" LastName="Tobey" FirstName="Mark"
     Nationality="United States" DateOfBirth="1890" DateDeceased="1976" />
<row ArtistID="18" LastName="Horiuchi" FirstName="Paul"
     Nationality="United States" DateOfBirth="1906" DateDeceased="1999" />
<row ArtistID="19" LastName="Graves" FirstName="Morris"
     Nationality="United States" DateOfBirth="1920" DateDeceased="2001" />
<row ArtistID="20" LastName="Anderson" FirstName="Guy"
     Nationality="United States" />
```

(c) FOR XML RAW Results in XML Document

FIGURE 11-48

Continued

Clicking this cell displays the results as shown in Figure 11-48(b). As expected, each column is placed as an attribute of the element named *row*. The complete output, edited as it would appear in an XML document (and with extra spaces in the attribute values removed), is shown in Figure 11-48(c). We will discuss the FOR XML clause in depth in Appendix K.

Summary

Today, database applications reside in rich and complicated environments. In addition to relational databases, there are nonrelational databases, VSAM and other file-processing data, email, and other types of data. To ease the job of the application programmer, various standards have been developed. The ODBC standard is for relational databases; the OLE DB standard is for relational databases and other data sources. ADO was developed to provide easier access to OLE DB data for the non-object-oriented programmer.

ODBC, or the Open Database Connectivity standard, provides an interface by which database applications can access and process relational data sources in a DBMS-independent manner. ODBC was developed by an industry committee and has been implemented by Microsoft and many other vendors. ODBC consists of an applications program, a driver manager, DBMS drivers, and data source components. Single- and multiple-tier drivers are defined. The three data source names are file, system, and user. System data sources are recommended for Web servers. The process of defining a system data source name involves specifying the type of driver and the identity of the database to be processed.

The Microsoft .NET Framework is Microsoft's comprehensive application development framework. The current version is .NET Framework 4.5 SP1, which is built on top of the .NET Framework 2.0 and .NET Framework 3.0 (and their service pack updates). It includes ADO.NET, ASP. NET, CLR, and the Base Class Library. Enhancements specific to .NET Framework 3.5 include the ADO.NET Entity Framework, which supports the EDM (Entity Data Model). The .NET Framework 4.0 added Parallel LINQ (PLINQ) and the Task Parallel Library (TPL). The .NET Framework 4.5 added support for Windows 8 Apps, including .NET for Windows Store Apps, Portable class libraries, and the Managed Extensibility Framework (MEF).

OLE DB is one of the foundations of the Microsoft data access world. It implements the Microsoft OLE and COM standards, and it is accessible to object-oriented programs through those interfaces. OLE DB breaks the features and functions of a DBMS into objects, thus making it easier for vendors to implement portions of functionality. Key object terms are *abstraction, methods, properties,* and *collections.* A rowset is an abstraction of a recordset, which, in turn, is an abstraction of a relation. Objects are defined by properties that specify their characteristics and by methods, which are the actions they can perform. A collection is an object that contains a group of other objects. An interface is a set of objects and the properties and methods they expose in that interface. Objects may expose different properties and methods in different interfaces. An implementation is how an object accomplishes its tasks. Implementations are hidden from the outside world and may be changed without affecting the users of the objects. An interface ought not to be changed ever.

Tabular data providers present data in the form of rowsets. Service providers transform data into another form; such providers are both consumers and providers of data. A rowset is equivalent to a cursor. Basic rowset interfaces are IRowSet, IAccessor, and IColumnsInfo. Other interfaces are defined for more advanced capabilities.

ADO.NET is a new, improved, and greatly expanded version of ADO that was developed for the Microsoft .NET initiative. ADO.NET incorporates all of the functionality of ADO but adds much more. In particular, ADO.NET facilitates the transformation of XML documents to and from database data.

A .NET data provider is a library of classes that provides ADO.NET services. A data provider data reader provides fast, forward-only access to data. A Command object can be processed to execute SQL and also to invoke stored procedures in a manner similar to but improved from that in ADO. The major new concept of ADO.NET is the DataSet. A DataSet is an in-memory database that is disconnected from any regular database but that has all the important characteristics of a regular database. DataSets can have multiple tables, relationships, referential integrity rules, referential integrity actions, views, and the equivalent of triggers. DataSet tables may have surrogate key columns (called auto-increment columns) and primary keys and may be declared unique.

DataSets are disconnected from the database(s) from which they are constructed, and they may be constructed from several different databases and possibly managed by different DBMS products. After a DataSet is constructed, an XML document of its contents and an XML Schema of its structure are easily produced. Further, the process works in reverse as well. XML Schema documents can be read to create the structure of the DataSet, and XML documents can be read to fill the DataSet.

DataSets are needed to provide a standardized, nonproprietary means to process database views. They are especially important for the processing of views with multiple multivalued paths. The potential downside of DataSets is that because they are disconnected, any updates against the databases they access must be performed using optimistic locking. In the case of conflict, either the DataSet must be reprocessed or the data change must be forced onto the database, causing the lost update problem.

JDBC is an alternative to ODBC and ADO that provides database access to programs written in Java. A JDBC driver is available for almost every conceivable DBMS product. Sun defines four driver types. Type 1 drivers provide a bridge between Java and ODBC. Types 2, 3, and 4 are written entirely in Java. Type 2 drivers rely on the DBMS product for intermachine communication, if any. Type 3 drivers translate JDBC calls into a DBMS-independent network protocol. Type 4 drivers translate JDBC calls into a DBMS-dependent network protocol.

An applet is a compiled Java bytecode program that is transmitted to a browser via HTTP and is invoked using the HTTP protocol. A servlet is a Java program that is invoked on the server to respond to HTTP requests. Type 3 and Type 4 drivers can be used for both applets and servlets. Type 2 drivers can be used only in servlets, and only then if the DBMS and Web server are on the same machine or if the DBMS vendor handles the intermachine communication between the Web server and the database server.

There are four steps when using JDBC: (1) load the driver, (2) establish a connection to the database, (3) create a statement, and (4) execute the statement.

Java Server Pages (JSP) technology provides a means to create dynamic Web pages using HTML (and XML) and Java. JSP pages provide the capabilities of a full object-oriented language to the page developer. Neither VBScript nor JavaScript can be used in a JSP page. JSP pages are compiled into machine-independent bytecode.

JSP pages are compiled as subclasses of the HTTPServlet class. Consequently, small snippets of code can be placed in a JSP page as well as complete Java programs. To use JSP, the Web server must implement the Java Servlet 2.1+ and JSP 1.0+ specifications. Apache Tomcat, an open source product from the Jakarta Project, implements these specifications. Tomcat can work in conjunction with Apache or as a stand-alone Web server for testing purposes.

When using Tomcat (or any other JSP processor), the JDBC drivers and JSP pages must be located in specified directories. When a JSP page is requested, Tomcat ensures that the most recent page is used. If an uncompiled newer version is available, Tomcat will automatically cause it to be parsed and compiled. Only one JSP page can be in memory at a time, and JSP requests are executed as a thread of the servlet processor, not as a separate process. The Java code in a JSP page can invoke a compiled Java bean, if desired.

PHP (PHP: Hypertext Processor) is a scripting language that can be embedded in Web pages. PHP is extremely popular and easy to learn, and it can be used in most Web server environments and with most databases.

For creating complex pages, you need an integrated development environment (IDE). An IDE gives you the most robust and user-friendly means of creating and maintaining Web pages. Microsoft Visual Studio, NetBeans for Java users, and the open source Eclipse IDE are all good IDEs. The NetBeans IDE provides a framework that can be modified by plug-in modules.

PHP now includes object-oriented features and PHP Data Objects (PDO), which simplify connecting Web pages to databases.

The confluence of database processing and document processing is one of the most important developments in information systems technology today. Database processing and document processing need each other. Database processing needs document processing for the representation and materialization (rendering Web pages for a specific device) of database views. Document processing needs database processing for the permanent storage of data.

SGML is as important to document processing as the relational model is to database processing. XML is a series of standards that were developed jointly by the database processing and document processing communities. XML provides a standardized yet customizable way to describe the contents of documents. XML documents can be automatically generated from database data, and database data can be automatically extracted from XML documents.

Although XML can be used to materialize Web pages, this is one of its least important uses. More important is its use for describing, representing, and materializing database views. XML is on the leading edge of database processing; see *www.w3.org* and *www.xml.org* for the latest developments.

XML is a better markup language than HTML, primarily because XML provides a clear separation between document structure, content, and materialization. Also, XML tags are not ambiguous.

SQL Server, Oracle Database, and MySQL can produce XML documents from database data. The Oracle Database facilities require the use of Java; see *www.oracle.com* for more information. SQL Server supports an add-on expression to the SQL SELECT statement, the FOR XML expression.

Key Terms

?php and ?	ADO.NET Data Provider	Apple iPad
.NET for Windows Store Apps	ADO.NET DataAdapter object	applet
.NET Framework	ADO.NET DataReader	application program interface (API)
abstraction	ADO.NET DataSet	ASP.NET
Active Data Objects (ADO)	ADO.NET Entity Framework	Base Class Library
Active Server Pages (ASP)	AMP	bytecode interpreter
ADO.NET	Apache Tomcat	Callable Statement object
ADO.NET Command object	Apache Web server	cell phone
ADO.NET Connection object	app	cellular network

client
client server architecture
collection
Common Language Runtime (CLT)
Component Object Model (COM)
Constraints
current values
cursor
data consumer
data provider
DataColumnCollection
DataRelationCollection
DataRelations
DataRowCollection
DataTable object
DataTableCollection
Default Web Site folder
DeleteCommand object
device
document type declaration (DTD)
Entity Data Model (EDM)
Extensible Markup Language (XML)
file data source
ForeignKeyConstraint
Google Android Operating System (OS)
Google Chrome
HTML document tags
HTML syntax rules
http://localhost
Hypertext Markup Language (HTML)
iisstart.htm
implementation
index.html
inetpub folder
InsertCommand object
integrated development environment
   (IDE)
interface
Internet
Internet Information Services (IIS)

Internet Information Services
   Manager
Java Data Objects (JDO)
Java Database Connectivity (JBDC)
Java platform
Java programming language
Java virtual machine
JavaScript
JavaServer Pages (JSP)
JDBC Connection object
JDBC DriverManager
JDBC ResultSet object
JDBC ResultSetMetaData object
JDBC Statement object
LAMP
Language Integrated Query (LINQ)
Managed Extensibility Framework
   (MEF)
method
Microsoft Internet Explorer
Microsoft Transaction Manager (MTS)
mobile phone
Mozilla Firefox
NetBeans IDE
object
object class
Object Linking and Embedding (OLE)
ODBC conformance levels
ODBC data source
ODBC Data Source Administrator
ODBC driver
ODBC driver manager
ODBC multiple-tier driver
ODBC single-tier driver
ODBC SQL conformance levels
OLE DB
Open Database Connectivity (ODBC)
original values
Parallel LINQ (PLINQ)
PHP

PHP concatenation operator (.=)
PHP Data Objects (PDO)
PHP plugin
PHP: Hypertext Processor
Portable Class Libraries
POST method
Prepared Statement objects
PrimaryKey property
properties
proposed values
recordset
routers
rowset
SelectCommand object
server
service
service provider
servlet
Simple Object Access Protocol
smartphone
SOAP
SQL injection attack
SQL SELECT…FOR XML statement
Standard Generalized Markup
   Language (SGML)
system data source
tablet
tabular data providers
Task Parallel Library (TPL)
three-tier architecture
two-tier architecture
UniqueConstraint
UpdateCommand object
user data source
WAMP
Web browser
World Wide Web (WWW or W3 or
   Web)
World Wide Web Consortium (W3C)
wwwroot folder

Review Questions

11.1 Describe why the data environment is complicated.

11.2 Explain how ODBC, OLE DB, and ADO are related.

11.3 Explain the author's justification for describing Microsoft standards. Do you agree?

11.4 Name the components of the ODBC standard.

11.5 What role does the driver manager serve? Who supplies it?

11.6 What role does the DBMS driver serve? Who supplies it?

11.7 What is a single-tier driver?

11.8 What is a multiple-tier driver?

11.9 Do the uses of the term *tier* in the three-tier architecture and its use in ODBC have anything to do with each other?

11.10 Why are conformance levels important?

11.11 Summarize the three ODBC API conformance levels.

11.12 Summarize the three SQL grammar conformance levels.

11.13 Explain how the three types of data sources differ.

11.14 Which data source type is recommended for Web servers?

11.15 What are the two tasks to be accomplished when setting up an ODBC data source name?

11.16 What is the Microsoft .NET Framework? What basic elements does it include?

11.17 What is the current version of the .NET Framework, and what new features does it include?

11.18 Why is OLE DB important?

11.19 What disadvantage of ODBC does OLE DB overcome?

11.20 Define *abstraction*, and explain how it relates to OLE DB.

11.21 Give an example of abstraction involving rowset.

11.22 Define *object properties* and *methods*.

11.23 What is the difference between an object class and an object?

11.24 Explain the role of data consumers and data providers.

11.25 What is an interface?

11.26 What is the difference between an interface and an implementation?

11.27 Explain why an implementation can be changed but an interface should not be changed.

11.28 Summarize the goals of OLE DB.

11.29 Explain the difference between a tabular data provider and a service provider. Which transforms OLE DB data into XML documents?

11.30 In the context of OLE DB, what is the difference between a rowset and a cursor?

11.31 What is ADO.NET?

11.32 What is a data provider?

11.33 What is a data reader?

11.34 How can ADO.NET be used to process a database without using DataReaders or DataSets?

11.35 What is an ADO.NET DataSet?

11.36 How do ADO.Net DataSets differ conceptually from databases?

11.37 List the primary structures of an ADO.NET DataSet as described in this chapter.

11.38 How do ADO.NET DataSets solve the problem of views with multivalued paths?

11.39 What is the chief disadvantage of ADO.NET DataSets? When is this likely to be a problem?

11.40 Why, in database processing, is it important to become an object-oriented programmer?

11.41 What is an ADO.NET Connection?

11.42 What is a DataAdapter?

11.43 What is the purpose of the SelectCommand property of a DataAdapter?

11.44 How is a data table relationship constructed in ADO.NET?

11.45 How is referential integrity defined in ADO.NET? What referential integrity actions are possible?

11.46 Explain how original, current, and proposed values differ.

11.47 How does an ADO.NET DataSet allow for trigger processing?

11.48 What is the purpose of the UpdateCommand property of a DataAdapter?

11.49 What are the purposes of the InsertCommand and DeleteCommand of a DataAdapter?

11.50 Explain the flexibility inherent in the use of the InsertCommand, UpdateCommand, and DeleteCommand properties.

11.51 What is the one major requirement for using JDBC?

11.52 What does JDBC stand for?

11.53 What are the four JDBC driver types?

11.54 Explain the purpose of Type 1 JDBC drivers.

11.55 Explain the purpose of Types 2, 3, and 4 JDBC drivers.

11.56 Define *applet* and *servlet*.

11.57 Explain how Java accomplishes portability.

11.58 List the four steps of using a JDBC driver.

11.59 What is the purpose of Java Server Pages?

11.60 Describe the differences between ASP and JSP.

11.61 Explain how JSP pages are portable.

11.62 What is the purpose of Tomcat?

11.63 Describe the process by which JSP pages are compiled and executed. Can a user ever access an obsolete page? Why or why not?

11.64 Why are JSP programs preferable to CGI programs?

11.65 What is Hypertext Markup Language (HTML), and what function does it serve?

11.66 What are HTML document tags, and how are they used?

11.67 What is the World Wide Web Consortium (W3C)?

11.68 Why is index.hmtl a significant file name?

11.69 What is PHP, and what function does it serve?

11.70 How is PHP code designated in a Web page?

11.71 How are comments designated in PHP code?

11.72 How are comments designated in HMTL code?

11.73 What is an integrated development environment (IDE), and how is it used?

11.74 What is the NetBeans IDE?

11.75 Show a snippet of PHP code for creating a connection to a database. Explain the meaning of the code.

11.76 Show a snippet of PHP code for creating a RecordSet. Explain the meaning of the code.

11.77 Show a snippet of PHP code for displaying the contents of a RecordSet. Explain the meaning of the code.

11.78 Show a snippet of PHP code for disconnecting from the database. Explain the meaning of the code.

11.79 With respect to http, what does *stateless* mean?

11.80 Under what circumstances does statelessness pose a problem for database processing?

11.81 In general terms, how are sessions managed by database applications when using http?

11.82 What are PHP Data Objects (PDO)?

11.83 What is the significance of PDOs?

11.84 Show two snippets of PHP Code that compare creating a connection to a database in standard PHP and in PDO. Discuss the similarities and differences in the code.

11.85 Why do database processing and document processing need each other?

11.86 How are HTML, SGML, and XML related?

11.87 Explain the phrase *standardized but customizable*.

11.88 What is SOAP? What did it stand for originally? What does it stand for today?

11.90 What are the problems in interpreting a tag such as in HTML?

11.91 What requirement is necessary for processing XML documents with Oracle?

11.92 Explain how SQL Server 2014 produces XML output using the FOR XML RAW clause.

Project Questions

11.93 In this exercise, you will create a Web page in the DBP folder and link it to the VRG Web page in the VRG folder.

   A. Figure 11-49 shows the HTML code for a Web page for the DBP folder. Note that the page is called *index.html*, the same name as the Web page in the VRG folder. This is not a problem because the files are in different folders. Create the index.html Web page in the DBP folder.

   B. Figure 11-50 shows some additional HTML to be added near the end of the code for the VRG Web page in the file index.html in the VRG folder. Update the VRG index.html file with the code.

   C. Try out the pages. Type **http://localhost/DBP** into your Web browser to display the DBP home page. From there, you should be able to move back and forth between the two pages by using the hyperlinks on each page. **Note:** You may need to click the Refresh button on your Web browser when using the VRG home page to get the hyperlink back to the DBP home page to work properly.

```
<!DOCTYPE html>
<html>
    <head>
        <meta http-equiv="Content-Type" content="text/html; charset=ISO-8859-1" />
        <title>DBP-e14 Home Page</title>
    </head>
    <body>
        <h1 style="text-align: center; color: blue">
            Database Processing (14th Edition) Home Page
        </h1>
        <hr />
        <h3 style="text-align: center">
            Use this page to access Web-based materials from Chapter 11 of:
        </h3>
        <h2 style="text-align: center; color: blue">
            Database Processing (14th Edition)
        </h2>
        <p style="text-align: center; font-weight: bold">
            David M. Kroenke
        </p>
        <p style="text-align: center; font-weight: bold">
            David J. Auer
        </p>
        <hr />
        <h3>Chapter 11 Demonstration Pages From Figures in the Text:</h3>
        <p>
            <a href="VRG/index.html">
                View Ridge Gallery Demonstration Pages
            </a>
        </p>
        <hr />
    </body>
</html>
```

FIGURE 11-49

The HTML Code for the index.html File in the DBP Folder

FIGURE 11-50

HTML Modifications for the index.html File in the VRG Folder

```
        <p>Example 4:   
                    <a href="ReadArtistPDO.php">
                        Display the ARTIST Table Using PHP PDO
                    </a>
            </p>
            <hr />
<!-- *********** NEW CODE STARTS HERE *********** -->
            <p style="text-align: center">
                    <a href="../index.html">
                        Return to the Database Processing Home Page
                    </a>
            </p>
            <hr />
<!-- *********** NEW CODE ENDS HERE *********** -->
            </body>
        </html>
```

Case Questions

Marcia's Dry Cleaning Case Question

If you have not already done so, create and populate the Marcia's Dry Cleaning (MDC) database for the DBMS you are using as described in:

- Chapter 10A for Microsoft SQL Server 2014
- Chapter 10B for Oracle Database
- Chapter 10C for Oracle MySQL 5.6

A. Add a new folder to the DBP Web site named MDC. Create a Web page for Marcia's Dry Cleaning in this folder, using the file name index.html. Link this page to the DBP Web page.

B. Create an appropriate ODBC data source for your database.

C. Add a new column Status to the INVOICE table. Assume that Status can have the values ['Waiting', 'In-process', 'Finished', 'Pending'].

D. Create a view called CustomerInvoiceView that has the columns LastName, FirstName, Phone, InvoiceNumber, DateIn, DateOut, Total, and Status.

E. Code a PHP page to display CustomerInvoiceView. Using your sample database, demonstrate that your page works.

F. Code two HTML/PHP pages to receive a date value AsOfDate and to display rows of CustomerInvoiceView for orders having DateIn greater than or equal to AsOfDate. Using your sample database, demonstrate that your pages work.

G. Code two HTML/PHP pages to receive customer Phone, LastName, and FirstName and to display rows for customers having that Phone, LastName, and FirstName. Using your sample database, demonstrate that your pages work.

H. Write a stored procedure that receives values for InvoiceNumber and NewStatus and that sets the value of Status to NewStatus for the row having the given value of InvoiceNumber. Generate an error message if no row has the given value of InvoiceNumber. Using your sample database, demonstrate that your stored procedure works.

I. Code two HTML/PHP pages to invoke the stored procedure created in part H. Using your sample database, demonstrate that your page works.

The Queen Anne Curiosity Shop

If you have not already done so, answer the questions for the Queen Anne Curiosity Shop (QACS) at the end of Chapter 7 (pages 383–389) and for the DBMS you are using as described in:

- Chapter 10A for Microsoft SQL Server 2014
- Chapter 10B for Oracle Database
- Chapter 10C for Oracle MySQL 5.6

A. Add a new folder to the DBP Web site named QACS. Create a Web page for the Queen Anne Curiosity Shop in this folder, using the file name index.html. Link this page to the DBP Web page.

B. Create an appropriate ODBC data source for your database.

C. Code a PHP page to display the data in the CUSTOMER table. Using your sample database, demonstrate that your page works.

D. Create a view called CustomerPurchasesView that has the columns CustomerID, LastName, FirstName, SaleID, SaleDate, SaleItemID, ItemID, ItemDescription, and ItemPrice.

E. Code a PHP page to display CustomerPurchasesView. Using your sample database, demonstrate that your page works.

F. Code two HTML/PHP pages to receive a date value AsOfDate and display rows of the CustomerPurchasesView for purchases having SaleDate greater than or equal to AsOfDate. Using your sample database, demonstrate that your pages work.

G. Write a stored procedure that receives values for SaleItemID and NewItemPrice and sets the value of ItemPrice to NewItemPrice for the row having the given value of SaleItemID. Generate an error message if no row has the given value of SaleItemID. Using your sample database, demonstrate that your stored procedure works.

H. Code two HTML/PHP pages to invoke the stored procedure created in part G. Using your sample database, demonstrate that your page works.

Morgan Importing

If you have not already done so, answer the questions for Morgan Importing (MI) at the end of Chapter 7 (pages 390–395) and for the DBMS you are using as described in:

- Chapter 10A for Microsoft SQL Server 2014
- Chapter 10B for Oracle Database
- Chapter 10C for Oracle MySQL 5.6

A. Add a new folder to the DBP Web site named MI. Create a Web page for Morgan Importing in this folder, using the file name index.html. Link this page to the DBP Web page.

B. Create an appropriate ODBC data source for your database.

C. Create a view called StorePurchasesView that has the columns StoreName, City, Country, Email, Contact, PurchaseDate, ItemDescription, Category, and PriceUSD.

D. Code a PHP page to display StorePurchasesView. Using your sample database, demonstrate that your page works.

E. Code two HTML/PHP pages to receive a date value AsOfDate and display rows of StorePurchases for purchases having PurchaseDate greater than or equal to AsOfDate. Using your sample database, demonstrate that your pages work.

F. Code two HTML/PHP pages to receive values of Country and Category and display rows of StorePurchases having values for input Country and Category values. Using your sample database, demonstrate that your pages work.

G. Write a stored procedure that receives values for PurchaseItemID and NewPriceUSD and sets the value of PriceUSD to NewPriceUSD for the row having the given value of PurchaseItemID. Generate an error message if no row has the given value of PurchaseItemID. Using your sample database, demonstrate that your stored procedure works.

H. Code two HTML/PHP pages to invoke the stored procedure created in part G. Using your sample database, demonstrate that your page works.

12

Big Data, Data Warehouses, and Business Intelligence Systems

Chapter Objectives

- To learn the basic concepts of Big Data, structured storage, and the MapReduce process
- To learn the basic concepts of data warehouses and data marts
- To learn the basic concepts of dimensional databases
- To learn the basic concepts of business intelligence (BI) systems

- To learn the basic concepts of online analytical processing (OLAP) and data mining
- To learn the basic concepts of distributed databases and object-relational databases
- To learn the basic concepts of virtual machines
- To learn the basic concepts of cloud computing

This chapter introduces topics that build on the fundamentals you have learned in the other chapters of this book. Now that we have designed and built a database, we are ready to put it to work. In Chapter 11, we built a Web database application for the View Ridge Gallery (VRG) Information System, and in this chapter, we will look at business intelligence (BI) systems applications. Additionally, this chapter looks at the problems associated with the rapidly expanding amount of data that is being stored and used in enterprise information systems and some of the technology that is being used to address those problems.

These problems are generally included in the need to deal with **Big Data** (also often written as *big data*), which is the current term for the enormous datasets generated by Web applications such as search tools (for example, Google and Bing) and Web 2.0 social networks (for example, Facebook, LinkedIn, and Twitter). Although these new and very visible Web applications are highlighting the problems of dealing with large datasets, these problems were already present in other areas, such as scientific research and business operations.[1]

---

[1] For more information, see the Wikipedia article on *Big Data* at *http://en.wikipedia.org/wiki/Big_data*.

FIGURE 12-1

Storage Capacity Terms

Name	Symbol	Approximate Value for Reference	Actual Value
Byte			8 bits [Store one character]
Kilobyte	KB	About 10^3	2^{10} = 1,024 bytes
Megabyte	MB	About 10^6	2^{20} = 1,024 KB
Gigabyte	GB	About 10^9	2^{30} = 1,024 MB
Terabyte	TB	About 10^{12}	2^{40} = 1,024 GB
Petabyte	PB	About 10^{15}	2^{50} = 1,024 TB
Exabyte	EB	About 10^{18}	2^{60} = 1,024 PB
Zettabyte	ZB	About 10^{21}	2^{70} = 1,024 EB
Yottabyte	YB	About 10^{24}	2^{80} = 1,024 ZB

Just how big is Big Data? Figure 12-1 defines some commonly used terms for data storage capacity. Note that computer storage is calculated based on binary numbers (base 2), not the usual decimal (base 10) numbers we are more familiar with. Therefore, a kilobyte is 1,024 bytes instead of the 1,000 bytes we would otherwise expect.

If we consider the desktop and notebook computers generally in use as this book is being written (early 2015), a quick check online of available computers shows notebooks being sold with hard drives up to 750 GB in capacity, whereas some desktops are available with 2 TB. That is just for one computer. Facebook is reported to handle more than 40 billion photos in its database.[2] If a typical digital photo is about 2 MB in size, that would require about 9.3 PB of storage!

As another measure of Big Data, Amazon.com reported that on November 29, 2010, orders for 13.7 million products were placed. This is an average of 158 product orders per second.[3] Amazon.com also reported that, on the peak day of the 2010 holiday season, its worldwide fulfillment network shipped more than 9 million items to 178 countries. This volume of both primary business transactions (item sales) and supporting transactions (shipping, tracking, and financial transactions) truly requires Amazon.com to handle Big Data.

The need to deal with larger and larger datasets has grown over time. We will look at some of the components of this growth. We will start with the need for business analysts to have large datasets available for analysis by business intelligence (BI) applications and briefly look at BI systems, particularly online analytical processing (OLAP), and the data warehouse structures that were designed for their use. We will then look at distributed databases, object-relational databases, clustered servers, and finally the evolving NoSQL non-relational systems.

---

[2]Wikipedia article on *Big Data* at *http://en.wikipedia.org/wiki/Big_data* (accessed February 2013).
[3]Amazon.com, "Third-Generation Kindle Now the Bestselling Product of All Time on Amazon Worldwide." News release, December 27, 2010. Available at *http://phx.corporate-ir.net/phoenix.zhtml?c=176060&p= irol-newsArticle&ID=1510745&highlight=* (accessed February 2015).

Business Intelligence Systems

Business intelligence (BI) systems are information systems that assist managers and other professionals in the analysis of current and past activities and in the prediction of future events. Unlike transaction processing systems, they do not support operational activities, such as the recording and processing of orders. Instead, BI systems are used to support management assessment, analysis, planning, control, and, ultimately, decision making.

The Relationship Between Operational and BI Systems

Figure 12-2 summarizes the relationship between operational and business intelligence systems. **Operational systems**—such as sales, purchasing, and inventory control systems—support primary business activities. They use a DBMS to both read data from and store data in the operational database. They are also known as **transactional systems** or **online transaction processing (OLTP) systems** because they record the ongoing stream of business transactions.

Instead of supporting the primary business activities, BI systems support management's analysis and decision-making activities. BI systems obtain data from three possible sources. First, they read and process data existing in the operational database—they use the operational DBMS to obtain such data, but they do not insert, modify, or delete operational data. Second, BI systems process data that are extracted from operational databases. In this situation, they manage the extracted database using a BI DBMS, which may be the same as or different from the operational DBMS. Finally, BI systems read data purchased from data vendors.

Reporting Systems and Data Mining Applications

BI systems fall into two broad categories: reporting systems and data mining applications. **Reporting systems** sort, filter, group, and make elementary calculations on operational data. **Data mining applications**, in contrast, perform sophisticated analyses on data, analyses that usually involve complex statistical and mathematical processing. The characteristics of BI applications are summarized in Figure 12-3.

Reporting Systems

Reporting systems filter, sort, group, and make simple calculations. All reporting analyses can be performed using standard SQL, though extensions to SQL, such as those used for **online analytical processing (OLAP)**, are sometimes used to ease the task of report production.

Reporting systems summarize the current status of business activities and compare that status with past or predicted future activities. Report delivery is crucial. Reports must be

FIGURE 12-2

Relationship Between
Operational and BI Systems

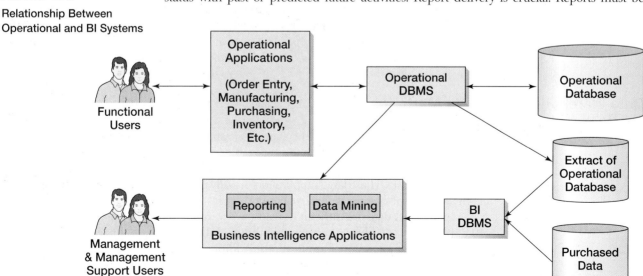

FIGURE 12-3

Characteristics of Business
Intelligence Applications

Characteristics of Business Intelligence Applications
• Reporting
– Filter, sort, group, and make simple calculations
– Summarize current status
– Compare current status to past or predicted status
– Classify entities (customers, products, employees, etc.)
– Report delivery crucial
• Data Mining
– Often employ sophisticated statistical and mathematical techniques
– Used for:
• What-if analyses
• Predictions
• Decisions
– Results often incorporated into some other report or system

delivered to the proper users on a timely basis in the appropriate format. For example, reports may be delivered on paper, via a Web browser, or in some other format.

Data Mining Applications

Data mining applications use sophisticated statistical and mathematical techniques to perform what-if analyses, to make predictions, and to facilitate decision making. For example, data mining techniques can analyze past cell phone usage and predict which customers are likely to switch to a competing phone company. Or data mining can be used to analyze past loan behavior to determine which customers are most (or least) likely to default on a loan.

Report delivery is not as important for data mining systems as it is for reporting systems. First, most data mining applications have only a few users, and those users have sophisticated computer skills. Second, the results of a data mining analysis are usually incorporated into some other report, analysis, or information system. In the case of cell phone usage, the characteristics of customers who are in danger of switching to another company may be given to the sales department for action. Or the parameters of an equation for determining the likelihood of a loan default may be incorporated into a loan approval application.

Data Warehouses and Data Marts

According to Figure 12-2, some BI systems read and process operational data directly from the operational database. Although this is possible for simple reporting systems and small databases, such direct reading of operational data is not feasible for more complex applications or larger databases. Those larger applications usually process a separate database constructed from an extract of the operational database.

Operational data are difficult to read for several reasons. For one, querying data for BI applications can place a substantial burden on the DBMS and unacceptably slow the performance of operational applications. Additionally, operational data have problems that limit their use for BI applications. Further, the creation and maintenance of BI systems require programs, facilities, and expertise that are not normally available from operations. Because of these problems, many organizations have chosen to develop data warehouses and data marts to support BI applications.

Components of a Data Warehouse

To overcome the problems just described, many organizations have created **data warehouses**, which are database systems that have data, programs, and personnel that specialize in the preparation of data for BI processing. Data warehouse databases differ from operational databases because the data warehouse data is frequently denormalized. Further, that data is never inserted, updated, or deleted by users, but only by data warehouse administrators. Data warehouses vary in scale and scope. They can be as simple as a sole employee processing a data extract on a part-time basis or as complex as a department with dozens of employees maintaining libraries of data and programs.

Figure 12-4 shows the components of a data warehouse. Data are read from operational databases by the **Extract, Transform, and Load (ETL) system**. The ETL system then cleans and prepares the data for BI processing. This can be a complex process.

First, the data may be problematic, which we will discuss in the next section. Second, data may need to be changed or transformed for use in a data warehouse. For example, the operational systems may store data about countries using standard two-letter country codes, such as US (United States) and CA (Canada). However, applications using the data warehouse may need to use the country names in full. Thus, the data transformation **{CountryCode →CountryName}** will be needed before the data can be loaded into the data warehouse.

The ETL stores the extracted data in a data warehouse database using a data warehouse DBMS, which can be different from the organization's operational DBMS. For example, an organization might use Oracle Database for its operational processing but use Microsoft SQL Server 2014 for its data warehouse. Other organizations might use Microsoft SQL Server 2014 for operational processing and data management programs from statistical package vendors such as SAS (SAS Analytics) or IBM (IBM SPSS Statistics) in the data warehouse.

Metadata concerning the data's source, format, assumptions and constraints, and other facts are kept in a **data warehouse metadata database**. The data warehouse DBMS extracts and provides data to BI tools, such as data mining programs.

BY THE WAY   Once problematic operational data have been cleaned in the ETL system, the corrected data can also be used to update the operational system to fix the original data problems.

FIGURE 12-4

Components of a Data Warehouse

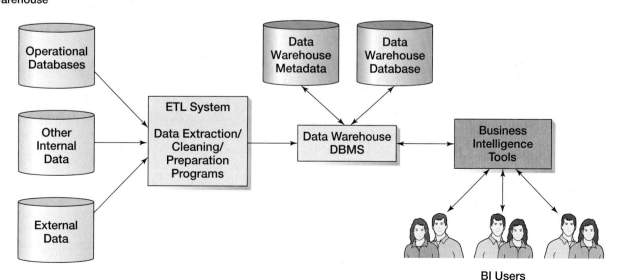

BI Users

FIGURE 12-5

FIGURE 12-5

Problems of Using
Transaction Data for
Business Intelligence

Problems of Using Transaction Data for Business Intelligence
• Dirty data
• Missing values
• Inconsistent data
• Data not integrated
• Wrong format
– Too fine
– Not fine enough
• Too much data
– Too many attributes
– Too much volume

Problems with Operational Data

Most operational databases have problems that limit their usefulness to all but the simplest BI applications. Figure 12-5 lists the major problem categories.

First, although data that are critical for successful operations must be complete and accurate, data that are only marginally necessary need not be. For example, some operational systems gather customer demographic data during the ordering process. However, because such data are not needed to fill, ship, or bill orders, the quality of the demographic data suffers.

Problematic data are termed **dirty data**. Examples are a value of "G" for customer sex and a value of "213" for customer age. Other examples are a value of "999-999-9999" for a U.S. phone number, a part color of "gren," and an e-mail address of "WhyMe@somewhereelseintheuniverse.who." All of these values pose problems for reporting and data mining purposes.

Purchased data often contain missing elements. In fact, most data vendors state the percentage of **missing values** for each attribute in the data they sell. An organization buys such data because, for some uses, some data are better than no data at all. This is especially true for data items whose values are difficult to obtain, such as the number of adults in a household, household income, dwelling type, and the education of the primary income earner. Some missing data are not too much of a problem for reporting applications. For data mining applications, however, a few missing or erroneous data points can actually be worse than no data at all because they bias the analysis.

Inconsistent data, the third problem in Figure 12-5, is particularly common for data that have been gathered over time. When an area code changes, for example, the phone number for a given customer before the change will differ from the customer's phone number after the change. Part codes can change, as can sales territories. Before such data can be used, they must be recoded for consistency over the period of the study.

Some data inconsistencies occur because of the nature of the business activity. Consider a Web-based order entry system used by customers around the world. When the Web server records the time of order, which time zone does it use? The server's system clock time is irrelevant to an analysis of customer behavior. Any standard time such as Universal Time Coordinate (UTC) time is also meaningless. Somehow, Web server time must be adjusted to the time zone of the customer.

Another problem is **nonintegrated data**. Suppose, for example, that an organization wants to report on customer orders and payment behavior. Unfortunately, order data are stored in a Microsoft Dynamics CRM system, whereas payment data are recorded in an

Oracle PeopleSoft financial management database. To perform the analysis, the data must somehow be integrated.

The next problem is that data can be **inappropriately formatted**. First, data can be too fine. For example, suppose that we want to analyze the placement of graphics and controls on an order entry Web page. It is possible to capture the customers' clicking behavior in what is termed **click-stream data**. However, click-stream data include *everything* the customer does. In the middle of the order stream, there may be data for clicks on the news, e-mail, instant chat, and the weather. Although all of this data might be useful for a study of consumer computer behavior, it will be overwhelming if all we want to know is how customers respond to an ad located on the screen. Because the data are too fine, the data analysts must throw millions and millions of clicks away before they can proceed.

Data can also be too coarse. A file of order totals cannot be used for a market basket analysis, which identifies items that are commonly purchased together. Market basket analyses require item-level data; we need to know which items were purchased with which others. This doesn't mean the order total data are useless; they can be adequate for other analyses, but they just won't do for a market basket analysis.

If the data are too fine, they can be made coarser by summing and combining. An analyst and a computer can sum and combine such data. If the data are too coarse, however, they cannot be separated into their constituent parts.

The final problem listed in Figure 12-5 concerns the issue of **too much data**. We can have an excess of columns, rows, or both. To illustrate the problem of too many columns (a synonym for attributes), suppose that we want to know the attributes that influence customers' responses to a promotion. Between customer data stored within the organization and customer data that can be purchased, we might have a hundred or more different attributes, or columns, to consider. How do we select among them? Because of a phenomenon called the **curse of dimensionality**, the more attributes there are, the easier it is to build a model that fits the sample data but that is worthless as a predictor. For this and other reasons, the number of attributes should be reduced, and one of the major activities in data mining concerns the efficient and effective selection of variables.

Finally, we may have too many instances, or rows, of data. Suppose that we want to analyze click-stream data on CNN.com. How many clicks does this site receive per month? Millions upon millions! To meaningfully analyze such data, we need to reduce the number of instances. A good solution to this problem is statistical sampling. However, developing a reliable sample requires specialized expertise and information system tools.

Purchasing Data from Vendors

Data warehouses often include data that are purchased from outside sources. A typical example is customer credit data. Figure 12-6 lists some of the consumer data than can be purchased from the KBM Group in their AmeriLINK database of consumer data. An amazing, and from a privacy standpoint frightening, amount of data is available just from this one vendor.

Data Warehouses Versus Data Marts

You can think of a data warehouse as a distributor in a supply chain. The data warehouse takes data from the data manufacturers (operational systems and purchased data), cleans and processes them, and locates the data on the shelves, so to speak, of the data warehouse. The people who work in a data warehouse are experts at data management, data cleaning, data transformation, and the like. However, they are not usually experts in a given business function.

A **data mart** is a collection of data that is smaller than that in the data warehouse and that addresses a particular component or functional area of the business. A data mart is like a retail store in a supply chain. Users in the data mart obtain data that pertain to a particular business function from the data warehouse. Such users do not have the data management expertise that data warehouse employees have, but they are knowledgeable analysts for a given business function. Figure 12-7 illustrates these relationships.

This data warehouse takes data from the data producers and distributes the data to three data marts. One data mart analyzes click-stream data for the purpose of designing Web pages.

AmeriLINK Data Categories
• Name, Address, Phone
• Age, Gender
• Ethnicity, Religion
• Income
• Education
• Marital Status, Life Stage
• Height, Weight, Hair and Eye Color
• Spouse's Name, Birth Date, etc.
• Kids' Names and Birth Dates
• Voter Registration
• Home Ownership
• Vehicles
• Magazine Subscriptions
• Catalog Orders
• Hobbies
• Attitudes

The second analyzes store sales data and determines which products tend to be purchased together. This information is used to train salespeople on the best way to up-sell customers. The third data mart analyzes customer order data for the purpose of reducing labor for item picking from the warehouse. A company such as Amazon.com, for example, goes to great lengths to organize its warehouses to reduce picking expenses.

FIGURE 12-7

Data Warehouses and Data
Marts

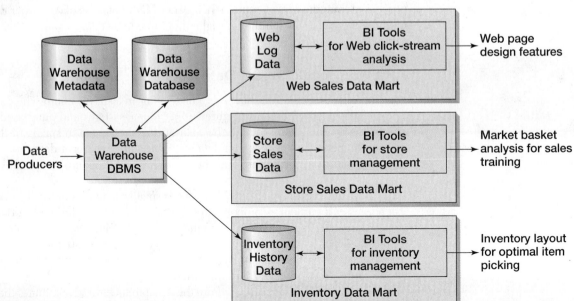

FIGURE 12-8

Characteristics of
Operational and Dimensional
Databases

Operational Database	Dimensional Database
Used for structured transaction data processing	Used for unstructured analytical data processing
Current data are used	Current and historical data are used
Data are inserted, updated, and deleted by users	Data are loaded and updated systematically, not by users

When the data mart structure shown in Figure 12-7 is combined with the data warehouse architecture shown in Figure 12-4, the combined system is known as an **enterprise data warehouse (EDW) architecture**. In this configuration, the data warehouse maintains all enterprise BI data and acts as the authoritative source for data extracts provided to the data marts. The data marts receive all their data from the data warehouse–they do not add or maintain any additional data.

Of course, it is expensive to create, staff, and operate data warehouses and data marts, and only large organizations with deep pockets can afford to operate a system such as an EDW. Smaller organizations operate subsets of this system. For example, they may have just a single data mart for analyzing marketing and promotion data.

Dimensional Databases

The databases in a data warehouse or data mart are built to a different type of database design than the normalized relational databases used for operational systems. The data warehouse databases are built in a design called a **dimensional database** that is designed for efficient data queries and analysis. A dimensional database is used to store historical data rather than just the current data stored in an operational database. Figure 12-8 compares operational databases and dimensional databases.

Because dimensional databases are used for the analysis of historical data, they must be designed to handle data that change over time. For example, a customer may have moved from one residence to another in the same city or may have moved to a completely different city and state. This type of data arrangement is called a **slowly changing dimension**, and in order to track such changes, a dimensional database must have a **date dimension** or **time dimension** as well.

The Star Schema

Rather than using the normalized database designs used in operational databases, a dimensional database uses a star schema. A **star schema**, so named because, as shown in Figure 12-9, it visually resembles a star, has a **fact table** at the center of the star and **dimension tables** radiating out from the center. The fact table is always fully normalized, but dimension tables may be non-normalized.

FIGURE 12-9

The Star Schema

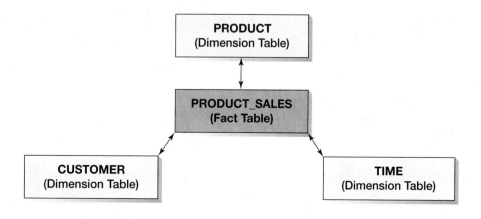

> **BY THE WAY** There is a more complex version of the star schema called the *snowflake schema*. In the snowflake schema, each dimension table is normalized, which may create additional tables attached to the dimension tables.

To illustrate a star schema for a dimensional database, we will build a (very) small data warehouse for Heather Sweeney Designs (HSD), a Texas company specializing in products for kitchen-remodeling services. HSD puts on seminars to attract customers and sell books and videos in addition to doing actual design work. For more information about Heather Sweeney Designs, see the Chapter 7 Heather Sweeney Designs Case Questions on pages 369–383. A database design for HSD is shown in Figure 12-10, and a Microsoft SQL Server 2014 database diagram for the HSD database is shown in Figure 12-11. In addition, the Chapter 7 Heather Sweeney Designs Case Questions show the HSD database column specifications in Figure 7-50, HSD database referential integrity constraint enforcement in Figure 7-51, the SQL statements to create the HSD database in Figure 7-52, and the SQL statements to populate the HSD database in Figure 7-53. The HSD database is the operational database for Heather Sweeney Designs. All production data is stored in the HSD database, and that data provides the source data that we will load into a dimensional database for BI work at Heather Sweeney Designs.

The actual dimensional database for BI use is named *HSD_DW*, and it is shown in Figure 12-12. Note that we use an underscore in the database name instead of a hyphen–DBMS systems seem to prefer the use of the hyphen (which, for example, is recognized in SQL Server 2014 in a GO statement) over the use of a underscore (which the SQL Server 2014 GO statement does *not* recognize). The SQL statements needed to create the tables in the HSD_DW database are shown in Figure 12-13, and the data for the HSD_DW database are shown in Figure 12-14. Compare the HSD_DW dimensional database model in Figure 12-12 to the HSD database diagram shown in Figure 12-11, and note how data in the HSD database have been used in the HSD_DW schema.

FIGURE 12-10

The HSD Database Design

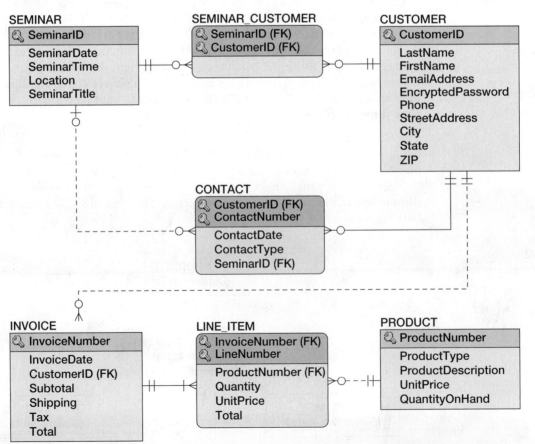

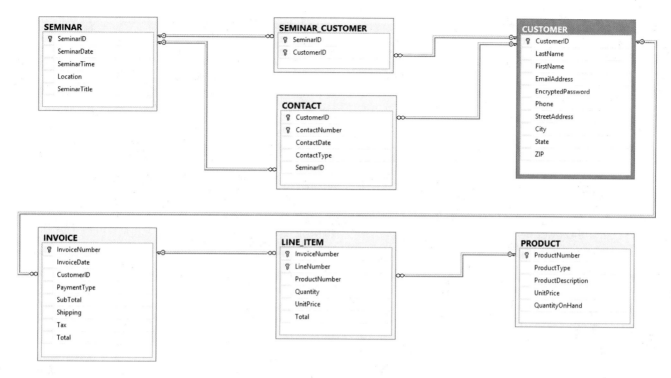

FIGURE 12-11

The HSD Database Diagram

BY THE WAY   You do not need to create the HSD database in order to create and use the HSD_DW database used in this chapter. However, because the HSD_DW database uses data extracted from the HSD database, it is worthwhile to study and understand the structure of the HSD database and data contained in the HSD database in order to appreciate how we transform that data for use in the HSD_DW database.

FIGURE 12-12

The HSD_DW Star Schema

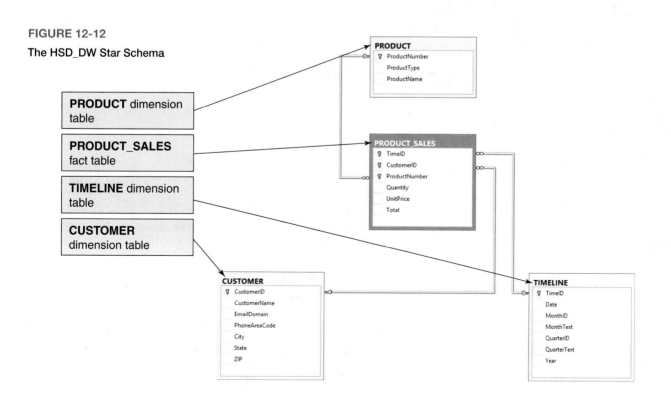

```
CREATE TABLE TIMELINE(
     TimeID                 Int              NOT NULL,
     [Date]                 Date             NOT NULL,
     MonthID                Int              NOT NULL,
     MonthText              Char(15)         NOT NULL,
     QuarterID              Int              NOT NULL,
     QuarterText            Char(10)         NOT NULL,
     [Year]                 Int              NOT NULL,
     CONSTRAINT             TIMELINE_PK      PRIMARY KEY(TimeID)
     );

CREATE TABLE CUSTOMER(
     CustomerID             Int              NOT NULL,
     CustomerName           Char(75)         NOT NULL,
     EmailDomain            VarChar(100)     NOT NULL,
     PhoneAreaCode          Char(6)          NOT NULL,
     City                   Char(35)         NULL,
     [State]                Char(2)          NULL,
     ZIP                    Char(10)         NULL,
     CONSTRAINT             CUSTOMER_PK      PRIMARY KEY(CustomerID)
     );

CREATE TABLE PRODUCT(
     ProductNumber          Char(35)         NOT NULL,
     ProductType            Char(25)         NOT NULL,
     ProductName            VarChar(75)      NOT NULL,
     CONSTRAINT             PRODUCT_PK       PRIMARY KEY(ProductNumber)
     );

CREATE TABLE PRODUCT_SALES(
     TimeID                 Int              NOT NULL,
     CustomerID             Int              NOT NULL,
     ProductNumber          Char(35)         NOT NULL,
     Quantity               Int              NOT NULL,
     UnitPrice              Numeric(9,2)     NOT NULL,
     Total                  Numeric(9,2)     NULL,
     CONSTRAINT             SALES_PK         PRIMARY KEY(TimeID, CustomerID, ProductNumber),
     CONSTRAINT             PS_TIMELINE_FK FOREIGN KEY(TimeID)
                                 REFERENCES TIMELINE(TimeID)
                                      ON UPDATE NO ACTION
                                      ON DELETE NO ACTION,
     CONSTRAINT             PS_CUSTOMER_FK FOREIGN KEY(CustomerID)
                                 REFERENCES CUSTOMER(CustomerID)
                                      ON UPDATE NO ACTION
                                      ON DELETE NO ACTION,
     CONSTRAINT             PS_PRODUCT_FK FOREIGN KEY(ProductNumber)
                                 REFERENCES PRODUCT(ProductNumber)
                                      ON UPDATE NO ACTION
                                      ON DELETE NO ACTION
     );
```

FIGURE 12-13

The HSD_DW SQL Statements

A fact table is used to store **measures** of business activity, which are quantitative or factual data about the entity represented by the fact table. For example, in the HSD_DW database, the fact table is PRODUCT_SALES:

```
PRODUCT_SALES (TimeID, CustomerID, ProductNumber, Quantity,
UnitPrice, Total)
```

In this table:

- Quantity is quantitative data that record how many of the item were sold.
- UnitPrice is quantitative data that record the dollar price of each item sold.
- Total (= Quantity * UnitPrice) is quantitative data that record the total dollar value of the sale of this item.

	TimeID	Date	MonthID	MonthText	QuarterID	QuarterText	Year
1	41927	2014-10-15	10	October	3	Qtr3	2014
2	41937	2014-10-25	10	October	3	Qtr3	2014
3	41993	2014-12-20	12	December	3	Qtr3	2014
4	42088	2015-03-25	3	March	1	Qtr1	2015
5	42090	2015-03-27	3	March	1	Qtr1	2015
6	42094	2015-03-31	3	March	1	Qtr1	2015
7	42097	2015-04-03	4	April	2	Qtr2	2015
8	42102	2015-04-08	4	April	2	Qtr2	2015
9	42117	2015-04-23	4	April	2	Qtr2	2015
10	42131	2015-05-07	5	May	2	Qtr2	2015
11	42145	2015-05-21	5	May	2	Qtr2	2015
12	42160	2015-06-05	6	June	2	Qtr2	2015

(a) TIMELINE Dimension Table

	CustomerID	CustomerName	EmailDomain	PhoneAreaCode	City	State	ZIP
1	1	Jacobs, Nancy	somewhere.com	817	Fort Worth	TX	76110
2	2	Jacobs, Chantel	somewhere.com	817	Fort Worth	TX	76112
3	3	Able, Ralph	somewhere.com	210	San Antonio	TX	78214
4	4	Baker, Susan	elsewhere.com	210	San Antonio	TX	78216
5	5	Eagleton, Sam	elsewhere.com	210	San Antonio	TX	78218
6	6	Foxtrot, Kathy	somewhere.com	972	Dallas	TX	75220
7	7	George, Sally	somewhere.com	972	Dallas	TX	75223
8	8	Hullett, Shawn	elsewhere.com	972	Dallas	TX	75224
9	9	Pearson, Bobbi	elsewhere.com	512	Austin	TX	78710
10	10	Ranger, Terry	somewhere.com	512	Austin	TX	78712
11	11	Tyler, Jenny	somewhere.com	972	Dallas	TX	75225
12	12	Wayne, Joan	elsewhere.com	817	Fort Worth	TX	76115

(b) CUSTOMER Dimension Table

	ProductNumber	ProductType	ProductName
1	BK001	Book	Kitchen Remodeling Basics For Everyone
2	BK002	Book	Advanced Kitchen Remodeling For Everyone
3	VB001	Video Companion	Kitchen Remodeling Basics Video Companion
4	VB002	Video Companion	Advanced Kitchen Remodeling Video Companion
5	VB003	Video Companion	Kitchen Remodeling Dallas Style Video Companion
6	VK001	DVD Video	Kitchen Remodeling Basics
7	VK002	DVD Video	Advanced Kitchen Remodeling
8	VK003	DVD Video	Kitchen Remodeling Dallas Style
9	VK004	DVD Video	Heather Sweeny Seminar Live in Dallas on 25-OCT-13

(c) PRODUCT Dimension Table

	TimeID	CustomerID	ProductNumber	Quantity	UnitPrice	Total
1	41927	3	VB001	1	7.99	7.99
2	41927	3	VK001	1	14.95	14.95
3	41937	4	BK001	1	24.95	24.95
4	41937	4	VB001	1	7.99	7.99
5	41937	4	VK001	1	14.95	14.95
6	41993	7	VK004	1	24.95	24.95
7	42088	4	BK002	1	24.95	24.95
8	42088	4	VK002	1	14.95	14.95
9	42088	4	VK004	1	24.95	24.95
10	42090	6	BK002	1	24.95	24.95
11	42090	6	VB003	1	9.99	9.99
12	42090	6	VK002	1	14.95	14.95
13	42090	6	VK003	1	19.95	19.95
14	42090	6	VK004	1	24.95	24.95
15	42090	7	BK001	1	24.95	24.95
16	42090	7	BK002	1	24.95	24.95
17	42090	7	VK003	1	19.95	19.95
18	42090	7	VK004	1	24.95	24.95
19	42094	9	BK001	1	24.95	24.95
20	42094	9	VB001	1	7.99	7.99
21	42094	9	VK001	1	14.95	14.95
22	42097	11	VB003	2	9.99	19.98
23	42097	11	VK003	2	19.95	39.90
24	42097	11	VK004	2	24.95	49.90
25	42102	1	BK001	1	24.95	24.95
26	42102	1	VB001	1	7.99	7.99
27	42102	1	VK001	1	14.95	14.95
28	42102	5	BK001	1	24.95	24.95
29	42102	5	VB001	1	7.99	7.99
30	42102	5	VK001	1	14.95	14.95
31	42117	3	BK001	1	24.95	24.95
32	42131	9	VB002	1	7.99	7.99
33	42131	9	VK002	1	14.95	14.95
34	42145	8	VB003	1	9.99	9.99
35	42145	8	VK003	1	19.95	19.95
36	42145	8	VK004	1	24.95	24.95
37	42160	3	BK002	1	24.95	24.95
38	42160	3	VB001	1	7.99	7.99
39	42160	3	VB002	2	7.99	15.98
40	42160	3	VK001	1	14.95	14.95
41	42160	3	VK002	2	14.95	29.90
42	42160	11	VB002	2	7.99	15.98
43	42160	11	VK002	2	14.95	29.90
44	42160	12	BK002	1	24.95	24.95
45	42160	12	VB003	1	9.99	9.99
46	42160	12	VK002	1	14.95	14.95
47	42160	12	VK003	1	19.95	19.95
48	42160	12	VK004	1	24.95	24.95

(d) PRODUCT_SALES Fact Table

FIGURE 12-14

The HSD_DW Table Data

The measures in the PRODUCT_SALES table are for *units of product per day*. We do not use individual sale data (which would be based on InvoiceNumber), but rather data summed for each customer for each day. For example, if you could compare the HSD database INVOICE data for Ralph Able for 6/5/15, you would see that Ralph made two purchases on that date (InvoiceNumber 35013 and InvoiceNumber 35016). In the HSD_DW database, however, these two purchases are summed into the PRODUCT_SALES data for Ralph (CustomerID = 3) for 6/5/15 (TimeID = 42160).

A dimension table is used to record values of attributes that describe the fact measures in the fact table, and these attributes are used in queries to select and group the measures in the fact table. Thus, CUSTOMER records data about the customers referenced by CustomerID in the SALES table, TIMELINE provides data that can be used to interpret the SALES event in time (which month? which quarter?), and so on. A query to summarize product units sold by Customer (CustomerName) and Product (ProductName) would be:

```
/* *** SQL-Query-CH12-01 *** */
SELECT       C.CustomerID, C.CustomerName,
             P.ProductNumber, P.ProductName,
             SUM(PS.Quantity) AS TotalQuantity
FROM         CUSTOMER AS C, PRODUCT_SALES AS PS, PRODUCT AS P
WHERE        C.CustomerID = PS.CustomerID
AND          P.ProductNumber = PS.ProductNumber
GROUP BY     C.CustomerID, C.CustomerName,
             P.ProductNumber, P.ProductName
ORDER BY     C.CustomerID, P.ProductNumber;
```

The results of this query are shown in Figure 12-15.

In Chapter 6, we discussed how an N:M relationship is created in a database as two 1:N relationships by use of an intersection table. We also discussed how additional attributes can be added to the intersection table in an association relationship.

In a star schema, the fact table is an association table—it is an intersection table for the relationships between the dimension tables with additional measures also stored in it. And, as with all other intersection and association tables, the key of the fact table is a composite key made up of all the foreign keys to the dimension tables.

Illustrating the Dimensional Model

When you think of the word *dimension*, you might think of "two dimensional" or "three dimensional." And the dimensional models can be illustrated by using a two-dimensional matrix and a three-dimensional cube. Figure 12-16 shows the SQL query results from Figure 12-15 displayed as a two-dimensional matrix of Product (using ProductNumber) and Customer (using CustomerID), with each cell showing the number of units of each product purchased by each customer. Note how ProductNumber and CustomerID define the two dimensions of the matrix: CustomerID labels what would be the *x*-axis, and ProductNumber labels the *y*-axis.

Figure 12-17 shows a three-dimensional cube with the same ProductNumber and CustomerID dimensions, but now with the added Time dimension on the *z*-axis. Now instead of occupying a two-dimensional box, the total quantity of products purchased by each customer on each day occupies a small three-dimensional cube, and all these small cubes combine to form a large cube.

As human beings, we can visualize two-dimensional matrices and three-dimensional cubes. Although we cannot visualize models with four, five, and more dimensions, BI systems and dimensional databases can handle such models.

Multiple Fact Tables and Conformed Dimensions

Data warehouse systems build dimensional models, as needed, to analyze BI questions, and the HSD_DW star schema in Figure 12-12 would be just one schema in a set of schemas. Figure 12-18 shows an extended HSD_DW schema.

	CustomerID	CustomerName	ProductNumber	ProductName	TotalQuantity
1	1	Jacobs, Nancy	BK001	Kitchen Remodeling Basics For Everyone	1
2	1	Jacobs, Nancy	VB001	Kitchen Remodeling Basics Video Companion	1
3	1	Jacobs, Nancy	VK001	Kitchen Remodeling Basics	1
4	3	Able, Ralph	BK001	Kitchen Remodeling Basics For Everyone	1
5	3	Able, Ralph	BK002	Advanced Kitchen Remodeling For Everyone	1
6	3	Able, Ralph	VB001	Kitchen Remodeling Basics Video Companion	2
7	3	Able, Ralph	VB002	Advanced Kitchen Remodeling Video Companion	2
8	3	Able, Ralph	VK001	Kitchen Remodeling Basics	2
9	3	Able, Ralph	VK002	Advanced Kitchen Remodeling	2
10	4	Baker, Susan	BK001	Kitchen Remodeling Basics For Everyone	1
11	4	Baker, Susan	BK002	Advanced Kitchen Remodeling For Everyone	1
12	4	Baker, Susan	VB001	Kitchen Remodeling Basics Video Companion	1
13	4	Baker, Susan	VK001	Kitchen Remodeling Basics	1
14	4	Baker, Susan	VK002	Advanced Kitchen Remodeling	1
15	4	Baker, Susan	VK004	Heather Sweeny Seminar Live in Dallas on 25-...	1
16	5	Eagleton, Sam	BK001	Kitchen Remodeling Basics For Everyone	1
17	5	Eagleton, Sam	VB001	Kitchen Remodeling Basics Video Companion	1
18	5	Eagleton, Sam	VK001	Kitchen Remodeling Basics	1
19	6	Foxtrot, Kathy	BK002	Advanced Kitchen Remodeling For Everyone	1
20	6	Foxtrot, Kathy	VB003	Kitchen Remodeling Dallas Style Video Compan...	1
21	6	Foxtrot, Kathy	VK002	Advanced Kitchen Remodeling	1
22	6	Foxtrot, Kathy	VK003	Kitchen Remodeling Dallas Style	1
23	6	Foxtrot, Kathy	VK004	Heather Sweeny Seminar Live in Dallas on 25-...	1
24	7	George, Sally	BK001	Kitchen Remodeling Basics For Everyone	1
25	7	George, Sally	BK002	Advanced Kitchen Remodeling For Everyone	1
26	7	George, Sally	VK003	Kitchen Remodeling Dallas Style	1
27	7	George, Sally	VK004	Heather Sweeny Seminar Live in Dallas on 25-...	2
28	8	Hullett, Shawn	VB003	Kitchen Remodeling Dallas Style Video Compan...	1
29	8	Hullett, Shawn	VK003	Kitchen Remodeling Dallas Style	1
30	8	Hullett, Shawn	VK004	Heather Sweeny Seminar Live in Dallas on 25-...	1
31	9	Pearson, Bobbi	BK001	Kitchen Remodeling Basics For Everyone	1
32	9	Pearson, Bobbi	VB001	Kitchen Remodeling Basics Video Companion	1
33	9	Pearson, Bobbi	VB002	Advanced Kitchen Remodeling Video Companion	1
34	9	Pearson, Bobbi	VK001	Kitchen Remodeling Basics	1
35	9	Pearson, Bobbi	VK002	Advanced Kitchen Remodeling	1
36	11	Tyler, Jenny	VB002	Advanced Kitchen Remodeling Video Companion	2
37	11	Tyler, Jenny	VB003	Kitchen Remodeling Dallas Style Video Compan...	2
38	11	Tyler, Jenny	VK002	Advanced Kitchen Remodeling	2
39	11	Tyler, Jenny	VK003	Kitchen Remodeling Dallas Style	2
40	11	Tyler, Jenny	VK004	Heather Sweeny Seminar Live in Dallas on 25-...	2
41	12	Wayne, Joan	BK002	Advanced Kitchen Remodeling For Everyone	1
42	12	Wayne, Joan	VB003	Kitchen Remodeling Dallas Style Video Compan...	1
43	12	Wayne, Joan	VK002	Advanced Kitchen Remodeling	1
44	12	Wayne, Joan	VK003	Kitchen Remodeling Dallas Style	1
45	12	Wayne, Joan	VK004	Heather Sweeny Seminar Live in Dallas on 25-...	1

FIGURE 12-15

The HSD_DW Query Results

Each cell shows the total quantity of each product that has been purchased by each customer

	CustomerID											
ProductNumber	1	2	3	4	5	6	7	8	9	10	11	12
BK001	1		1	1			1		1			
BK002			1	1		1	1					1
VB001	1		2	1	1				1			
VB002			2						1		2	
VB003						1		1			2	1
VK001	1		2	1	1				1			
VK002			2	1		1			1		2	1
VK003						1	1	1			2	1
VK004				1		1	2	1			2	1

FIGURE 12-16

The Two-Dimensional ProductNumber–CustomerID Matrix

In Figure 12-18, a second fact table named SALES_FOR_RFM has been added:

`SALES_FOR_RFM (TimeID, CustomerID, InvoiceNumber, PreTaxTotalSale)`

This table shows that fact table primary keys do not need to be composed solely of foreign keys that link to dimension tables. In SALES_FOR_RFM, the primary key includes the InvoiceNumber attribute. This attribute is necessary because the composite key (TimeID, CustomerID) will not be unique and thus cannot be the primary key. Note that SALES_FOR_RFM links to the same CUSTOMER and TIMELINE dimension tables as PRODUCT_SALES. This is done to maintain consistency within the data warehouse, and when a dimension table links to two or more fact tables, it is called a **conformed dimension**.

Why would we add a fact table named SALES_FOR_RFM? To explain that, we need to discuss reporting systems.

Reporting Systems

The purpose of a reporting system is to create meaningful information from disparate data sources and to deliver that information to the proper users on a timely basis. As stated earlier, reporting systems differ from data mining because they create information using the simple operations of sorting, filtering, grouping, and making simple calculations. We begin this section with a description of a typical reporting problem: RFM analysis.

RFM Analysis

RFM analysis is a way of analyzing and ranking customers according to their purchasing patterns. It is a simple technique that considers how *recently* (**R score**) a customer ordered, how *frequently* (**F score**) a customer orders, and how much *money* (**M score**) the customer spends per order. RFM is summarized in Figure 12-19.

To produce an RFM score, we need only two things: customer data and sales data for each purchase (the date of the sale and the total amount of the sale) made by each customer. If you

Each cell will show the total quantity of each product that has been purchased by each customer on a specific date

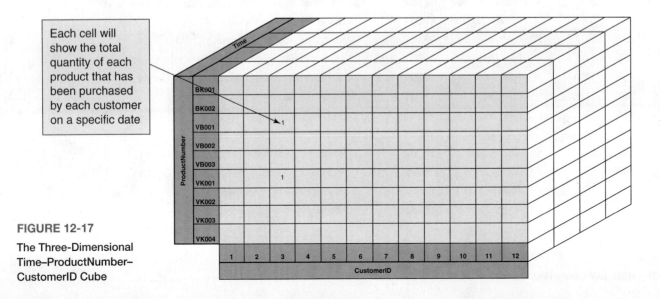

FIGURE 12-17

The Three-Dimensional Time–ProductNumber–CustomerID Cube

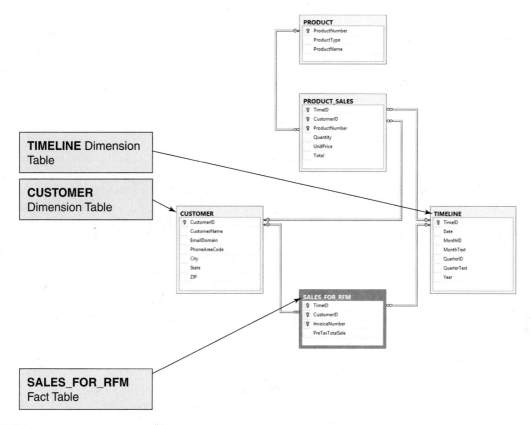

FIGURE 12-18

The Extended HSD_DW Star Schema

look at the SALES_FOR_RFM table and its associated CUSTOMER and TIMELINE dimension tables in Figure 12-18, you see that we have exactly those data: The SALES_FOR_RFM table is the starting point for RFM analysis in the HSD_DW BI system.

To produce an RFM score, customer purchase records are first sorted by the date of their most recent (R) purchase. In a common form of this analysis, the customers are divided into five groups, and a score of 1 to 5 is given to customers in each group. Thus, the 20 percent of the customers having the most recent orders are given an R score of 1, the 20 percent of the customers having the next most recent orders are given an R score of 2, and so forth, down to the last 20 percent, who are given an R score of 5.

The customer records are then sorted on the basis of how frequently they order. The 20 percent of the customers who order most frequently are given an F score of 1, the next 20 percent most frequently ordering customers are given a score of 2, and so forth, down to the least frequently ordering customers, who are given an F score of 5.

Finally, the customers are sorted again according to the amount of their orders. The 20 percent who have placed the most expensive orders are given an M score of 1, the next 20 percent are given an M score of 2, and so forth, down to the 20 percent who spend the least, who are given an M score of 5.

Figure 12-20 shows sample RFM data for Heather Sweeney Designs. (Note that these data have *not* been calculated and are for illustrative purposes only.) The first customer, Ralph Able, has a score of {1 1 2}, which means that he has ordered recently and orders frequently.

FIGURE 12-19

RFM Analysis

RFM Analysis
• Simple report-based customer classification scheme
• Score customers on recentness, frequency, and monetary size of orders
• Typically, divide each criterion into 5 groups and score from 1 to 5

FIGURE 12-20

The RFM Score Report

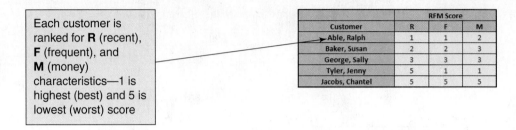

Each customer is ranked for **R** (recent), **F** (frequent), and **M** (money) characteristics—1 is highest (best) and 5 is lowest (worst) score

Customer	RFM Score		
	R	F	M
Able, Ralph	1	1	2
Baker, Susan	2	2	3
George, Sally	3	3	3
Tyler, Jenny	5	1	1
Jacobs, Chantel	5	5	5

His M score of 2 indicates, however, that he does not order the most expensive goods. From these scores, the salespeople can surmise that Ralph is a good customer but that they should attempt to up-sell Ralph to more expensive goods.

Susan Baker (RFM score of {2 2 3}) is above average in terms of how frequently she shops and how recently she has shopped, but her purchases are average in value. Sally George (RFM score of {3 3 3}) is truly in the middle. Jenny Tyler (RFM score of {5 1 1}) is a problem. Jenny has not ordered in some time, but, in the past, when she did order, she ordered frequently and her orders were of the highest monetary value. These data suggest that Jenny might be going to another vendor. Someone from the sales team should contact her immediately. However, no one on the sales team should be talking to Chantel Jacobs (RFM score of {5 5 5}). She has not ordered for some time, she doesn't order frequently, and when she does order, she only buys inexpensive items and not many of them.

OLAP

OLAP provides the ability to sum, count, average, and perform other simple arithmetic operations on groups of data. OLAP systems produce **OLAP reports**. An OLAP report is also called an **OLAP cube**. This is a reference to the dimensional data model, and some OLAP products show OLAP displays using three axes, like a geometric cube. The remarkable characteristic of an OLAP report is that it is dynamic: The format of an OLAP report can be changed by the viewer, hence the term *online* in the name online analytical processing.

OLAP uses the dimensional database model discussed earlier in this chapter, so it is not surprising to learn that an OLAP report has measures and dimensions. A measure is a dimensional model *fact*—the data item of interest that is to be summed or averaged or otherwise processed in the OLAP report. For example, sales data may be summed to produce Total Sales or averaged to produce Average Sales. The term *measure* is used because you are dealing with quantities that have been or can be measured and recorded. A dimension, as you have already learned, is an attribute or a characteristic of a measure. Purchase date (TimeID), customer location (City), and sales region (ZIP or State) are all examples of dimensions, and in the HSD_DW database, you saw how the time dimension is important.

In this section, we will generate an OLAP report by using an SQL query from the HSD_DW database and a Microsoft Excel **PivotTable**.

> **BY THE WAY**   We use Microsoft SQL Server 2014 and Microsoft Excel 2013 to illustrate this discussion of OLAP reports and PivotTables. For other DBMS products, such as MySQL, you can use the DataPilot feature of the Calc spreadsheet application in the OpenOffice.org product suite.

There are three ways we can proceed:

- Manually copy and format an SQL query as a formatted table in a Microsoft Excel worksheet:
    - Copy the SQL query results into an Excel worksheet.
    - Add column names to the results.
    - Format the query results as an Excel table (optional).
    - Select the Excel range containing the results with column names.
    - Create the PivotTable.

- *or* connect to a DBMS data source using the Microsoft Excel Get External Data Command:
  - Click the Get External Data command on the DATA command tab.
  - Select an Microsoft SQL Server 2014 database as the data source.
  - Specify that the data should go into a Microsoft Excel table.
  - Create the PivotTable.
- *or* use the Microsoft PowerPivot for Excel 2013 add-in feature to connect to a DBMS data source and then create the PivotTable.

The purpose of our OLAP report is to analyze the sales of Heather Sweeney Designs products based on selected dimensions in the HSD_DW database. For example, we might want to see how product sales vary based on the city the customer lives in. We begin by writing an SQL query to gather the required information from the dimensional database. We then use the results of this query if we *copy* the data into an Excel worksheet. The SQL query, as used in SQL Server 2014 is:

```
/* *** SQL-Query-CH12-02 *** */

SELECT      C.CustomerID, CustomerName, C.City,

            P.ProductNumber, P.ProductName,

            T.[Year], T.QuarterText,

            SUM(PS.Quantity) AS TotalQuantity

FROM        CUSTOMER C, PRODUCT_SALES PS, PRODUCT P, TIMELINE T

WHERE       C.CustomerID = PS.CustomerID

    AND     P.ProductNumber = PS.ProductNumber

    AND     T.TimeID = PS.TimeID

GROUP BY    C.CustomerID, C.CustomerName, C.City,

            P. ProductNumber, P.ProductName,

            T.QuarterText, T.[Year]

ORDER BY    C.CustomerName, T.[Year], T.QuarterText;
```

However, because SQL Server 2014 (and other SQL-based DBMS products, such as Oracle Database and MySQL) can store views but not queries, we need to create and use an SQL view if we are going to use an Excel data connection. The SQL query to create the HSDDWProductSalesView, as used in SQL Server 2014 is:

```
/* *** SQL-CREATE-VIEW-CH12-01 *** */

CREATE VIEW HSDDWProductSalesView AS

SELECT      C.CustomerID, C.CustomerName, C.City,

            P.ProductNumber, P.ProductName,

            T.[Year], T.QuarterText,

            SUM(PS.Quantity) AS TotalQuantity

FROM        CUSTOMER C, PRODUCT_SALES PS, PRODUCT P, TIMELINE T

WHERE       C.CustomerID = PS.CustomerID

    AND     P.ProductNumber = PS.ProductNumber

    AND     T.TimeID = PS.TimeID

GROUP BY    C.CustomerID, C.CustomerName, C.City,

            P. ProductNumber, P.ProductName,

            T.QuarterText, T.[Year];
```

We can now use the HSDDWProductSalesView when we connect to the database as the data source for an OLAP report. We will do this using the standard Microsoft Excel 2013 tools on the DATA command tab, and Figure 12-21(a) shows our starting point, a blank Microsoft Excel 2013 workbook (named DBP-e13-HSD-BI.xlsx) with the Microsoft SQL Server 2012 SP1 Data Mining Add-Ins for Office (downloadable from

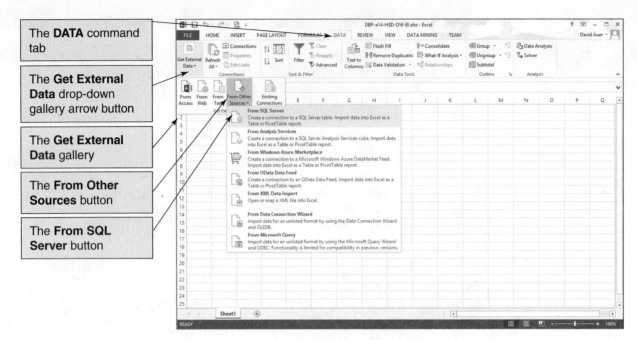

The **DATA** command tab

The **Get External Data** drop-down gallery arrow button

The **Get External Data** gallery

The **From Other Sources** button

The **From SQL Server** button

(a) The Get External Data Command

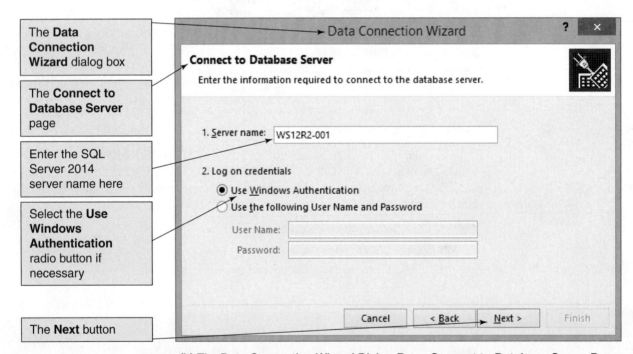

The **Data Connection Wizard** dialog box

The **Connect to Database Server** page

Enter the SQL Server 2014 server name here

Select the **Use Windows Authentication** radio button if necessary

The **Next** button

(b) The Data Connection Wizard Dialog Box—Connect to Database Server Page

FIGURE 12-21

OLAP Reports

www.microsoft.com/en-us/download/details.aspx?id=35578)). There is currently no updated version for SQL Server 2014, but this version does work with SQL Server 2014.

> **BY THE WAY**   The Microsoft SQL Server 2012 SP1 PowerPivot for Microsoft Excel 2010 add-in is downloadable from *www.microsoft.com/en-us/download/details .aspx?id=29074*). PowerPivot provides additional tools and the ability to work with larger datasets than can be handled by Microsoft Excel 2013 itself. It is a useful tool and well worth looking into. Again, there is no version specifically updated for SQL Server 2014 and Excel 2013, but the provided tools do work with the newer versions.

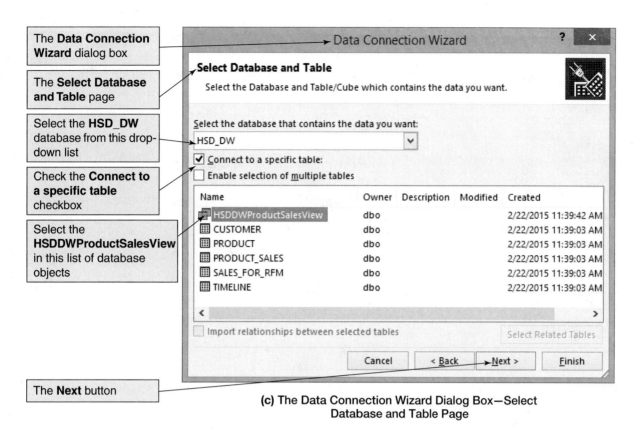

(c) The Data Connection Wizard Dialog Box—Select
Database and Table Page

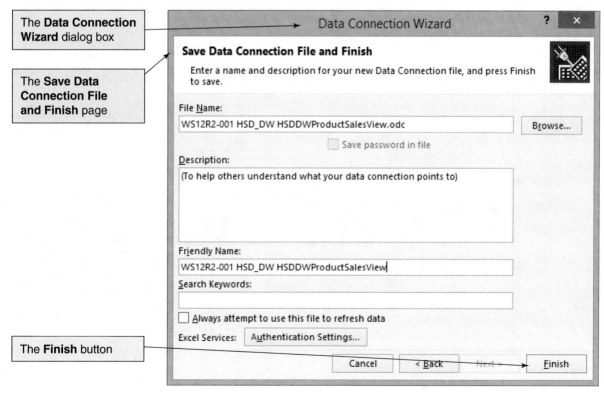

(d) The Data Connection Wizard Dialog Box—Save Data
Connection File and Finish Page

FIGURE 12-21   *(continued)*

Continued

The **Import Data** dialog box

Select the **Table** radio button if necessary

Select the **Existing worksheet** radio button if necessary

The **OK** button

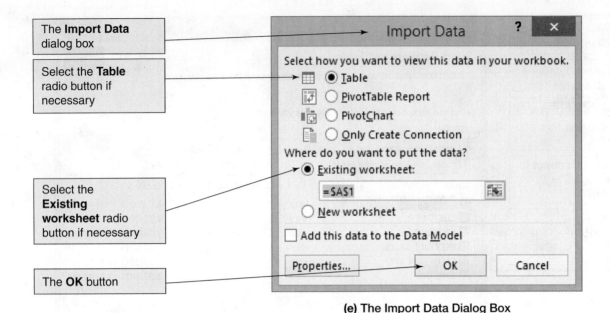

(e) The Import Data Dialog Box

The **TABLE TOOLS** contextual command tab

The **INSERT** command tab

The **ANALYZE** command tab

The HSD_DW database data is now in the worksheet

Name the worksheet **HSDDWProductSalesView**

(f) The HSDDWProductSalesView Data in the Worksheet

FIGURE 12-21

Continued

To connect to the HSD_DW data, we click the **Get External Data** drop-down gallery arrow button on the DATA command tab. As shown in Figure 12-21(a), this displays the Get External Data gallery. Here we click the **From Other Sources** button, which gives us a list of data sources that includes SQL Server.

Clicking the **From SQL Server** button starts the **Data Connection Wizard** shown in Figure 12-21(b). In the **Connect to Database Server** page of the wizard, we select the SQL Server we want to use and ours means of authentication and then click the **Next** button.

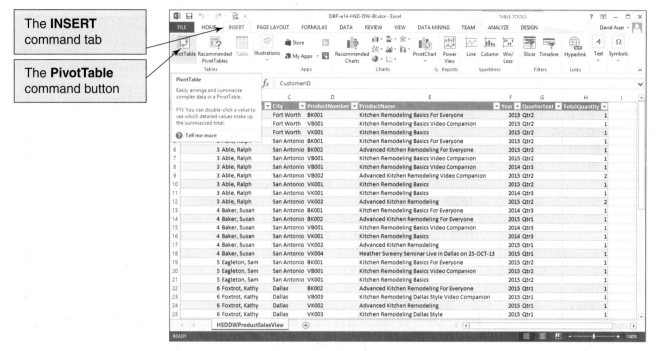

The **INSERT** command tab

The **PivotTable** command button

(g) The PivotTable Command

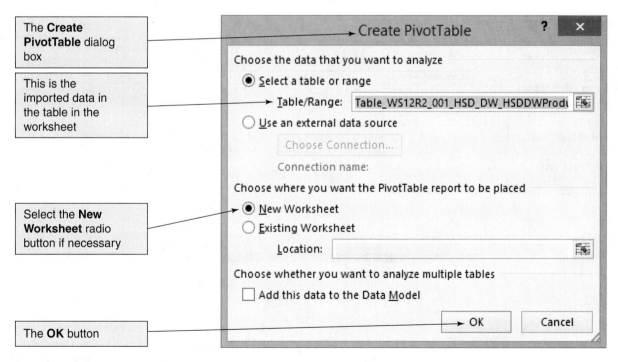

The **Create PivotTable** dialog box

This is the imported data in the table in the worksheet

Select the **New Worksheet** radio button if necessary

The **OK** button

(h) The Create Pivot Table Dialog Box

FIGURE 12-21

Continued

(continued)

The **PivotTable Fields List** pane—select the report elements to be displayed here

The **PivotTable** report area—the Pivot Table will be displayed in this area, which can be extended as necessary to accommodate the PivotTable

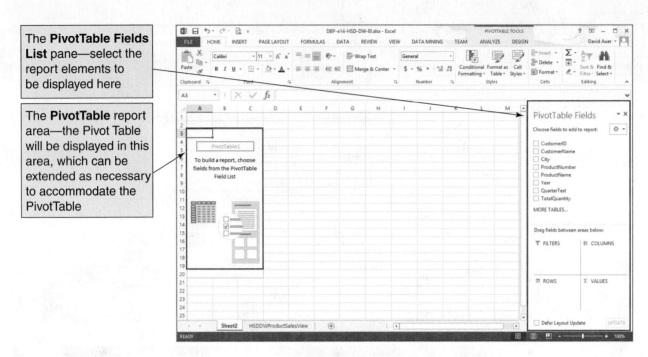

(i) The PivotTable in the New Worksheet

The **PivotTable Field List** pane—the elements have been selected and are now displayed here

The **PivotTable** report

The PivotTable worksheet has been named the **HSD-DW-BI-Pivot-Table**

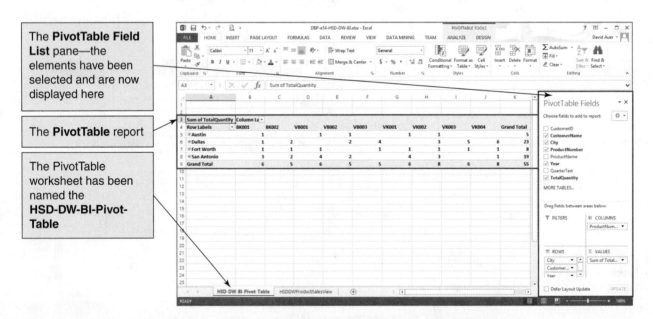

(j) The ProductNumber by City OLAP Report

FIGURE 12-21

Continued

> **BY THE WAY**   If the Microsoft SQL Server 2014 instance is on your local machine (your own computer) and is installed as the default (unnamed) instance, type in only your computer name. For example, WS12-001 in Figure 12-21(b) is our computer, and we have installed Microsoft SQL Server 2014 on it as a default instance; we simply type in WS12-001.
>
> If you are connecting to a non-default, named instance of Microsoft SQL Server 2014, type in both the computer name and the SQL Server 2014 instance name. For example, if we installed an additional version of Microsoft SQL Server 2014 such as SQL Server 2014 Express Advanced on our computer, we would type in WS12-001\ SQLEXPRESS to connect to this named instance.

As shown in Figure 12-21(c), in the **Select Database and Table** page of the wizard, we select the **HSD_DW** database and **HSDDWProductSalesView** as the source of our data–note how useful the SQL-CREATE-VIEW-CH12-01 statement and the resulting HSDDWProductSalesView view are in making it easy to get exactly the data we want for the PivotTable. After selecting the database and view, we click the **Next** button to display the **Save Data Connection File and Finish** wizard page as shown in Figure 12-21(d). This step simply saves the data connection we have created for future use, and there is nothing we need to do on this page, so we click the **Finish** button.

As shown in Figure 12-21(e), the **Import Data** dialog box is displayed. Because we want to store our data in a worksheet in our Microsoft Excel workbook *before* we create the PivotTable, the correct selections are shown here. Click the **OK** button.

In Figure 12-21(f), we see the data formatted as a table in the worksheet, which we now name as **HSSDWProductSalesView**. Microsoft Excel has opened the ANALYZE command tab in the TABLE TOOL contextual command tab, but we actually need the INSERT command tab at this point. Click the INSERT command tab to display the commands on the INSERT command tab as shown in Figure 12-21(g).

On the INSERT command tab, click the **PivotTable** button. The **Create Pivot Table** dialog box is displayed, as shown in Figure 12-21(h). The correct table range is selected, and we select the New Worksheet radio button because we want the PivotTable in a new, separate worksheet. Click the **OK** button to create the PivotTable structure, as shown in Figure 12-21(i). Selecting the appropriate fields in the **PivotTable Fields** pane then creates the PivotTable itself, as seen in Figure 12-21(j).

In Figure 12-21(j), the measure is quantity sold, and the dimensions are ProductNumber and City. This report shows how quantity varies by product and city. For example, four copies of VB003 (Kitchen Remodeling Dallas Style Video Companion) were sold in Dallas, but none were sold in Austin.

We generated the OLAP report in Figure 12-21(j) by using a simple SQL query (run using the Microsoft PowerPivot for Microsoft Excel add-in) and Microsoft Excel, but many DBMS and BI products include more powerful and sophisticated tools. For example, Microsoft SQL Server 2014 includes SQL Server Analysis Services.[4] It is possible to display OLAP cubes in many ways besides with Excel. Some third-party vendors provide more sophisticated graphical displays, and OLAP reports can be delivered just like any of the other reports described for report management systems.

The distinguishing characteristic of an OLAP report is that the user can alter the format of the report. Figure 12-22 shows an alteration in which the user added two additional dimensions, customer and year, to the horizontal display. Quantity sold is now broken out by customer and, in one case, by year. With an OLAP report, it is possible to **drill down** into the data–that is, to further divide the data into more detail. In Figure 12-22, for example, the user has drilled down into the San Antonio data to display all customer data for that city and to display year sales data for Ralph Able.

In an OLAP report, it is also possible to change the order of the dimensions. Figure 12-23 shows city quantities as vertical data and ProductID quantities as horizontal data. This OLAP report shows quantity sold by city and by product, customer, and year.

Both displays are valid and useful, depending on the user's perspective. A product manager might like to see product families first (ProductID) and then location data (city). A sales manager might like to see location data first and then product data. OLAP reports provide both perspectives, and the user can switch between them while viewing a report.

Unfortunately, all of this flexibility comes at a cost. If the database is large, doing the necessary calculating, grouping, and sorting for such dynamic displays will require substantial

---

[4]Up to this point in this book, we have been able to do everything in this book using Microsoft SQL Server 2014 Express Edition. Unfortunately, Microsoft SQL Server 2014 Express Edition does not include SQL Server Analysis Services, so you will have to use the Microsoft SQL Server 2014 Standard Edition or better if you want to use the SQL Server Analysis Services. Although OLAP reports *can* be done without SQL Server Analysis Services, Server Analysis Services adds a lot of functionality, and the Microsoft SQL Server 2012 SP1 Data Mining Add-ins for Microsoft Office (used in this text) will not function without it.

FIGURE 12-22

OLAP ProductNumber by City, Customer, and Year Report

The City = San Antonio data are also showing customer data

The Customer = Able, Ralph data are also showing year data

Sum of TotalQuantity	Column La...									
Row Labels	BK001	BK002	VB001	VB002	VB003	VK001	VK002	VK003	VK004	Grand Total
Austin	1		1	1			1	1		5
Pearson, Bobbi	1		1	1			1	1		5
Dallas	1	2		2	4		3	5	6	23
Foxtrot, Kathy		1			1		1	1	1	5
George, Sally	1	1						1	2	5
Hullett, Shawn					1			1	1	3
Tyler, Jenny				2	2		2	2	2	10
Fort Worth	1	1	1		1	1	1	1	1	8
Jacobs, Nancy	1		1			1				3
Wayne, Joan		1		1			1	1	1	5
San Antonio	3	2	4	2		4	3		1	19
Able, Ralph	1	1	2	2		2	2			10
2014			1			1				2
2015	1	1	1	2		1	2			8
Baker, Susan	1	1	1			1	1		1	6
Eagleton, Sam	1		1			1				3
Grand Total	6	5	6	5	5	6	8	6	8	55

computing power. Although standard, commercial DBMS products do have the features and functions required to create OLAP reports, they are not designed for such work. They are designed to provide rapid response to transaction processing applications, such as those for order entry or manufacturing planning.

Accordingly, special-purpose products called **OLAP servers** have been developed to perform OLAP analyses. As shown in Figure 12-24, an OLAP server reads data from an operational database, performs preliminary calculations, and stores the results of those calculations in an OLAP database. For performance and security reasons, the OLAP server and the DBMS usually run on separate computers. The OLAP server would normally be located in the data warehouse or a data mart.

FIGURE 12-23

OLAP City by ProductNumber, Customer, and Year Report

The city variable is on the column designator

The ProductID variable is on the primary row designator

The ProductID = VB001 data are also showing **Customer** data

The Customer = Able, Ralph data are also showing year data

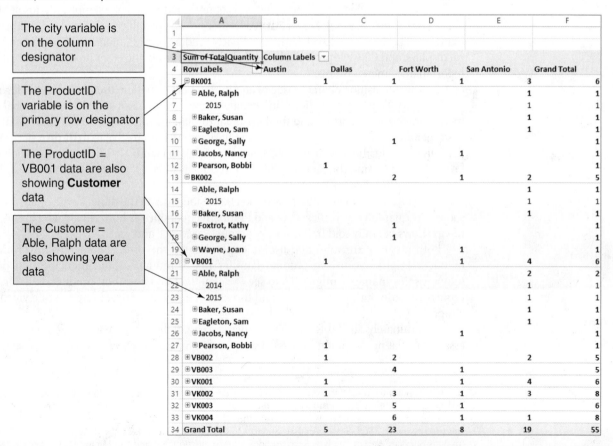

Sum of TotalQuantity	Column Labels				
Row Labels	Austin	Dallas	Fort Worth	San Antonio	Grand Total
BK001	1	1	1	3	6
Able, Ralph				1	1
2015				1	1
Baker, Susan				1	1
Eagleton, Sam				1	1
George, Sally		1			1
Jacobs, Nancy			1		1
Pearson, Bobbi	1				1
BK002		2	1	2	5
Able, Ralph				1	1
2015				1	1
Baker, Susan				1	1
Foxtrot, Kathy		1			1
George, Sally		1			1
Wayne, Joan			1		1
VB001	1		1	4	6
Able, Ralph				2	2
2014				1	1
2015				1	1
Baker, Susan				1	1
Eagleton, Sam				1	1
Jacobs, Nancy			1		1
Pearson, Bobbi	1				1
VB002	1	2		2	5
VB003		4	1		5
VK001	1		1	4	6
VK002	1	3	1	3	8
VK003		5	1		6
VK004		6	1	1	8
Grand Total	5	23	8	19	55

FIGURE 12-24

Role of the OLAP Server
and OLAP Database

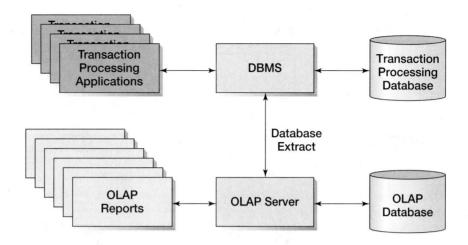

Data Mining

Instead of the basic calculations, filtering, sorting, and grouping used in reporting applications, data mining involves the application of sophisticated mathematical and statistical techniques to find patterns and relationships that can be used to classify data and predict future outcomes. As shown in Figure 12-25, data mining represents the convergence of several phenomena. Data mining techniques have emerged from the statistical and mathematics disciplines and from the artificial intelligence and machine-learning communities. In fact, data mining terminology is an odd combination of terms used by these different disciplines.

Data mining techniques take advantage of developments for processing enormous databases that have emerged in the past dozen or so years. Of course, all these data would not have been generated were it not for fast and inexpensive computers, and without such computers, the new techniques would be impossible to compute.

Most data mining techniques are sophisticated and difficult to use. However, such techniques are valuable to organizations, and some business professionals, especially those in finance and marketing, have developed expertise in their use. Almost all data mining techniques require specialized software. Popular data mining products are Enterprise Miner from SAS Corporation, SPSS Modeler from IBM, and Insightful Miner from Insightful Corporation.

FIGURE 12-25

Convergence of Disciplines
for Data Mining

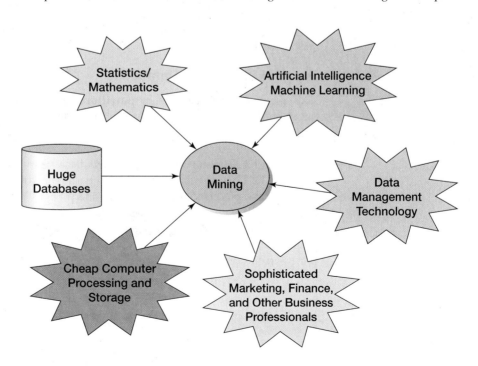

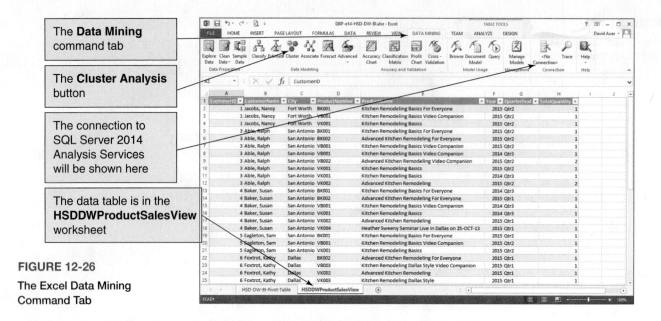

The **Data Mining** command tab

The **Cluster Analysis** button

The connection to SQL Server 2014 Analysis Services will be shown here

The data table is in the **HSDDWProductSalesView** worksheet

FIGURE 12-26

The Excel Data Mining Command Tab

However, there is a movement to make data mining available to more users. For example, Microsoft has created the Microsoft SQL Server 2012 SP1 Data Mining Add-ins for Microsoft Office—this package runs with both Microsoft Office 2010 and Microsoft Office 2013.[5] Figure 12-26 shows Microsoft Excel 2013 with the Data Mining command tab and command groups. With this add-in, data stored in Microsoft Excel are sent to SQL Server Analysis Services for processing, and the results are returned to Microsoft Excel for display.

Distributed Database Processing

One of the first solutions to increase the amount of data that could be stored by a DBMS system was to simply spread the data among several database servers instead of just one. A group of associated servers are known as a **server cluster**,[6] and the database shared between them is called a distributed database. A **distributed database** is a database that is stored and processed on more than one computer. Depending on the type of database and the processing that is allowed, distributed databases can present significant problems. Let us consider the types of distributed databases.

Types of Distributed Databases

A database can be distributed by **partitioning**, which means breaking the database into pieces and storing the pieces on multiple computers; by **replication**, which means storing copies of the database on multiple computers; or by a combination of replication and partitioning. Figure 12-27 illustrates these alternatives.

Figure 12-27(a) shows a nondistributed database with four pieces labeled W, X, Y, and Z. In Figure 12-27(b), the database has been partitioned but not replicated. Portions W and X are stored and processed on Computer 1, and portions Y and Z are stored and processed on Computer 2. Figure 12-27(c) shows a database that has been replicated but not partitioned. The entire database is stored and processed on Computers 1 and 2. Finally, Figure 12-27(d) shows a database that is partitioned and replicated. Portion Y of the database is stored and processed on Computers 1 and 2.

---

[5]For more information and to download the Microsoft SQL Server 2012 SP1 Data Mining Add-ins for Microsoft Office package, go to *www.microsoft.com/en-us/download/details.aspx?id=35578*. Note, however, that these add-ins will not work with Microsoft SQL Server 2014 Express Edition—you have to have a version of SQL Server with SQL Server Analysis Services.

[6]For more information on computer clusters, see the Wikipedia article at *http://en.wikipedia.org/wiki/Server_cluster*.

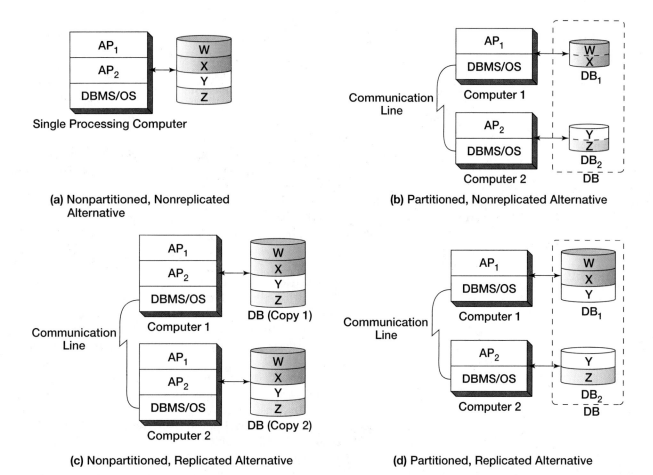

(a) Nonpartitioned, Nonreplicated Alternative

(b) Partitioned, Nonreplicated Alternative

(c) Nonpartitioned, Replicated Alternative

(d) Partitioned, Replicated Alternative

FIGURE 12-27

Types of Distributed Databases

The portions to be partitioned or replicated can be defined in many different ways. A database that has five tables (for example, CUSTOMER, SALESPERSON, INVOICE, LINE_ITEM, and PART) could be partitioned by assigning CUSTOMER to portion W, SALESPERSON to portion X, INVOICE and LINE_ITEM to portion Y, and PART to portion Z. Alternatively, different rows of each of these five tables could be assigned to different computers, or different columns of each of these tables could be assigned to different computers.

Databases are distributed for two major reasons: performance and control. Having a database on multiple computers can improve throughput, either because multiple computers are sharing the workload or because communications delays can be reduced by placing the partitions closer to their users. Distributing the database can improve control by segregating different portions of the database to different computers, each of which can have its own set of authorized users and permissions.

Challenges of Distributed Databases

Significant challenges must be overcome when distributing a database, and those challenges depend on the type of distributed database and the activity that is allowed. In the case of a fully replicated database, if only one computer is allowed to make updates on one of the copies, then the challenges are not too great. All update activity occurs on that single computer, and copies of that database are periodically sent to the replication sites. The challenge is to ensure that only a logically consistent copy of the database is distributed (no partial or uncommitted transactions, for example) and to ensure that the sites understand that they are processing data that might not be current because changes could have been made to the updated database after the local copy was made.

If multiple computers can make updates to a replicated database, then difficult problems arise. Specifically, if two computers are allowed to process the same row at the same time, they can cause three types of error: They can make inconsistent changes, one computer can delete a row that another computer is updating, or the two computers can make changes that violate uniqueness constraints.

To prevent these problems, some type of record locking is required. Because multiple computers are involved, standard record locking does not work. Instead, a far more complicated locking scheme, called **distributed two-phase locking**, must be used. The specifics of the scheme are beyond the scope of this discussion; for now, just know that implementing this algorithm is difficult and expensive. If multiple computers can process multiple replicas of a distributed database, then significant problems must be solved.

If the database is partitioned but not replicated [Figure 12-27(b)], then problems will occur if any transaction updates data that span two or more distributed partitions. For example, suppose the CUSTOMER and SALESPERSON tables are placed on a partition on one computer and that INVOICE, LINE_ITEM, and PART tables are placed on a second computer. Further suppose that when recording a sale all five tables are updated in an atomic transaction. In this case, a transaction must be started on both computers, and it can be allowed to commit on one computer only if it can be allowed to commit on both computers. In this case, distributed two-phase locking also must be used.

If the data are partitioned in such a way that no transaction requires data from both partitions, then regular locking will work. However, in this case, the databases are actually two separate databases, and some would argue that they should not be considered a distributed database.

If the data are partitioned in such a way that no transaction updates data from both partitions but that one or more transactions read data from one partition and update data on a second partition, then problems might or might not result with regular locking. If dirty reads are possible, then some form of distributed locking is required; otherwise, regular locking should work.

If a database is partitioned and at least one of those partitions is replicated, then locking requirements are a combination of those just described. If the replicated portion is updated, if transactions span the partitions, or if dirty reads are possible, then distributed two-phase locking is required; otherwise, regular locking might suffice.

Distributed processing is complicated and can create substantial problems. Except in the case of replicated, read-only databases, only experienced teams with a substantial budget and significant time to invest should attempt distributed databases. Such databases also require data communications expertise. Distributed databases are not for the faint of heart.

Object-Relational Databases

Object-oriented programming (OOP) is a technique for designing and writing computer programs. Today, most new program development is done using OOP techniques. Java, C++, C#, and Visual Basic.NET are object-oriented programming languages.

Objects are data structures that have both **methods**, which are computer programs that perform some task, and **properties**, which are data items particular to an object. All objects of a given class have the same methods, but each has its own set of values for its data items. When using OOP, the properties of the object are created and stored in main memory. Storing the values of properties of an object permanently is called **object persistence**. Many different techniques have been used for object persistence. One of them is to use some variation of database technology.

Although relational databases can be used for object persistence, using this method requires substantial work on the part of the programmer. The problem is that, in general, object data structures are more complicated than the rows of a table. Typically, several, or even many, rows of several different tables are required to store object data. This means the OOP programmer must design a mini-database just to store objects. Usually, many objects are involved in an information system, so many different mini-databases need to be designed and processed. This method is so undesirable that it is seldom used.

In the early 1990s, several vendors developed special-purpose DBMS products for storing object data. These products, which were called **object-oriented DBMSs (OODBMSs)**, never achieved commercial success. The problem was that by the time they were introduced, billions of bytes of data were already stored in relational DBMS format, and no organization wanted to convert its data to OODBMS format to be able to use an OODBMS. Consequently, such products failed in the marketplace.

However, the need for object persistence did not disappear. Some vendors, most notably Oracle Corporation, added features and functions to their relational DBMS products to create **object-relational databases**. These features and functions are basically add-ons to a relational DBMS that facilitate object persistence. With these features, object data can be stored more readily than with a purely relational database. However, an object-relational database can still process relational data at the same time.[7]

Although OODBMSs have not achieved commercial success, OOP is here to stay, and modern programming languages are object-based. This is important because these are the programming languages that are being used to create the latest technologies that are dealing with Big Data.

Virtualization

One major development in computing occurred when systems administrators realized that the hardware resources (CPU, memory, input/output from/to disk storage) were very underutilized. For example, as shown in Figure 12-28, most of the time the CPU is not busy, and there may be a lot of available memory not being used by the CPU for application processing.

This realization led to the idea of sharing the hardware resources with more than one computer. But how could that possibly be done—how can more than one computer share hardware resources?

The answer was to have one physical computer host one or more **virtual computers**, more commonly known as **virtual machines**. To do this, the actual computer hardware, now called the **host machine**, runs an application program known as a **virtual machine manager** or **hypervisor**. The hypervisor creates and manages the virtual machines and controls the interaction between the virtual machine and the physical hardware.[8] For example, if a virtual machine has been allocated two Gigabytes of main memory for its use, the hypervisor is responsible for making sure the actual physical memory is allocated and available to the virtual machine.

Although there are many variants on exactly how virtual machines are implemented,[9] Figure 12-29 illustrates two standard generic physical/virtual machine setups. Figure 12-29(a) shows the situation where the host machine is *not* dedicated solely to hosting virtual machines

FIGURE 12-28

The Underutilization of Computer Resources

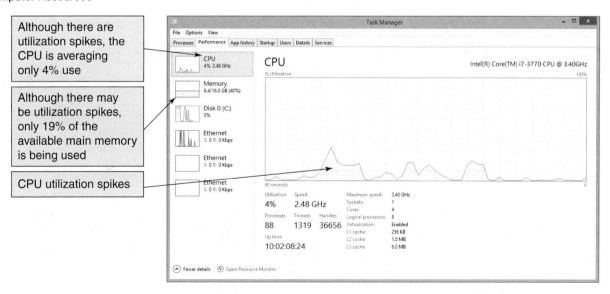

Although there are utilization spikes, the CPU is averaging only 4% use

Although there may be utilization spikes, only 19% of the available main memory is being used

CPU utilization spikes

---

[7]To learn more about object-relational databases, see the Wikipedia article at *http://en.wikipedia.org/wiki/Object-relational_database*.

[8]For more information on computer virtualization, see the Wikipedia article on virtualization at *http://en.wikipedia.org/wiki/Virtualization*.

[9]See the Wikipedia article on comparison of platform virtual machines at *http://en.wikipedia.org/wiki/Comparison_of_platform_virtual_machines*

FIGURE 12-29

The Virtual Machine
Environment

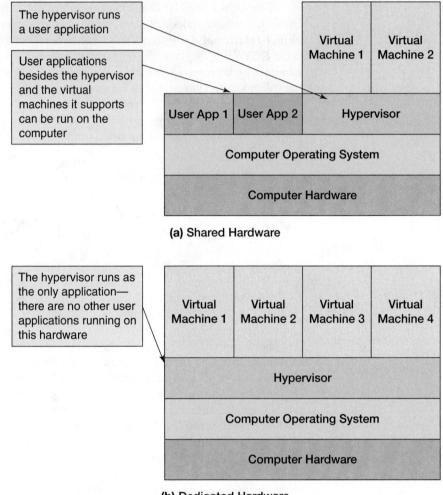

The hypervisor runs
a user application

User applications
besides the hypervisor
and the virtual
machines it supports
can be run on the
computer

Virtual
Machine 1

Virtual
Machine 2

User App 1 | User App 2 | Hypervisor

Computer Operating System

Computer Hardware

(a) Shared Hardware

The hypervisor runs as
the only application—
there are no other user
applications running on
this hardware

Virtual
Machine 1

Virtual
Machine 2

Virtual
Machine 3

Virtual
Machine 4

Hypervisor

Computer Operating System

Computer Hardware

(b) Dedicated Hardware

but also runs other user applications. This is typical of a desktop computer where the user wants to use, for example, a spreadsheet application (such as Microsoft Excel 2013) and a word processing application (such as Microsoft Word 2013) while being able to host virtual machines at the same time. This can be done using a product such as VMware Workstation (see *www.vmware.com/products/workstation/overview.html*), which is available for the Windows and Linux operating systems.

Figure 12-29(b) shows the situation where the host machine *is* dedicated to hosting virtual machines but does not run other user applications. This is typical of network servers where the goal is to maximize overall utilization of the hardware resources by sharing them among many servers but there are no users running applications on the host machine.

One of the advantages of virtual machines is that in many products you can run various operating systems in different virtual machines and none of them has to be the same operating system that is running on the underlying hardware and supporting the hypervisor. Thus, a desktop running Microsoft Windows 8.1 can run the Linux and FreeBSD operating systems in virtual machines. Figure 12-30 shows a desktop computer running Microsoft Windows 8.1 supporting a virtual machine running the Microsoft Server 2012 R2 operating system. This virtual machine has Microsoft SQL Server 2014 installed and is, in fact, one of the virtual machines that we used to obtain all the SQL Server 2014 screenshots.

Cloud Computing

For many years, systems administrators and database administrators knew exactly where their servers (physical or virtual) were located—in a dedicated, secure machine room on the company premises. With the advent of the Internet, companies started offering hosting services

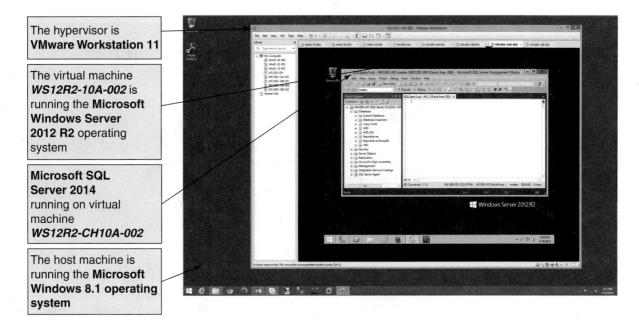

The hypervisor is **VMware Workstation 11**

The virtual machine ***WS12R2-10A-002*** is running the **Microsoft Windows Server 2012 R2** operating system

Microsoft SQL Server 2014 running on virtual machine ***WS12R2-CH10A-002***

The host machine is running the **Microsoft Windows 8.1 operating system**

FIGURE 12-30

SQL Server 2014 Running in a Microsoft Windows Server 2012 R2 Virtual Machine

on servers (physical or virtual) that were located somewhere else—in a location (sometimes known but sometimes unknown) away from the company premises. And as long as these hosting companies provide the services we want (and at a price we want to pay), we really don't care about exactly where the hosting servers are located.

This configuration of servers and services hosted for us over the Internet is known as **cloud computing**. As shown in Figure 12-31, our Internet customer sees us by our presentation at our company Web site and related e-commerce services on the Internet at *www.ourcompany.com*. They don't care whether the servers that provide the services they want (being able to see and buy the latest versions of our *Class A Widget*) are located physically at our company or somewhere else "in the cloud" as long as those services are available to them and work reliably.

Hosting services in the cloud has become an established and lucrative business. Hosting companies range from Web site hosting companies such as eNom and Yahoo! Small Business to companies that offer complete business support packages such as Microsoft Office 365 and Google Business Solutions to companies that make various components such as complete virtual servers, file storage, DBMS services, and much more.

In this last category, significant players include Microsoft with **Windows Azure** (*http://azure.microsoft.com/en-us/*) and Amazon.com with **Amazon Web Services (AWS)** (*http://aws.amazon.com/*). Of course, there are others, but these two provide a good starting point. Windows Azure, like any Microsoft product, is Microsoft centric and not currently as expansive in its product offerings as AWS.

Of particular interest in AWS are the **EC2 service**, which provides complete virtual servers, the **DynamoDB database service**, which provides a NoSQL data store (discussed later in this chapter), and the **RDS (Relational DBMS Service)**, which provides online instances of Microsoft SQL Server, Oracle Database, and MySQL database services.

At this point, we will use RDS to illustrate how we can use online database services similar to what we have been doing in this book. We have created one RDS instance of SQL Server Express (it is actually SQL Server 2014 Express) named *kamssqlex01*. Although hosted by AWS, if we connect to this DB instance with normal SQL Server management tools, it will appear to us just like any other SQL Server instance we are running.

Figure 12-32 illustrates this by showing the kamssqlex01 database instance in the Microsoft SQL Server Management Studio. We have created and populated the VRG database discussed in Chapter 7 and Chapter 10A and have run an example query against the database. Everything we see here is exactly the same as if the database was located on our own desktop computer or local database server. This shows how easy it is to set up computing resources hosted "in the cloud," and there is no doubt that we will see more and more use of cloud computing.

FIGURE 12-31

The Cloud Computing
Environment

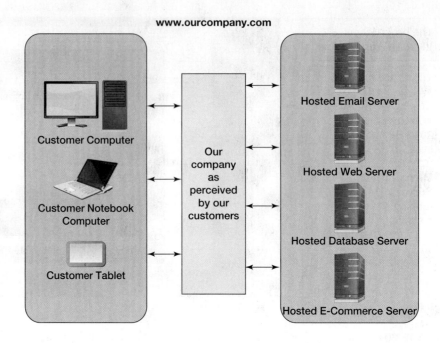

Big Data and the Not Only SQL Movement

We have used the relational database model and SQL throughout this book. However, there is another school of thought that has led to what was originally known as the **NoSQL** movement but now is usually referred as the **Not only SQL** movement.[10] It has been noted that most, but not all, DBMSs associated with the NoSQL movement are nonrelational DBMSs.[11]

A NoSQL DBMS is often a distributed, replicated database, as described earlier in this chapter, and used where this type of a DBMS is needed to support large datasets. There have been several classification systems proposed for grouping and classifying NoSQL databases. For our purposes, we will adopt and use a set of four categories of NoSQL databases:[12]

- **key-value**–examples are **Dynamo** and **MemcacheDB**
- **document**–examples are **Couchbase** and **MongoDB**
- **column family**–examples are Apache **Cassandra** and **HBase**
- **graph**–examples are **Neo4J** and **AllegroGraph**

NoSQL databases are used by widely recognized Web applications–both Facebook and Twitter use the Apache Software Foundation's Cassandra database. In this chapter, we discuss column family databases, and we discuss the other three types in Appendix K–*Big Data*.

Column Family Databases

The basis for much of the development of column family databases was a structured storage mechanism developed by Google named **Bigtable**, and column family databases are now widely available, with a good example being the Apache Software Foundation's Cassandra project. Facebook did the original development work on Cassandra and then turned it over to the open source development community in 2008.

A generalized column family database storage system is shown in Figure 12-33. The structured storage equivalent of a relational DBMS (RDBMS) table has a very different construction. Although similar terms are used, they do *not mean* the same thing that they mean in a relational DBMS.

---

[10]For a good overview, see the Wikipedia article on *NoSQL* available at *http://en.wikipedia.org/wiki/NoSQL*.
[11]See the Wikipedia article on *NoSQL* at *http://en.wikipedia.org/wiki/NoSQL*.
[12]Wikipedia article on *NoSQL* (accessed February 22, 2015).

The **kamssqlex01** DB instance is Microsoft SQL Server 2014 Express at AWS

The **VRG** database showing the tables

An example SQL query and results

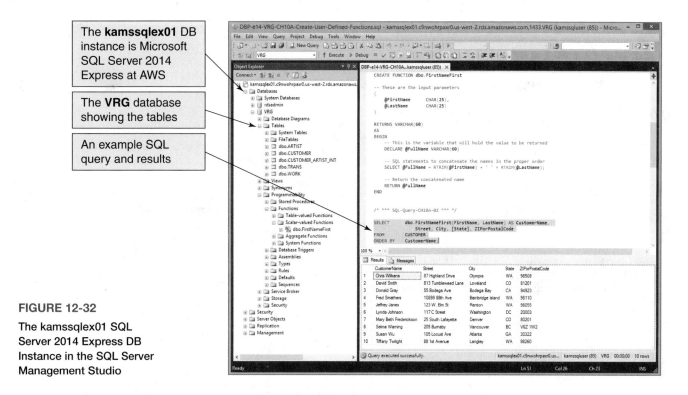

FIGURE 12-32

The kamssqlex01 SQL Server 2014 Express DB Instance in the SQL Server Management Studio

The smallest unit of storage is called a *column*, but it is really the equivalent of an RDBMS table cell (the intersection of an RDBMS row and column). A column consists of three elements: the *column name*, the *column value* or datum, and a *timestamp* to record when the value was stored in the column. This is shown in Figure 12-33(a) by the LastName column, which stores the LastName value Able.

Columns can be grouped into sets referred to as *super columns*. This is shown in Figure 12-33(b) by the CustomerName super column, which consists of a FirstName column and a LastName column and which stores the CustomerName value Ralph Able.

Columns and super columns are grouped to create *column families*, which are the structured storage equivalent of RDBMS tables. In a column family, we have rows of grouped columns, and each row has a RowKey, which is similar to the primary key used in an RDBMS table. However, unlike an RDBMS table, a row in a column family does not have to have the same number of columns as another row in the same column

FIGURE 12-33

A Generalized Structured Storage System

Name: LastName
Value: Able
Timestamp: 40324081235

(a) A Column

Super Column Name:	CustomerName	
Super Column Values:	Name: FirstName	Name: LastName
	Value: Ralph	Value: Able
	Timestamp: 40324081235	Timestamp: 40324081235

(b) A Super Column

(continued)

Column Family Name:	Customer			
RowKey001	Name: FirstName Value: Ralph Timestamp: 40324081235	Name: LastName Value: Able Timestamp: 40324081235		
RowKey002	Name: FirstName Value: Nancy Timestamp: 40335091055	Name: LastName Value: Jacobs Timestamp: 40335091055	Name: Phone Value: 817-871-8123 Timestamp: 40335091055	Name: City Value: Fort Worth Timestamp: 40335091055
RowKey003	Name: LastName Value: Baker Timestamp: 40340103518	Name: EmailAddress Value: Susan.Baker@elsewhere.com Timestamp: 40340103518		

(c) A Column Family

Super Column Family Name:	Customer			
Rowkey001	Customer Name		CustomerPhone	
	Name: FirstName Value: Ralph Timestamp: 40324081235	Name: LastName Value: Able Timestamp: 40324081235	Name: Areacode Value: 210 Timestamp: 40335091055	Name: PhoneNumber Value: 281–7987 Timestamp: 40335091055
Rowkey002	Customer Name		Customer Phone	
	Name: FirstName Value: Nancy Timestamp: 40335091055	Name: LastName Value: Jacobs Timestamp: 40335091055	Name: Areacode Value: 817 Timestamp: 40335091055	Name: PhoneNumber Value: 871–8123 Timestamp: 40335091055
Rowkey003	Customer Name		Customer Phone	
	Name: FirstName Value: Susan Timestamp: 40340103518	Name: LastName Value: Baker Timestamp: 40340103518	Name: Areacode Value: 210 Timestamp: 40340103518	Name: PhoneNumber Value: 281–7876 Timestamp: 40340103518

(d) A Super Column Family

FIGURE 12-33

Continued

family. This is illustrated in Figure 12-33(c) by the Customer column family, which consists of three rows of data on customers.

Figure 12-33(c) clearly illustrates the difference between structured storage column families and RDBMS tables: Column families can have variable columns and data stored in each row in a way that is impossible in an RDBMS table. This storage column structure is definitely *not* in 1NF as defined in Chapter 2, let alone BCNF! For example, note that the first row has no Phone or City columns, while the third row not only has no FirstName, Phone, or City columns but also contains an EmailAddress column that does not exist in the other rows.

Finally, all the column families are contained in a *keyspace*, which provides the set of RowKey values that can be used in the data store. RowKey values from the keyspace are shown being used in Figure 12-33(c) to identify each row in a column family. While this structure may seem odd at first, in practice it allows for great flexibility because columns to contain new data may be introduced at any time without modifying an existing table structure.

As shown in Figure 12-33(d), a **super column family** is similar to a column family but uses super columns (or a combination of columns and super columns) instead of columns. Of course, there is more to column family database storage than discussed here, but now you should have an understanding of the basic principles of column family databases.

MapReduce

While structured storage provides the means to store data in a Big Data system, the data themselves are often analyzed using the **MapReduce** process. Because Big Data involve extremely large datasets, it is difficult for one computer to process data by itself. Therefore, a set of clustered computers are used with a distributed processing system similar to the distributed database system discussed previously in this chapter.

The MapReduce process is used to break a large analytical task into smaller tasks, assign each smaller task to a separate computer in the cluster, gather the results of each of those tasks, and combine them into the final product of the original tasks. The term *Map* refers to the work done on each individual computer, and the term *Reduce* refers to combining the individual results into the final result.

A commonly used example of the MapReduce process is counting how many times each word is used in a document. This is illustrated in Figure 12-34, where we can see how the original document is broken into sections and then each section is passed to a separate computer in the cluster for processing by the Map process. The output from each of the Map processes is then passed to one computer, which uses the Reduce process to combine the results from each Map process into the final output, which is the list of words and how many times each appears in the document. Most NoSQL database systems support MapReduce and other, similar processes.

FIGURE 12-34

MapReduce

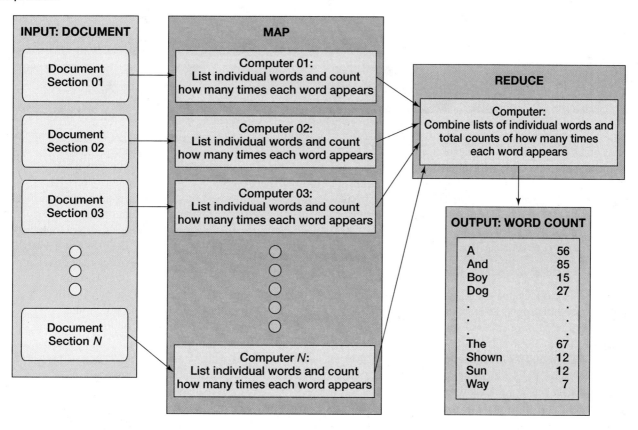

Hadoop

Another Apache Software Foundation project that is becoming a fundamental Big Data development platform is the **Hadoop Distributed File System (HDFS)**, which provides standard file services to clustered servers so their file systems can function as one distributed file system. Hadoop originated as part of Cassandra, but the Hadoop project has spun off a nonrelational data store of its own called **HBase** and a query language named **Pig**.

Further, all the major DBMS players are supporting Hadoop. Microsoft is planning a Microsoft Hadoop distribution and has teamed up with HP and Dell to offer the **SQL Server Parallel Data Warehouse**. Oracle Corporation has developed the **Oracle Big Data Appliance** that uses Hadoop. A search of the Web on the term "MySQL Hadoop" quickly reveals that a lot is being done by the MySQL team as well.

The usefulness and importance of these Big Data products to organizations such as Facebook demonstrate that we can look forward to the development of not only improvements to the relational DBMSs but also a very different approach to data storage and information processing. Big Data and products associated with Big Data are rapidly changing and evolving, and you should expect many developments in this area in the near future.

BY THE WAY   The NoSQL world is an exciting one, but you should be aware that, if you want to participate in it, you will need to sharpen your OOP programming skills. Whereas we can develop databases in Microsoft Access, Microsoft SQL Server, Oracle Database, and MySQL using management and applications development tools that are very user friendly (Microsoft Access itself, Microsoft SQL Server Management Studio, Oracle SQL Developer, and MySQL Workbench), application development in the NoSQL world is currently done in programming languages.

This, of course, may change, and we look forward to seeing the future developments in the NoSQL realm. For now, you'll need to sign up for that programming course!

Summary

Business intelligence (BI) systems assist managers and other professionals in the analysis of current and past activities and in the prediction of future events. BI applications are of two major types: reporting applications and data mining applications. Reporting applications make elementary calculations on data; data mining applications use sophisticated mathematical and statistical techniques.

BI applications obtain data from three sources: operational databases, extracts of operational databases, and purchased data. BI systems sometimes have their own DBMS, which may or may not be the operational DBMS. Characteristics of reporting and data mining applications are listed in Figure 12-3.

Direct reading of operational databases is not feasible for all but the smallest and simplest BI applications and databases for several reasons. Querying operational data can unacceptably slow the performance of operational systems, operational data have problems that limit their usefulness for BI applications, and BI system creation and maintenance require programs, facilities, and expertise that are normally not available for an operational database.

Problems with operational data are listed in Figure 12-5. Because of these, many organizations have chosen to create and staff data warehouses and data marts. Data warehouses extract and clean operational data and store the revised data in data warehouse databases. Organizations may also purchase and manage data obtained from data vendors. Data warehouses maintain metadata that describes the source, format, assumptions, and constraints about the data they contain. A data mart is a collection of data that is smaller than that held in a data warehouse and that addresses a particular component or functional area of the business. In Figure 12-7, the data warehouse distributes data to three smaller data marts. Each data mart services the needs of a different aspect of the business.

Operational databases and dimensional databases have different characteristics, as shown in Figure 12-8. Dimensional databases use a star schema with a fully normalized fact table that connects to dimension tables that may be non-normalized. Dimensional databases must deal with slowly changing dimensions, and therefore a time dimension is important in a dimensional database. Fact tables hold measures of interest, and dimension tables hold attribute values used in queries. The star schema can be extended with additional fact tables, dimension tables, and conformed dimensions.

The purpose of a reporting system is to create meaningful information from disparate data sources and to deliver that information to the proper users on a timely basis. Reports are produced by sorting, filtering, grouping, and making simple calculations on the data. RFM analysis is a typical reporting application. Customers are grouped and classified according to how recently they have placed an order (R), how frequently they order (F), and how much money (M) they spend on orders. The result of an RFM analysis is three scores. In a typical analysis, the scores range from 1 to 5. An RFM score of $\{1\ 1\ 4\}$ indicates that the customer has purchased recently and purchases frequently but does not purchase large-dollar items.

Online analytical processing (OLAP) is a generic category of reporting applications that enable users to dynamically restructure reports. A measure is the data item of interest. A dimension is a characteristic of a measure. An OLAP cube is an arrangement of measures and dimensions. With OLAP, users can drill down and change the order of dimensions. Because of the high processing requirements, some organizations designate separate computers to function as OLAP servers.

Data mining is the application of mathematical and statistical techniques to find patterns and relationships and to classify and predict. Data mining has arisen in recent years because of the confluence of factors shown in Figure 12-25.

A distributed database is a database that is stored and processed on more than one computer. A replicated database is one in which multiple copies of some or all of the database are stored on different computers. A partitioned database is one in which different pieces of the database are stored on different computers. A distributed database can be replicated and partitioned.

Distributed databases pose processing challenges. If a database is updated on a single computer, then the challenge is simply to ensure that the copies of the database are logically consistent when they are distributed. However, if updates are to be made on more than one computer, the challenges become significant. If the database is partitioned and not replicated, then challenges occur if transactions span data on more than one computer. If the database is replicated and if updates occur to the replicated portions, then a special locking algorithm called distributed two-phase locking is required. Implementing this algorithm can be difficult and expensive.

Objects consist of methods and properties or data values. All objects of a given class have the same methods, but they have different property values. Object persistence is the process of storing object property values. Relational databases are difficult to use for object persistence. Some specialized products called object-oriented DBMSs were developed in the 1990s but never received commercial acceptance. Oracle Database and others have extended the capabilities of their relational DBMS products to provide support for object persistence. Such databases are referred to as object-relational databases.

The NoSQL movement (now often read as "not only SQL") is built upon the need to meet the Big Data storage needs of companies such as Amazon.com, Google, and Facebook. The tools used to do this are nonrelational DBMSs known as structured storage. Early examples were Dynamo and Bigtable; a more recent popular example is Cassandra. These products use a non-normalized table structure built on columns, super columns, and column families tied together by rowkey values from a keyspace. Data processing of the very large datasets found in Big Data is often done by the MapReduce process, which breaks a data processing task into many parallel tasks done by many computers in the cluster and then combines these results to produce a final result. An emerging product that is supported by Microsoft and Oracle Corporation is the Hadoop Distributed File System (HDFS), with its spinoffs HBase, a nonrelational storage component, and Pig, a query language.

Key Terms

AllegroGraph	conformed dimension	distributed database
Amazon Web Services (AWS)	Couchbase	distributed two-phase locking
Big Data	curse of dimensionality	dirty data
Bigtable	data mart	document [NoSQL database category]
business intelligence (BI) system	data mining application	drill down
Cassandra	data warehouse	Dynamo
click-stream data	data warehouse metadata database	DynamoDB database service
cloud computing	date dimension	EC2 service
column family [NoSQL database category]	dimension table	enterprise data warehouse (EDW) architecture
	dimensional database	

Extract, Transform, and Load (ETL)
  System
F score
fact table
graph [NoSQL database category]
Hadoop Distributed File System
  (HDFS)
HBase
host machine
hypervisor
key-value [NoSQL database category]
M score
MapReduce
measure
MemcacheDB
method
Microsoft Azure
MongoDB

Neo4J
nonintegrated data
NoSQL
Not only SQL
object
object-oriented DBMS (OODBMS)
object-oriented programming (OOP)
object persistence
object-relational database
OLAP cube
OLAP report
OLAP server
online analytical processing (OLAP)
online transaction processing (OLTP)
  system
operational system
Oracle Big Data Appliance
partitioning

Pig
PivotTable
property
R score
RDS (Relational DBMS Service)
replication
reporting system
RFM analysis
server cluster
slowly changing dimension
SQL Server Parallel Data Warehouse
star schema
super column family
time dimension
transactional system
virtual computer
virtual machine
virtual machine manager

Review Questions

12.1 What are BI systems?

12.2 How do BI systems differ from transaction processing systems?

12.3 Name and describe the two main categories of BI systems.

12.4 What are the three sources of data for BI systems?

12.5 Explain the difference in processing between reporting and data mining applications.

12.6 Describe three reasons why direct reading of operational data is not feasible for BI applications.

12.7 Summarize the problems with operational databases that limit their usefulness for BI applications.

12.8 What are dirty data? How do dirty data arise?

12.9 Why is server time not useful for Web-based order entry BI applications?

12.10 What is click-stream data? How is it used in BI applications?

12.11 Why are data warehouses necessary?

12.12 Why do the authors describe the data in Figure 12-6 as "frightening"?

12.13 Give examples of data warehouse metadata.

12.14 Explain the difference between a data warehouse and a data mart. Use the analogy of a supply chain.

12.15 What is the enterprise data warehouse (EDW) architecture?

12.16 Describe the differences between operational databases and dimensional databases.

12.17 What is a star schema?

12.18 What is a fact table? What type of data is stored in fact tables?

12.19 What is a measure?

12.20 What is a dimension table? What type of data is stored in dimension tables?

12.21 What is a slowly changing dimension?

12.22 Why is the time dimension important in a dimensional model?

12.23 What is a conformed dimension?

12.24 State the purpose of a reporting system.

12.25 What do the letters *RFM* stand for in RFM analysis?

12.26 Describe, in general terms, how to perform an RFM analysis.

12.27 Explain the characteristics of customers having the following RFM scores: {1 1 5}, {1 5 1}, {5 5 5}, {2 5 5}, {5 1 2}, {1 1 3}.

12.28 What does OLAP stand for?

12.29 What is the distinguishing characteristic of OLAP reports?

12.30 Define *measure, dimension,* and *cube.*

12.31 Give an example, other than one in this text, of a measure, two dimensions related to your measure, and a cube.

12.32 What is drill down?

12.33 Explain how the OLAP report in Figure 12-23 differs from that in Figure 12-22.

12.34 What is the purpose of an OLAP server?

12.35 Define *distributed database.*

12.36 Explain one way to partition a database that has three tables: T1, T2, and T3.

12.37 Explain one way to replicate a database that has three tables: T1, T2, and T3.

12.38 Explain what must be done when fully replicating a database but allowing only one computer to process updates.

12.39 If more than one computer can update a replicated database, what three problems can occur?

12.40 What solution is used to prevent the problems in Review Question 12.39?

12.41 Explain what problems can occur in a distributed database that is partitioned but not replicated.

12.42 What organizations should consider using a distributed database?

12.43 Explain the meaning of the term *object persistence.*

12.44 In general terms, explain why relational databases are difficult to use for object persistence.

12.45 What does OODBMS stand for, and what is its purpose?

12.46 According to this chapter, why were OODBMSs not successful?

12.47 What is an object-relational database?

12.48 What is virtualization?

12.49 What is cloud computing?

12.50 What is Big Data?

12.51 Based on Figure 12-1, what is the relationship between 1 MB of storage and 1 EB of storage?

12.52 What is the NoSQL movement? What are the four categories of NoSQL databases used in this book?

12.53 What were the first two nonrelational data stores to be developed, and who developed them?

12.54 What is Cassandra, and what is the history of the development of Cassandra to its current state?

12.55 As illustrated in Figure 12-33, what is column family database storage, and how are column family database storage systems organized? How do structured storage systems compare to RDBMS systems?

12.56 Explain MapReduce processing.

12.57 What is Hadoop, and what is the history of the development of Hadoop to its current state? What are HBase and Pig?

Project Questions

12.58 Based on the discussion of the Heather Sweeney Designs operational database (HSD) and dimensional database (HSD_DW) in the text, answer the following questions.

A. Using the SQL statements shown in Figure 12-13, create the HSD_DW database in a DBMS.

B. What possible transformations of data were made before HSD_DW was loaded with data? List some possible transformations, showing the original format of the HSD data and how they appear in the HSD_DW database.

C. Write the complete set of SQL statements necessary to load the transformed data into the HSD_DW database.

D. Populate the HSD_DW database using the SQL statements you wrote to answer part C.

E. Figure 12-35 shows the SQL code to create the SALES_FOR_RFM fact table shown in Figure 12-18. Using those statements, add the SALES_FOR_RFM table to your HSD_DW database.

F. What possible transformations of data are necessary to load the SALES_FOR_RFM table? List some possible transformations, showing the original format of the HSD data and how they appear in the HSD_DW database.

FIGURE 12-35

The HSD_DW SALES_FOR_RFM SQL CREATE TABLE Statement

```
CREATE TABLE SALES_FOR_RFM(
        TimeID              Int                 NOT NULL,
        CustomerID          Int                 NOT NULL,
        InvoiceNumber       Int                 NOT NULL,
        PreTaxTotalSale     Numeric(9,2)        NOT NULL,
        CONSTRAINT          SALES_FOR_RFM_PK
                            PRIMARY KEY (TimeID, CustomerID, InvoiceNumber),
        CONSTRAINT          SRFM_TIMELINE_FK FOREIGN KEY(TimeID)
                            REFERENCES TIMELINE(TimeID)
                                ON UPDATE NO ACTION
                                ON DELETE NO ACTION,
        CONSTRAINT          SRFM_CUSTOMER_FK FOREIGN KEY(CustomerID)
                            REFERENCES CUSTOMER(CustomerID)
                                ON UPDATE NO ACTION
                                ON DELETE NO ACTION
);
```

G. Write an SQL query similar to SQL-Query-CH12-02 on page 551 that uses the total dollar amount of each day's product sales as the measure (instead of the number of products sold each day).

H. Write the SQL view equivalent of the SQL query you wrote to answer part G.

I. Create the SQL view you wrote to answer part H in your HSD_DW database.

J. Create a Microsoft Excel 2013 workbook named HSD-DW-BI-Exercises.xlsx.

K. Using either the results of your SQL query from part G (copy the results of the query into a worksheet in the HSD-DW-BI-Exercises.xlsx workbook and then format this range as a worksheet table) or your SQL view from part I (create an Excel data connection to the view), create an OLAP report similar to the OLAP report shown in Figure 12-32. (*Hint:* If you need help with the needed Microsoft Excel actions, search in the Microsoft Excel help system for more information.)

L. Heather Sweeney is interested in the effects of payment type on sales in dollars.

    1. Modify the design of the HSD_DW dimensional database to include a PAYMENT_TYPE dimension table.

    2. Modify the HSD_DW database to include the PAYMENT_TYPE dimension table.

    3. What data will be used to load the PAYMENT_TYPE dimension table? What data will be used to load foreign key data into the PRODUCT_SALES fact table? Write the complete set of SQL statements necessary to load these data.

    4. Populate the PAYMENT_TYPE and PRODUCT_SALES tables using the SQL statements you wrote to answer part 3.

    5. Create the SQL queries or SQL views needed to incorporate the PaymentType attribute.

    6. Create a Microsoft Excel 2013 OLAP report to show the effect of payment type on product sales in dollars.

Case Questions

Marcia's Dry Cleaning Case Questions

If you have not already done so, create and populate the Marcia's Dry Cleaning (MDC) database for the DBMS you are using as described in:

- Chapter 10A for Microsoft SQL Server 2014
- Chapter 10B for Oracle Database
- Chapter 10C for MySQL 5.6

A. You need about 20 INVOICE transactions with supporting INVOICE_ITEMs in the database. Write the needed SQL statements for any needed additional INVOICE transactions, and insert the data into your MDC database.

B. Design a data warehouse star schema for a dimensional database named MDC_DW. The fact table measure will be ExtendedPrice.

C. Create the MDC_DW database in your DBMS product.

D. What transformations of data will need to be made before the MDC_DW database can be loaded with data? List all the transformations, showing the original format of the MDC data and how it appears in the MDC_DW database.

E. Write the complete set of SQL statements necessary to load the transformed data into the MDC_DW database.

F. Populate the MDC_DW database using the appropriate MDC data or transformations of that data.

G. Write an SQL query similar to SQL-Query-CH12-02 on page 551 that uses the ExtendedPrice as the measure.

H. Write the SQL view equivalent of the SQL query you wrote to answer part G.

I. Create the SQL view you wrote to answer part H in your MDC_DW database.

J. Create the Microsoft Excel 2013 workbook named MDC-DW-BI-Exercises.xlsx.

K. Using either the results of your SQL query from part G (copy the results of the query into a worksheet in the MDC-DW-BI.xlsx workbook and then format this range as a worksheet table) or your SQL view from part I (create a Microsoft Excel data connection to the view), create an OLAP report similar to the OLAP report shown in Figure 12-21(j). (*Hint:* If you need help with the needed Microsoft Excel actions, search in the Microsoft Excel help system for more information.)

L. Describe how an RFM analysis could be useful in Marcia's business.

The Queen Anne Curiosity Shop Project Questions

If you have not already implemented the Queen Anne Curiosity Shop database shown in Chapter 7 in a DBMS product, create and populate the QACS database now in the DBMS of your choice (or as assigned by your instructor).

A. You need about 30 PURCHASE transactions in the database. Write the needed SQL statements for any needed additional PURCHASE transactions, and insert the data into your QACS database.

B. Design a data warehouse star schema for a dimensional database named QACS_DW. The fact table measure will be ItemPrice.

C. Create the QACS_DW database in a DBMS product.

D. What transformations of data will need to be made before the QACS_DW database can be loaded with data? List all the transformations, showing the original format of the QACS database and how it appears in the QACS_DW database.

E. Write the complete set of SQL statements necessary to load the transformed data into the QACS_DW database.

F. Populate the QACS_DW database using the appropriate QACS database data or transformations of that data.

G. Write an SQL query similar to SQL-Query-CH12-02 on page 551 that uses retail price as the measure.

H. Write the SQL view equivalent of the SQL query you wrote to answer part G.

I. Create the SQL view you wrote to answer part H in your QACS_DW database.

J. Create a Microsoft Excel 2013 workbook named QACS-DW-BI-Exercises.xlsx.

K. Using either the results of your SQL query from part G (copy the results of the query into a worksheet in the QACS-DW-BI.xlsx workbook and then format this range as a worksheet table) or your SQL view from part I (create a Microsoft Excel data connection to the view), create an OLAP report similar to the OLAP report shown in Figure 12-21(j). (*Hint:* If you need help with the needed Microsoft Excel actions, search in the Microsoft Excel help system for more information.)

L. Describe how an RFM analysis could be useful to the Queen Anne Curiosity Shop.

Morgan Importing

If you have not already implemented the Morgan Importing database shown in Chapter 7 in a DBMS product, create and populate the MI database now in the DBMS of your choice (or as assigned by your instructor).

James Morgan wants to analyze shipper performance based on the difference between a shipment's scheduled departure date and the actual departure date. This value will be named DepartureDelay, with the values measured in days. The values of Days can be positive (the shipment departed later than the scheduled departure date), zero (the shipment departed on the scheduled departure date), or negative (the shipment departed before the scheduled departure date).

Since Morgan Importing purchasing agents are responsible for contacting the shippers and arranging the shipments, James also wants an analysis of purchasing agents' performance based on the same measure.

A. You need about 30 SHIPMENT transactions in the database. Write the needed SQL statements for any needed additional SHIPMENT transactions, and insert the data into your MI database.

B. Design a data warehouse star schema for a dimensional database named MI_DW. The fact table measure will be DepartureDelay (the difference between ScheduledDepartureDate and ActualDepartureDate). Dimension tables will be TIMELINE, SHIPMENT, SHIPPER, and PURCHASING_AGENT (PURCHASING_AGENT is a subset of EMPLOYEE containing data on only the employees who are purchasing agents).

C. Create the MI_DW database in a DBMS product.

D. What transformations of data will need to be made before the MI_DW database can be loaded with data? List all the transformations, showing the original format of the MI database and how it appears in the MI_DW database.

E. Write the complete set of SQL statements necessary to load the transformed data into the MI_DW database.

F. Populate the MI_DW database using the appropriate MI database data or transformations of that data.

G. Write an SQL query similar to SQL-Query-CH12-02 text on page 551 that uses DepartureDelay as the measure.

H. Write the SQL view equivalent of the SQL query you wrote to answer part G.

I. Create the SQL view you wrote to answer part H in your MI_DW database.

J. Create a Microsoft Excel 2013 workbook named MI-DW-BI-Exercises.xlsx.

K. Using either the results of your SQL query from part G (copy the results of the query into a worksheet in the MI-DW-BI.xlsx workbook and then format this range as a worksheet table) or your SQL view from part I (create a Microsoft Excel data connection to the view), create an OLAP report similar to the OLAP report shown in Figure 12-21(j). (*Hint:* If you need help with the needed Microsoft Excel actions, search in the Microsoft Excel help system for more information.)

Online Appendices

Complete versions of these appendices are available on this textbook's Web site.

Go to *www.pearsonhighered.com/kroenke* and select the Companion Website for this book.

Appendix A

Getting Started with Microsoft Access 2013

Appendix B

Getting Started with Systems Analysis and Design

Appendix C

E-R Diagrams and the IDEF1X Standard

Appendix D

E-R Diagrams and the UML Standard

Appendix E

Getting Started with the MySQL Workbench Data Modeling Tools

Appendix F

Getting Started with Microsoft Visio 2013

Appendix G

Data Structures for Database Processing

Appendix H

The Semantic Object Model

Appendix I

Getting Started with Web Servers, PHP, and the NetBeans IDE

Appendix J

Business Intelligence Systems

Appendix K

Big Data

Web Links

News

CNET News.com: *www.news.com*
Wired: *www.wired.com*
ZDNet: *www.zdnet.com*

Data Mining

IBM SPSS Software: *http://www-01.ibm.com/software/analytics/spss*
KDnuggets: *www.kdnuggets.com*
SAS Enterprise Miner: *www.sas.com/technologies/analytics/datamining/miner*
Microsoft SQL Server 2012 Data Mining Add-Ins for Office 2010: *http://www.microsoft.com/en-us/download/details.aspx?id=29061*

DBMS and Other Vendors

Oracle Database 12*c*: *www.oracle.com/database/index.html*
Oracle Database Express Edition 11*g* Release 2: *www.oracle.com/ technetwork/database/database-technologies/express-edition/overview/ index.html?ssSourceSiteId=ocomen*
SQL Server 2014: *www.microsoft.com/en-us/sqlserver/default.aspx*
SQL Server 2014 Express Edition: *http://www.microsoft.com/en-us/ server-cloud/products/sql-server-editions/sql-server-express.aspx*
MySQL: *www.mysql.com*
Eclipse IDE: *www.eclipse.org*
PHP: *http://us.php.net*
NetBeans: *www.netbeans.org/index.html*
Microsoft Visual Studio Express Editions: *www.microsoft.com/Express/*

Standards

JDBC: *www.oracle.com/technetwork/java/javase/jdbc/index.html* and *http://en.wikipedia.org/wiki/JDBC*
ODBC: *http://en.wikipedia.org/wiki/Open_Database_Connectivity*
World Wide Web Consortium (W3C): *www.w3.org*
XML: *www.w3.org/XML*, *www.xml.org*, and *http://en.wikipedia.org/wiki/XML*

Online Publications

Database Journal: *http://www.databasejournal.com*

Classic Articles and References

ANSI X3. *American National Standard for Information Systems–Database Language SQL*. ANSI, 1992.

Bruce, T. *Designing Quality Databases with IDEF1X Information Models*. New York: Dorset House, 1992.

Chamberlin, D. D., et al. "SEQUEL 2: A Unified Approach to Data Definition, Manipulation, and Control." *IBM Journal of Research and Development* 20 (November 1976).

Chen, P. "The Entity-Relationship Model: Toward a Unified Model of Data." *ACM Transactions on Database Systems* 1 (March 1976).

Chen, P. *Entity-Relationship Approach to Information Modeling*. E-R Institute, 1981.

Coar, K. A. L. *Apache Server for Dummies*. Foster City, CA: IDG Books, 1997.

Codd, E. F. "A Relational Model of Data for Large Shared Data Banks." *Communications of the ACM* 13 (June 1970).

Codd, E. F. "Extending the Relational Model to Capture More Meaning." *Transactions on Database Systems* 4 (December 1979).

Date, C. J. *An Introduction to Database Systems*, 8th ed. Upper Saddle River, NJ: Pearson Education, 2003.

Embley, D. W. "NFQL: The Natural Forms Query Language." *ACM Transactions on Database Systems* 14 (June 1989).

Eswaran, K. P., J. N. Gray, R. A. Lorie, and I. L. Traiger. "The Notion of Consistency and Predicate Locks in a Database System." *Communications of the ACM* 19 (November 1976).

Fagin, R. "A Normal Form for Relational Databases That Is Based on Domains and Keys." *Transactions on Database Systems* 6 (September 1981).

Fagin, R. "Multivalued Dependencies and a New Normal Form for Relational Databases." *Transactions on Database Systems* 2 (September 1977).

Hammer, M., and D. McLeod. "Database Description with SDM: A Semantic Database Model." *Transactions on Database Systems* 6 (September 1981).

Keuffel, W. "Battle of the Modeling Techniques." *DBMS Magazine* (August 1996).

Kroenke, D. "Waxing Semantic: An Interview." *DBMS Magazine* (September 1994).

Moriarty, T. "Business Rule Analysis." *Database Programming and Design* (April 1993).

Muller, R. J. *Database Design for Smarties: Using UML for Data Modeling*. San Francisco: Morgan Kaufmann, 1999.

Nijssen, G., and T. Halpin. *Conceptual Schema and Relational Database Design: A Fact-Oriented Approach*. Upper Saddle River, NJ: Prentice Hall, 1989.

Nolan, R. *Managing the Data Resource Function*. St. Paul: West Publishing, 1974.

Ratliff, C. Wayne, "dStory: How I Really Developed dBASE." *Data Based Advisor* (March 1991).

Rogers, D. "Manage Data with Modeling Tools." *VB Tech Journal* (December 1996).

Ross, R. *Principles of the Business Rule Approach*. Boston: Addison-Wesley, 2003.

Zloof, M. M. "Query by Example." *Proceedings of the National Computer Conference, AFIPS* 44 (May 1975).

Useful Books

Atkinson, Paul, and Robert Vieira. *Beginning Microsoft SQL Server 2012 Programming*. Indianapolis: John Wiley & Sons, Inc., 2012.

Ben-Gan, Itzik, Dejan Sarka, and Ron Talmage. *Querying Microsoft SQL Server 2012: Exam 70-461 Training Kit*. Sebastopol: O'Reilly Media, Inc., 2012.

Berry, M., and G. Linoff. *Data Mining Techniques for Marketing, Sales, and Customer Support*. New York: Wiley, 1997.

Bordoloi, Bijoy, and Douglas Bock. *Oracle SQL*. Upper Saddle River: Prentice Hall, 2004.

Bordoloi, Bijoy, and Douglas Bock. *SQL for SQL Server*. Upper Saddle River: Prentice Hall, 2004.

Celko, J. *SQL for Smarties*, 2nd ed. San Francisco: Morgan Kaufmann, 2000.

Celko, J. *SQL Puzzles and Answers*. San Francisco: Morgan Kaufmann, 1997.

Conger, Steve. *Hands-On Database: An Introduction to Database Design and Development*. Upper Saddle River: Prentice Hall, 2012.

Fields, D. K., and M. A. Kolb. *Web Development with Java Server Pages*. Greenwich, CT: Manning Press, 2000.

Garcia-Molina, Hector, Jeffrey D. Ullman, and Jennifer Widom. *Database Systems: The Complete Book*, 2nd ed. Upper Saddle River: Prentice Hall, 2009.

Harold, E. R. *XML: Extensible Markup Language*. New York: IDG Books Worldwide, 1998.

Hoffer, Jeffrey A., V. Ramesh, and Heikki Topi. *Modern Database Management*, 11th ed. Upper Saddle River: Prentice Hall, 2013.

Jorgensen, Adam, Steven Wort, Ross LoFortre, and Brian Knight. *Professional Microsoft SQL Server 2012 Administration*. Indianapolis: John Wiley & Sons, Inc., 2012.

Jukić, Nenad, Susan Vrbsky, and Svetlozar Nestrorov. *Database Systems: Introduction to Databases and Data Warehouses*. Upper Saddle River: Prentice Hall, 2013.

Kay, M. *XSLT: Programmer's Reference*. Birmingham, United Kingdom: WROX Press, 2000.

Kendall, Kenneth E., and Julie E. Kendall. *Systems Analysis and Design*, 9th ed. Upper Saddle River: Prentice Hall, 2014.

Loney, K. *Oracle Database 11g: The Complete Reference*. Berkeley, CA: Osborne/McGraw-Hill, 2008.

Muench, S. *Building Oracle XML Applications*. Sebastopol, CA: O'Reilly, 2000.

Muller, R. J. *Database Design for Smarties: Using UML for Data Modeling*. San Francisco: Morgan Kaufmann, 1999.

Mundy, J., W. Thornthwaite, and R. Kimball. *The Microsoft Data Warehouse Toolkit*. Indianapolis, IN: Wiley, 2006.

Nixon, Robin. *Learning PHP, MySQL, Javascript, CSS & HTML5*, 3rd ed. Sebastopol: O'Reilly Media, Inc., 2014.

Perry, James, and Gerald Post. *Introduction to Oracle 10g*. Upper Saddle River: Prentice Hall, 2007.

Perry, James, and Gerald Post. *Introduction to SQL Server 2005*. Upper Saddle River: Prentice Hall, 2007.

Pyle, D. *Data Preparation for Data Mining*. San Francisco: Morgan Kaufmann, 1999.

Sarka, Dejan, Matija Lah, and Grega Jerkic. *Implementing a Data Warehouse with Microsoft SQL Server 2012: Exam 70-463 Training Kit*. Sebastopol: O'Reilly Media, Inc., 2012.

Thomas, Orin, Peter Ward, and Bob Taylor. *Administering Microsoft SQL Server 2012 Databases: Exam 70-462 Training Kit*. Sebastopol: O'Reilly Media, Inc., 2012.

Although this section defines many of the key terms in the book, it is not meant to be exhaustive. Terms related to a specific DBMS product, for example, should be referenced in Chapter 10A for Microsoft SQL Server 2014, Chapter 10B for Oracle Database, and Chapter 10C for MySQL 5.6. These references can be found in the index. Similarly, SQL concepts are included, but details of SQL commands and syntax should be referenced in the chapter that discusses those details.

.NET Framework. Microsoft's comprehensive application development platform. It includes such components as ADO.NET, ASP.NET, and .NET for Windows Store Apps.

.NET for Windows Store Apps. An extension to the .NET framework that supports the applications (apps) developed for Microsoft Windows 8 devices.

<?php and ?>. The symbols used to indicate blocks of PHP code in Web pages.

/* and */. The symbols used to indicate a comment line in an SQL script in SQL Server 2014, Oracle Database 12*c*, and MySQL 5.6.

<?php and ?>. The symbols used to indicate blocks of PHP code in Web pages.

Abstraction. A generalization of something that hides some unimportant details but enables work with a wider class of types. A recordset is an abstraction of a relation. A rowset is an abstraction of a recordset.

ACID transaction. ACID stands for "atomic, consistent, isolated, and durable." An *atomic* transaction is one in which all of the database changes are committed as a unit; either all are done or none is. A *consistent* transaction is one in which all actions are taken against rows in the same logical state. An *isolated* transaction is one that is protected from changes by other users. A *durable* transaction is one that is permanent after it is committed to the database, regardless of subsequent failures. There are different levels of consistency and isolation. *See also* statement-level consistency, transaction isolation level, transaction-level consistency.

Action. As used in this book, a shorter term for *minimum cardinality enforcement action. See also* minimum cardinality enforcement action.

Active Data Objects (ADO). An implementation of OLE DB that is accessible via object- and non-object-oriented languages. It is used primarily as a scripting-language (JScript, VBScript) interface to OLE DB.

Active repository. Parts of the systems development processes where metadata is created automatically as the system components are created. *See also* data repository.

Active Server Pages (ASP). A file containing markup language, server script, and client script that is processed by the Active Server Processor in Microsoft Internet Information Server (IIS).

Ad-hoc query. A query created by a user as and when needed, as compared to a predefined and stored query.

ADO.NET. A data access technology that is part of Microsoft's .NET initiative. ADO.NET provides the capabilities of ADO but with a different object structure. ADO.NET also includes new capabilities for the processing of datasets. *See also* ADO.NET DataSet.

ADO.NET Command object. The ADO.NET object that mimics an SQL statement or stored procedure. It is run against the data in the DataSet.

ADO.NET Connection object. The ADO.NET object responsible for connecting to a data source.

ADO.NET Data Provider. A class library that provides ADO.NET services. There are Data Providers for ODBC, OLE.DB, SQL Server, and EDM applications.

ADO.NET DataAdapter object. The ADO.NET object that is the connector between a Connection object and a DataSet object.

It uses four command objects: SelectCommand, InsertCommand, UpdateCommand, and DeleteCommand.

ADO.NET DataReader. An ADO.NET object that is similar to a read-only, forward only cursor and that can be used only by an ADO.NET Command object's Execute method.

ADO.NET DataSet. A representation of data from a database that is stored in computer memory for immediate use. It is distinct and disconnected from the data in the database.

ADO.NET Entity Framework. An extension to ADO.NET that supports the Microsoft EDM. *See also* Entity Data Model (EDM).

After image. A record of a database entity (normally a row or a page) after a change. Used in recovery to perform rollforwards.

Aggregate function. A built-in or user-defined SQL function that operates on a set of column values and returns a single value.

Alert. In reporting systems, a type of report that is triggered by an event.

AllegroGraph. A nonrelational graph DBMS product.

Alternate key (AK). In entity-relationship models, a synonym for candidate key.

Amazon Web Services (AWS). A cloud computing environment provided by Amazon.com.

American National Standards Institute (ANSI). The American standards organization that creates and publishes the SQL standards. *See also* Structured Query Language (SQL).

AMP. An abbreviation for Apache, MySQL, and PHP/Pearl/Python. *See also* Apache Web Server, PHP.

Android operating system. An operating system (OS) developed by Google and widely used on tablets and smartphones.

Anomaly. An undesirable consequence of a data modification. The term is used in normalization discussions. With an insertion anomaly, facts about two or more different themes must be added to a single row of a relation. With a deletion anomaly, facts about two or more themes are lost when a single row is deleted.

Apache Tomcat. An application server that works in conjunction with the Apache Web server. *See also* Apache Web server.

Apache Web server. A popular Web server that runs on most operating systems, particularly Windows and Linux.

API. *See* application program interface (API).

App. A short term for *application;* normally applied to applications running on tablets and smartphones.

Apple II. A pioneering PC introduced in 1977 by Apple Inc.

Apple iPad. A pioneering tablet computer introduced in 2010 by Apple Inc.

Apple OS X. A personal computer operating system developed by Apple Inc. and used on Apple personal computers.

Applet. A compiled, machine-independent Java bytecode program that is run by the Java virtual machine embedded in a browser.

Application. A business computer system that processes a portion of a database to meet a user's information needs. It consists of menus, forms, reports, queries, Web pages, and application programs.

Application program. A custom-developed program for processing a database. It can be written in a standard procedural language, such as Java, C#, Visual Basic .NET, or C++, or in a language unique to the DBMS, such as PL/SQL or T-SQL.

Application program interface (API). A set of program procedures or functions that can be called to invoke a set of services. The API includes the names of the procedures and functions and a description of the name, purpose, and data type of parameters to be provided. For example, a DBMS product can provide a library of functions to call for database services. The names of procedures and their parameters constitute the API for that library.

Archetype/version object. A two-object structure that represents multiple versions of a standardized item; for example, a SOFTWARE-PRODUCT (the archetype) and PRODUCT-RELEASE (the version of the archetype). The identifier of the version always includes the identifier of the archetype object.

ARPANET. A network forerunner of the Internet that was created by the Advanced Research Projects Agency at the Department of Defense in 1969.

ASP. *See* Active Server Pages (ASP).

ASP.NET. The updated version of ASP for the .NET Framework. *See also* Active Server Pages (ASP), .NET Framework.

Association entity. As used in a data model, an entity that links two other entities and also contains attributes that apply to the relationship between those two entities rather than to either entity itself. *See also* associative entity.

Association object. An object that represents the combination of at least two other objects and that contains data about that combination. It is often used in contracting and assignment applications.

Association pattern. In database design, a table pattern where an intersection table contains additional attributes beyond the attributes that make up the composite primary key.

Association table. As used in a database design, a table that links two other tables and also contains columns that apply to the relationship between those two tables rather than to either table itself.

Associative entity. As used in a data model, an entity that links two other entities and also contains attributes that apply to the relationship between those two entities rather than to either entity itself. *See also* association entity.

Asterisk (*) wildcard character. A character used in Microsoft Access 2013 queries to represent one or more unspecified characters. *See also* SQL percent sign (%) wildcard character.

Atomic. A set of actions that is completed as a unit. Either all of the actions are completed or none of them is.

Atomic transaction. A group of logically related database operations that is performed as a unit. Either all of the operations are performed or none of them is.

Attribute. (1) A column of a relation; also called a *column, field,* or *data item.* (2) A property in an entity.

Authorization rules. A set of processing permissions that describes which users or user groups can take particular actions against particular portions of the database.

AUTO_INCREMENT attribute. In MySQL, the data attribute used to create surrogate keys.

AutoNumber. In Access 2013, the data type used to create surrogate keys.

AVG. In SQL, a function that computes the average of a set of numbers. *See also* SQL built-in functions.

Base Class Library. A component of the Microsoft .NET Framework that provides support for the programming languages used with the .NET Framework.

Base domain. In IDEF1X, a domain definition that stands alone. Other domains may be defined as subsets of a base domain.

Before image. A record of a database entity (normally a row or a page) before a change. Used in recovery to perform rollback.

Big Data. The established term for the enormous datasets created by Web applications, such as search tools (e.g., Google and Bing), and by Web 2.0 social networks, such as Facebook, LinkedIn, and Twitter.

Bigtable. A nonrelational unstructured data store developed by Google.

BI. *See* business intelligence (BI) systems.

Binary relationship. A relationship between exactly two entities or tables.

Boyce-Codd normal form (BCNF). A relation in which every determinant is a candidate key.

Business intelligence (BI) systems. Information systems that assist managers and other professionals in the analysis of current and past activities and in the prediction of future events. Two major categories of BI systems are reporting systems and data mining systems.

Bytecode interpreter. For an application written in Java, the program used by a specific operating system to execute the application. Bytecode interpreters are known as Java virtual machines. *See also* Java virtual machine.

Callable Statement object. A JDBC object used to invoke database compiled queries and stored procedures.

Candidate key. An attribute or group of attributes that identifies a unique row in a relation. One of the candidate keys is chosen to be the primary key.

Cardinality. In a binary relationship, the maximum or minimum number of elements allowed on each side of the relationship. The maximum cardinality can be 1:1, 1:N, N:1, or N:M. The minimum cardinality may be optional-optional, optional-mandatory, mandatory-optional, or mandatory-mandatory.

Cartesian product. The SQL operation of paring each and every row in one table with each and every row in another table. The Cartesian product is the first step in an SQL join operation.

Cascading deletion. A referential integrity action specifying that when a parent row is deleted, related child rows should be deleted as well.

Cascading update. A referential integrity action specifying that when the key of a parent row is updated, the foreign keys of matching child rows should be updated as well.

Cassandra. A nonrelational unstructured data store from the Apache Software Foundation.

Casual relationship. A relationship that is created without a foreign key constraint. This is useful if the tables are missing data values.

Categorization cluster. In IDEF1X, a group of mutually exclusive category entities. *See also* complete category cluster.

Category entity. In IDEF1X, a subtype that belongs to a category cluster.

Cell phone. A term for a *mobile phone,* which is a device that connects to the telephone system via radio signals. *See also* mobile phone.

Cellular network. A wireless telephone network divided into geographical areas named *cells.*

Character strings. Database data composed of letters, numbers and special characters such as @, #, $, and %.

CHECK constraint. In SQL, a constraint that specifies what data values are allowed in a particular column.

Checkpoint. The point of synchronization between a database and a transaction log. All buffers are force-written to external storage. The term is sometimes used in other ways by DBMS vendors.

Child. An entity or row on the many side of a one-to-many relationship.

Class attributes. In the uniform modeling language (UML), attributes that pertain to the class of all entities of a given type.

Click-stream data. Data about a customer's clicking behavior on a Web page; such data are often analyzed by e-commerce companies.

Client. In client-server architecture, the software that resides on the user's computer, tablet, or smartphone. *See also* client-server architecture.

Client-server architecture. A computer application architecture that divides the application into two parts: the *client,* which resides on the users' device, and the *server,* which resides on a centralized server computer.

Cloud computing. The use of networks, such as the Internet, to deliver services to users, where users are unconcerned about exactly where the servers delivering the services are located. Thus, the servers are said to be "in the cloud."

Cluster analysis. A form of unsupervised data mining in which statistical techniques identify groups of entities that have similar characteristics.

CODASYL DBTG. The Conference on Database Systems Languages (CODASYL) Database Task Group (DBTG). The network database model was created by this group.

Collection. An object that contains a group of other objects. Examples are the ADO Names, Errors, and Parameters collections.

Column. A logical group of bytes in a row of a relation or a table. The meaning of a column is the same for every row of the relation.

Column family [NoSQL database category]. A nonrelational database structure based on columns of data. The structure may be based on columns, super columns, column families, and super column families.

COM. *See* Component Object Model (COM).

Command-line utility. A character user interface program that presents a command prompt to the user. The user then types a command and presses the Enter key for execution. Each major DBMS product has a command-line utility.

Commit. A command issued to the DBMS that makes database modifications permanent. After the command has been processed, database changes are written to the database and to a log so they will survive system crashes and other failures. A commit is usually used at the end of an atomic transaction. Contrast this with rollback.

Common Language Runtime (CLT). A component of the Microsoft .NET Framework that provides support for the programming languages used with the .NET Framework.

Complete category cluster. A category cluster in which all possible category entities are defined. The generic entity must also be one of the category entities.

Compliment. In mathematical set theory, the result of a logical operation using the NOT logical operator. *See also* set theory.

Component design. The third step in the systems development life cycle (SDLC) model. The system is designed based on specific hardware and software. The database design is created in this step. *See also* systems development life cycle (SDLC).

Component Object Model (COM). A Microsoft specification for the development of object-oriented programs.

Composite determinant. In functional dependencies, a determinant consisting of two or more attributes.

Composite identifier. In data modeling, an identifier consisting of two or more attributes.

Composite key. In database design, a key with two or more attributes.

Composite primary key. In database design and actual databases, a primary key with two or more attributes.

Computed value. A column of a table that is computed from other column values. Values are not stored but are computed when they are to be displayed.

Concurrency. A condition in which two or more transactions are processed against the database at the same time. In a single CPU system, the changes are interleaved; in a multi-CPU system, the transactions may be processed simultaneously, and the changes on the database server are interleaved.

Concurrent processing. The sharing of the CPU among several transactions. The CPU is allocated to each transaction in a round robin or in some other fashion for a certain period of time. Operations are performed so quickly that they appear to users to be simultaneous. In local area networks (LANs) and other distributed applications, concurrent processing is used to refer to the (possibly simultaneous) processing of applications on multiple computers.

Concurrent transactions. Two transactions that are being processed at the same time.

Concurrent update problem. An error condition in which one user's data changes are overwritten by another user's data changes. Same as lost update problem.

Confidence. In market basket analysis, the probability of a customer's buying one product, given that the customer has purchased another product.

Conformed dimension. In a dimensional database design, a dimension table that has relationships to two or more fact tables.

Connection relationship. In IDEF1X, a HAS-A relationship.

Consistency. Two or more concurrent transactions are consistent if the result of their processing is the same as it would have been if they had been processed in some serial order.

Consistent. In an ACID transaction, either statement-level or transaction-level consistency. *See also* ACID transaction, consistency, statement-level consistency, transaction-level consistency.

Consistent backup. A backup file from which all uncommitted changes have been removed.

Constraints. A part of the ADO.NET DataTableCollection.

Control-of-flow statements. Procedural program statements that direct the execution of the program depending upon an existing condition. Control-of-flow statements include, for example, IF…THEN…ELSE logic and DO WHILE logic.

Correlated subquery. A type of subquery in which an element in the subquery refers to an element in the containing query. A subquery that requires nested processing.

Couchbase. A nonrelational document DBMS product.

COUNT. In SQL, a function that counts the number of rows in a query result. *See also* SQL built-in functions.

Crow's foot model. Formally known as the Information Engineering (IE) Crow's Foot model, it is a system of symbols used to construct E-R diagrams in data modeling and database design.

Crow's foot symbol. A symbol in the IE Crow's Foot E-R model that indicates a many side of the relationship. It visually resembles a bird's foot, thus the name *crow's foot*.

CRUD. An acronym for create, read, update, and delete. It is used to describe the four actions done to data by a DBMS.

Curse of dimensionality. In data mining applications, the phenomenon that the more attributes there are, the easier it is to build a model that fits the sample data but that is worthless as a predictor.

Cursor. An indicator of the current position in a pseudofile for an SQL SELECT that has been embedded in a program; it shows the identity of the current row.

Cursor type. A declaration on a cursor that determines how the DBMS places implicit locks. Four types of cursor discussed in this text are forward only, snapshot, keyset, and dynamic.

Data. The values stored in database tables.

Data administration. The enterprise-wide function that concerns the effective use and control of the organization's data assets. Data administration may be handled by an individual, but it is usually handled by a group. Specific functions include setting data standards and policies and providing a forum for conflict resolution. *See also* database administrator (DBA).

Data constraint. A limitation on a data value. *See also* domain constraint, interrelation constraint, intrarelation constraint, range constraint

Data consumer. A user of OLE DB functionality.

Data control language (DCL). A language used to describe the permissions granted in a database. SQL DCL is that portion of SQL that is used to grant and revoke database permissions.

Data definition language (DDL). A language used to describe the structure of a database. SQL DDL is that portion of SQL that is used to create, modify, and drop database structures.

Data dictionary. A user-accessible catalog of database and application metadata. The contents of an *active* data dictionary are automatically updated by the DBMS whenever changes are made in the database or application structure. The contents of a *passive* data dictionary must be updated manually when changes are made.

Data integrity. The state of a database in which all constraints are fulfilled. Usually refers to interrelation constraints in which the value of a foreign key is required to be present in the table having that foreign key as its primary key.

Data integrity problems. A table that has inconsistencies that create insert, update, or deletion anomalies is said to have *data integrity problems*.

Data Language/I (DL/I). An early DBMS product that used hierarchies or trees to represent data.

Data manipulation language (DML). A language used to describe the processing of a database. SQL DML is that portion of SQL that is used to query, insert, update, and modify data.

Data mart. A facility similar to a data warehouse but with a restricted domain. Often, the data are restricted to particular types, business functions, or business units.

Data mining application. Business intelligence systems that use sophisticated statistical and mathematical techniques to perform what-if analyses, to make predictions, and to facilitate decisions. Contrast with reporting systems.

Data model. A model of the users' data requirements usually expressed in terms of the entity-relationship model.

Data provider. A provider of OLE DB functionality. Examples are tabular data providers and service data providers.

Data repository. Collections of metadata about databases, database applications, Web pages, users, and other application components.

Data sublanguage. A language for defining and processing a database to be embedded in programs written in another language, in most cases a procedural language such as Java, C#, Visual Basic, or C++. A data sublanguage is an incomplete programming language because it contains only constructs for data access.

Data warehouse. A store of enterprise data that is designed to facilitate management decision making. A data warehouse includes not only data but also metadata, tools, procedures, training, personnel information, and other resources that make access to the data easier and more relevant to decision makers.

Data warehouse DBMS. The DBMS product used by the data warehouse. See also data warehouse.

Data warehouse metadata. In a data warehouse, metadata concerning the data, its source, its format, its assumptions and constraints, and other facts about the data.

Data warehouse metadata database. The database used to store the data warehouse metadata.

Database. A self-describing collection of integrated records.

Database administration. The function that concerns the effective use and control of a particular database and its related applications.

Database administrator (DBA). The person or group responsible for establishing policies and procedures to control and protect a database. The database administrator works within guidelines set by data administration to control the database structure, manage data changes, and maintain DBMS programs.

Database application. An application that uses a database to store the data needed by the application.

Database data. The portion of a database that contains data of interest and use to the application end users. See also data.

Database design. A diagram that represents that database as it will be implemented in a DBMS product.

Database integrity. The result of implementing domain integrity, entity integrity, and referential integrity in a database.

Database management system (DBMS). A set of programs used to define, administer, and process the database and its applications.

Database migration. Adapting a database to new or changing requirements.

Database redesign. The process of changing the structure of a database to adapt the database to changing requirements or to fix it so it has the structure it should have had in the first place.

Database save. A copy of database files that can be used to restore the database to some previous consistent state.

Database schema. (1) The logical design of a database structure. (2) In MySQL, the functional equivalent of a database in Microsoft Access or Microsoft SQL Server.

Database system. An information system composed of users, database applications, a database management system (DBMS), and a database.

DataColumnsCollection. An ADO.NET DataTable object.

DataRelations. Act as relational links between tables in an ADO.NET DataRelationCollection.

DataRelationCollection. The ADO.NET structure that stores DataRelations.

DataRowCollection. An ADO.NET DataTable object.

Dataset. In ADO.NET, an in-memory collection of tables that is not connected to any database. Datasets have relationships, referential integrity constraints, referential integrity actions, and other important database characteristics. They are processed by ADO.NET objects. A single dataset may be materialized as tables, as an XML document, or as an XML Schema.

DataTable object. The ADO.NET structure that mimics a relational database table.

DataTableCollection. The ADO.NET structure that stores DataTables.

Date dimension. In a dimensional database, a dimension that stores date and time values. See also dimensional database.

DBA. See database administrator (DBA).

DBMS. See database management system (DBMS).

DBMS reserved word. A word that has a special meaning in the DBMS and should not be used as a table, column, or other name in a database.

DDL. See data definition language (DDL).

Deadlock. A condition that can occur during concurrent processing in which each of two (or more) transactions is waiting to access data that the other transaction has locked. Also called a deadly embrace.

Deadly embrace. See deadlock.

Decision support system (DSS). One or more applications designed to help managers make decisions. An earlier name for business intelligence (BI).

Decision tree analysis. A form of unsupervised data mining that classifies entities of interest into two or more groups according to values of attributes that measure the entities' past history.

DEFAULT keyword. In SQL, the word used to specify a default value for an attribute.

Default value. A value assigned to an attribute if there is no other value assigned to it when a new row is created in a table.

Default namespace. In an XML Schema document, the namespace that is used for all unlabeled elements.

Default Web Site folder. On a Web server, the folder (or directory) at the base of the Web site structure.

Degree. For relationships in the entity-relationship model, the number of entities participating in the relationship. In almost all cases, such relationships are of degree two.

Deletion anomaly. In a relation, the situation in which the removal of one row of a table deletes facts about two or more themes.

Delimited identifier. A reserved word placed in special symbols to distinguish it from the DBMS reserved word so it can be used as a table, column, or other name in a database.

Denormalize. To intentionally create a set of database tables that are not normalized to BCNF and 4NF.

Dependency graph. A network of nodes and lines that represents the logical dependencies among tables, views, triggers, stored procedures, indexes, and other database constructs.

Determinant. One or more attributes that functionally determine another attribute or attributes. In the functional dependency (A, B) → C, the attributes (A, B) are the determinant.

Device. Any equipment, such as a personal computer, that is connected to the Internet.

Differential backup. A backup file that contains only changes made since a prior backup.

Digital dashboard. In reporting systems, a display that is customized for a particular user. Typically, a digital dashboard has links to many different reports.

Dimension table. In a star schema dimensional database, the tables that connect to the central fact table. Dimension tables hold attributes used in the organizing queries in analyses such as those of OLAP cubes.

Dimensional database. A database design that is used for data warehouses and is designed for efficient queries and analysis. It contains a central fact table connected to one or more dimension tables.

Dirty data. In a business intelligence system, data with errors. Examples are a value of "G" for customer sex and a value of "213" for customer age. Other examples are a value of "999-999-9999" for a U.S. phone number, a part color of "gren," and an email address of "WhyMe@somewhereelseintheuniverse.who." Dirty data pose problems for reporting and data mining applications.

Dirty read. Reading data that have been changed but not yet committed to the database. Such changes may later be rolled back and removed from the database.

Discriminator. In the entity-relationship model, an attribute of a supertype entity that determines which subtype pertains to the supertype.

Distributed database. A database that exists, either by partitioning or replication, on more than one database server.

Distributed two-phase locking. A locking mechanism used with distributed databases.

DK/NF. *See* domain/key normal form.

DML. *See* data manipulation language (DML).

Document [NoSQL database category]. A nonrelational database structure based on data stored as documents. The structure is commonly based on Extensible Markup Language (XML) or JavaScript Object Notation (JSON).

Document Object Model (DOM). An API that represents an XML document as a tree. Each node of the tree represents a piece of the XML document. A program can directly access and manipulate a node of the DOM representation.

Document type declaration (DTD). A set of markup elements that defines the structure of an XML document.

DOM. *See* Document Object Model (DOM).

Domain. A named set of all possible values that an attribute can have. Domains can be defined by listing allowed values or by defining a rule for determining allowed values.

Domain integrity constraint. Also called a *domain constraint*, a data constraint that limits data values to a particular set of values. *See also* data constraint, interrelation constraint, intrarelation constraint, range constraint.

Domain/key normal form (DK/NF). A relation in which all constraints are logical consequences of domains and keys.

Drill down. User-directed disaggregation of data used to break higher-level totals into components.

DTD. *See* document type declaration (DTD).

Durable. In an ACID transaction, the database changes are permanent. *See also* ACID transaction.

Dynamic cursor. A fully featured cursor. All inserts, updates, deletions, and changes in row order are visible to a dynamic cursor.

Dynamic report. In reporting systems, a report that reads the most current data at the time of the report's creation. Contrast with static report.

Dynamo. A nonrelational unstructured data store developed by Amazon.com.

DynamoDB database service. A nonrelational key-value DBMS product.

Empty set. In an SQL query, a query response that contains no records, indicating that there is no data in the database that matches the query.

Enterprise-class database system. A DBMS product capable of supporting the operating requirement of large organizations.

Enterprise data warehouse (EDW) architecture. A data warehouse architecture that links specialized data marts to a central data warehouse for data consistency and efficient operations.

Entity. (1) In the entity-relationship model, a representation of something that users want to track. *See also* entity class, entity instance. (2) In a generic sense, something that users want to track. In the relational model, an entity is stored in one row of a table.

Entity class. In the entity-relationship model, a collection of entities of a given type; for example, EMPLOYEE and DEPARTMENT. The class is described by its attributes.

Entity Data Model (EDM). An emerging Microsoft data modeling technology that is part of the .NET Framework.

Entity instance. A particular occurrence of an entity; for example, Employee 100 and the Accounting Department. An entity instance is described by values of its attributes.

Entity integrity constraint. The constraint that the primary key column or columns must have unique values so that each row can be uniquely identified.

Entity-relationship (E-R) data modeling. Creating a data model using E-R diagrams. *See also* entity-relationship (E-R) diagram

Entity-relationship (E-R) diagram. A graphic used to represent entities and their relationships. In the traditional E-R model, entities are shown as squares or rectangles, and relationships are shown as diamonds. The cardinality of the relationship is shown inside the diamond. In the crow's foot model, entities are shown in rectangles, and relationships are shown by lines between the rectangles. Attributes are generally listed within the rectangle. The many side of many relationships is represented by a crow's foot.

Entity-relationship (E-R) data modeling. A set of constructs and conventions used to create data models. The things in the users' world are represented by entities, and the associations among those things are represented by relationships. The results are usually documented in an entity-relationship (E-R) diagram.

Ethernet networking technology. A commonly used network standard.

Equijoin. The process of joining relation A containing attribute A1 with B containing attribute B1 to form relation C, so for each row in C, A1 = B1. Both A1 and B1 are represented in C.

E-R diagram. *See* entity-relationship (E-R) diagram.

Exclusive lock. A lock on a data resource such that no other transaction can either read or update that resource.

Exclusive subtype. A subtype in which a supertype instance is related to at most one subtype in a set of possible subtypes.

Existence-dependent entity. Same as a weak entity. An entity that cannot appear in the database unless an instance of one or more other entities also appears in the database. A subclass of existence-dependent entities is ID-dependent entities.

Explicit join. An SQL join statement that used the SQL JOIN ON syntax. *See also* SQL JOIN ON syntax.

Explicit lock. A lock requested by command from an application program.

Extended E-R model. The entity-relationship (E-R) model extended with subtypes. *See also* entity-relationship (E-R) model

Extensible Markup Language (XML). *See* XML (Extensible Markup Language).

Extensible Style Language. *See* XSLT (Extensible Style Language: Transformations).

Extract. A portion of an operational database downloaded to a local area network (LAN) or personal computer for local processing. Extracts are created to reduce communication cost and time when querying and creating reports from data created by transaction processing.

Extract, Transform, and Load (ETL) system. The portion of a data warehouse that converts operational data to data warehouse data.

F score. In RFM analysis, the "how frequently" score, which reflects how often a customer makes a purchase. *See also* RFM analysis.

Fact table. In a dimensional database, the central table that contains numerical values.

Field. (1) A logical group of bytes in a record such as Name or PhoneNumber. (2) In the relational model, a synonym for attribute.

Fifth normal form (5NF). A normal form necessary to eliminate an anomaly where a table can be split apart but not correctly joined back together. Also know as Project-Join Normal Form (PJ/NF).

File data source. An ODBC data source stored in a file that can be emailed or otherwise distributed among users.

First normal form (1NF). Any table that fits the definition of a relation.

Flat file. A file that has only a single value in each field. The meaning of the columns is the same in every row. Typically, the file has no indices, and fields are delimited by commas or tab characters.

Foreign key. An attribute that is a key of one or more relations other than the one in which it appears. Used to represent relationships.

FOREIGN KEY constraint. In SQL, the constraint used to create relationships and referential integrity between tables.

Fourth normal form (4NF). A relation in Boyce-Codd normal form in which there are no multivalued dependencies or in which all attributes participate in a single multivalued dependency.

Functional dependency. A relationship between attributes in which one attribute or group of attributes determines the value of another. The expression $X \rightarrow Y$ means that given a value of X, we can determine the value of Y. A given value of X may appear in a relation more than once, but if so, it is always paired with the same value of Y. Also, if $X \rightarrow (Y, Z)$, then $X \rightarrow Y$ and $X \rightarrow Z$. However, if $(X, Y) \rightarrow Z$, then, in general, $X \text{ Not} \rightarrow Z$ and $Y \text{ Not} \rightarrow Z$.

Functionally dependent. The term that describes the right-hand side of a functional dependency. The right-hand side values of a functional dependency are said to be functionally dependent upon the left-hand side values of the functional dependency. In the expression $X \rightarrow Y$, Y is functionally dependent upon X. *See also* functional dependency

Generic entity. In IDEF1X, an entity that has one or more category clusters. The generic entity takes the role of a supertype for the category entities in the category cluster.

Google Chrome. Google's Web browser.

Graph [NoSQL database category]. A nonrelational database structure based on graph theory. The structure is based on nodes, properties, and edges.

Graphical user interface (GUI). A user interface that uses graphical elements for interaction with a user.

Granularity. The size of the database resource that is locked. Locking the entire database is large granularity; locking a column of a particular row is small granularity.

Growing phase. The first stage in two-phase locking in which locks are acquired but not released.

Hadoop. *See* Hadoop Distributed File System (HDFS).

Hadoop Distributed File System (HDFS). An open source file distribution system that provides standard file services to clustered servers so their file systems can function as one distributed file system.

HBase. A nonrelational unstructured data store developed as part of the Apache Software Foundation's Hadoop project. *See also* Hadoop Distributed File System (HDFS).

HAS-A relationship. A relationship between two entities or objects that are of different logical types; for example, EMPLOYEE HAS-A(n) AUTO. Contrast this with an IS-A relationship.

Host machine. For networking, any device connected to the network. For Web site, the server that stores and serves the Web pages.

HTML. *See* Hypertext Markup Language (HTML).

HTML document tags. The tags in HTML documents that indicate the structure of the document.

HTML syntax rules. The standards that are used to create HTML documents.

HTTP. *See* Hypertext Transfer Protocol (HTTP).

http://localhost. For a Web server, a reference to the user's computer.

Hypertext Markup Language (HTML). A standardized set of text tags for formatting text, locating images and other nontext files, and placing links or references to other documents.

Hypertext Transfer Protocol (HTTP). A standardized means for using TCP/IP to communicate over the Internet.

Hypervisor. The software that creates, controls, and communicates with virtual machines.

IBM Personal Computer (IBM PC). A personal computer developed by the IBM Corporation.

ID-dependent entity. An entity whose identifier contains the identifier of a second entity. For example, APPOINTMENT is ID-dependent on CLIENT, where the identifier of APPOINTMENT is (Date, Time, ClientNumber) and the identifier of CLIENT is ClientNumber. An ID-dependent entity is weak, meaning that it cannot logically exist without the existence of that second entity. Not all weak entities are ID-dependent, however.

IDEF1X (Integrated Definition 1, Extended). A version of the entity-relationship model, adopted as a national standard but difficult to understand and use. Most organizations use a simpler E-R version like the crow's foot model.

Identifier. An attribute that names, or identifies, an entity.

Identifying connection relationship. In IDEF1X, a 1:1 or 1:N HAS-A relationship in which the child entity is ID-dependent on the parent.

Identifying relationship. A relationship that is used when the child entity is ID-dependent upon the parent entity.

IDENTITY ({StartValue}, {Increment}) property. For Microsoft SQL Server 2014, the attribute that is used to create a surrogate key.

IE Crow's Foot model. James Martin's version of the Information Engineering (IE) model for diagramming data models, which uses a crow's foot symbol to indicate the many side of a relationship. *See also* Information Engineering (IE) model.

IIS. *See* Internet Information Server (IIS).

iisstart.htm. The default Web page used by the Microsoft Internet Information Server Web server. *See also* Internet Information Server (IIS).

Implementation. In object-oriented programming, a set of objects that instantiates a particular object-oriented interface.

Implicit join. In SQL statements, a join that does not use the SQL JOIN ON syntax. *See also* SQL JOIN ON syntax.

Implicit lock. A lock that is automatically placed by the DBMS.

Inclusive subtype. In data modeling and database design, a subtype that allows a supertype entity to be associated with more than one subtype.

Inconsistent backup. A backup file that contains uncommitted changes.

Inconsistent read problem. In a transaction, a series of reads of a set of rows in which some of the rows have been updated by a second transaction and some of the rows have not been updated by that second transaction. Can be prevented by two-phase locking and other strategies.

Index. Data created by the DBMS to improve access and sorting performance. Indexes can be constructed for a single column or groups of columns. They are especially useful for columns used by WHERE clauses, for conditions in joins, and for sorting.

index.html. A default Web page name provided by most Web servers.

Inetpub folder. In Windows operating systems, the root folder for the IIS Web server.

Information. (1) Knowledge derived from data, (2) data presented in a meaningful context, or (3) data processed by summing, ordering, averaging, grouping, comparing, or other similar operations.

Information Engineering (IE) model. An E-R model developed by James Martin.

Inner join. Synonym for join. Contrast with outer join.

InsertCommand object. The ADO.NET DataAdapter object used to insert new data from a DataSet back to the actual DBMS data.

Insertion anomaly. In a relation, the condition that exists when, to add a complete row to a table, one must add facts about two or more logically different themes.

Instance. A specific occurrence of an object of interest.

Instance failure. A failure in the operating system or hardware that causes the DBMS to fail.

Integrated Definition 1, Extended (IDEF1X). A version of the E-R model issued by the National Institute of Standards and Technology in 1993. *See also* Entity-relationship (E-R) model.

Integrated development environment (IDE). An application that provides a programmer or application developer with a complete set of development tools in one package.

Integrated tables. Database tables that store both data and the relationships among the data.

Interface. (1) The means by which two or more programs call each other; the definition of the procedural calls between two or more programs. (2) In object-oriented programming, the design of a set of objects that includes the objects' names, methods, and attributes.

International Organization for Standardization (ISO). The international standards organization that works on SQL standards, among others.

Internet. The network that connects the entire Earth, and the basis for much of modern computing.

Internet Information Server (IIS). A Microsoft product that operates as an HTTP server.

Internet Information Services Manager. The application used to manage Microsoft's IIS Web server.

Intersection. A set theory operation similar to a logical AND operation. *See also* set theory.

Intersection table. A table (relation) used to represent a many-to-many relationship. It contains the keys of the tables (relations) in the relationship. The relationships from the parent tables to the intersection tables must have a minimum cardinality of either mandatory-optional or mandatory-mandatory.

Interrelation constraint. A data constraint between two tables. *See also* data constraint, domain integrity constraint, intrarelation constraint, range constraint.

Intrarelation constraint. A data constraint within one table. *See also* data constraint, domain integrity constraint, interrelation constraint, range constraint.

iPhone. A smartphone built by Apple Inc.

IS-A relationship. A relationship between a supertype and a subtype. For example, EMPLOYEE and ENGINEER have an IS-A relationship.

Isolated. One of the four qualities needed for an ACID transaction: The four qualities are atomic, consistent, isolated and durable. *See also* ACID transaction, transaction isolation level.

Isolation level. *See* transaction isolation level.

Java. An object-oriented programming language that has better memory management and bounds checking than C++. It is used primarily for Internet applications, but it also can be used as a general-purpose programming language. Java compilers generate Java bytecode that is interpreted on client computers. Many believe that Microsoft C# is a near-copy of Java.

Java Data Objects (JDO). Part of the Oracle Corporation's Java Platform. *See also* Java, Java Platform.

Java Database Connectivity (JDBC). A standard interface by which application programs written in Java can access and process SQL databases (or table structures such as spreadsheets and text tables) in a DBMS-independent manner. While originally it did not stand for Java Database Connectivity, it does now and is an acronym. *See also* Java, Java Platform.

Java platform. The complete set of Java tools provided by Oracle Corporation. *See also* Java.

Java Programming Language. *See* Java, Java Platform.

Java Runtime Environment (JRE). Part of the Oracle Corporation's Java Platform that must be installed on individual computers to enable the use of Java applications. *See also* Java, Java Platform.

Java servlet. *See* servlet.

Java virtual machine. A Java bytecode interpreter that runs on a particular machine environment; for example, Intel or AMD. Such interpreters are usually embedded in browsers, included with the operating system, or included as part of a Java development environment.

JavaScript. A proprietary scripting language originally created by Netscape but now owned by Oracle Corporation. The Microsoft version is called JScript; the standard version is called ECMA-262. These are easily learned interpreted languages that are used for both Web server and Web client application processing. Sometimes written as *Java Script*.

JavaServer Pages (JSP). A combination of HTML and Java that is compiled into a Java servlet that is a subclass of the HttpServlet class. Java code embedded in a JSP has access to HTTP objects and methods. JSPs are used similarly to ASPs, but they are compiled rather than interpreted, as ASP pages are.

JDBC. *See* Java Database Connectivity (JDBC).

JDBC Connection Object. One of a set of objects created by a Java application to connect to a database using JDBC. *See also* Java, Java Database Connectivity (JDBC).

JDBC DriverManager. The JDBC application that routes program calls for JDBC objects to the proper JDBC driver to connect to the database. *See also* Java, Java Database Connectivity (JDBC).

JDBC ResultSet object. One of a set of objects created by a Java application to connect to a database using JDBC. *See also* Java, Java Database Connectivity (JDBC).

JDBC ResultSetMetaData Object. One of a set of objects created by a Java application to connect to a database using JDBC. *See also* Java, Java Database Connectivity (JDBC).

JDBC Statement Object. One of a set of objects created by a Java application to query or update a database using JDBC. *See also* Java, Java Database Connectivity (JDBC).

Joining the two tables. In SQL, the process of combining data rows from two tables. *See* SQL join operation.

JScript. A proprietary scripting language owned by Microsoft. The Netscape/Oracle version is called JavaScript; the standard version is called ECMAScript-262. These are easily learned interpreted languages used for both Web server and Web client application processing.

JSP. *See* JavaServer Pages (JSP).

Key. (1) A group of one or more attributes identifying a unique row in a relation. Because relations may not have duplicate rows, every relation must have at least one key, which is the composite of all of the attributes in the relation. A key is sometimes called a logical key. (2) With some relational DBMS products, an index on a column used to improve access and sorting speed. It is sometimes called a physical key.

Key-value [NoSQL database category]. A nonrelational database structure based on data values identified by key values.

Keyset cursor. An SQL cursor that combines some of the features of static cursors with some of the features of dynamic cursors. *See also* cursor, cursor type.

Knowledge worker. An information system user who prepares reports, mines data, and does other types of data analysis.

Labeled namespace. In an XML Schema document, a namespace that is given a name (label) within the document. All elements preceded by the name of the labeled namespace are assumed to be defined in that labeled namespace.

LAMP. A version of AMP that runs on Linux. *See also* AMP.

Language Integrated Query (LINQ). A Microsoft .NET Framework component that allows SQL queries to be run directly from application programs.

LEFT OUTER join. A join that includes all the rows of the first table listed in the SQL statement (the "left" table) regardless of whether they have a matching row in the other table.

Lift. In market basket analysis, confidence divided by the base probability of an item purchase.

Linux. An open-source personal computer operating system (OS) associated with one of its main creators, Linus Torvalds.

Local Area Network (LAN). A computer network that operates with computers in a definable small area, such as a business or university.

Lock. The process of allocating a database resource to a particular transaction in a concurrent-processing system. The size of the resource locked is known as the lock granularity. With an exclusive lock, no other transaction may read or write the resource. With a shared lock, other transactions may read the resource, but no other transaction may write it.

Lock granularity. The size of a locked data element. The lock of a column value of a particular row is a small granularity lock, and the lock of an entire table is a large granularity lock.

Locking behavior. How a DBMS controls locks on database elements such as tables during SQL operations.

Log. A file containing a record of database changes. The log contains before images and after images.

Logical unit of work (LUW). An equivalent term for transaction. *See also* transaction.

Login name. The character string that a user uses to log into a computer.

Logistic regression. A form of supervised data mining that estimates the parameters of an equation to calculate the odds that a given event will occur.

Lost update problem. Same as concurrent update problem.

M score. In RFM analysis, the "how much money" score, which reflects how much a customer spends per purchase. *See also* RFM analysis.

Managed Extensibility Framework (MEF). An extension to the Microsoft .NET Framework added in version 4.5 to provide support for Windows 8 apps.

Mandatory. In a relationship, when the minimum number of entity instances that *must* participate in a relationship is one, then participation in the relationship is said to be *mandatory*. *See also* minimum cardinality, optional.

Mandatory-to-mandatory (M-M) relationship. A relationship in which entity instances are required on both sides of the relationship.

Mandatory-to-optional (M-O) relationship. A relationship in which an entity instance is required on the left-hand side of the relationship but not on the right-hand side.

Many-to-many (N:M) relationship. A relationship in which one parent entity instance (or row in the parent table) can be associated with many child entity instances (or rows in the child table). At the same time, one child entity instance (or row in the child table) can be associated with many parent entity instances (or rows in the parent table). In an actual database, these relationships are transformed into two one-to-many relationships between the original entities (tables) and an intersection table.

Market basket analysis. A type of data mining that estimates the correlations of items that are purchased together. *See also* confidence, lift.

MapReduce. A Big Data processing technique that breaks a data analysis into many parallel processes (the Map function) and then combines the results of these processes into one final result (the Reduce function).

MAX. In SQL, a function that determines the largest value in a set of numbers. *See also* SQL built-in functions.

Maximum cardinality. (1) In a binary relationship in the entity-relationship data model, the maximum number of entities on each side of the relationship. Common values are 1:1, 1:N, and N:M. (2) In a relationship in the relational model database design, the maximum number of rows on each side of the relationship. Common values are 1:1 and 1:N. An N:M relationship is not possible in the relational model database design, where an additional intersection relation (table) must be used to link the two relations (tables) via two 1:N relationships.

Measure. In OLAP, the source data for the cube—data that are displayed in the cells. They may be raw data, or they may be functions of raw data, such as SUM, AVG, or other computations.

Media failure. A failure that occurs when the DBMS is unable to write to or read from a disk. Usually caused by a disk head crash or other disk failure.

MemcachDB. A nonrelational key-value DBMS product.

Metadata. Data concerning the structure of data that are used to describe tables, columns, constraints, indexes, and so forth. Metadata is data about data.

Method. A program attached to an object-oriented programming (OOP) object. A method can be inherited by lower-level OOP objects.

Microsoft Access 2013. Microsoft's personal database product.

Microsoft Internet Explorer. Microsoft's Web browser.

Microsoft SQL Server 2014 Management Studio. The GUI utility that is used with Microsoft SQL Server 2014.

Microsoft Transaction Manager (MTS). Part of Microsoft's OLE DB. *See also* OLE DB.

Microsoft Windows. A Microsoft operating system (OS) for personal computers.

Microsoft Windows PowerShell. A Microsoft command-line utility.

Microsoft Windows Server. A Microsoft operating system (OS) for server computers.

MIN. In SQL, a function that determines the smallest value in a set of numbers. *See also* SQL built-in functions.

Minimum cardinality. (1) In a binary relationship in the entity-relationship model, the minimum number of entities required on each side of a relationship. (2) In a binary relationship in the relational model, the minimum number of rows required on each side of a relationship. Common values of minimum cardinality for both definitions are optional to optional (O-O), mandatory to optional (M-O), optional to mandatory (O-M), and mandatory to mandatory (M-M).

Minimum cardinality enforcement actions. Activities that must be taken to preserve minimum cardinality restrictions.

Mobile phone. A handheld device that connects to the telephone system via radio signals. *See also* cell phone.

Modification anomaly. In a relation, the situation that exists when the storage of one row records facts about two or more entities or when the deletion of one row removes facts about two or more entities.

MongoDB. A nonrelational document DBMS product.

Mozilla Firefox. Mozilla's open source Web browser.

Multivalued dependency. A condition in a relation with three or more attributes in which independent attributes appear to have relationships they do not have. Formally, in a relation R (A, B, C), having key (A, B, C) where A is matched with multiple values of B (or of C or both), B does not determine C, and C does not determine B. An example is the relation EMPLOYEE (EmpNumber, EmpSkill, DependentName), where an employee can have multiple values of EmpSkill and DependentName. EmpSkill and DependentName do not have any relationship, but they do appear to in the relation.

MUST constraint. A constraint that requires one entity to be combined with another entity.

MUST COVER constraint. The binary relationship indicates all combinations that must appear in the ternary relationship.

MUST NOT constraint. The binary relationship indicates combinations that are not allowed to occur in the ternary relationship.

MySQL AUTO_INCREMENT property. In MySQL, the method used to generate surrogate primary key values of sequenced numbers.

MySQL Workbench. The GUI utility used with MySQL 5.6.

Natural join. A join of a relation A having attribute A1 with relation B having attribute B1, where A1 equals B1. The joined relation, C, contains either column A1 or B1 but not both. Contrast this with equijoin.

Neo4J. A nonrelational graph DBMS product.

NetBeans IDE. An open-source GUI integrated development environment (IDE) from Oracle Corporation.

Neural networks. A form of supervised data mining that estimates complex mathematical functions for making predictions. The name is a misnomer. Although there is some loose similarity between the structure of a neural network and a network of biological neurons, the similarity is only superficial.

N:M. The abbreviation for a many-to-many relationship between two entities or relations.

Nonidentifying connection relationships. In IDEF1X, 1:1 and 1:N HAS-A relationships that do not involve ID-dependent entities.

Nonidentifying relationship. In data modeling, a relationship between two entities such that one is *not* ID-dependent on the other. *See also* identifying relationship.

Nonintegrated data. Data that are stored in two incompatible information systems.

Non-prime attribute. In normalization, an attribute that is not contained in any candidate key.

Nonrepeatable read. The situation that occurs when a transaction reads data it has previously read and finds modifications or deletions caused by a committed transaction.

Nonspecific IDEF1X relationships. In IDEF1X, an N:M relationship.

Normal form. A rule or set of rules governing the allowed structure of relations. The rules apply to attributes, functional dependencies, multivalue dependencies, domains, and constraints. The most important normal forms are first normal form, second normal form, third normal form, Boyce-Codd normal form, fourth normal form, fifth normal form, and domain/key normal form.

Normalization. (1) The process of constructing one or more relations such that in every relation the determinant of every functional dependency is a candidate key (BCNF). (2) The process of removing multivalued dependencies (4NF). (3) In general, the process of evaluating a relation to determine whether it is in a specified normal form and of converting it to relations in that specified normal form, if necessary.

NoSQL. *See* Not only SQL.

NoSQL movement. *See* Not only SQL.

NOT NULL constraint. In SQL, a constraint that specifies that a column must contain a value in every row.

Not only SQL. Actually referring to the creation and use of nonrelational DBMS products instead of just not using the SQL language, this movement was originally mislabeled as the NoSQL movement. It is now recognized that both relational and nonrelational DBMS products are needed in management information systems and that they must interact with each other. Thus, the term *not only SQL*.

Not-type-valid document. An XML document that either does not conform to its document type declaration (DTD) or does not have a DTD. *See also* schema-valid document, type-valid document.

NULL constraint. In SQL, a constraint that specifies that a column may have empty cells in some or all rows.

Null status. Whether the column has a NULL constraint or a NOT NULL constraint. *See also* NOT NULL constraint, NULL constraint.

Null value. An attribute value that has never been supplied. Such values are ambiguous and can mean that (a) the value is unknown, (b) the value is not appropriate, or (c) the value is known to be blank.

Object. In object-oriented programming, an abstraction that is defined by its properties and methods. *See also* object-oriented programming (OOP).

Object class. In object-oriented programming, a set of objects with a common structure. *See also* object-oriented programming (OOP).

Object Linking and Embedding (OLE). Microsoft's object standard. OLE objects are Component Object Model (COM) objects and support all required interfaces for such objects.

Object persistence. In object-oriented programming, the characteristic that an object can be saved to nonvolatile memory, such as a disk. Persistent objects exist between executions of a program.

Object-oriented DBMS (OODBMS or ODBMS). A DBMS that can store the objects similar to those used in OOP. *See also* object-oriented programming (OOP).

Object-oriented programming (OOP). A programming methodology that defines objects and the interactions between them to create application programs.

Object-relational databases. DBMS products that support both relational and object-oriented programming data structures, such as Oracle Database.

ODBC. *See* Open Database Connectivity (ODBC) standard.

ODBC conformance level. In ODBC, definitions of the features and functions that are made available through the driver's application program interface (API). A driver API is a set of functions that the application can call to receive services. There are three conformance levels: Core API, Level 1 API, and Level 2 API.

ODBC data source. In the ODBC standard, a database and its associated DBMS, operating system, and network platform.

ODBC Data Source Administrator. The application used to create ODBC data sources.

ODBC driver. In ODBC, a program that serves as an interface between the ODBC driver manager and a particular DBMS product. Runs on the client machines in a client-server architecture.

ODBC driver manager. In ODBC, a program that serves as an interface between an application program and an ODBC driver. It determines the required driver, loads it into memory, and coordinates activity between the application and the driver. On Windows systems, it is provided by Microsoft.

ODBC multiple-tier driver. In ODBC, a two-part driver, usually for a client-server database system. One part of the driver resides on the client and interfaces with the application; the second part resides on the server and interfaces with the DBMS.

ODBC single-tier driver. In ODBC, a database driver that accepts SQL statements from the driver manager and processes them without invoking another program or DBMS. A single-tier driver is both an ODBC driver and a DBMS. It is used in file-processing systems.

ODBC SQL conformance levels. ODBC SQL conformance levels specify which SQL statements, expressions, and data types an OBDC driver can process. Three SQL conformance levels are defined: Minimum SQL Grammar, Core SQL Grammar, Extended SQL Grammar.

OLAP. *See* online analytical processing (OLAP).

OLAP cube. In OLAP, a presentation structure having axes upon which data dimensions are placed. Measures of the data are shown in the cells of the cube. Also called a hypercube.

OLAP report. The output of an OLAP analysis in tabular format. For example, this can be an Excel Pivot Table. *See also* OLAP cube.

OLAP server. A server specifically developed to perform OLAP analyses.

OLE DB. The COM-based foundation of data access in the Microsoft world. OLE DB objects support the OLE object standard. ADO is based on OLE DB.

1:N. The abbreviation for a one-to-many relationship between two entities or relations.

One-to-many (1:N) relationship. A relationship in which one parent entity instance (or row in the parent table) can be associated with many child entity instances (or rows in the child table). At the same time, one child entity instance (or row in the child table) can be associated with only one parent entity instance (or row in the parent table).

One-to-one (1:1) relationship. A relationship in which one parent entity instance (or row in the parent table) can be associated with only one child entity instance (or row in the child table). At the same time, one child entity instance (or row in the child table) can be associated with only one parent entity instance (or row in the parent table).

Online analytical processing (OLAP). A form of dynamic data presentation in which data are summarized, aggregated, deaggregated, and viewed in the frame of a table or a cube.

Online transaction processing (OLTP) system. An operational database system available for, and dedicated to, transaction processing.

Open Database Connectivity (ODBC). A standard interface by which application programs can access and process relational databases, spreadsheets, text files, and other table-like structures in a DBMS or in a program-independent manner. The driver manager portion of ODBC is incorporated into Windows. ODBC drivers are supplied by DBMS vendors, by Microsoft, and by third-party software developers.

Operational system. A database system in use for the operations of the enterprise, typically an OLTP system, *See also* online transaction processing (OLTP) system.

Optimistic locking. A locking strategy that assumes no conflict will occur, processes a transaction, and then checks to determine whether conflict did occur. If conflict did occur, no changes are made to the database and the transaction is repeated. *See also* pessimistic locking.

Optional. In a relationship, when the minimum number of entity instances that *must* participate in a relationship is zero, then participation in the relationship is said to be *optional. See also* mandatory, minimum cardinality

Optional-to-mandatory (O-M) relationship. A relationship in which an entity instance is required on the right-hand side of the relationship but not on the left-hand side.

Optional-to-optional (O-O) relationship. A relationship in which an entity instance is not required on either side of the relationship.

Oracle SQL Developer. The GUI utility for Oracle Database 12*c*.

Outer join. A join in which all of the rows of a table appear in the join result, regardless of whether they have a match in the join condition. In a left outer join, all of the rows in the left-hand relation appear; in a right outer join, all of the rows in the right-hand relation appear.

Overlapping candidate keys. Two candidate keys are said to be overlapping candidate keys if they have one or more attributes in common.

Parameter. A data value that is passed as input to a stored procedure or other application.

Parent. An entity or row on the one side of a one-to-many relationship.

Parent mandatory and child mandatory (M-M). A relationship where the minimum cardinality of the parent is 1 and the minimum cardinality of the child is 1.

Parent mandatory and child optional (M-O). A relationship where the minimum cardinality of the parent is 1 and the minimum cardinality of the child is 0.

Parent optional and child mandatory (O-M). A relationship where the minimum cardinality of the parent is 0 and the minimum cardinality of the child is 1.

Parent optional and child optional (O-O). A relationship where the minimum cardinality of the parent is 0 and the minimum cardinality of the child is 0.

Partially dependent. In normalization, a condition where an attribute is dependent on only part of a composite primary key instead of on the whole key.

Partitioning. For databases, separating a database into parts, which will normally be stored on separate DBMS servers.

Passive repository. Repositories that are filled only when someone takes the time to generate the needed metadata and place it in the repository. *See also* data repository.

Persistent object. In object-oriented programming, an object that has been written to persistent storage.

Persistent Stored Modules. *See* SQL/Persistent Stored Modules (SQL/PSM).

Personal Computer (PC). Also known as a *micro-computer*, a small computer intended for use by one person as his or her own computer.

Personal database system. A DBMS product intended for use by an individual or small workgroup. Such products typically include application development tools such as form and report generators in addition to the DBMS. For example, Microsoft Access 2013.

Pessimistic locking. A locking strategy that prevents conflict by locking data resources, processing the transaction, and then unlocking the data resources. *See also* deadlock, optimistic locking.

Phantom read. The situation that occurs when a transaction reads data it has previously read and finds new rows that were inserted by a committed transaction.

PHP. A Web page programming language that runs routines on the Web server rather than on the user's client device. *See aslo* PHP: Hypertext Processor (PHP).

PHP Data Objects (PDO). A consistent data-access specification for PHP that allows a programmer to use the same functions independent of which DBMS is being used.

PHP: Hypertext Processor (PHP). A Web page scripting language used to create dynamic Web pages. It now includes an object-oriented programming component and PHP Data Objects (PDO). *See also* PHP Data Objects (PDO).

Pig. The database query language created as part of the Hadoop suite and used to query the HBase nonrelational DBMS. *See also* Hadoop, Hbase.

PivotTable. Microsoft's name for its OLAP client, as used in Microsoft Excel 2013. *See also* OLAP.

PL/SQL. *See* Procedural Language/SQL (PL/SQL).

PL/SQL SEQUENCE object. An Oracle Database object used to implement surrogate primary keys by providing sequences of numbers.

Portable Class Libraries. An extension to the Microsoft .NET Framework added in version 4.5 to provide support for Windows 8 apps.

POST method. In PHP, a method of passing data values from one Web page to another for processing.

PowerShell sqlps utility [MSSQL]. In Microsoft SQL Server 2014, an add-in to the Microsoft PowerShell command-line utility that allows it to work with Microsoft SQL Server.

Prepared Statement object. A JDBC object used to invoke database compiled queries and stored procedures.

Primary key. A candidate key selected to be the key of a relation; the primary key is used as a foreign key for representing relationships.

PRIMARY KEY constraint. In SQL, a constraint statement used to create a primary key for a table.

PrimaryKey property. The ADO.NET DataSet object used to enforce row uniqueness in a DataTable object.

Procedural programming language. A programming language where each step necessary to obtain a result must be specified. The language may have the ability to contain sets of steps in structures called procedures or subprocedures.

Procedural Language/SQL (PL/SQL). An Oracle-supplied language that augments SQL with programming language structures such as while loops, if-then-else blocks, and other such constructs. PL/SQL is used to create stored procedures and triggers.

Processing rights and responsibilities. Organizational policies regarding which groups can take which actions on specified data items or other collections of data.

Program/data independence. The condition existing when the structure of the data is not defined in application programs. Rather, it is defined in the database and then the application programs obtain it from the DBMS. In this way, changes can be made in the data structures that may not necessarily be made in the application programs.

Programmer. A person who creates application programs in a programming language.

Project-Join normal form (PJ/NF). Another name for 5NF. *See also* Fifth normal form (5NF).

Property. Same as attribute.

Proposed values. One type of ADO.NET DataSet object data values stored in a DataRow collection in a DataTable object.

Prototype. A quickly developed demonstration of an application or portion of an application.

Pseudofile. The term used to describe the results of an SQL statement, used in conjunction with a cursor. *See also* cursor.

Pull report. In reporting systems, a report that must be requested by users.

Push report. In reporting systems, a report that is sent to users according to a schedule.

QBE. *See* query by example (QBE).

Query. A request for database data that meets specific criteria. This can be thought of as asking the database a question and getting an answer in the form of the data returned.

Query by example (QBE). A style of query interface, first developed by IBM but now used by Microsoft Access 2013 and other DBMS products, that enables users to express queries by providing examples of the results they seek.

Question mark (?) wildcard character. A character used in Access 2013 queries to represent a single unspecified character. *See also* SQL underscore (_) wildcard character.

R score. In RFM analysis, the "how recently" score, which reflects how recently a customer made a purchase. *See also* RFM analysis.

Range constraint. A data constraint that specifies that data values must be within a specific range of values. *See also* data constraint, domain integrity constraint, interrelation constraint, intrarelation constraint.

Read committed isolation level. A level of transaction isolation that prohibits dirty reads but allows nonrepeatable reads and phantom reads.

Read uncommitted isolation level. A level of transaction isolation that allows dirty reads, nonrepeatable reads, and phantom reads.

Record. (1) In a relational model, a synonym for row and tuple. (2) A group of fields pertaining to the same entity; used in file-processing systems.

Recordset. An ADO.NET object that encapsulates a relation; created as the result of the execution of an SQL statement or a stored procedure.

Recovery via reprocessing. Recovering a database by restoring the last full backup and then re-creating each transaction since the backup.

Recovery via rollback/rollforward. Recovering a database by restoring the last full backup and then using data stored in a transaction log to modify the database as needed by either adding transactions (rollforward) or removing erroneous transactions (rollback).

Recursive relationship. A relationship among entities or rows of the same type. For example, if CUSTOMERs refer to other CUSTOMERs, the relationship is recursive.

ReDo files. In Oracle Database, backups of rollback segments used for backup and recovery. ReDo files may be online or offline.

Referential integrity (RI) actions. In general, rules that specify the activities that must take place when insert, update, or delete actions occur on either the parent or child entities in a relationship. In this text, we use referential integrity actions only to document activities needed to preserve required parents. Other actions can be defined as part of the database design. *See also* minimum cardinality enforcement actions, Figure 6-29.

Referential integrity constraint. A relationship constraint on foreign key values. A referential integrity constraint specifies that the values of a foreign key must be a subset of the values of the primary key to which it refers.

Regression analysis. A form of supervised data mining in which the parameters of equations are estimated by data analysis.

Relation. A two-dimensional array containing single-value entries and no duplicate rows. Values for a given entity are shown in rows; values of attributes of that entity are shown in columns. The meaning of the columns is the same in every row. The order of the rows and columns is immaterial.

Relational database. A database consisting of relations. In practice, relational databases contain relations with duplicate rows. Most DBMS products include a feature that removes duplicate rows when necessary and appropriate. Such a removal is not done as a matter of course because it can be time-consuming to enforce.

Relational model. A data model in which data are stored in relations and relationships between rows are represented by data values.

Relational schema. A set of relations with interrelation constraints.

Relationship. An association between two entities or rows.

Relationship cardinality constraint. A constraint on the number of rows that can participate in a relationship. Minimum cardinality constraints determine the number of rows that must participate; maximum cardinality constraints specify the largest number of rows that can participate. *See also* maximum cardinality, minimum cardinality.

Relationship class. An association between entity classes.

Relationship instance. (1) An association between entity instances; (2) a specific relationship between two tables in a database.

Repeatable read isolation level. A level of transaction isolation that disallows both dirty reads and nonrepeatable reads. Phantom reads can occur.

Replication. For both Oracle Database, Microsoft SQL Server, and MySQL, a term that refers to maintaining accurate copies of data on databases that are distributed on more than one computer.

Report. A formatted set of information created to meet a user's need.

Report authoring. In a reporting system, connecting to the data source, creating the report structure, and formatting the report.

Report delivery. In a reporting system, pushing the reports to users or allowing them to pull the reports as needed.

Report management. In a reporting system, defining who receives which reports, when, and by what means.

Reporting system. A business intelligence system that processes data by filtering, sorting, and making simple calculations. OLAP is a type of reporting system. Contrast with data mining systems.

Repository. A collection of metadata about database structure, applications, Web pages, users, and other application components. Active repositories are maintained automatically by tools in the application-development environment. Passive repositories must be maintained manually.

Requirements analysis. The second step in the systems development life cycle (SDLC) model. User requirements are gathered and analyzed, and a set of user approved project requirements are created. The data model is created in this step.

Reserved word. A word that has a special meaning in the DBMS or ODBC and should not be used as a table, column, or other name in a database. *See also* DBMS reserved word.

Resource locking. *See* lock.

Reverse engineered (RE) data model. The structure that results from reverse engineering. It is not really a data model because it includes physical structures such as intersection tables. It is, instead, a thing unto itself; midway between a data model and a relational database design.

Reverse engineering. The process of reading the structure of an existing database and creating a reverse-engineered data model from that schema.

RFM analysis. A type of reporting system in which customers are classified according to how recently (R), how frequently (F), and how much money (M) they spend on their orders.

RIGHT OUTER constraint. A join that includes all the rows of the second table listed in the SQL statement (the "right" table) regardless of whether they have a matching row in the other table.

Role. In database administration, a defined set of permissions that can be assigned to users or groups.

Rollback. The process of recovering a database in which before images are applied to the database to return to an earlier checkpoint or other point at which the database is logically consistent.

Rollforward. The process of recovering a database by applying after images to a saved copy of the database to bring it to a checkpoint or other point at which the database is logically consistent.

Root. (1) In MySQL, the name of the DBMS administrator account. (2) The top record, row, or node in a tree. A root does not have a parent.

Routers. Networking devices used to move messages across the Internet and other connected networks.

Row. A group of columns in a table. All the columns in a row pertain to the same entity. A row is the same as a tuple and a record.

Rowset. In OLE DB, an abstraction of data collections such as recordsets, email addresses, and nonrelational and other data.

SAX. Simple API (Application Program Interface) for XML. An event-based parser that notifies a program when the elements of an XML document have been encountered during document parsing.

Scalar-valued function. A user-defined function that operates on a single row of data and returns a single value.

Schema. (1) In MySQL, a synonym for *database*. (2) A complete logical view of the database.

Schema-valid document. An XML document that conforms to its XML Schema definition.

SCN. *See* system change number.

Scrollable cursor. A cursor type that enables forward and backward movement through a recordset. Three scrollable cursor types discussed in this text are snapshot, keyset, and dynamic.

Second normal form (2NF). A relation in first normal form in which all nonkey attributes are dependent on all of the key attributes.

SelectCommand object. The ADO.NET DataAdapter object used to query data in a DataSet.

Self-describing. In a database, the characteristic of including data about the database in the database itself. Thus, the data that define a table are included in a database along with the data that are contained in that table. These descriptive data are called *metadata*. *See also* metadata, relation, table.

Semantic object model. The constructs and conventions used to create a model of the users' data. The things in the users' world are represented by semantic objects (sometimes called objects). Relationships are modeled in the objects, and the results are usually documented in object diagrams.

Sequence. The Oracle Database 12*c* SQL statement used to create surrogate key values.

Serializable isolation level. A level of transaction isolation that disallows dirty reads, nonrepeatable reads, and phantom reads.

Server. A robust computer operated by information systems staff and used to run the server portion of client-server application such as Web pages and email. Servers are thus said to provide services to users. *See also* service, client-server architecture.

Server cluster. A group of servers that communicate and coordinate with each other.

Service. The provision of some utility to users. For example, a Web server provides the Web service, which is providing Web pages to users. *See also* server.

Service provider. An OLE DB data provider that transforms data. A service provider is both a data consumer and a data provider.

Servlet. A compiled, machine-independent Java bytecode program that is run by a Java virtual machine located on a Web server.

Set. In mathematical set theory, a collection of things (often referred to as *objects*). *See also* set theory.

Set operators. In mathematical set theory, the symbols for the operations that may be done with sets. In SQL, the SQL set operators that mimic set operations are specifically UNION, INTERSECT and EXCEPT. The SQL logical operators AND, OR, and NOT also implement some set theory functionality. *See also* set theory.

Set theory. The area of mathematics that works with sets. *See also* set.

SGML. *See* Standard Generalized Markup Language (SGML).

Shared lock. A lock against a data resource in which only one transaction may update the data but many transactions can concurrently read that data.

Shrinking phase. In two-phase locking, the stage at which locks are released but no lock is acquired.

Sibling. A record or node that has the same parent as another record or node.

Simple Object Access Protocol. A standard used for remote procedure calls. It uses XML for definition of the data and HTTP for transport. Contrast with SOAP.

Slowly changing dimension. In a dimensional database, a data column with values that change occasionally but irregularly over time; for example, a customer's address or phone number.

Smartphone. A cell phone that is capable of running user client applications (apps) in a client-server environment. *See also* cell phone, client-server architecture.

Snowflake schema. In a dimensional database or an OLAP database, the structure of tables such that dimension tables may be several levels away from the table storing the measure values. Such dimension tables are usually normalized. Contrast with star schema.

SOAP. Originally, Simple Object Access Protocol. Today, it is a protocol for remote procedure calls that differs from the Simple Object Access Protocol because it involves transport protocols in addition to HTTP. It is no longer an acronym.

Software development kit (SDK). A group of development tools provided to programmers to help them create applications.

SQL. *See* Structured Query Language (SQL).

SQL ALTER TABLE statement. The SQL command used to change the structure of a database table.

SQL AND operator. The SQL operator used to combine conditions in an SQL WHERE clause.

SQL built-in aggregate functions. In SQL, the functions COUNT, SUM, AVG, MAX, or MIN.

SQL CMD utility. A command-line utility used with SQL Server 2008.

SQL CREATE TABLE statement. The SQL command used to create a database table.

SQL CREATE VIEW statement. The SQL command used to create a database view.

SQL Data Control Language (DCL). The SQL statements to grant and/or revoke user permissions to perform operations on tables and other database components.

SQL DROP TABLE statement. The SQL command used to remove a table from a database.

SQL expression. A formula or set of values that determines the exact results of an SQL query. We can think of an SQL expression as anything that follows an actual or implied equal to (=) character (or any other relational operator, such as greater than [>], less than [<], and so on) or that follows certain SQL keywords, such as LIKE and BETWEEN.

SQL FROM clause. The part of an SQL SELECT statement that specifies conditions used to determine which tables are used in a query.

SQL GROUP BY clause. The part of an SQL SELECT statement that specifies conditions for grouping rows when determining the query results.

SQL HAVING clause. The part of an SQL SELECT statement that specifies conditions used to determine which rows are in the groupings in a GROUP BY clause.

SQL injection attack. The use of hacker-modified SQL statements, usually by manipulating input data in Web forms, to attack and infect an SQL database attached to a Web site. Preventable by careful application coding. The Lizamoon SQL injection attack in March 2011 affected more than 1.5 million URLs.

SQL join operation. In SQL, the process of combining data rows from two tables by using a relational algebra operation on two relations, A and B, which produces a third relation, C. A row of

A is concatenated with a row of B to form a new row in C if the rows in A and B meet a restriction concerning their values. Normally, the restriction is that one or more columns of A equal one or more columns of B. For example, suppose that A1 is an attribute in A and B1 is an attribute in B. The join of A with B in which A1 = B1 will result in a relation, C, having the concatenation of rows in A and B in which the value of A1 equals the value of B1. In theory, restrictions other than equality are allowed; a join could be made in which A1 > B1. Such nonequal joins are not used in practice, however.

SQL JOIN ON syntax. The SQL syntax used to create an explicit join.

SQL logical operators. The operators AND, OR, and NOT.

SQL MERGE statement. This SQL command is essentially a combination of the SQL INSERT and SQL UPDATE statements, where an INSERT or UPDATE is performed depending upon existing data.

SQL OR operator. The SQL operator used to specify alternate conditions in an SQL WHERE clause.

SQL ORDER BY clause. The part of an SQL SELECT statement that specifies how the query results should be sorted when they are displayed.

SQL outer join. An SQL join operation that include all rows from one of the tables in the join regardless of whether or not they match associated rows in the other table.

SQL percent sign (%) wildcard character. The standard SQL wildcard character used to specify multiple characters. Microsoft Access 2013 uses an asterisk (*) character instead of the percent character.

SQL/Persistent Stored Modules (SQL/PSM). SQL statements that extend SQL by adding procedural programming capabilities, such as variables and flow-of-control statements, and thus provide some programmability within the SQL framework. SQL/PSM is used to create user-defined functions, stored procedures, and triggers. *See also* trigger, stored procedure, user-defined function.

SQL/PSM. *See* SQL/Persistent Stored Modules (SQL/PSM).

SQL query. An SQL statement that uses the SQL SELECT/FROM/WHERE framework to "ask" a question that can be "answered" using database data. *See also* SQL SELECT/FROM/WHERE framework

SQL script. A set of SQL statements that are intended to be executed as a group.

SQL script comment. A comment in an SQL script. *See also* SQL script.

SQL script file. A file that holds an SQL script for repeated use. *See also* SQL script.

SQL SELECT clause. The part of an SQL SELECT statement that specifies which columns are in the query results.

SQL SELECT * statement. A variant of an SQL SELECT query that returns all columns for all tables in the query.

SQL SELECT...for XML statement. A variant of an SQL SELECT query that returns the query results in XML format.

SQL SELECT/FROM/WHERE framework. The basic structure of an SQL query. *See also* SQL SELECT clause, SQL FROM clause, SQL WHERE clause, SQL ORDER BY clause, SQL GROUP BY clause, SQL HAVING clause, SQL AND operator, SQL OR operator.

SQL Server IDENTITY ({StartValue}, {Increment}) expression. The Microsoft SQL Server syntax used to provide surrogate key values of sequential numbers.

SQL set operators. The operators UNION, INTERSECT, and EXCEPT.

SQL Transaction Control Language (TCL). The SQL statements used to create and control SQL managed transactions and thus protect database data.

SQL TRUNCATE TABLE statement. The SQL TRUNCATE TABLE command removes all data from a database table while leaving the table structure in place.

SQL underscore (_) wildcard character. The standard SQL wildcard character used to match a single character. Microsoft Access 2013 uses a question mark (?) character instead of the underscore character.

SQL WHERE clause. The part of an SQL SELECT statement that specifies conditions used to determine which rows are in the query results.

SQL view. A relation that is constructed from a single SQL SELECT statement. The term *view* in most DBMS products, including MySQL, Oracle Database, and Microsoft SQL Server, means SQL view.

SQL*Plus. A command-line utility in Oracle Database 12*c*.

Standard Generalized Markup Language (SGML). A standard means for tagging and marking the format, structure, and content of documents. HTML is an application of SGML. XML is a subset of SGML.

Star schema. In a dimensional database or an OLAP database, the structure of tables such that every dimension table is adjacent to the table storing the measure values. In the star schema, the dimension tables are often not normalized. Contrast with snowflake schema.

Statement-level consistency. All rows affected by a single SQL statement are protected from changes made by other users during the execution of the statement. Contrast with transaction-level consistency.

Static cursor. A cursor that takes a snapshot of a relation and processes that snapshot.

Static report. In reporting systems, a report that is prepared once from underlying data and does not change when the underlying data change. Contrast with dynamic report.

Stock-keeping unit (SKU). A unique identifier for each product available from a vendor.

Stored function. *See* user-defined function.

Stored procedure. A collection of SQL statements stored as a file that can be invoked by a single command. Usually, DBMS products provide a language for creating stored procedures that augments SQL with programming language constructs. Oracle Database provides PL/SQL for this purpose; Microsoft SQL Server provides T-SQL; MySQL also adds procedural capabilities but does not use a separate name for these additions. With some products, stored procedures can be written in a standard language such as Java. Usually, stored procedures are stored within the database itself.

Strong entity. In an entity-relationship model, any entity whose existence in the database does not depend on the existence of any other entity. *See also* ID-dependent entity, weak entity.

Strong password. A password that meets requirements intended to make it difficult to guess or unencrypt.

Structured Query Language (SQL). A language for defining the structure and processing of a relational database. It can be used as a stand-alone language, or it may be embedded in application programs. SQL has been adopted as a national standard by the American National Standards Institute (ANSI). The most common version used today is SQL-92, the version adopted by ANSI in 1992. SQL was originally developed by IBM.

Stylesheet. A document used by XSLT to indicate how to transform the elements of an XML document into another format.

Subquery. In SQL, a SELECT statement within another SELECT statement.

Subset. In mathematical set theory, a portion of a set. *See also* set.

Subtype. In generalization hierarchies, an entity or object that is a subspecies or subcategory of a higher-level type, called a supertype. For example, ENGINEER is a subtype of EMPLOYEE.

SUM. In SQL, a function that adds up a set of numbers. *See also* SQL built-in functions.

Supertype. In generalization hierarchies, an entity or object that logically contains subtypes. For example, EMPLOYEE is a supertype of ENGINEER, ACCOUNTANT, and MANAGER.

Supervised data mining. A form of data mining in which an analyst creates a prior model or hypothesis and then uses the data to test that model or hypothesis.

Support. In market basket analysis, the probability that two items will be purchased together.

Surrogate key. A unique, system-supplied identifier used as the primary key of a relation. It is created when a row is created, it never changes, and it is destroyed when the row is deleted. The values of a surrogate key have no meaning to the users and are usually hidden within forms and reports.

System change number (SCN). In Oracle Database, a database-wide value that is used to order changes made to database data. The SCN is incremented whenever database changes are committed.

System data source. An ODBC data source that is local to a single computer and can be accessed by that computer's operating system and select users of that operating system.

System maintenance. The fifth step in the systems development life cycle (SDLC) model. The implemented system is modified to correct errors and to implement new changes, and user responses and requests are gathered for the next iteration of the SDLC. *See also* systems development life cycle (SDLC).

Systems analysis and design. The process of studying business processes, and designing management information systems to support those processes. *See also* systems development life cycle (SDLC).

Systems development life cycle (SDLC). The five-stage cycle used to develop management information systems.

Table. A database structure of rows and columns to create cells that hold data values. Also known as a *relation* in a relational database, although strictly only tables that meet specific conditions can be called relations. *See also* relation.

TableName.ColumnName syntax. A syntax used to indicate which table a column is associated with. For example, CUSTOMER.LastName indicates the LastName column in the CUSTOMER table.

Tablet. A handheld user device that can run user client applications. Similar to a cell phone, but generally larger and without the telephone capability.

Table-valued function. In SQL/PSM, a user-defined function that returns a table of values.

Tabular data provider. An OLE DB data provider that presents data in the form of rowsets.

Ternary relationship. A relationship between three entities.

Third normal form (3NF). A relation in second normal form that has no transitive dependencies.

Three-tier architecture. A system of computers having a database server, a Web server, and one or more client computers. The database server hosts a DBMS, the Web server hosts an HTTP server, and the client computer hosts a browser. Each tier can run a different operating system.

Time dimension. A required dimension table in a dimensional database. The time dimension allows the data to be analyzed over time.

Transaction. (1) A group of actions that is performed on the database automatically; either all actions are committed to the database or none of them is. (2) In general, the record of an event in the business world.

Top level query. The first SELECT statement in an SQL query using a subquery.

Transaction control language (TCL). SQL statements that are used to mark transaction boundaries and control transaction behavior.

Transaction isolation level. The degree to which a database transaction is protected from actions by other transactions. The 1992 SQL standard specified four isolation levels: Read Uncommitted, Read Committed, Repeatable Reads, and Serializable.

Transaction-level consistency. All rows affected by any of the SQL statements in a transaction are protected from changes during the entire transaction. This level of consistency is expensive to enforce and reduces throughput. It may also mean that a transaction cannot see its own changes. Contrast with statement-level consistency.

Transact-SQL (T-SQL). A Microsoft-supplied language that is part of Microsoft SQL Server. It augments SQL with programming language structures such as while loops, if-then-else blocks, and other such constructs. Transact-SQL is used to create stored procedures and triggers.

Transitive dependency. In a relation having at least three attributes, for example, R (A, B, C), the situation in which A determines B, B determines C, but B does not determine A.

Transactional system. A database dedicated to processing transactions such as product sales and orders. It is designed to make sure that only complete transactions are recorded in the database. *See also* OLTP.

Tree. A collection of records, entities, or other data structures in which each element has at most one parent, except for the top element, which has no parent.

Trigger. A special type of stored procedure that is invoked by the DBMS when a specified condition occurs. BEFORE triggers are executed before a specified database action, AFTER triggers are executed after a specified database action, and INSTEAD OF triggers are executed in place of a specified database action. INSTEAD OF triggers are normally used to update data in SQL views.

T-SQL. *See* Transact-SQL (T-SQL).

Tuple. Same as row.

Two dashes (- -). Symbols used to indicate a single-line comment in a stored procedure or a trigger in SQL Server 2014, Oracle Database 12*c*, and MySQL 5.6.

Two-phase locking. The procedure by which locks are obtained and released in two phases. During the growing phase, the locks are obtained; during the shrinking phase, the locks are released. After a lock is released, no other lock will be granted for that transaction. Such a procedure ensures consistency in database updates in a concurrent-processing environment.

Two-tier architecture. In a Web-based database processing environment, the Web server and the DBMS are running on the same computer. One tier is for the Web browsers, and one is for the Web server/DBMS computer.

Type domain. In IDEF1X, a domain that is defined as a subset of a base domain or another type of domain.

Type-valid XML document. An XML document that conforms to its document type declaration (DTD). Contrast with not-type-valid document.

UML. *See* Unified Modeling Language (UML).

Unary relationship. A relationship between a table and itself. Also call a recursive relationship.

Unified Modeling Language (UML). A set of diagrams, structures, and techniques for modeling and designing object-oriented programs and applications. It is a set of tools for object-oriented development that has led to a development methodology. UML incorporates the entity-relationship model for data modeling.

Union. A set operation similar to a logical OR operation. *See also* set theory.

UNIQUE constraint. In SQL, a constraint that specifies that the values in a column must be unique.

Unsupervised data mining. A form of data mining in which analysts do not create a prior model or hypothesis but rather let the data analysis reveal a model.

Updatable view. An SQL view that can be updated. Such views are usually very simple, and the rules that allow updating are normally quite restrictive. Nonupdatable views can be made updatable by writing application-specific INSTEAD OF triggers.

Update anomaly. A data error created in a non-normalized table when an update action modifies one data value without modifying another occurrence of the same data value in the table.

UpdateCommand object. The ADO.NET DataAdapter object used to update existing data from a DataSet back to the actual DBMS data.

User. A person using an application.

User-defined function (stored function). A stored set of SQL statements that is *called by name* from another SQL statement, that may have *input parameters* passed to it by the calling SQL statement, and that *returns an output value* to the SQL statement that called the function.

User data source. An ODBC data source that is available only to the user who created it.

User group. A group of users. *See also* user.

Username. The set of characters that a user identifies himself/herself with for authentication purposes to log onto a computer.

Variable. A value that may be assigned or calculated by a stored procedure or a trigger in SQL Server 2014, Oracle Database 12*c*, and MySQL 5.6.

VBScript. An easily learned, interpreted language created by Microsoft that is used for both Web server and Web client applications processing.

Venn diagram. In mathematical set theory, the visual diagrams used to represent sets and their interactions.

Virtualization. A technique for sharing the hardware resources of one computer by having that one physical computer host one or more virtual computers, more commonly known as virtual machines. To do this, the actual computer hardware, now called the host machine, runs an application program known as a virtual machine manager or hypervisor. The hypervisor creates and manages the virtual machines and controls the interaction between the virtual machine and the physical hardware. For example, if a virtual machine has been allocated two Gigabytes of main memory for its use, the hypervisor is responsible for making sure the actual physical memory is allocated and available to the virtual machine.

WAMP. AMP running on a Windows operating system. *See also* AMP.

Weak entity. In an entity-relationship model, an entity whose logical existence in the database depends on the existence of another entity. All ID-dependent entities are weak, but not all weak entities are ID-dependent.

Web (the). A synonym for the World Wide Web. *See also* World Wide Web.

Web 2.0. Web sites that allow users to contribute content.

Web browser. The client application used to view and interact with Web sites. *See also* client-server architecture, web site.

Web portal. A Web page designed to be an entrance point for a Web site. It may display information from several sources and may require authentication to access.

Web site. A location on the World Wide Web. *See also* World Wide Web.

World Wide Web. The set of interconnected hypertext objects accessible on the Internet, organized into Web sites.

World Wide Web Consortium (W3C). The group that creates, maintains, revises, and publishes standards for the World Wide Web including HTML, XML, and XHTML.

WWW. A synonym for the World Wide Web. *See also* World Wide Web.

wwwroot folder. The root folder or base directory of a Web site on a Microsoft IIS Web server.

x..y cardinality format [UML]. The symbology format used in UML E-R diagrams to document minimum and maximum cardinalities. X records the minimum cardinality, and y records the maximum cardinality.

XML (Extensible Markup Language). A standard markup language that provides a clear separation between structure, content, and materialization. It can represent arbitrary hierarchies and hence can be used to transmit any database view.

XML Namespaces. A standard for assigning names to defined collections. X:Name is interpreted as the element Name as defined in namespace X. Y:Name is interpreted as the element Name as defined in namespace Y. Useful for disambiguating terms.

XML Schema. An XML document that defines the structure of other XML documents. Extends and replaces document type declarations (DTDs).

XPath. A sublanguage within XSLT that is used to identify parts of an XML document to be transformed. Can also be used for calculations and string manipulation. Commingled with XSLT.

XPointer. A standard for linking one document to another. XPath has many elements from XPointer.

XQuery. A standard for expressing database queries as XML documents. The structure of the query uses XPath facilities, and the result of the query is represented in an XML format. Currently under development and likely to be important in the future.

XSL (XSLT Stylesheet). The document that provides the {match, action} pairs and other data for XSLT to use when transforming an XML document.

XSLT (Extensible Style Language: Transformations). A program (or process) that applies XSLT Stylesheets to an XML document to produce a transformed XML document.

Index